Second Language Learning and Teaching

Series Editor

Mirosław Pawlak

For further volumes:
http://www.springer.com/series/10129

About the Series

The series brings together volumes dealing with different aspects of learning and teaching second and foreign languages. The titles included are both monographs and edited collections focusing on a variety of topics ranging from the processes underlying second language acquisition, through various aspects of language learning in instructed and non-instructed settings, to different facets of the teaching process, including syllabus choice, materials design, classroom practices and evaluation. The publications reflect state-of-the-art developments in those areas, they adopt a wide range of theoretical perspectives and follow diverse research paradigms. The intended audience are all those who are interested in naturalistic and classroom second language acquisition, including researchers, methodologists, curriculum and materials designers, teachers and undergraduate and graduate students undertaking empirical investigations of how second languages are learnt and taught.

Mirosław Pawlak
Editor

New Perspectives on Individual Differences in Language Learning and Teaching

 Springer

Mirosław Pawlak
Department of English Studies
Faculty of Pedagogy and Fine Arts
Adam Mickiewicz University
Nowy Swiat 28–30
62-800 Kalisz
Poland

ISBN 978-3-642-20849-2   e-ISBN 978-3-642-20850-8
DOI 10.1007/978-3-642-20850-8
Springer Heidelberg New York Dordrecht London

Library of Congress Control Number: 2011943321

Cover design: eStudio Calamar, Berlin/Figueres

Printed on acid-free paper

Springer is part of Springer Science+Business Media (www.springer.com)

Acknowledgments

The editor would like to express his gratitude to Professor Jan Majer (University of Łódź, Poland) who kindly agreed to review the papers included in the present volume. His invaluable comments and suggestions have without doubt greatly enhanced the quality of this work.

Contents

Contributors

Alwan, Fatma She has experience in TEFL as a teacher (8 years), supervisor and teacher trainer (16 years) and text-book writer (3 years) in the United Arab Emirates (UAE) Ministry of Education since 1985. She holds an Ed.D in TESOL from Exeter University and an M.A. in Educational Management from Bath University, UK. She is a certified trainer of NLP by the International NLP Trainers Association (INLPTA). She has multiple research interests related to teaching English as a foreign language, and has presented and published in areas of improving learning outcomes with NLP, teacher evaluation and curriculum development. She is a member of the Editorial Advisory Board of the Journal of Asia TEFL. Ministry of Education, Abu Dhabi, UAE, e-mail: alwan99@hotmail.com

Aronin, Larissa She received her Ph.D. in Moscow, is currently based at Oranim Academic College of Education, Israel and is affiliated to the Trinity College, Dublin. Dr. Aronin has published in a range of international journals on a wide array of topics connected with multilingualism-notably, complexity and multilingual education, individual multilingualism, the language awareness of multilinguals, and TLA. She serves as a Secretary of the International Association of Multilingualism. Aronin is an Editorial Board member of *Studies in Second Language Learning and Teaching* (Adam Mickiewicz University) and an Advisory Board Member of *Language Teaching* (CUP). Trinity College Dublin, Dublin, Ireland; Oranim Academic College of Education, Haifa, Israel; Bar Ilan University, Ramat-Gan, Israel

Baran-Łucarz, Małgorzata She holds an M.A. and Ph.D. in applied linguistics. She is an Assistant Professor at the University of Wrocław and has been since 1998 a teacher at the Teacher Training College in Wrocław. Apart from running classes in methodology, second language acquisition and phonetics at these institutes she also teaches phonetics in workshops organized by the Teacher Development Center for pre-service and in-service FL teachers. Her main areas of interest are methodology, SLA (particularly the issue of individual learner differences, such as field independence, aptitude, personality and affective factors), psycholinguistics, phonetics and pronunciation pedagogy. Institute of English Studies, University of Wroclaw, Wroclaw, Poland, e-mail: mbaran-lucarz@ifa.uni.wroc.pl

Bawardi, Basilius He teaches and researches modern Arabic Literatureat Bar Ilan University in Israel. He is also the head of Teaching Languages program (M.Ed. program) at the Oranim Academic College of Education. He holds an M.A. and Ph.D. in modern Arabic literature from Haifa University. He publishes on Modern Arabic poetry, teaching modern Arabic poetry, Arabic Ideological text, the formation and development of genres in Modern Arabic literature (nineteenth and twentieth centuries) and the development of modern Arabic narrative fiction in nineteenth century. Trinity College Dublin, Dublin, Ireland; Oranim Academic College of Education, Haifa, Israel; Bar Ilan University, Ramat-Gan, Israel

Biedroń, Adriana Pomeranian Academy in Słupsk, Słupsk, Poland, e-mail: biedron@apsl.edu.pl

Chunhong, Zhou She is a lecturer from Beijing Sport University. She graduated with an M.A. degree in English Language and Literature from Zhongshan University in 2005 and began her teaching career after graduation. Her research field is British and Irish literature and second language acquisition. In her three-year career as an English teacher, in addition to her classroom work she has acted as liaison person for international teachers and engaged in translation work. She has compiled two series of English textbooks in collaboration with her colleagues and participated in several international language teaching conferences including the 5th Asia TEFL Conference in Malaysia. Ti Yu Da Xue, Beijing Sports University, Beijing, China

Cohen, Andrew D. He was a Peace Corps Volunteer in rural development with the Aymara Indians on the High Plains of Bolivia, taught at the University of California at Los Angeles and at the Hebrew University of Jerusalem, was a Fulbright Scholar in Brazil and a Visiting Scholar at the University of Auckland, New Zealand, and has been teaching in the Program in Second Language Studies at the University of Minnesota, where he was Scholar of the College of Liberal Arts (2002–2005). Cohen was the recipient of the 2006 American Association for Applied Linguistics Distinguished Scholarship and Service Award. He has published numerous research articles on language teaching, language learning, language testing, and research methods, as well as books on bilingual education, on language learning strategies, and on language assessment and research methods. He co-edited *Studying speaking to inform second language learning* with Diana Boxer (Multilingual Matters, 2004) and *Language learner strategies: 30 years of research and practice* with Ernesto Macaro (Oxford University Press, 2007), is co-author of *Teaching and learning pragmatics: Where language and culture meet* (Pearson Education, 2010), and author of *Strategies in learning and using a second language* (Pearson Education, 2011). He is also author of an online course on assessing language ability in adults and young adults in the *ELT Advantage* series with Heinle Cengage Learning. University of Minnesota, MN, USA, e-mail: adcohen@umn.edu

Crisfield, Eowyn She holds a B.A. in TESL, and an M.A. in applied linguistics, both from Concordia University (Canada). She has over 10 years experience teaching ESL/EFL at the post-secondary/adult education level, mainly in Canada and in France. In addition to heading a research project on motivation, she has also been involved in research projects in the fields of teacher-training and sociolinguistics, as well as in curriculum development for ESP courses. She is presently working as a freelance consultant in the Netherlands, where her areas of specialization include teacher-training for non-native immersion teachers and language/educational planning for bilingual children. Concordia University, Montreal, Canada, e-mail: ecrisfield@yahoo.ca

Csizér, Kata She is Assistant Professor at the Department of English Applied Linguistics, School of English and American Studies, Eötvös Loránd University, Budapest. She holds a Ph.D. in language pedagogy and her main field of research interest focuses on the socio-psychological aspects of second language learning and teaching as well as second and foreign language motivation. She has published over 30 academic papers on L2 motivation and related issues and a book titled *Motivation, language attitudes and globalisation* (2006, Multilingual Matters, co-authored by Zoltán Dörnyei and Nóra Németh). Eötvös University, Budapest, Hungary, e-mail: weinkata@yahoo.com

Gabryś-Barker, Danuta She works as Professor at the Institute of English, University of Silesia, Poland. Her major academic interests lie in lexical multilinguality, psycholinguistics, language processing and introspective research methods as applied in SLA, and action research in the context of teacher training at the pre-service level. She published a book on a multilingual mental lexicon *Aspects of multilingual storage, processing, and retrieval* (University of Silesia Press, 2005), edited a volume on *Morphosyntactic issues in second language acquisition* (Multilingual Matters, 2008). She is also the author of numerous articles on various aspects of SLA, and teacher training published in Poland in such journals as *Linguistica Silesiana* or *Neofilolog*, and abroad in *International Journal of Multilingualism*. University of Silesia, Katowice, Poland, e-mail: danutagabrys@hotmail.com

Griffiths, Carol She has considerable experience as a teacher and manager of English for Speakers of Other Languages (ESOL). She graduated with a Ph.D. from the University of Auckland after researching language learning strategy use by ESOL students. She has presented papers at a number of conferences and has had a number of publications. Her book entitled *Lessons from Good Language Learners* (April, 2008) looks at how language is learnt successfully from various perspectives. Carol is currently working as a teacher trainer for the British Council in North Korea (DPRK) and continues to research the question of how students successfully learn language. Yeditepe University, Istanbul, Turkey, e-mail: carolgriffiths5@gmail.com

Jedynak, Małgorzata She works as an academic in English Studies Department, University of Wrocław. In 2004 she obtained her Ph.D. degree in applied linguistics with the thesis entitled *Critical period revisited: the Impact of age on the final attainment in L2 pronunciation.* She expanded her linguistic interests covering a post-graduate course on methodology of teaching the visually impaired learners. Her research papers are related to the acquisition of phonology/phonetics by L2 learners. The recent research she is involved in concerns different aspects related to the acquisition of L1 and L2 by the visually impaired learners: the choice and use of learning strategies, the role of autonomy in the learning process, teaching techniques implemented in an L2 classroom, the issue of giftedness in a foreign language. Institue of English Studies, University of Wrocław, Wrocław, Poland, e-mail: gosiajedynak@poczta.onet.pl

Kębłowska, Magdalena She is a teacher of EFL and ELT methodology at the Teacher Training College, Adam Mickiewicz University, Poznań. She runs B.A. and M.A. seminars as well as post-graduate courses at the College and the School of English, AMU. Her research areas include roles of teachers and affect in SLA. She is an author of a number of syllabuses for English language courses at Polish schools. Teacher Training College, Adam Mickiewicz University, Poznan, Poland, e-mail: magdalenakeblowska@tlen.pl

Leśniewska, Justyna Jagiellonian University, Kraków, Poland

Mercer, Sarah She has a Ph.D. in applied linguistics from the University of Lancaster and currently teaches English language at the University of Graz, Austria. Her research interests cover various aspects of the psychology surrounding the foreign language learning experience including self-concept, motivation, attributions, mindsets and strategies. University of Graz, Graz, Austria, e-mail: sarah.mercer@uni-graz.at

Michońska-Stadnik, Anna She works in the Institute of English Studies at the University of Wrocław, Poland. She teaches mostly graduate students and runs M.A. seminars in applied linguistics and English language teaching methodology. She also teaches EFL methodology to undergraduate students in Karkonosze College in Jelenia Góra. Apart from applied linguistics and ELT methodology, her research interests include: teacher training and development, psycholinguistics and neuro-linguistics. She has published more than 40 research papers and three books, and has taken part in numerous scientific conferences in Poland and abroad. She is currently the Head of Applied Linguistics Section in the Institute of English Studies in Wrocław. University of Wrocław, Wrocław, Poland, e-mail: michsta@uni.wroc.pl

Nava, Andrea He is a Lecturer in English Language and Linguistics in the Faculty of Letters and Philosophy, Università degli Studi di Milano. His main research interests include second language acquisition, grammaticography and the history of language teaching. University of Milan, Milan, Italy, e-mail: andrea.nava@unimi.it

Nijakowska, Joanna She is an Assistant Professor in the Chair of Pragmatics, Institute of English, University of Łódź, Poland. She holds a Ph.D. in linguistics.

A specialist in psycholinguistics, foreign language acquisition and didactics, and learning difficulties, she runs teacher training courses for ELT students and practitioners. She has authored and edited books and papers on EFL and dyslexia and presented her research at European and American academic centers. Her research interests include pragmatics and language learning as well as pragmatic language disorders. Chair of Pragmatics, University of Łódź, Łódź, Poland, e-mail: jnijak@wp.pl

Nikolov, Marianne She is Professor of English Applied Linguistics at University of Pécs, Hungary, where she teaches in the undergraduate and graduate programs of TEFL and Applied Linguistics. She has coordinated a number of large scale national and international projects, has taught abroad in the UK and US, and she has received a Fulbright award. She has published on early start programs, language testing, classroom research, language policy, and teacher education both in English and Hungarian. Her articles have been published in edited volumes and International *Review of Applied Linguistics, Language Learning, Language Teaching Research, Magyar Pedagógia, Modern Nyelvoktatás, NovELTy*, and *System*. University of Pécs, Pécs, Hungary, e-mail: nikolov.marianne@pte.hu

Niżegorodcew, Anna Anna Niżegorodcew Ph.D. is Professor in Applied Linguistics, Chair of the Applied Linguistics Section of the English Studies Department of the Jagiellonian University, Kraków, Poland. She also worked at the Centre for Foreign Teacher Training and European Education of the University of Warsaw. She was Head of the Jagiellonian University Foreign Language Teachers' College. She has published many articles and several books in the field of applied linguistics, psycholinguistics and foreign language teacher training. Her book *Input for instructed L2 learners: The relevance of relevance* (Multilingual Matters, 2007) applies relevance theory to foreign language classroom discourse. Her most recent interests focus on intercultural communication (Niżegorodcew et al, forthcoming). Jagiellonian University, Kraków, Poland, e-mail: annanizegorodcew@gmail.com

Ottó, István He teaches statistics in the graduate program of TEFL and applied linguistics at the University of Pécs, Hungary. He has taken part in a number of large scale national and international projects. He has published on various aspects of individual learner differences including age, language aptitude, motivation, creativity, and language testing, both in English and Hungarian. He developed a localized version of the Modern Language Aptitude Test for Hungarian L2 learners. His articles have been published in edited volumes and *TESOL Quarterly, Language Teaching Research, Magyar Pedagógia, Modern Nyelvoktatás, NovELTy*. Regional Public Administration Office for Southern Transdanubia, Pécs, Hungary, e-mail: iotto@freemail.hu

Pawlak, Mirosław He received his doctoral and postdoctoral degrees from Adam Mickiewicz University in 1999 and 2006, respectively. He is now Head of the Department of English Studies at the Faculty of Pedagogy and Fine Arts in Kalisz of Adam Mickiewicz University, Poznań, Poland, and Professor the

Institute of Modern Languages of the State School of Higher Professional Education in Konin, Poland. His main areas of interest are SLA theory and research, form-focused instruction, classroom discourse, learner autonomy, communication and learning strategies, individual learner differences and pronunciation teaching. His recent publications include *The place of form-focused instruction in the foreign language classroom* (2006, Kalisz–Poznań: Adam Mickiewicz University Press) and several edited collections on learner autonomy, language policies of the Council of Europe, form-focused instruction, individual learner differences, and instructed acquisition of speaking. Adam Mickiewicz University, Kalisz, Poland, e-mail: pawlakmi@amu.edu.pl

Pedrazzini, Luciana She is a Lecturer in English and TEFL Methodology in the Faculty of Letters and Philosophy, Università degli Studi di Milano. Her main research interest are in the area of lexis and include Second Language Acquisition, learner corpora and teacher education University of Milan, Milan, Italy, e-mail: luciana.pedrazzini@unimi.it

Piechurska-Kuciel, Ewa She works at the Department of English, Opole University. She teaches applied linguistics and ELT courses. Her main interests are connected with the role of affective factors in the process of FL acquisition, especially with language anxiety. Opole University, Opole, Poland, e-mail: epiech@uni.opole.pl

Robinson, Peter He is Professor of Linguistics and Second Language Acquisition at Aoyama Gakuin University in Tokyo. His recent publications include *Task complexity, the cognition hypothesis and second language instruction: Special issue of the International Review of Applied Linguistics* (2007), Mouton deGruyter (guest-edited with Roger Gilbart); *The handbook of cognitive linguistics and second language acquisition* (2008), Routledge (co-edited with Nick Ellis); and *Second language task complexity: Researching the cognition hypothesis of language learning and peformance* (2011), John Benjamins. Aoyama Gakuin University, Shibuya-ku, Japan, e-mail: peterr@cl.aoyama.ac.jp

Singleton, David Trinity College Dublin, Dublin, Ireland, e-mail: dsnglton@tcd.ie

White, Joanna She is Professor of Applied Linguistics at Concordia University, and a prolific researcher in the areas of immersion education and child second language acquisition. Concordia University, Montreal, Canada

Wróbel, Szymon He is Professor of Philosophy at the Institute of Philosophy and Sociology of Polish Academy of Sciences in Warsaw and Professor at the Faculty of Pedagogy and Fine Arts of Adam Mickiewicz University in Kalisz. He is a psychologist and philosopher who is interested in contemporary social theory and philosophy of language and mind. His main spheres of scientific interest are the theory of social power, contemporary linguistics and the receptions of psychoanalysis ideas in political theory. Since 2003 Wróbel has been involved in the research project of the British Academy of Sciences and the Polish Academy of

Sciences entitled *Post-Structuralism. Psychoanalysis. Politics.* At present he is preparing his new book entitled *The limits of the political.* Professor Wróbel has published three books and over 60 articles in academic journals. His books include: *Power and reason: The reflective stages of the critical social theory,* Poznań: Adam Mickiewicz University Press 2002; *The galaxies, libraries, ashes. The cartography of monstrous literature.* Kraków: Universitas Press 2001; *The discovery of the unconscious or destruction of the cartesian concept of mind?* Foundation for the Polish Science, Warsaw 1997. Faculty of Pedagogy and Fine Arts, Adam Mickiewicz University, Kalisz, Poland; Institute of Philosophy and Sociology, Polish Academy of Sciences, Warsaw, Poland, e-mail: wrobelsz@gmail.com

Individual Differences in Language Learning and Teaching: Achievements, Prospects and Challenges

Mirosław Pawlak

Abstract There is a consensus that the rate of second/foreign language acquisition and the ultimate level of attainment are to a large extent affected by individual variation among learners, with a range of cognitive, affective and social variables accounting for the fact that some of them are highly successful and others barely move beyond the level of rudimentary communication. Controversy arises, however, when it comes to the identification, description and classification of such factors, determining their influence on attainment, showing how they relate to each other and the processes of language acquisition, or offering consistent and feasible pedagogical recommendations for classroom practice. The present paper, which serves as an introduction to this edited collection, provides an overview of the field by highlighting the most significant accomplishments of research conducted to date, discussing its main shortcomings and presenting the challenges that will have to be confronted in the near future. It also describes the organization of the volume and briefly summarizes the focus of the contributions included in each of the five parts that the book comprises.

Introduction

Even though individual variation plays a significant role in both first and second/foreign language acquisition, determining the rate at which learners master the different components of communicative competence, the crucial difference between these two processes lies in the fact that, barring cases of brain damage or environmental depravation, the former is always successful whereas the latter is not. As Ellis points out, individuals learning an additional language "(…) vary not only in the speed of acquisition but also in their ultimate level of attainment, with a few achieving native-like competence and others stopping far short" (2004: 526). While these differences in achievement can be attributed to a number of factors, such as the amount and quality of naturalistic exposure, the duration and intensity of instruction, teachers' dedication, skills and abilities, the choice of teaching methodology, textbooks and supplementary materials, or the size, composition and dynamics of a particular group, it is individual learner differences that appear to be of vital importance when it comes to deciding success or failure in learning another language. To quote Cohen and Dörnyei, "[w]hen learners embark on the study of an L2, (…) they carry a considerable 'personal baggage' (…) that will have a significant bearing on how learning proceeds. Past research (…) has identified a number of key components of this learner 'baggage' and has also provided clear evidence that these components determine how fast and how well we are likely to master the L2" (2002: 170). Indeed, as shown in recent state-of-the-art publications (e.g. Robinson 2002a; Dörnyei and Skehan 2003; Ehrman et al. 2003; Ellis 2004; Dörnyei 2005; Ellis 2008), such factors as age, aptitude, motivation or strategy use have been found to manifest a strong positive relationship with attainment, thus being potent predictors of success. Although it is clear that these factors interact with one another as well as a number of contextual variables (e.g. the task in hand or the nature of pedagogic intervention), and it is this interaction rather than the contribution of a single trait that eventually accounts for learning outcomes, their importance in the process of studying an L2 cannot be overestimated.

Such encouraging research findings notwithstanding, individual characteristics have traditionally remained on the sidelines of the field of second language acquisition (SLA), which has mainly been preoccupied with establishing similarities between learners with an eye to exploring those processes of language learning which are universal and, once identified and understood, can provide a basis for making concrete recommendations for classroom practice (Skehan 1989; Dörnyei and Skehan 2003; Dörnyei 2005; Ellis 2008). Although recent years have seen signs of a major reversal in this respect, with researchers gaining fresh insights into the nature and impact of some individual characteristics, numerous areas remain in need of further investigation, the latest developments in SLA have to be taken into account, stronger links with psychology have to be forged, interactions between different variables must be explored, and the impact of different traits on learning outcomes should be determined, not only in isolation but also in combination with mediating factors. This edited volume seeks to contribute to all these lines of enquiry by bringing together papers by internationally famous scholars and Polish researchers which take stock of the key developments in research into individual characteristics, and attempt to offer fresh insights in this area, touching upon such neglected issues as individual variation among teachers and learning difficulties. The main aim of this introductory chapter is to provide a backdrop for the specific issues investigated in the articles included in the collection by briefly outlining various approaches to defining and classifying individual differences (ID), discussing the major trends in research methodology, highlighting the most significant developments in the field, identifying the challenges that will have to be tackled in the near future and commenting on the organization of the book.

Definitions and Classifications of Individual Differences

Gaining in-depth understanding of the contributions of individual differences in language learning and teaching is bound to pose a formidable challenge even for experienced scholars not only because of the complex, multifaceted and inter-disciplinary nature of the field, but also on account of the inconsistency with which specific concepts are defined, characterized, classified and measured. According to Dörnyei (2005: 4), individual differences "(...) refer to dimensions of enduring personal characteristics that are assumed to apply to everybody and on which people differ by degrees (...) in other words, they concern stable and systematic deviations from a normal blueprint". On the face of it, such a definition appears to be rather uncontroversial and it resonates in many other accounts of the charac-teristics that learners bring to the task of learning foreign languages. Still, even in this case, questions arise as to the impact of the genetic endowment and the environment, the aggregate or differentiated nature of these variables, the extent to which they are indeed stable and can be subject to external manipulation, the likelihood that learners are capable of manifesting opposite dimensions of the same trait in different contexts, or the assumption that the role of IDs may vary depending on the aspect of target language proficiency. Even more acute problems are discernible when it comes to the definition of specific individual variables, which is evident, for example, in the lack of consensus as to whether cognitive styles and learning styles refer to the same concepts or perhaps should be differ-entiated, the degree to which intelligence overlaps the notion of language aptitude, or the controversy as to whether learning strategies can be distinguished from ordinary learning activities (cf. Brown 2001; Dörnyei and Skehan 2003; Dörnyei 2005; Ellis 2008). Inevitably, conceptual difficulties of this kind translate into serious problems involved in designing and conducting research projects, they may affect their findings and make comparisons between different studies difficult, if not impossible.

Another major woe of the study of individual differences is reflected in the attempts undertaken by theorists and researchers to classify the diverse variables which may influence the rate of learning and ultimate levels of achievement. Even a cursory look at the literature reveals that there is enormous variation in this respect, with different scholars proposing competing taxonomies, including dif-fering sets of variables, assigning them to quite disparate categories and labeling similar concepts in various ways. In his textbook intended for teacher education programs, for example, Brown (2001), chooses to make a distinction between *styles and strategies*, *personality factors* and *sociocultural aspects* but decides to discuss such crucial aspects as age, aptitude and intelligence in separate chapters devoted to acquisition and human learning. In addition, he seems to equate cog-nitive styles with learning styles, views motivation as a personality variable and has little to say about the impact of gender or socioeconomic factors. In another methodology coursebook, Johnson (2001) introduces a rather confusing division of individual differences into *cognitive*, *affective* and *personality variables* as well as *learning strategies*, making such controversial decisions as classifying attitudes as affective rather than sociocultural factors, viewing cognitive styles as personality variables or ignoring age altogether. A very different approach is evident in the latest edition of the textbook for language teachers authored by Cook (2008), who deliberately eschews a comprehensive taxonomy and focuses primarily on such variables as *motivation, attitudes, aptitude* and *age*, offering only very brief comments on the contribution of cognitive styles, personality factors, intelligence, gender, first language level and empathy.

Somewhat surprisingly, such problems are also evident in more comprehensive and detailed state-of-the-art overviews of research into individual differences, penned by leading figures in the field and functioning as a source of inspiration and reference for students and scholars interested in pursuing this line of enquiry. Cohen and Dörnyei (2002), for example, frame their discussion around the distinction between those *learner characteristics that are beyond the teacher's control*, such as age, gender and aptitude, and *those which can be actively shaped to increase the effectiveness of instruction*, such as motivation, learning styles and learner strategies. Several important factors (e.g. intelligence, personality) are omitted in this review, others (age, gender, aptitude, cognitive styles) are only given scant attention, which is perhaps reflective of the interests of the authors themselves, and the degree to which external manipulation may indeed be effective in some cases is anybody's guess. Ellis (2004), in turn, groups what he views as a daunting array of individual factors according to whether they represent *abilities* (i.e. relatively immutable cognitive capabilities for language learning), such as intelligence, aptitude or memory, *propensities* (i.e. changeable cognitive and affective qualities which manifest learner preparedness or orientation to language learning), such as learning style, motivation, anxiety, personality and willingness to communicate, *learner cognitions about L2 learning* (i.e. their beliefs and, arguably, also their expectations and preferences about learning and teaching), and *learner actions* (i.e. learning strategies). While several learner characteristics are missing from this overview (e.g. empathy, inhibition), it is the absence of age that is the most conspicuous, a choice that Ellis (2004: 529) justifies by saying that it "(…) does not belong to any of the four categories; rather, it potentially affects learners' abilities, propensities, cognitions and actions (as do other factors such as previous learning experiences and the learning situation)". He adopts a similar approach in his latest overview of SLA research (Ellis 2008) where age is considered at the outset rather than in the chapter dealing with IDs, and so does Dörnyei (2005: 8) in his cutting-edge book on learner characteristics, on grounds that age and gender are demographic variables which "(….) affect every aspect of the SLA process, including virtually all the other ID variables".

Generally speaking, there has been a marked tendency in many recent publications on individual differences to be selective in the choice of variables to be discussed and to avoid classifying the different factors into broader categories perhaps in recognition of the fact that some of them are the outcome of the complex interaction between cognition, affect and social influences. This approach, somewhat reminiscent of the one taken by Skehan (1989) in his landmark book on IDs, is visible in the volumes by Dörnyei (2005) and Ellis (2008), where some issues are purposefully omitted or discussed in a context other than individual factors and the different variables are dealt with separately rather than neatly compartmentalized into discrete subdivisions. It is also embraced by Dörnyei and Skehan (2003), who elect to focus on variables which are considered to have considerable potential in predicting success in L2 learning, namely *aptitude, cognitive and learning styles, learning strategies* and *motivation*, Ehrman et al. (2003), who confine their discussion to *learning styles, learning strategies* and *affective variables*, as well as Gass and Selinker (2008), who discuss individual variation in a chapter devoted to factors falling beyond the language domain, looking at *affect, social distance, age, aptitude, motivation, personality, learning styles* and *learning strategies*. Yet another interesting trend is that most such overviews tend to ignore the impact of learning deficits and typically pay little heed to the fact that individual differences apply not only to learners but also to their teachers, most of whom are non-native speakers and thus learners themselves, and who are bound to make instructional decisions in accordance with their own personal characteristics. Rare exceptions in this respect are the edited volume by Robinson (2002b), which features a paper by Grigorenko (2002) addressing the impact of first language disabilities on L2 acquisition, and the article by Ehrman et al. (2003: 324) who admit that "(…) just as students vary, so do teachers: in motivation, in overall aptitude, in self-efficacy as teachers, in teaching/learning styles, and in preferred strategies". Although these are welcome signs that the present research agenda is being extended, there is a need to conduct studies in these two neglected but vitally important areas, a problem that some papers included in this publication seek to rectify. All things considered, it seems that more rigor is needed in describing individual differences to impose order on the numerous factors that have been identified as predictors of success, and to propose a comprehensive framework which can serve as a point of reference for further theorizing and research in this area.

Issues in Research Methodology

Following the distinction introduced by McLaughlin (1987), Skehan (1989) proposes two contrasting approaches which can be drawn upon in the investigation of individual differences that he calls the *hierarchical approach* and the *concatenative approach*. While the former adopts a theory-then-research position, predicts how a specific variable might affect language learning, allows hypothesis formation and testing, and aspires to have explanatory power, the latter takes as its point of departure the identification of a relatively circumscribed area that may provide insights into the interaction between IDs and learning outcomes, explores the relationships between numerous factors and success, and then uses the facts detected in this way to construct theoretical models. While much of the early research into individual factors was concatenative in nature, prime examples thereof being the good language learner studies of the 1970s (Rubin 1975; Stern 1975; Naiman et al. 1996/1978), more recently researchers have manifested a proclivity for the hierarchical approach in an attempt to explore hypotheses concerning the impact of specific variables, as is the case with numerous studies examining the relationship between strategy use and proficiency (see Dörnyei 2005; Cohen and Macaro 2007; Ellis 2008, for reviews) (cf. Ellis 2008). Whether such a shift should be perceived as unequivocally beneficial is a contentious issue since more principled and systematic as it undoubtedly is, the theory-then-research perspective may lack adequate depth to provide the so much needed insights into the genuine contributions of specific variables or account for the intricate relationships between them, which implies that it should at least be complemented with research of the concatenative type. In fact, it was the importance of this kind of research that Skehan (1989: 150) emphasized twenty years ago when he commented that research on individual differences "(...) is necessary from a theory-building perspective since it is more likely to enable the broad outlines of second and foreign language research to be established, and consequently to provide an evaluative framework for more small-scale and theory-driven work to be located". Although we currently know much more about learner characteristics then we did then, the difficulty in establishing a coherent taxonomy of these variables suggests that the hierarchical and concatenative perspectives should indeed be combined if significant progress is expected to be made in the near future.

As regards data collection and analysis in ID research, it has primarily been quantitative in nature and only recently have more qualitative approaches started to gain ground and be employed with more frequency, either in their own right or alongside the usual numerical procedures (cf. Ellis 2004, 2008). In the case of quantitative research, information about the variable in question is typically collected by means of a self-report questionnaire which more often than not draws upon some variation of Likert-scale items. Whereas some of these data-collection instruments, such as the *Group Embedded Figures Test* (Witkin et al. 1971), the *Myers-Briggs Type Indicator* (MBTI) (Myers and Briggs 1976) or the *Learning Style Inventory* (Kolb 1984), have been borrowed from general psychology, others have been specifically designed to explore the characteristics of language learners, with such examples as the *Attitude/Motivation Test Battery* (Gardner 1985), the *Strategy Inventory for Language Learning* (Oxford 1990), the *Perceptual Learning Style Preference Questionnaire* (Reid 1987), the *Learning Strategy Use Inventory and Index* (Cohen and Chi 2002), or the *Learning Style Questionnaire* (Ehrman and Leaver 2003). As Skehan (1989) emphasizes, the design of such research tools must involve informed operationalization of the construct to be examined, careful choice and wording of specific items, and determining their reliability and validity, a procedure that is rigorously followed in the construction of well-established instruments such as those listed above. However, this should not be taken to mean that they are free from shortcomings, since, as Dörnyei (2005) argues, even some of those very frequently used may fail to provide an adequate picture of the factors they purport to tap. Since many quantitative studies seek to determine the relationship between a specific variable and learning outcomes, another crucial issue is the choice of achievement measures which range from subjects' self-assessments to their scores on standardized proficiency tests, and can substantially affect the findings. Once such data have been obtained, statistical procedures, such as Pearson product moment correlation, Spearman's rank order correlation, factor analysis or multiple regression are employed with a view to establishing the strength of relationships between variables or a specific ID and target language proficiency. Since the existence of strong, significant positive correlations does not provide a basis for making claims about cause-and-effect relationships, some studies employ such statistical tools as the analysis of variance (ANOVA) or structural equation modeling (SEM) in order to establish the direction of causality (cf. Ellis 2008).

Apart from the inherent difficulty in determining by means of correlational techniques whether a particular factor causes or influences another, yet another problem of quantitative research is that it provides rather general and oversimplified information that may not reflect learners' attitudes, feelings, thoughts or behaviors as they deal with different tasks in different contexts. For example, when responding to the Likert-scale items concerning strategy use included in the SILL (Oxford 1990), such as 'I look for patterns in the new language' or 'I ask other people to correct my pronunciation', learners may be in a quandary over which answer to indicate since their actions are bound to vary according to circumstances (e.g. the amount of time available, access to adequate language data, familiarity with another learner, degree of self-confidence). There are also serious doubts surrounding the validity of some of even the most established and frequently used data collection tools, as is the case with the *Embedded Figures Test* (EFT) which aims to measure the degree of field independence but, according to Dörnyei (2005: 139), its overall score "(...) is more like an ability score, ranging from bad to good, than a bipolar cognitive style score". Similar reservations have been voiced concerning the immensely popular SILL since factor analysis has failed to verify the distinct character of the various categories (e.g. Robson and Midorikawa 2001) and, to quote Dörnyei (2005: 182) again, "the scales are not cumulative and computing mean scale scores is psychometrically not justifiable". It is such shortcomings that have prompted researchers to turn to qualitative procedures, with some of them going as far as to advocate total rejection of questionnaires as viable data collection tools (e.g Spielman and Radnofsky 2001). Among others, qualitative research has addressed such issues as motivation (e.g. Ushioda 2001; Kim 2009), anxiety (e.g. Spielman and Radnofsky 2001; Gregersen and Horwitz 2002), beliefs (e.g. Hosenfeld 2003; Kramsch 2003), or learning strategies (e.g. Gao 2003; Pawlak 2008a).

While the merits of such studies are undeniable since they provide valuable insights into the situated, context-dependent nature of individual characteristics as well as the intricate ways in which they interact with each other, it would appear, however, that the application of quantitative procedures is inevitable when researchers wish to move beyond the stage of identification, description or classification. This is because qualitative analysis alone is simply too impressionistic and subjective when it comes to exploring such issues as the strength of the relationship between variables, the link between a specific ID factor and attainment, or the value of learner training programs. For this reason, perhaps the best solution is to combine the quantitative and qualitative approach, either within a single study, by, for example, employing several data collection instruments (e.g. diaries, interviews, test scores, surveys) or at the very least including open-ended items in self-report questionnaires, or across different studies, so that their findings complement each other and eventually furnish a more accurate, detailed and reliable picture of the relevant trait. The need for hybrid research of this kind is emphasized by Spolsky (2000) and Ellis (2004), the latter of whom mentions the studies conducted by Abraham and Vann (1987) and Schumann (1997) as prime illustrations of this approach, and argues that it "(…) is likely to provide a much richer and personalized account of the factors responsible for learner difference" (2004: 529). He hastens to add, however, that "(…) there are few examples in the published literature on individual differences, doubtless because this kind of research is very time consuming" (2008: 648).

Overview of Key Developments in Research into Individual Differences

The literature on individual differences in language learning and teaching is so extensive and rich, it touches upon such a huge array of diverse factors and adopts such distinct theoretical perspectives that any attempt to provide a comprehensive and exhaustive account of the latest developments in the field, let alone give justice to its evolution over that last few decades in this limited space would be doomed to failure. Apart from this, many of the articles included in this collection contain sometimes quite detailed summaries of the main research findings in the areas they explore and, thus, it would make little sense to attempt a necessarily much less extensive and in-depth overview at this point. Nevertheless, it seems warranted to highlight in this introductory chapter some of the most significant developments in the field, especially those related to factors the investigation of which holds considerable promise for explicating the causes of success and failure in learning additional languages, such that have only recently been identified as potential predictors of attainment as well as those that are of particular relevance to practitioners. For this reason, the discussion in the present section will mainly be confined to such factors as *age, intelligence, aptitude, cognitive* and *learning* styles, *learning strategies, motivation, anxiety, beliefs* and *willingness to communicate*. Some comments will also be offered on the ways in which these traits may impact learners' preferences concerning different aspects of instruction, their behaviors during a lesson and their performance, as well as how they may influence teachers' classroom practices.

It is perhaps fitting to start this brief overview with a glance at three factors which can be regarded as cognitive in nature, remain largely beyond the control of teachers and learners, and have traditionally been perceived as major influences on ultimate attainment, namely *age*, *intelligence* and *aptitude*. As regards the first of these variables, evidence has accumulated that, in contrast to first language acquisition, in the case of second language learning, it is better to talk about a *sensitive* rather than a *criticalperiod* on account of the fact that ability to learn does not abruptly cease to exist but, rather, gradually deteriorates over a period of time and does allow a degree of success (cf. Harley and Wang 1997; Eubank and Gregg 1999). As Ellis comments, "[o]verall (…) the research indicates no clear discontinuity in learning as a result of age. Rather, the ability to learn an L2 declines gradually with age. Also, there is growing evidence that some learners who start learning as adults can achieve native-like competence" (2008: 31). On the other hand, however, there are studies indicating that lack of exposure in the first months of life may result in subtle differences in some aspects of proficiency. This led Hyltenstam and Abrahamson to suggest that "(…) absolute native-like command of an L2 may be impossible for any learner" (2003: 575), and Long to hypothesize that "(…) the effect of early exposure to one or more additional languages beyond the L1 is neurophysiological, and a neurophysiological change that is lasting, persisting at least throughout the normal first language acquisition period (…) continues into the early teens (…)" (2007: 74). Still, whether or not such assumptions offer support for *the younger the better principle* is debatable since few learners strive after native-like proficiency anyway, some exceptional adult learners are capable of becoming almost indistinguishable from native speakers, and the discrepancies are mostly visible in pronunciation which is not the sole or the most important measure of success. Moreover, a very early start may be of little relevance in foreign language contexts where scant exposure has to be compensated for by conscious study in which older learners are likely to excel and individual characteristics such as aptitude or motivation may come to the fore, especially after the critical period closes (Cohen and Dörnyei 2002; Ioup 2005; Muñoz and Singleton 2011).

While the findings of research into maturational constraints have not dramatically modified the earliest claims about the existence of a critical or sensitive period, the developments in the area of intelligence have been far more groundbreaking. It is clear, for instance, that the traditional notion of intelligence, measured in terms of linguistic and logical-mathematical abilities, is inadequate to account for success or failure in all aspects of second language learning because although IQ test scores are related to what Cummins (1980) described as *cognitive/academic language proficiency* (CALP), they do not correlate with what he labeled *basic interpersonal communicative skills* (BICS) (Genesee 1976; Brown 2001; Johnson 2001). One approach to dealing with this apparent limitation was proposed by Gardner (1983) in his *multiple intelligences theory*, which posits that instead of viewing intelligence as a unitary concept we should recognize different types of intelligences that learners may possess, that is not only linguistic and mathematical-logical but also spatial, musical, bodily-kinesthetic, interpersonal, intrapersonal and naturalistic. However, while this idea has an understandable appeal to language teachers who can use it as a basis for planning activities which cater to the strengths of particular learners, it has little empirical support and it is quite difficult to implement in a typical classroom (cf. Waterhouse 2006). Somewhat more promising perhaps appears to be Sternberg's (1988, 2002) *theory of successful intelligence*, which deemphasizes mental speed and distinguishes *analytical intelligence* (i.e. the ability to analyze, compare and evaluate), *creativeintelligence* (i.e. the ability to find novel solutions), and *practical intelligence*, (i.e. the ability to manipulate the environment). In fact, the second of these has recently started to be explored by second language acquisition researchers, with the studies conducted by Ottó (1998) and Albert and Kormos (2004) identifying a positive relationship between creativity and target language performance.

Closely related to the concept of intelligence is the notion of *language aptitude*, or "(...) a specific talent for learning foreign languages which exhibits considerable variation between learners" (Dörnyei and Skehan 2003: 590), an attribute which does not determine the ultimate level of proficiency which an individual can accomplish but, rather, affects the *rate* at which he or she will progress in mastering an L2. Also in this case huge advances have been made since the first unscientific prognosis tests appeared in the US between 1925 and 1930 (Spolsky 1995) and then two commercial aptitude batteries for adolescents and adults were developed in the form of Carroll and Sapon's (1959) *Modern Language Aptitude Test* (MLAT) and Pimsleur's (1966) *Language Aptitude Battery* (PLAB). In the first place, although it was argued from the very beginning that aptitude is not a unitary factor but rather a composite of different abilities, Carroll's (1981) conceptualization of the notion in terms of *phonetic coding ability*, *grammatical sensitivity*, *rote learning ability* and *inductive language learning ability* has been subject to considerable modifications. For instance, Skehan (1989) collapsed the original model into a three-way distinction between *auditory ability*, *linguistic ability* and *memory ability*, Sasaki (1996) found that it comprises both *general cognitive abilities* and *specific linguistic ones*, Grigorenko et al. (2000), drawing upon the theory of successful intelligence, operationalized it as five *acquisition processes* performed in the visual and oral mode at the level of lexis, morphology, semantics and syntax, while Robinson (2005) proposed an aptitude complex consisting of ten basic cognitive abilities drawn upon in different learning conditions. Naturally, such new conceptualizations necessitated the development of alternative aptitude batteries, good examples of which are Parry and Child's (1990) VORD, Grigorenko et al. (2000) *Cognitive Ability for Novelty in Acquisition of Language as applied to foreign language test* (CANAL-FT) or Kiss and Nikolov's (2005) aptitude test for children. None of these tests, however, has proved superior to MLAT in predicting proficiency with respect to both explicit and implicit learning (Sawyer and Ranta 2001). Other key advances in the field of language aptitude research include the *linguistic coding differences hypothesis* (Sparks et al. 1995), which links the capacity for second language learning with first language literacy skills such as phonological/orthographic processing or word recognition/decoding, the recognition of the potential of working memory capacity to predict TL proficiency (Miyake and Friedman 1998; Sawyer and Ranta 2001; Mackey et al. 2002; Ortega 2009; DeKeyser and Koeth 2011), research into the interaction of aptitude complexes, task demands, and learning outcomes (Robinson 2001a, 2002a, 2007; DeKeyser and Koeth 2011), or an attempt to relate the components of language aptitude to different phases of the process of acquisition (Skehan 2002). Irrespective of which of these lines of enquiry will eventually prove the most illuminating or when it will become possible to integrate the different approaches, it is as clear as it was almost fifty years ago that, to quote Gardner and MacIntyre (1992: 215), "(…) in the long run language aptitude is probably the single best predictor of achievement in a second language".

Another two individual variables that are also largely cognitive in nature but are open to some degree of external manipulation are *cognitive styles*, often referred to as *learning styles*, and *learning strategies*. As regards the former, they are an attractive concept to researchers and practitioners alike because distinct predispositions to process information, solve problems and deal with learning situations have their own strengths and weaknesses and may contribute in different ways to the mastery of various aspects of the target language, which indicates that an approach which may be a liability in one context can prove advantageous in another. Equally important is the fact that, although learning styles are relatively stable characteristics, teachers can modify classroom activities in such a way that they are more compatible with the style preferences of particular learners or at least ensure greater variety, and, in the course of time, learners themselves may be induced to engage in *style stretching* by experimenting with new ways of approaching learning tasks (Oxford 2001; Cohen and Dörnyei 2002; Dörnyei and Skehan 2003). The promise of the concept of learning style, however, may be somewhat exaggerated in view of the fact that, according to Dörnyei (2005: 120), "(…) the area is a real quagmire: There is a confusing plethora of labels and style dimensions; there is a shortage of valid and reliable measurement instruments; there is a confusion in the underlying theory; and the practical implications put forward in the literature are scarce and rather mixed, and rarely helpful". For one thing, there is a tendency to equate cognitive and learning styles and combine them in various classifications, which is misleading since, as Dörnyei and Skehan (2003: 602) explain, "the former (…) is more restricted to information-processing preferences while the latter embraces all aspects of learning". Secondly, cognitive and learning styles have been conceptualized in disparate ways and various descriptive models have been proposed, only some of which aim to specifically investigate language learning. The most influential of these include Witkin et al.'s (1971) distinction between *field-independence* and *field-dependence*, Reid's (1987) identification of *perceptual learning modalities* (i.e. visual, auditory, kinesthetic and tactile), Willing's (1987) differentiation between *concrete, analytical, communicative* and *authority-oriented learning styles*, Riding's (1991) taxonomy based on the superordinate dimensions of the *wholist-analytic* and *verbal-imagery style*, Skehan's (1998) description of learners as *analysis-oriented* or *memory-oriented*, and Ehrman and Leaver's (2003) construct differentiating between *ectasis* and *synopsis* (i.e. need for conscious or unconscious learning, respectively).

Unavoidably, the emergence of all these descriptive systems was accompanied by the development of related assessments tools, which makes it difficult to compare research findings across studies or offer sound pedagogical proposals. Thirdly, and perhaps most importantly, as Ellis (2008: 672) points out, "(…) there is very little evidence to show that learning styles (as currently conceptualized) are strongly related to proficiency and (…) none to show how they relate to the process of learning", a major limitation which casts doubt on the rationale behind giving this line of enquiry such a high profile. It remains to be seen whether recently developed instruments intended to tap into style preferences, such as the *Learning Style Survey* (Cohen and Chi 2002) or the *Learning Style Questionnaire* (Ehrman and Leaver 2003) will enable us to more precisely define and categorize learning styles, explicate their complex nature and interactions with other IDs, or understand their contributions to language learning.

If cognitive and learning styles can be modified in only extremely limited ways, there is copious evidence that learners can be successfully trained in effective application of learning strategies which Oxford defines as "(…) specific actions taken by the learner to make learning easier, faster, more enjoyable, more self-directed, more effective, and more transferrable to new situations" (1990: 8). Considerable effort has been expended on investigating different facets of strategic devices since Rubin (1975) spearheaded research into the characteristics of good language learners and the advances in this area can hardly be overestimated. Among other things, a number of individual, group and situational variables affecting strategy choice and use (age, gender, motivation, personality, culture, goals, learning situation, etc.) have been identified (Takeuchi et al. 2007), a positive relationship between the application of strategies and achievement has been established (Anderson 2005), different forms of strategies-based instruction have been devised (Rubin et al. 2007), and the research methods employed in empirical investigations have been refined and considerably improved (White et al. 2007; Oxford 2011). Given such undeniable accomplishments, it must come as a surprise that despite all the research endeavors specialists have not so far been able to resolve some fundamental issues regarding the definition, classification, distinctive characteristics and value of strategic behaviors (cf. Grenfell and Macaro 2007; Cohen 2011). For example, whereas Oxford's (1990) conceptualization stresses their functional dimension and recognizes the totality of an individual's contributions to the learning process (i.e. intellectual, social, emotional and physical), O'Malley and Chamot (1990) place a premium on cognitive aspects of strategy use, a view which is supported by Macaro (2006) who opposes considering strategies in terms of overt behavior. Such problems, in turn, result in difficulties connected with classifying strategic devices, with some specialists making a distinction between *learning*, *production* and *communication strategies* (Tarone 1980), others combining the three groups in a single taxonomy which includes the category of *compensation strategies* (Oxford 1990), others differentiating between *language learning* and *language use strategies* (Cohen and Dörnyei 2002), and others yet dividing strategic devices according to language skills and subsystems. There is also no consensus as to the level of consciousness and attention involved in strategy use, the merits of viewing strategies on a micro- or macro-level, the basis for distinguishing strategic learning from ordinary learning, or the belief that their frequent application leads to enhanced TL proficiency (Dörnyei 2005; Cohen 2007; Takeuchi et al. 2007; Ellis 2008). Ambiguities of this kind have led some scholars (Dörnyei and Skehan 2003; Dörnyei 2005) to call into question the very existence of strategy as a psychological construct, and to advocate abandoning the term altogether in favor of the notion of *self-regulation*, understood as the extent to which learners actively participate in their own learning and comprising the diverse cognitive, metacognitive, motivational, behavioral or environmental resources they can apply to enhance this process. Griffiths (2008a: 85) argues, however, that "the self-regulation concept does not remove the need for a strategy concept, neither does it do anything to resolve battles over definition". She brings together the areas of consensus and proposes a conceptualization of language learning strategies as "[a]ctivities consciously chosen by learners for the purpose of regulating their own learning" (2008a: 87). This approach might indeed be salutary given the tangibility of strategic behaviors for teachers and learners or the fact that training students in their use is likely to enhance learning, lead to better outcomes and foster autonomy. Combined with the latest developments in the field which include examining strategies in the context of specific tasks, focusing on the quality rather than quantity of strategy use or exploring the application of strategies in such neglected areas as grammar and pronunciation, adopting this operational definition may be a point of departure for disentangling at least some of the complexities discussed above.

Also highly amenable to outside influences is *motivation* which, as Leaver, Ehrman and Shekhtman so aptly put it, "(...) is behind all the choices you make and everything you do" (2005: 104), and which, quite unsurprisingly, has been found to account for almost as much variance in learners' achievement as aptitude (cf. Ellis 2004, 2008). Over the last few decades this factor has been addressed in numerous studies, a phenomenon that can be ascribed to its considerable relevance to both practitioners and researchers as an attribute which aids learners in sustaining their efforts to confront the often arduous, long and tedious challenge of learning a foreign language, has the potential to compensate at least to some extent for maturational constraints, low aptitude or unfavorable learning conditions, and can be consciously promoted in the classroom. Dörnyei (2005) divides research into L2 motivation into three phases: (1) *the social-psychological period*, which lasted from 1959 to 1990 and was dominated by the work conducted within the framework of Gardner (1985) *socio-educational model of second language acquisition* and Clément's (1980) *theory of linguistic self-confidence*, (2) *the cognitive-situated period*, which was in its heyday in the 1990s and was marked by empirical investigations taking as a point of reference cognitive theories in educational psychology, such as *self-determination theory* (Deci and Ryan 1985, 2002) and *attribution theory* (Weiner 1992), or those which examined motivation in specific learning situations, and (3) *the process-oriented period*, which was initiated with the beginning of the new millennium and emphasizes the dynamic nature of motivation (Dörnyei 2000, 2001a, 2001b). Since Gardner's theory of motivation failed to take into account the classroom context (Crookes and Schmidt

1991) and thus "(...) the angle of enquiry it promoted yielded few genuinely useful insights for teachers and learners" (Ushioda 2008: 20), it seems warranted to confine our discussion to the key developments of the last two decades. One potentially fruitful line of enquiry is the study of the construction of motivation in the performance of communicative tasks (e.g. Dörnyei and Kormos 2000; Kormos and Dörnyei 2004), which led Dörnyei (2005) to propose a *dynamic task processing system* composed of the interrelated mechanisms of *task execution, appraisal* and *action control*. A related but far more consequential development is the recognition of the *dynamic nature* and *temporal variation* of motivation, which was first voiced in the work of Williams and Burden (1997) who view motivation on a continuum and distinguish between three stages of the motivational process, that is *reasons for doing something, deciding to do something* and *sustaining the effort or persisting*. This proposal is further explored in the *process model of motivation* put forward by Dörnyei and Ottó (1998) and later extended by Dörnyei (2001a, 2001b), which depicts the progression of learner motivation in terms of the *preactional stage* (i.e. *choice motivation*), the *actional stage* (i.e. *executive motivation*), and the *postactional stage* (i.e. *motivational retrospection*), associates the three phases with the different motives posited by various motivational theories, and identifies the motivational strategies which may be associated with each stage. Also of interest are attempts to shed light on the ways in which social processes and influences shape individuals' motivations (Norton and Toohey 2001), in particular those drawing upon *sociocultural theory* (e.g. Bronson 2000; Ushioda 2007), as well as the investigation of the efforts learners make to sustain their motivation and stay focused on their goals, intentions and tasks, referred to as *self-motivating strategies* (Dörnyei 2001a), *anxiety management* (Horwitz 2001), *efficacy management* (Wolters 2003) or *motivational self-regulation* (Ushioda 2003; Dörnyei 2005; Ushioda 2008). The latest and perhaps very promising research direction is the *theory of L2 motivational self-esteem* (e.g. Dörnyei and Csizér 2002; Csizér and Dörnyei 2005; Dörnyei 2005; Dörnyei 2009). It reinterprets the notion of *integrativeness* as a second language-related facet of *anideal self*, defined as "(...) the representation of the attributes that one would ideally like to possess (i.e. representation of hopes, aspirations, or wishes)" (Dörnyei 2009: 13), and is based on the assumption that "(....) if proficiency in the target language is part and parcel of one's ideal or *ought-to self*, this will serve as a powerful motivator to learn a language because of our psychological desire to reduce the discrepancy between our current and possible future selves" (Ushioda and Dörnyei 2009: 4).

The last three individual factors to be discussed in this section, namely *anxiety*, *beliefs* and *willingness to communicate*, are also of immediate concern to practitioners and can be to some extent addressed in everyday teaching practice. *Language anxiety*, which is a situation specific type of anxiety and involves "(...) the worry and negative emotional reaction aroused when learning or using a second language" (MacIntyre 1999: 27), is intricately related to such factors as self-esteem, inhibition or risk-taking, and may be a major influence on achievement. The research conducted to date has mainly focused upon pinpointing the sources of anxiety (e.g. Gregersen and Horwitz 2002), the relationship between anxiety and learning outcomes (e.g. Horwitz 2001), the impact of language anxiety on the process of learning (e.g. MacIntyre and Gardner 1991), and some studies have combined all of these foci examining in addition the characteristics of learners with high levels of language anxiety (e.g. Piechurska-Kuciel 2008). A crucial insight deriving from such empirical investigations is that anxiety is a dynamic factor which interacts with other variables and, depending on a particular learner, it can facilitate the learning process, impede it, be the result rather than the cause of learning difficulties, or have no effect on attainment (Ellis 2008). As regards *learner beliefs*, Dörnyei (2005) expresses doubts as to whether they constitute enduring learner traits and should be included in the discussion of individual variables, a view that is challenged by Ellis (2008: 699) who argues that "(…) clearly learners do vary considerably in their beliefs about language and language learning and it is reasonable to assume that their beliefs influence both the process and product of learning". Over the years, researchers have identified various types of beliefs, with Wenden (1991) linking them with metacognitive knowledge, Benson and Lor (1999) making a distinction between *higher-order conceptions* (quantitative/analytic vs. qualitative/experiential) and *lower-order beliefs* (about the nature of language and language learning), and Mori (1999) identifying such dimensions as *perception of the difficulty of language learning, the effectiveness of approaches to or strategies for language learning* and *the source of linguistic knowledge*. As is the case with motivation and anxiety, it has been found that learner beliefs are also content-dependent and subject to considerable modification over time, likely under the influence of predominant instructional practices (e.g. Kern 1995; Tanaka 2004). There have been few studies seeking to establish the link between beliefs and learning outcomes, and they have yielded mixed results (e.g. Mori 1999; Tanaka and Ellis 2003), which, however, should come as no surprise since "(…) the fact that learners hold a particular belief is no guarantee they will act on it" (Ellis 2008: 703). Finally, *willingness to communicate*, can be defined as "the intention to initiate communication, given a choice" (MacIntyre et al. 2001: 369) and, as such, it is of pivotal significance to communicative approaches where learners' readiness to speak is a major factor affecting learning outcomes. While this attribute is relatively stable in the first language, in second language learning it is influenced by a number of linguistic and psychological variables (cf. MacIntyre et al. 1998, 2003), such as *communication anxiety, perceived communication competence, perceived behavioral control*, including *opportunities for L2 communication*, or *international posture* (cf. MacIntyre et al. 2001; Yashima 2002; Clément et al. 2003). There is also evidence that willingness to communicate is in a constant state of flux, changing on a moment-to-moment basis as opportunities to speak arise in different communicative tasks, as demonstrated in a recent study conducted by MacIntyre and Legatto (2011). Since lowering anxiety levels in language lessons, shaping belief systems in such a way that they will result in the selection of the most advantageous strategies or creating conditions in which learners will be eager to engage in TL communication are all tasks that teachers are invariably confronted with, there is a clear need for further theorizing and research in these areas.

Even if the available research findings are sometimes inconclusive, it stands to reason that the factors discussed above are bound to interact with each other and affect both learners and teachers, often in quite complex, intricate and unpredictable ways. For example, although age or aptitude are undoubtedly powerful predictors of success, caution should be exercised in claiming that learners who are past the critical period or manifest little talent for languages are necessarily at a disadvantage since these unpropitious circumstances can in many cases be compensated for by creativity, motivation, beliefs or expert strategy use. Conversely, as most teachers would testify, even a very early start or an exceptional gift for language learning do not guarantee high levels of achievement if learners are not sufficiently motivated, they do not receive adequate guidance or are confronted with unfavorable learning conditions. In a similar vein, although research shows that some cognitive styles are more characteristic of successful learners than others (e.g. field-independence), given the complexity and multidimensionality of language learning, it would appear that a much more significant trait is the capacity to adjust one's stylistic preferences in response to contextual factors such as the requirements of a specific task (cf. Chapelle and Roberts 1986; Nel 2008). It should also be kept in mind that many individual variables are intertwined and interrelated (e.g. aptitude, intelligence and cognitive styles), they may be determined by other factors (e.g. learning strategies or willingness to communicate), they may be composed of more specific abilities (e.g. aptitude or motivation), and it is often hard to determine to what extent they contribute to attainment or are themselves generated by success (e.g. beliefs, self-esteem, motivation, beliefs). The interconnectedness and changeability of different variables is in fact recognized by complex systems theories which hold that language learning is an adaptive, non-linear, self-organizing, feedback-sensitive and emergent process (cf. Larsen-Freeman and Cameron 2008). Moreover, individual characteristics such as those discussed above are bound to impact to a considerable degree learners' preferences concerning different aspects of teaching and learning as well as their classroom behaviors and response to different instructional practices. Even though this line of enquiry still remains in its infancy (e.g. Nagata, Aline and Ellis 1999; Mackey et al. 2002; Trofimovich et al. 2007; Griffiths 2008b), it stands to reason that, for example, working memory, the degree of field independence or field dependence or preferred learning strategies may determine the effect of various techniques of grammar teaching and error correction, whereas motivation, beliefs or anxiety are likely to influence participation in group work activities. Finally, it should also be kept in mind, as the papers by Gabryś-Barker and Michońska-Stadnik included in this volume demonstrate, that individual factors have to be considered from the perspective of teachers who are language learners themselves and who plan and conduct their lessons in accordance with their own beliefs, capabilities and style preferences. As Nel (2008: 55) points out, "[b]y understanding students' learning styles and by being flexible regarding their own teaching styles, teachers can heighten their awareness and be more sensitive in their listening, observation, preparation, presentation, and interaction".

The Future of Research into Individual Learner Differences

Taking into account the enormity and complexity of the field as well as the fragmentary and often inconclusive research findings, a pertinent question to pose at this juncture is what lies ahead in the study of individual differences. In conclusion to his comprehensive overview of IDs, Ellis (2008) comments that substantial advances have been made in the last two decades which are evident, for example, in greater diversity of research methods used, improvements in the measurement of individual difference variables, increasing emphasis on theoretically-driven research and the use of advanced statistical tools, attempts to explore the relationships between various factors, confirmation that aptitude and motivation account for most of the variance in achievement, recognition of the situated and dynamic nature of propensity factors (e.g. motivation, beliefs, learning styles), and insights into the relationship between individual variables and a processing model of second language acquisition. At the same time, however, he echoes Skehan's (1991) concern that so far no successful attempt has been made to offer a comprehensive theory of the role of IDs in second/foreign language learning, understood as "(…) a theory that would explain the interrelationships of the different factors, how they affect the behavioral and cognitive processes involved in L2 acquisition and their combined effect on achievement (…)" (Ellis 2008: 547). He argues that a theory of this kind would need to: (1) acknowledge the situated nature of language learning, (2) account for the impact of individual variables on opportunities for learning and the process of acquisition, (3) spell out how learners' abilities and propensities feed into their cognitions about different aspects of language learning and how these cognitions affect strategy use, (4) specify the role of consciousness in mediating the influence of individual factors, and (5) explain how such factors affect different aspects of proficiency (cf. Ellis 2004). Dissatisfaction with our current knowledge about the contribution of individual variables has also been expressed by other specialists who point out that many concepts that have been subjected to careful scrutiny have failed to live up to researchers' expectations and, therefore, there is a need to revise some of the theoretical models and ground claims in research rather than base them on hunches or pure conjecture (cf. Dörnyei and Skehan 2003; Dörnyei 2005).

While it would be difficult to take issue with such common-sense recommendations, it seems obvious that they will amount to little more than wishful thinking if they are not guided by copious empirical evidence obtained from studies that are appropriately focused, carefully designed and easily comparable in terms of data collection tools, research methodology and analytical procedures. One key dilemma is whether to channel our energies into indentifying new variables which can influence the process of learning or rather focus on those which have been shown to hold the most promise, with some scholars adopting the latter position and suggesting that research into different aspects of aptitude and motivation should be the first priority (Dörnyei and Skehan 2003; Ellis 2008). Such narrowing of the research agenda, however, would seem to be imprudent in view of the fact that many individual factors are interrelated, they may be influenced by other variables and they comprise a number of more specific abilities, which suggests that addressing a range of different issues in a systematic and varied way is likely to provide more valuable insights into the domains that the theory postulated by Ellis (2004, 2008) should grapple with. A related, yet distinct, problem are the principles that future research should adhere to as well as the more general directions it should take and, in this case, the recommendations offered by scholars are more palatable and should at least in part be heeded. Dörnyei (2005), for instance, stresses the importance of viewing ID factors as context-dependent and dynamic rather than absolute and fixed, abandoning the search for linear relationships in favor of investigating the effect of combinations of various traits under different circumstances, and relating individual characteristics to the processes of SLA, a stance that is somewhat in line with the tenets of complex system theories mentioned in the previous section (Larsen-Freeman and Cameron 2008). Also here, however, circumspection should be exercised about downright abandonment of studies which investigate single variables and seek linear relationships since such research endeavors have the potential to uncover the missing pieces of the puzzle and enhance our understanding of the intricacies of individual variation in language learning and teaching. In addition, although the notion of aptitude complexes advanced so vigorously by Robinson (2002a, 2007, this volume) is appealing, there are doubts as to the usefulness and feasibility of the pedagogical implications that research in this area might generate. This being the case, in the opinion of the present author, it still makes sense to examine the effect of single variables, focusing in particular on areas that have been conspicuously neglected (e.g. strategies used for learning grammar or pronunciation), the interaction between individual difference factors and the value of instructional practices (e.g. aspects of aptitude and various forms of practice), or the ways in which teachers' individual characteristics affect their classroom practices (e.g. the compatibility of teachers' and students' style preferences). Such an approach might help us, as Dörnyei and Skehan (2003: 622) postulate, "(…) to show how the ideas which may be relevant to educational settings generate reliable and robust findings in such settings".

The value of insights provided by future empirical investigations as well as the extent to which they can contribute to resolving the dilemmas addressed by a comprehensive theory of individual differences also hinge upon the research methodology employed. For one thing, as was emphasized above, if such studies are expected to produce meaningful findings, it is necessary to combine quantitative and qualitative approaches as a way of acknowledging the situated and dynamic nature of the process of language learning and the variables which affect it. This suggests, in turn, that we should set less store by applying increasingly more elaborate statistical procedures with a view to identifying correlations or cause-and-effect relationships and more often opt instead for a fine-grained analysis of qualitative data obtained by means of interviews, diaries or think-aloud protocols, collected on several occasions over a longer period of time. Yet another challenge is the development of valid and reliable data collection tools that would enable more accurate measurement of specific factors and could gradually replace currently used, often seriously flawed instruments, thus allowing comparisons between studies and producing a more complete picture of the variable in question. Last but not least, there is a need to move beyond one-shot investigations of traits that happen to be of interest to researchers at a particular time and devise long-term research programs which would examine specific IDs in a principled and step-by-step manner, as this would help us avoid situations in which, for example, claims are made about the impact of a given variable on proficiency even though this variable as such is still poorly understood. A program of this kind was outlined by Pawlak (2008b) with respect to the study of pronunciation learning strategies, whereby in the initial stages emphasis should be placed on identifying, describing and classifying these strategic devices, and only later should it shift to examining intervening variables, investigating the effect on attainment or exploring the value of training programs. Obviously, such a solution does not mean that relationships between variables should not be explored from the outset as the results of such studies are likely to inform existing descriptive schemes and contribute to the development of better taxonomies and research tools.

A Brief Overview of This Volume

The papers included in the anthology testify to the complexity and multidimensionality of the field of individual variation in language learning and teaching, touching upon a multiplicity of variables affecting learners and teachers and adopting diverse theoretical perspectives. For this reason, the task of grouping the contributions into separate chapters and deciding on the order in which they should appear posed a considerable dilemma which the editor was able to resolve only after much deliberation and consultation. In the end, it was decided to preface the contributions with an overview of the key developments in individual difference research and to divide the volume into five parts, devoted to theoretical perspectives, cognitive variables, affective and social factors, the impact of individual characteristics on learning and teaching, and learning deficits. In each chapter, the articles are sequenced according to the theme they deal with rather than alphabetical order, which will hopefully enhance the overall clarity and coherence of the collection and make it more approachable to readers who will find it easier to locate the issues and problems that are of interest to them. Although there are some key ID areas that the contributions fail to address (e.g. ambiguity tolerance, gender), an undeniable merit of the volume is that it tackles a number of neglected factors such as interfaces between individual variation and instructional practices, grammar learning strategies, individual differences in teachers or the demands of teaching learners with special needs.

Part I, entitled *Changing perspectives on individual learner differences*, brings together three contributions which seek to illustrate how individual variation can be approached within the framework of different theoretical paradigms and distinct research traditions. The chapter opens with a contribution by Anna Niżegorodcew who emphasizes the benefits of a context-embedded approach to the study of individual differences and argues that sociocultural and sociolinguistic accounts of SLA can afford most valuable insights in this area. A similar view is embraced by Larissa Aronin and Basilius Bawardi who discuss individual variation within the context of contemporary global and sociolinguistic changes, and express the opinion that there is a need to reassess and restructure more traditional theoretical paradigms and empirical enquiries in the light of the latest developments of this kind. Finally, István Ottó and Marianne Nikolov attempt to explain adults' failure to master foreign languages despite their superior ability to deal with rules in terms of the connectionist framework and present the results of a set of simulations which support the model they propose.

Part II, *Cognitive factors and instructed language acquisition*, has six papers seeking to shed light on the impact of aptitude, age, intelligence and cognitive processes on language learning and teaching. In the article opening this part, Peter Robinson argues that the concept of aptitude needs to be revised to take account of clusters of abilities which are drawn upon in the performance of pedagogic tasks under different instructional conditions, and argues that new aptitude batteries must be devised as a basis for assessing learners' strengths and weaknesses in such aptitude complexes. In the following paper, Adriana Biedroń reports the results of a study in which she compared the short-term and working memory abilities of gifted and regular foreign language learners, finding that they were higher for the former than the latter and concluding that the phonological loop and the central executive are components of working memory that may determine the outcomes of foreign language learning. Emphasis subsequently shifts to the role of the age factor as David Singleton and Justyna Leśniewska demonstrate that the evidence for the existence of a critical period in language learning is far from convincing and conclude that, even if maturational constraints did exist, it would still be difficult to propose an optimal age for starting formal second/foreign language instruction. The next two contributions by Szymon Wróbel and Anna Michońska-Stadnik deal with the concept of intelligence and its contributions to language learning, with the former seeking to determine whether there exists a separate linguistic intelligence and the latter setting out to explore the relationship between teachers' multiple intelligences profiles and their teaching styles. The last article in this part, authored by Fatma Alwan, attempts to show how different meta-programs indentified within the framework of neurolinguistic programming underpin learners' personality types and can explain differential success of various instructional practices, advocating that variety is the best way of dealing with such individual preferences.

The focus of the six papers included in Part III, *Affective and social factors in language learning*, is on the role of affect in different sociopolitical, socioeconomic and educational contexts. First, Magdalena Kębłowska provides an overview of the role of affective variables in second language acquisition, discusses how they impact classroom learning and stresses the need for raising awareness of this crucial area among teacher trainees. Next, Ewa Piechurska-Kuciel presents the findings of a study which explored anxiety levels in urban, suburban and rural grammar school students, and found that although this problem is most acute in the last group, the place of residence ceases to be a significant factor at the end of the educational experience when anxiety levels tend to decrease for all students. In another research-based contribution, Danuta Gabryś-Barker investigates the origins and nature of the belief and value systems held by pre-service teachers and stresses the importance of reflection in the initial stages of becoming a reflective practitioner. Sarah Mercer, in turn, explores the notion of self-concept in foreign language pedagogy, demonstrates on the basis of the results of a case study that it encompasses both stable and dynamic components, and discusses possible pedagogical implications. Subsequently, Eowyn Crisfield and Joanna White address motivational factors by reporting the findings of an empirical investigation which confirmed the existence of a link between student-perceived usefulness of a course and the levels of interest and motivation, but found that its strength may vary as a function of level. In the last paper in this part, Kata Csizér overviews the main achievements and shortcomings of motivation research in Hungary over the past twenty years and suggests that researchers should focus to a greater extent on the motivational impact of specific instructional contexts, take account of the dynamic nature of motivation and investigate the motivational profiles of special needs learners.

Part IV, entitled *Individual differences in learning and teaching practices*, consists of five papers which deal with the issue of individual variation within the context of learners' efforts to gain greater control of various language subsystems and their preferences regarding instructional choices. In the first paper, Andrew Cohen addresses the issue of comprehension and production of pragmatic features and discusses a range of individual variables which may influence the degree of success in this respect. This is followed by a contribution by Mirosław Pawlak who uses the descriptive scheme proposed by Oxford et al. (2007) to explore the use of grammar learning strategies by advanced learners of English and concludes that there is an urgent need to devise a comprehensive classification of such strategic devices as well as a valid and reliable data collection instrument. Małgorzata Baran-Łucarz focuses on the influence of cognitive and affective variables on learning foreign language pronunciation, arguing that success in mastering this subsystem is facilitated by field-independence, auditory preference or musical talent, but motivated learners lacking in these predispositions can also succeed if they receive the optimal kind of instruction. Subsequently, Carol Griffiths and Zhou Chunhong demonstrate that while there is individual variation in preferences concerning the source, timing and type of error correction, all learners view the provision of corrective feedback as indispensable for making progress in a second language. The chapter closes with a paper by Luciana Pedrazzini and Andrea Nava who present the results of a study examining individual differences in dictionary use and report that the employment of this strategy is a function of proficiency level and the degree of language awareness.

Finally, Part V, *Learners with special needs in foreign language*, which is the shortest in the anthology and consists of only two contributions, addresses the somewhat neglected area of learning deficits and their impact on language learning. First, Małgorzata Jedynak focuses on the issue of giftedness in visually impaired learners, discusses difficulties in indentifying these individuals, and offers a range of pedagogic implications for teachers who wish to fully exploit the potential of such learners. The article by Joanna Nijakowska, in turn, is devoted to the ways in which developmental dyslexia manifests itself in learners, the various difficulties in reading and spelling that such learners encounter, and the different emotional-motivational disorders that problems in these areas are likely to generate.

References

Abraham, R., and R. Vann. 1987. Strategies of two language learners: A case study. In eds. A. Wenden and J. Rubin, 85–102.

Albert, À., and J. Kormos. 2004. Creativity and narrative task performance: An exploratory study. *Language Learning* 54: 277–310.

Anderson, N.J. 2005. L2 learning strategies. In ed. E. Hinkel, 757–771.

Benson, P., ed. 2007. *Learner autonomy 8: Teacher and learner perspectives*. Dublin: Authentik.

Benson, P., and W. Lor. 1999. Conceptions of language and language learning. *System* 27:459–472.

Birdsong, D., ed. 1999. *Second language acquisition and the critical period hypothesis*. Mahwah: Lawrence Erlbaum.

Bronson, M. 2000. *Self-regulation in early childhood: Nature and nurture*. New York: Guilford Press.

Brown, H.D. 2001. *Principles of language learning and teaching* (fourth edition). White Plains: Pearson Education.

Carroll, J.B. 1981. Twenty five years of research in foreign language aptitude. In ed. K.C. Diller, 83–118.

Carroll, J.B., and A. Sapon. 1959. *The Modern Language Aptitude Test*. San Antonio: Psychological Corporation.

Celce-Murcia, M., ed. 2001. *Teaching English as a second or foreign language* (third edition). Boston: Heinle & Heinle.

Chapelle, C., and C. Roberts. 1986. Ambiguity tolerance and field independence as predictors of proficiency in English as a second language. *Language Learning* 36: 27–45.

Clément, R. 1980. Ethnicity, contact and communicative competence in a second language. In eds. H. Giles, W.P. Robinson, and P.M. Smith, 147–154.

Clément, R., S.C. Baker, and P.D. MacIntyre. 2003. Willingness to communicate in a second language: The effects of contexts, norms and vitality. *Journal of Language and Social Psychology* 22: 190–209.

Cohen, A.D. 2007. Coming to terms with language learner strategies: Surveying the experts. In ed. A.D. Cohen, and E. Macaro, 29–45.

Cohen, A.D. 2011. Second language learner strategies. In ed. E. Hinkel, 681-698.

Cohen, A.D., and J.C. Chi. 2002. Language strategy use inventory and index. In eds. R.M. Paige, A.D. Cohen, B. Kappler, J.C. Chi, and J.P. Lassegard, 16–28.

Cohen, A.D., and Z. Dörnyei. 2002. Focus on the language learner: Motivation, styles and strategies. In ed. N. Schmitt, 170–190.

Cohen, A.D., and E. Macaro, eds. 2007. *Language learner strategies*. Oxford: Oxford University Press.

Cook, V. 2008. *Second language learning and language teaching*. London: Edward Arnold.

Crookes, G., and R. Schmidt. 1991. Motivation: Reopening the research agenda. *Language Learning* 41: 469–512.

Csizér, K., and Z. Dörnyei. 2005. The internal structure of language learning motivation: Results of structural equation modeling. *Modern Language Journal* 89: 19–36.

Davies, A., and C. Elder, eds. 2004. *The handbook of applied linguistics*. Oxford: Blackwell Publishing.

DeKeyser, R.M., ed. 2007. *Practice and second language learning: Perspectives from applied linguistics and cognitive psychology*. New York: Cambridge University Press.

DeKeyser, R.M., and J. Koeth. 2011. Cognitive aptitudes for second language learning. In ed. E. Hinkel, 395–406.

Deci, E.L., and R.M. Ryan. 1985. *Intrinsic motivation and self-determination in human behavior*. New York: Plenum.

Deci, E.L., and R.M. Ryan, eds. 2002. *Handbook of self-determination*. Rochester: University of Rochester Press.

De Groot, A.M.B., and J.F. Kroll, eds. 1997. *Tutorials in bilingualism: Psycholinguistic perspectives*. London: Lawrence Erlbaum.

Diller, K.C., ed. 1981. *Individual differences and universals in language learning aptitude*. Rowley: Newbury House.

Dörnyei, Z. 2000. Motivation in action: Towards a process-oriented conceptualization of student motivation. *British Journal of Educational Psychology* 70: 519–538.

Dörnyei, Z. 2001a. *Motivational strategies in the language classroom*. Cambridge: Cambridge University Press.

Dörnyei, Z. 2001b. *Teaching and researching motivation*. Harlow: Pearson Education.

Dörnyei, Z. 2005. *The psychology of the language learner: Individual differences in second language acquisition*. Mahwah: Lawrence Erlbaum.

Dörnyei, Z. 2009. The L2 motivational self-esteem. In eds. Z. Dörnyei, and E. Ushioda, 9–42.

Dörnyei, Z., and K. Csizér. 2002. Some dynamics of language attitudes and motivation: Results of a longitudinal nationwide study. *Applied Linguistics* 23: 421–462.

Dörnyei, Z., and J. Kormos. 2000. The role of individual and social variables in oral task performance. *Language Teaching Research* 4: 275–300.

Dörnyei, Z., and I. Ottó. 1998. Motivation in action: A process model of L2 motivation. *Working Papers in Applied Linguistics* 4: 43–69.

Dörnyei, Z., and R. Schmidt, eds. 2001. *Motivation and second language acquisition*. Honolulu: University of Hawaii Press.

Dörnyei, Z., and P. Skehan. 2003. Individual differences in L2 learning. In eds. C.J. Doughty, and M.H. Long, 589–630.

Dörnyei, Z., and E. Ushioda, eds. 2009. *Motivation, language identity and L2 self*. Bristol, Buffalo, Toronto: Multilingual Matters.

Doughty, C.J., and M.H. Long, eds. 2003. *The handbook of second language acquisition*. Oxford. Blackwell Publishing.

Ehrman, M.E., and B.L. Leaver, 2003. Cognitive styles in the service of language learning. *System* 31: 391–415.

Ehrman, M.E., B.L. Leaver, and R.L. Oxford. 2003. A brief overview of individual differences in second language learning. *System* 31: 313–330.

Ellis, R., ed. 1999. *Learning a second language through interaction*. Amsterdam, Philadelphia: John Benjamins.

Ellis, R. 2008. *The study of second language acquisition* (second edition). Oxford: Oxford University Press.

Ellis, R. 2004. Individual differences in second language learning. In eds. A. Davies, and C. Elder, 525–551.

Eubank, L., and K.R. Gregg. 1999. Critical periods and (second) language acquisition: Divide et impera. In ed. D. Birdsong, 65–99.

Gao, X. 2003. Changes in Chinese students' learner strategy use after arrival in the UK: A qualitative inquiry. In eds. D. Palfreyman, and R. Smith, 41–57.

Gardner, H. 1983. *Frames of mind. The theory of multiple intelligences*. New York: Basic Books.

Gardner, R.C. 1985. *Social psychology and second language learning. The role of attitudes and motivation*. London: Edward Arnold.

Gardner, R.C., and P.D. MacIntyre. 1992. A student's contributions to second language learning. Part I: Cognitive variables. *Language Teaching* 25. 211–220.

Gass, S.M., and L. Selinker. 2008. *Second language acquisition: An introductory course*. New York and London: Routledge

Genesee, F. 1976. The role of intelligence in second language learning. *Language Learning* 26: 267–280.

Giles, H., W.P. Robinson, and P.M. Smith, eds. 1980. *Social psychological perspectives*. Oxford: Pergamon.

Gregersen, T., and E. Horwitz. 2002. Language learning and perfectionism: Anxious and non-anxious language learners' reactions to their own oral performance. *Modern Language Journal* 86: 562–570.

Grenfell, M., E. Macaro. 2007. Claims and critiques. In eds. A.D. Cohen, and E. Macaro, 9–28.

Griffiths, C. 2008a. Strategies and good language learners. In ed. C. Griffiths, 83–98.

Griffiths, C. 2008b. Age and good language learners. In ed. C. Griffiths, 35–48

Griffiths, C., ed. 2008c. *Lessons from good language learners*. Cambridge: Cambridge University Press.

Grigorenko, E.L. 2002. Foreign language acquisition and language-based learning disabilities. In ed. P. Robinson, 95–112.

Grigorenko, E., R.J. Sternberg, and M.E. Ehrman. 2000. A theory-based approach to the measurement of foreign language learning ability: The Canal-F theory and test. *Modern Language Journal* 84: 390–405.

Harley, B., and W. Wang. 1997. The critical period hypothesis: Where are we now? In ed. A.M.B. De Groot, and J.F. Kroll, 19–51.

Healy, A.F., and L.E. Bourne, eds. 1998. *Foreign language learning: Psycholinguistic studies on training and retention*. Mahwah: Lawrence Erlbaum.

Hinkel, E. ed. 2005. *Handbook of research in second language teaching and learning*. Mahwah: Lawrence Erlbaum.

Hinkel, E. ed. 2011. *Handbook of research in second language teaching and learning. Volume II*. Mahwah: Lawrence Erlbaum.

Horwitz, E. 2001. Language anxiety and achievement. *Annual Review of Applied Linguistics* 21: 112–126.

Hosenfeld, C. 2003. Evidence of emergent beliefs of a second language learner: A diary study. In eds. P. Kalaja, and A.M.F. Barcelos, 37–55.

Hyltenstam, K., and N. Abrahamsson. 2003. Maturational constraints in SLA. In: eds. C.J. Doughty, and M.H. Long, 539–588.

Ioup, G. 2005. Age in second language development. In: ed. E. Hinkel, 419-435.

Johnson, K. 2001. *An introduction to foreign language learning and teaching*. Harlow: Pearson Education.

Kalaja, P., and A.M.F. Barcelos, eds. 2003. *Beliefs about SLA: New research approaches.* Dordrecht: Kluwer Academic Publishers.

Kern, R. 1995. Students' and teachers' beliefs about language learning. *Foreign Language Annals* 28: 71–91.

Kim, T.-J. 2009. The sociocultural interface between ideal self and ought-to self: A case study of two Korean students' ESL motivation. In eds. Z. Dörnyei, and E. Ushioda, 274–294.

Kiss, C., and M. Nikolov. 2005. Developing, piloting and validating an instrument to measure young learners' aptitude. *Language Learning* 55: 99–150.

Kolb, D.A. 1984. *Experiential learning: Experience as the source of learning and development.* Englewood Cliffs: Prentice Hall.

Kormos, J., and Z. Dörnyei. 2004. The interaction of linguistic and motivational variables in second language task performance. *Zeitschrift für Interkulturellen Fremdsprachenunterricht* [Online] 9. http://www.ualberta.ca/ ~ german/ejournal/kormos2.htm

Kramsch, C. 2003. Metaphor and the subjective construction of beliefs. In eds. P. Kalaja, and A.M.F. Barcelos, 109–128.

Larsen-Freeman, D., and L. Cameron. 2008. *Complex systems and applied linguistics.* Oxford: Oxford University Press.

Leaver, B.L., M.E. Ehrman, and B. Shekhtman. 2005. *Achieving success in second language acquisition.* Cambridge: Cambridge University Press.

Little, D., J. Ridley, and E. Ushioda, eds. 2003. *Learner autonomy in the foreign language classroom: Teacher, learner, curriculum and assessment.* Dublin: Authentik.

Long, M.H. 2007. *Problems in SLA.* Mahwah: Lawrence Erlbaum.

Macaro, E. 2006. Strategies for language learning and for language use: Revising the theoretical framework. *Modern Language Journal* 90: 320–337.

MacIntyre, P.D. 1999. Language anxiety: A review of the research for language teachers. In ed. D.J. Young, 24–45.

MacIntyre, P.D., and R. Gardner. 1991. Language anxiety: Its relationship to other anxieties and to processing in native and second language. *Language Learning* 41: 513–534.

MacIntyre, P.D. and J.J. Legatto. 2011. A dynamic system approach to willingness to communicate: Developing an idiodynamic method to capture rapidly changing affect. *Applied Linguistics* 32: 149–171.

MacIntyre, P.D., R. Clément, Z. Dörnyei, and K.A. Noels. 1998. Conceptualizing willingness to communicate in a L2: A situated model of confidence and affiliation. *Modern Language Journal* 82: 545–562.

MacIntyre, P.D., S.C. Baker, R. Clément, and S. Conrod. 2001. Willingness to communicate, social support, and language learning orientations of immersion students. *Studies in Second Language Acquisition* 23: 369–388.

MacIntyre, P.D., S.C. Baker, R. Clément, and L.A. Donovan. 2003. Talking in order to learn: Willingness to communicate and intensive language programs. *Canadian Modern Language Review* 59: 589–607.

Mackey, A. ed. 2007. *Conversational interaction in second language acquisition.* Oxford: Oxford University Press.

Mackey, A., J. Philip, T. Egi, A. Fujii, and T. Tatsumi. 2002. Individual differences in working memory, noticing of interactional feedback and L2 development. In ed. P. Robinson, 181–209.

McLaughlin, B. 1987. *Theories of second language learning.* London: Edward Arnold.

Miyake, A., and D. Friedman. 1998. Individual differences in second language proficiency: Working memory as language aptitude. In eds. A.F. Healy, and L.E. Bourne, 339–364.

Mori, Y. 1999. Epistemological beliefs and language learning beliefs: What do language learners believe about their learning? *Language Learning* 49: 377–415.

Muñoz, C., and D. Singleton. 2011. A critical review of age-related research on L2 ultimate attainment. *Language Teaching* 44: 1–35.

Myers, I., and K. Briggs. 1976. *The Myers-Briggs Type Indicator, Form G.* Palo Alto: California Consulting Psychology Press.

Nagata, H., D. Aline, and R. Ellis, 1999. Modified input, language aptitude and the acquisition of word meanings. In ed. R. Ellis, 133–149.

Naiman, N., M. Fröhlich, H.H. Stern, and A. Todesco. 1996 (1978). *The good language learner.* Clevedon: Multilingual Matters.

Nel, C. 2008. Learning style and good language learners. In ed. C. Griffiths, 49–60.

Norton, B., and K. Toohey. 2001. Changing perspectives on good language learners. *TESOL Quarterly* 35: 307–322.

O'Malley, J.M., and A.U. Chamot. 1990. *Learning strategies in second language acquisition.* Cambridge: Cambridge University Press.

Ortega, L. 2009. *Understanding second language acquisition.* London: Hodder Education.

Ottó, I. 1998. The relationship between individual differences in learner creativity and language learning success. *TESOL Quarterly* 32: 763–773.

Oxford, R.L. 1990. *Language learning strategies: What every teacher should know.* Boston: Heinle.

Oxford, R.L. 2001. Language learning styles and strategies. In ed. M. Celce-Murcia, 359–366.

Oxford, R.L. 2011. *Teaching and researching language learning strategies.* Pearson: Harlow Education.

Oxford, R., K. Rang Lee, and G. Park. 2007. L2 grammar strategies: The second Cinderella and beyond. In eds. A.D. Cohen, and E. Macaro, 117–139.

Paige, R.M., A.D. Cohen, B. Kappler, J.C. Chi, and J.P. Lassegard, eds. 2002. *Maximizing study abroad.* Minneapolis: Center for Advanced Research for Language Acquisition, University of Minnesota.

Palfreyman, D., and R. Smith, eds. 2003. *Learner autonomy across cultures: Language education perspectives.* Basingstoke: Palgrave Macmillan.

Parry, T.S., and J.R. Child. 1990. Preliminary investigation of the relationship between VORD, MLAT, and language proficiency. In eds. T.S. Parry, and C.W. Stansfield, 30–66.

Parry, T.S., and C.W. Stansfield, eds. 1990. *Language aptitude reconsidered.* Englewood Cliffs: Prentice Hall.

Pawlak, M. 2008a. *Advanced learners' use of strategies for learning grammar: A diary study.* In ed. M. Pawlak, 109–125.

Pawlak, M. 2008b. Another look at the use of pronunciation learning strategies: An advanced learner's perspective. In ed. E. Waniek-Klimczak, 304–322.

Pawlak, M., ed. 2008c. *Investigating English language learning and teaching.* Poznań–Kalisz: Adam Mickiewicz University Press.

Piechurska-Kuciel, E. 2008. *Language anxiety in secondary grammar school students.* Opole: University of Opole Press.

Pimsleur, p. 1966. *The Pimsleur Language Aptitude Battery.* New York: Hartcourt Brace Jovanovic.

Reid, J. 1987. The learning style preferences of ESL students. *TESOL Quarterly* 21: 87–111.

Riding, R. 1991. *Cognitive styles analysis.* Birmingham: Learning and Training Technology.

Robinson, p. 2001a. Individual differences, cognitive abilities, aptitude complexes, and learning conditions in SLA. *Second Language Research* 17: 268–392.

Robinson, P. ed. 2001b. *Cognition and second language acquisition.* Cambridge: Cambridge University Press.

Robinson, p. 2002a. Learning conditions, aptitude complexes and SLA: A framework for research and pedagogy. In ed. P. Robinson, 113–133.

Robinson, P., ed. 2002b. *Individual differences and instructed language learning*. Amsterdam, Philadelphia: John Benjamins.

Robinson, p. 2005. Aptitude and second language acquisition. *Annual Review of Applied Linguistics* 25: 46–73.

Robinson, p. 2007. Aptitude, abilities, contexts and practice. In ed. R.M. DeKeyser, 256–287.

Robson, G., and H. Midorikawa. 2001. How reliable and valid is the Japanese version of the Strategy Inventory for Language Learning? *JALT Journal* 23: 202–226.

Rubin, J. 1975. What the 'Good Language Learner' can teach us. *TESOL Quarterly* 9: 41–51.

Rubin, J., A.U. Chamot, V. Harris, and N.J. Anderson. 2007. Intervening in the use of strategies. In eds. A.D. Cohen, and E. Macaro, 141–160.

Sasaki, M. 1996. *Second language proficiency, foreign language aptitude and intelligence: Quantitative and qualitative analyses*. New York: Peter Lang.

Sawyer, M., and L. Ranta. 2001. Aptitude, individual differences, and instructional design. In ed. P. Robinson, 319–353.

Schmitt, N., ed. 2002. *An introduction to applied linguistics*. London: Edward Arnold.

Schumann, J. 1997. *The neurobiology of affect in language*. Malden: Blackwell.

Skehan, p. 1989. *Individual differences in second language learning*. London: Edward Arnold.

Skehan, p. 1991. Individual differences in second language learning. *Studies in Second Language Acquisition* 13: 275–298.

Skehan, p. 1998. *A cognitive approach to language learning*. Oxford: Oxford University Press.

Skehan, p. 2002. Theorizing and updating aptitude. In ed. P. Robinson, 69–93.

Sparks, R.L., L. Ganschow, and J. Patton. 1995. Prediction of performance in first-year foreign language courses: Connections between native and foreign language learning. *Journal of Educational Psychology* 87: 638–655.

Spielman, G., and M. Radnofsky. 2001. Learning language under tension: New directions from a qualitative study. *Modern Language Journal* 85: 259–278.

Spolsky, B. 1995. Prognostication and language aptitude testing, 1925-1962. *Language Testing* 12: 321–340.

Spolsky, B. 2000. Anniversary article: Language motivation revisited. *Applied Linguistics* 21: 157–169.

Stern, H.H. 1975. What can we learn from the good language learner? *Canadian Modern Language Review* 31: 304–318.

Sternberg, R.J. 1988. *The triarchic mind: A new theory of human intelligence*. New York: Viking Press.

Sternberg, R.J. 2002. The theory of successful intelligence and its implications for language aptitude testing. In ed. P. Robinson, 13–43.

Takeuchi, O., C. Griffiths, and D. Coyle. 2007. Applying strategies to contexts: The role of individual, situational and group differences. In A.D. Cohen, and E. Macaro, 69–92.

Tanaka, K. 2004. Changes in Japanese students' beliefs about language learning and English language proficiency in a study-abroad context. Unpublished doctoral dissertation, University of Auckland.

Tanaka, K., and R. Ellis. 2003. Study abroad, language proficiency, and learner beliefs about language learning. *JALT Journal* 9: 81–102.

Tarone, E. 1980. Communication strategies, foreigner talk, and repair in interlanguage. *Language Learning* 30: 417–431.

Trofimovich, P., A. Ammar, and E. Gatbonton. 2007. How effective are recasts? The role of attention, memory and analytical ability. In ed. A. Mackey, 171–195.

Ushioda, E. 2001. Language learning at university: Exploring the role of motivational thinking. In eds. Z. Dörnyei, and R. Schmidt, 91–124.

Ushioda, E. 2003. Motivation as a socially mediated process. In eds. D. Little, J. Ridley, and E. Ushioda, 90–102.

Ushioda, E. 2007. Motivation, autonomy and sociocultural theory. In ed. P. Benson, 5–24.

Ushioda, E. 2008. Motivation and good language learners. In ed. C. Griffiths, 19–34.

Ushioda, E., and Z. Dörnyei. 2009. Motivation, language identities and the L2 self: A theoretical overview. In Z. Dörnyei, and E. Ushioda, 1–8.

Waniek-Klimczak, E., ed. 2008. *Issues in accents of English*. Newcastle upon Tyne: Cambridge Scholars Publishing.

Waterhouse, L. 2006. Multiple intelligences, the Mozart effect, and emotional intelligence: A critical review. *Educational Psychologist* 41: 207–225.

Weiner, B. 1992. *Human motivation: Metaphors, theory and research*. Newbury Park: Sage.

Wenden, A. 1991. *Learner strategies for learner autonomy*. Englewood Cliffs: Prentice Hall.

Wenden, A., and J. Rubin. 1987. *Learner strategies in language learning*. Englewood Cliffs: Prentice Hall.

White, C., K. Schramm, and A.U. Chamot. 2007. Research methods in strategy research: Reexamining the toolbox. In eds. A.D. Cohen, and E. Macaro, 93–116.

Williams, M., and R. Burden. 1997. *Psychology for language teachers*. Cambridge: Cambridge University Press.

Willing, K. 1987. *Learning styles and adult migrant education*. Adelaide: National Curriculum Resource Center.

Witkin, H.A., P.K. Oltman, E. Raskin, and S.A. Karp. 1971. *A manual for the Embedded Figures Test*. Palo Alto: California Consulting Psychology Press.

Wolters, C. 2003. Regulation of motivation: Evaluating the underemphasized aspect of self-regulated learning. *Educational Psychologist* 34: 189–205.

Yashima, T. 2002. Willingness to communicate in a second language: The Japanese EFL context. *Modern Language Journal* 86: 54–66.

Young, D.J., ed. 1999. *Affect in foreign language and second language learning*. Boston: McGraw-Hill.

Part I
Changing Perspectives on Individual Learner Differences

L2 Learners' Individual Differences and the Changing SLA Perspective

Anna Niżegorodcew

Abstract This paper reflects upon L2 learners' individual differences against the background of the changing second language acquisition (SLA) theory paradigm. In the first part of the article, the focus is on the present changing status of SLA theory, from the exclusively cognitive approach to the sociolinguistic/sociocultural one. It is claimed that both approaches can be encompassed by the expanding the concept of communicative competence. In the second part, some examples of the author's past research and of her students' more recent studies are presented to exemplify the influence of contextually embedded individual differences on EFL learning and use. In conclusion, it is claimed that such a treatment of individual differences is closer to the sociolinguistic and sociocultural SLA theory than the traditional understanding of individual differences as stable traits.

1 Introduction

The goal of the present paper is to reflect upon L2 learners' individual differences against the background of the changing SLA theory. According to Zoltan Dörnyei (2005), the most characteristic feature of recent individual differences (IDs) research is its concern with the context in which the research studies have been carried out. "Scholars have come to reject the notion that the various [individual] traits are context-independent and absolute, and are now increasingly proposing new dynamic conceptualizations in which ID factors enter into some interaction with the situational parameters" (Dörnyei 2005: 218). According to Ellis

A. Niżegorodcew (✉)
Jagiellonian University, Kraków, Poland
e-mail: annanizegorodcew@gmail.com

M. Pawlak (ed.), *New Perspectives on Individual Differences in Language Learning and Teaching*, Second Language Learning and Teaching, DOI: 10.1007/978-3-642-20850-8_1, © Springer-Verlag Berlin Heidelberg 2012

(2004: 547), the contextualized ID research takes into account specific settings in which L2 learning takes place as well as the tasks learners are requested to perform.

Such an approach is markedly different from the traditional psychological treatment of IDs as stable traits responsible for individual learning and performance. My own research on L2 learning aptitude at the end of the 70s (Niżegorodcew 1979, 1980a, 1980b) was conducted in that traditional psychological vein, following Carroll and Sapon's *Modern Language Aptitude Test* (Carroll and Sapon 1959) and Pimsleur's *Language Aptitude Battery* (Pimsleur 1966). It consisted in designing various aptitude tests and correlating their results with L2 learning achievements of more and less successful learners. Following Carroll, L2 aptitude was treated as a cluster of linguistic performance abilities based on underlying linguistic competencies. Yet, in my research conclusion, in line with some other L2 aptitude studies at that time (see Skehan 1989), I claimed that under different teaching conditions, L2 teaching methods and classroom techniques, the abilities assessed by a particular set of aptitude tests could be irrelevant for L2 learning success. In other words, the idea that L2 learning aptitude should be studied in a more situated way was already present in more traditional L2 aptitude studies of the 70s and 80s.

In this paper an attempt is made to combine reflections on L2 learners' IDs as they impact on the SLA processes in their situational complexity. Such an attempt is in line with the changing understanding of SLA. Consequently, the first part of this paper is focussed on the discussion on the present changing status of SLA theory, from the cognitive only approach to the sociolinguistic/sociocultural approach. In the second part of the paper, I present some examples of my own and my students' research studies in the light of the impact of IDs on L2 learning and use in the sociocultural context of learning and using English as a second/foreign language by children, adolescents and adults.

2 From the Psycholinguistic to the Sociolinguistic/Sociocultural Approach to SLA Theory

It can be claimed that the debate between the psycholinguistic and the sociocultural approach to second language acquisition (SLA) theory started in 1997 with the publication of Firth and Wagner's (1997) critique of the cognitive only approach to SLA. They criticized the distinction made by SLA mainstream researchers between L2 use and L2 learning/acquisition. At that time, fourteen years ago, in spite of a few supporters of Firth and Wagner's critique, such as Hall (1997) and Liddicoat (1997), most of the mainstream SLA theorists who responded to Firth and Wagner's paper, such as Kasper (1997), Poulisse (1997), Long (1997) or Gass (1998), claimed that internal psycholinguistic processes of L2 acquisition should be distinguished from their sociocultural context and that SLA theory is concerned with the psycholinguistic processes, not with the external circumstances in which they occur. Gass formulated the claim in a clear way: "there are apples and oranges, and apples do not need to be orange" (Gass 1998: 83).

In order to define the present scope of SLA theory, it is necessary to place it in a historical perspective. About 50 years ago linguists and psychologists interested in second or foreign language acquisition found a common ground in psycholinguistic research. After Chomsky's revolution in linguistics, linguists led the way in psycholinguistic theory. The focus being mainly on language structures, psychologists working in the psycholinguistic framework mostly tried to validate linguistic theories on grounds of the claimed psychological reality of universal linguistic processes (see Kurcz 1976). Although in Hatch's (1983) survey *second language psycholinguistics* was still used as a general term, since that time *SLA theory* seems to have replaced *second language psycholinguistic theory* as an umbrella concept in studies of the cognitive aspects of L2 acquisition, comprehension and production. According to Zuengler and Miller (2006), the SLA theorists representing the cognitive approach treat L2 acquisition/learning as getting a knowledge from the external input, which is demonstrated in L2 learners' increasingly target-like performance. This knowledge involves grammatical rules and lexical structures being assimilated by the individual mind. SLA is treated as the assimilation of linguistic data isolated from the context of its use. Since the late 60s the language of the language learner or the interlanguage (Corder 1967; Selinker 1972) has become focus of SLA research. One of the discovered characteristic features of interlanguage was its instability. Variability in the language of the language learner has been accounted for both by the psycholinguistic and sociolinguistic models (see Ellis 1994). The psycholinguistic perspective focused on planned and unplanned speech, as well as on monitored and unmonitored performance. In other words, the psycholinguistic approach tried to account for the psychological processes responsible for the variable control L2 users have over the linguistic knowledge they have acquired.

The approach to the interface between the external linguistic knowledge provided in the input and the internal psycholinguistic processes determines whether SLA researchers take the context of acquisition into consideration or whether their focus is purely cognitive. Those who take second and foreign language teaching into account do not have doubts that teaching/learning contexts exert a deep influence on the accessibility of the linguistic input, both in the physical and psychological sense of the word. On the other hand, those who, like the followers of the cognitive *focus-on-form* (FonF) approach, focus their attention only on the meaning and form of utterances as the input source (see Doughty 2001) may disregard the context in which the utterances have been produced.

The sociolinguistic SLA models are concerned with environmental factors affecting L2 learners' competence, such as the situation in which groups of people, e.g. immigrants, acquire a second language in naturalistic circumstances. An example of a sociolinguistic SLA model is John Schumann's *Acculturation Theory* (McLaughlin 1987). Its proponents equated L2 acquisition with acculturation and they claimed that people acquire L2 to the extent they successfully acculturate, that is, adopt cultural norms of a L2 community. The sociolinguistic

SLA perspective perceives L2 learning as gradually becoming a member of the target language community, which is demonstrated in acquiring its verbal and non-verbal norms. In consequence, according to Larsen-Freeman (2002), the object of SLA theory in the sociolinguistic perspective has a different ontological position from the object of SLA theory in the psycholinguistic perspective, and the two perspectives cannot meet. Zuengler and Miller (2006) also claim that the debate between the psycholinguistic and the sociolinguistic perspectives is irresolvable. However, they give examples of some research studies which seem to argue for the commensurability of the two approaches (see Block 2003). Their authors believe that non-native L2 learners in collaborative tasks help each other by providing input which gradually becomes part of their L2 knowledge.

The question arises, however, what kind of knowledge is being developed due to collaborative tasks, whether it is grammatical knowledge, that is, linguistic competence, or sociolinguistic knowledge, that is, sociolinguistic competence (see Hymes 1972). The question how long-lasting this knowledge is remains beyond the scope of the present discussion, although, obviously, this is a fundamental question in language acquisition theory.

Let us then recapitulate what seems to be the present state of affairs in SLA theory. There exist two distinct SLA theoretical perspectives: the *psycholinguistic* and the *sociolinguistic* one, the former focused on individual cognitive processes in L2 acquisition and the latter on the social context of L2 use. The sociolinguistic perspective is also referred to as *sociocultural theory* (Lantolf and Pavlenko 1994). Both perspectives can be encompassed by the expanding concept of communicative competence, including linguistic, sociolinguistic and pragmalinguistic competence. In such an understanding of SLA theory, processes of L2 acquisition and use are viewed both as cognitive processes (the psycholinguistic approach) and the communicative ones (the sociolinguistic approach). Moreover, a number of researchers believe, like Larsen-Freeman, that it is not psycholinguistic and sociolinguistic theory but rather *social constructivism theory*, e.g. the *Vygotskian dialogical theory of meaning construction*, that should inform the field of L2 learning and teaching (Larsen-Freeman 1995). It seems that SLA sociolinguistic/sociocultural theory has developed into a fully-fledged research field. The field draws among others on *Vygotskian theory*, *language socialization perspective*, *dialogic perspective* and *critical theory* (Zuengler and Miller 2006).

3 Individual Differences Research Meets SLA Theory: Evidence from My Own and My Students' Research Projects

In his monograph on individual differences in second language acquisition, Dornyei concludes his discussion on IDs with a description of three common features he has discovered in recent research. The first common aspect is the importance of context and, consequently, qualitative rather quantitative research methods. The second common theme is treating IDs as complex rather than isolated traits. And the third connecting feature of recent research is an attempt on the part of applied linguists to relate IDs to SLA processes (Dörnyei 2005: 218–219). Let us focus on these common aspects of ID research, illustrated by my own and my students' research.

In line with Dörnyei's warning against simplifications in applying psychological models in applied linguistic research, one of the tendencies which is most annoying and frustrating for the supervisor and harmful for the undergraduates is their naive belief that they can easily apply psychological models and use methods of psychological research in their applied linguistic studies. Research on ID features is one of the primary themes of such simplistic approaches. Among the ID factors undergraduates are mainly interested in are L2 learners' motivation, personality, aptitude, learning strategies and learning anxiety. The questions undergraduates wish to ask are in fact traditional research questions of ID psychology—how do relatively stable individual traits correlate with L2 learning success?

The proposed projects usually lack construct validity. For instance, an undergraduate wishing to correlate L2 learning aptitude with musical abilities had only very vague ideas about the complexity of the very concept of L2 learning aptitude. She was drawn to her initial thesis proposal by her musical interests and a few articles she read on L2 aptitude batteries. She lacked basic statistical knowledge on calculating correlations and was not able to connect her proposed ID theme with L2 classroom teaching. Another undergraduate, comparing L2 learning motivation of two very different groups of students, one group attending a state school and the other—a private language school, did not control for other interfering conditions—the fact that the state school was in a small town and the private school in a big city. Her effort in adaptation of a well-known motivation questionnaire in order to compare learners' motivation in state and private schools was partly wasted in a carelessly designed study. Such examples indicate that classical quantitative ID research is most frequently beyond the scope of applied linguistics undergraduates. What seems much more accessible is qualitative ID research, based on semi-structured interviews, observation and diaries. In this respect ID research questions can refer to L2 acquisition/learning informed by sociocultural SLA theory.

My research on the use of communication strategies by low proficiency EFL adolescents learning English at school (Niżegorodcew 1991, 1993) showed among other things that learners used different strategies while trying to describe a picture story without sufficient linguistic resources. The most common strategic pattern involved active searching for the required lexical items by appealing for the interlocutor's help. The pattern was nearly equally common in higher and lower proficiency students. Conversely, the second most common pattern of strategic behaviour consisted in passive repetition of parts of the interlocutor's questions to make an impression of taking part in conversation. The pattern was most common among less proficient students.

The distribution of active and passive strategies indicates that it is not only the level of proficiency that affects the use of particular strategic behaviour. Although L2 proficiency was found to be the most important factor correlating with

communicative success in describing the picture story, I speculated that personality features and previous experiences involving L2 learning and use could
influence the choice of particular strategies—the active or the passive ones.
Besides, I claimed that "underlying communication patterns, common in a given
language and culture can favourably or unfavourably affect the choice of more
'active' or 'passive' communication strategies" (Niżegorodcew 1993: 356).

From our present perspective, such speculations can be interpreted as linking
strategic language use research with the sociocultural context in which picture
story descriptions and accompanying conversations were taking place. The
microscale context involved the learners' previous experiences with L2 learning
and use, undoubtedly affecting such personality features as risk-taking, willingness
to speak to strangers and tolerance of ambiguity. Some adolescents could be more
outgoing, risk-taking and willing to converse with strangers than others because
they travelled abroad, met L2 speakers and were challenged by their teachers. The
macroscale context, in turn, involved communication patterns characteristic of a
particular society, a particular community, or even a particular family. Underlying
communication patterns characteristic of the Polish society and the Polish school,
according to which it is the adult/the teacher who is responsible for maintaining
conversation with the adolescent/the student, can affect limited and restrained L2
use. It could be speculated that the observed passive strategic behaviour resulted
both from lack of personal experiences in using L2 and lack of more active
communication patterns in the students' environment.

Another study I wish to refer to was my own longitudinal observational study of
two very young learners, Mikołaj and Zosia, acquiring English in the same low
intensity courses (Niżegorodcew 2002, 2006) for a period of over two years. At the
final assessment time Mikolaj was 4;2 and Zosia 3;7 respectively. Although the
children came from similar family background and were taught by the same
teachers, their approach to L2 learning and use was different and changed considerably during the observation period. Mikołaj at 4;2 was very attentive and
cooperative, which stood in sharp contrast to his uncooperativeness and passivity
two years before. On the other hand, Zosia at 3;7 was much less attentive and
cooperative than what she was like when she started learning English two years
before. The longitudinal study made me realize that the children's approach to
learning English was different not only due to their individual differences (e.g.
more active and spontaneous behaviour matching willingness to use English) but
that it also changed over time as the children's parents paid more or less attention
to the L2 learning process.[1]

---

[1] Both children, Mikołaj and Zosia (at present approximately 12 years old), are continuing learning
English at school. However, the novelty and enthusiasm of the first years of learning English has
worn off. Their parents are more concerned with their musical achievements since they both attend a
musical school. The children are treating English like other school subjects. It seems that the English
teacher has treated all children as if they were absolute beginners in English at the beginning of the
school course and she did not provide a continuation course for children like Mikołaj and Zosia. The
effect of such an undifferentiated approach was detrimental for the children's motivation.

Such a conclusion was also drawn by my former doctoral student Joanna Rokita (2007) on the basis of her longitudinal and cross-sectional studies on lexical development in English taught as a foreign language to very young children (2;0-4;0). Rokita concludes her studies saying that the only child, who at 3;7 was able to communicate in English, apparently did it due to her mother's support and dedication. She speculates that parental involvement in child L2 learning is indispensable if the child is to achieve success at such an early age. In other words, the context in which L2 is learned by very young learners undoubtedly affects L2 acquisition. L2 taught as a foreign language is gradually acquired owing to a cluster of sociocultural and socioaffective circumstances, primarily, of the parental support and their L2 proficiency enabling them to use L2 while talking to their children on the daily basis over a long period of time. It could be speculated that my subjects, Mikołaj and Zosia, were first provided with much parental support to learn English, which was later partly withdrawn.

As can be seen from the above studies, the L2 learning process viewed from the sociocultural perspective meets ID research in its complex understanding of human differentiation being a combined result of genetic endowment and environmental influences (Strelau 2000a, 2000b). The children and adolescents learned English as a foreign language in similar formal circumstances (school, language course) according to similar syllabuses. However, their use of communication strategies in the described cross-sectional study (in the case of the adolescents) and their spontaneous use of the acquired L2 in the longitudinal study (in the case of the children) varied a lot.

Adults also vary in their approaches to L2 learning and use, depending on their IDs, involving personality features, life histories, beliefs and attitudes. Two MA theses written in 2008 under my supervision can serve as examples of qualitative exploratory research studies. They are Agata Kita's "ERASMUS students' experiences during the mobility period: an exploratory study" (Kita 2008) and Agnieszka Smagieł's "The acculturation process of Polish immigrants in Great Britain" (Smagieł 2008).

Kita explored the perceptions of study periods abroad reported by nine students of the English Department of the Jagiellonian University. The students spent the study periods in different European countries (Germany, France, Spain, Great Britain and Sweden) under the ERASMUS mobility scheme. Among different aspects of the perceptions were the subjects' self-observations of changes in personal qualities and of changes in their L2 (English) and L3 (German, French, Spanish or Swedish) competence. The reports were based on a semi-structured interview which provided qualitative data on different individual perceptions of study periods abroad, depending on the study setting, rapport with the hosts, other ERASMUS students' support, quality of the academic courses in the host country and L1, L2 and L3 use opportunities. The author provided a sociocultural analysis of reasons underlying satisfaction or dissatisfaction with the study periods abroad. Such a study, notwithstanding its limited scope and exploratory character, approaches IDs research in a complex and contextualized way, drawing on personal accounts and opinions of the interviewees. One of the conclusions that can be drawn from Kita's study is that the ERASMUS mobility scheme provides undergraduates with diverse experiences, which are assessed as more satisfactory if the culture of the host university and country is more congruent with the culture of the student and her university. Some diversity, however, is welcome, since it extends international students' horizons and makes them more tolerant of cultural differences. The answers concerning undergraduates' L2/L3 development indicate that students also become more tolerant with regard to their L2/L3 accuracy. They develop their identity as ERASMUS students, that is, multilingual European students, who are likely to draw on all of their multilingual resources in the face of a threatening communication breakdown. Thus, SLA perceived rather as becoming a member if a given speech community than getting an accurate linguistic knowledge from the experts has clearly become the student researcher's focus.

A similar focus has motivated Agnieszka Smagieł in her MA thesis "The acculturation process of Polish immigrants in Great Britain" (Smagieł 2008). The student used both quantitative and qualitative research methods to explore changes in attitudes, interests, motivation and anxiety of a group of 24 young Polish immigrants in a British town. In the quantitative study she compared her subjects' opinions and beliefs at the beginning of their stay in Great Britain with those after a period of six months. In the qualitative research she focused on two persons chosen from the Polish immigrants' group to carry out an in-depth exploration of their English language proficiency development, their readiness to use English in everyday contacts with native speakers, their beliefs about L2 learning and their attitudes towards the British. The study was based on the student researcher's observations and talks with the subjects over a period of one year.

In the questionnaire study Smagieł found a significant increase in Polish immigrants' positive attitudes towards the British, in the interest and motivation to learn English and a decrease in the level of anxiety. Furthermore, being able to observe two people she shared her accommodation with, Smagieł provided a wealth of observations on two different approaches to the host country, including English language learning and use, which after a year resulted in very different levels of fluency, readiness to speak English and behavioural patterns. In the case of the more successful female subject in Smagieł's study, she changed her attitude towards English, started socializing with English speaking people and greatly improved her communicative competence. The other subject remained rather restrained in social contacts and treated them purely instrumentally. Consequently, his communicative competence after a year developed to a much lesser extent than the female subject's. Undoubtedly, the woman's greater success can be ascribed to her more outgoing personality. However, also her past language learning history (she was a student of Russian philology) must have affected her interest in learning another foreign language and her readiness to seek contacts with English speaking people.

Smagieł's research is a model study in which sociocultural SLA theory informed the student researcher what aspects of her subjects' behaviour and attitude she should take into account in her observations. The study results are also interesting for SLA sociocultural theory because they support the claim that SLA can be treated as developing a new identity and becoming a member of a new community.

4 Conclusion

It is possible to draw a conclusion on the basis of the recent research that contemporary IDs studies, which treat individual characteristics in a situated and complex way, can be much more easily related to sociolinguistic/sociocultural SLA theory than the traditional IDs studies could be related to psycholinguistic theory. Such an insight can also be gained from qualitative small scale research studies on foreign/second language learning and use, which are accessible to applied linguists, including teachers in training, Master Degree and PhD students.

In my view, IDs research meets sociocultural/sociolinguistic SLA theory whenever the sociocultural/sociolinguistic context of language learning and use is taken into consideration in accounting for learners' different level of L2 attainment. The traditional IDs research focuses on learners' aptitude, motivation, cognitive style, learner strategies etc., and correlates the results with classroom attainment. Such an approach, however, treats IDs in isolation. Even if a high correlation is found between, e.g. aptitude and school grades, the researcher does not know whether in different learner groups and with different learning tasks the correlation coefficients would be equally high. In group L2 learning, and in particular in the so-called 'mixed ability' classes, the support or rejection of an individual student by the teacher or by the peer group can result in their greater or smaller readiness to use L2, their fluency and discourse patterns. In turn, L2 patterns are taken into account while assessing students, and consequently, they affect L2 grades.

IDs research which combines a thorough description of contextual factors and L2 teaching tasks provides the researchers with descriptive data that could be classified according to recurrent patterns of behaviour into particular types. Such a classification does not treat IDs as completely stable and unchanging traits. It rather links L2 learners' patterns of behaviour with environmental influences, parents' and teachers' styles, peer group pressure and other social group influences in the case of immigrants. L2 learners are viewed as becoming part of a culture of the classroom and/or a community. Their past histories, personalities and abilities are analysed together with their level of attainment in different L2 learning situations and tasks. The outcomes of such a research perspective seems to be promising both for the sake of teachers' and teacher trainees' research projects, as well as for the advancement of a more integrated treatment of IDs.

References

Alatis, J., C. Straehle, B. Gallenberger, and M. Ronkin, eds. 1995. *Georgetown University round table on languages and linguistics.* Washington, DC: Georgetown University Press.

Arabski, J., ed. 2002. *Time for words: Studies in foreign language vocabulary acquisition.* Frankfurt am Main: Peter Lang.

Arabski, J., ed. 2006. *Cross-linguistic influences in the second language lexicon.* Clevedon: Multilingual Matters.

Block, D. 2003. *The social turn in second language acquisition*. Edinburgh: Edinburgh University Press.

Carroll, J.B., and S. Sapon. 1959. *Modern Language Aptitude Test. Form A*. New York: The Psychological Corporation.

Corder, S.P. 1967. The significance of learners' errors. *IRAL* 5: 161–169.

Davies, A., and C. Elder, eds. 2004. *The handbook of applied linguistics*. Oxford: Blackwell.

Dörnyei, Z. 2005. *The psychology of the language learner*. Mahwah, NJ: Lawrence Erlbaum.

Doughty, C.J. 2001. Cognitive underpinnings of focus on form. In ed. P. Robinson, 206–257.

Ellis, R. 1994. *The study of second language acquisition*. Oxford: Oxford University Press.

Ellis, R. 2004. Individual differences in second language learning. In eds. A. Davies, and C. Elder, 525–551.

Firth, A., and J. Wagner. 1997. On discourse, communication and (some) fundamental concepts in SLA research. *Modern Language Journal* 81: 285–300.

Gass, S. 1998. Apples and oranges: or, why apples are not orange and don't need to be. *Modern Language Journal* 82: 83–90.

Hall, J. 1997. A consideration of SLA as a theory of practice. *Modern Language Journal* 81: 301–306.

Hatch, E. 1983. *Psycholinguistics: A second language perspective*. Rowley, MA: Newbury House.

Hymes. 1972. On communicative competence. In eds. J. Pride, and J. Holmes, 269–293.

Kasper, G. 1997. 'A' stands for acquisition. *Modern Language Journal* 81: 307–312.

Kettemann, B., and W. Wieden, eds. 1993. *Current issues in European second language acquisition research*. Tubingen: Gunter Narr.

Kita, A. 2008. ERASMUS students' experiences during the mobility period: An exploratory study. Unpublished MA thesis, Jagiellonian University, Kraków.

Kramsch, C., ed. 2002. *Language acquisition and language socialization: Ecological perspectives*. London: Continuum.

Kurcz, I. 1976. Psycholingwistyka [Psycholinguistics]. Warszawa: Państwowe Wydawnictwo Naukowe.

Lantolf, J., and A. Pavlenko. 1994. Sociocultural theory and second language learning. *Annual Review of Applied Linguistics* 15: 108–124.

Larsen-Freeman, D. 1995. On the changing role of linguistics in the education of second language teachers. In eds. J. Alatis, C. Straehle, B. Gallenberger, and M. Ronkin, 711–724.

Larsen-Freeman, D. 2002. Language acquisition and language use from a chaos/complexity perspective. In ed. C. Kramsch, 33–46.

Liddicoat, A. 1997. Interaction, social structure, and second language use. *Modern Language Journal* 81: 313–317.

Long, M.H. 1997. Construct validity in SLA research. *Modern Language Journal* 81: 318–323.

McLaughlin, B. 1987. *Theories of second language learning*. London: Edward Arnold.

Niżegorodcew, A. 1979. Rola specjalnych uzdolnień w nauce języków obcych w szkole [The role of language aptitude in learning foreign languages in school]. *Przegląd Glottodydaktyczny* 3: 31–42.

Niżegorodcew, A. 1980a. Zdolności do nauki języka obcego w świetle badań testowych [Languages aptitude in the light of test studies]. *Zeszyty Naukowe UJ* 31: 137–155.

Niżegorodcew, A. 1980b. The role of aptitude in foreign language learning in secondary grammar school pupils. *Glottodidactica* 13: 37–48.

Niżegorodcew, A. 1991. *Dyskurs interakcyjny a kompetencja komunikacyjna w języku obcym [Interactive discourse and communicative competence in a foreign language]*. Kraków: Jagiellonian University Press.

Niżegorodcew, A. 1993. The structure of foreign language discourse and the use of communication strategies by low proficiency foreign language learners. In ed. B. Kettemann, and W. Wieden, 349–357.

Niżegorodcew, A. 2002. Initial stages in L2 lexical acquisition. In ed. J. Arabski, 267–275.

Niżegorodcew, A. 2006. Assessing L2 lexical development in early L2 learning: A case study. In ed. J. Arabski, 167–176.

Niżegorodcew, A., Y. Bystrov, and M. Kleban, eds. Forthcoming. Developing intercultural competence through English: Focus on Ukrainian and Polish cultures.

Pimsleur, P. 1966. *Language Aptitude Battery*. New York: Harcourt, Brace and World.

Poulisse, N. 1997. Some words in defense of the psycholinguistic approach. *Modern Language Journal* 81: 324–328.

Pride, J., and J. Holmes, eds. 1972. *Sociolinguistics*. Harmondsworth: Penguin.

Robinson, P., ed. 2001. *Cognition and second language instruction*. Cambridge: Cambridge University Press.

Rokita, J. 2007. *Lexical development in early L2 acquisition*. Kraków: Wydawnictwo Naukowe Akademii Pedagogicznej.

Schmidt, R. 1990. The role of consciousness in second language learning. *Applied Linguistics* 11: 129–158.

Selinker, L. 1972. Interlanguage. *IRAL* 10: 209–231.

Skehan, P. 1989. *Individual differences in second language learning*. London: Edward Arnold.

Smagieł, A. 2008. The acculturation process of Polish immigrants in Great Britain. Unpublished MA thesis, Jagiellonian University, Kraków.

Strelau, J. 2000a. Różnice indywidualne: Opis, determinanty i aspekt społeczny [Individual differences: Description, determinants and social aspect]. In ed. J. Strelau, 653–681.

Strelau, J. 2000b. *Psychologia: Podręcznik akademicki [Psychology: An academic textbook]*. Gdańsk: Gdańskie Wydawnictwo Psychologiczne.

Zuengler, J., and E. Miller. 2006. Cognitive and sociocultural perspectives: Two parallel SLA worlds? *TESOL Quarterly* 40: 35–58.

Individual Differences in the Light of New Linguistic Dispensation

Larissa Aronin and Basilius Bawardi

Abstract This article offers some theoretical considerations on the issue of individual differences within the context of contemporary global and sociolinguistic conditions. The essential changes in the field of second language learning and use are treated in connection with global shifts. In the first section the paper provides a description of the new linguistic dispensation as well as its emergent properties and developments. This section is followed by the analysis of the most salient current issues in individual differences such as the reassessment of factors explaining individual variation in view of recent developments, the increase and diversification of language learner populations, the limitless diversification and expansion of the factors deemed responsible for variety in the process and outcomes of language learning, the appearance of new categories of determinants for language learning and consequent re-assessment and restructuring of teaching methodology.

1 Introduction

The aim of this paper is to put forward some theoretical considerations on the issue of individual differences within the context of contemporary global and sociolinguistic conditions. To that end we shall, (1) first describe the essential changes

L. Aronin (✉) · B. Bawardi
Trinity College Dublin, Dublin, Ireland
e-mail: larisa@research.haifa.ac.il

L. Aronin · B. Bawardi
Oranim Academic College of Education, Haifa, Israel

L. Aronin · B. Bawardi
Bar Ilan University, Ramat-Gan, Israel

M. Pawlak (ed.), *New Perspectives on Individual Differences in Language Learning and Teaching*, Second Language Learning and Teaching, DOI: 10.1007/978-3-642-20850-8_2, © Springer-Verlag Berlin Heidelberg 2012

in the field of second language learning and use which have taken place due to and along with global shifts. In particular, we will refer to the new linguistic dispensation of multilingualism as well as its properties and developments. Next, (2) we shall discuss the consequent changes which have occured in the theoretical understanding of individual differences and show how each particular property and development of the new linguistic dispensation is related to various aspects of individual differences. Finally, we will (3) point to some implications of individual differences for the practice of second language learning. For the purposes of the present discussion we understand *second language* as any additional language other than one's mother tongue, that is, as a cover term for second, foreign, third, and subsequent language be it in terms of use, attitude or order of acquisition. Where the distinction between the terms *foreign, second or third* language proves necessary (Sect. 2 of this article) we will specify these languages as such. *Multilingualism* is treated here as the acquisition and use of two or more languages hence multilingualism subsumes bilingualism.

2 Contemporary Sociolinguistic Arrangements in Light of Global Shifts

2.1 Contemporary Multilingualism: The New Linguistic Dispensation

The global linguistic arrangements of modern times are predominantly connected with the use of more than one language. Bi- and multilingualism are ubiquitous in the planet and it is believed that there are more people using more than one language than those using only one (Graddol 1997; Fishman 1998). Further, language patterns have changed so significantly that sets of languages, rather than single languages, now perform the essential functions of communication, cognition and identity for both individuals and the global community (Aronin 2005). Therefore, in this article we will refer to the contemporary sociolinguistic situation as *multilingualism*.

Contemporary multilingualism is considered an ineluctable concomitant of all dimensions of globalization inextricably intertwined with all the major attributes of the dramatic social changes currently occurring in the world. These changes include the compression and expansion of time and space (cf. Giddens 1990; Eriksen 2001), the transcendence of territorial, physical and social boundaries, global mobility, manifested in rapid acceleration in movement of people, goods, trends, and ideas (cf. Bauman 1999; Urry 2000, 2003) in addition to the shift from the social topology of structure (communities, groups, states), via 'horizontal groups' (Friedman 1999), towards the fluid social topology of human society (Urry 2003). Critical globalization writers debate the emergence of global consciousness (O'Byrne 2005) as well as abstract and subjective forms of rationality where knowledge, self-discovery, and emancipation are associated with the concept of *lifeworld* (Habermas 1987). Roudometoff (2005, p. 84) believes that the component structures of lifeworld, namely, culture, society, and personality have undergone significant developments. The issue of identity has become remarkably important in general scientific discourse as compared with its profile in pre-globalization times (cf. Castells 1997). According to Friedman (2000), globalization has its own defining structure of power built around three balances, "(...) which overlap and affect one another" (Friedman 2000, p. 13). Besides the traditional balance between nation-states and the more recent balance between nation-states and global markets, the third and "the one that is really newest of all" is that between individuals and nation-states (Friedman 2000, p. 14). Friedman believes that with the advent of mobility and permeable borders of different kinds, the simultaneous wiring into various networks yields more power to individuals than ever before to the extent that "[i]ndividuals can increasingly act on the world stage directly—unmediated by a state" (Friedman 2000, p. 14).

The above and other changes have resulted in cardinal shifts in the realm of language use in individuals and society and have entailed the recognition that contemporary patterns of language use prove different from those characteristic of previous sociolinguistic contexts (Fishman 1998; Maurais 2003; Aronin and Hufeisen 2009). Although multilingual individuals and societies have existed throughout the history of humankind, the present stage of global sociolinguistic arrangements constitutes a novel development. To emphasize its difference from *historical multilingualism* it is referred to as *a new linguistic dispensation* (see more on this in Aronin and Singleton 2008a). This new dispensation is marked by the ubiquity of multilingualism, the increasing breadth and depth of the effect of multilingualism and its relationship to modifications of human experience. In general terms, researchers agree on the two trends broadly distinguishing today's world linguistic situation (Fishman 1998; Maurais 2003): the wide diversification of recognized languages in use accompanied by a troubling decline in the vigour and, indeed, danger of extinction of many languages and the other, an unprecedented spread of the use of English (Graddol 1997; Graddol 2006; Fishman 1998). Despite the simultaneity of these trends they appear *prima facie* to be in contradiction with each other.

2.2 The **Properties** *and the* **Developments** *of Contemporary Multilingualism*

The intricate interplay of the above two trends accounts for the three distinctive specific qualities inherent in the new linguistic dispensation (that is, current multilingualism): *suffusiveness, complexity* and *liminality*. These *properties*, separately and together, in turn, lead to the specific *developments* (processes and phenomena) unfolding in the realities of global society. The developments involve but are not limited to shifts in norms, an ambience of awareness, the emergence of

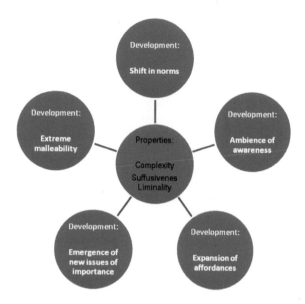

Fig. 1 The properties and developments of the current global linguistic dispensation (Aronin and Singleton 2008c)

new focal issues, extreme malleability and an expansion of affordances (Aronin and Singleton 2008c; Aronin and Singleton, Submitted) (see Fig. 1). The properties and developments of contemporary multilingualism relate prominently to individual differences and may account for significant emerging factors for learning and teaching languages today. These properties will now be discussed in further detail.

The property of *suffusiveness* manifests itself in the world wide permeation of multilingualism evident in the existence of multilingual populations, geographical areas, business, culture and other activity domains where multilingual practices prevail. *Suffusiveness* is supported and propagated by modern technology through the wide diversity of multilingual populations, countries and individuals. Multilingualism 'is based' on the ever rising number of languages—the most accepted figures ranging from 6,000 to 14,000 (Graddol 1997; Fishman 1998; Gnutzmann 2005). Technology, more specifically, computerization, miniaturization, digitization, satellite communication, and the Internet allow for and ensure integrative processes and spread languages and multilingual practices around the world. Multilingualism is suffusive not only due to its permeability but, crucially, on account of its being integral to the construction of a modern reality. Vital societal processes and salient characteristics of contemporary society are inseparably linked with multilingualism. While 'historical multilingualism' was largely supplementary to the development and maintenance of previous societies, virtually every facet of contemporary human life depends on multilingual social arrangements and multilingual individuals (Aronin and Singleton 2008a; Aronin and Singleton, Submitted).

The property *of complexity* relates to the multifaceted nature and dimensions of multilingualism which interact in intricate ways. The dynamic nature of

	Second language acquisition	Multilingual language acquisition
Table 1 Second language acquisition vs. multilingual acquisition (Cenoz 2000, p. 40)	1. L1 → L2 2. Lx + Ly	1. 1. L1 → L2 → L3 1. L1 → Lx/Ly 2. Lx/Ly → L3 3. Lx/Ly/Lz 4. L1 → L2 → L3 → L4 5. L1 → Lx/Ly → L4 6. L1 → L2 → Lx/Ly 7. L1 → Lx/Ly/Lz 8. Lx/Ly → L3 → L4 9. Lx/Ly → Lz/Lz1 10. Lx/Ly/Lz → L4 11. Lx/Ly/Lz/Lz1

multilingualism makes it impossible to account for it as a sum of its parts. Multilingualism in general and the processes of second language acquisition and second language instruction are characterized by fuzziness, irregularity, fragmentariness and at times even chaos. Sociolinguists and educators have to consider multiple agents like number of languages, variety of speakers, modes of use, levels of mastery in relation to an immense variety of interactions resulting in a linguistic reality of language use perceived as unpredictable behaviour, often 'on the verge of the chaotic' (Larsen-Freeman 2002; Aronin and Singleton 2008b). The contact between thousands of languages of various standing and nominations (e.g. official, minority, heritage languages; on nominations see Aronin et al. 2011) carrying out various functions (e.g. mother tongue, second/foreign language) spoken by linguistically diverse populations with a variety of formal and informal educational experiences generates diversity.

As for factors influencing second language acquisition, these are many. Among them are, for instance, educational context, formal or informal and the particular goals of language learning: which and how many languages are taught? Are they taught as disciplines or as means of education? Which language skills are emphasized and what levels form the objectives? Other factors cover: the order of language acquisition, methods and techniques, specific aims and programs and teacher qualification. In regard to individual factors, these are numerous and include the origins of multilinguality, personal experiences and reasons for multilingualism, needs and affordances, world outlook, preferences, emotions and metalinguistic awareness.

To exemplify the complexity of second language acquisition we refer here to the frequently cited table by Cenoz (2000, p. 40) (Table 1). The table shows only one factor in multiple language acquisition, that of acquisition order, but clearly demonstrates how this order gives rise to variation and the leap in complexity and diversity between second language acquisition and acquisition of a third and additional languages. With two languages involved in the acquisition process we may consider only two possible acquisition orders: the second language can be acquired either after L1 (L1 → L2) or at the same time as the L1 (Lx + Ly). In the case of third language acquisition there are already at least four possible acquisition orders. The three languages can be acquired consecutively (L1 → L2 → L3) or with a simultaneous component: the simultaneous acquisition of two languages (Lx/Ly) could take place after the L1 has been acquired (L1 → Lx/Ly,) or before the L3 is acquired (Lx/Ly → L3). Or there could be simultaneous contact with all three languages (Lx/Ly/Lz). This diversity can be further increased where the acquisition process is interrupted by the acquisition of an additional language and then restarted (L1 → L2 → L3 → L2).

Lately, one may note increasing recognition of the complexity of multilingualism in general, and of second/multiple language acquisition in particular. Larsen-Freeman (1997, 2002) pointed to striking similarities between chaos/complexity and second language acquisition. Herdina and Jessner placed the focus of their dynamic model of multilingualism (DMM) on "(…) the variability and dynamics of the individual speaker system" (Herdina and Jessner 2002, p. 2). Gabryś-Barker (2005) analysing quantitative studies on multilingual development, lexical storage, processing and retrieval, adopted the perspective of the complexity of multilingualism and of the fuzziness of multilingual lexicon as her frame of reference. Aronin and Tikhiy (2005) demonstrated the remarkable parallel between the concepts of complexity and the recent key findings in multilingualism. The crucial novel approaches in multilingualism testify to the emergent qualities, that is, new properties and behaviours not contained in the essence of the constituent elements. Further, these new characteristics and behaviours cannot be predicted from knowledge of initial conditions. The recent view adopted by multilingualism studies asserts that:

- Multilingualism is not only quantitatively, but also qualitatively different from bilingualism, and possesses characteristics not found in bilingualism (see for example, Hoffmann 2001a, 2001b; Herdina and Jessner 2002).
- A bilingual is not the sum of two monolinguals and a multilingual is not the sum of multiple monolinguals but possesses very special characteristics not found in less-linguals. Following Grosjean (1985, 1992) and Cook (1992, 1993), bilinguals are now viewed as possessing a special constellation of language competencies which allow communication in various and multiple social contexts. Thus, multilinguals are represented as possessing "a configuration of linguistic competences that is distinct from that of bilinguals and monolinguals" (Cenoz and Genesee 1998, p. 19).
- Second, third and subsequent language acquisition processes do not exactly replicate the processes operative in previous language acquisition (Grosjean 1985, 1992). This means that trilingual education, for example, is not just a simple matter of the mechanical addition of one or more languages in the curriculum.
- Complexity presupposes sensitivity to initial conditions. Sensitivity to initial conditions of chaotic systems means that the slightest change in those conditions can produce radically different results.

Fig. 2 Graphic model of Lorenz's butterfly (the figure is taken from http://www.wiley.com/legacy/wileychi/systemsengineering/Systems_Engineering/page3/page3.html)

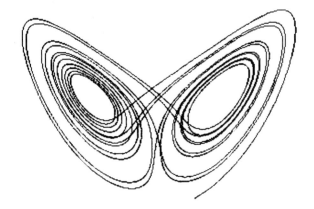

Lorenz's butterfly can serve not only as a model demonstrating infinite diversity and unpredictability of the possible outcomes of second language learning but may also symbolize the issue of individual differences (see Fig. 2—Graphic model of Lorenz's butterfly). In practice, in the domain of second/multiple language teaching sensitivity to initial conditions proves familiar to anyone who observes the variety of language profiles of every individual student in a given class. Thus, variations will be observed in early or late onset of study, sufficient or insufficient exposure to a language, encounters which may spark or enhance interest in a particular language. As indicated above, all these may result in significant diversions from any particular expected outcome. Discussions of the age factor in second/third language exposure, decisions regarding the sequence of language learning in childhood, school, as well as emigration conditions, all constitute attempts to cope with the impact of initial conditions.

The last property of contemporary multilingualism labeled *liminality* addresses the observation that many language related processes and phenomena have, of late, become especially discernible due to recent societal shifts and changes and in particular to those in the domain of language use. In other words, under current sociolinguistic dispensation, issues which previously were impossible to single out, are now becoming apparent. Spolsky (1999) provided a clear instance of liminality. Describing second/foreign language teaching and learning, he noted that "[t]hose of us concerned with the field of second language learning have been forced by the ethnic revival and by our new appreciation of language and ethnicity to extend our concerns to embrace the social context in which the teaching takes place" (Spolsky 1999, p. 182). This new concern forms a contrast with the purely linguistic approach to second language learning prevalent before. Another illustration of liminality may serve to clarify the property in question. Multilingualism, now increasingly perceived as subsuming bilingualism, was initially considered a case of bilingualism and developed within the framework of bilingualism. In fact, this position is still held today by some researchers and lay people. Recently however, research has supplied findings testifying to and clarifying the special nature of tri/multilingual users as distinct from bilinguals (Cenoz and Genesee 1998; Cenoz et al. 2001; Herdina and Jessner 2002).

To sum up, the three *properties* of contemporary multilingualism, *suffusiveness, complexity* and *liminality,* materialize in the concrete *developments* taking place in the current global linguistic dispensation (Aronin and Singleton 2008c). In section two we will examine the changes in the domain of individual differences as they are connected with properties and developments of the new linguistic dispensation.

3 Individual Differences in the Context of the New Linguistic Dispensation

3.1 A Brief Overview of Traditional Perspectives on Individual Differences

The topic of individual differences in second language acquisition has been dealt with by a range of disciplines among them cognitive psychology and applied linguistics. Serious research into bilingualism which emerged in the 1970s and 1980s, (see for example, Gal 1979; Baetens Beardsmore 1982; Genesee 1983; Romaine 1989), focused on individual language behavior, including the psychology of language learning and the intricacy of the bilingual mind (Paradis 1985; Obler 1989). The cognitive effect of the contact between two languages, as well as advantages and disadvantages of bilingualism were widely discussed (cf. Skutnabb-Kangas 1981; Hamers and Blanc 1983). From that time on the focal points in individual differences include age, often considered within the topic of the critical period hypothesis (Marinova-Todd et al. 2000; Singleton and Ryan 2004; Singleton 2005), learners' cognitive abilities (cf. Ackerman 1988, Ackerman 1989) and motivation (Gardner and Lambert 1959, 1972).

In 1994 Ellis directed attention to the three large classes of variables that may be implicated in determining individual differences in second language acquisition: *learner differences*, *learner strategies* and *performance outcomes* Ellis 1994. In 1997 Ellis referred to learners' characteristics as *psychological dimensions* as opposed to *social* (which include conditions of learning). Segalowitz (1997, p. 86) noted that a cognitive linguistics approach "overlooks the social and communicative dimensions that necessarily affect the course of language development" and notably, called for "explicit recognition of the complexity of the perceptual, memory, attentional, and other demands made on the individual's cognitive resources, demands felt at every level, from the perception of basic linguistic units to the handling of communicative negotiations" (Segalowitz 1997, 86). Segalowitz formulated the problem of how to account for individual differences specific to second language development in the following way: "What are the psychological complexities of communication that underlie L2 skill development, what cognitive resources are required to deal with these complexities, and why do individuals differ in the way they organize and manage their resources?"

Lightbown and Spada (2006) acknowledged the importance of the social and educational settings in which learners find themselves. Under the umbrella of individual differences they included intelligence, aptitude, learning styles, personality, motivation and attitudes, identity and ethnic group affiliation, learner beliefs, age of acquisition and the critical period hypothesis. In addition, these writers addressed the difficulties and challenges in assessing the relationship between individual learner characteristics and second language learning.

3.2 Individual Differences and the New Linguistic Dispensation

The global transformation and modification in language arrangements including language use and language learning has resulted in a shift in the perception of individual differences calling for a fresh look at which differences impact second language acquisition and the extent to which they do so.

The suffusiveness and ubiquity of multilingualism in accordance with the unprecedented spread of English and the diversification of languages in use resulted in the increase of language learner populations of all ages, abilities and statuses of citizenship. Increased physical and social mobility and the expansion of affordances have led to a surge in migrant populations characterized by diversity in relation to which and how many languages are learnt and used, in which role they are learned, as well as the level of mastery of the languages at one's disposal. Migrants represent a category of language learners with multiple subcategories. Walker (2006, p. 1), for example, in her study of multilingual migrants who use various minority languages in addition to English in Aotearoa, New Zealand notably, emphasized "(...) the complex interconnections between cognitive, sociolinguistic and social-psychological dimensions associated with language learning". She concluded that viewing often already bilingual migrants as language learners in the process of renegotiating their identity carries implications for language learning pedagogy. From this perspective, second language learning and teaching methods and their outcome depend on particular learner characteristics, in other words, specific individual differences.

Amharic speaking illiterate adult Ethiopian immigrants to Israel learning Hebrew and English as second or additional languages possess distinctive characteristics which present special challenges to language teachers (Osmolovsky 2008). These immigrants study Hebrew in the framework of a specially organized course tailored for the needs of this population. Osmolovsky notes that the success of the project "depends on the right combination and application of linguistic and cultural context and includes, among other things, the students moving around the class as well as manipulating moving objects rather than learning only from verbal material".

The beneficiaries of multilingual teaching projects in Europe such as EuroCom and projects funded by the European Centre of Modern languages (ECML) form a different group of language learners. In addition to differences in aptitude, cognitive abilities and age these European citizens are characterized by other important variables that impact language learning. These include the particular mother tongue or habitually spoken language and the typological distance between it and the target language. Since the aim of EuroCom, is "to provide European citizens with a solid linguistic basis for understanding each other, at least within their own language family" (Jessner 2008a, p. 36) teaching concentrates on specifically developed materials which practice inferencing techniques in typologically-related languages like Romance, Germanic and Slavonic languages (see more on EuroCom in Jessner 2008a; Hufeisen and Marx 2007b and EuroCom http://eurocom-frankfurt.de accessed 20.04.2011).

An even more narrowly identified group of European additional language learners are the speakers of Scandinavian languages. Receptive multilingualism recently has been officially introduced as a goal although the practices of inter-Scandinavian comprehension, have long been in existence (see for example, Braunmüller 2007). For Scandinavians learning a linguistically related neighbouring language, the ease and outcome of the learning process depend on perceived and real linguistic distance between the two related languages, and the extent to which the latter corresponds to the former. Other relevant factors include mastery of their own languages and exposure to the target neighbouring languages. Notably, for successful receptive multilingual communication such factors as phonological and linguistic awareness, metalinguistic and intercultural understanding, readiness for communication all need to be on significantly high levels (Zeevaert and ten Thije 2007).

In an attempt to level individual differences in receptive multilingual communication, facilitate the learning process and work towards better results, Möller (2007) explored lexical possibilities of inter-comprehension through the investigation of German cognates of Dutch words. In another study, Lutjeharms (2007) showed the importance of teaching learners to organize their comprehension by exploiting transfer and syntactic cues from more proficient languages to 'correct' the perceived structural similarity of the languages in question. Both studies along with others demonstrate that didactic implementations of the receptive multilingual approach to Germanic languages are under way (Hufeisen and Lutjeharms 2005; Hufeisen and Marx 2007a; Marx 2010).

The examples presented above were provided to illustrate the increase and diversification of language learner populations and how this expansion and branching out render diversity in the factors that have an impact on language learning processes and outcomes. To further exemplify the point we will now consider two most prominent lines of research which we identified as contributing the most into our knowledge about the individual differences. The first explores a variety of interactions between languages used by individuals. The second embraces studies which share the interest in various identity aspects of language learners as factors of influence on second language acquisition.

Research investigating the interaction between languages used by an individual is providing new data and important insights. Studies in the framework of second language acquisition (SLA) focus on multiple language acquisition, tri- and multilingual education and, in particular, cross-linguistic influences (Cenoz et al. 2001; Jessner 2008a) including cross-linguistic transfer between L2 and L3, i.e. not from L1, which was the previous focus (cf. De Angelis and Selinker 2001; De Angelis 2005; De Angelis and Dewaele 2009). The studies on cross-linguistic influences present an enormous variety of language learning situations and outcomes. Thus, being a mono-, bi-, tri- or multilingual learner/speaker adds dimensions of individual differences which, in turn, diversify exponentially.

Typologies and classifications of multilinguals capture differences between learners which in the long run determine their proficiency and may be seen as attempts to organise and consider the novel dimensions of differences between learners and speakers of multiple languages. For example, Skutnabb-Kangas (1981, p. 75) divided bilinguals into four sub groups—élite bilinguals, children from linguistic majorities, children from bilingual families, and children from linguistic minorities. Baetens Beardsmore (1982) provided a wide-ranged typology of bilingualism and bilinguals, in which he made distinctions between societal and individual bilingualism and receptive and productive bilingualism. These typologies may be extended to multilinguals. Li Wei (2000a, pp. 6–7) identified thirty-seven types of bilingualism, including, for example, balanced, incipient, dormant and receptive bilinguals. Hoffmann (2001a, pp. 18–19) classified trilinguals into five groups, taking into account both the circumstances and the social context under which the subjects became speakers of three languages. She noted that:

> One could also establish other typologies reflecting, as criteria, features related to acquisition such as age, acquisition process (simultaneous, successive or a combination of them), acquisition context (home, community, classroom, school), language competence and skills attained, among others (Hoffmann 2001a, p. 19).

Other distinctions between bi- and multilinguals are found in learner strategies. Kemp (2007) reported that multilingual learners use different strategies than monolingual students learning their first foreign language. She also noted the variation in multilinguals' use of strategies. Previous linguistic knowledge constitutes a factor believed to be significant in learning subsequent languages. Most of the models used in research on multilingualism which developed from a psycholinguistic perspective on multilingualism take into account prior linguistic knowledge. Hufeisen's factor model serves a good example. The model clearly describes the processes of L1 acquisition, L2 learning, L3 learning and learning of the next language as consecutive stages showing the difference between each previous and following stage. Thus, it demonstrates that the groups of factors responsible for language learning and acquisition vary depending on whether the first, the second or the consecutive language is being learnt (Hufeisen 1998; Hufeisen and Marx 2007b). Another example comes from Gallardo del Puerto (2007) who reported that the acquisition of linguistic aspects in L3, in particular, phonological acquisition, does not follow the same route as the acquisition of grammar or vocabulary of the third language. While acquiring the sounds of their tertiary language learners did not benefit from their bilingual proficiency in a significant way. Jessner (2008b) explicitly associates qualitative differences between L2 and L3 learning with the shift in norms language learners relate to:

> Changes of quality between second and third language learning are based on the differences in norms that the language learners relate to, that is a bilingual norm in third language learning as opposed to a monolingual norm in second language learning. In addition, in most contexts, third language learning assumes that the learner has already gained experience in learning a first foreign language.

The second current development in the area of individual differences concerns the apparent emphasis on identity traits, both inborn and acquired through the societal circumstances a person finds himself/herself in. Among these factors are psychotypology (cf. Ó Laoire and Singleton 2009), emotions (cf. Dewaele 2005), affordances (cf. Singleton and Aronin 2007; Aronin and Singleton 2010b) and learner autonomy (cf. Little 2007). Language learner identity has become, in accordance with the current universal interest in identity, the point of departure for language teaching.

Aronin and Ó Laoire (2004) singled out the notion of *multilinguality* and defined it as "(...) a personal characteristic that can be described as an individual *store of languages* at any level of proficiency including partial competence— incomplete fluency as well as metalinguistic awareness, learning strategies, opinions and preferences and passive or active knowledge on languages, language use and language learning/acquisition" (Aronin and Ó Laoire 2004, pp. 17–18). Another definition of multilinguality by the same authors emphasizes that "multilinguality is a facet of a self, activated and expressed through language and language related phenomena, which influences the social and private life of an individual. Multilinguality is expressed through actions, perceptions, attitudes and abilities" (Aronin and Ó Laoire 2003). The identity of the contemporary language learner, his/her multilinguality in its multiple manifestations in the long run accounts for the speed, ease or difficulty and the outcome of second and consequent language acquisition.

The transition in attention from the monolingual perspective to the norm of using and mastering two or more languages led to increased appreciation of specific abilities exclusive to bi- and multilingual language users. One can note in this respect Baker's (1993) concept of *communicative sensitivity,* characteristic of bilinguals (which may be extended to trilinguals) who navigate through complex pragmatic situations. However, the most unique and specific feature differentiating bi- and multilingual language users/learners from monolinguals is captured in the concept of multicompetence (Cook 1992, 1993, 1996).

Kecskés and Papp (2000a) proposed the notions of *Common Underlying Conceptual Base (CUCB)* and multilingual *Language Processing Device (LPD)* which, according to these authors, make the speaker multicompetent. Kecskés and Papp speak about individual variation in those who enjoy the affordance of multicompetence. They explain that crossing a proficiency threshold is the prerequisite for developing CUCB: "If this threshold has not been reached, the learning of subsequent languages is merely an educational enhancement (...)" (Kecskés and Papp 2000b). Not only do monolinguals differ from bilinguals and those mastering their second language from those acquiring their third. In addition to the differentiation between monolinguals and multicompetent language users, the divergence between bilinguals and trilinguals is also under scrutiny.

Taking the idea of multicompetence further and looking at multicompetence from a psycholinguistic perspective, Cenoz and Genesee (1998, p. 19) state that "multilinguals possess a configuration of linguistic competencies that is distinct from that of monolinguals and bilinguals". To close this section we wish to reiterate that multicompetence with its various interpretations deals with yet one additional dimension of language learner individual differences. As more concrete aspects of this quality of multilingual speakers crystallize it is becoming apparent that multicompetence comprises multiple dimensions going beyond those initially identified. The recognition of multicompetence as a crucially influential factor of language learning has practical implications since multicompetence approaches to language proficiency make a difference in multilingual education (Hufeisen and Neuner 2004; Jessner 2008b).

4 Conclusions

Globalization has shaped a new world of language practices and ideologies manifested in a distinctly new global linguistic dispensation, where constellations of languages rather than one single language are prerequisite for society's functioning and progress on a world scale. The new linguistic dispensation, i.e. contemporary multilingualism, is characterized by special properties and developments. Singled out for theoretical purposes of understanding the contemporary global sociolinguistic settings, the properties of suffusiveness, complexity and liminality, and the developments of change of norms, emergence of new topics of importance, ambience of awareness, extreme malleability and expansion of affordances take effect jointly or each in cooperation with another or several others to make for the changes referred to in this article.

Alongside the continuing traditional inquiries into individual differences, the focus of interest in this area has moved towards the factors determined by recent global social changes. The new global linguistic dispensation has resulted in shifts in the domain of second language acquisition in general, and, in particular, has brought about an essential reconsideration of factors influencing individual variation in learning additional languages. In that context we have pointed to the increase and diversification of language learner populations, the limitless diversification and expansion of the factors deemed responsible for variety in the process and outcome of language learning and the appearance of new categories of determinants for language learning. Factors of individual variation that already enjoyed researchers' attention are undergoing revision and reassessment as a result of developments in contemporary sociolinguistic arrangements. More attention has been channeled to cross-linguistic influence, transfer of language knowledge, learning strategies and developing linguistic and metalinguistic awareness. Further, there is notable recognition of the interactions between L2 and L3/Ln rather than the unidirectional transfer from L1 to L2. Variables determined by identity of a learner receive particular attention and research into diverse identity-related factors is on the rise. Consequent re-assessment and restructuring of teaching and learning methods have taken place, finding their practical outcome in the development of the concepts of tertiary language didactics, plurilingualism didactics and language learning projects taking advantage of specific character-istics of multilingual learners.

To conclude, the new global linguistic dispensation has led to the recognition of additional factors impacting individual differences. This development has reper-cussions for language pedagogy. As new insights emerge further implications will require consideration.

References

Ackerman, P. 1988. Determinants of individual differences during skill acquisition: Cognitive abilities and information processing. *Journal of Experimental Psychology: General* 117: 288–318.

Ackerman, P. 1989. Individual differences and skill acquisition. In eds. P. Ackerman, R. Sternberg, and R. Glaser, 165–217.

Ackerman, P., R. Sternberg, and R. Glaser, eds. 1989. *Learning and individual differences.* New York: Freeman.

Appelbaum, R., and W. Robinson, eds. 2005. *Critical globalization studies.* New York and London: Routledge.

Aronin, L. 2005a. Theoretical perspectives of trilingual education. *International Journal of the Sociology of Language* 171: 7–22.

Aronin, L., and B. Hufeisen, eds. 2009. *The exploration of multilingualism: Development of research on L3, multilingualism and multiple languages.* Amsterdam: John Benjamins.

Aronin, L., and M. Ó Laoire. 2003. Multilinguality in multilingual research. Paper presented at the Third International Conference on Third Language Acquisition and Trilingualism 2003, Tralee.

Aronin, L., and D. Singleton. 2008a. Multilingualism as a new linguistic dispensation. *International Journal of Multilingualism* 5: 1–16.

Aronin, L., and D. Singleton. 2008b. The complexity of multilingual contact and language use in times of globalization. *Conversarii. Studi Linguistici* 2: 33–47.

Aronin, L., and D. Singleton. 2008c. English as a constituent of Dominant Language Constellation. Paper presented at the GlobEng conference, 2008, Verona.

Aronin, L., and D. Singleton (guest eds). 2010a. Special Issue: The Diversity of Multilingualism. *International Journal of the Sociology of Language,* J.A. Fishman (general ed). Mouton de Gruyter.

Aronin, L., and D. Singleton. 2010b. Affordances and the diversity of multilingualism. In J. A. Fishman (general ed), September 2010, L. Aronin & D. Singleton (guest eds), 105–129. Mouton de Gruyter.

Aronin, L., and D. Singleton. Submitted. *Multilingualism.* Amsterdam: John Benjamins.

Aronin, L., and V. Tikhiy. 2005. Applying complexity science to multilingual education. Paper presented at Complexity, Science and Society Conference, 2005, Liverpool.

Aronin, L., and M. ÓLaoire. 2004. Exploring multilingualism in cultural contexts: Towards a notion of multilinguality. In eds. C. Hoffmann, and J. Ytsma, 11–29.

Aronin, L., M. ÓLaoire, and D. Singleton. 2011. The Multiple Faces of Multilingualism: Language Nominations. In *Applied Linguistics Review*. Mouton: De Gruyter.

Baetens Beardsmore, H. 1982. *Bilingualism: Basic principles*. Clevedon: Tieto Ltd.

Baker, C. 1993. *Foundations of bilingual education and bilingualism*. Clevedon: Multilingual Matters.

Bauman, Z. 1999. *Globalization: The human consequences*. Cambridge: Polity Press.

Braunmüller, K. 2007. Receptive multilingualism in Nothern Europe in the Middle Ages: A description of a scenario. In eds. J. Thije, and L. Zeevaert, 25–47.

Brown, G., K. Malmkjaer, and J. Williams, eds. 1996. *Performance and competence in second language acquisition*. Cambridge: Cambridge University Press.

Castells, M. 1997. *The power of identity*. Oxford: Blackwell.

Cenoz, J. 2000. Research on multilingual acquisition. In eds. J. Cenoz, and U. Jessner, 39–53.

Cenoz, J., and F. Genesee, eds. 1998. *Beyond bilingualism: Multilingualism and multilingual education*. Clevedon: Multilingual Matters.

Cenoz, J., and U. Jessner, eds. 2000. *English in Europe: The acquisition of a third language*. Clevedon: Multilingual Matters.

Cenoz, J., B. Hufeisen, and U. Jessner, eds. 2001. *Cross-linguistic influence in third language acquisition: Psycholinguistic perspectives*. Clevedon: Multilingual Matters.

Cook, V. 1992. Evidence for multi-competence. *Language Learning* 42: 557–591.

Cook, V. 1993. *Linguistics and second language acquisition*. London: Macmillan.

Cook, V. 1996. Competence and multi-competence. In eds. G. Brown, K. Malmkjaer, and J. Williams, 57–69.

Cummins, J., and Hornberger, N., eds. 2008. *Encyclopedia of language and education. Volume 5: Bilingual education*. 2nd ed. Springer Science+Business Media LLC.

De Angelis, G. 2005. Multilingualism and non-native lexical transfer: An identification problem. *International Journal of Multilingualism* 2: 1–25.

De Angelis, G., and J.-M. Dewaele. Under Revision. The development of psycholinguistic research on cross-linguistic influence. In eds. L. Aronin, and B. Hufeisen.

De Angelis, G., and L. Selinker. 2001. Interlanguage transfer and competing linguistic systems in the multilingual mind. In eds. U. Jessner, B. Hufeisen, and J. Cenoz, 42–58.

De Groot, A., and J. Kroll, eds. 1997. *Tutorials in bilingualism: Psycholinguistic perspectives*. Mahwah: Lawrence Erlbaum.

Dewaele, J.-M. 2005. Investigating the psychological and emotional dimensions in instructed language learning: obstacles and possibilities. *Modern Language Journal* 89: 367–380.

Doyé, P., and F.-J. Meissner, eds. 2010. *Lernerautonomie durch Interkomprehension: Projekte und Perspektiven*. Tübingen: Narr.

Ellis, R. 1994. *The study of second language acquisition*. Oxford: Oxford University Press.

Ellis, R. 1997. *Second language acquisition*. Oxford: Oxford University Press.

EuroCom http://eurocom-frankfurt.de. Accessed 20 April 2011.

Eriksen, T. 2001. *Tyranny of the moment: Fast and slow time in the information age*. London: Pluto Press.

Fishman, J. 1998. The new linguistic order. *Foreign Policy* 113: 26–40.

Fishman, J., ed. 1999. *Handbook of language and ethnic identity*. Oxford: Oxford University Press.

Friedman, L. 1999. *The horizontal society*. Newhaven: Yale University Press.

Friedman, T. 2000. *The lexus and the olive tree: Understanding globalization*. New York: Anchor Books.

Gabryś-Barker, D. 2005. *Aspects of multilingual storage, processing and retrieval*. Katowice: Wydawnictwo Uniwersytetu Śląskiego.

Gal, S. 1979. *Language shift: Social determinants of linguistic change in bilingual Australia.* New York: Academic Press.

Gallardo del Puerto, F. 2007. Is L3 phonological competence affected by the learner's level of bilingualism? *International Journal of Multilingualism* 4: 1–16.

Gardner, R., and W. Lambert. 1959. Motivational variables in second language acquisition. *Canadian Journal Psychol* 13: 266–272.

Gardner, R., and W. Lambert. 1972. *Attitudes and motivation in second language learning.* Rowley: Newbury House.

Gass, S., C. Madden, D. Preston, and L. Selinker, eds. 1989. *Variation in second language acquisition: Vol II. Psycholinguistic issues.* Clevedon: Multilingual Matters.

Genesee, F. 1983. Bilingual education of majority-language children: The immersion experiments in review. *Applied Psycholinguistics* 4: 1–6.

Giddens, A. 1990. *The consequences of modernity.* Cambridge: Polity Press.

Gnutzmann, C. 2005. Standard English and world standard English. Linguistic and pedagogical considerations. In eds. C. Gnutzmann, and F. Intemann, 107–118.

Gnutzmann, C., and F. Intemann, eds. 2005. *The globalisation of English and the English language classroom.* Tübingen: Narr.

Graddol, D. 1997. *The future of English?* London: The British Council.

Graddol, D. 2006. *English next.* London: British Council.

Grosjean, F. 1985. The bilingual as a competent but specific speaker-learner. *Journal of Multilingual and Multicultural Development* 6: 467–477.

Grosjean, F. 1992. Another view if bilingualism. In ed. R. Harris, 51–62.

Habermas, J. 1987. *The theory of communicative action. Vol. 2. Lifeworld and system: A critique of functionalist reason.* Cambridge: Polity.

Hamers, J., and M. Blanc. 1983. *Bilinguality and bilingualism.* Cambridge: Cambridge University Press.

Harris, R., ed. 1992. *Cognitive processing in bilinguals.* Amsterdam: Elsevier Science Publishers.

Herdina, P., and U. Jessner. 2002. *A dynamic model of multilingualism: Perspectives of change in psycholinguistics.* Clevedon: Multilingual Matters.

Hoffmann, C. 2001a. The status of trilingualism in bilingualism Studies. In eds. J. Cenoz, B. Hufeisen, and U. Jessner, 13–25.

Hoffmann, C., and J. Ytsma, eds. 2004. *Trilingualism in family, school and community.* Clevedon: Multilingual Matters.

Hufeisen, B. 1998. L3–Stand der Forschung–Was bleibt zu tun? In eds. B. Hufeisen, and D. Lindemann, 169–183.

Hufeisen, B., and D. Lindemann, eds. 1998a. *Tertiärsprachen. Theorien, Modelle, Methoden.* Tübingen: Stauffenburg.

Hufeisen, B., and D. Lindemann, eds. 1998b. *Trilingualism in family, school and community.* Clevedon: Multilingual Matters.

Hufeisen, B., and M. Lutjeharms, eds. 2005. *Gesamtsprachencurriculum–Integrierte Sprachen-didaktik–Common Curriculum. Theoretische Überlegungen und Beispiele der Umsetzung.* Tubingen: Gunter Narr.

Hufeisen, B., and N. Marx, eds. 2007a. *EuroComGerm–Die sieben Siebe: Germanische Sprachen lessen lernen.* Aachen: Shaker.

Hufeisen, B., and N. Marx. 2007b. How can DaFnE and EuroComGerm contribute to the concept of receptive multilingualism? Theoretical and practical considerations. In eds. J. Thije, and L. Zeevaert, 307–321.

Hufeisen, B., and G. Neuner. 2004. *The plurilingualism project: Tertiary language learning—German after English.* Strasbourg: Council of Europe Publishing.

Jessner, U. 2008a. Teaching third languages: Findings, trends and challenges. *Language Teaching* 41: 15–56.

Jessner, U. 2008b. Multicompetence approaches to language proficiency development in multilingual education. In eds. J. Cummins, and N. Hornberger, 1–13.

Jessner, U., B. Hufeisen, and J. Cenoz, eds. 2000. *Cross-linguistic aspects of L3 acquisition.* Clevedon: Multilingual Matters.

Kecskés, I., and T. Papp. 2000a. *Foreign language and mother tongue.* Hillsdale, MJ: Lawrence Erlbaum.

Kecskés, I., and T. Papp. 2000b. Metaphorical competence in trilingual language production. In eds. J. Cenoz, and U. Jessner, 99–120.

Kemp, C. 2007. Strategic processing in grammar learning: Do multilinguals use more strategies? *International Journal of Multilingualism* 4: 241–261.

Kramsch, C., ed. 2002. *Language acquisition and language socialization: Ecological perspectives.* London: Continuum.

Ó Laoire, M., ed. 2006. *Multilingualism in educational settings.* Hohengehren: Schneider Verlag.

Ó Laoire, M., and D. Singleton. 2009. The role of prior knowledge in L3 learning and use: further evidence of a psychotypological dimension. In eds. L. Aronin, and B. Hufeisen, 79–102.

Larsen-Freeman, D. 1997. Chaos/complexity science and second language acquisition. *Applied Linguistics* 18: 141–165.

Larsen-Freeman, D. 2002. Language acquisition and language use from a chaos/ complexity theory perspective. In ed. C. Kramsch, 33–46.

Lightbown, P., and N. Spada. 2006. *How languages are learned*, 3rd ed. Oxford: Oxford University Press.

Little, D. 2007. Language learner autonomy: Some fundamental considerations revisited. *Innovation in Language Learning and Teaching* I(1): 14–29.

Li, Wei. 2000a. Dimensions of multilingualism. In ed. Wei Li, 3–25.

Li, Wei, ed. 2000b. *The bilingualism reader.* London and New York: Routledge.

Lutjeharms, M. 2007. Processing levels in foreign-language reading. In eds. J. Thije, and L. Zeevaert, 265–284.

Marinova-Todd, S., B. Marshall, and C. Snow. 2000. Three misconceptions about age and L2 learning. *TESOL Quarterly* 34: 9–34.

Marx, N. 2010. Eag and multilingualism pedagogy. An empirical study on students' learning processes on the internet platform English after German. In eds. P. Doyé, and F.-J. Meissner.

Maurais, J. 2003. Towards a new linguistic world order. In eds. J. Maurais, and M. Morris, 13–36.

Maurais, J., and M. Morris, eds. 2003. *Languages in a globalizing world.* Cambridge: Cambridge University Press.

Möller, R. 2007. A computer-based exploration of the lexical possibilities of intercomprehension: Finding German cognates of Dutch words. In eds. J. Thije, and L. Zeevaert, 285–305.

O'Byrne, D. 2005. Toward a critical theory of globalization: A Habermasian approach. In eds. R. Appelbaum, and W. Robinson, 75–87.

Obler, L. 1989. Exceptional second language learners. In eds. S. Gass, C. Madden, D. Preston, and L. Selinker, 141–159.

Osmolovsky, A. 2008. Social tuning of illiterate adult immigrants through the selective connecting of Amharic and Hebrew languages and cultures. Poster presentation at the 17 Sociolinguistic Symposium, Amsterdam.

Paradis, M. 1985. On the representation of two languages in one brain. *Language Sciences* 61: 1–40.

Romaine, S. 1989. *Bilingualism.* London: Blackwell.

Roudometoff, V. 2005. Transnationalism and cosmopolitanism: Errors of globalism. In eds. R. Appelbaum, and W. Robinson, 65–74.

Segalowitz, N. 1997. Individual differences in second language acquisition. In eds. A. de Groot, and J. Kroll, 85–112.

Singleton, D. 2005. The Critical Period Hypothesis: A coat of many colours. *International Review of Applied Linguistics in Language Teaching* 43: 269–285.

Singleton, D., and L. Aronin. 2007. Multiple language learning in the light of the theory of affordances. *Innovation in Language Teaching and Learning* 1: 83–96.

Singleton, D., and L. Ryan. 2004. *Language acquisition: The age factor*, 2nd ed. Clevedon: Multilingual Matters.

Skutnabb-Kangas, T. 1981. *Bilingualism or not: The education of minorities.* Clevedon: Multilingual Matters.

Spolsky, B. 1999. Second language learning. In ed. J. Fishman, 181–192.

Thije, J., and L. Zeevaert, eds. 2007. *Receptive multilingualism: Linguistic analyses, language policies and didactic concepts.* Amsterdam: John Benjamins.

Urry, J. 2000. *Sociology beyond societies: Mobilities for the twenty-first century.* London: Routledge.

Urry, J. 2003. *Global complexity.* Cambridge: Polity Press.

Walker, U. 2006. The role of bi/multilingual selves among multilingual migrants on Aotearoa/ New Zealand: Implications for language learning and teaching. In ed. M. Ó Laoire, 1–19.

Zeevaert, L., and J. ten Thije. 2007. Introduction. In eds. J. Thije, and L. Zeevaert, 1–21.

Extra Input Biased Learning: a Connectionist Account of the Adult Language Learning Paradox

István Ottó and Marianne Nikolov

Abstract In this paper we offer one possible resolution of the Adult Language Learning (ALL) Paradox (Sokolik 1990), which posits that notwithstanding adults' higher ability in dealing with rules and their initial advantage over younger learners, they generally fail to achieve high levels of L2 proficiency, in spite of the fact that natural languages are rule-governed systems. We briefly review some existing explanations from a variety of perspectives and conclude that neither of them takes into account both adults' initial advantage and children's higher ultimate attainment. We propose a connectionist model as an explanation for the ALL Paradox and present the results of a set of simulations which were based on this theory. The results supported the theory.

1 Introduction

A recurring theme in second language acquisition (SLA) research is the notion of a certain critical period for learning second languages (Harley 1986; Scovel 1988; Singleton 1989; Long 1990; Harley and Wang 1997; Birdsong 1999; Scovel 2000; Paradis 2004; Singleton and Ryan 2004; Birdsong 2005; Bongaerts 2005; DeKeyser and Larson-Hall 2005; Singleton 2005; Nikolov and Mihaljevic Djigunovic 2006; Slabakova 2006). After this period the learning of an L2 becomes problematic, and ultimate attainment in L2 proficiency can generally be

I. Ottó
Regional Public Administration Office for Southern Transdanubia, Pécs, Hungary
e-mail: iotto@freemail.hu

M. Nikolov (✉)
University of Pécs, Pécs, Hungary
e-mail: nikolov.marianne@pte.hu

M. Pawlak (ed.), *New Perspectives on Individual Differences in Language Learning and Teaching*, Second Language Learning and Teaching, DOI: 10.1007/978-3-642-20850-8_3, © Springer-Verlag Berlin Heidelberg 2012

expected to be lower than what could have been achieved had the acquisition process started before the onset of the critical period. The *strong version* of the critical period hypothesis (CPH) is often formulated as *the younger the better position*, which postulates that younger learners are more efficient and successful than older learners and puberty marks the onset of a decline in SLA capacity. Other findings, however, indicate that older learners have an initial edge in acquiring L2s (e.g. Burstall 1980; Patkowski 1980; Harley 1986; García Mayo and García Lecumberri 2003; Muñoz 2003).

In the present paper we take the consensus view, which has emerged out of a plethora of studies (see the reviews by Larsen-Freeman and Long 1991; Ellis 1994; Harley and Wang 1997; Paradis 2004; Singleton and Ryan 2004; DeKeyser and Larson-Hall 2005); this view acknowledges that in general starting earlier is better in the long run, but older is better in the sense that, initially, late beginners outperform younger learners. This standpoint leads to an interesting controversy between the initial advantage of late beginners and the higher ultimate attainment of younger learners. In the present paper we offer a possible explanation for the existence of this phenomenon.

2 Background

2.1 The Critical Period Hypothesis

The term *critical period* is used to refer to the general phenomenon of declining competence over increasing age of exposure and is used to state that there is a period when language acquisition can take place naturally and effortlessly, but after a certain age the brain is no longer able to process language input in this way (Ellis 1985: 107). The most frequently understood period referred to is reflected in Scovel's (1988: 2) definition: "In brief, the critical period hypothesis is the notion that language is best learned during the early years of childhood, and that after about the first dozen years of life, everyone faces certain constraints in the ability to pick up a new language". That there exists an air of uncertainty in the literature about the term *critical* is signified by the fact that different authors have also used *optimal* (e.g. Asher and Garcia 1969) and *sensitive* (e.g. Patkowski 1980) as an alternative. We use these terms interchangeably.

The critical period issue has attracted wide interest from researchers, and while some argue that even its existence is controversial, others try to prove its effects. The enormous literature on the CPH reveals a number of standpoints with regards to age-related differences in SLA. The first position states that only children can hope to attain native-like L2 proficiency (Dulay et al. 1982; Scovel 1988; Larsen-Freeman and Long 1991; Johnson 1992); the second finds that the data are ambiguous: "(...) one can say that there is some good supportive evidence and that there is no actual counterevidence" (Singleton 1989: 137). The third position denies the existence of the critical period and states that "(...) the learning situation in combination with age-related affective and cognitive factors could account for some of the variation in success between child and adult L2 learning" (van Els et al. 1984: 109).

2.2 An Emerging Consensus on the CPH

Most of the research that has been done on the CPH up to now has centered around at least two questions: whether age-related differences affect *ultimate attainment* in L2 proficiency, and whether they affect *rate of acquisition*. The seemingly inconsistent findings in the literature appear to be the result of a failure on researchers' part to separate the two issues (Ellis 1994; DeKeyser and Larson-Hall 2005).

Possibly the most exciting question with regards to the role of age in SLA is whether ultimate attainment can become native-like when exposure to the target language begins after a postulated critical period. According to public wisdom or 'folk linguistics' (Rixon 1992: 75), an early start in SLA can be only beneficial because of the experience parents have that the majority of children pick up language very quickly and easily when exposed to it. This position derives directly from the critical period concept developed in first language acquisition research (Lenneberg 1967). In addition to first language acquisition data, supporting evidence for this position comes both from research on foreign language learning and studies on immigrant SLA (for a review see Singleton 1989; or, more recently, Nikolov and Mihaljevic Djigunovic 2006).

A problem for the strong version of the CPH (which states that an early start is inevitable for native-like proficiency) is that an increasing number of studies find that native-like attainment seems possible in the case of some exceptional learners (see e.g. Ioup et al. 1994; Bongaerts et al. 1997; Moyer 1999; Nikolov 2002; Marinova-Todd 2003; Moyer 2004; Urponen 2004). The significance of these studies is that, in our opinion, the strong version of the CPH does not bear out even a single case where late SLA results in native-like L2 proficiency. What is not clear, however, is whether the exceptional learners identified in the above studies actually represent counterexamples for the CPH. We return to this point towards the end of this paper. Meanwhile, it is worth citing Singleton's (1989: 137) summary, which, due to its careful wording, is probably still valid with regard to children's higher ultimate attainment in SLA:

> Concerning the hypothesis that those who begin learning a second language in childhood in the long run *generally* achieve a higher level of proficiency than those who begin later in life, one can say that there is some good supportive evidence and that there is no actual counterevidence [emphasis added].

Another point that has gained wide acceptance among researchers is that even though most children are ultimately more successful than adults in SLA, they are not always faster. A number of studies show that older learners tend to outperform younger learners with regards to the *initial rate of acquisition* of the target language (for a review, see e.g. Larsen-Freeman and Long 1991). Probably the most frequently cited investigation to support this view was conducted by Snow and Hoefnagel-Höhle (1978), who tested English-speaking subjects living in the Netherlands. They tested participants on a number of measures including Dutch pronunciation, auditory discrimination, morphology, sentence repetition, sentence translation, sentence judgment, vocabulary, story comprehension and story-telling. The results of these tests revealed little age-related difference in relation to phonetic/phonological skills, but in the area of general competence adult and adolescent beginners had a distinct initial advantage over younger learners, the adolescents achieving the highest scores. However, this initial advantage progressively *diminished* with longer residence in the host environment and some younger learners overtook older ones.

2.3 The Adult Language Learning Paradox

While the initial debate over whether younger or older is better for language acquisition and the seemingly inconsistent findings of early studies appear to have been resolved by this time, we seem to have arrived at a baffling conclusion which posits that older learners, who progress faster, will eventually end up at a lower proficiency level than younger learners. This paradoxical situation has been termed the *adult language learning (ALL) paradox* (Sokolik 1990: 390–391):

> Given the superior ability of adult humans in comparison to children to generalize and extract rules from their experience (Inhelder and Piaget 1958), and given that human language is rule-governed, it would follow that adults should be better able to learn a second language than are children. However, our observations of actual second language learning contradict this inference.

In the following sections we briefly outline a number of theoretical explanations for the existence of a critical period in SLA and evaluate them on the basis of their compatibility with the ALL Paradox formulation of the CPH.

3 Theoretical Explanations

Explanations for the existence of a critical period for SLA have focused on roughly four theoretical perspectives: (1) neurolinguistic explanations; (2) cognitive explanations; (3) social-psychological explanations; and (4) linguistic explanations. We present a brief summary of the various arguments below.

3.1 The Neurological Argument

The first discussion concerning the existence of a neurologically based optimal age for language acquisition was published by Penfield and Roberts (1959). They argued that the child's greater ability to learn a language was explained by the greater plasticity of its brains. The evidence cited referred to the child's capacity to recover after injury of the speech areas of the left hemisphere, whereas adults often did not recover normal speech. Later, Lenneberg (1967) also argued that the left and right hemispheres of the human brain become specialized for different functions roughly between the age of two and puberty. This process is called *lateralization*, and according to the hypothesis, the end of lateralization coincides with the child's puberty, after which language acquisition becomes more problematic.

The same area of inquiry was further extended by Scovel (1969), who tried to argue the validity of three claims: (1) that even relatively unsophisticated native speakers can identify nonnative speakers by their accent; (2) that the inability to sound like a native speaker might stem from SLA taking place after lateralization is completed; and (3) that a critical period is defensible only for phonological learning. The original claim that lateralization might be responsible for the existence of the critical period has been extended to other neurophysiological changes: "(...) hemispheric specialization, the proportionately rapid growth of the brain compared to body growth, increased production of neurotransmitters, the process of myelinization, the proliferation of nerve pathways in the cerebral cortex, and the speeding up of synaptic transmission" Scovel (1988: 62) are listed among the possible factors causing child/adult differences in SLA. According to Jacobs and Schumann (1992), however, the brain remains plastic for the lifetime and the hypothesis that there are multiple critical periods of language acquisition has recently found neurobiological support. In their interpretation, "(...) the cerebral cortex prefers novel stimuli and (...) neurons tend to habituate (i.e. cease responding) to repetitive and/or non-meaningful stimuli (...)" (Jacobs and Schumann 1992: 291).

Most researchers who argue for the existence of a critical period for SLA interpret the data accumulated in neuroscience as supportive: "(...) the idea that there exist biological constraints on SLA currently seems the most tenable (...)" (Larsen-Freeman and Long 1991: 166); or "the ultimate explanation for the existence of foreign accents is that they are biologically based: they cannot be explained by variables that are derived from personality or environment" (Scovel 1988: 101), while others conclude their review of the literature by stating that there is a "(...) lack of convincing evidence for a biological barrier to second language acquisition by adults (...)" (Dulay et al. 1982: 90) and turn their attention to the cognitive, linguistic and socio-psychological explanations.

As pointed out by Pulvermüller and Schumann (1994), an important problem with the neurological explanation is that it cannot account for successful late SLA. In our opinion, irrespective of the outcome of the debate over a yet unidentified neurological factor causing a loss of plasticity in the brain, a further issue with the neurological perspective is that it ignores adults' initial edge in language learning and therefore it cannot in itself account for the existence of the ALL Paradox.

3.2 The Cognitive Explanation

The most frequently mentioned cognitive explanation for child/adult differences is the onset of Piaget's formal operations stage, which is supposed to affect SLA negatively. Dulay et al. (1982) hypothesized that formal operations relate directly to conscious language learning only, and as the Monitor Model emphasizes the importance of acquisition, in their view cognitive differences between children and adults can explain only some of the child/adult differences, although cognitive considerations would not explain why children typically outperform adults in SLA in the long run. Larsen-Freeman and Long (1991: 163) characterize the same process as a 'trade-off': adults benefit from the ability to think abstractly in the areas of problem solving, but at the same time lose their ability to make use of the LAD for SLA. Cummins (1980) distinguishes between basic interpersonal communicative skills (which are context-embedded and relatively undemanding cognitively) and cognitive/academic skills (which are related to context-reduced, cognitively demanding communication). In his view, cognitive maturity interacting with the accumulation of experience in the literate uses of the mother tongue facilitates the acquisition of second language cognitive/academic skills, and this is why adults are found more accurate than children in SLA.

In sum, cognitive considerations presuppose that child and adult SLA involves different processes: unconscious or LAD type, as opposed to conscious processes utilizing general problem-solving abilities. Pronunciation is not referred to in the cognitive explanations for the existence of a critical period. Ellis (1985: 109), however, mentions the possibility that of all aspects of language pronunciation is the least amenable to conscious manipulation. This explanation might provide an answer for the existence of the 'Joseph Conrad phenomenon'.

3.3 Social-psychological Explanations

The sociolinguistic arguments for the existence of the critical period in SLA focus mainly on the role of attitudes and peer pressure. According to these explanations, young children are not developed enough cognitively to possess attitudes toward races, cultures and languages, as "(...) most of these attitudes are 'taught', consciously or unconsciously, by parents, other adults, and peers" (Brown 1976: 51). The negative attitudes toward the speakers of the target language or the language itself develop gradually during the school years. Consequently, child SLA is less influenced by negative attitudes, as children tend to be open to any new learning experience.

Peer pressure also plays a different role in child and adult SLA. Children in the host environment are usually aware of the pressure on them to be like the rest of the kids, and this pressure extends to language, as well. Adults also experience some peer pressure but their peers tend to tolerate linguistic differences more than children. Native adults provide more positive feedback in foreigner talk than children do (Brown 1987).

A similar explanation can be drawn from Schumann's (1976, 1990) Acculturation/Pidginization Model. Success in SLA depends on the extent and quality of contact between the learner and the target language culture, which in turn depends on the degree of social and psychological distance between the learner and the language and culture. As children are less aware of social and psychological distance, they bridge the gap with ease, and find many ways of contacting the teacher and other peers.

Krashen's Monitor Model provides a different explanation for child/adult differences in the form of the *affective filter*. As he claims,

> While the filter may exist for the child second language acquirer, it is rarely, in natural informal language acquisition situations, high enough to prevent native-like levels of attainment. For the adult it rarely goes low enough to allow native-like attainment (Krashen 1985: 13).

Singleton points out a logical problem involved in tying the inhibition of SLA to the affective dimension of the onset of formal operations. He contrasts Krashen's claim that SLA difficulties are occasioned by the self-consciousness and sense of vulnerability to the judgment of others, which Piagetians associate with the formal operations stage, with their further claim, that these feelings tend to diminish by the age of 15 or 16 (Singleton 1989: 191). In his view, the implication would be that learners are less inhibited at the age of 16 than at 14.

The effects of anxiety have also been hypothesized to account for child/adult differences in SLA. Younger children are less worried as they are less aware of language forms and the possibility of making mistakes in these forms. Also, once they focus on the message, mistakes do not concern them greatly. In the host environment it has been found that learners with lower levels of anxiety tend to learn better, volunteer more in the classroom and socialize with the target language group more easily (MacIntyre and Gardner 1991: 530).

In any case, the study of L2 motivation is a complex issue, and we should not be content with a simplistic explanation based on one or a few motivational components. As pointed out recently by Dörnyei and Ottó 1998 see also (Dörnyei 2001, 2005), motivation is a dynamically changing entity which is influenced by a multitude of factors. Thus, discussing one or two of these factors in isolation is clearly underestimating the question at hand; however, when it comes to specifying the actual ingredients of motivation that might differ for child and adult language learners, we soon find out that there are differences which aid child SLA, and others which do not (e.g. children are probably less worried about past failures, but they might lack long-term goals such as a well-paying job). Also, there might be substantial individual variation in both groups with regards to many of the components. The above mentioned argument for lower levels of anxiety in children as a general advantage in SLA is a case in point: it is not unthinkable that a number of adult learners are less anxious than some particularly shy children.

3.4 Linguistic Explanations

The linguistic explanations concerning the age factor focus on differences in the input children and adults experience during SLA. One of these arguments claims that children typically engage in different kinds of interaction than adults. Some researchers say that children get more 'here and now' and less complex input than adults (Hatch 1978), while others argue that older learners have an advantage as they are better at obtaining appropriate input. The amount of input is also claimed to be larger for children in research based on the distinction between 'age of arrival' and 'length of residence' in the host environment (e.g. Johnson and Newport 1989; Johnson 1992). Again, it is unclear from these explanations how the ALL Paradox comes about, as both perspectives focus on the advantage of one of the groups, which leaves us with a general advantage for either adults or children rather than an initial advantage for adults and a long-term advantage for children.

4 A Connectionist Resolution of the All Paradox

4.1 Connectionist Models

Connectionism (also known as parallel distributed processing, or the study of neural networks) is a relatively novel approach to modeling cognition (for an introduction see e.g. Bechtel and Abrahamsen 1991). Models in this paradigm rely on our current knowledge of the structure and functioning of the brain. Connectionist models are made up of units, and connections which carry information between the units. These elements form networks which are in some ways similar to those in the brain. Although there are various questions that arise with regards to the biological plausibility of these networks, the performance of numerous models approximates that of humans, which makes them very attractive to those studying human behavior and cognition (McLeod et al. 1998).

The units in a network are usually arranged in layers (see Fig. 1). In addition to an input and an output layer, there might be several hidden layers, which allow the network to work out an internal representation of the stimulus it is presented with during training. The flow of information in the network is from the input layer to the output layer. When a pattern of activation appears on the input layer (this is equivalent to assigning a value other than zero to some of the units), activity is

Fig. 1 Sample neural
network architecture

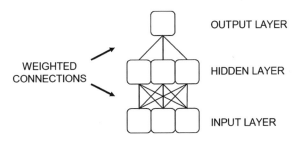

propagated forward to the output units through the weighted connections and the
hidden units. The activation of a unit is determined by its net input from the
previous layer, which is then altered by an activation function. The net input to a
unit is usually computed as:

$$netinput_i = \sum_j a_j w_{ij}$$

where a_j is the activation of the jth unit in the preceding layer and w_{ij} is the
weighted connection from that unit to the unit whose net input we are interested in.
Various activation functions can be applied to the net input; one of the most
common is the logistic activation function (also known as the 'squashing'
function), which is computed as follows:

$$a_i = \frac{1}{1 + e^{-netinput_i}}$$

where a_i is the activation value of unit i, and $netinput_i$ is the net input to the unit
(see above).

The training of a connectionist network usually happens as follows:

Step 1 A training pair (an input pattern and a corresponding output pattern which
is also called a target pattern) is randomly selected from the training set.

Step 2 The network is presented with the input, that is, the appropriate units are
assigned a value 1 in the input layer, while the rest of the units are assigned
a value 0.

Step 3 Activity is propagated forward to the output units through the weighted
connections and the hidden units according to the formulas above.

Step 4 The pattern of activity that appears in the output layer is compared to the
target pattern, and the difference between the two patterns is used as an
error term to modify the connections between the layers of units. This
modification happens in a way that makes it more likely that the network
will produce the correct output the next time it is presented with the same
input. An often used algorithm is called the Delta Rule, which causes the
weights in a network to change as follows:

$$w_{ij}(t) = w_{ij}(t - 1) + r_{learning} e_i a_j$$

where $w_{ij}(t)$ is the new weight from unit j to unit i, $w_{ij}(t-1)$ is the old weight from unit j to unit i, e_i is the error on unit i, and a_j is the activation value of unit j. The error on unit i is in turn computed as follows:

$$e_i = d_i - a_i$$

where d_i is the desired activation of unit i and a_i is its actual activation.

Step 5   The above process (Steps 1–4) is iterated until all the input-output pairings are learnt by the network.

Connectionist models have been applied to various aspects of language acquisition (see Gasser 1990; Elman 1993; Sokolik and Smith 1992; Plunkett and Marchman 1993; Jensen and Ulbaek 1994; Rumelhart and McClelland 1994; Plunkett 1995; Kempe and MacWhinney 1998; McLeod et al. 1998, Chap. 9) and—a particular interest to us—to the resolution of the ALL Paradox (Sokolik 1990). This latter application is discussed below in some detail.

4.2 Connectionism and the ALL Paradox

Sokolik (1990) proposed a connectionist model as an alternative explanation for solving the ALL Paradox. According to Sokolik's explanation, a certain *nerve growth factor* (NGF) in the brain controls the learning rate, a parameter that determines how much a learning trial affects the connections in the network (at Step 4 above). Children are expected to have higher levels of NGF, which may be responsible for the difference in learning rate.

The problem is illustrated by a hypothetical example: a three-year-old English speaking child and a 25-year-old English speaking parent are in France, they are both acquiring feature X_f of French. The starting weight for both learners is arbitrarily said to be 0.2, whereas complete knowledge of feature X_f would be represented by a connection weight of 1. The learning rate value associated with the availability of NGF for the three-year-old is posited at 0.25, and at 0.05 as available to the 25-year-old. These parameter settings result in two different learning curves as depicted in Fig. 2 where the x-axis represents the number of epochs (the amount of time at an identical pace of exposure) taken to complete the task. The shorter line illustrates the hypothetical three-year-old, whose NGF and learning rate are higher, whereas the longer line illustrates the 25-year-old learner. As it is illustrated, the younger learner has acquired feature X_f after 10 exposures to the data, while the adult takes 55 epochs to reach the same point (Sokolik 1990).

To summarize briefly, the explanation provided by Sokolik suggests that the decreased availability of NGF after puberty is to blame for the child/adult differences in SLA. In our opinion, in spite of the new terminology, Sokolik's explanation is merely a reformulation of the neurological explanation and it leaves

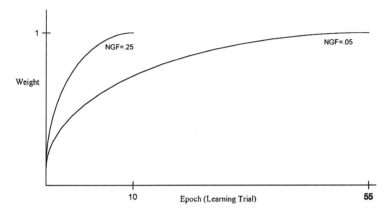

Fig. 2 The effect of a *nerve growth factor* (NGF) on learning (based on Sokolik 1990: 692)

the ALL Paradox unresolved in a very obvious way: the model fails to give an account of the fact that initially adults develop faster than children. This is probably due to the fact that Sokolik's model does not take into consideration adult humans' reliance on a variety of rules when learning an L2. It must be noted that this was most likely the outcome of the way of thinking that still characterizes much of the work carried out under the umbrella term of connectionism; in an effort to demonstrate the capabilities of networks which "learn without rules", researchers seem to forget that humans do learn with the help of rules. In the sections that follow, we outline a connectionist account of the ALL Paradox which we believe might provide a more plausible model of child/adult differences in SLA.

5 The Theory of Extra Input Biased Learning

5.1 *Target Language Descriptors and the Acquisition/Learning Hypothesis*

The theory of extra input biased learning rests on the assumption that adult SLA happens through two complementary processes: (1) *acquisition*, which is the same process that guides child SLA, and (2) a companion *learning* process, which relies heavily on rules, that is, explicit formulations of the observed regularities in the target language. This distinction in SLA research is often attributed to Krashen's Acquisition/Learning Hypothesis (e.g. Krashen 1981, 1982, 1985, 1987). Although Krashen has been given due criticism because of his vagueness about how exactly learning differs from acquisition (see e.g. Gregg 1984; McLaughlin 1987), even the fiercest critiques acknowledge that this is a valid distinction, at least on the level of product, where a distinction between explicit and implicit knowledge is widely accepted. As we point out below, within the theory of extra input biased learning, acquisition and learning have very specific meanings.

In order to see the difference between acquisition and learning, it seems useful to introduce a new term at this point, the notion of *Target Language Descriptors* (TLDs). We define a TLD as a piece of explicit information which is used to characterize target language phenomena. This is a general definition which allows TLDs to take a variety of forms: they can be, for instance, grammatical categories (e.g. 'feminine noun'), clarification of semantic meaning (e.g. 'dog = X' where X stands for the first language equivalent of dog), descriptions of phonemes (e.g. 'to pronounce the voiceless 'th' [Θ] sound in English put your tongue between your teeth'), etc. The origin of these bits of information is at least twofold: (1) TLDs can come in the form of pedagogical grammars/rules as part of instruction, or (2) they can be discovered by the language learner himself/herself. Thus, TLDs are not necessarily an outcome of formal instruction; they are also the result of the human tendency to explain new phenomena in light of old experiences. The more experience one has, the more likely it seems that s/he will be able to and will relate new information to some knowledge s/he is already possessing.

Acquisition is seen here as a TLD-free process which does not make use of explicit information about the target language. Learning, on the other hand, is the process whereby new information becomes augmented with TLDs. The application of rules, for example, usually requires some sort of categorization of target language phenomena. By way of illustration, the past tense form of irregular English verbs is commonly learned together with the infinitive forms by language learners (e.g. 'drink'–'drank'), and regular verbs are learned as 'regular' or together with some mnemonic (e.g. '-ed' verbs). This labeling process enables the application of explicit rules, such as 'to get the past tense form of regular English verbs add '-ed' to the stem'. To be able to apply such a rule the learner must know which verbs are regular and which are not. While these categories remain opaque when the language is entirely acquired—as is the case with the mother tongue— the experience of *learning* a language is shaped by the extra input in the form of TLDs. With the appearance of TLDs in language learning the task of acquiring a language is no longer that of distilling the regularities in new information, but rather that of finding a relationship between the new information and TLDs. In our opinion, this is the most fundamental difference between child and adult SLA on the level of process. In the following sections we describe how this distinction helps explain the ALL Paradox.

5.2 The Effects of Extra Information on the Learning Process

The basic idea of extra input biased learning comes from a technique called extra *output* biased learning (Yu and Simmons 1990), which has been developed in computer science with the aim of finding a way for speeding up the training of

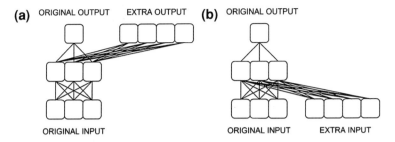

Fig. 3 Networks with **a** extra output and **b** extra input units

neural networks. The above researchers argued that pattern associator neural
networks might be viewed as *mapping functions* from the input space to the output
space. A serious challenge facing most networks is that in most cases there might
exist several possible weight configurations (functions) which would enable a
network to carry out its task successfully (Yu and Simmons 1990). As the network
moves through training and is presented with the individual training patterns, so
changes the network's idea of this mapping function. Each training pair directs the
search in a way as to increase the probability that the network will produce the
correct output the next time it is presented with the same input. The competing
tendencies (i.e. varying input–output pairs) will make it difficult for the network to
settle on one of the solutions.

Extra output biased learning is a technique that takes into account the importance of the training patterns themselves and thus offers a way of helping the
network find a correct weight configuration more rapidly. The idea in short (for a
more technical description, see Yu and Simmons 1990) is to attach a number of
extra units and connections to the network (see Fig. 3a), which reduce the training
time considerably. The reduction in training time is the result of the constraints
specified on the extra units, which the network will have to satisfy in addition to
the constrains set by the original units. When we set a new requirement to the
network in the form of extended output patterns, the network is allowed to continue its search with less degrees of freedom, which means that there are fewer
possible solutions to choose from. The fewer the alternatives resulting from the
channeling effect of the extra output, the faster the network can converge on a
solution.

5.3 Extra Input Biased Learning and the ALL Paradox

We have seen how extra output biased learning can speed up the learning
process. We have also argued that TLDs provide extra input to the adult
language learner, which modifies the learning experience. This extra input can
be modeled in a connectionist architecture by adding some extra units at the

input layer (see Fig. 3b). The result is similar to what is happening when we add extra output to a network: the extra input exerts a constraining effect on the learning process and, due to this 'guidance', the system homes in on a solution faster. What we have to notice, however, is that placing the extra units at the input layer rather than at the output layer has crucial consequences for the network's performance.

One nice thing about extra output biased learning is that once the training of the network is over, the extra units and the extra connections can be removed from the model, because they do not influence the output of the original network (Yu and Simmons 1990). After removing the extra units, the path of the activation to the original output remains intact (you can verify this by looking at the extra connections in Fig. 3a, none of which feeds into any of the original units). Once we relocate the extra units, however, and place them at the input layer, their removal can no longer be done without a serious decrease in the network's performance since the activations of the extra input units influence the output of the original network. If no input is given to the network on the extra units, the hidden units in the network will receive less activation and, as a consequence, a different pattern of activation appears on the output layer than what would be expected.

How does all this relate to the ALL Paradox? It is a reasonable suggestion that if the child's competence develops through acquisition, which is a TLD-free process, then the child's language use will not be influenced by TLDs as this extra information is simply not included in the child's L2 competence; children acquire and use L2s without TLDs, that is, the application of the acquired knowledge relies on the same information that was available during learning. We have argued, however, that a crucial feature of adult SLA is that it depends also on a learning process which involves TLDs, and as a result, adults might use the L2 both with and without relying on TLDs. In the former case, that is, during spontaneous naturalistic language use, TLDs that were present during the learning process are not retrieved, which means that the resulting performance reflects the outcome of the TLD-free acquisition process. Although an initial advantage is gained from the use of TLDs which cause a speed-up in the learning process, the fact that this extra information becomes built into the L2 system carries the risk that a failure to recall such information will result in reduced performance.

Initially this is not a problem, as there are few TLDs, and at the early stages of learning, TLDs might be readily available in a textbook, in students' notebooks or diaries, or in the form of teacher feedback, all of which can be regarded as external storage devices which the student can rely on to aid his/her L2 use. Notwithstanding the initial benefits of this approach, adults have to pay dearly for the advantage they gain from the learning process: acquisition, which would guarantee long-term success, is set back, and in the long run, when TLDs become greater in number and no external help is available, L2 use will be impaired. It is possible, of course, that after enough exposure to the target language the acquisition process

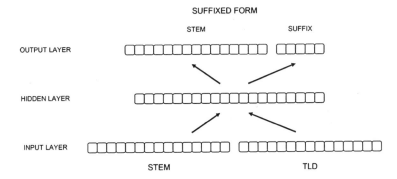

Fig. 4 Network used in simulations

can recover from the overwhelming effect of a TLD-loaded learning environment, just how much exposure is needed for that purpose is unclear.

6 An Example Simulation

6.1 The Task

To illustrate how the theory of extra input biased learning might account for the ALL Paradox, we show here a simple example which simulates the acquisition of a morphosyntactic feature (denoted by X_f following Sokolik 1990) of an hypothetical language. This feature is derived from word stems by adding one out of three suffixes. Each word in the language has a single representation of feature X_f, that is, a word cannot be suffixed using two different suffixes at different times. Note that we are not in the least proposing this as a model of SLA, but as a simple example of how extra input might lead to the phenomenon that has been called the ALL Paradox.

6.2 Description of the Network

For the simulations we used a simple feed-forward neural network with one layer of hidden units (see Fig. 4). There was full connectivity between the layers, that is, every unit in the input layer was connected to every unit in the hidden layer, and every unit in the hidden layer was connected to every unit in the output layer. The input layer consisted of 30 units, 15 units representing the stem and 15 units representing an optional TLD. The output layer consisted of 20 units representing the suffixed forms, 15 units representing the stem, and 5 units representing the suffix. The input and output layers were separated by a layer of 20 hidden units.

Table 1 Sample training pairs

	INPUT		OUTPUT	
	STEM	*TLD*	*STEM*	*SUFFIX*
CHILD AND	000111110011100	000000000000000	000111110011100	10010
ADULT/ACQUISITION	000000111001111	000000000000000	000000111001111	10010
	100111001100110	000000000000000	100111001100110	01001
	011110100110110	000000000000000	011110100110110	01001
	101000000101010	000000000000000	101000000101010	10110
	100011010111100	000000000000000	100011010111100	10110
	.	.	.	.
	.	.	.	.
	.	.	.	.
ADULT/LEARNING	000111110011100	100011011111101	000111110011100	10010
	000000111001111	100011011111101	000000111001111	10010
	100111001100110	110011010101011	100111001100110	01001
	011110100110110	110011010101011	011110100110110	01001
	101000000101010	111101100001011	101000000101010	10110
	100011010111100	111101100001011	100011010111100	10110
	.	.	.	.
	.	.	.	.
	.	.	.	.

6.3 Stimulus

The training data consisted of a set of 30 stems and the corresponding 30 suffixed forms for the child simulation. For the adult simulations the training data consisted of two sets of 30 input–output patterns: the first set was identical to the child training data, and the other set included input patterns augmented by a TLD. The stems, the suffixes and the TLDs were all random binary vectors with differing lengths as described above. A random binary vector is a series of 1s and 0s, thus a random binary vector of length 5 might be [10011]. Table 1 presents sample training pairs.

6.4 Training

The training of the network was done using the backpropagation learning algorithm, which is one of the most widely used algorithms in current connectionist models. It is also called the generalized Delta Rule, as it is an extension of the delta rule to multilayered networks, that is, networks with at least one layer of hidden units.

To simulate the fact that there are child/adult differences in the use of TLDs, two different types of training took place. For the child simulation there was one process, which simulated acquisition. The network was presented with a stem as input (TLD units were set to zero) and it was to provide the suffixed form of the stem as output. The learning rate (or, rather, acquisition rate) was set to $r_{acquisition} = 1$.

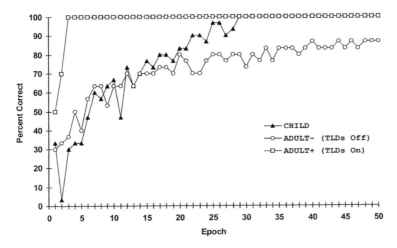

Fig. 5 Percentage of correctly suffixed stems for the three simulations

For the adult simulations there were two complementary processes, that is, the network was trained on two types of training pairs during each epoch. The first type of training pair was used to simulate the learning situation, when the task of the network was to discover the relationship between the stem and a TLD as input and the suffixed form as output, while the second type of training pairs was used to simulate the process of acquisition whereby the relationship between stem and suffixed forms had to be worked out without TLDs. These latter training pairs were identical to what the child simulation was exposed to. To simulate the fact that learning and acquisition are complementary processes in adults and learning is the primary process, we used an alternating learning rate: when the network was presented with a training pair where the input included a TLD (i.e. when the network was in *learning* mode), the learning rate was set to $r_{learning} = 0.9$, and when the network was exposed to a TLD-free training pair (i.e. when the network was in acquisition mode) we defined an *acquisition* rate as $r_{acquisition} = 1 - r_{learning}$, which after the substitution of the value for the learning rate was $r_{acquisition} = (1 - 0.9) = 0.1$.

6.5 Results and Discussion

The results of the simulations are depicted in Fig. 5. The three lines represent the performance of the CHILD run, and the performance of the ADULT run when it was tested with and without TLDs. The percentage of the correctly suffixed stems is plotted against the number of epochs, that is, the number of times the network was exposed to the training set. The line with the small triangles depicts the performance of the hypothetical child language learner (CHILD). The line marked by squares represents the performance of a hypothetical adult language learner when s/he is able to make use of TLDs (ADULT+). The line with the circles shows the performance of the same hypothetical adult language learner when s/he is not able to rely on TLDs (ADULT−).

6.5.1 Rate of Acquisition

The results of the simulations supported our discussion of the ALL Paradox in that an initial advantage is clearly visible in the case of the ADULT+ run over the CHILD run. When the network was allowed to make use of TLDs during the testing phase, it was able to correctly suffix the stems in the training set after only three exposures to the data. In contrast, the CHILD run needed 30 epochs to reach error-free performance. These results are consistent with our everyday experience that in the presence of rules adults can clearly outperform children. What is important to note, however, is that this advantage is dependent on the availability of TLDs.

6.5.2 Ultimate Attainment

Similarly to rate of acquisition, the discussion of ultimate attainment has to be considered with reference to TLDs. Our results indicate that child (i.e. acquisition-only) SLA is more successful than adult SLA when TLDs are not available during language use. This result is in line with findings which predict higher ultimate attainment in naturalistic L2 use for children.

Furthermore, our results are also consistent with studies that find exceptional language learners who can perform at a native-like level. These studies, however, do not explain how this might be possible. The simulations suggest that there are at least three ways in which adults might exhibit native-like proficiency. One is to directly provide them with the appropriate TLD, which is a technique that has been applied in the form of drills in foreign language classrooms. The problem with this technique, however, is that once students walk out of the classroom TLDs provided by the teacher or the textbook are no longer available and communication is bound to break down when naturalistic language use is the norm. On the other hand, it might be possible to associate TLDs with the source feature (the stem in our case) to such a degree that they will be recalled when needed and the computation of the target feature becomes possible. Although this might work for a number of features, it is highly unlikely that during language production all of the necessary TLDs become available and the targets can be computed without substantial time-consuming effort. This would help explain why pronunciation is the most problematic area when the goal is native-like attainment: during language use, the primary aim is to communicate and this can be achieved without a 100% accuracy in pronunciation, whereas other features (e.g. word order) are more important and are assigned higher priority by the speaker. As the TLDs related to pronunciation are probably given lower priority, they are not recalled and performance will reflect the speaker's acquired competence.

This takes us to the third possibility, namely, that adults can *acquire* the target language just as children do. According to the results of the simulations, it is indeed a possibility as the ADULT- run reached error-free performance at epoch 176. Therefore, at least in theory, it is possible that adults can acquire the target language and reach native-like performance, but we have to take caution in interpreting this result. We cannot predict based on the present simulation just how much exposure to TLD-free data is needed for this. It is possible that 'Epoch 176' translates into something well beyond a mortal language learner's lifetime.

In our opinion, reality is somewhere between the three types of outcomes. An adult language learner's competence might be made up of some features which have been acquired to a near-native level, while others are part of a TLD-dependent competence, and finally some features can only be applied successfully with a sophisticated grammar of the target language in one hand and a dictionary in the other.

7 Conclusion

In this paper we have described the Adult Language Learning Paradox, which posits that notwithstanding adults' higher ability in dealing with rules, they generally fail to achieve high levels of L2 proficiency in spite of the fact that natural languages are rule-governed systems. We have reviewed some existing explanations from a variety of perspectives and concluded that neither of them accounts for both adults' initial advantage and children's higher ultimate attainment. We have proposed a connectionist theory as an explanation for the ALL Paradox, and we presented the results of a set of simulations, which were based on this theory. The network used in the simulations exhibited an initial advantage for a hypothetical adult language learner and higher ultimate attainment for an hypothetical child language learner.

An interesting feature of our model is that it blends two of the perspectives discussed previously. It is essentially a cognitive theory in that it refers to a learning process which presupposes a certain degree of cognitive maturity, but a special role is assigned to differences in the input older learners deal with, which lies at the heart of the theory. The difference between existing explanations which put the blame on some aspect of the linguistic input and extra input biased learning is that our model seeks to answer the ALL Paradox not only by looking at the amount of input (more exposure to the data) but also by examining the role of extra input in biasing individual learning trials. The conclusion we can draw is that although the bias coming from extra input favors faster development, it prepares the language learner for a different task than what is expected in everyday situations demanding L2 use, and therefore a trade-off between speed and ultimate attainment remains a necessity in adult SLA.

References

Asher, J., and R. Garcia. 1969. The optimal age to learn a foreign language. *Modern Language Journal* 38: 334–341.

Bechtel, W., and A. Abrahamsen. 1991. *Connectionism and the mind: an introduction to parallel processing in networks*. Cambridge: Basil Blackwell.

Birdsong, D., ed. 1999. *Second language acquisition and the critical period hypothesis*. Mahwah: Lawrence Erlbaum.

Birdsong, D. 2005. Interpreting age effects in second language acquisition. In eds. J.F. Kroll, and A.M.B. De Groot, 109–127.

Bloom, P., ed. 1994. *Language acquisition: Core readings*. Cambridge: MIT Press.

Bongaerts, T. 2005. Introduction: ultimate attainment and the critical period hypothesis for second language acquisition. *International Review of Applied Linguistics in Language Teaching* 43: 259–267.

Bongaerts, T., C. van Summeren, B. Planken, and E. Schills. 1997. Age and ultimate attainment in the pronunciation of a foreign language. *Studies in Second Language Acquisition* 19: 447–465.

Brown, D. 1987. *Principles of language learning and teaching*. Englewood Cliffs: Prentice Hall Regents.

Burstall, C. 1980. Primary French in the balance. In ed. S. Holden, 86–90.

Cummins, J. 1980. The cross-lingual dimensions of language proficiency: Implications for bilingual education and the optimal age issues. *TESOL Quarterly* 14: 175–187.

de Groot, A.M.B., and J. F. Kroll, eds. *Tutorials in bilingualism: Psycholinguistic perspectives*. Mahwah, NJ: Lawrence Erlbaum.

DeKeyser, R., and J. Larson-Hall. 2005. What does the critical period really mean? In eds. J.F. Kroll, and A.M.B. de Groot, 88–108.

Dörnyei, Z. 2001. *Teaching and researching motivation*. London: Longman.

Dörnyei, Z. 2005. *The psychology of the language learner: Individual differences in second language acquisition*. Mahwah: Lawrence Erlbaum.

Dörnyei, Z., and I. Ottó. 1998. Motivation in action: A process model of L2 motivation. *Working Papers in Applied Linguistics, Thames Valley University, London* 2: 203–229.

Dulay, H., M. Burt, and S. Krashen. 1982. *Language two*. Oxford: Oxford University Press.

Ellis, R. 1985. *Understanding second language acquisition*. Oxford: Oxford University Press.

Ellis, R. 1994. *The study of second language acquisition*. Oxford: Oxford University Press.

Elman, J.L. 1993. Learning and development in neural networks: The importance of starting small. *Cognition* 48: 71–99.

Fletcher, P., and B. MacWhinney, eds. 1995. *The handbook of child language*. Cambridge: Blackwell.

García Mayo, M.P., and M.L. García Lecumberri, eds. 2003. *Age and the acquisition of English as a foreign language*. Clevedon, Avon: Multilingual Matters.

Gasser, M. 1990. Connectionism and universals of second language acquisition. *Studies in Second Language Acquisition* 12: 179–199.

Gregg, K. 1984. Krashen's monitor and occam's razor. *Applied Linguistics* 5: 79–100.

Harley, B. 1986. *Age in second language acquisition*. Clevedon, Avon: Multilingual Matters.

Harley, B., and W. Wang. 1997. The critical period hypothesis: Where are we now? In eds. A.M.B. de Groot, and J.F. Kroll, 19–51.

Hatch, E.M., ed. 1978. *Second language acquisition: A book of readings*. Rowley: Newbury House.

Holden, S., ed. 1980. *Teaching children*. London: Modern English Publications.

Inhelder, B., and J. Piaget. 1958. *The growth of logical thinking from childhood to adolescence*. New York: Basic Books.

Ioup, G., E. Boustagui, M. El Tigi, and M. Moselle. 1994. Reexamining the critical period hypothesis: A case study of successful adult SLA in a naturalistic environment. *Studies in Second Language Acquisition* 16: 73–98.

Jacobs, B., and J. Schumann. 1992. Language acquisition and the neurosciences: Towards a more integrative perspective. *Applied Linguistics* 13: 282–301.

Jensen, K.A., and I. Ulbaek. 1994. The learning of the past tense of Danish verbs: Language learning in neural networks. *Applied Linguistics* 15: 15–35.

Johnson, J. 1992. Critical period effects in second language acquisition: The effect of written versus auditory materials on the assessment of grammatical competence. *Language Learning* 42: 217–248.

Kempe, V., and B. MacWhinney. 1998. The acquisition of case marking by adult learners of Russian and German. *Studies in Second Language Acquisition* 20: 543–587.

Krashen, S. 1981. *Second language acquisition and second language learning*. Oxford: Pergamon Press.

Krashen, S. 1982. *Principles and practice in second language acquisition*. Oxford: Pergamon Press.

Krashen, S. 1985. *The input hypothesis: Issues and implications*. London: Longman.

Krashen, S. 1987. *Principles and practice in second language acquisition*, new ed. London: Prentice Hall.

Kroll, J.F., and A.M.B. de Groot, eds. 2005. *Handbook of bilingualism: Psycholinguistic approaches*. Oxford: Oxford University Press.

Larsen-Freeman, D., and M. Long. 1991. *An introduction to second language acquisition research*. London: Longman.

Lenneberg, E. 1967. *Biological foundations of language*. New York: Wiley.

Long, M.H. 1990. The least a second language acquisition theory needs to explain. *TESOL Quarterly* 24: 649–666.

MacIntyre, P., and R. Gardner. 1991. Language anxiety: Its relationship to other anxieties and to processing in native and second languages. *Language Learning* 41: 513–534.

Marinova-Todd, S.H. 2003. Comprehensive analysis of ultimate attainment in adult second language acquisition. Unpublished doctoral dissertation, Harvard University.

McLaughlin, B. 1987. *Theories of second-language learning*. London: Edward Arnold.

McLeod, P., K. Plunkett, and E.T. Rolls. 1998. *Introduction to connectionist modelling of cognitive processes*. Oxford: Oxford University Press.

Moyer, A. 1999. Ultimate attainment in L2 phonology: The critical factors of age, motivation, and instruction. *Studies in Second Language Acquisition* 21: 81–108.

Moyer, J. 2004. *Age accent and experience in second language acquisition*. Clevedon, Avon: Multilingual Matters.

Muñoz, C. 2003. Variation in oral skills development and age of onset. In eds. M.P. García Mayo, and M.L. García Lecumberri, 161–181.

Johnson, J., and E. Newport. 1989. Critical period effects in second language learning: The influence of maturational state on the acquisition of English as a second language. *Cognitive Psychology* 21: 60–99.

Nikolov, M. 2002. *Issues in English language education*. Bern: Peter Lang.

Nikolov, M., and J. Mihaljevic Djigunovic. 2006. Recent research on age, second language acquisition, and early foreign language learning. *Annual Review of Applied Linguistics* 26: 234–260.

Paradis, M. 2004. *A neurolinguistic theory of bilingualism*. Amsterdam: John Benjamins.

Patkowski, M. 1980. The sensitive period for the acquisition of syntax in a second language. *Language Learning* 30: 449–472.

Penfield, W., and L. Roberts. 1959. *Speech and brain mechanisms*. New York: Atheneum Press.

Plunkett, K. 1995. Connectionist approaches to language acquisition. In eds. P. Fletcher, and B. MacWhinney, 36–72.

Plunkett, K., and V. Marchman. 1993. From rote learning to system building: Acquiring verb morphology in children and connectionist nets. *Cognition* 48: 21–69.

Pulvermüller, F., and J. Schumann. 1994. Neurobiological mechanisms of language acquisition. *Language Learning* 44: 681–734.

Rixon, S. 1992. English and other languages for younger children: Practice and theory in a rapidly changing world. *Language Teaching* 25: 73–93.

Rumelhart, D.E., and J.L. McClelland. 1994. On learning the past tenses of English verbs. In ed. P. Bloom, 423–471.

Schumann, J.H. 1976. Second language acquisition: The pidginization hypothesis. *Language Learning* 26: 391–408.

Schumann, J.H. 1990. Extending the scope of the acculturation/pidginization model to include cognition. *TESOL Quarterly* 24: 664–684.

Scovel, T. 1969. Foreign accents, language acquisition and cerebral dominance. *Language Learning* 19: 245–253.

Scovel, T. 1988. *A time to speak: A psycholinguistic inquiry into the critical period for human speech*. New York: Newbury House/Harper & Row.

Scovel, T. 2000. A critical review of the critical period research. *Annual Review of Applied Linguistics* 20: 213–223.

Singleton, D. 1989. *Language acquisition: The age factor*. Clevedon, Avon: Multilingual Matters.

Singleton, D. 2005. The critical period hypothesis. *International Review of Applied Linguistics in Language Teaching* 43: 269–285.

Singleton, D., and L. Ryan. 2004. *Language acquisition: The age factor*. 2nd ed. Clevedon, Avon: Multilingual Matters.

Slabakova, R. 2006. Is there a critical period for semantics? *Second Language Research* 22: 302–338.

Snow, C., and M. Hoefnagel-Höhle. 1978. The critical period for language acquisition: Evidence from second language learning. *Child Development* 49: 1114–1128.

Sokolik, M.E. 1990. Learning without rules: PDP and a resolution of the adult language learning paradox. *TESOL Quarterly* 24: 685–696.

Sokolik, M.E., and M.E. Smith. 1992. Assignment of gender to French nouns in primary and secondary language: A connectionist model. *Second Language Research* 8: 39–58.

Urponen, M.I. 2004. Ultimate attainment in postpuberty second language acquisition. Unpublished doctoral dissertation. Boston University.

van Els, T., T. Bongaerts, F. Extra, C. van Os, and A.J. van Dieten. 1984. *Applied linguistics and the learning and teaching of foreign languages*. London: Edward Arnold.

Yu, Y.-H., and F.H. Simmons. 1990. Extra output biased learning. Technical report [No. AI90–128]. Austin, TX: University of Texas.

Part II
Cognitive Factors and Instructed Language Acquisition

Individual Differences, Aptitude Complexes, SLA Processes, and Aptitude Test Development

Peter Robinson

Abstract Aptitude for second or foreign language learning is the ability to successfully adapt to and profit from instructed, or naturalistic exposure to the L2. Attention allocation, control, rehearsal in memory, self-regulation, analogical reasoning and many more processes combine to facilitate adaptation and learning in instructed settings, and during participation in instructional tasks. The cognitive processing, emotional and behavioural challenges various settings and tasks pose draw on subtly differentiated clusters of abilities and other personal factors. This paper argues research is needed into these in order to identify 'complexes' of abilities or 'aptitudes' for 'types' of situated pedagogic activity. An aptitude battery that assessed strengths and weaknesses in such complexes would be of great diagnostic value in matching learners to optimal learning contexts. Currently available aptitude tests cannot be used to this end, and so new aptitude batteries must be developed.

1 Introduction

Since the 1950 and 1960s when existing aptitude batteries were first researched, piloted, and then published there has been a great deal of first, and second language acquisition (SLA) research (see e.g. Fletcher and MacWhinney 1995; Doughty and Long 2003; Tomasello 2003; Robinson and Ellis 2008). These early aptitude batteries were developed without the benefit of findings from this research. Similarly, important psychological constructs and phenomena such as priming

P. Robinson (✉)
Aoyama Gakuin University, Shibuya-ku, Japan
e-mail: peterr@cl.aoyama.ac.jp

M. Pawlak (ed.), *New Perspectives on Individual Differences in Language Learning and Teaching*, Second Language Learning and Teaching, DOI: 10.1007/978-3-642-20850-8_4, © Springer-Verlag Berlin Heidelberg 2012

(Kinoshita and Lupker 2003), task switching (Monsell 2003), implicit (Bowers and Marsolek 2003), episodic (Baddeley et al. 2002) and working memory (Baddeley 2007; Conway et al. 2007) were simply not conceived of, theorised and researched at that time. There is therefore a clear need to update our current measures of, and theories of, aptitude, accommodating, where necessary, these recent findings from SLA and cognitive psychology research. In the first part of this paper I describe views of the relationship of aptitude to instructional processes, and how current second language acquisition research, and research into second language (L2) pedagogy and the effectiveness of different kinds of instruction have the potential to further clarify this relationship. I then describe two very recently proposed models of L2 aptitude which draw on these areas of research, and which can be used for the purposes of selection, as well as diagnosis and instructional option/ ability matching, (I think these are complementary purposes) pointing out throughout where these recent views and models are similar to, and diverge from older models and conceptions of aptitude, such as those represented by the *Modern Language Aptitude Test* (MLAT, Carroll and Sapon 1959), Pimsleur's *Language Aptitude Battery* (PLAB, Pimsleur 1966) and the US Defense Language Institute's (DLI) *Defense Language Aptitude Battery* (DLAB, Petersen and Al Haik 1976).

2 Aptitude and Effects of Instruction

Research and theorizing about the nature of foreign language aptitude has been a relatively neglected area of applied linguistic, and SLA research over the last 20 years. There are signs, however, that this situation is changing somewhat—and hopefully this will be reflected in new attempts at aptitude test development. Two, quite different, reasons for the state of neglect of aptitude research, and lack of aptitude test development, have been the following.

Firstly, for quite some time, throughout the 1970s and a large part of the 1980s, many applied linguists and SLA researchers were convinced that unconscious, universal processes available to child L1 learners were heavily influential on adult SLA, and therefore that aptitude measures, which identify differences in cognitive abilities and processes largely (at least in the initial stages of L2 learning) under executive control, were as irrelevant to predicting successful SLA as they seem, in principle, to be in predicting L1 acquisition. In Krashen's terms, it was felt that aptitude predicted only formal, and limited scope, classroom learning, and was not influential on unconscious, universal learning processes, or acquisition—the process he (and others) argued is primarily responsible for successful long-term SLA. Krashen's work dominated much theorizing and educational practice throughout the 1980s, and continued to be influential into the 1990s.

Secondly, there has been a belief that aptitude is what currently available aptitude tests measure—tests largely developed over 30 years ago (in the case of MLAT and PLAB), before SLA research into cognitive processing and effects of classroom instruction had substantially begun. Aptitude has therefore been untheorized—it is simply equated with a score obtained by using existing, and available conventional tests, such as MLAT, or PLAB. New tests, consequently, have not been developed. The implicit assumption has often been, too, that there is one aptitude, equated with that same MLAT or PLAB score, and that aptitude is largely unmodifiable, and so attempts to characterize different aptitudes for L2 learning, or to train and develop aptitude, have not been pursued.

2.1 Questioning Reason 1

Leaving aside theoretical issues which I will not describe in great detail here, Reason 1 has largely been discredited and the acquisition-learning distinction abandoned. In its place contemporary SLA research at the pedagogy-interface emphasizes the critical role of awareness (noticing) and attention to language form and content, in context, as well as the role of memory processes, i.e. elaboration and rehearsal of attended information in working memory prior to encoding in long-term memory (for SLA reviews of these areas see Hulstijn 1989, 2001; Schmidt 1990, 2001; Tomlin and Villa 1994; Robinson 1995a, 2003; Ellis 2001). Consequently, research has been progressing into what level of attention to, and processing of, input is necessary for successful retention, and subsequent development of L2 form and meaning relationships. This research has made specific links between such cognitive processing requirements and a variety of instructional, interventionist classroom pedagogic techniques.

These links can best be summarized by adapting a distinction made by Long (1991) between (1) focus on form (FonF), or brief shifts of attention from communicative meaning to formal aspects of the L2 online during communicative activity; (2) focus on forms (FonFS), or offline preteaching of grammatical forms prior to communication, or interruptions to communicative activity to deliver explicit metalinguistic feedback; and (3) focus on meaning (FM), in which no deliberate attempt is made to direct the focus of learner attention to language as object, leaving form to be 'picked up', incidentally, from exposure alone to input during communicative activity (see Doughty and Williams 1998a; Long and Robinson 1998; Muranoi 2000). The concern of this research, then, has been to match the particular form, meaning, or functional linguistic pattern, to the most appropriate interventionist technique, as well as to assess the relative effectiveness of these three overall treatment types (see Norris and Ortega 2000, for an overview and meta analysis of the findings to date). Briefly put, over and above meaningful exposure alone (FM), pedagogic techniques can be ranged along a continuum in terms of their attentional demands, and intrusiveness on the communicative act (see Doughty and Williams 1998a, p. 258, 1998b). At the least explicit, intrusive end, simple flooding of input with exemplars of a particular form can be designed (White 1998); more intrusively, and to increase attentional allocation to form in context, such exemplars can be enhanced in some way, such as by underlining, or other ways of making visual input salient (Leeman et al. 1995); while the most intrusive option, online, or offline pedagogic rule explanation has also been examined for its interaction with morphological, syntactic, phonological, semantic, or otherwise defined processing complexity (see DeKeyser 1995; Robinson 1996b; VanPatten 2004).

One important point about this research, which has to date gone largely untreated (though see Robinson 1995b, 1997a, 2001a, b, 2002a, b, 2005a, b, 2007) is that the effectiveness of these various focus on form techniques and interventions is likely to be mediated by very different sets of cognitive abilities. Options in instructional, interventionist techniques must be matched to the cognitive resources and abilities learners bring to the classroom to be optimally effective. So learning from pedagogic rule instruction would draw on a different set of abilities than purely incidental learning, or learning from enhanced input floods. I return to these issues in some detail below.

At this point, suffice it to say that developments in language pedagogy and SLA research assume cognitive processes, largely under executive control, are fundamentally important to L2 success, and that variation between learners in L2 success in instructed environments can likely be explained in part by differences between them in the cognitive abilities that such processes draw on. And these are measurable differences. In this way, I will argue below, as does Sternberg (1985, 2002), successful L2 learning can now be seen as the result of an interaction between a learner's pattern of abilities in relevant areas for L2 processing, and the instructional interventions and techniques that are adopted in the L2 classroom. Techniques that may work for one learner, will often, therefore, not be so effective for another. This brings me to the second reason raised above for the neglect of aptitude research in recent years.

2.2 Questioning Reason 2

While it is obviously to be hoped that aptitude is what aptitude tests measure, for reasons just given, it is likely that currently available aptitude tests (MLAT, PLAB), and others like them, such as DLAB, are insufficient to capture the range of abilities drawn on by the interventionist L2 pedagogic techniques described above. After all, it is aptitude for learning in instructional context that we hope to measure—aptitude does not exist independently of these in an educationally useful way, one could say, as did Richard Snow (I will not go into detail here about Snow's complex metatheory of cognitive, affective, context interactions, though see Corno et al. 2002, and Shavelson et al. 2002 for concerted work in his framework, and Robinson 2007, for discussion of its relevance to SLA). Certainly, such aptitude tests as MLAT were developed long before the SLA research described above had begun, or had even begun to be conceptualized. Therefore there is clearly a need to examine, and likely supplement available aptitude tests if they are to be optimally effective predictors of learning from the contemporary instructional options briefly summarized above.

John B. Carroll, it must be said, was clearly of the same mind when he developed the tests that became the MLAT. In 1981, he wrote, of one of the antecedents to the MLAT, the Iowa Foreign Language Aptitude test, that "it seemed to reflect too formal and rigid a conception of foreign language learning as a process of deciphering and translating written materials" (Carroll 1981, p. 89). That is, it was developed to predict success in learning following the then predominant Grammar Translation methodology. Carroll went on to comment that "I noted the need for measures of foreign language learning aptitude that would be appropriate for predicting success in the oral-aural and in many cases intensive language courses that were then being conducted in schools, colleges and governmental military organizations" (Carroll 1981, p. 89). That is, Carroll had in mind the kinds of abilities necessary to learning in classrooms and programs following Audiolingual courses of instruction in the late 1950s and early 1960s.

Audiolingualism (AL) is quite rightly treated by Lightbown and Spada (1999, pp. 118–120) as an approach to pedagogy that emphasizes correct imitation, and explicit instant oral correction, of largely mechanical oral drills, or what they call the Get it right from the beginning approach to L2 instruction. Audiolingual methodology was a precursor of the very different communicative, immersion and latterly task-based classrooms of the 1970, 1980, and 1990s which emphasize meaningful input; attempt accommodate learnability and teachability constraints; and which Lightbown and Spada call Get it right in the end approaches. No wonder, then, that Carroll's subtests do seem to validly measure the abilities necessary to learning in AL classrooms; grammatical sensitivity (the words in sentences subtest); rote memory (the paired associates subtest); mastery of oral language and aurally presented patterns (the phonemic sensitivity subtest). But while, I will argue, some of the MLAT subtests (e.g. the first two mentioned) may be valid measures of the ability to learn from metalinguistic correction, or rule explanation, there is seemingly little (i.e. not much, I don't mean nothing at all) in the MLAT which would be a valid measure of the ability to learn from input floods, or from orally delivered recasts of learner utterances, or from incidental learning from meaningful exposure alone (though see recent work on the effectiveness of MLAT type subtests as predictors of learning in some communicative programs, e.g. Harley and Hart 1997, 2002; Ranta 2002). This does not mean that incidental learning from comprehended input, say, is aptitude independent (Krashen's claim), but rather that the MLAT does not seem to be a valid measure of the abilities which differentiate successful, from less successful purely incidental learners. And Carroll did not intend it to be, either.

Underlying the points made above then, is the larger objection to Reason 2 for abandoning work on aptitude. As in work on intelligence testing, by Sternberg, Gardner and others, which has questioned the monolithic conception of intelligence in favor of (particularly in Sternberg's case) constrained theories of multiple intelligences, so recent views of aptitude, such as my own described below, see it as a multiple construct. Learners have sets of aptitudes, or what following Snow (1994) I call aptitude complexes for learning from classroom instruction, which can, importantly, be matched to specific instructional options to help ensure the optimal learning conditions for any specific learner, or group of learners with similar aptitude profiles.

A further issue I will raise here, but not dwell on, since research is quite simply lacking, is the issue of trainability. It may be that certain sets of abilities, as opposed to others, are more or less amenable to training. Sternberg has shown this to be so, to some extent, in the area of intelligence (see Sternberg 2002, for a summary), and the same may well be true for language aptitude components. At the moment, we don't know, but the sets of aptitude complexes I will propose certainly suggest that some, as opposed to others, may be relatively susceptible to training. Finally, an important issue related to this one, again not discussed in detail here, is the issue of static versus dynamic testing of abilities. Aptitude tests are to date delivered to learners who are 'cold', unprepared, and lacking in experience of the activities the test requires them to perform. Dynamic testing of abilities, in which the extent of learners' adaptation to the testing task, after they have been 'warmed up', has been developed, and is reported to have had some success, over and above static tests, as predictors of later learning (see Sternberg and Grigorenko 2000 for review). In this view, a dynamic measure of inductive language learning ability, for example, would not consist of a paper and pencil test following timed/brief exposure to a set of representative stimuli, but would take place over time, and inductive learning would be assessed on the basis of more lengthy 'trial exposure' to, and feedback on hypotheses about, the learning stimuli.

These latter two issues, of trainability, and of dynamic testing, may seem somewhat irrelevant to institutions which use aptitude tests primarily with a view to selecting the most able students into instructional programs (e.g. the DLI, as opposed to high schools)—but they need not be. If some learners can be trained, in a short time, to substantially improve their L2 learning abilities, or if some learners, given a dynamic test, can be shown to adapt quickly and well (outperforming initially fast starters) to the test/task demands imposed (i.e. after getting over the initial test/task shock) then this information is also important to candidate selection, I would argue.

Having gone this far in describing how I feel the construct of aptitude could benefit from further theoretical development, let me make three broad points, before describing two current models of aptitude which have the potential to meet a number of the concerns I have raised above about the construct, treatment and so predictive validity of existing measures.

Point 1. Aptitude(s) are sets, or 'complexes' of abilities which enable learners to profit from instructional interventions, particularly such activities as task-work, communicative pair-work, provision of implicit and explicit negative oral feedback, staged grammar rule instruction, input-based learning from extensive reading and listening, etc. I describe how I see these complexes being structured, and interrelated in more detail below.

Point 2. If instructional options are many and varied a 'comprehensive' battery is needed if the rate of 'overall' learning from the variety of options is to be successfully predicted.

Point 3. The battery should be capable of matching students to SPECIFIC instructional options—both in and out of classrooms (to options available for giving corrective feedback, for self-study, practice, and homework activities, for example)—which are best suited to their different patterns of abilities.

3 Two Proposals for New Measures of Aptitude

3.1 Why Parsimony is Not Necessarily to be Desired in Aptitude Tests

If the three points made above are incorporated into a rationale for developing an effective aptitude test, then there are likely to be a greater number of subtests than is currently the case with traditional tests, such as the MLAT, PLAB or DLAB, and so it will become even more unlikely than at present that any particular learner, or group of learners, will do well on all of them. Sampling a wider range of abilities, that is, will incur greater variation in performance than is currently the case with MLAT, PLAB or DLAB. This variation does not mean that total scores cannot still be used for selection purposes, but it does provide a means of more accurately profiling differences in acquisition-relevant abilities between learners, which can be used to instructional effect. One major argument for parsimony, or few aptitude subtests, has been ease of administration. Clearly, in the 1950, 1960 and 1970s, when current aptitude tests, such as MLAT and PLAB were developed, testing had to take place at one sitting, in groups, using paper and pencil formats. But the situation has now dramatically changed. On-line computer delivered subtests, completed over a period of time, at the individual candidate's convenience, is now an available option— making more exhaustive testing of abilities possible, without the additional inconvenience, and fatigue, that this might have caused in the past.

The following proposals therefore describe models of aptitude that could be developed into tests, consisting of a number of subtests, which could be used as the basis of candidate selection, while at the same time providing information which is pedagogically useful about diagnosed areas of likely weakness, and also information which can be used to match learners to optimally effective instructional options. Aptitude, as I have argued above, does not have its effects alone, it has its effects in those instructional contexts (see Sternberg and Wagner 1994; Robinson 2001a, b, 2002a, 2007) which draw, differentially, on the numerous sets of abilities that aptitude tests measure.

3.2 Skehan's 'Processing Stage' Model of Aptitude

Skehan (2002) proposes that the components of aptitude for instructed learning must be differentiated according to the SLA processing stage they correspond to

SLA Processing Stage	Aptitude Component
1. Noticing	Auditory segmentation
	Attention management
	Working memory
	Phonemic coding
2. Pattern identification	Fast analysis/working memory
	Grammatical sensitivity
3. Extending	Inductive language learning ability
4. Complexifying	Grammatical sensitivity
	Inductive language learning ability
5. Integrating	Restructuring capacity
6. Becoming accurate, avoiding terror	Automatisation
	Proceduralisation
7. Creating a repertoire, achieving salience	Retrieval processes
8. Automatising rulebased language, achieving fluency	Automatising, proceduralisation
9. Lexicalising, dual-coding	Memory, chunking, retrieval processes

Fig. 1 Processing stages and potential aptitude components (from Skehan 2002)

(see Fig. 1), and he identifies four broad stages; noticing the input; patterning the input to facilitate further analysis and generalization; controlling the analyzed knowledge in production; and lexicalising, or variegating the patterns learned to suit different communicative, and situational contexts.

Each proposed stage in Fig. 1 is matched by a hypothetical description of the cognitive abilities and resources a complementary aptitude component would measure. Skehan notes that in the approach he describes, "we are not taking existing aptitude tests and seeing if SLA relevance can be perceived for each of them. Rather we are taking SLA stages, and exploring whether aptitude would be relevant for each of these stages" (Skehan 2002, pp. 89–90). While some stages do relate quite clearly to the abilities measured by current MLAT, PLAB and DLAB subtests, in other cases the model "reveals where it would be useful to produce aptitude tests if we are to be able to predict effectively in acquisition-rich contexts" (Skehan 2002, p. 90).

The first stage concerns noticing and registration of the input, and in addition to measures of attentional management and working memory Skehan identifies the phonetic sensitivity component of MLAT as a particularly relevant measure. Stages 2–5 in Fig. 1 broadly concern pattern analysis. Here the grammatical sensitivity and inductive language learning measures of MLAT are proposed to capture some of the abilities contributing to these aspects of language processing, but Skehan notes that Stage 5, labeled integrating the analyzed knowledge, involves capacity for 'restructuring'—an aptitude component not well matched by any existing tests.

Similarly, current aptitude subtests do not capture well the abilities contributing to control of analyzed knowledge in Stages 6–8, and the cumulative proceduralisation of knowledge in fluent performance over time. One suggestion is that—as in dynamic tests of other aptitudes, which involve an authentic trial learning session, as I have mentioned above—a cumulative measure of ability to profit while engaged in learning would be appropriate here. In such tests (see Feuerstein 1979; Budoff 1987; Guthke 1992; Sternberg and Grigorenko 2000), aptitudes for learning are assessed—at least in part—in terms of pre-post test performance on some learning activity. One option that may be suitable, as in Grigorenko et al. (2000) *CANAL-F Aptitude Test*, and Sick and Irie's (2001) *Lunic Language Marathon*, is to develop an aptitude component which involves actual learning of—and also being tutored in while learning—a miniature artificial language. This is very similar to one current subtest of DLAB, which I will discuss in more detail in the following section. Such a subtest would involve two stages: an initial (timed, computer delivered) self-study (no feedback) stage, where learners attempt to understand the rules of the artificial language alone and are then tested. Following this there would be a period of instruction (again, timed, computerized in its delivery, but with computerized feedback on performance) in the language, followed by a further test. Performance on the second part of the test would be assessed by measuring gain from the first test of unaided self-study, to results of learning following tutored, computerized instruction on the second test. Gain may then be taken as a measure of what Skehan calls "the capacity to proceduralise with linguistic material" (Skehan 2002, p. 92) while profiting from tutored exposure, as happens in real time teaching and learning classroom environments. There are precedents for such computerized delivery of instruction in artificial, as well as natural languages, in the SLA literature, and some of these are referred to below (e.g. DeKeyser 1995; Robinson 1996a, b, 1997b, 2002a, 2005b; de Graaff 1997; and see DeKeyser 2003, for a summary).

Finally, the last of Skehan's processing stages, lexicalising, involves 'going beyond rule-based processing' to build a fluent lexical repertoire. Since this involves an aptitude component that measures storage and retrieval memory processes that provide on-line access, current aptitude measures such as MLAT and DLAB again are not appropriate here, since they measure only paired associate, rote memorization abilities, if any. Relevant here, from the SLA research literature, has been research which has studied the effects of multiple exposure to instances of a particular form, and automatic access of instances in making judgements about grammatical acceptability (Robinson and Ha 1993; Robinson 1997b) drawing on seminal work on instance theory and access during decision making by Logan (1988). While the findings regarding the applicability of Logan's instance theory of automatic access to L2 acquisition are not yet clear (see DeKeyser 2001, for review) it is clear that the memory component of current aptitude tests is the one most in need of revision to accommodate findings from cognitive psychology and SLA research about different forms of memory, as they are implicated in learning, and access to learned material. Relevant here is work on working memory (see Daneman and Carpenter 1980; Miyake and Friedman 1998; Robinson 2002c, 2005b; Baddeley 2007), implicit and explicit tests of memory (Merickle and Reingold 1991; Robinson 1995a, 2002c, 2005b; Bowers and Marsolek 2003) and possibly too, episodic memory for the learning context, and the contextual coordinates with which language is often tagged (see Baddeley 2000; Baddeley et al. 2002; and also Ellis 2001, 2003).

Skehan's programmatic proposal suggests that some components of existing aptitude tests may be useful for capturing the abilities involved at different stages of L2 processing (particularly those involving language analysis, such as the MLAT's words in sentences), but that further development of complementary subtests will be necessary. As with my own approach, described below, aptitude subtests are also seen to operate in differentiated clusters to determine the complexes of L2 processing abilities appropriate to each of the four broad noticing, patterning, controlling and lexicalising stages.

The validity of aptitude tests as theoretically motivated measures of fine-grained SLA processes is thus prioritized in this approach to aptitude test design and development in contrast to the traditional concerns of parsimony, i.e. have as few subtests as possible, and so pragmatism, i.e. ensure brevity of administration. As noted above, while the tension between validity and thoroughness, versus parsimony and pragmatism, was understandable in the 1960s and 1970s when aptitude tests could only be administered at one sitting in classrooms, in the present day computerized, self-paced delivery and scoring of aptitude subtests has become a very feasible alternative—relaxing the traditional concerns over feasible test administration.

3.3 Robinson's 'Aptitude Complex/Ability Differentiation' Model of Aptitude

Robinson, adopting the interactionist approach of Snow (1987, 1994) identifies a number of aptitude-complexes, or combinations of cognitive abilities, that he argues are differentially related to processing under different conditions of instructional exposure to L2 input, and therefore that strengths in one or another of these complexes of abilities can be expected to be important to learning from one instructional technique, or under one condition, versus another. Sternberg has commented on his own attempts to learn three different languages—with very different degrees of success—that "(...) my aptitude was not internal to me, but in the interaction between my abilities and the way I was being taught" (Sternberg 2002, p. 13). Robinson's model of L2 aptitude for instructed learning is an attempt to specify the information processing details of this observation, and to relate them to current issues in SLA theory and pedagogy. There are two closely related hypotheses that define Robinson's basic framework, and he attempts to show how, taken together, they make predictions about how to optimally match learners to instructional options (for expanded discussions of the framework see Robinson 2001a, b, 2001c, 2002a, 2005a, 2007).

3.4 The Aptitude Complex Hypothesis

The first Aptitude Complex Hypothesis (based on proposals by Snow 1987, 1994) claims that certain sets or combinations of cognitive abilities are drawn on in learning under one condition of instructional L2 exposure, versus another. Figure 2 operationalizes instructional options, and options in types of practice condition, in terms of techniques for intervening during classroom activity to focus on form, either by recasting, providing orally or typographically salient input floods to enhance forms and so facilitate incidental learning, or via rule explanation, as it may occur during Input Processing instruction. Not all learners can be expected to have equivalent aptitudes for learning from each of these options. It follows therefore that if the effects of instruction and practice are to be optimized for individual learners, then these should take place under those conditions to which their aptitudes are best matched. The details of how aptitude complexes can be matched to these instructional options are motivated in part by findings from the recent SLA research into the effects of focus on form (FonF), forms (FonFs) and meaning (FM), described briefly above, as the following discussion illustrates.

Figure 2 describes four aptitude complexes, each made up of different combinations of ability factors. Aptitude complex 1, for learning from recasting, is made up of the abilities for noticing the gap (NTG) between the recast and the learner's prior utterance (see Doughty 2001), as well as memory for contingent speech (MCS). These two abilities are argued to be important to holding the interlocutor's recast in memory, while comparing it to the learner's prior utterance, and also noticing critical formal differences between the two. These second order ability (NTG and MCS) factors contributing to this L2 aptitude complex are themselves combinations of domain neutral primary abilities such as perceptual speed and pattern recognition (in the case of noticing the gap) and phonological working memory capacity and speed (in the case of memory for contingent speech). This model, then, is hierarchical in its organization of the structure of abilities, in the tradition of Cattell (1971) and Carroll (1993), while also capturing the insight of Snow (1994), that specific combinations of abilities (aptitude complexes) may be related to specific options in L2 instructional exposure.

Figure 2 also relates primary abilities hypothesized, for example, to underlie the second order ability to notice the gap (NTG), to specific tests of these primary abilities. In the case of perceptual or basic processing speed a test of inspection time, as described in Anderson's (1992) work, is proposed, while in the case of pattern recognition, the sound symbol correspondence—or phonetic sensitivity—subtest of Sasaki's LABJ aptitude battery is proposed. Evidence for the strong relationship between performance on the LABJ sound symbol test of phonetic sensitivity and learning from recasts has been found (e.g. findings of Robinson and Yamaguchi 1999). In the case of memory for contingent speech, the listening span test of working memory used by Mackey et al. (2002) is proposed as a suitable test of phonological working memory capacity—one of the contributory primary abilities. This measure has also been shown to positively predict the ability to notice and learn from recasts during L2 interaction by Mackey et al. (2002), and working memory in general has been argued to be strongly implicated in aptitude for L2 processing and language learning (see Miyake and Friedman 1998; Ellis 2001; Robinson 2002b, c, 2005b; Williams and Lovatt 2003).

The second aptitude complex in Fig. 2, for incidental learning from oral input containing a flood of particular forms, is made up of the ability factor memory for contingent speech (MCS) described above, and also deep semantic processing (DSP). This second DSP factor contributes the ability to process the semantic content of input containing the flooded item(s) deeply—and may be measured by tests of the primary ability to infer word meaning (see de Graaff 1997) or to construct analogical representations of meaning, and so establish greater semantic coherence between aspects of the input (see e.g. discussion by Sternberg 1985 of analogical reasoning, and tests of these). The third aptitude complex, for incidental learning from floods provided in written input differs only in that memory for contingent text (MCT), rather than speech, combines with DSP to contribute to this complex of abilities for learning. Finally, Fig. 2 illustrates a fourth aptitude complex—aptitude for learning from a brief rule explanation, supplemented by examples written on a classroom board, and then applying the rule (while remembering and rehearsing it) in subsequent comprehension (as in input processing instruction) or production activities. This aptitude complex is made up of the secondary abilities memory for contingent text, as well as metalinguistic rule rehearsal (MRR). This last MRR ability factor is proposed to be measured well by two existing subtests of aptitude: the MLAT words in sentences/grammatical sensitivity and paired associates/rote memory subtests, and findings for strong significant positive correlations of rule instructed learning with performance on these subtests in a study by Robinson (1997a) support this claim. The findings for low, nonsignificant correlations of performance on these subtests and incidental learning in Robinson (1997a) also support the separation of this MRR ability from aptitude complexes 2 and 3 for incidental learning and practice in meaning focused conditions, as shown in Fig. 2.

3.5 The Ability Differentiation Hypothesis

The second part of this framework, the Ability Differentiation Hypothesis, is based on findings described by Deary et al. (1996) as well as work on language-based learning abilities and disabilities by, amongst others, Ganschow and Sparks (1993) and Grigorenko (2002). Work on language-based learning disabilities and developmental dyslexia (see the review in Grigorenko 2002) has shown that some learners have extensive L1-based impairment to, for example, phonological working memory capacity, or specific difficulties in mastering morphosyntactic paradigms in their native language, and Ganschow and Sparks (1993) further argue that such L1-based disabilities underlie poor aptitude for L2 learning. Deary et al. (1996) have also shown, in the field of general intelligence research, that when comparing adults and children, or high IQ with low IQ groups, performance on the subtests of traditional measures of intelligence (such as the Wechsler Adult Intelligence Scale) is more differentiated (i.e. there are multiple abilities, and a weaker general factor, or 'g') for adults and high IQ groups than their child, and

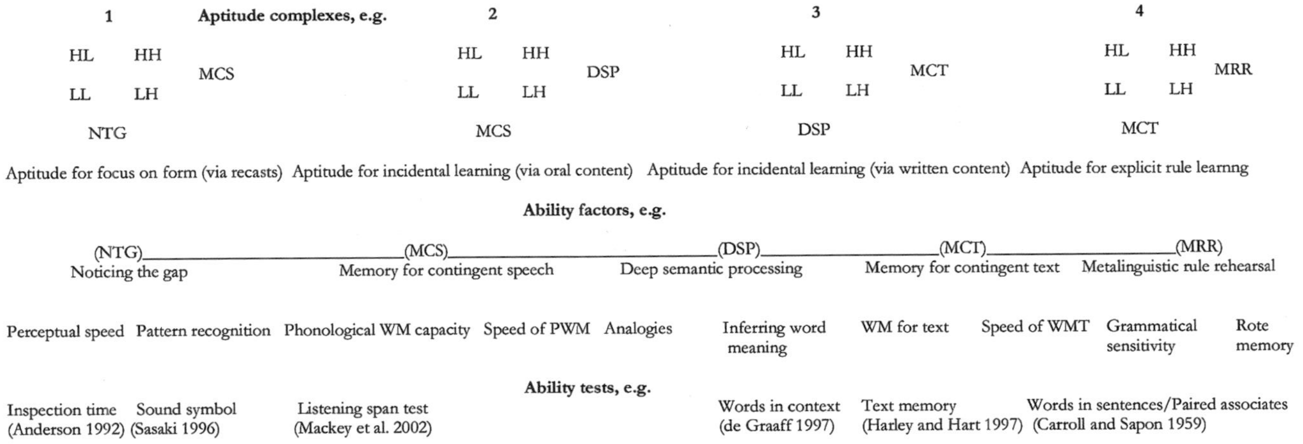

Aptitude complexes, e.g.

	1	2	3	4
	HL HH	HL HH	HL HH	HL HH
	LL LH	LL LH	LL LH	LL LH
	MCS	DSP	MCT	MRR
	NTG	MCS	DSP	MCT

Aptitude for focus on form (via recasts)   Aptitude for incidental learning (via oral content)   Aptitude for incidental learning (via written content)   Aptitude for explicit rule learning

Ability factors, e.g.

(NTG)	(MCS)	(DSP)	(MCT)	(MRR)
Noticing the gap	Memory for contingent speech	Deep semantic processing	Memory for contingent text	Metalinguistic rule rehearsal
Perceptual speed Pattern recognition	Phonological WM capacity Speed of PWM Analogies	Inferring word meaning Words in context	WM for text Speed of WMT	Grammatical sensitivity Rote memory

Ability tests, e.g.

Inspection time   Sound symbol
(Anderson 1992) (Sasaki 1996)

Listening span test
(Mackey et al. 2002)

Words in context
(de Graaff 1997)

Text memory
(Harley and Hart 1997)

Words in sentences/Paired associates
(Carroll and Sapon 1959)

Key: HH = high, high; LH = low, high; HL = high, low; LL = low, low; NTG = noticing the gap; MCS = memory for contingent speech; DSP = deep semantic processing; MCT = memory for contingent text; MRR = metalinguistic rule rehearsal; WM = working memory; PWM = phonological working memory.

Fig. 2 Hierarchical model of cognitive abilities showing two levels of ability factors (primary abilities, and second order ability factors for language learning aptitude), and ability tests used as markers for the central ability. Aptitude complexes at the top are intended to suggest combinations of abilities drawn on under particular learning conditions (based on Snow 1994, p. 10, Fig. 1)

lower IQ counterparts (see also Carroll 1993, pp. 677–681). These findings suggest, then, that patterns of strengths in abilities contributing to aptitude complexes in Fig. 2 may also be very differentiated for some adult L2 learners, such that the noticing the gap ability is high, while the memory for contingent speech ability is low. This possibility is captured in the top right HL quadrant in aptitude complex 1 in Fig. 2. Alternatively, strengths in both NTG and MCS may be high (HH), meaning recasting is a particularly suitable option for focussing on form for these learners; or strengths in both of these factors may be much lower (LL), suggesting that either alternative focus on form techniques are more suitable, or that some remediative training in developing the abilities in question may be (if possible) a necessary option.

4 Conclusion: Aptitude Tests—Selection, Diagnosis and Matching to Instructional Options as Purposes

Where the purpose of the aptitude test is selection, e.g. in the case of the DLI's DLAB, then learners who have high abilities in all of the areas described in Robinson's model would most sensibly be preferred. However, such individuals would likely be rare, and so it would more likely be the case that learners high in some, or many areas, but low in one or two, were selected, and subsequently instruction could be tailored so as to avoid the instructional options, feedback techniques, etc., that they are most likely to have problems in learning from or responding to. The sequential, processing stage approach taken by Skehan also suggests that aptitudes for learning at each stage may differ, with the consequence that some learners may have poor aptitude for input processing and noticing (Stage 1) but stronger strengths in aptitudes for patterning the input (Stages 2–5); or for proceduralising and automatizing analyzed input (Stages 6–8); or for lexicalising learned rules of narrow domain applicability (Stage 9). In Skehan's model, where the purpose of the aptitude test is selection, as with the DLAB, then clearly learners high in aptitude at each stage would be preferred, but again, it is likely such learners would be few and far between. Where learners are selected who are weak in some capacities for L2 processing, then the resulting subtest profile can be used to support areas of weakness through supplementary, more structured and extensive practice activities.

Both Robinson's and Skehan's models can therefore form the basis of an aptitude test whose primary function is selection, but both also have diagnostic value, which can be used to identify areas of needed support in processing for L2 learning. However, beyond this it is not clear whether Skehan's proposed aptitude test could be used to match learners to more specific options in classroom activity, such as decisions about optimally learner effective focus on form techniques, or decisions about matching learners to optimally effective task types during accuracy, fluency and interaction practice in communicative classrooms. That is, Skehan takes different stages of global L2 information processing, rather than the specific conditions of instructed L2 exposure, as his operational platform for proposing aptitude components.

In contrast, considerations of the relationship of aptitude(s) to the specific conditions of instructed L2 classroom exposure and options for pedagogic interventions within them are the major motivation for, and operational platform of Robinson's framework. The Ability Differentiation Hypothesis claims that some L2 learners may have more clearly differentiated abilities—and so strengths in corresponding aptitude complexes—than others, and further that it is particularly important to match these learners to instructional conditions, and conditions of practice which favor their strengths in aptitude complexes, in contrast to other learners who may have less differentiated abilities, and equivalent strengths and aptitudes for learning under a variety of conditions of exposure and classroom practice. Both of the models of aptitude described above, complementary as they are, though with different emphases, offer researchers the opportunity to engage with aptitude test development in a way that incorporates findings from SLA and cognitive psychology. It is only natural that as research in these fields progresses we should turn our attention to revising the not-so-Modern Language Aptitude Test, and others, and hopefully this will be done in the coming years ahead.

References

Ackerman, P.L., R.J. Sternberg, and R. Glaser, eds. 1989. *Learning and individual differences.* New York: Freeman.

Anderson, M. 1992. *Intelligence and development: A cognitive theory.* Oxford: Blackwell.

Baddeley, A. 2000. The episodic buffer: A new component of working memory? *Trends in Cognitive Sciences* 4: 417–423.

Baddeley, A. 2007. *Working memory thought, and action.* Oxford: Oxford University Press.

Baddeley, A., M. Conway, and J. Aggelton, eds. 2002. *Episodic memory: New directions for research.* Oxford: Oxford University Press.

Bowers, J., and C. Marsolek, eds. 2003. *Rethinking implicit memory.* Oxford: Oxford University Press.

Budoff, M. 1987. The validity of learning potential assessment. In ed. C.S. Lidz, 52–81.

Carroll, J.B. 1962. The prediction of success in intensive foreign language training. In ed. R. Glaser, 87–136.

Carroll, J.B. 1981. Twenty five years of research on foreign language aptitude. In ed. K.C. Diller, 83–118.

Carroll, J.B. 1993. *Human cognitive abilities: A survey of factor-analytic studies.* New York: Cambridge University Press.

Carroll, J.B., and S.M. Sapon. 1959. *Modern language aptitude test.* New York: The Psychological Corporation/Harcourt Brace Jovanovich.

Cattell, R.B. 1971. *Abilities: Their structure growth and action.* Boston: Houghton Nefflin.

Conway, A., C. Jarrold, M. Kane, A. Miyake, and J. Towse, eds. 2007. *Variation in working memory.* Oxford: Oxford University Press.

Corno, L., L.J. Cronbach, H. Kupermintz, D.F. Lohman, E.B. Mandinach, A.W. Porteus, and J.E. Talbert. 2002. *Remaking the concept of aptitude: Extending the legacy of Richard E. Snow.* Mahwah: Lawrence Erlbaum.

Cornwell, S., and P. Robinson, eds. 2001. *Individual differences in foreign language learning: Effects of aptitude, intelligence and motivation.* Tokyo: Aoyama Gakuin University.

Daneman, M., and P.A. Carpenter. 1980. Individual differences in working memory and reading. *Journal of Verbal Learning and Verbal Behaviour* 19: 450–466.

De Bot, K., R.B. Ginsberg, and C. Kramsch, eds. 1991. *Foreign language research in cross-cultural perspective*. Amsterdam: Benjamins.

de Graaff, R. 1997. *Differential effects of explicit instruction on second language acquisition*. The Hague: Holland Institute of Generative Linguistics.

Deary, I., V. Egan, G. Gibson, E. Austin, R. Brand, and T. Kellaghan. 1996. Intelligence and the differentiation hypothesis. *Intelligence* 23: 105–132.

Dechert, H., and M. Raupach, eds. 1989. *Interlingual processing*. Tubingen: Gunter Narr.

DeKeyser, R.M. 1995. Learning second language grammar rules: An experiment with a miniature linguistic system. *Studies in Second Language Acquisition* 17: 379–410.

DeKeyser, R.M. 1997. Beyond explicit rule learning: Automatizing second language syntax. *Studies in Second Language Acquisition* 19: 195–221.

DeKeyser, R.M. 2003. Implicit and explicit learning. In eds. C.J. Doughty, and M.H. Long, 469–498.

DeKeyser, R.M., ed. 2007. *Practice and second language learning: Perspectives from applied linguistics and cognitive psychology*. New York: Cambridge University Press.

Diller, K.C., ed. 1981. *Individual differences and universals in language learning aptitude*. Rowley: Newbury House.

Doughty, C.J. 2001. Cognitive underpinnings of focus on form. In ed. P. Robinson, 206–257.

Doughty, C.J., and M.H. Long, eds. 2003. *The handbook of second language acquisition*. Oxford: Blackwell.

Doughty, C.J., and E. Varela. 1998. Communicative focus on form. In eds. C.J. Doughty, and J. Williams, 114–138.

Doughty, C.J., and J. Williams. 1998a. Pedagogical choices in focus on form. In eds. C.J. Doughty, and J. Williams, 197–262.

Doughty, C.J., and J. Williams, eds. 1998b. *Focus on form in classroom second language acquisition*. New York: Cambridge University Press.

Ellis, N.C. 2001. Memory for language. In ed. P. Robinson, 34–68.

Ellis, N.C. 2003. Constructions, chunking and connectionism. In eds. C.J. Doughty, and M.H. Long, 63–103.

Feuerstein, R. 1979. *The dynamic assessment of retarded performers: The learning potential assessment device: Theory instruments, and techniques*. Baltimore: University Park Press.

Fletcher, P., and B. MacWhinney, eds. 1995. *The handbook of child language*. Oxford: Blackwell.

Ganschow, L., and R.L. Sparks. 1993. Foreign language learning disabilities: Issues, research, and teaching implications. In eds. S.A. Vogel, and P.B. Adelman, 282–317.

Glaser, R., ed. 1962. *Training research and education*. New York: Wiley.

Grigorenko, E.L. 2002. Language-based learning disabilities. In ed. P. Robinson, 95–113.

Grigorenko, E.L., R.J. Sternberg, and M. Ehrman. 2000. A theory-based approach to the measurement of foreign language aptitude: The CANAL-F theory and test. *Modern Language Journal* 84: 390–405.

Guthke, J. 1992. Learning tests: The concept, main research findings, problems and trends. *Learning and Individual Differences* 4: 137–151.

Harley, B., and D. Hart. 1997. Language aptitude and second language proficiency in classroom learners of different starting ages. *Studies in Second Language Acquisition* 19: 379–400.

Harley, B., and D. Hart. 2002. Age, aptitude, and second language learning on a bilingual exchange. In ed. P. Robinson, 301–330.

Harrington, M. 2001. Sentence processing. In ed. P. Robinson, 91–124.

Healy, A., and L. Bourne, eds. 1998. *Foreign language learning: Psycholinguistic studies on training and retention*. Mahwah: Lawrence Erlbaum.

Hulstijn, J.H. 1989. Implicit and incidental language learning: Experiments in the processing of natural and partly artificial input. In eds. H. Dechert, and M. Raupach, 49–73.

Hulstijn, J.H. 2001. Intentional and incidental second language vocabulary learning: A reappraisal of elaboration, rehearsal and automaticity. In ed. P. Robinson, 258–286.

Hulstijn, J.H., and R.M. DeKeyser, eds. 1997. Second language acquisition research in the laboratory: Special Issue. *Studies in Second Language Acquisition* 19.

Kinoshita, S., and S. Lupker, eds. 2003. *Masked priming: The state of the art*. Hove: Psychology Press.

Knorr, E., and A. Neubauer. 1996. Speed of information processing in an inductive reasoning task and its relationship to psychometric intelligence. *Personality and Individual Differences* 20: 653–660.

Krashen, S.D. 1981. Aptitude and attitude in relation to second language acquisition and learning. In ed. K.C. Diller, 155–175.

Leeman, J., I. Artegoitia, B. Fridman, and C.J. Doughty. 1995. Integrating attention to form with meaning: focus on form in content-based Spanish instruction. In ed. R. Schmidt, 217–258.

Lidz, C.S., ed. 1987. *Dynamic assessment: An interactional approach to evaluating learning potential*. New York: Guilford Press.

Lightbown, P., and N. Spada. 1999. *How languages are learned*. Oxford: Oxford University Press.

Logan, G.D. 1988. Towards an instance theory of automatization. *Psychological Review* 95: 492–527.

Long, M.H. 1991. Focus on form: A design feature in language teaching methodology. In eds. K. De Bot, R.B. Ginsberg, and C. Kramsch, 39–52.

Long, M.H., and P. Robinson. 1998. Focus on form: Theory, research, practice. In eds. C.J. Doughty, and J. Williams, 15–41.

Mackey, A., J. Philp, T. Egi, A. Fujii, and T. Tatsumi. 2002. Individual differences in working memory, noticing of interactional feedback and L2 development. In ed. P. Robinson, 181–210.

MacWhinney, B. 2001. The competition model: The input, the context, and the brain. In ed. P. Robinson, 69–90.

Merickle, P.M., and E.M. Reingold. 1991. Comparing direct (explicit) and indirect (implicit) measures to study unconscious memory. *Journal of Experimental Psychology: Learning, Memory and Cognition* 17: 224–233.

Miyake, A., and N. Friedman. 1998. Individual differences in second language proficiency: Working memory as language aptitude. In eds. A. Healy, and L. Bourne, 339–364.

Monsell, S. 2003. Task switching. *Trends in Cognitive Sciences* 7: 134–140.

Muranoi, H. 2000. Focus on form through interaction enhancement: Integrating formal instruction into a communicative task in EFL classrooms. *Language Learning* 50: 617–673.

Norris, J.M., and L. Ortega. 2000. Effectiveness of L2 instruction: A research synthesis and quantitative meta-analysis. *Language Learning* 50: 417–528.

Petersen, C., and A. Al Haik. 1976. The development of the defense language aptitude battery. *Educational and Psychological Measurement* 36: 369–380.

Pimsleur, P. 1966. *Pimsleur language aptitude battery (PLAB)*. New York: The Psychological Corporation.

Ranta, L. 2002. The role of learners' analytic abilities in the communicative classroom. In ed. P. Robinson, 159–180.

Reber, A.S. 1993. *Implicit learning and tacit knowledge: An essay on the cognitive unconscious*. Oxford: Clarendon Press.

Robinson, P. 1995a. Attention, memory and the 'noticing' hypothesis. *Language Learning* 45: 283–331.

Robinson, P. 1995b. Aptitude, awareness, and the fundamental similarity of implicit and explicit second language learning. In ed. R. Schmidt, 1995, 303–357.

Robinson, P. 1996a. Learning simple and complex second language rules under implicit, incidental, rule-search and instructed conditions. *Studies in Second Language Acquisition* 18: 27–67.

Robinson, P. 1996b. *Consciousness rules and instructed second language acquisition*. New York: Lang.

Robinson, P. 1997a. Individual differences and the fundamental similarity of implicit and explicit adult second language learning. *Language Learning* 47: 45–99.

Robinson, P. 1997b. Automaticity and generalizability of second language learning under implicit, incidental, enhanced and rule-search conditions. *Studies in Second Language Acquisition* 19: 223–247.

Robinson, P. 2001a. Individual differences, cognitive abilities, aptitude complexes, and learning conditions in SLA. *Second Language Research* 17: 268–392.

Robinson, P., ed. 2001b. *Cognition and second language instruction.* Cambridge: Cambridge University Press.

Robinson, P. 2002a. Learning conditions, aptitude complexes and SLA: A framework for research and pedagogy. In ed. P. Robinson, 113–133.

Robinson, P. 2002b. Individual differences in intelligence, aptitude and working memory during adult incidental second language learning: A replication and extension of Reber, Walkenfield and Hernstadt (1991). In ed. P. Robinson, 211–266.

Robinson, P., ed. 2002c. *Individual differences and instructed language learning.* Amsterdam, Philadelphia: Benjamins.

Robinson, P. 2003. Attention and memory in SLA. In eds. C.J. Doughty, and M.H. Long, 631–679.

Robinson, P. 2005a. Aptitude and second language acquisition. *Annual Review of Applied Linguistics* 25: 46–73.

Robinson, P. 2005b. Cognitive abilities, chunk-strength and frequency effects in implicit artificial grammar and incidental L2 learning: Replications of Reber, Walkenfeld and Hernstadt (1991) and Knowlton and Squire (1996) and their relevance for SLA. *Studies in Second Language Acquisition* 27: 235–268.

Robinson, P. 2007. Aptitude, abilities, contexts and practice. In ed. R.M. DeKeyser, 256–287.

Robinson, P., and N.C. Ellis, eds. 2008. *The handbook of cognitive linguistics and second language acquisition.* New York/London: Routledge.

Robinson, P., and M. Ha. 1993. Instance theory and second language rule learning under explicit conditions. *Studies in Second Language Acquisition* 15: 413–438.

Robinson, P., and Y. Yamaguchi. 1999. Aptitude, task feedback and generalizability of focus on form: A classroom study. Paper presented at the 12th AILA World Congress, Waseda University, Tokyo, August.

Sasaki, M. 1996. *Second language proficiency foreign language aptitude, and intelligence.* New York: Lang.

Schaeken, W., G. De Vooght, A. Vandierendonck, and G. Y'deWalle, eds. 2002. *Deductive reasoning and strategies.* Mahwah: Lawrence Erlbaum.

Schmidt, R. 1990. The role of consciousness in second language learning. *Applied Linguistics* 11: 127–158.

Schmidt, R., ed. 1995. *Attention and awareness in foreign language learning.* Honolulu: University of Hawai'i Press.

Schmidt, R. 2001. Attention. In ed. P. Robinson, 1–32.

Shavelson, R.J., et al. 2002. Richard Snow's remaking of the concept of aptitude and multidimensional test validity: Introduction to the special issue. *Educational Assessment* 8: 77–99.

Sick, J., and K. Irie. 2001. The Lunic Language Marathon: A new language aptitude instrument for Japanese foreign language learners. In eds. S. Cornwell, and P. Robinson, 173–186.

Skehan, P. 1998. *A cognitive approach to language learning.* Oxford: Oxford University Press.

Skehan, P. 2002. Theorising and updating aptitude. In ed. P. Robinson, 69–94.

Snow, R.E. 1987. Aptitude complexes. In eds. R.E. Snow, and M.J. Farr, 11–34.

Snow, R.E. 1989. Aptitude-treatment interaction as a framework for research on learning and individual differences. In eds. P.L. Ackerman, R.J. Sternberg, and R. Glaser, 13–59.

Snow, R.E. 1994. Abilities in academic tasks. In eds. R.J. Sternberg, and R.K. Wagner, 3–37.

Snow, R.E., and M.J. Farr, eds. 1987. *Aptitude, learning and instruction.* Hillsdale: Lawrence Erlbaum.

Stanovitch, K.E. 1999. *Who is rational? Studies of individual differences in reasoning.* Mahwah: Lawrence Erlbaum.

Sternberg, R.J. 1985. *Beyond IQ: a triarchic theory of human intelligence.* New York: Cambridge University Press.

Sternberg, R.J. 2002. The theory of successful intelligence and its implications for language aptitude testing. In ed. P. Robinson, 13–44.

Sternberg, R.J., and E.L. Grigorenko. 2000. *Dynamic testing: The nature and measurement of learning potential.* New York: Cambridge University Press.

Sternberg, R.J., and R.K. Wagner, eds. 1994. *Mind in context: Interactionist perspectives on human intelligence.* New York: Cambridge University Press.

Tomasello, M. 2003. *Constructing a language: A usage-based theory of language acquisition.* Boston: Harvard University Press.

Tomlin, R., and V. Villa. 1994. Attention in cognitive science and second language acquisition. *Studies in Second Language Acquisition* 15: 183–203.

VanPatten, B., ed. 2004. *Processing instruction: Theory, research and commentary.* Mahwah: Lawrence Erlbaum.

Vogel, S.A., and P.B. Adelman, eds. 1993. *Success for college students with learning disabilities.* New York: Springer-Verlag.

White, J. 1998. Getting the learners' attention: A typographical input enhancement study. In eds. C.J. Doughty, and J. Williams, 85–113.

Williams, J.N., and P. Lovatt. 2003. Phonological memory and rule learning. *Language Learning* 53: 67–121.

Memory Abilities in Gifted Foreign Language Learners

Adriana Biedroń

Abstract This paper addresses the problem of the role of memory abilities in second language acquisition. In particular, it focuses on short-term and working memory abilities in gifted foreign language learners. Contemporary researchers agree that working memory may be a concept that will revolutionize research on foreign language aptitude (Miyake and Friedman 1998; Ellis 2001; Sawyer and Ranta 2001; Dörnyei 2005). If attention is necessary for learning and if it is limited by working memory capacity, there must be a close relationship between working memory capacity and learning outcomes (Sawyer and Ranta 2001). The present study investigated the role of short-term memory and working memory in gifted foreign language learners. The results of 44 gifted foreign language learners were compared to the results of 82 normal foreign language learners (mainstream philology students). Three instruments were used in the study: the *Modern Language Aptitude Test—MLAT* (Carroll and Sapon 2002), the *Wechsler Adult Intelligence Scale—WAIS-R (PL)*—an adaptation for use with the Polish population by Brzezinski et al. (1996) and the *Polish Reading Span—PRSPAN* (Biedroń and Szczepaniak 2011). The analysis revealed that short-term memory and working-memory abilities in the gifted foreign language learners were higher than in the normal foreign language learners. A tentative conclusion based on the results of the study is that two components of working memory, namely the phonological loop and the central executive, are significant variables in determining the outcome of learning a foreign language.

Preparation of this research project was supported by the Polish Ministry of Science and Higher Education in 2009–2011, project no. 1231/B/HO3/2009/37.

A. Biedroń (✉)
Pomeranian Academy in Słupsk, Słupsk, Poland
e-mail: biedron@apsl.edu.pl

M. Pawlak (ed.), *New Perspectives on Individual Differences in Language Learning and Teaching*, Second Language Learning and Teaching, DOI: 10.1007/978-3-642-20850-8_5, © Springer-Verlag Berlin Heidelberg 2012

1 Introduction

Empirical research in the fields of second language acquisition (SLA) and cognitive psychology offers convincing evidence to believe that working memory (WM) is "one of the greatest accomplishments of human mind" (Conway et al. 2008: 3) and a significant source of individual variation in performing cognitive tasks. WM measures are an indicator of intellectual ability. WM plays an important role in a number of complex cognitive abilities, such as language learning, reasoning, comprehension and cognitive control. Two subsystems of WM are especially significant in SLA: the phonological loop and the central executive (Baddeley and Hitch 1974). The *phonological loop*, termed as a language acquisition device, plays a crucial role in learning the novel phonological forms of new words. The *central executive*, in turn, directs attentional processes that create conditions for goal-directed behavior by maintaining relevant information in an active state or retrieving that information under conditions of interference, distraction, or conflict. WM capacity underlies the noticing ability which facilitates SLA in general (Miyake and Friedman 1998; Ellis 2001; Sawyer and Ranta 2001; Dörnyei 2005; Conway et al. 2008; Robinson and Ellis 2008; Robinson 2009). Although there is a large body of research on individual differences that contribute to success in the learning of foreign languages (i.e., Dörnyei 2005, 2009; Griffiths 2008; Dewaele 2009), there is a marked lack of research on the memory abilities of gifted foreign language learners.

The purpose of the present study was to analyze the characteristics of WM and short-term memory (STM) abilities of gifted foreign language learners (learners were characterized as gifted if they spoke at least one foreign language at level C1/C2). Emphasis was placed on the extent to which WM capacity can serve a predictor of foreign language learning success. The opening section of the present paper presents a definition of linguistic talent and provides an overview of the research on gifted foreign language learners. The subsequent sections are intended as an outline of the empirical research aiming to investigate the role of STM and WM in learning a foreign language. This is followed by a description of empirical research on memory abilities of gifted and normal foreign language learners. In the closing section, some problematic issues are discussed and suggestions concerning the role of the phonological loop and the central executive in foreign language learning are offered.

2 Gifted Foreign Language Learners

Foreign language learning aptitude is a concept deeply rooted in SLA research tradition (cf. Carroll 1981), but its evolution has always been significantly affected by developments in cognitive psychology. Recently, the knowledge of human cognitive abilities has expanded owing to new discoveries in related domains such as cognitive science, genetics and neurology. The discussion of the role of foreign language aptitude in SLA would be seriously impoverished if these important discoveries were excluded from it by applied linguists. Taking into consideration advancements in research on such cognitive abilities as working memory, noticing or learning from recasting in the last decade (cf. Robinson 2002), it becomes evident that the concept of foreign language aptitude has changed a lot since its origination and is continually evolving.

So far, little research addressing exceptionally talented foreign language learners has been conducted and cognitive factors probed generally. All the studies on exceptional L2 learners can be roughly divided into two groups. The first group comprises early research on gifted individuals (cf. Schneiderman and Desmarais 1988; Obler 1989; Smith and Tsimpli 1991; Ioup et al. 1994) whereas the second includes more up-to-date research on accomplished L2 postpuberty learners (cf. Moyer 1999; Bongaerts et al. 2000; Marinova-Todd 2003; van Boxtel et al. 2003; Birdsong, 2004, 2007; Bongaerts 2005; Abrahamsson and Hyltenstam 2008, 2009). Within this group, the most in-depth multiple-domain study is the one conducted by Swedish researchers, Abrahamsson and Hyltenstam. Nonetheless, all these group studies mainly address the problem of the possibility of native-like attainment after the critical period, rather than the role of memory in determining the outcome of learning a foreign language.

A definition of talent in early research on gifted L2 learners was adopted from psychology. Fein and Obler (1988), defined the performance of a talented individual as outstanding in one of two ways: either it is outstanding by comparison to the performance of others in society, or it is outstanding for the individual in question. Most researchers in the 1980s and 1990s upheld Selinker's (1972) position that 5% of the adult population is capable of attaining native-like competence in languages after puberty. More recently, this statement has been challenged. As Abrahamsson and Hyltenstam argue, "there are researchers who have doubted Selinker's (1972) and others' quite optimistic estimations and have instead suggested that the actual incidence of nativelikeness should approach zero" (Abrahamsson and Hyltenstam 2008: 484).

Despite the marked scarcity of research on exceptional foreign language learners, Skehan (1998: 207) emphasized its significance in applied linguistics. As he commented, "analyses of aptitude are relevant to some fundamental issues in applied linguistics, since aptitude can be seen as a rare window on the nature of the talent for language learning". According to Skehan, very talented learners are not qualitatively different from simply high aptitude learners. The most significant characteristic of exceptionally successful learners is the fact that they possess unusual verbal memory (Skehan 1998). In the view of Schneiderman and Desmarais (1988), linguistic talent can be defined as an exceptional ability to achieve native-like competence in a foreign language after puberty. This definition is consistent with Skehan's (1998) position that exceptional foreign language learners master a foreign language relatively quickly, postpubertly and to a native-like level.

Nevertheless, research in the field of linguistic talents somehow contrasted with these claims as far as criteria of choice, methods of investigation and evaluation of talented individuals are concerned. Different criteria were chosen by different researchers and operationalizations of talent varied. For example, a talented polyglot savant, Christopher, age 45, examined by Smith and Tsimpli (1991) and Morgan et al. (2007) was presented as a person able to read, write, understand and translate 20 languages. However, his ability ranged from fluency to mastery only in the bare elements of the languages. What is more, analysis of excerpts of his translations, as well as his very low intelligence quotient, cast doubt on his abilities, in particular in the field of pragmatics. The researchers (Morgan et al. 2007) admitted that it is rather the range of languages he learned, not the depth of mastery of them that is impressive. Totally different criteria were chosen by Ioup et al. (1994), who examined a woman who learned Arabic as an adult in a natural environment. Her knowledge of Arabic was scrupulously examined by linguists and native speakers, and evaluated as native-like in all respects: pronunciation, grammar, vocabulary and accent recognition. At the moment of the research she had lived in Egypt for 25 years, was married to an Egyptian and her children were native speakers of Arabic. Although her mastery of Arabic was unquestionable, the criterion of rate of learning is doubtful in this case.

Early research on exceptional linguistic abilities concentrated on the neuro-logical bases underlying linguistic talent (Fein and Obler 1988; Schneiderman and Desmarais 1988; Obler 1989). Schneiderman and Desmarais (1988) proposed a neuropsychological substrate for talent described in terms of greater neurocogni-tive flexibility. Owing to this special brain feature, gifted individuals were supposed not to process L2 input in terms of the rigid parameters they had set for an L1, but to set new parameters or neural connections for an L2. The researchers defined talented foreign language learners as those basically indistinguishable from native speakers. In line with Selinker (1972), they argued that only 5% in a population is able to achieve such a level of proficiency in all aspects of a foreign language. They separated phonological talent, which they considered a talent to mimic dialects, from other talents, such as those for grammar and lexis.

On the basis of case studies of talented foreign language learners described in the literature (Schneiderman and Desmarais 1988; Obler 1989; Smith and Tsimpli 1991; Ioup et al. 1994), it is evident that linguistic talent is not precisely defined; however, certain features can be found in all the cases. The most striking factor is excellent memory, especially verbal memory. Besides, the characteristics common to the subjects include: a very good command of at least one foreign language, high phonological abilities, high analytic abilities for dealing with simple codes, and rich vocabulary. Their IQ is within the average range; however, they perform higher on verbal than performance scales. These characteristics were univocally attributed to a specific brain organization.

Interesting conclusions as well as controversies result from rare studies com-paring L2-learners' and native speakers' linguistic knowledge across multiple domains of performance (cf. Marinova-Todd 2003; Abrahamsson and Hyltenstam 2008, 2009). Marinova-Todd (2003) examined 30 late learners of English on nine tasks, including measures of pronunciation, vocabulary, morphosyntax, and language use. Three learners performed within the native range on all the tasks. What is significant, all three of them were immersed in the target language at the age of 21; besides, two of them represented Slavic languages typologically distant from English. Interestingly, Marinova-Todd concluded that foreign language aptitude does not explain the phenomenon of native-like accomplishment of L2 learners. Marinova-Todd's study accords well with Bongaerts's (2005) and Birdsong's (2005) strong conviction that it is possible to attain native-like proficiency postpubertly, and that such an outcome is not restricted to learners whose languages are typologically related to the target language.

This opinion remains in a sharp contrast with Abrahamsson and Hyltenstam's (2003, 2008, 2009) conclusion drawn as a result of their ongoing study on near-native postpuberty learners, as well as their critical analysis of relevant studies on this topic. The researchers formulated two claims based on their research results: (1) adult native-like L2 learners should be termed as near-native, because scrupulous linguistic analyses for broad-based proficiency reveals that they fail to achieve a level that overlaps with that of native speakers (cf. Bley-Vroman 1989; Gregg 1996; Long and Robinson 1998), and (2) the few individuals who manage to reach a level of proficiency indistinguishable from that of native speakers have a high degree of foreign language aptitude (cf. DeKeyser 2000). In all the group studies there is little, or no information about memory abilities of the participants.

3 Short-Term and Working Memory

The terms *short-term memory* and *working memory* are sometimes used interchangeably, because of the alleged difficulty in making a distinction between them (Schumann 2004; Robinson 2007). However, most researchers discriminate between these two terms (Baddeley et al. 1998; Engle et al. 1999; Baddeley 2003; Conway et al. 2008; Kane et al. 2008). The term *short-term memory* (STM) refers to a sort of static memory that is held for a short period of time (less than 20 s). In contrast, *working memory* (WM) involves the temporary storage and manipulation of information that is necessary for the performance of a wide range of cognitive tasks (Baddeley 2003: 189). According to Conway et al. (2008: 3), WM is seen as "fundamentally a form of memory, but it is more than memory, for it is memory at work". WM includes a number of components that contain mechanisms for the storage of information and mechanisms for executive control of information. The mechanisms of executive control separate WM from STM.

The multicomponent WM model that is now accepted in SLA theory and research was formulated by Baddeley and Hitch (1974). They originally proposed dividing memory into three subsystems: (1) *the phonological loop*, which processes verbal and acoustic information, (2) *the visuospatial sketchpad*, which processes visual information, and (3) *the central executive*, which is a supervisory attention-limited control system. Later, they proposed a fourth component, *the episodic buffer*, which stores information (Baddeley 2000). In subsequent research on WM, the findings of correlation analyses provided evidence that WM plays an important role in a number of complex cognitive abilities, such as language learning, reasoning, comprehension and cognitive control, and that WM measures are an indicator of intellectual ability (Kane et al. 2008). WM has limited capacity, which constrains cognitive performance. Individuals differ with respect to their WM capacity. People with greater WM capacity perform better on a variety of complex cognitive tasks than people with smaller WM capacity (Conway et al. 2008).

According to Engle et al. (1999: 309), WM and STM are separate, but considerably correlated constructs (correlation 0.68). The researchers found that the correlation was based on the shared feature representing storage, coding and rehearsal, although some shared variance was also likely to be due to executive attention. It was the increased demand on executive attention that was found to cause the unique, residual variance in WM. As a result, the accuracy of measures of WM capacity and STM span is debatable. Some STM span tasks seem to measure executive control, a good example being some spatial STM tasks or STM tasks that include long lists of verbal items. Due to the fact that STM can hold only four items at a time and the phonological loop can hold items for only 2 s, tests with more than four items would require some degree of executive attention, which means that in fact, they measure WM capacity. What is more, a test of STM for one person can be a test of WM for another, which is the result of different cognitive and maturational factors, including general cognitive ability.

Kane et al. (2008) found that WM and STM were much more domain-specific in people in high-IQ groups than in lower-IQ groups, in that verbal and spatial WM abilities were correlated much less in high-IQ than in lower-IQ groups. They concluded that such differences between verbal and spatial WM abilities might result from testing subjects from a group in which general cognitive ability is high and in which the range of ability is small, for example, the majority of university students. The researchers suggest that when the range of general cognitive ability is narrow, any variability in cognitive performance results from other factors, such as domain-specific abilities, skills, or strategies.

3.1 Baddeley's Model of Working Memory

According to Baddeley (2003), the system of WM encompasses two main mechanisms: for storage of information and for cognitive control. The element of executive attention represented by the central executive is the most important part of the system.

3.1.1 The Central Executive

The central executive in the estimation of Baddeley et al. (1998) is the system responsible for the attentional control of WM. Neurologically, it is situated in the frontal lobes. It performs executive processes which are principal in determining individual differences in WM span. WM span measures are typically tests in which strings of sentences are aurally or visually presented to subjects who are required to remember the last word in each sentence for subsequent immediate recall (Daneman and Carpenter 1980). Therefore, the subjects are requested to combine simultaneous storage and processing of information. WM span seems to be a good predictor of a variety of cognitive tasks such as, for example, reading comprehension. There is also a high positive correlation with standard intelligence tests (Baddeley 2003).

The theory of the central executive was further explored by Kane et al. (2008) who proposed that the extent to which executive attention is engaged by a task is critically determined by the degree of interference or conflict presented by the context (cf. Oberauer et al. 2008). Working memory capacity refers to the attentional processes that create conditions for goal-directed behavior by maintaining relevant information in an active state or retrieving that information under conditions of interference, distraction, or conflict. Executive attention mechanisms are engaged to block or inhibit goal-irrelevant information. Executive attention processes, measured by WM span tasks, are believed to be primarily domain-general and only secondarily represent domain-specific rehearsal and storage processes. In contrast, STM span tasks primarily represent domain-specific storage and rehearsal skills, and only secondarily executive attention processes. According to Kane et al. (2008), WM span tasks requiring subjects to maintain or recover access to target information under interference are generally better measures of a domain-general attentional capability than STM span tasks. Summarizing, the researchers propose that WM capacity variation is driven by individual differences in executive attention processes.

3.1.2 The Phonological Loop

The phonological loop is the most theoretically grounded aspect of WM; moreover, it seems most relevant to the theory of individual differences in SLA. The phonological loop is a temporary verbal-acoustic storage system, necessary in performing different cognitive tasks. It comprises two components: a phonological store which represents material in a phonological code and which decays over seconds unless it is refreshed by the second component, the subvocal rehearsal system. This component registers and maintains visual information within the store, provided the items can be named. Neurologically, the phonological loop is situated in the left hemisphere, with separate storage and rehearsal systems. Storage is associated with the cortical area (Brodmann area 44), whereas the rehearsal system is situated in Broca's area (Brodmann areas 6 and 40) (Baddeley 2003: 192).

3.2 The Phonological Loop as a Language Acquisition Device

The hypothesis that WM is designed to support complex cognitive tasks (Baddeley and Hitch 1974) was extended by Baddeley et al. (1998) who attempted to explore its evolutionary development and define its role in human cognitive functioning. Baddeley et al. (1998: 158) propose that the purpose for which the phonological loop evolved is to store unfamiliar sound patterns while more permanent memory records are being constructed. Its role in memorizing familiar words is secondary. They hypothesize that the system might have evolved in order to facilitate the acquisition of language.

The phonological loop is a limited-capacity system cooperating with long-term memory (LTM). The sensitivity of the task of learning of nonwords to the pho-nological loop constraints can be reduced by partial reliance on LTM knowledge. In other words, the phonological loop is capable of exploiting prior learning. This explains why nonword repetition is highly correlated with vocabulary knowledge. It is easier to remember wordlike nonwords[1] drawing on the knowledge of either similar words in the native language or generalized knowledge of the acoustic properties of the language. Therefore, learning of new words seems to be mediated by both the phonological loop and long-term knowledge of the native language. LTM represents the residue of accumulated long-term phonological knowledge that is not easily modified by the input from WM. The acquisition of new words requires prolonged learning, especially in the case of the acquisition of a phono-logically novel material by adults with a mature phonological system. It is possible that polyglots have the ability to draw heavily on the knowledge of all the languages they know, which facilitates the learning of subsequent languages (cf. Papagno and Vallar 1995).

Baddeley et al. (1998: 166) labeled the phonological loop as a language acquisition device. As they hold, "the case of gifted language learners suggests that a natural talent for language learning may arise directly as a consequence of excellent phonological loop function". In line with Baddeley et al. (1998), Skehan (1998) concluded that it is excellent memory abilities that underlie linguistic talent. He based his conclusions on the results of research on talented foreign language learners to the effect that such learners do not have exceptional intelligence but all possess exceptional verbal memory (cf. Schneiderman and Desmarais 1988; Obler 1989; Ioup et al. 1994; Sawyer and Ranta 2001). In the words of Skehan (1998: 233), "exceptionally successful foreign language learners consistently seem to be characterized by the possession of unusual memories, particularly for the retention of verbal material".

WM is often treated as a key component of foreign language aptitude. For example, Miyake and Friedman (1998) emphasize its central role in language processing in both language production and language comprehension. Language processing is a linear process that requires the simultaneous integration and storage of incoming sequences of symbols (cf. Ellis 1996). According to Miyake and Friedman (1998), Baddeley's WM theory matches this SLA model perfectly, in that it contains both the storage and the processing component. A cumulative body

---

[1] Wordlike nonwords are words that closely resemble the phonological structure of a native language.

of evidence demonstrates a strong correlation between L1 WM capacity and L2 WM capacity, and between WM capacity and L2 proficiency (Daneman and Carpenter 1980; Harrington and Sawyer 1992; Osaka et al. 1993; Papagno and Vallar 1995; Berquist 1998; Miyake and Friedman 1998; Miyake et al. 1998; Sagarra 1998; Robinson 2002; Mackey et al. 2002). Moreover, a positive relationship was found between L1 WM and L2 WM, which suggests that performance on WM measures may be language independent (Mackey et al. 2002). This finding upholds the general assumption in cognitive science that WM is not domain-specific (Kane et al. 2008).

Biedroń and Szczepaniak (2011) tested short-term and working memory abilities in gifted foreign language learners (accomplished multilinguals). Twenty-seven accomplished multilinguals were compared to 36 mainstream philology students. The following instruments were used in the study: three memory subtests of the Wechsler Intelligence Scale (Digit Span, Digit-Symbol Coding, and Arithmetic, which constitute the Memory and Resistance to Distraction index); two short-term memory tests of the Modern Language Aptitude Test [MLAT 1 (Number learning) and MLAT 5 (Paired associates)], and a working memory test, the Polish Reading Span (PRSPAN) designed by the authors of the study. The results of the accomplished multilinguals were compared to the results of first-year English philology students (mainstream). The analysis revealed that short-term memory and working-memory abilities in the accomplished multilinguals were higher than in the mainstream philology students. Moreover, the accomplished multilinguals obtained higher scores than the mainstream philology students on memory tests that are based on linguistic material than on tests based on numerical material. There were stronger correlations between the general MLAT, MLAT 1, MLAT 4 and MLAT 5, and the memory scales than the other IQ scales. The researchers attributed the success in learning a foreign language to the two components of working memory (i.e. the phonological loop and the central executive).

There is still no consensus as regards the problem whether cognitive individual differences are equally influential in all learning conditions. Mackey et al. (2002) and Zobl (1992) suggest that WM abilities, which require simultaneous input storage and processing, might be differently influential in different learning conditions. This position is challenged by Robinson (2003) who considers all conditions of adult learning, that is explicit, implicit and incidental 'fundamentally similar'. Learning in all conditions requires an active engagement of attention and rehearsal of input in WM, which is subject to individual variation; however, in the case of incidental learning, individual differences will have a delayed effect. According to Robinson, individual differences in WM capacity cause different learning outcomes. As he comments, "measures of working memory capacity, which affects the extent and efficiency of focal attention allocation, are closely and positively related to second language proficiency and skill development" (Robinson 2003: 660).

As indicated by the results of the studies presented in this section, there is abundant evidence that individual differences in WM affect SLA. In general, there is consensus among researchers on the adequacy of Baddeley's model of WM, with its phonological loop and central executive components as subsystems that are critical in learning a foreign language.

4 Study

4.1 Objectives

The purpose of the study reported here was to examine STM and WM abilities in 44 accomplished multilinguals (termed as 'gifted L2 learners'). The selection criteria for the study were both qualitative and quantitative. Qualitative criteria included: proficiency scores confirmed by certificates or other documents, the number of languages they had learned including at least one language at level C1/C2 in the case of younger (<23 years) and at least 2 languages at level C1/C2 in the case of older (23–35 years) L2 learners, language learning history and the recommendation of their teachers. All the participants represented an advanced level of English (C1/C2). The quantitative criteria included: the *Modern Language Aptitude Test* (Carroll and Sapon 2002) score (at least 95 percentile) and the *Test Zdolności Językowych*—TZJ (*Language Ability Test*) (Wojtowicz 2006) score (at least 80% of correct answers). The sample of the gifted L2 learners was compared to a group of mainstream English philology students (termed as 'normal L2 learners').

4.2 Hypotheses

Two research hypotheses were formulated:
1. Gifted L2 learners will obtain high scores on all STM and WM tests.
2. Their scores on memory tests will be significantly higher than the scores of 'normal' learners, that is mainstream English philology students.

4.3 Subjects

There were two groups of learners: accomplished multilinguals (termed as 'gifted L2 learners' and mainstream philology students (termed as 'normal L2 learners'). The gifted group consisted of 44 students who were identified as gifted based on proficiency scores, the number of languages they had learned, language learning history, recommendation of their teachers, the MLAT score, and the TZJ score. They were either appointed by their teachers or encouraged by co-workers or class-mates to participate; some responded to an invitation to participate in the study sent via e-mail. Their age varied from 20 to 35 years; the mean was 24.5. All the participants were experienced language learners. The normal L2 learners were 82 first-year English philology students at Polish university—the Pomeranian Academy in Słupsk. They were intermediate learners of English as a foreign language. Their age varied from 20 to 23 years; the mean was 22. At the time the study was conducted, they had been learning English for 7–10 years.They completed only parts 1 and 5 of the MLAT which do not require an advanced level of English, and the PRSPAN.

4.4 Instruments

The following instruments were used in this study:

1. *Modern Language Aptitude Test—MLAT* (Carroll and Sapon 2002). This is a language aptitude test that is useful for predicting success in learning a foreign language (Skehan 1998). The MLAT is entirely in English and is suitable for native and near-native speakers of English. Only parts 1 (Number learning) and 5 (Paired associates) measuring STM were taken into account in the analysis.
2. *Wechsler Adult Intelligence Scale—WAIS-R (PL)*. This is an adaptation of the Weschler Intelligence Scale for use with the Polish population by Brzezinski et al. (1996). The Polish version of the Wechsler scales is composed of 11 subtests (six verbal and five performance) comprising the full test. Three subtests embracing the *Memory and Resistance to Distraction index* measure memory: (a) *Arithmetic*—tests WM, attention and numerical reasoning (e.g. "How many months are in three quarters of a year?"), (b) *Digit Span*—tests attention, concentration and mental control. In this subtest, subjects are given sets of digits to repeat initially forwards then backwards (e.g. "Repeat the numbers 2, 4, 9 in reverse order"), and (c) *Digit Symbol Coding*—tests visual-motor speed and short-term visual memory. The subtest involves copying a coding pattern. Symbols are matched with numbers according to a key.
3. *Polish Reading Span—PRSPAN* (Biedroń and Szczepaniak 2011) a Polish adaptation of the American Reading Span (RSPAN) (Engle et al. 1999), designed by the author of the study in cooperation with a psychologist. The RSPAN is referred to as a prototypical WM test, which is a modified version of the reading span task (Daneman and Carpenter 1980).[2]

---

[2] A detailed description of the subjects and instruments can be found in Biedroń and Szczepaniak (2011).

Table 1 Descriptive statistics for the gifted L2 learners $N = 44$

Variable	Mean	Minimum	Maximum	SD
MLAT 1	41.090	28.000	43.000	2.900
MLAT 5	22.227	13.000	24.000	2.429
Digit span	15.068	10.000	19.000	2.527
Arithmetic	14.045	8.000	18.000	2.605
Digit symbol coding	14.409	11.000	19.000	2.049
Memory index	128.454	102.000	150.000	10.285
Working memory	39.000	23.000	52.000	7.246

4.5 Results and Interpretation

Descriptive statistics for the gifted L2 learners are presented in Table 1. The results for all the memory tests indicate high, although not homogenous, abilities in this field. Very high results were obtained in MLAT 1 (95.5%), MLAT 5 (92.6%), and PRSPAN (75%). The results for the Wechsler memory subscales (Digit Span, Arithmetic, Digit Symbol Coding) are high; hence, the Memory and Resistance to Distraction index is also high, but not as high as in the MLAT results. Evidently, the gifted L2 learners perform better on memory tests based on verbal than on numerical material. The results for the PRSPAN that measured WM capacity are varied (mean = 39; SD = 7.2); however, some of the participants managed to recollect about 90% of the words, the highest result being 100%. This score was recorded by two participants. One of these was a 28-year-old university lecturer, a polyglot working in a Sinology department. This person knows one language at level C2 (near-native) (Chinese), three languages at level C1 (advanced) (English, Turkish and German), and is able to communicate in six other languages: Japanese, Hebrew, Swedish, Russian, Croatian, and French. It is worth mentioning that she started to learn Chinese at the age of 19. The other participant was a 21-year-old Japanese philology student, learning five languages. Her MLAT score was 175 (91% of correct answers). Both participants completed the Wechsler Intelligence Scale well ahead of time.

The parametric correlation (the Pearson product–moment correlation coefficient) was applied to measure the correlation (linear dependence) between MLAT 1, MLAT 5, the Wechsler Intelligence Scales measuring memory and the WM test, the PRSPAN. The inspection of the results showed that positive correlations exist between the MLAT and the Memory and Resistance to Distraction index. MLAT 1 correlates with Arithmetic ($r = 0.45$) and Memory and Resistance to Distraction index ($r = 0.48$); MLAT 5 correlates with Memory and Resistance to Distraction index ($r = 0.37$), $p < 0.05$. Correlations between MLAT 1 and 5 and WM are close to significant ($r = 0.29$) and ($r = 0.28$), respectively. This accords with the previous study results, namely, that there is a positive correlation between the MLAT subtests and WM.

Since the Wechsler scales have norms, it was decided to compare the gifted L2 learners' scores on intelligence tests measuring memory to the norm—the results

Table 2 t-test of differences in the memory abilities between the gifted L2 learners and the normal L2 learners

Variable	Mean gifted	Mean normal	t	df	p	N gifted	N normal	SD gifted	SD normal
MLAT 1	41.090	29.768	7.250	124.000	0.001	44.000	82.000	2.900	10.120
MLAT 5	22.227	16.720	6.210	124.000	0.001	44.000	82.000	2.429	5.598
WM	39.000	27.543	6.680	119.000	0.001	40.000	81.000	7.246	9.568

of the normal Polish population. A one-sample t-test confirmed that there exist statistically significant differences in memory scores between the gifted L2 learners and the norm in the population, with those of the gifted learners being higher (cf. Biedroń 2011).

The results of the gifted L2 learners were compared to the results of the normal L2 learners. It was decided to compare MLAT 1, MLAT 5 and the PRSPAN (WM). The factors of age and gender were not taken into consideration as variables, because most of the tests used in the study have age and gender norms. The purpose of this comparison was to demonstrate whether there are any differences in the memory abilities between the two groups of learners.

The results for comparison are presented in Table 2. As expected, there are big differences in the memory abilities of the two groups (MLAT 1, MLAT 5, WM), with those of the gifted L2 learners being higher. Moreover, despite the high level of differentiation of the group of the gifted learners (ages, languages and professions), the standard deviations of this group are lower than those of the normal learners for all memory factors, which indicates a balanced high level among members of the gifted group. The difference in the PRSPAN (WM) is significant: 22.11%. Figure 1 shows the results of the t-test of differences in WM between the gifted and the normal L2 learners.

The previous study by the present author (Biedroń and Szczepaniak 2011) revealed that there were statistically significant differences between the gifted L2 learners and the normal L2 learners in Digit Span and Digit Symbol Coding, but not as striking as in MLAT 1, 5 and the PRSPAN. This is interpreted as evidence that gifted L2 learners' memory for verbal material is better that their memory for numerical material. The results of the present study confirm the results of this previous research project.

5 Discussion and Conclusions

The first hypothesis formulated with regard to memory abilities assumed that the gifted L2 learners will obtain very high scores on all the STM and WM tests, that is the Wechsler Intelligence subscales: Arithmetic, Digit Span and Digit Symbol Coding (the Memory and Resistance to Distraction index), MLAT 1, MLAT 5 and the PRSPAN. These subtests measure STM and WM, focusing of attention and resistance to distraction—abilities important in learning a foreign

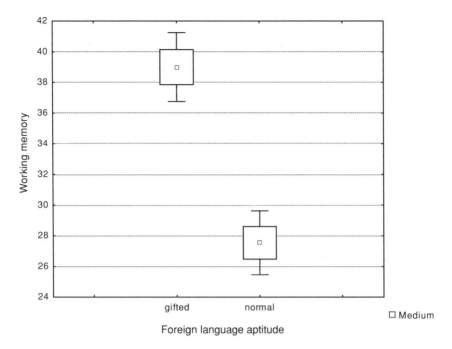

Fig. 1 Gifted L2 learners–normal L2 learners group differences for WM

language (cf. Robinson 2002; Skehan 2002). This hypothesis was confirmed; The results on all the memory subtests were high, but the results of the subtests based on linguistic material were higher than those based on numerical material. It is possible that emotional factors had an impact on the participants' performance on some intelligence tests. The most difficult subtest was Arithmetic, which was probably the result of emotional tension. Some of the subjects' low confidence with respect to mathematical abilities evoked anticipation of failure. This discouraged them and negatively influenced their performance (cf. Hornowska 2004). However, the memory abilities as measured by the Wechsler Scale are high and in some talented L2 learners amazingly high. Half of the participants scored over 130 points in the Memory and Resistance to Distraction index, which is a very high result—the third standard deviation above the mean. Four participants whose scores were close to the maximal (between 144 and 150 points) were very advanced polyglots, the highest scoring in the MLAT.

Hypothesis 2 stated that the scores of the gifted L2 learners will be significantly higher than the scores of the normal L2 learners, that is the mainstream English philology students. In the previous study, Biedroń and Szczepaniak (2011) tested STM and WM abilities in gifted foreign language learners. The analysis revealed that STM and WM abilities in the gifted L2 learners were higher than in the normal L2 learners. Moreover, the gifted L2 learners obtained higher scores than the normal L2 learners on memory tests that are based on linguistic material than on tests based on numerical material. In the present study the results of the gifted L2 learners in MLAT 1, MLAT 5 and the PRSPAN which measures WM, were compared to those of normal L2 learners. As expected, the previous study results were confirmed. In all the memory tests significant differences between the groups were noticed, with those of the gifted L2 learners being much higher. Therefore, hypothesis 2 is corroborated. As has already been mentioned, the gifted L2 learners possess very high verbal memory capacity, which fully conforms to the theoretical corpus (cf. Schneiderman and Desmarais 1988; Obler 1989; Ioup et al. 1994; Miyake and Friedman 1998; Skehan 1998; Sawyer and Ranta 2001; Robinson 2002). The results of both studies conducted by the present author are in line with Kane et al.'s (2008) hypothesis that WM and STM are much more domain-specific in people with high IQ, for example university students, than in those from lower IQ groups. The group of the gifted L2 learners comprised highly selected foreign language learners, characterized by high general and high verbal IQ.

A strong correlation between L1 WM capacity and L2 WM capacity, and between WM capacity and L2 proficiency has been consistently reported by researchers, but generally, evidence for such a correlation with STM is scarce. On the other hand, the accuracy of measures of WM capacity and STM span is debatable. Kane et al. (2008) argue that some STM span tasks seem to measure executive control, which is a part of WM.

The results of the present study accord with Engle et al.'s (1999) conclusion that neither STM nor WM tasks are pure reflections of these constructs. To the extent that STM tasks demand controlled attention, they also reflect the WM construct. Moreover, the tests results reflect individual differences between the participants with regard to their intelligence or level of cognitive development. As a result, what is clearly a STM task for one participant could be a WM task for another. This can be observed in MLAT 1, MLAT 5, Digit Span backward and the PRSPAN—the tests in which a participant has to hold in memory an item for a period of time from a few seconds to a few minutes and perform some operations on the material at the same time. It is possible that some of the participants relied on efficient mnemonic strategies worked out in the process of learning languages, which can be used unconsciously. Given the foregoing, great caution should be exercised in analyzing data and drawing conclusions regarding measurements of memory capacity.

On the basis of the memory tests, it is concluded that the participants have a highly efficient phonological loop, whose function is to store unfamiliar sound patterns while more permanent memory records are being constructed (Baddeley et al. 1998: 158). The phonological loop is a limited-capacity system relying on LTM and the knowledge of an L1. The research project seems to confirm the advantage of polyglots over less advanced learners to rely on the knowledge of all the languages they know, which facilitates learning of subsequent languages, however, this conclusion is tentative. The problem whether gifted L2 learners are born with greater memory capacity or if, rather, their memory capacity extends due to the multiple language learning experience is still to be resolved.

The high score in the PRSPAN, a test of WM which requires a great amount of attention, confirms that the central executive works more efficiently in gifted L2 learners. Variation in WM capacity causes significant variation in general intelligence and executive attention is the central factor in this variation (cf. Kane et al. 2008). Central executive triggers and sustains goal-directed behavior by maintaining relevant information in an active state or retrieving that information under conditions of interference or distraction. This means that the learners who score high on WM capacity tests, like the PRSPAN, have better abilities to notice and select relevant information and to inhibit irrelevant information, which can make them more capable of noticing of corrective feedback (cf. Mackey et al. 2002; Robinson 2002). Summing up, the extraordinary memory abilities of the gifted L2 learners confirm Skehan's (1998) assumption that the most significant characteristic of exceptionally successful learners is the possession of unusual verbal memory.

References

Abrahamsson, N., and K. Hyltenstam. 2008. The robustness of aptitude effects in near-native second language acquisition. *Studies in Second Language Acquisition* 30: 481–509.

Abrahamsson, N., and K. Hyltenstam. 2009. Age of onset and nativelikeness in a second language: listener perception versus linguistic scrutiny. *Language Learning* 59: 249–306.

Baddeley, A.D. 2000. The episodic buffer: A new component of working memory? *Trends in Cognitive Sciences* 4: 417–123.

Baddeley, A.D. 2003. Working memory and language: an overview. *Journal of Communication Disorders* 36: 189–208.

Baddeley, A.D., and G.J. Hitch. 1974. Working memory. In ed. G. Bower, 47–90.

Baddeley, A.D., S. Gathercole, and C. Papagno. 1998. The phonological loop as a language acquisition device. *Psychological Review* 105: 158–173.

Berquist, B. 1998. Working memory models applied to second language acquisition. Paper presented at the annual conference of the American Association of Applied Linguistics, Seattle, March.

Biedroń, A. 2011. Intelligence in gifted L2 learners. In ed. M. Pawlak, 129–142.

Biedroń, A., and A. Szczepaniak. 2011. Working-memory and short-term memory abilities in accomplished multilinguals. *Modern Language Journal*. In press.

Birdsong, D. 2004. Second language acquisition and ultimate attainment. In eds. A. Davies, and C. Elder, 82–105.

Birdsong, D. 2005. Nativelikeness and non-nativelikeness in L2A research. *IRAL* 43: 319–328.

Birdsong, D. 2007. Nativelike pronunciation among late learners of French as a second language. In eds. O.S. Bohn, and M.J. Munro, 99–116.

Bley-Vroman, R. 1989. What is the logical problem of foreign language learning? In eds. S. Gass, and J. Schachter, 41–68.

Bohn, O.S., and M.J. Munro, eds. 2007. *Language experience in second language speech learning*. Amsterdam: John Benjamins Publishing Company.

Bongaerts, T. 2005. Introduction: Ultimate attainment and the critical period hypothesis for second language acquisition. *IRAL* 43: 259–267.

Bongaerts, T., S. Mennen, and F. van der Silk. 2000. Authenticity of pronunciation in naturalistic second language acquisition: The case of very advanced late learners of Dutch as a second language. *Studia Linguistica* 54: 298–308.

Bower, G., ed. 1974. *The psychology of learning and motivation*. 8 vols. New York: Academic Press.

Brzezinski, J., M. Gaul, E. Hornowska, A. Machowski, and M. Zakrzewska. 1996. *Skala Inteligencji D. Wechslera Dla Dorosłych. Wersja Zrewidowana. WAIS-R (Pl). Podręcznik*. Warszawa: Pracownia Testów Psychologicznych PTP.

Carroll, J.B. 1981. Twenty-five years of research on foreign language aptitude. In ed. K.C. Diller, 83–118.

Carroll, J.B., and S. Sapon. 2002. *Modern language aptitude test (MLAT) manual 2002 edition*. North Bethesda, MD: Second Language Testing Inc.

Conway, A.R.A., C. Jarrold, M.J. Kane, A. Miyake, and J.N. Towse. 2008. Variation in working memory: An introduction. In eds. A.R.A. Conway, Ch. Jarrold, M.J. Kane, A. Miyake, and J.N. Towse, 3–17.

Conway, A.R.A., Ch. Jarrold, M.J. Kane, A. Miyake, and J.N. Towse, eds. 2008. *Variation in working memory*. Oxford: Oxford University Press.

Daneman, M., and P. Carpenter. 1980. Individual differences in working memory and reading. *Journal of Verbal Learning and Verbal Behavior* 19: 450–466.

Davies, A. and C. Elder, eds. 2004. *Handbook of applied linguistics*. London: Blackwell Publishing.

DeKeyser, R.M. 2000. The robustness of critical period effects in second language acquisition. *Studies in Second Language Acquisition* 22: 499–533.

DeKeyser R.M., ed. 2007. *Practice in second language*. Cambridge: Cambridge University Press.

Dewaele, J.-M. 2009. Individual differences in second language acquisition. In eds. W.C. Ritchie, and T.K. Bhatia, 623–646.

Diller, K.C., ed. 1981. *Individual differences and universals in language learning aptitude*. Rowley: Newbury House.

Dörnyei, Z. 2005. *The psychology of the language learner: Individual differences in second language acquisition*. Mahwah, NJ: Lawrence Erlbaum.

Dörnyei, Z. 2009. *The psychology of second language acquisition*. Oxford: Oxford University Press.

Doughty, C.J., and M.H. Long, eds. 2003. *The handbook of second language acquisition*. Oxford: Blackwell Publishing.

Doughty, C., and J. Williams, eds. 1998. *Focus on form in classroom second language acquisition*. Cambridge: Cambridge University Press.

Ellis, N.C. 1996. Sequencing and SLA: Phonological memory, chunking and points of order. *Studies in Second Language Acquisition* 18: 91–129.

Ellis, N.C. 2001. Memory for language. In ed. P. Robinson, 33–68.

Engle, R.W., J.E. Laughlin, S.W. Tuholski, and A.R.A. Conway. 1999. Working memory, short-term memory, and general fluid intelligence: a latent-variable approach. *Journal of Experimental Psychology: General* 128(3): 309–331.

Fein, D., and L.K. Obler. 1988. Neuropsychological study of talent: A developing field. In eds. L.K. Obler, and D. Fein, 3–15.

Foster-Cohen, S., and S. Pekarek-Doehler, eds. 2003. *Eurosla yearbook 3*. Amsterdam: John Benjamins Publishing Company, University of Canterbury/University of Basel.

Gass, S., and J. Schachter, eds. 1989. *Linguistic perspectives on second language acquisition*. New York: Cambridge University Press.

Gass, S., C. Madden, D. Preston, and L. Selinker, eds. 1989. *Variation in second language*. Clevedon, Avon: Multilingual Matters.

Gass, S., and L. Selinker, eds. 1992. *Language transfer in language learning*. Amsterdam/Philadelphia: John Benjamins Publishing Company.

Gregg, K.R. 1996. The logical and developmental problems of second language acquisition. In eds. W.C. Ritchie, and T.K. Bhatia, 49–81.

Griffiths, C., ed. 2008. *Lessons from good language learners*. Cambridge: Cambridge University Press.

Harrington, M., and M. Sawyer. 1992. L2 working memory capacity and L2 reading skill. *Studies in Second Language Acquisition* 14: 25–38.

Healy, A., and L. Bourne, eds. 1998. *Foreign language learning.* Mahwah: Lawrence Erlbaum.

Hornowska, E. 2004. *Skala inteligencji dla dorosłych Davida Wechslera WAIS-R oraz WAIS-III.* Warszawa: Wydawnictwo Naukowe Scholar.

Hyltenstam, K., and N. Abrahamsson. 2003. Maturational constraints in SLA. In eds. C.J. Doughty, and M.H. Long, 539–589.

Ioup, G., E. Boustagui, M. El Tigi, and M. Moselle. 1994. Re-examining the CPH: a case study of successful adult SLA in a naturalistic environment. *Studies in Second Language Acquisition* 16: 73–98.

Kane, M.J., A.R.A. Conway, D.Z. Hambrick, and R.W. Engle. 2008. Variation in working memory capacity as variation in executive attention and control. In eds. A.R.A. Conway, C. Jarrold, M.J. Kane, A. Miyake, and J.N. Towse, 21–49.

Long, M., and P. Robinson. 1998. Focus on form: theory, research, and practice. In eds. C. Doughty, and J. Williams, 15–63.

Mackey, A., J. Philip, T. Egi, A. Fujii, and T. Tatsumi. 2002. Individual differences in working memory, noticing interactional feedback and L2 development. In ed. P. Robinson, 181–209.

Marinova-Todd, S.H. 2003. Comprehensive analysis of ultimate attainment in adult second language acquisition. Unpublished doctoral dissertation, Harvard University, Massachusetts.

Miyake, A., and N.P. Friedman. 1998. Individual differences in second language proficiency: Working memory as language aptitude. In eds. A. Healy, and L. Bourne, 339–364.

Miyake, A., N.P. Friedman, and M. Osaka. 1998. Cue acquisition and syntactic comprehension in second language learning. Findings reported in Miyake A, Friedman NP (1998) Individual differences in second language proficiency: Working memory as language aptitude. In eds. A. Healy, and L. Bourne, 339–364.

Morgan, G., N. Smith, I. Tsimpli, and B. Woll. 2007. Classifier learning and modality in a polyglot savant. *Lingua* 117: 1339–1353.

Moyer, A. 1999. Ultimate attainment in L2 phonology. *Studies in Second Language Acquisition* 21: 81–108.

Oberauer, K., H. Süß, O. Wilhelm, and N. Sander. 2008. Individual differences in working memory capacity and reasoning ability. In eds. A.R.A. Conway, C. Jarrold, M.J. Kane, A. Miyake, and J.N. Towse, 49–76.

Obler, L.K., and D. Fein, eds. 1988. *The exceptional brain: Neuropsychology of talent and special abilities.* London: The Guilford Press.

Obler, L. 1989. Exceptional second language learners. In eds. S. Gass, C. Madden, D. Preston, and L. Selinker, 141–159.

Osaka, M., N. Osaka, and R. Groner. 1993. Language-independent working memory: Evidence from German and French span tests. *Bulletin of the Psychonomic Society* 31: 117–118.

Papagno, C., and G. Vallar. 1995. Verbal short-term memory and vocabulary learning in polyglots. *Quarterly Journal of Experimental Psychology* 38A: 98–107.

Pawlak, M., ed. 2009. *Studies in pedagogy and fine arts: new perspectives on individual differences in language learning and teaching.* 8 vols. Poznań-Kalisz: Faculty of Pedagogy and Fine Arts in Kalisz Adam Mickiewicz University in Poznan.

Pawlak, M., ed. 2011. *Extending the boundaries of research in second language learning and teaching.* Heidelberg: Springer.

Ritchie, W.C., and T.K. Bhatia, eds. 1996. *Handbook of second language acquisition.* San Diego: Academic Press.

Ritchie, W.C., and T.K. Bhatia, eds. 2009. *The new handbook of second language acquisition.* Bingley, UK: Emerald.

Robinson, P., ed. 2001. *Cognition and second language instruction.* Cambridge: Cambridge University Press.

Robinson, P., ed. 2002. *Individual differences and instructed language learning.* Philadelphia: John Benjamins Publishing Company.

Robinson, P. 2002. Learning conditions, aptitude complexes and SLA: A framework for research and pedagogy. In ed. P. Robinson, 113–133.

Robinson, P. 2003. Attention and memory during SLA. In eds. C.J. Doughty, and M.H. Long, 631–679.

Robinson, P. 2007. Aptitudes, abilities, contexts, and practice. In ed. R.M. DeKeyser, 256–286.

Robinson, P., and N.C. Ellis, eds. 2008. *Handbook of cognitive linguistics and second language acquisition*. New York: Routledge.

Robinson, P. 2009. Individual differences, aptitude complexes, SLA processes and aptitude test development. In ed. M. Pawlak, 89–109.

Robinson, P., and N.C. Ellis. 2008. Conclusion: Cognitive linguistics, second language acquisition and L2 instruction—issues for research. In eds. P. Robinson, and N.C. Ellis, 489–545.

Sagarra, N. 1998. The role of working memory in adult L2 development: A longitudinal study. Paper presented at the annual conference of the American Association for Applied Linguistics, Seattle, March.

Sawyer, M., and L. Ranta. 2001. Aptitude, individual differences, and instructional design. In ed. P. Robinson, 319–354.

Schneiderman, E.I., and C. Desmarais. 1988. The talented language learner: Some preliminary findings. *Second Language Research* 4: 91–109.

Schumann, J.H. 2004. Introduction. In eds. J.H. Schumann, S.E. Crowell, N.E. Jones, N. Lee, S.A. Schuchert, and L.A. Wood, 1–21.

Schumann, J.H., S.E. Crowell, N.E. Jones, N. Lee, S.A. Schuchert, and L.A. Wood, eds. 2004. *The neurobiology of learning: Perspectives from second language acquisition*. Mahwah: Lawrence Erlbaum.

Selinker, L. 1972. Interlanguage. *IRAL* 10: 209–231.

Skehan, P. 1998. *A cognitive approach to language learning*. Oxford: Oxford University Press.

Skehan, P. 2002. Theorising and updating aptitude. In ed. P. Robinson, 69–95.

Smith, N., and I. Tsimpli. 1991. Linguistic modularity? A case study of 'savant' linguist. *Lingua* 84: 315–351.

Van Boxtel, S., T. Bongaerts, and A.-P. Coppen. 2003. Native-like attainment in L2 syntax. In eds. S. Foster-Cohen, and S. Pekarek-Doehler, 157–181.

Wojtowicz, M. 2006. *Test zdolności językowych TZJ*. Warszawa: Pracownia Testów Psychologicznych PTP.

Zobl, H. 1992. Prior linguistic knowledge and the conservation of the learning procedure: Grammaticality judgments of unilingual and multilingual learners. In eds. S. Gass, and L. Selinker, 176–196.

Age and SLA: Research Highways and Bye-Ways

David Singleton and Justyna Leśniewska

Abstract This article addresses the issue of the role of age factors in second language acquisition. Specifically, it takes a critical look at the notion that the second language acquisition process is maturationally constrained—the proposition commonly labelled the Critical Period Hypothesis—and the practical implications of this proposition. The article begins by reviewing some of the oft-cited evidence concerning the critical period hypothesis (CPH), coming to the conclusion that the evidence in question falls short of establishing its veracity. In its second part, the article turns to some less well-trodden approaches in the critical period area, summarizing some recent qualitative research which does not particularly favor the CPH, and going on to survey the kinds of inferences researchers have drawn from the critical period discussion for the stage at which second languages should be introduced into the school curriculum. On this last point, the article concludes that even if the existence or non-existence of a critical period for language acquisition were clearly demonstrated, this would not necessarily answer the question of what age should constitute the starting-point for formal second language instruction.

D. Singleton (✉)
Trinity College Dublin, Dublin, Ireland
e-mail: dsnglton@tcd.ie

J. Leśniewska
Jagiellonian University, Kraków, Poland

M. Pawlak (ed.), *New Perspectives on Individual Differences in Language Learning and Teaching*, Second Language Learning and Teaching, DOI: 10.1007/978-3-642-20850-8_6, © Springer-Verlag Berlin Heidelberg 2012

1 Introductory: The Notion of a Critical Period for Language Acquisition

When the age factor is discussed in the context of language development, the inevitable question that arises is whether there is a 'critical period' for language acquisition—a question that was first raised explicitly in the work of Lenneberg (1967) but which was pre-figured in Penfield's publications (e.g. Penfield and Roberts 1959). For biologists a critical period is a limited phase in the development of an organism during which a particular capacity must be established if it is to be established at all. An example frequently cited in this connection is that of imprinting in ducklings, which, for a limited time after hatching, become bonded to the first moving object they perceive—which is usually, to their great good fortune, their mother. De Villiers and De Villiers (1978) refer to following behaviour of newly-hatched Mallard ducklings:

> This following behavior only occurs within a certain time period after hatching, after which point the ducklings develop a fear of strange objects and retreat instead of following. Within these time limits is the critical period for the following behavior. (De Villiers and De Villiers 1978: 210)

Another example relates to the development of binocularity:

> A critical period for the development of binocularity may begin when central nervous system cells driven by each eye grow and compete for cortical synapses (Wiesel and Hubel 1963). ... The critical period for development of binocularity may take place between weeks 4 and 12 in the cat; 1 and 9 in certain monkeys; and years 1 and 3 in man. (Almli and Finger 1987: 126)

If the language development process in humans is constrained by the limits of a critical period in this kind of sense, the implication is that it cannot get under way before the onset of the period in question and that unless it begins before the end of the period it will not happen at all. There may also be an implication that, even if language acquisition *begins* within the critical period, it may be arrested at the point of offset of that period. Attempts to apply the critical period notion to language development along these kinds of lines have been collectively labelled the critical period hypothesis (henceforth CPH).

In what follows we first review the debate about the critical period and SLA in terms of studies that are fairly well known and in terms of arguments that have been rather frequently rehearsed. We then go on to refer to some research which may be seen as exploring less well-trodden paths. In particular we look, on the one hand, at two recent studies which have attempted to bring a qualitative perspective to bear on CPH-related issues, and, on the other, at research and discussion bearing on the complexities of the debate relating to the connection between the CPH and the question of early L2 instruction.

2 The CPH and SLA: Research Highways

As well as forming the basis of much investigation and discussion in the L1 research domain (see e.g. Singleton and Ryan 2004: Chaps. 2, 3), the CPH has been extensively explored in relation to the process of acquiring additional languages. L2-related interpretations of the CPH can be briefly summarized as follows: after a certain maturational point the L2 learner is no longer capable of attaining to native-like levels of proficiency, and/or needs to expend more conscious effort than in earlier L2 acquisition and/or makes use of different mechanisms from those deployed in L2 acquisition during childhood, and, in any case, there is a sharp decline in L2 learning potential (different in nature from the more gradual age-related declines in the organism's general learning capacity) beyond a particular maturational stage. It has to be said that none of the above notions is unproblematic, as the following discussion makes clear. At a general level it is worth bearing in mind that, as Aram et al. (1997:. 85) point out, "the end of the critical period for language in humans has proven... difficult to find, with estimates ranging from 1 year of age to adolescence", and that, in addition, there is much dispute about what kinds of capacities are supposed to be affected by the critical period (see Singleton 2005).

With regard to attaining native-like levels of proficiency, Scovel (1988: 185) suggests that those who begin to be exposed to an L2 after age 12 cannot ever "pass themselves off as native speakers phonologically" (a position since slightly qualified—Scovel 2000, 2006). Long (1990: 274) follows Scovel in his interpretation of the phonological evidence, but goes on to claim that for the acquisition of L2 morphology and syntax to reach native levels exposure to the L2 must begin before age 15 (cf. also Long 2007). Such claims have been called into question by studies focused on older beginners attaining to very high levels of L2 proficiency—e.g. Birdsong 1992; Ioup et al. 1994; Bongaerts et al. 1995, 1997, 2000; Ioup 1995; Palmen et al. 1997; Bongaerts 1999, 2003; Moyer 1999; Muñoz and Singleton 2007, Kinsella 2009). Hyltenstam and Abrahamsson (2000: 155) affirm that there is no recorded case of a post-pubertal L2 beginner behaving in every detail like a native speaker (cf also Hyltenstam and Abrahamsson 2003a, b), but they also note that very early L2 beginners tend to differ too at the level of fine linguistic detail from monoglot native speakers. The maturational issue may be a good deal less important in this connection than the fact of possessing knowledge of another language (cf., e.g. Grosjean 1982; Cook 1995; McDonald 2000).

Concerning the effortfulness of later language learning, Lenneberg (1967: 176) makes the claim that post-pubertal L2 learning requires "conscious and labored effort", a claim which some researchers (e.g. Hyltenstam and Abrahamsson 2000: 152) have seen as an essential dimension of the CPH. Many professionals and researchers involved in one way or another with language have simply assumed that later L2 learning requires more effort. Thus, we find an article in an Irish medical journal (Breathnach 1993) largely echoing Lenneberg's (1967) views— speaking of a "transitory sensitive period" for language (Breathnach 1993: 43) and claiming that "the infant learns to pronounce and use the language he hears around him with ease and perfection", while adult L2 learning "demands a systematic and determined effort" (Breathnach 1993: 44). Bongaerts also seems to show some sympathy for this point of view when he comments that his results may be partly explicable in terms of the very intensive training received by his subjects (e.g. Bongaerts 1999: 154–155). However, such 'input enhancement' may not be indispensable for successful late L2 learning. For example, one of Ioup's highly successful adult learners of Arabic was untutored, and her performance was native-like even in areas of which she was unaware—e.g. subtle aspects of syntax and morphophonology (Ioup 1995: 118). Even if later L2 learning *is* more effortful, this may have absolutely nothing to do with the ending of a putative critical period for language. After all, the conscious, deliberate dimension of learning increases in *all* domains as cognitive development advances (cf. Feldman 2009).

In relation to the idea that children and adults may have fundamentally different language-learning mechanisms at their disposal, some Chomskyans (e.g. Bley-Vroman 1989) have claimed that post-pubertal L2 language learning has no access to UG (for discussion, see e.g. Cook and Newson 2007: 237f); the empirical basis for this perspective was never very solid (cf. e.g. Flynn 1987; Martohardjono and Flynn 1995; see also Hawkins 2001: 353–359), and different researchers working in the Chomskyan paradigm take very different perspectives on this issue (see, e.g. Mitchell and Myles 2004: 78f). As Braidi (1999: 67) points out, the still ongoing evolution of Chomskyan theory renders evaluation of earlier studies extremely difficult, although she also notes that "L2 learners do not seem to exhibit grammars that are not sanctioned by UG". Much research appears to indicate that post-pubertal L2 learners deal in the same way as L1 acquirers with linguistic features purportedly having a UG basis (see, e.g. Dekydtspotter et al. 1998; Bruhn de Garavito 1999). Similarly, Rothman (2008) reports on late L2 acquirers who seem to have continued access to UG.

Some non-UG-oriented research has also been interpreted as pointing to different mechanisms subserving language learning in later years. Liu et al.'s (1992) investigation of Chinese learners of English suggests that, whereas those whose exposure to English began after age 20 applied Chinese sentence-processing strategies to English, those whose learning of English began before age 13 deployed the same processing strategies as monolingual English speakers. In fact, this finding does not require a 'different mechanisms' explanation. It can be explained in terms of the increasing extent to which the L1 influences L2 processing as a function of years of experience of the L1 and the degree to which it is entrenched. Harley and Hart (1997: 395) found that the early beginners' L2 outcomes "were much more likely to be associated with a memory measure than with a measure of language ability", whereas the reverse was true of the later beginners, and DeKeyser's (2000) study yielded not dissimilar results: the adult beginners in his study who scored within the range of the child beginners manifested high levels of verbal analytical ability, an ability which seemed to play no role in the performance of the child beginners. Some other studies also emphasise the role of language ability in late L2 acquisition: Abrahamsson and Hyltenstam (2008) found that those late acquirerers of Swedish who reached native-like levels of attainment possessed unusually high levels of language aptitude. They treat such individuals as exceptions to the CPH, who for some reason have continued access to UG. DeKeyser's reading of his results is that maturational constraints apply only to implicit language learning mechanisms (cf. DeKeyser 2003a, b, 2006). Harley and Hart for their part point to the possible influence of primary versus secondary-level instructional styles. A further possibility is that such results reflect general cognitive changes which impact on language learning but not *only* on language learning.

Yet another approach has been to claim that late language acquisition makes use of different areas of the brain as compared with early acquisition. For example, an investigation of the spatial representation of L1 and L2 in the cerebral cortex of early and late bilinguals during a sentence-generation task carried out by Kim et al. (1997) revealed little or no age-related separation of activity in Wernicke's area, but did reveal differences in respect of activity in Broca's area: among the late bilinguals two distinct but adjacent centres of activation showed up for L1 and L2, whereas in the early bilinguals there appeared to be a single area of activation for both languages. Marinova-Todd et al. (2000) note that in Kim et al.'s study there was no control of the proficiency level of the later beginners and evoke the possibility "that the adult learners assessed (…) were poorly selected and do not represent highly proficient adult bilinguals" (Marinova-Todd et al. 2000: 17–18). If this were the case, the neurological divergences observed might simply reflect differences in proficiency level, which some studies have found to be more important than age of onset in determining brain organization in respect of additional languages (cf. Perani et al. 1998; Abutalebi et al. 2001). For a detailed account of the L2 neural localization controversy, see Abutalebi (2008) (cf. Muñoz and Singleton 2011).

Turning to the question of whether there is a sharp decline in the language-acquiring capacity, findings from studies investigating 'naturalistic' L2 acquisition favour the notion that, while adolescent and adult subjects may have an initial advantage, in the long run younger beginners are more likely to attain to native-like levels of proficiency (cf. Oyama 1976, 1978; Snow and Hoefnagel-Höhle 1978; Krashen et al. 1979; Patkowski 1980; Johnson and Newport 1989; Hyltenstam 1992). On the other hand, research into primary-level L2 programmes in schools where the general medium of instruction is the L1 (see e.g. Burstall et al. 1974; Oller and Nagato 1974) shows that pupils who are exposed early to an L2 and then integrated into classes containing pupils without such experience tend not to maintain a clear advantage for long.

This last finding may relate to blurring/stagnating/de-motivating effects resulting from mixing non-beginners with beginners in the same classes and/or to differences in exposure time between naturalistic and instructed learners (see, e.g. Singleton 1992; Singleton and Ryan 2004: Chaps 4, 6; Stern 1976). On the basis of such considerations, both naturalistic evidence and formal instructional evidence may bear an interpretation which is consistent with the view that the younger one starts the better one's eventual level of proficiency is likely to be. Muñoz (2006a), however, suggests, on the basis of a long-term comparative study of younger and older formally instructed L2 learners, that younger learners may have a fundamentally different (disadvantaging) cognitive relationship with classroom L2 learning as compared with adolescents and adults (cf Muñoz 2008a, 2008b). In any case:

(i) the evidence does not support the simplistic 'younger = better in all circumstances over any timescale' optique which underlies some early treatments (e.g. Tomb 1925; Stengel 1939; Penfield and Roberts 1959; Lenneberg 1967);

(ii) even the 'younger = better in the long run' view is sustainable only as a general tendency; an early start in an L2 is neither a strictly necessary nor a sufficient condition for the attainment of very high proficiency; age of first encounter is only one of the determinants of the ultimate level of proficiency attained. As mentioned earlier, even very young L2 beginners diverge at the level of fine linguistic detail from native speakers (see e.g. Flege 1999; Hyltenstam and Abrahamsson 2000: 161);

(iii) there is a question-mark over the existence of an abrupt cut-off point— or 'elbow' (Bialystok and Hakuta 1999; Flege 1999; Birdsong 2004)—such as would normally be associated with a critical period as classically understood. While such an effect was indeed observed in some classic studies such as that of Johnson and Newport (1989) and similar discontinuities were noted in some more recent studies—notably by DeKeyser et al. (2010) with respect to morphosyntax—other studies report a continuous decline. Bialystok and Hakuta's re-analysis of Johnson and Newport's data (Bialystok and Hakuta 1994; Bialystok 1997) suggests "that the tendency for proficiency to decline with age projects well into adulthood and does not mark some defined change in learning potential at around puberty" (Bialystok 1997: 122); Bialystok and Hakuta (1999) have also analysed census data on age of arrival in an English (L2) speaking environment and reported English proficiency; what emerges is a steady linear decline of reported proficiency as age of arrival increases but no indication of a dramatically sharper rate of decline at any point between infancy and senescence; data on the relationship between L2 accent and age of arrival show a similarly continuous decline (cf. also Flege 1999). Recent studies by Reichle (2010a, 2010b), employing acceptability judgment tests to investigate information structure, also report a steady linear decline, characteristic of the general cognitive deterioration caused by aging.

In sum, it appears that any decline in L2-learning capacity that occurs at the end of childhood varies from individual to individual, which is not what one would expect if the underlying cause of the decline were a critical period for language; it also appears that any decline in L2-learning capacity with age is continuous and linear, which, again, is not in keeping with the usual understanding of the notion of critical period.

3 The CPH and SLA: Research Bye-Ways

3.1 Qualitative Research Bearing on the CPH

Much recent research on age-related differences shows a tendency to shift attention from purely neurobiological maturational factors to a combination of social, environmental and affective variables (see Singleton and Muñoz 2011 for an overview), to an approach, in other words, that recognizes the complexity of the language acquisition process. Such studies focus on the role of input and the quality of the target language experience in ultimate attainment (Moyer 2004, 2005, 2009; Hellman 2008; Flege 2009), on the complex interplay of environmental and social factors that influence individual choices (Jia et al. 2002; Jia and Aaronson 2003), and on the influence of learners' orientations on ultimate attainment (Marinova-Todd 2003; Moyer 2004; Gatbonton et al. 2007; Gatbonton and Trofimovich 2008; Segalowitz et al. 2009; Kinsella 2009). Whereas the bulk of research carried out under the general aegis of the age factor has been quantitative in orientation, under the impetus of the perceived need to attend to issues such as those outlined above, there have in recent times, been attempts to bring a more qualitative perspective to bear. The two studies presented below represent and illustrate this development. Both studies focus on L2 accent acquisition, and both yield findings which are less than favourable to the CPH.

In the first study (Muñoz and Singleton 2007) the subjects under scrutiny were twelve female late L2 learners of English resident in Ireland whose average age of learning (AOL) (i.e., age of initial significant L2 exposure) was 22.5 years (range 18–28), whose average length of residence (LOR) was 10 years (range 6–20), and whose average age at the time of testing was 35 (age range 28–47). All had Spanish and/or Catalan as their L1(s). Also participating in the study were two groups of native speakers of Irish English. The first group comprised five native speakers—with a similar age, sex and education profile to the non-native speaker group—who functioned in the study as the control group. A second group of four native speakers of English acted as judges, blindly rating the oral production of the learners and the native speakers. All the judges were postgraduate students of applied linguistics, who could be considered expert raters (Piske et al. 2001). None of them knew Spanish (or Catalan).

Speech in English was elicited by means of an oral film-retelling task. An extract from each of the non-native and native participants, seventeen in all, was transferred to a CD for presentation (in randomized order) to the judges. In order to eliminate possible differences in the content of the extracts, all were taken from the descriptions of the same sequence. The mean number of syllables in each extract was 9.9, and the range was from 8 to 11 syllables. The judges were asked to rate each extract on a 5-point scale.

The L2 informants were interviewed by an English-speaking researcher in English on the basis of an adaptation of the language background questionnaire used in Piske et al. (2001). The questions concerned temporal aspects of participants' experience, such as age of arrival in Ireland, length of residence, age of first immersion in English, and age of formal learning of English. It also included questions in respect of informants' knowledge of English and their L1 (Spanish or Catalan or both) and their use of the various languages at their disposal over different periods and in different contexts. A third group of questions concerned their education, both in Spain and in Ireland, including their experience of formally learning English.

As expected, a significant difference overall emerged between native speakers and non-natives in terms of foreign accent ratings. However, two of the non-natives scored within the native-speaker range. The qualitative discussion, which constitutes the more interesting dimension of the study, profiles in some detail these two very successful learners, who, according to at least some interpretations of the CPH, seemed to have, in a limited domain and to a limited degree, 'beaten' the critical period. The profiles which emerged were in some ways very different; however, they did share some characteristics. Both of the successful learners both spoke English at home (one lived with her English-speaking husband and the other with English-speaking friends), whereas all the other participants spoke Spanish at home. The two successful learners also had in common the fact that they enjoyed and took satisfaction from learning and using English. They in addition both evinced a certain dissatisfaction with the level of English they had so far achieved; their thirst for becoming native-like seemed to induce lower self-estimations of ability than in the case of most of the other informants. Finally, they were also the youngest participants, and they are among those whose age of arrival in Ireland was at the lower end of the scale (although still well beyond puberty).

The greatest difference between the two was the relative importance of formal instruction in English: while in one case this had been very extensive, the individual in question representing the typical example of an advanced formal learner of English, in the other case instruction in English had played a much more modest role. Another difference worth noting is that, while the first of the above learners had one L1 (Spanish), some command of Italian and very little French, apart from English, the second has effectively two L1s (Catalan and Spanish) as well as English and some French. Given what we know about the way in which bilingualism promotes language awareness and sensitivity, it is at least conceivable that the more languages in which an individual has a substantial proficiency, other things being equal, the higher the level of his/her language awareness and sensitivity is likely to be (cf. Singleton and Aronin 2007). The authors of the study speculated, accordingly, that those metalinguistic skills into which the first learner had been inducted via formal instruction the second learner might have evolved through her multilinguality.

In the second study under scrutiny in the present section (Kinsella and Singleton 2008) the focus was on L2 regional accent recognition by late acquirers of French as an additional language. The study was part of a larger piece of research (Kinsella 2009) involving 20 native English speakers who had been raised monolingually and who had not begun learning French before the age of 11, but who were now resident in France and reported occasionally passing for native speakers of French. In the larger study these subjects were asked to perform three tasks: (i) to engage in a semi-structured interview surveying biological-experiential, social-psychological and instructional data; (ii) to identify the regional French accents instantiated in three spoken texts; (iii) to complete a test incorporating lexical and grammatical elements. The latter two tasks were also performed by a native-speaker control group. The data reported in Kinsella and Singleton's (2008) paper are drawn from the results of the first two of the above procedures.

The non-natives were fairly successful with two of the regional accents. 80% identified the accent of Alsace and Provence (compared with a 100% success rate among native speakers) but were less successful with the accent of the Touraine region, only 20% of participants identifying this one. It is noteworthy, however, that this accent also defeated 60% of the natives. Four of the twenty non-natives scored within the best native-speaker range, identifying all three of the accents. As in the case of the Muñoz and Singleton study, the profiles of these very successful late learners were explored in detail.

It transpired that their mean age at the time of the study was somewhat higher (55.25 years) than that of the group as a whole (41.1 years), that their mean length of residence in France was markedly longer (30 years vs. 14.1 years), but that their average age of arrival in France was comparable to that of the entire sample (25 years compared with 28.6 years). The length of residence aspect is obviously worthy of note. A closer look at the interview data revealed a number of further common elements: all the successful subjects had a French partner; all conducted their social life primarily through French; all identified themselves closely with the Francophone community; and all considered it important to pass for a native speaker of French.

Putting the above two sets of results together, we can say that the qualitative dimensions of the studies brought out some possible success factors in overcoming any age-related contra-indications to high levels of L2 performance that might not have so readily have emerged from less fine-grained exploration of individual profiles. Common success factors across the two studies include large quantities of interaction in the L2 and a very serious desire to speak the language well. However, specifically individual factors—or possible factors—are also revealed by such profiling. Thus, for example, in one case extensive formal instruction comes to the fore, in another multilinguality.

3.2 Critical Period Research and Early L2 Instruction

As Stern (1983: 132) notes, the movement advocating the introduction of foreign languages into the primary school curriculum in the 1950s and 1960s was much influenced by the 'younger = better' ideas of Penfield and the neurological evidence he adduced in their support. It has been suggested that Penfield's notions about early L2 learning owe more to his personal experience of immersing his own children in foreign languages at an early age than to his work as a scientist

(Dechert 1995). Nevertheless the fact remains that the advocacy of the CPH, or at least its immediate forerunner, was a major contributor to decisions concerning the early introduction of L2s into the classroom. Although this issue is somewhat on the periphery of academic debate about the existence of a critical period for language, given its importance in practical, educational terms, and the amount of discussion it provokes among non-specialists, it certainly merits attention.

The notion of a critical period continues to figure in the argumentation of those who wish to put the case for early L2 instruction. Many SLA researchers who subscribe to the CPH have no hesitation in claiming that it constitutes an argument for early L2 instruction. For example, in a interview published seven years ago, Nina Spada had the following to say:

> If the goal for learning/teaching a foreign language is to obtain the highest level of second language skills... there is support for the argument that 'earlier is better'. This support, found in the critical period hypothesis literature, is based on the claim that biological and maturational factors constrain language learning beyond a certain age (ReVEL 2004).

In Poland, the CPH is very often brought up when the case is made for the early introduction of foreign language instruction. Polish publications for language teachers usually recommend early foreign language instruction, focusing mostly on the phonetic aspects of the CPH, and the supposedly greater flexibility of the vocal organs before the onset of puberty (Wieszczeczyńska 2000: 8), but also stressing the psychological and developmental advantages of early L2 learning (creativity, willingness to imitate, natural curiosity, the positive influence of foreign language learning on the intellectual development of the child and on his/her personality—in terms of the openness to new cultures, ideas etc.). Rzewólska's (2008: 17) overview of the age factor for Polish readers ends with the conclusion that, as a rule, only children are able to acquire native-like pronunciation, though she does quote studies that question the CPH by providing other explanations for the lack of native-like pronunciation in adult L2 learners.

As Jedynak (2005: 198), for her part, points out, the widespread advertising for early foreign language courses in Poland almost always echoes a CPH perspective, generating a widespread belief that post-pubertal learners are, if not doomed to failure, then faced with severely limited chances. Jedynak (2005, 2009) focuses on finding adult L2 learners who achieve native-like proficiency as far as pronunciation is concerned; the existence of such learners is widely taken as undermining the CPH (identified in Jedynak's study with the Lennebergian assumption that the critical period is co-terminous with cerebral lateralization). She is inclined to link older beginners' successes with the context of learning: the setting, the intensity of phonological training, and the length of learning. Bongaerts (e.g. 1999), as we have seen, also adverts to the role of training in this context, but much more tentatively.

Jedynak (2005, 2009) herself investigated some subjects who had had no significant contact with the L2 before the age of 15 (in her study assumed to be the cut-off point for the critical period) and then began their L2 learning in either a naturalistic or an instructional setting, subsequently reaching a good or excellent level of proficiency. She investigated 35 learners of English as L2 and 10 learners of Polish as L2 via questionnaire, interview, and audio-recording of their reading a text and giving a short speech in the L2. All speech samples were rated by qualified judges in terms of their approximation to native pronunciation. Nine of the subjects (seven learning English and two learning Polish) were rated as native speakers. Length of learning seemed to emerge as the dominant factor relative to level of attainment, with phonetic training, contrary to Jedynak's expectation, not really featuring as an element. Such findings are clearly not very supportive of a CPH perspective in general, never mind the kind of educational implications derived from it by Spada and others. Nevertheless, Jedynak (2005: 204) concludes that the critical period probably does play a role in restricting the language learning ability of the "overwhelming majority" of adult language learners, but that there are some learners who are 'phenomenal' in that they are "not bound by the constraints of the CP", having a higher degree of neurocognitive flexibility and/or certain learner characteristics (such as having an insight into one's learning styles and preferences, or a powerful motivation to speak an accentless L2) which "override the disadvantages of a late start". It has to be said that the notion of a species-wide critical period to which some privileged souls are immune might not go down terribly well in the biological sciences.

Other advocates of the CPH take a different line. Thus, Johnson and Newport (1989: 81) note that the crucial measure in their study was age of arrival in the L2 environment rather than age of onset of formal L2 instruction in their subjects' home country, and conclude that this means "that the learning which occurs in the formal language classroom may be unlike the learning which occurs during immersion, such that early instruction does not necessarily have the advantage for ultimate performance that is held by early immersion". DeKeyser (2003a, b) broadly agrees. He argues that school-based L2 learning is mostly explicit in nature and is therefore largely unaffected by maturational constraints. His position is as follows:

> Rather than suggesting the importance of starting early, [age differences] indicate that the instructional approach should be different depending on age: full-scale immersion is necessary for children to capitalize on their implicit learning skills, and formal rule teaching is necessary for adults to draw on their explicit learning skills (DeKeyser 2003a: 335).

DeKeyser's notion that learning a foreign language as a subject in a formal instructional setting is not particularly in tune with children's capacities seems to be supported by Rokita's (2006) research. This compared the early L2 lexical development of Polish children aged two to four learning English in naturalistic and instructional settings. Rokita found the results of instructed learning to be very modest in comparison with the progress observable in a naturalistic setting. In a longitudinal study, she found that the achievements of instructed L2 learners were far inferior to those of naturalistic learners, both in quantitative and qualitative terms, that in the former case the L2 was very rarely used spontane- ously for communicative purposes (it was mostly elicited), and also that early exposure to the L2 did not have a discernible effect on the further learning of lexis (Rokita 2006: 81). Such findings lead Rokita to doubt the usefulness of such programmes as those run by the Helen Doron language school, because of the fast forgetting of learnt material, the lack of any communicative use of the foreign language, and absence of evidence of any covert acquisition of the target language.

Interestingly, just as there are supporters of the CPH who do not necessarily argue for early L2 instruction, there are CPH sceptics who are all in favour of the introduction of L2s into the primary school curriculum. For instance, Ekstrand (1971), Genesee (1978), and Hatch (1983), all of whom have expressed themselves unpersuaded of the existence of a critical period for language acquisition, have argued for early L2 instruction on the basis, not of the influence of maturational constraints, but in consideration of factors such as the general desirability of as long an exposure to the L2 as possible and the importance of laying an early foundation to L2 learning so that ground can later covered that might otherwise be neglected.

In short, research and discussion in recent decades have moved us rather a long way from the simple idea of the 1950s and 1960s that there were maturational constraints on language acquisition and that these implied the desirability of an early introduction of L2 instruction into the school curriculum. Not only are the reality and nature of the posited maturational constraints highly controversial, but it is not at all clear if the answer to the question of whether or not a critical period exists gives us any clear direction in relation to L2 educational policy with respect to young children.

4 Concluding Remarks

The 'research highways' part of the above discussion has run through a representative selection of fairly oft-cited age related L2 studies to end with the suggestion that the current state of the mainline evidence is not such as to persuade the sceptical mind of the reality of a critical period for SLA.

With regard to the 'research bye-ways' part, this has offered two collections of bye-ways: on the one hand, recent qualitative work bearing on the CPH, and, on the other, an overview of discussion of the relationship between the CPH and language educational thinking. With regard to the first, the findings of the studies reviewed proved not particularly favourable to the CPH perspective, but their qualitative dimensions yielded interesting insights regarding the roles of quantity of L2 use and motivation. With regard to the second, the picture revealed of the dissensions among researchers—both between CPH advocates and sceptics and within each group—leave us with very little hope of any kind of consensus on this issue for a very long time to come.

References

Abello-Contesse, C., R. Chacón-Beltrán, M.D. López-Jiménez, and M.M. Torreblanca-López, eds. 2006. *Age in L2 acquisition and teaching.* Bern: Peter Lang.

Abrahamsson, N., and K. Hyltenstam. 2008. The robustness of aptitude effects in near-native second language acquisition. *Studies in Second Language Acquisition* 30: 481–509.

Abutalebi, J. 2008. Neural aspects of second language representation and language control. *Acta Psychologica* 128: 466–478.

Abutalebi, J., S.F. Cappa, and D. Perani. 2001. The bilingual brain as revealed by functional neuroimaging. *Bilingualism: Language and Cognition* 4: 179–190.

Almli, C.R., and S. Finger. 1987. Neural insult and critical period concepts. In ed. M.H. Bornstein, 123–143.

Arabski J., and A. Wojtaszek, eds. 2010. *Neurolinguistic and psycholinguistic perspectives on SLA.* Bristol: Multilingual Matters.

Aram, D., E. Bates, J. Eisele, J. Fenson, R. Nass, D. Thal, and D. Trauner. 1997. From first words to grammar in children with focal brain injury. *Developmental Neuropsychology* 13: 275–343.

Bialystok, E. 1997. The structure of age: In search of barriers to second language acquisition. *Second Language Research* 13: 116–137.

Bialystok, E., and K. Hakuta. 1994. *In other words: The science and psychology of second language acquisition.* New York: Basic Books.

Bialystok, E., and K. Hakuta. 1999. Confounded age: Linguistic and cognitive factors in age differences for second language acquisition. In ed. D. Birdsong, 161–181.

Birdsong, D. 1992. Ultimate attainment in second language acquisition. *Language* 68: 706–755.

Birdsong, D., ed. 1999. *Second language acquisition and the critical period hypothesis.* Mahwah: Lawrence Erlbaum.

Birdsong, D. 2004. Second language acquisition and ultimate attainment. In ed. A. Davies, and C. Elder, 82–105.

Bley-Vroman, R. 1989. What is the logical problem of foreign language learning? In ed. S.M. Gass, and J. Schachter, 41–68.

Bongaerts, T. 1999. Ultimate attainment in L2 pronunciation: the case of very advanced late L2 learners. In ed. D. Birdsong, 133–159.

Bongaerts, T. 2003. Effets de l'âge sur l'acquisition de la prononciation d'une seconde langue. *Acquisition et Interaction en Langue Étrangère* 18: 79–98.

Bongaerts, T., B. Planken, and E. Schils. 1995. Can late starters attain a native accent in a foreign language: a test of the critical period hypothesis. In ed. D. Singleton, and Z. Lengyel, 30–50.

Bongaerts, T., C. van Summeren, B. Planken, and E. Schils. 1997. Age and ultimate attainment in the pronunciation of a foreign language. *Studies in Second Language Acquisition* 19: 447–465.

Bongaerts, T., S. Mennen, and F. Van der Slik. 2000. Authenticity of pronunciation in naturalistic second language acquisition: The case of very advanced late learners of Dutch as a second language. *Studia Linguistica* 54: 298–308.

Bornstein, M.H., ed. 1987. *Sensitive periods in development: Interdisciplinary perspectives.* Hillsdale: Lawrence Erlbaum.

Braidi, S.M. 1999. *The acquisition of second language syntax.* London: Edward Arnold.

Breathnach, C. 1993. Temporal determinants of language acquisition and bilingualism. *Irish Journal of Psychological Medicine* 10: 41–47.

Bruhn de Garavito J (1999) Adult SLA of *se* constructions in Spanish: evidence against pattern learning. In Proceedings of the Boston university conference on language development. 23 vols. 112–119

Burstall, C., M. Jamieson, S. Cohen, and M. Hargreaves. 1974. *Primary French in the balance.* Windsor: NFER.

Cook, V. 1995. Multicompetence and effects of age. In ed. D. Singleton, and Z. Lengyel, 51–66.

Cook, V., and M. Newson. 2007. *Chomsky's universal grammar: an introduction.* 3rd ed. Oxford: Blackwell.

Davies, A., and C. Elder, eds. 2004. *The handbook of applied linguistics*. London: Blackwell.
De Villiers, J., and P. De Villiers. 1978. *Language acquisition*. Cambridge: Harvard University Press.
Dechert, H. 1995. Some critical remarks concerning Penfield's theory of second language acquisition. In ed. D. Singleton, and Z. Lengyel, 67–94.
DeKeyser, R. 2000. The robustness of critical period effects in second language acquisition. *Studies in Second Language Acquisition* 22: 499–534.
DeKeyser, R. 2003a. Implicit and explicit learning. In eds. C. Doughty, and M.H. Long, 313–348.
DeKeyser, R. 2003b. Confusion about confounding: the critical period and other age-related aspects of second language learning. Paper presented at ELIA VIII (Encuentros de Linguistica Inglesa Aplicada), El factor edad en la adquisición y enseñanza de L2, Seville.
DeKeyser, R. 2006. A critique of recent arguments against the critical period hypothesis. In eds. C. Abello-Contesse, R. Chacón-Beltrán, M.D. López-Jiménez, and M.M. Torreblanca-López, 49–58.
DeKeyser, R., I. Alfi-Shabtay, and D. Ravid. 2010. Cross-linguistic evidence for the nature of age effects in second language acquisition. *Applied Psycholinguistics* 31: 413–438.
Dekydtspotter, L., R.A. Sprouse, and R. Thyre. 1998. Evidence of full UG access in L2 acquisition from the interpretive interface: quantification at a distance in English–French interlanguage. In Proceedings of the Boston university conference on language development. 22 vols. 141–152.
Dörnyei, Z., and E. Ushioda, eds. 2009. *Motivation, language identity and the L2 self*. Bristol: Multilingual Matters.
Doughty, C., and M.H. Long, eds. 2003. *The handbook of second language acquisition*. Malden: Blackwell.
Ekstrand, L.H. 1971. Varför engelska redan in åk 3? (Why begin English as early as grade 3?). In eds. S. Jakobson, and L. Mellgren.
Feldman, R.S. 2009. *Development across the lifespan*. 5th ed. Upper Saddle River: Prentice Hall.
Flege, J.E. 1999. Age of learning and second language speech. In ed. D. Birdsong, 101–131.
Flege, J.E. 2009. Give input a chance! In eds. T. Piske, and M. Young-Scholten, 175–190.
Flynn, S. 1987. *A parameter-setting model of l2 acquisition: Experimental studies in anaphora*. Dordrecht: Reidel.
Gass, S.M., and J. Schachter, eds. 1989. *Linguistic perspectives on second language acquisition*. Cambridge: Cambridge University Press.
Garcia-Mayo, M.P. and M.L. Garcia-Lecumberri, eds. 2003. *Age and the acquisition of English as a foreign language: theoretical issues and field work*. Clevedon: Multilingual Matters.
Gatbonton, E., and P. Trofimovich. 2008. The ethnic group affiliation and L2 proficiency link: empirical evidence. *Language Awareness* 17: 229–248.
Gatbonton, E., P. Trofimovich, and N. Segalowitz. 2007. *Language and identity: does ethnic group affiliation affect L2 performance? Paper presented at the international symposium on bilingualism (ISB6)*. Germany: Hamburg (June).
Genesee, F. 1978. Is there an optimal age for starting second language instruction? *McGill Journal of Education* 13: 145–54.
Grosjean, F. 1982. *Life with two languages*. Cambridge: Harvard University Press.
Harley, B., and D. Hart. 1997. Language aptitude and second language proficiency in classroom learners of different starting ages. *Studies in Second Language Acquisition* 19: 379–400.
Harris, R.J., ed. 1992. *Cognitive processing in bilinguals*. New York: Elsevier.
Hatch, E. 1983. *Psycholinguistics: A second language perspective*. Rowley: Newbury House.
Hawkins, R. 2001. *Second language syntax: A generative introduction*. Oxford: Blackwell.
Hellman, A.B. 2008. The limits of eventual attainment in adult-onset second language acquisition. Ed.D. dissertation: Boston University, Boston.
Hinkel E. ed. 2011. *Handbook of research in second language teaching and learning*. 2 vols. London: Routledge

Hyltenstam, K. 1992. Non-native features of non-native speakers: On the ultimate attainment of childhood L2 learners. In ed. R.J. Harris, 351–368.

Hyltenstam, K., and N. Abrahamsson. 2000. Who can become native-like in a second language? all, some or none? on the maturational constraints controversy in second language acquisition. *Studia Linguistica* 54: 150–166.

Hyltenstam, K., and N. Abrahamsson. 2003a. Maturational constraints in SLA. In eds. C. Doughty, and M.H. Long, 539–588.

Hyltenstam, K., and N. Abrahamsson. 2003b. Ñge de l'exposition initiale et niveau terminal chez les locuteurs du suédois L2. *Acquisition et Interaction en Langue Étrangère* 18: 99–127.

Ioup, G. 1995. Evaluating the need for input enhancement in post-critical period language acquisition. In eds. D. Singleton, and Z. Lengyel, 95–123.

Ioup, G., E. Boustagui, M. Tigi, and M. Moselle. 1994. Reexamining the critical period hypothesis: A case study of successful adult SLA in a naturalistic environment. *Studies in Second Language Acquisition* 16: 73–98.

Jakobson, S. and L. Mellgren, eds. 1971. *Metodik och Praktisk Språkfärdighet 2*. Kristianstad: Hermods.

Jedynak, M. 2005. The impact of age on ultimate attainment in the pronunciation of English as a foreign language. In *Acta Universitatis Wratislaviensis 2782: Anglica Wratislaviensia XLIII*, 195–205. Wrocław: Wydawnictwo Uniwersytetu Wrocławskiego.

Jedynak, M. 2009. *Critical period hypothesis revisited: The impact of age on ultimate attainment in the pronunciation of a foreign language*. Frankfurt am Main: Peter Lang.

Jia, G., and D. Aaronson. 2003. A longitudinal study of Chinese children and adolescents learning English in the United States. *Applied Psycholinguistics* 24: 131–161.

Jia, G., D. Aaronson, and Y. Wu. 2002. Long-term language attainment of bilingual immigrants: Predictive variables and language group differences. *Applied Psycholinguistics* 23: 599–621.

Johnson, J.S., and E.L. Newport. 1989. Critical period effects in second language learning: The influence of maturational state on the acquisition of ESL. *Cognitive Psychology* 21: 60–99.

Kim, K.H.S., N.R. Relkin, K.M. Lee, and J. Hirsch. 1997. Distinct cortical areas associated with native and second languages. *Nature* 388: 171–174.

Kinsella, C. 2009. An investigation into the proficiency of successful late learners of French. Ph.D. dissertation, Trinity College Dublin.

Kinsella, C., and D. Singleton. 2008. Phonological attainment in late acquirers of French as an L2. Paper presented at the 20th international conference on foreign/second language acquisition, Szczyrk, May.

Krashen, S., M. Long, and R. Scarcella. 1979. Age, rate and eventual attainment in second language acquisition. *TESOL Quarterly* 9:573–582. (Reprinted in Krashen SD, Scarcella RC, Long MH, eds. Child–adult differences in second language acquisition, 161–72. Rowley: Newbury House)

Krashen, S.D., R.C. Scarcella, and M.H. Long, eds. 1982. *Child–adult differences in second language acquisition*. Rowley: Newbury House.

Lenneberg, E.H. 1967. *Biological foundations of language*. New York: Wiley.

Leśniewska, J., and E. Witalisz, eds. 2006. *Language and identity: English and American studies in the age of globalization*. Krakow: Jagiellonian University Press.

Liu, H., E. Bates, and P. Li. 1992. Sentence interpretation in bilingual speakers of English and Chinese. *Applied Psycholinguistics* 12: 451–484.

Long, M.H. 1990. Maturational constraints on language development. *Studies in Second Language Acquisition* 12: 251–285.

Long, M.H. 2007. *Problems in SLA*. Mahwah: Lawrence Erlbaum.

Marinova-Todd, S.H. 2003. Know your grammar: what the knowledge of syntax and morphology in an L2 reveals about the critical period for second/foreign language acquisition. In eds. M.P. Garcia-Mayo, and M.L. Garcia-Lecumberri, 59–73.

Marinova-Todd, S.H., D.B. Marshall, and C.E. Snow. 2000. Three misconceptions about age and L2 learning. *TESOL Quarterly* 34: 9–34.

Martohardjono, G., and S. Flynn. 1995. Is there an age factor for universal grammar? In eds. D. Singleton, and Z. Lengyel, 135–153.

McDonald, J. 2000. Grammaticality judgments in a second language: Influences of age of acquisition and native language. *Applied Psycholinguistics* 21: 395–423.

Mitchell, R., and F. Myles. 2004. *Second language learning theories*. 2nd ed. London: Arnold.

Moyer, A. 1999. Ultimate attainment in L2 phonology: The critical factors of age, motivation and instruction. *Studies in Second Language Acquisition* 21: 81–108.

Moyer, A. 2004. *Age, accent and experience in second language acquisition: An integrated approach to critical period inquiry*. Clevedon: Multilingual Matters.

Moyer, A. 2005. Formal and informal experiential realms in German as a foreign language: A preliminary investigation. *Foreign Language Annals* 38: 377–387.

Muñoz, C. ed. 2006. *Age and the rate of foreign language learning*. Clevedon: Multilingual Matters.

Moyer, A. 2009. Input as a critical means to an end: quantity and quality of experience in L2 phonological attainment. In eds. T. Piske, and M. Young-Scholten, 159–174.

Muñoz, C. 2006a. The effects of age on foreign language learning: the BAF project. In ed. C. Muñoz, 1–40.

Muñoz, C. ed. 2006b. *Age and the rate of foreign language learning*. Clevedon: Multilingual Matters.

Muñoz, C. 2008a. Symmetries and asymmetries of age effects in naturalistic and instructed L2 learning. *Applied Linguistics* 24: 578–596.

Muñoz, C. 2008b. Age-related differences in foreign language learning: Revisiting the empirical evidence. *International Review of Applied Linguistics in Language Teaching* 46: 197–220.

Muñoz, C., and D. Singleton. 2007. Foreign accent in advanced learners: Two successful profiles. *The EUROSLA Yearbook* 7: 171–190.

Muñoz, C., and D. Singleton. 2011. A critical review of age-related research on L2 ultimate attainment, state of the art article. *Language Teaching* 44: 1–35.

Oller, J., and N. Nagato. 1974. The long-term effect of FLES: an experiment. *Modern Language Journal* 58: 15–19.

Oyama, S. 1976. A sensitive period for the acquisition of a nonnative phonological system. *Journal of Psycholinguistic Research* 5: 261–285. Reprinted in Krashen, S.D., R.C. Scarcella, and M.H. Long, eds. *Child–adult differences in second language acquisition*, 20–38. Rowley: Newbury House.

Oyama, S. 1978. The sensitive period and comprehension of speech. *Work Papers Biling* 16:1–17. Reprinted in Krashen, S.D., R.C. Scarcella, M.H. Long, eds. *Child–adult differences in second language acquisition*, 39–51. Rowley: Newbury House.

Palmen, M.-J., T. Bongaerts, and E. Schils. 1997. L'authenticité de la prononciation dans l'acquisition d'une langue étrangère au-delà de la période critique: des apprenants parvenus à un niveau très avancé en français. *Acquisition et Interaction en Langue Etrangère* 9: 173–191.

Patkowski, M.S. 1980. The sensitive period for the acquisition of syntax in a second language. *Language Learning* 30: 449–472.

Penfield, W., and L. Roberts. 1959. *Speech and brain mechanisms*. Princeton: Princeton University Press.

Perani, D., E. Paulesu, N.S. Galles, E. Dupoux, S. Dehaene, V. Bettinardi, S.F. Cappa, F. Fazio, and J. Mehler. 1998. The bilingual brain: proficiency and age of acquisition of the second language. *Brain* 121: 1841–1852.

Piske, T., and M. Young-Scholten, eds. 2009. *Input matters*. Clevedon: Multilingual Matters.

Piske, T., I. MacKay, and J. Flege. 2001. Factors affecting degree of foreign accent in an L2: A review. *Journal of Phonetics* 29: 191–215.

Piske, T. and M. Young-Scholten eds. 2009. *Input matters*. Clevedon: Multilingual Matters

Reichle, R.V. 2010a. The critical period hypothesis: Evidence from information structural processing in French. In eds. J. Arabski, and A. Wojtaszek, 17–29.

Reichle, R.V. 2010b. Judgments of information structure in L2 French: Nativelike performance and the critical period hypothesis. *International Review of Applied Linguistics in Language Teaching* 48: 53–85.

ReVEL. 2004. Interview. *Revista Virtual de Estudos de Linguagem* 2. http://planeta.terra.com.br/educacao/revel/edicoes/num_2/interview_l2.htm.

Rokita, J. 2006. Comparing early L2 lexical development in naturalistic and instructional settings. In eds. J. Leśniewska, and E. Witalisz, 70–82.

Rothman, J. 2008. Why all counter-evidence to the critical period hypothesis is not equal or problematic. *Language and Linguistics Compass* 2: 1063–1088.

Rzewólska, A. 2008. Kluczowe czynniki w procesie uczenia się języków obcych—wiek rozpoczynania nauki, wpływ języka pierwszego. *Języki Obce w Szkole* 3: 15–21.

Scovel, T. 1988. *A time to speak: A psycholinguistic inquiry into the critical period for human language*. Rowley: Newbury House.

Scovel, T. 2000. A critical review of the critical period hypothesis. *Annual Review of Applied Linguistics* 20: 213–223.

Scovel, T. 2006. Age, acquisition, and accent. In eds. C. Abello-Contesse, R. Chacón-Beltrán, M.D. López-Jiménez, and M.M. Torreblanca-López, 31–48.

Segalowitz, N., E. Gatbonton, and P. Trofimovich. 2009. Links between ethnolinguistic affiliation, self-related motivation and second language fluency: Are they mediated by psycholinguistic variables? In eds. Z. Dörnyei, and E. Ushioda, 172–192.

Singleton, D. 1992. Second language instruction: the when and the how. *AILA Review* 9: 46–54.

Singleton, D. 2005. The critical period hypothesis: a coat of many colours. *International Review of Applied Linguistics in Language Teaching* 43: 269–285.

Singleton, D., and L. Aronin. 2007. Multiple language learning in the light of the theory of affordances. *Innovation in Language Learning and Teaching* 1: 83–96.

Singleton, D., and Z. Lengyel, eds. 1995. *The age factor in second language acquisition*. Clevedon: Multilingual Matters.

Singleton, D., and C. Muñoz. 2011. Around and beyond the critical period hypothesis. In ed. E. Hinkel, 407–425.

Singleton, D., and L. Ryan. 2004. *Language acquisition: the age factor*. 2nd ed. Clevedon: Multilingual Matters.

Snow, C., and M. Hoefnagel-Höhle. 1978. The critical period for language acquisition: Evidence from second language learning. *Child Development* 49: 1114–1128.

Stengel, E. 1939. On learning a new language. *International Journal of Psycho-Analysis* 20: 471–479.

Stern, H. 1976. Optimal age: myth or reality? *Canadian Modern Language Review* 32: 283–94.

Stern, H.H. 1983. *Fundamental concepts of language teaching*. Oxford: Oxford University Press.

Tomb, J.W. 1925. On the intuitive capacity of children to understand spoken languages. *British Journal of Psychology* 16: 53–54.

Wiesel, T.N., and D.H. Hubel. 1963. Single-cell responses in striate cortex of kittens deprived of vision in one eye. *Journal of Neurophysiology* 26: 1003–1017.

Wieszczeczyńska, E. 2000. Dlaczego warto rozpoczynać naukę języka obcego w okresie wczesnoszkolnym? *Języki Obce w Szkole* 6: 6–11.

The Concept of Linguistic Intelligence and Beyond

Szymon Wróbel

Abstract Four unresolved issues will dominate the discussion of intelligence: whether intelligence is singular, or consists of various more or less independent intellectual faculties, whether intelligence is inherited, and whether any of its elements can accurately be measured? The fourth question is linked more with psycholinguistic investigations than with general psychology: do children learn language using a mental organ, some of whose principles of organization are not shared with other cognitive systems such as perception, motor control, and reasoning? Or is language acquisition just another problem to be solved by general intelligence, in this case, the problem of how to communicate with other humans over the auditory channel? In this paper, I will try to outline what kind of argumentation reinforce the suspicion that there is a special kind of intelligence (mental organ/module)—linguistic one. I try to test the hypothesis of linguistic intelligence in the light of the very idea of multiple intelligences.

1 Introduction

A century ago the French psychologist Alfred Binet was asked by the Ministry of Education to help determine who would experience difficulty in school. Proceeding in an empirical manner, Binet posed many questions to youngsters of different ages. He ascertained which questions, when answered correctly, would

S. Wróbel (✉)
Faculty of Pedagogy and Fine Arts, Adam Mickiewicz University, Kalisz, Poland
e-mail: wrobelsz@gmail.com

S. Wróbel
Institute of Philosophy and Sociology, Polish Academy of Sciences, Warsaw, Poland

M. Pawlak (ed.), *New Perspectives on Individual Differences in Language Learning and Teaching*, Second Language Learning and Teaching, DOI: 10.1007/978-3-642-20850-8_7, © Springer-Verlag Berlin Heidelberg 2012

predict success in school, and which questions, when answered incorrectly, would foretell school difficulties. The items that discriminated most clearly between the two groups became, in effect, the first test of intelligence (Binet and Simon 1916/ 2007). Binet devised the instrument that is often considered psychology's greatest success story. Millions of people who have never heard Binet's name have had aspects of their fate influenced by the instrumentation that the French psychologist inspired. And thousands of psychometricians—specialists in the measurement of psychological variables—earn their living courtesy of Binet's invention.

Although it has persisted over the long run, the version of intelligence proposed by Binet is now facing its biggest threat. Many scholars and observers feel that intelligence is too important to be left to the psychometricians. Experts are extending the breadth of the concept, proposing many specific intelligences such as, for example, *emotional intelligence* and *moral intelligence*. They are experimenting with new methods of determining the degree of intelligence, including those that avoid tests altogether in favor of direct measures of brain activity. They are forcing individuals everywhere to confront a number of questions: what is intelligence? How ought it to be assessed? And how do our notions of intelligence fit with what we value about human beings?

The outline of the psychometricians' success story is well known (Sternberg 1994). Binet's colleagues in England and Germany contributed to the conceptualization and instrumentation of intelligence testing, which soon became known as IQ tests. An IQ, or *intelligence quotient*, designates the ratio between mental age and chronological age. Clearly, we would prefer a child in our care to have an IQ of 120, making him or her smarter than an average child at this age, rather than that of 80, making him or her older than an average possessor of this IQ. Like other Parisian fashions of the period, the intelligence test migrated easily to the United States. First used to determine who was feeble-minded, they soon started to be used to assess normal children, to identify the gifted, and to determine who was fit to serve in the Army. By the 1920s the intelligence test had become a fixture in educational practice in the United States and much of Western Europe.

Perhaps surprisingly, the conceptualization of intelligence did not advance much in the decades following Binet's (1916/2007) and Terman's (1916) pioneering contributions. Intelligence tests came to be seen, rightly or wrongly, as primarily a tool for selecting people to fill academic or vocational niches. In one of the most famous remarks about intelligence testing, the influential Harvard psychologist Boring (1923: 123) declared: "Intelligence is what the tests test". So long as these tests did what they were supposed to do (that is, give some indication of school success), it did not seem necessary or prudent to probe too deeply into their meaning or to explore alternative views of the human intellect.

Psychologists who study intelligence have mainly disagreed about three questions. The first one: is intelligence singular, or does it consist of various more or less independent intellectual faculties? The purists—together with the turn-of-the-century English psychologist Spearman (1923)—defend the notion of a single overarching 'g', or *general intelligence*. The pluralists—ranging from Thurstone (1924/1973) of the University of Chicago, who posited seven vectors of the mind, to Guilford (1967) of the University of Southern California, who discerned 150 factors of the intellect—construe intelligence as composed of some, or even many, dissociable components. In Guilford's (1967) structure of intellect theory, intelligence is viewed as comprising *operations*, *contents*, and *products*. There are five kinds of operations (i.e. cognition, memory, divergent production, convergent production, evaluation), six kinds of products (i.e. units, classes, relations, systems, transformations, and implications), and five kinds of contents (i.e. visual, auditory, symbolic, semantic, behavioral). Since each of these dimensions is independent, there are theoretically 150 different components of intelligence.

Still, the public is more interested in the second question: is intelligence (or are intelligences) largely inherited? Studies of identical twins reared apart provide surprisingly strong support for the heritability of psychometric intelligence. That is, if one wants to predict someone's score on an intelligence test, the scores of the biological parents (even if the child has not had appreciable contact with them) are more likely to prove relevant than the scores of the adoptive parents. By the same token, the IQs of identical twins are more similar than the IQs of fraternal twins. And, contrary to common sense (and political correctness), the IQs of biologically related people grow closer in the later years of life. Still, because of the intricacies of behavioral genetics and the difficulties of conducting valid experiments with human child-rearing, a few defend the proposition that intelligence is largely environmental rather than heritable, and some believe that we cannot answer the question at all (cf. Plomin et al. 2001).

One other question has intrigued both laypeople and psychologists alike: are intelligence tests biased? Cultural assumptions are evident in early intelligence tests. Some class biases are obvious—who except the wealthy could readily answer a question about polo? Others are more subtle. Suppose the question is what one should do with money found on the street. Although ordinarily one might turn it over to the police, what if one had a hungry child? Or what if the police were known to be hostile to members of one's ethnic group? Only the canonical response to such a question would be scored as correct.

Psychometricians have striven to remove the obviously biased items from such measures. But biases that are built into the test situation itself are far more difficult to deal with. For example, a person's background affects his or her reaction to being placed in an unfamiliar locale, being instructed by someone dressed in a certain way, and having a printed test booklet thrust into his or her hands. And, as the psychologist Steele (1992) has argued, the biases prove even more acute when people know that their academic potential is being measured and that their racial or ethnic group is widely considered to be less intelligent than the dominant social group.

The idea of bias touches on the common assumption that tests in general, and intelligence tests in particular, are inherently conservative instruments—tools of the establishment. It is therefore worth noting that many testing pioneers thought of themselves as progressives in the social sphere. They were devising instruments that could reveal people of talent even if those people came from remote and apparently inferior backgrounds. And, occasionally, the tests did discover intellectual diamonds in the rough. More often, however, they picked out the privileged. The still unresolved question of the causal relationship between IQ and social privilege has stimulated many a dissertation across the social sciences.

Paradoxically, one of the clearest signs of the success of intelligence tests is that they are no longer widely administered. In the wake of legal cases about the propriety of making consequential decisions about education on the basis of IQ scores, many public school officials have become test-shy. By and large, the testing of IQ in the schools is restricted to cases involving a recognized problem (such as a learning disability) or a selection procedure (determining eligibility for a program that serves gifted children).

2 The Idea of Multiple Intelligences

The concept of intelligence has in recent years undergone its most robust challenge since the days of Alfred Binet. Some who are informed by psychology but not bound by psychometric assumptions have invaded this formerly sacrosanct territory. They have put forth their own ideas of what intelligence is, how (and whether) it should be measured, and which values should be invoked in considerations of the human intellect. For the first time in many years the intelligence establishment is clearly on the defensive—and the new century seems likely to usher in quite different ways of thinking about intelligence.

One evident factor in the rethinking of intelligence is the perspective introduced by scholars who are not psychologists. Anthropologists have commented on the parochialism of the Western view of intelligence. Some cultures do not even have a concept called intelligence, and others define intelligence in terms of traits that we in the West might consider odd—obedience, good listening skills, or moral fiber, for example. Neuroscientists are skeptical that the highly differentiated and modular structure of the brain is consistent with a unitary form of intelligence. Computer scientists have devised programs deemed intelligent; these programs often go about problem-solving in ways quite different from those embraced by human beings or other animals.

Even within the field of psychology the natives have been getting restless. For example Sternberg (1985) in his books on the subject began with the strategic goal of understanding the actual mental processes mobilized by standard test items, such as the solving of analogies. But he soon went beyond standard intelligence testing by insisting on two hitherto neglected forms of intelligence: the practical ability to adapt to varying contexts (as we all must in these days of divorcing and downsizing), and the capacity to automate familiar activities so that we can deal effectively with novelty and display creative intelligence.

Sternberg has gone to greater pains than many other critics of standard intelligence testing to measure these forms of intelligence with the paper-and-pencil laboratory methods favored by the profession. And he found that a person's ability to adapt to diverse contexts or to deal with novel information can be differentiated from success with standard IQ-test problems. His efforts to create a new intelligence test have not been crowned with easy victory. Most psychometricians are conservative—they like the tests that have been in use for decades, and if new ones are to be marketed, these must correlate well with existing instruments. So much for openness to novelty within psychometrics.

Others in the field seem less bound by its strictures. The psychologist and journalist Goleman (1996) has achieved worldwide success with his book *emotional intelligence*. Contending that this new concept, sometimes called EQ, may matter as much as or more than IQ, Goleman draws attention to such pivotal human abilities as controlling one's emotional reactions and 'reading' the signals of others. In the view of the noted child psychiatrist Coles (1997), we should prize character over intellect. He decries the amorality of our families, hence our children; he shows how we might cultivate human beings with a strong sense of right and wrong, who are willing to act on that sense even when it runs counter to self-interest. Other fairly popular accounts deal with *leadership intelligence* (LQ), *executive intelligence* (EQ or ExQ), and even *financial intelligence*.

The most important conclusions of these investigations are: (1) intelligence is not a single entity, (2) it does not result from a single factor, and (3) it cannot be measured simply via IQ tests. Gardner (1993), the proponent of the concept of multiple intelligences began his research by asking two questions: How did the human mind and brain evolve over millions of years? and How can we account for the diversity of skills and capacities that are or have been valued in different communities around the world? Armed with these questions and a set of eight criteria, he concluded that all human beings possess at least eight intelligences: *linguistic* and *logical–mathematical* (the two most prized in school and the ones central to success on standard intelligence tests), *musical, spatial, bodily-kinesthetic, naturalistic, interpersonal*, and *intrapersonal* (Gardner 1993).

Gardner makes two complementary claims about intelligence. The first is universal. We all possess these eight intelligences—and possibly more. Indeed, rather than seeing us as rational animals, Gardner offers a new definition of what it means to be a human being, cognitively speaking: *Homo sapiens* is the animal that possesses these eight forms of mental representation. His second claim concerns individual differences. Owing to the accidents of heredity, environment, and their interactions, no two of us exhibit the same intelligences in precisely the same proportions. Our profiles of intelligence differ from one another. This fact poses intriguing challenges and opportunities for our education systems. We can ignore these differences and pretend that we are all the same; historically, that is what most education systems have done. Or we can fashion an education system that tries to exploit these differences, individualizing instruction and assessment as much as possible.

The idea of multiple intelligences is so overwhelming, and the notion of mind so disintegrated, that some philosophy and psychology scholars go as far as to claim that we can no longer refer to mind as a substance but merely a quality, function, or a condition of human psyche. This process is parallel to the disintegration of the notion of intelligence. For instance, we now speak of *ecological intelligence*, meaning that species do not need mathematical algorithms enabling them to solve all kinds of esoteric problems. There exists no formal logic system nor general intelligence that would be crucial for our survival, but instead we use practised patterns of thinking and highly specialized partial intelligence. In this kind of architecture, linguistic intelligence plays an important role. According to Gardner, this kind of intelligence involves sensitivity to spoken and written language, the ability to learn languages, and the capacity to use language to accomplish certain goals. This intelligence includes the ability to effectively use language to express oneself rhetorically or poetically, as well as language as a means to remember information. In the next step, I would like to examine the sources of linguistic intelligence.

3 The Nature of Linguistic Intelligence

Language acquisition is one of the central topics in cognitive science. Every theory of cognition has tried to explain it and probably no other topic has aroused such controversy. Possessing a language is the quintessentially human trait: all normal humans speak, no nonhuman animal does. Language is the main vehicle by which we learn about other people's thoughts, and the two must be intimately related. Every time we speak, we are revealing something about language, so the facts of language structure are easy to come by; these data hint at a system of extraordinary complexity. Nonetheless, learning a first language is something every child does successfully, in a matter of a few years and without the need for formal lessons. With language so close to the core of what it means to be human, it is not surprising that children's acquisition of language has received so much attention. Anyone with strong views about the human mind would like to show that children's first few steps are steps in the right direction.

Adopting the perspective of multiple intelligences I would like to ask what kind of evidence we have to postulate the existence such a specific type of intelligence as linguistic intelligence? In a way we go back to the well known question of the theory of language acquisition: do children learn language using a mental organ, some of whose principles of organization are not shared with other cognitive systems such as perception, motor control, and reasoning (Chomsky 1975; Fodor 1983; Chomsky 1991)? Or is language acquisition just another problem to be solved by general intelligence; in this case, the problem of how to communicate with other humans over the auditory channel (Putnam 1971; Bates 1989)?

Humans evolved brain circuitry that appears to be designed for language mostly in the left hemisphere surrounding the sylvian fissure, though how exactly their internal wiring gives rise to rules of language is unknown. The brain mechanisms underlying language are not just those allowing us to be smart in general. Strokes often leave adults with catastrophic losses in language (Pinker 1994), though not necessarily impaired in other aspects of intelligence, such as those measured on the nonverbal parts of IQ tests. Similarly, there is an inherited set of syndromes called specific language impairment (Gopnik and Crago 1991) which is marked by delayed onset of language, difficulties in articulation in childhood, and lasting difficulties in understanding, producing, and judging grammatical sentences. By definition, specifically language impaired people show such deficits despite the absence of cognitive problems like retardation, sensory problems like hearing loss, or social problems like autism.

More interestingly, there are syndromes showing the opposite dissociation, where intact language coexists with severe retardation. These cases show that language development does not depend on fully functioning general intelligence. One example comes from children with Spina Bifida, a malformation of the vertebrae that leaves the spinal cord unprotected, often resulting in hydrocephalus, an increase in pressure in the cerebrospinal fluid filling the ventricles (large cavities) of the brain, distending the brain from within. Hydrocephalic children occasionally end up significantly retarded but can carry on long, articulate, and fully grammatical conversations, in which they earnestly recount vivid events that are, in fact, products of their imaginations (Curtiss 1989; Cromer 1992; Pinker 1994). Another example is Williams Syndrome, an inherited condition involving physical abnormalities, significant retardation (the average IQ is about 50), incompetence at simple everyday tasks (tying shoelaces, finding one's way, adding two numbers, and retrieving items from a cupboard), social warmth and gregariousness, and fluent, articulate language abilities (Bellugi et al. 1990).

The input to language acquisition consists of sounds and situations; the output is a grammar specifying, for that language, the order and arrangement of abstract entities like nouns, verbs, subjects, phrase structures, control, and c-command. Somehow the child must discover these entities to learn the language. We know that even preschool children have an extensive unconscious grasp of grammatical structure, but how has the child managed to go from sounds and situations to syntactic structure?

Innate knowledge of grammar in itself is not sufficient. It does no good for the child to have written down in his or her brain 'There exist nouns'; children need some way of finding them in parents' speech, so that they can determine, among other things, whether the nouns come before the verb, as in English, or after, as in Irish. Once the child finds nouns and verbs, any innate knowledge would immediately be helpful, because the child could then deduce all kinds of implications about how they can be used. But finding them is the crucial first step, and it is not an easy one.

To understand how X is learned, you first have to understand what X is. Linguistic theory is thus an essential part of the study of language acquisition. Linguistic research tries to do two things. First, it must characterize the facts of English and all the other languages whose acquisition we are interested in explaining. Second, since children are not predisposed to learn English or any other language, linguistics has to examine the structure of other languages. In particular, linguists attempt to determine which aspects of grammar are universal, prevalent, rare, and nonexistent across languages. Contrary to early suspicions, languages do not vary arbitrarily and without limit; there is by now a large catalogue of language universals, properties shared exactly, or in a small number of variations, by all languages (see Greenberg 1978; Comrie 1981). This obviously bears on what children's language acquisition mechanisms find easy or hard to learn.

And one must go beyond a mere list of universals. Many universal properties of language are not specific to language but are simply reflections of universals of human experience. All languages have words for 'water' and 'foot' because all people need to refer to water and feet; no language has a word a million syllables long because no person would have time to say it. But others might be specific to the innate design of language itself. For example, if a language has both derivational suffixes (which create new words from old ones, like '-ism') and inflectional suffixes (which modify a word to fit its role in the sentence, like plural '-s'), then the derivational suffixes are always closer to the word stem than the inflectional ones. Universals, which are specifically linguistic, should be captured in a theory of Universal Grammar (Chomsky 1981, 1991). Universal Grammar specifies the allowable mental representations and operations that all languages are confined to use. The theory of universal grammar is closely tied to the theory of the mental mechanisms children use in acquiring language; their hypotheses about language must be couched in structures sanctioned by Universal Grammar.

4 Conclusions and Implications for Education

By individual differences many scholars mean the 'general' and 'specific' factors of intelligence. The general factor of intelligence, indexed by intelligence quotient (IQ), reflects the fact that individuals tend to show a positive correlation on performance across a range of intellectual tasks. At a given age, the general factor accounts for much of the variability between individuals. In addition to the general factor, there are domain-specific factors such as verbal and spatial ability, which may vary independently within an individual. The exact number of domain-specific abilities is controversial. Individual differences in IQ tend to be relatively stable over time, and IQ in early childhood is predictive of adult IQ level (Hindley and Owen 1978). This fact suggests that IQ corresponds to some inherent property of the cognitive system. A clue as to the nature of this property might be gained from the fact that performance on elementary cognitive tasks with very low knowledge content correlates with performance on intellectual tasks requiring extensive use of knowledge.

On the other hand, by cognitive development we often mean the phenomenon whereby within an individual, the reasoning ability tends to improve with age roughly in parallel across many intellectual domains. Although there may be some mismatch in abilities in different tasks at a given time, by and large children's performance on a wide range of intellectual tasks can be predicted from their age. However, at a certain point in development, children's performance can only be improved to a limited extent by practice and instruction (Siegler 1978a), suggesting that development may not be identical to learning or to the acquisition of more knowledge.

Davis and Anderson (1999) offer a detailed consideration of the theoretical relation of these two forms of cognitive variability. Here I would like to highlight two claims. First, the idea that having a higher IQ is equivalent to having a 'bit more cognitive development' is challenged by the fact that when older children with a lower IQ are matched to younger children with a higher IQ, performance appears qualitatively different. The older children show stronger performance on tasks with a high knowledge component while the younger children show stronger performance on tasks involving abstract reasoning (Spitz 1982).

Second, several theoretical mechanisms have been proposed to underlie individual differences and cognitive development. In terms of mechanisms that might underlie differences in IQ, several authors have proposed differences in speed of processing among basic cognitive components, on the grounds that speed of response in simple cognitive tasks predicts performance on complex reasoning tasks, and that neurophysiological measures such as latency of average evoked potentials and speed of neural conductivity correlate with IQ (Eysenck 1986; Nettelbeck 1987; Anderson 1999). Sternberg (1983) has proposed differences in the ability to control and co-ordinate the basic processing mechanisms, rather than in the functioning of the basic components themselves. Finally, Dempster (1991) has proposed differences in the ability to inhibit irrelevant information in lower cognitive processes, since individuals can show large neuroanatomical differences in the frontal lobes, the neural bases of executive function.

In terms of mechanisms that might underlie cognitive development, we once more find speed of processing offered as a factor that may drive improvement in reasoning ability. Case (1985) suggested that an increase in speed of processing aids development via an effective increase in short term storage space, allowing more complex concepts to be represented. Halford (1999) proposed that the construction of representations of higher dimensionality or greater complexity is driven by an increase in processing capacity, where processing capacity is a measure of the cognitive resources allocated to a task.

On the one hand, then, previous theories relating individual differences to cognitive development proposed that cognitive development is not equivalent to 'more IQ' and thus that development and intelligence are variations on different cognitive dimensions. On the other hand, the lists of hypothetical mechanisms postulated to drive variability in each domain show several overlaps (speed, inhibition), suggesting that development and intelligence could represent variations on the same cognitive dimension(s). There is no current consensus in this respect.

The last conclusion could be: in the psychometric and behaviorist eras, it was generally believed that intelligence was a single entity that was inherited, and that human beings—initially a blank slate—could be trained to learn anything, provided that it was presented in an appropriate way. Nowadays an increasing number of researchers believe precisely the opposite, namely that there exists a multitude of intelligences, quite independent of each other, that each intelligence has its own strengths and constraints, that the mind is far from blank at birth, and that it is unexpectedly difficult to teach things that go against early naive theories that challenge the natural lines of force within an intelligence and its matching domains.

As Gardner (1993) repeatedly points out, Western perceptions of intelligence are often limited to tests which assess verbal-linguistic or mathematical–logical skills. Historically, programs that serve students who are designated as gifted are reflective of this narrow cultural and educational mindset. Multiple intelligence dramatically broadens categories of giftedness. Thus, programs based on Multiple intelligence have the potential to include students having gifts, or combinations of gifts, from Gardner's other categories—bodily-kinesthetic, musical, spatial, interpersonal, intrapersonal, and, soon to be elaborated, naturalistic intelligence. This broadened array greatly appeals to those teachers and parents who hold a more egalitarian or comprehensive view that every child has a gift or combined gifts.

While, generally, teachers seem to accept the underlying philosophical constructs of inclusion, their major concerns appear to be related to questions of implementation, to administrative levels of support, or to their own standards of professional training. But one of the more common philosophical views that is continually voiced is that inclusive practices serve only limited numbers of teachers—those who fall into narrowly prescribed categories at both ends of the intellectual spectrum. Graduates speaking out on related issues point to the fact that special, categorical designations provide for unequal funding and time commitments and leave the majority of students unserved or supported by special programs, specialists, federal or state mandates or funds, enrichment programs, and the like. Teachers appear to hold the opinion that the lack of support for differentiated instruction for average pupils is one of the glaring inequities in educational practices. In these instances, many teachers believe that Multiple intelligence has the potential to serve as a foundation for justifying expanded notions of giftedness and for extending the definition of giftedness to cover broader populations.

While there are many reasons for the educational popularity of Multiple Intelligence, the key to comprehending the theory's burgeoning acceptance seem to be the basic needs of teachers as they try to provide more inclusive, affective and effective instruction. These basic teaching needs are primarily related to promoting understanding and appreciation among students, creating classrooms where learners experience a sense of loving and belonging, fostering pupils' self-esteem, personal intellectual empowerment and self-motivation, and helping teachers employ more diversified instructional techniques. Multiple intelligence Theory has taken hold in classrooms because it helps educators meet the needs of many different types of learners easily, and because it reflects teachers' and parents' deeply-rooted conviction that all children possess gifts and that the most important mission of schools is to foster positive personal development.

References

Anderson, M., ed. 1999. *The development of intelligence*. Hove: Psychology Press.

Bates, E. 1989. Functionalism and the competition model. In eds. B. MacWhinney, and E. Bates, 3–73.

Bellugi, U., A. Bihrle, T. Jernigan, D. Trauner, and S. Doherty. 1990. Neuropsychological, neurological, and neuroanatomical profile of Williams Syndrome. *American Journal of Medical Genetics Supplement* 6: 115–125.

Binet, A., and T. Simon. 1916/2007. *The development of intelligence in children*. Trans. E. Kit. Williams and Wilkins (original). Baltimore: Kessinger Publishing (reprint).

Boring, E.G. 1923. Intelligence as the tests test it. *New Republic* 35: 35–37.

Bornstein, A., and J. Bruner, eds. 1989. *Interaction in human development*. Hillsdale: Lawrence Erlbaum.

Case, R. 1985. *Intellectual development: Birth to adulthood*. Orlando: Academic Press.

Chomsky, N., ed. 1975. *Reflections on language*. New York: Random House.

Chomsky, N. 1981. *Lectures on government and binding*. Dordrecht: Foris Publications.

Chomsky, N. 1991. Linguistics and cognitive science: Problems and mysteries. In ed. A. Kasher, 26–53.

Coles, R. 1997. *The moral intelligence of children*. New York: Random House.

Comrie, B. 1981. *Language universals and linguistic typology*. Chicago: University of Chicago Press.

Cromer, R.F. 1992. *Language and thought in normal and handicapped children*. Cambridge: Blackwell.

Curtiss, S. 1989. The independence and task-specificity of language. In eds. A. Bornstein, and J. Bruner, 105–137.

Davis, H., and Anderson, M. 1999. Individual differences and development—one dimension or two? In ed. M. Anderson, 161–191.

Dempster, F.N. 1991. Inhibitory processes: A neglected dimension of intelligence. *Intelligence* 15: 157–173.

Eysenck, H. 1986. The theory of intelligence and the psychophysiology of cognition. In eds. R.J. Sternberg, and D.K. Detterman, 1–34.

Fodor, J.A. 1983. *Modularity of mind*. Cambridge: Bradford Books, MIT Press.

Gardner, H. 1993. *Frames of mind: The theory of multiple intelligences*. Britain: Fontana Press.

Goleman, D. 1996. *Emotional intelligence: Why it can matter more than IQ*. New York: Bantam Books.

Gopnik, J., and M. Crago. 1991. Familial aggregation of a developmental language disorder. *Cognition* 39: 1–50.

Greenberg, J., ed. 1978. *Universals of human language*. 4 vols syntax. Stanford: Stanford University Press.

Guilford, J.P. 1967. *The nature of human intelligence*. New York: McGraw-Hill.

Halford, G. 1999. The development of intelligence includes the capacity to process relations of greater complexity. In ed. M. Anderson, 193–214.

Hindley, C.B., and C.E. Owen. 1978. The extent of individual changes in IQ for ages between 6 months and 17 years in a British longitudinal sample. *Journal of Child Psychology and Psychiatry* 19: 329–350.

Kasher, A., ed. 1991. *The Chomskyan turn*. Cambridge: Blackwell.

MacWhinney, B., and E. Bates, eds. 1989. *The crosslinguistic study of sentence processing*. New York: Cambridge University Press.

Nettelbeck, T. 1987. Inspection time and intelligence. In ed. P.A. Vernon, 295–346.

Pinker, S. 1994. *The language instinct*. New York: Morrow.

Plomin, R., J.C. DeFries, G.E. McClearn, and P. McGuffin. 2001. *Behavioral genetics*. New York: Freeman.

Putnam, H. 1971. The 'innateness hypothesis' and explanatory models in linguistics. In ed. J. Searle, 12–23.

Searle, J., ed. 1971. *The philosophy of language*. New York: Oxford University Press.

Siegler, R.S. 1978a. The origins of scientific reasoning. In ed. R.S. Siegler, 109–149.

Siegler, R.S., ed. 1978b. *Children's thinking: What develops?*. Hillsdale: Lawrence Erlbaum.

Spearman, C. 1923. *The nature of 'intelligence' and the principles of cognition*. London: Macmillan.

Spitz, H.H. 1982. Intellectual extremes, mental age, and the nature of human intelligence. *Merrill-Palmer Quarterly* 28: 167–192.

Steele, C.M. 1992. Race and the schooling of black Americans. *The Atlantic Monthly*, 68–78.

Sternberg, R.J. 1983. Components of human intelligence. *Cognition* 15: 1–48.

Sternberg, R.J. 1985. *Beyond IQ: A triarchic theory of human intelligence*. New York: Cambridge University Press.

Sternberg, R.J. 1994. *Encyclopedia of human intelligence*. New York: Macmillan.

Sternberg, R.J., and D.K. Detterman, eds. 1986. *What is intelligence: Contemporary viewpoints on its nature and definition*. Norwood: Ablex.

Terman, M.L. 1916. *The measurement of intelligence: An explanation of and a complete guide for the use of the Stanford revision and extension of the Binet-Simon Intelligence Scale*. Boston: Houghton Mifflin.

Thurstone, L.L. 1924/1973. *The nature of intelligence*. London: Routledge.

Vernon, P.A., ed. 1987. *Speed of information-processing and intelligence*. Norwood: Ablex.

The Relationship Between Multiple Intelligences and Teaching Style

Anna Michońska-Stadnik

Abstract The aim of this article is to present a piece of research devoted to the relationship between teachers' teaching style and their multiple intelligences profile. The theory of Multiple Intelligences, as it was presented by Howard Gardner, tries to prove that human beings are characterized by several types of intelligences, with a few of them clearly dominating. In this way, earlier theories describing the construct in question appear to be invalid, at least to some extent. The IQ tests, which measure only a few separate abilities, cannot represent the whole construct of intelligence. The teaching styles chosen for the study were established on the basis of earlier descriptions by different authors. For the purpose of this research three teaching styles were compiled: the counseling style, the authoritarian style and the affective style. By means of observations, a questionnaire and Multiple Intelligences Inventory, the existing relationship was revealed to show that all teachers were characterized by linguistic intelligence and other personal intelligences varied depending on their teaching style.

1 Early Concepts of Intelligence and Intelligence Measurements

Together with the development of modern psychology at the beginning of the twentieth century, scholars started to make efforts to define what it means to be intelligent. Initially, intelligence was understood as a unified concept; a human feature which is genetic in its origin. Gardner (1993) mentions theories of Lewis

A. Michońska-Stadnik (✉)
University of Wrocław, Wrocław, Poland
e-mail: michsta@uni.wroc.pl

M. Pawlak (ed.), *New Perspectives on Individual Differences in Language Learning and Teaching*, Second Language Learning and Teaching, DOI: 10.1007/978-3-642-20850-8_8, © Springer-Verlag Berlin Heidelberg 2012

Madison Terman and Charles Spearman from the first half of the twentieth century who viewed intelligence as a general human capacity for developing concepts and solving problems. In 1949 Donald O. Hebb (see Gardner 1993) distinguished between two types of intelligence: *type A* and *type B*. Intelligence A is an innate capacity depending completely on an individual's neurological faculties. This ability should enable an individual to develop intelligent responses to stimuli from the environment. If such an interaction occurs, the level of development of intelligent responses is what constitutes intelligence B. In 1964 Philip E. Vernon (see Williams and Burden 1997) supplemented this theory with the third type of intelligence—*type C*, which is measured by IQ tests. It can be assumed, then, that IQ tests measure a separate construct of intelligence, different from both the innate type and the environmental type.

Another concept of intelligence was introduced in 1985 by Robert Sternberg. In his *triarchic theory of intelligence* the emphasis is mainly put on the idea of intelligent behavior as the appropriate use of cognitive skills and strategies within a specific context. Sternberg (1985) viewed intelligence in terms of people's purposeful adaptation to the real world, and consequently it was supposed to consist of three components. Thus, *metacomponents* are those cognitive skills which are employed in planning and decision-making. Thanks to these abilities people can recognize the existence of a given problem and are aware of different strategies which can be used to solve it. They are then able to decide which particular strategies should be used in a given real-life context and which should be abandoned, at least for the time being. *Performance components* actually execute a strategy for solving a task, encode information, include the basic operations involved in inferential thinking and drawing comparisons. *Knowledge-acquisition components* are the processes used while acquiring new knowledge; they determine how fast a new task becomes routine, help in selecting relevant information and integrate new knowledge in a meaningful way with what is already known (Williams and Burden 1997: 20). Later, as Ronald Kellogg (1995: 401) reports, Sternberg additionally proposed two more subcomponents of intelligence: *experiential* and *contextual*. Experiential intelligence tells us how well individuals can cope with novelty and familiarity. Sternberg assumes that people differ in their ability to cope with new situations and to handle routine tasks. The experiential component is an attempt to define these differences. On the other hand, the contextual component tells us how well people can pertain and adjust to the surrounding environment. In the light of Sternberg's theory, intelligent behavior is concerned with being able to adapt to the requirements of the environment. It is also possible to adapt the environment to suit the needs and demands of an individual.

Since IQ tests have been mentioned above, it seems necessary to devote some space to early measurements of intelligence. In 1904 the Ministry of Public Instruction in Paris appointed a commission to establish procedures for the education of mentally impaired children attending primary schools in the city. The purpose of those procedures was to make a clear and reliable distinction between the children who could and those who could not succeed in mainstream school education, and a special program was to be prepared for the latter. In 1905 the psychologist Alfred Binet in cooperation with Paul Simon (cf. Eysenck 1990) constructed his first measurement instrument, afterwards called the *Binet–Simon scale*. It contained a set of thirty problems which concentrated on such mental faculties as judgment, comprehension and reasoning (Eysenck 1990: 11). These tasks were constructed in such a way that they could be understood without the benefit of school learning. If it appeared that a child whose chronological age was eight was able to solve problems appropriate for the age of ten, the mental age of the child was higher than his/her chronological age. The IQ (intelligence quotient) is the proportion of mental age and chronological age multiplied by one hundred to get rid of the decimal point. Consequently, $10:8 = 1.25 \times 100 = 125$, which means that the child referred to earlier represented the IQ of 125. Afterwards, it so happened that a test for children became associated with the construct itself, i.e. the IQ scale started to represent the notion of general intelligence.

Since most psychologists agree that intelligence testing was one of their greatest achievements, it is necessary to point out several complications connected with measuring intelligence. First of all, some specialists (e.g. Stern 1983) admit that IQ test results are a powerful predictor of success in classroom education, including foreign language learning. On the other hand, it appears that they have relatively little predictive power outside the school setting since more influential factors such as the economic and social background should be taken into account. This view is represented by Gardner (1993). Similarly, Michael Long (2000: 77) presents contrasting evidence as regards IQ tests as predictors of academic achievement. He argues that many research findings indicate only a limited relationship between these two measures. Any correspondence which does exist can yield many alternative interpretations. One of those is that the academic skill itself might have some effect on IQ, or that the tests might be influenced by a variety of other general factors, for example by motivation or lack of concentration. IQ tests are also heavily reliant on verbal abilities, and even the other, seemingly non-verbal test items are strongly affected by verbal processes. It appears that verbal knowledge is an important basis for academic progress. Consequently, there must be a strong correlation between school attainment tests and IQ tests because they both depend on the same ability.

The results of intelligence tests, as Kellogg (1995) claims, have also been dissatisfying when it comes to helping teachers understand the behavior of particular children. The IQ estimates a child's mental abilities at a given moment and it varies over time, which means that it has low predictive power as regards the child's future cognitive achievements.

One more difficulty with IQ tests arises when we consider measuring adult intelligence. The original tests were intended for children. With time, the use of standardized tests became widespread also among adults. The question remains how to relate the adult mental age to chronological age, when chronological age increases and mental age remains constant after adolescence. Theoretically, it would mean a constant decrease of an individual's IQ level, which in fact does not happen until very late in life, together with the lowering of cognitive processing capacity. All in all, what we need to remember is the fact that IQ tests are good measures of what most people recognize as intelligence, but it does not mean that a single IQ score can be considered a definite measurement of the competence of an individual.

There are also more sophisticated versions of the IQ test and one of them is the Scholastic Aptitude Test (SAT), used excessively in the United States (Gardner 1993: 6). It is a similar kind of measure, where a person is evaluated on the basis of their verbal and math score. Both scores are added up and in this way an individual is rated along a single intellectual dimension. When somebody scores more than 130, he/she can be admitted to a special program for gifted students.

In reference to foreign/second language learning, special attention should be focused on the relationship between intelligence and language aptitude. Gass and Selinker (2008) report that there seems to be no straightforward relationship between these two constructs. Some researchers claim that "language aptitude is simply due to intelligence in general" (Gass and Selinker 2008: 420). Others, however, state that "statistical investigations have demonstrated that language aptitude cannot be explained simply on the basis of the most common measurement of intelligence, IQ scores. There are clearly many overlapping traits, but there is not a one-to-one correspondence between measures on a general IQ test and measures of aptitude" (Gass and Selinker 2008: 420).

2 Multiple Intelligences: An Alternative View

The idea of a multiplicity of intelligences as we know it in the form presented by Gardner in his book entitled *Frames of mind: the theory of multiple intelligences* first published in 1983, is a contribution to the pluralistic tradition which began in the 1960s. Gardner (1993: xvi) extended these theories and suggested that "intelligences are always expressed in the context of specific tasks, domains, and disciplines". Gardner is currently Professor of Cognition and Education at the Harvard Graduate School of Education and adjunct professor of neurology at the Boston University School of Medicine. His work connected with multiple intelligences (MI) has had a profound impact on thinking and practice in education, including foreign language learning and teaching.

The MI theory proposes an alternative definition of intelligence based on a radically different view of the mind. Gardner suggests a pluralistic view of the mind, "acknowledging that people have different cognitive strengths and contrasting cognitive styles" (Christison 1998: 3). These styles allow people to solve problems and offer products according to their intellectual preferences. Therefore, the same real-life situation may provoke completely different reactions from different people.

Gardner also proposed the distinction among *intelligences, domains* and *fields*. Human intelligences are part of our birthright. We are born into cultures which are characterized by a number of domains, be it crafts and disciplines in which a person becomes acculturated and has the ability to pass beyond the novice level.

If a person achieves a certain competence, the field, which includes people, institutions, etc. becomes important for it secures judgment whether a person is successful in practicing.

Gardner's propositions were convincing and supported by 20 years of thorough psychological research. Although mainstream psychology either criticized or ignored his ideas at the beginning, nowadays more and more researchers are inclined to be in favor of the existence of a multitude of intelligences which appear to be quite independent of each other, and each has its own characteristic components. It so happened that the usefulness of the concept was first recognized by applied linguists and second language acquisition specialists, even before it was appreciated by psychologists. The MI theory seems to provide a basis for a number of educational implications that are worthy of serious consideration.

As it appears, very little research has been done in connection with adult intelligence. Therefore, the aim of this paper is to find out whether there is any relationship between teachers' prevailing intelligence types and their teaching styles. Most research on multiple intelligences concerned learners and classroom presentation techniques suitable for different intelligence types. The research described here focuses on teachers and their instruction preferences correlated with their MI spectrum.

2.1 The Eight Intelligences

Initially, Gardner defined seven intelligences: linguistic (verbal), logical–mathematical, spatial, musical, kinesthetic, interpersonal and intrapersonal. In 1999 naturalistic intelligence was added but, as Mary Ann Christison (1998: 4) says, "the list is not meant to be final or exhaustive. We differ in the particular intelligence profiles with which we are born and the ways in which we develop them". In the course of life some individuals develop particular intelligences more than others, which may be caused either by different training or inheritance of certain characteristics from parents. The cognitive capacities are used concurrently and usually complement each other as individuals develop skills and solve problems. The description of the eight intelligence types presented below has been taken from Gardner (1993).

Linguistic intelligence is the ability to use language to convey a variety of different meanings, the ability to memorize information, to show sensitivity to the meaning of words, their order, sounds and rhythms. *Musical intelligence* is referred to as the ability to distinguish meaning and importance in a collection of pitches arranged in a rhythmical way, and to produce such sets. This competence starts developing as the first of all the intelligences in children. *Logical–mathematical* intelligence enables people to confront the world of objects, to order and reorder them, and to assess their quantity. It entails the ability to use numbers effectively and reason well. For *spatial intelligence*, the most essential are the abilities to see the visual world accurately, to transform and modify one's initial perceptions, to produce a graphic likeness of spatial information. It is characteristic of people with *bodily-kinesthetic intelligence* that they use their body in various skilled ways, to work skillfully with different objects, involving movements of fingers and hands. Generally, this intelligence allows us to control body motions. *Intrapersonal intelligence* helps to build an accurate mental model of oneself, and to draw upon this model while making decisions about one's life. It is the ability to engage in self-analysis and reflection. *Interpersonal intelligence*, on the other hand, entails the capacity to discriminate among other individuals and their moods. These skills permit us to read other people's intentions and desires, to understand their behaviors and motivations. Finally, *naturalistic intelligence* enables people to recognize, categorize and draw upon certain features of the surrounding environment. It includes such abilities as recognizing and classifying plants, minerals, and animals.

2.2 Criteria for Recognition of Intelligences

Gardner isolated his eight types of intelligences on the basis of several groups of evidence. He concentrated on those activities which were affected by damage in different parts of the brain, and on this ground he established that those intelligences are independent faculties in the human mind. For instance, it is said that the most crucial site for spatial processing are the posterior parts of the right hemisphere. It has been documented that a brain stroke or other kinds of trauma lesions to the right parietal regions of the brain will cause problems in visual attention, spatial representation and orientation, memory and imagery production. Hence a conclusion that spatial intelligence is a separate faculty the responsibilities of which cannot be taken over to the same degree by any other intelligence.

To support his theories, Gardner also paid attention to the activities which were represented by exceptional people, namely prodigies and idiot savants. Both types of individuals exhibit one particular ability at a very high level of competence, and performance in other domains may be average, mediocre or even nonexistent (cf. autistic children). This kind of behavior enables us to see human intelligences in isolation and it proves that specific brain regions are responsible for specific intelligences.

Further evidence for the existence of seven distinct types of intelligences comes from operations. Gardner argues for the presence of basic information processing mechanisms which are able to deal with various kinds of input from the environment. Unfortunately, because of a lack of appropriate tools that would prove helpful in establishing that core operations exist, their identification is a matter of guesswork. Still, it is believed that, for instance, sensitivity to pitch is a core of musical intelligence, and the ability to imitate movement is a core of bodily intelligence.

Each intelligence has its own developmental history—its time of arising in childhood, its time of peaking during one's lifetime, and its time of gradual decline. Musical intelligence, for example, peaks early, but linguistic or logical–

mathematical intelligence can peak very late. A true intelligence can have its development traced through the evolution of homo sapiens. Yet another argument which Gardner used to isolate the eight intelligences is supported by the results of experimental psychological tasks and psychometric findings. Experiments provided support for the assertion that certain abilities are, or are not, manifestations of the same intelligences.

The last but not least criterion by which an intelligence can be judged comes from the idea that much of human representation of knowledge takes place through symbol systems like language, pictures or mathematics. Humans have developed many kinds of symbol systems for various disciplines of life. A true intelligence has its own set of images it uses, which are unique to it and important in completing certain kinds of tasks.

The eight intelligences are usually assessed by means of checked statement tests (cf. Christison 1998: 11–13), where each ability is described by ten statements. The testees are to check all the statements which seem to be true about them. In this way, individuals may plot their intelligence profile as in most cases people possess more than one dominating intelligence. Christison's survey was prepared especially for teachers of a foreign language and therefore it was used in the reported study to be correlated with teaching styles.

3 Teaching Styles

Teaching style may be defined as "the manner in which the teacher interprets his or her role within the context of the classroom" (Katz 1996: 58). Styles are created on the basis of theories of teaching and learning and the kind of classroom interaction teachers believe best supports these theories. Numerous divisions of teaching styles have been created and it is beyond the scope of this paper to describe all of them in detail. It is enough to mention Katz's (1996) metaphorical teaching styles: *the choreographer, the earth mother, the entertainer* and *the professor*, as well as Komorowska's (2001) *autocratic style, laissez-faire style, paternalistic style, consultative style, partaking style* and *democratic style*. On the basis of these and other classifications, the following division of teaching styles has been developed by researchers (Strojna 2004).

3.1 The Authoritarian Style

Teachers whose classroom behavior can be described in terms of the authoritarian style act like experts and disciplinarians. Their style consists in taking over the whole control over the group, independent formulation of goals and plans without consulting the students, giving orders and demanding their precise and obedient fulfillment. This type of teacher is characterized by broad knowledge of the subject taught and the lack of interest in the techniques and methodology of teaching it. They rely on a small range of individual and intuitive techniques, and are rather inflexible. They do not check learning progress systematically, they neither give nor get feedback from their learners. Hence, they have difficulties with responding to learners' styles and needs. A teacher of this kind stresses class attendance by establishing procedures concerning absences and lateness, sets basic rules of behavior during the lessons, including those which are connected with the way the learners sit in the room. Authoritarian teachers believe that each subject has got a certain content to be passed from the teacher to learners and this is what they concentrate on. In their opinion the subject they teach is central and the teacher 'embodies' the subject. The teacher's main responsibility is to evaluate and correct learners' performance on tasks where high standards are set. An authoritarian teacher is the source and the organizer of everything that happens in class. The lessons are structured in such a way that teacher-class interaction, like questions and answers, is the prevailing type of class talk. This allows teachers to preserve control over the content and the direction of tasks. If any explanation, summary or description is required during the lesson, they supply all the answers themselves, not letting students detract from the route they set.

3.2 The Affective Style

It is a contradiction of the authoritarian style. It is characterized by a complete liberty of learners and almost complete lack of any limitations. Teachers make their decisions on the basis of previously gained knowledge of their students, taking it into consideration while working out the final solutions. This type of teachers encourage their learners to state their opinions and they listen to them carefully. They try to involve learners in the process of decision-making, hence learners may have influence on the choice of tasks they are to complete or the deadlines for those tasks. However, it does not always mean that those decisions reflect the learners' point of view. Regardless of the final outcome, learners always participate in the process of decision-making. The most important task for the teacher is to be able to take into account what learners think without losing the position of the leader at the same time. Teachers employ this style of teaching if they want to build an atmosphere of mutual respect in the classroom, if they want to get to know their learners well, and if they want them to cooperate harmoniously.

Unlike the previous type of teachers, affective teachers do not only have the knowledge of the topic they teach, but are also acquainted with a variety of methods and techniques helpful in the process of teaching. They are able to employ them in their classrooms and thus they can come into better contact with their learners, their learning processes and needs. They seek opportunities for professional development, such as workshops and training courses as well as for exchanging ideas and experiences with their colleagues.

While in the previously described teaching style control over learners' behavior and their learning was most important for the teacher, the affective style is mainly concerned with maintaining good human relationships. The affective teacher is usually lenient with the lateness policy so as not to create any unnecessary tension between him/her and the learners. These teachers do their best to show the learners the importance of interpersonal contact, make sure no one stays anonymous during the school year, encourage students to help each other, to share ideas and exchange information. They are interested in students' family life, problems they have, and want to know their learners as well as they can.

Since the emphasis is put on communication among learners, the lessons are so structured as to ensure group interaction. If the teacher addresses a question to the class, he/she expects volunteers to answer rather than force students. The affective teacher tries to inspire learners to share responsibility for everything that happens in class. He/she provides information and procedures to help learners go through the assigned material at the same time making sure that the atmosphere they are to work in is conducive to their development. He/she wants to make room for some unpredictability, to leave space for learners' own ideas which they can incorporate in the course of the lesson.

3.3 The Counseling Style

This is the most infrequent style practiced by teachers. It consists in delineating very precise and strict lines within which learners are allowed to behave. The basic goals which are to be realized are stated clearly by the teacher; he/she also sets the minimum of didactic and educational requirements. The rest is a question of agreement between the members of the group and their teacher. This style guarantees order and realization of educational goals but also gives learners freedom of choice of the form and speed of work. It prepares them to be autonomous learners of the foreign language, teaches responsibility and self-dependence.

The counseling teacher is the one who has the knowledge of the subject-matter, is familiar with teaching methods and techniques, but also pays much attention to the learning atmosphere concentrating on individual differences between learners. Such a teacher is aware of the fact that the feeling of close relationship between the group members, security felt by individuals, teacher's sensitivity to learners' needs and self-esteem are conducive to high quality learning. For them, knowledge is the ability to organize one's thoughts, to interpret facts and to act on them.

These teachers are not such strict disciplinarians, control is maintained not by setting strict rules to be obeyed, but by persuasion. The teacher's main task is to create such atmosphere which would enable their learners to reorganize their state of knowledge, develop their comprehension of the subject and improve their personalities.

4 Description of the Study

As was stated before, the aim of the study was to see if there exists any relationship between the teaching style represented by individual teachers and their dominating multiple intelligence types. There were eight female teachers who agreed to participate in the study (A–H). All of them were non-native teachers of English as a second language in secondary schools in Wrocław. They were all experienced teachers who had been working for at least five years, each of them around the age of thirty. The oldest teacher was 42 years old. The research method used in the study can be referred to as cross-sectional focused description. There were three data collecting instruments used: the Multiple Intelligences Inventory for English language teachers, adapted form Christison (1998: 11–13), an observation chart, and a questionnaire for establishing teaching styles. The observation chart consisted of four main groups of issues: ways of maintaining discipline in the classroom, class grouping structure, classroom interaction structure and creating positive classroom atmosphere. The main issues were divided into more detailed examples of behaviors and the observers were to mark the occurrences of a particular behavior on the chart. Each teacher was observed twice and they were not informed about the purpose of observation. The last instrument was the questionnaire, where the teachers were to answer 19 questions. These questions were formulated on the basis of the characteristics of the three teaching styles described in the previous part (see Appendix). The questionnaires were distributed after the observations had been completed.

5 Research Results

Table 1 above presents the results of the research project. The individual teaching styles were established on the basis of observations and completed teachers' questionnaires. On the basis of the observation charts and the questionnaire, four teachers were described as representing the counseling teaching style, two could be classified as authoritarian and the remaining two as affective. The MI profiles they possessed included mostly three types of intelligence: linguistic, interpersonal and intrapersonal. It may be presumed that the teaching activities themselves develop linguistic intelligence as the verbal abilities are supposed to be inherent in the profession. There are, however, differences among individual teachers as far as other elements of their intelligence profiles are concerned. It can be noticed that the counseling teaching style is characterized by interpersonal intelligence, i.e. these teachers seem to relate well with other people. On the other hand, authoritarian teachers represent the intrapersonal MI type, i.e. they are directed inwards, caring more for their own mental and affective well-being than for other people (e.g. learners and their emotions). Affective teachers are also characterized by intrapersonal intelligence.

Table 1 Research results

Teacher	Teaching style	Dominating intelligences
A	Counseling	Linguistic, interpersonal, spatial
B	Authoritarian	Linguistic, intrapersonal
C	Counseling	Linguistic, interpersonal, bodily-kinesthetic
D	Affective	Intrapersonal, interpersonal, linguistic
E	Counseling	Linguistic, interpersonal, naturalistic
F	Authoritarian	Linguistic, intrapersonal, musical
G	Affective	Linguistic, intrapersonal, interpersonal
H	Counseling	Linguistic, spatial, interpersonal

After having analyzed the obtained data, we may intend to ask a question: had all these teachers been linguistic before they chose that occupation or did they become linguistic after they had chosen it? Another interesting issue is whether the teachers who have already developed a particular teaching style chose this one over the others because they were influenced by the traits of their intelligence, or is the teaching style responsible for a particular type of intelligence to develop? These and other questions may be addressed in further research on the same issue. The study described above, without going into deeper psychological analysis, was only able to confirm the existing relationship between the teaching style and the profile of multiple intelligences.

Appendix

Questionnaire for ESL teachers

1. Do you prepare lesson plans?

   Yes
   No
   Sometimes

2. If your answer is 'yes', do you manage to carry out all the tasks you included in your lesson plan?

   Yes
   No
   Sometimes

3. Do you clearly state goals at the beginning of the lesson?

   Yes
   No
   Sometimes

4. If your answer is 'yes', are you able to say at the end of the lesson that you completed all the goals?

Yes
No
Sometimes

5. What is the dominating type of interaction during your lessons?

Teacher-class
Teacher-student
Student-student

6. What is the dominating type of students' grouping in your lessons?

Individual work
Pairwork
Groups of three
Groups of four and more
Whole class interaction
Other ....

7. Teacher talking time occurs during

Presentation
Practice
Production
Other parts of the lesson

8. Do you encourage your students to participate actively in the lesson?

Yes
No
Sometimes

9. How do you encourage your students to participate actively?

By asking questions
By including interesting topics
By praising students
Other ....

10. Do you provide your students with feedback?

Yes
No
Sometimes

11. What forms of feedback do you use?

Individual written comments
Individual oral comments

Immediate feedback
Delayed feedback
Informative feedback
Other forms ....

12. Do you encourage volunteers to answer questions in your lessons?

Yes
No
Sometimes

13. In what situations?

When nobody starts the discussion
When some students have specific information on particular topics
When asking a volunteer student may encourage others to speak
Other situations ....

14. Do you try to pass on responsibility to the learners for their own learning?

Yes
No
I don't know

15. In what ways do you do this?

I guide them to be aware of their language learning needs
I teach them how to plan their own learning process
I teach them how to find and use additional sources and materials
I encourage them to cooperate
I make them aware of the existence of various learning strategies and encourage their usage
Other ways ....

16. Do you have problems with maintaining classroom discipline?

Yes
No
Sometimes

17. How do you try to maintain classroom discipline?

I give bad marks for improper behavior
I administer tests as punishment
I use voice and gestures
I shout at my students
Other ways ....

18. Do you think your personality plays a role in shaping classroom relationships?

Yes
No

I don't know

19. Your role in the teaching process:

Instructing
Controlling
Organizing
Facilitating
Participating
Modeling
Evaluating
Motivating
Other roles ....

References

Bailey, K.M., and D. Nunan, eds. 1996. *Voices from the language classroom*. Cambridge: Cambridge University Press.

Christison, M.A. 1998. Applying multiple intelligences theory. *English Language Teaching Forum* 36: 9–13.

Eysenck, H.J. 1990 [1962]. *Know your own IQ*. London: Penguin Books.

Gardner, H. 1993. *Frames of mind: The theory of multiple intelligences*, (second edition). London: Fontana Press.

Gass, S.M., and L. Selinker. 2008. *Second language acquisition: An introductory course*, (third edition). New York and London: Routledge/Taylor and Francis Group.

Katz, A. 1996. Teaching style: A way to understand instruction in language classrooms. In eds. K.M. Bailey, and D. Nunan, 57–87.

Kellogg, R.T. 1995. *Cognitive psychology*. London: SAGE Publications.

Komorowska, H. 2001. *Metodyka nauczania języków obcych*. [*Methodology of foreign language teaching*]. Warszawa: Fraszka Edukacyjna.

Long, M. 2000. *The psychology of education*. London and New York: Routledge/Falmer.

Stern, H.H. 1983. *Fundamental concepts of language teaching*. Oxford: Oxford University Press.

Sternberg, R. 1985. *Beyond IQ: A triarchic theory of human intelligence*. Cambridge: Cambridge University Press.

Strojna, K. 2004. *The influence of multiple intelligences on teaching style*. Unpublished M. A. thesis. Uniwersytet Wrocławski: Instytut Filologii Angielskiej.

Williams, M., and R. Burden. 1997. *Psychology for language teachers*. Cambridge: Cambridge University Press.

Individual Differences: A Question of Meta Program Variety

Fatma Alwan

Abstract Personality types are determined by thinking styles known in Neuro-Linguistic Programming (NLP) as 'meta programs'. These programs work as filters, determine our perception of experiences and underpin the personality type of each individual. They are context specific and may change with time. This article discusses personality types according to five complex meta programs and aims to enable teachers to deal with students according to their individual differences from this perspective. The five meta programs are presented according to the type of filter they relate to. First, the motivation direction filter consists of two meta programs: 'towards' and 'away from'. It indicates values that direct people's actions. Second, the relationship filter which determines how people process new information contains two meta programs: 'sameness' and 'difference'. Third, the way work is carried out, or operation filter has two meta programs: 'options' and 'procedures'. Fourth, the frame of reference filter indicates the decision making process and consists of the 'internal' and 'external' meta programs. Finally, according to the chunk-size filter, there are two ways in which people present information as in the 'specific' and 'global' meta programs. This paper also aims to equip teachers with a theoretical knowledge base that would make them tolerate certain behaviors from students since they will recognize the underpinning cognitive reasons that justify them.

F. Alwan (✉)
Ministry of Education, Abu Dhabi, UAE
e-mail: alwan99@hotmail.com

M. Pawlak (ed.), *New Perspectives on Individual Differences in Language Learning and Teaching*, Second Language Learning and Teaching, DOI: 10.1007/978-3-642-20850-8_9, © Springer-Verlag Berlin Heidelberg 2012

1 Introduction

One of the main tenets of NLP is that people have different models of the world. This view of the world is affected by the individual's past experiences that have shaped his or her beliefs and values, and continue to affect perception of reality (Bandler and Grinder 1975). In experiencing the world, people tend to 'delete' portions of reality; they also 'distort' facts as well as 'generalize' findings (O'Connor and Seymour 1995). These tendencies to delete, distort and generalize vary from one context to another but tend to follow certain patterns within the same context (Hall and Bodenhamer 2005). These ways of thinking are known in NLP as meta programs. These programs direct our mental processes by working as filters, and, consequently, determine our perception of experiences (Woodsmall 1988). Essentially, each person uses a combination of meta programs that is unique and that is reflected in his or her language and behaviour (Charvet 1997).

When people interact, they display certain behavior traits which are determined by meta programs. As James and Woodsmall (1988: 91) put it, "[m]eta programs are the most unconscious filters to our perception (...) they are powerful determinants of personality". They vary in their intensity and can be perceived on a continuum (Charvet 1997). Understanding meta programs does not only contribute to improving communication but it is also a guide in motivating people and building rapport with them by using the appropriate language that matches their preferred types of meta programs. As Revell and Norman (1999: 121) put it, "[i]f you know what the possible patterns are, you can make sure that you stimulate your students in a variety of different and relevant ways".

There are simple meta programs and complex ones. Simple meta programs include the well-known personality types of introvert/extrovert, intuitor/sensor, thinker/feeler, and judger/perceiver. These have been identified by Carl Jung and form the basis for the Myers-Briggs Personality Profile (Woodsmall 1988). As Hall and Bodenhamer (2005) acknowledge, complex meta programs have been identified initially by Leslie-Cameron Bandler and Richard Bandler as factors that interfere with the results of therapy with NLP. Bodenhamer and Hall have further identified 51 meta programs. James and Woodsmall (1988) posit that meta programs can be detected through simple questions in minutes. Nonetheless, behavioral information is a more accurate indicator than verbal answers to identification questions when they seem to contradict each other. In essence, they are context-specific and depend on our physical and emotional state. Hence an individual may prefer certain meta programs at work and different ones at home.

This article explores individual differences on the basis of five perceptual filters, and discusses ways of identifying individual differences in the light of five types of complex meta programs, through the person's language and behaviour. It also suggests what procedures to follow and language to use in the classroom to establish rapport and communicate effectively with the students to match their model of the world.

2 Direction Filter: 'Towards' and 'Away From' Meta Programs

When people act, they are driven by values. Woodsmall (1988: 17) defines values as "those things which a person is willing to invest time, energy and resources to either achieve or avoid". Some people are motivated by positive outcomes and these are said to prefer a 'towards' meta program while others are spurred to action so as to avoid certain negative consequences. Such people are known to favor an 'away from' meta program. In general, as mentioned above, a person may prefer a 'towards' pattern in one aspect of life and an 'away from' pattern in another depending on contextual factors.

In order for teachers to motivate their students, it is recommended to know their preferred motivation direction; whether it is 'towards' or 'away from' and what specific things they seek to gain or avoid. This is essential in making decisions with regard to rewards and punishments. Statistically, people who prefer a towards meta program constitute about 40% of the community, and those who prefer an away from pattern are 40% too. On the other hand, there are people who prefer both towards and away from meta programs and they constitute 20% of the community (Bailey, cited in Woodsmall 1988 and in Charvet 1997). Hence, it pays off to balance the language used in addressing the class to cater for both groups.

When working with individual students, these meta programs can be identified by asking such questions as: 'What do you want (from a teacher) (in a lesson)?', and follow up with: 'What will having (this) do for you?' (Woodsmall 1988). With students who prefer a 'towards' pattern, possible answers could be: 'I want a teacher who is generous with marks', 'I want a lesson that is exciting', or 'I want my teacher to treat me with respect'. With students who tend to prefer an 'away from' pattern, responses like: 'I donot want a teacher who shouts at mistakes', 'I donot want a boring lesson' or 'I donot want a teacher who is strict', it is necessary to indicate clearly that they seek to stay away from certain negative emotions that come as a result of a certain behavior. In whole-class teaching, when it is hard to extract individual information about them, it is beneficial to simply balance verbal communication using 'towards' and 'away from' language.

2.1 'Towards' Meta Program

Students with a preferred 'towards' motivation direction filter are goal-driven. They talk about their wants, achievements and gains, and compete for good grades. They go to school because they "want to learn" (Woodsmall 1988: 19). They respond to rewards and can set priorities and manage them. They are happy when they win or succeed but they become frustrated when they do not get what they want. However, they are not able to recognize what should be avoided or what is wrong.

Teachers should focus on what they can do to help students obtain their goals. They ought to explain how a particular way of teaching or how an activity in the lesson will benefit them. Moreover, it is beneficial to emphasize to these students their future gains as a result of what they are learning. They should be made to experience the pleasure of having what they want in the future, praised, given additional grades and offered prizes or other rewards. To pace their language, teachers can use words like: 'get', 'attain', 'accomplish' and 'attract' (James and Woodsmall 1988; Woodsmall 1988; Charvet 1997; Woodsmall and Woodsmall 1998; Hall and Bodenhamer 2005).

2.2 'Away From' Meta Program

Students who prefer an 'away from' motivation direction seek to avoid problems by moving away from painful outcomes. They come to school because "they have to" (Woodsmall 1988: 19). They always talk about problems and about what they do not want, what they are avoiding and what they want to get rid of. They are motivated to study or work well in class when you threaten or punish them. Such students are not able to organize priorities and it is difficult for them to focus on a goal.

To deal successfully with students who prefer this pattern, a teacher needs to anticipate the problems that they may come up with, and to be prepared to comfort them by telling them that the problems can be eliminated or at least minimized. An appropriate way to motivate students who prefer an 'away from' meta program, in addition, would be to threaten them about the negative consequences if they do not study, pay attention in class, or do their homework, etc. Feel free to use punishments and threats of deducting marks with this type. Talking to them about the dangers of their actions and the future disadvantages is a successful strategy, too. Effective language to use includes words like: 'avoid', 'keep away from', 'prevent' and 'get rid of' (James and Woodsmall 1988; Woodsmall 1988; Charvet 1997; Woodsmall and Woodsmall 1998; Hall and Bodenhamer 2005).

3 Relationship Filter: 'Sameness' and 'Difference' Meta Programs

When encountering new information, people tend to focus on either how it is similar to what they know or different from what they already know. This meta program plays a vital role in affecting our perception of the world. While some people focus on what is present, others pay attention to what is missing, and what is wrong with everything. On the other hand, some people are mixed types, giving attention to similarities and then differences or differences and then similarities. This article focuses on the extreme types of sameness and difference with their exception patterns. According to Bailey (cited in Charvet 1997), people who prefer a sameness filter comprise 5–10% of the community. Similarly, people with a difference relationship filter make up 5–10% of the community, too. In addition, sameness with exception people make up 55–65% and difference with exception individuals represent 20–25% of the community.

When working with individual students, it is feasible for the teacher to identify this filter by asking the question: 'What is the relationship between (…) and (…)?'. Students who filter relationships through sameness will respond with: 'They are the same', 'They are similar' and 'There are common features'. By contrast, those who focus on differences will respond with: 'It has really changed', 'They are different' and 'Everything is new'. To maintain rapport with a large class, teachers should use a mixture of sameness and difference language (Charvet 1997; Woodsmall 1988).

3.1 'Sameness' Meta Program

Students who sort information by similarities tend to talk about common features among things, simplify what they are learning and hate difficulty. Thus they emphasize how the current lesson is similar to a previous one. They accept routine without variety or change and expect others to be like them. As they cannot cope with change and cannot recognize differences, they like to have the same teacher every year, and want the lessons to go in the same way. Nonetheless, the majority of the people are of the less extreme group who tend to filter relationship first through sameness then they recognize exceptions or differences. These people like things to stay the same with a little variety only. They have the ability to cope with slow, gradual change but not the sudden type (James and Woodsmall 1988; Charvet 1997; Woodsmall 1988; Woodsmall and Woodsmall 1998; Hall and Bodenhamer 2005).

When selecting activities, teachers should make sure that their lesson contains activities that students who prefer 'sameness' are familiar with. If they introduce a new activity, they should explain how it is similar to something learners have done before. Routines suit this type. When teachers are new to the class, they should explain that they will make sure that they teach students in the same way they are used to, and there may be some changes in some areas only. It is advisable to use matching language like: 'as you always do', 'exactly as before', 'same as' and 'in common'. Students who prefer a 'sameness with exception' meta program can be addressed with language like: 'the same except', 'better' and 'advanced' (Charvet 1997: 79).

3.2 'Difference' Meta Program

Also known as 'mismatchers', students who prefer to filter relationships from a difference perspective are argumentative, critical of everything, and tend to do the opposite of what they are told. They also focus on reasons why things do not work. Such individuals are perfectionists since they notice what is out of place and can think of exceptions. They love change and complexity but are not able to recognize similarities (James and Woodsmall 1988; Woodsmall 1988; Charvet 1997; Woodsmall and Woodsmall 1998; Hall and Bodenhamer 2005). James and Shephard (2002) posit that teenagers tend to assert their identity through mismatching and that in some cases, this meta program continues into their life as adults.

The teacher should explain to them how what they are learning is different from what they have learned before and make sure to introduce variety into the classroom. At the same time, learners can be expected to give negative feedback about their friends and about the teacher. Fortunately, mismatching language builds rapport with students who prefer this type and thus it is beneficial to use words like: "new, different, revolutionary, unique, radical" (Woodsmall 1988: 33), "totally different, unlike anything else (…) one of a kind, shift, switch, a complete turn around, brand new, unheard of, the only one" (Charvet 1997: 80). James and Shephard (2002) explain that such children tend to disagree with everything said to them and the best way make use of their tendency to mismatch is to ask them to do the opposite.

The less extreme types focus on differences first and then recognize similarities. These individuals are like people who prefer a difference pattern but they also accept some routine and look for exceptions. That is, they focus on differences but also mention similarities casually. To cater for the difference with exception pattern, it is also advisible to mention common features in addition to differences and use language that reflects both difference and similarity (see Sect. 2.1). When addressing them, teachers should emphasize how things are the same first and explain that there is a slight change or improvement on what they are doing.

4 Operation Filter: 'Options' and 'Procedures' Meta Programs

This filter indicates the way work is carried out and whether it is predictable or spontaneous. There are individuals who cannot learn or perform a job without having someone tell them how to do it exactly. There are others, on the other hand, who hate to be told that there is one way of carrying out the job or activity. Thus when students respond to procedures, they are either good at procedures and enjoy following them, or tend to change procedures and figure out other ways to do things. Statistics show that people with a preferred options meta program form

40% of the community, as well as those who prefer a procedures pattern (40%). In addition, there are balanced individuals who prefer both options and procedures types and they make up 20% of the population (Bailey, in Woodsmall 1988).

To identify how individual students prefer to perform, teachers could ask: 'Why did you choose (…)?' (Woodsmall 1988: 33; Charvet 1997: 64). For people with a preferred 'options' meta program, the answer will contain a list of criteria, and for people with a preferred 'procedures' meta program, the answer will consist of a story, or 'how' they did this. For example, a student who favors an 'options' meta program may answer the question: 'Why didnot you do your homework?' by saying 'to gain more time in preparing for the science exam.' A 'procedures' favoring student will explain 'how' and will tell you a story, e.g., 'I arrived home late after school as my father forgot to pick me up on his way back home, and I had to wait for him to arrange for someone else to drive me home. When I reached home, I spent the evening studying for the science exam'.

4.1 'Options' Meta Program

Students who prefer this meta program focus on options and possibilities and tend to justify their actions (Woodsmall 1988). They believe that there is always a better alternative. They also recognize that what they are doing is a choice and there are other options as to what they could do (Woodsmall and Woodsmall 1998). While they are good at designing a process, they are not good at following the steps they have designed themselves as they hate following procedures. Most of all, they hate regulations and routine actions (Woodsmall 1988). Consequently, they like breaking or bending rules and they like variety. As they see it, committing themselves to do something means they have fewer options. However, they may commit themselves to do something till something else comes up (Charvet 1997). They are also interested in theory, not practice (Woodsmall 1988).

To establish rapport with this type, it is advisable to talk about bending rules especially for them and explain how the lesson will expand their options and give them a variety of activities to provide alternatives. It is also necessary to "stress that they are a special case" Woodsmall (1988: 36). Overall, there is a need to use language that emphasizes choice such as: 'other ways', 'choices', 'possibilities' and 'alternatives' (Woodsmall 1988: 20; Charvet 1997: 65).

4.2 'Procedures' Meta Program

Students who prefer this meta program think that there is a correct way of doing a task or of answering a question. They repeat the same procedure again and again in the same way (Charvet 1997) and do not talk about alternatives (Woodsmall 1988). Once they start a procedure, they feel compelled to follow through (Charvet 1997). They have a perception that they are forced to do something and that they do not have a choice in the matter (Woodsmall 1988). However, they are good at following procedures (Woodsmall and Woodsmall 1998). They are stuck when the procedure fails, and do not know how to generate another procedure. They cannot cope when procedures do not work as they cannot recognize variations. Moreover, they like routines and rules but do not like options as they feel stuck with them. As a result, they want teachers to tell them how to carry out an activity, answer a question or even how to study.

When dealing with this type of students, it is necessary to make the procedures of the lesson and the tasks they are required to do clear to them. For instance, it is a good idea to show them in steps how to study vocabulary or write a composition. Instead of providing options, teachers should mention which step they are at. It is better to avoid options or limit them to the minimum. To pace their language, it is advisable to "speak in procedures" (e.g., 'first', 'second', 'then', 'after that', etc.) (Charvet 1997: 66), and use words like: 'procedure', 'the only way', 'correct way' (Woodsmall 1988: 37).

5 Frame of Reference Filter: 'Internal' and 'External' Meta Programs

The decision making process of the individual can be understood if we recognize this Meta program. It indicates the locus of control according to the individual. It also indicates the location of the person's values when evaluating people or experiences (Valentino 2000). The frame of reference filter indicates how people evaluate things or other people. When individuals evaluate anything or anybody, they do this from two perspectives; either they base their judgment on what they think is right or on what others think is right (Woodsmall 1988).

People make judgments and decisions according to either inside or outside standards (Charvet 1997). Based on their responses, we can make predictions about how people would evaluate something (Valentino 2000). It is possible for a teacher to identify a student's frame of reference filter by asking: 'How do you know you are right/have done a good job?' (Woodsmall 1988: 21; Charvet 1997: 50), or 'How would you react to feedback from (…)?', or 'Whom do you involve when you make a decision?' (Charvet 1997: 51). A student who favors an internal (or a self-referent) meta program will respond with: "'I just know', 'I know inside', 'I feel it inside', 'it feels right', 'I decide' (Woodsmall 1988: 21); while a student who prefers an external (or other-referent) meta program responds with: '(my teacher/friend) tells me' or 'my grades show my standard'.

It is worth noting that children start their lives with an external frame of reference and they either keep the frame or develop an internal frame according to their experiences in life (Woodsmall 1988). A teacher should help students to develop an internal check, if not an internal frame through critical thinking tasks.

Teachers who balance their language to cater for both types will maintain rapport with their students. Statistically, people who prefer an internal frame of reference constitute 40% of the community, and those who prefer an external one 40%. Besides, there are people who prefer a combination of the internal and external meta program, and they constitute 20% of the community (Bailey, in Charvet 1997).

5.1 'Internal' Meta Program

Students with an internal frame of reference have their own opinion of what is right and what is not, decide on their own, and use language that indicates their autonomy in decision-making (Woodsmall 1988). They may gather information from different sources but they have the final word about making their decision. As a result, it is difficult for them to accept instructions or feedback from others (Woodsmall and Woodsmall 1998). They do not care to know how others are doing or how they are doing compared to others. If they think that they know more than the teacher, they will not learn. Students who prefer this meta program are self-motivators. In addition, they do not require supervision as they judge the quality of their work by themselves (Charvet 1997). On the other hand, they have relationship difficulties since they do not care to take other people's views into consideration and question what they are told (Woodsmall 1988). Apparently, this is a challenge for the teacher during group work.

To develop rapport with students who prefer an 'internal' frame of reference, teachers should avoid mentioning what other people say about them and, rather, focus on what they think about themselves. They should be told that they need to think for themselves or decide for themselves and given the chance to work independently more often. Further, it is advisable to explain to them why they need to do a task in a certain way (James and Woodsmall 1988; Woodsmall 1988; Charvet 1997; Woodsmall and Woodsmall 1998; Hall and Bodenhamer 2005). Pacing language includes such phrases as: 'Your mind will tell you that I am right', 'Deep inside you will agree with me' (Woodsmall 1988: 22), 'only you can decide' or 'the final decision is yours'.

5.2 'External' Meta Program

Students with an external frame of reference require external feedback and directions. They look for feedback from others like teachers, parents or friends to tell them if they are right or wrong. They even depend on other people to produce their judgments or make their decisions. Basically, they need the opinion of others to decide as they cannot decide on their own (Woodsmall 1988), and they tend to accept what others say without questioning. They are mostly influenced by celebrities or significant others. As a result, they want to know how others are doing or how they are doing compared to others. Thus they are concerned about what their teacher thinks of them. In consequence, they are not able to produce critical judgment (Woodsmall and Woodsmall 1998).

In order to pace students who prefer an external frame of reference, we can tell them what other people think about them, provide them with data and show them statistics. Since they care a lot about teachers' opinions about them and are interested in learning about other students, they should be praised, criticized, given feedback and told what to do. Pacing language includes such phrases as: "other people think, the facts show, this is the way it is, here is some feedback, I will let you know" (Woodsmall 1988: 25).

6 Chunk Size Filter: 'Specific' and 'Global' Meta Program

The ability to break information into different chunk sizes is known as chunking. As pieces of information can be large or small (Valentino 2000), there are two ways in which people present information: some individuals are detailed oriented while others prefer to be global. Similarly, some people can deal with details while others can handle large chunks (Charvet 1997).

There is no specific question for identifying this pattern; however, it can be recognized when the student speaks by simply listening to the amount of detail mentioned. To explore this pattern we can simply prop them to talk about something with: 'Tell me about (…)', or 'Tell me what you want' (Woodsmall 1988: 38). We should also expect the majority of the students to have a preference for large chunks of information as, statistically, people with a preferred small chunk-size filter form 15% of the population while people with a general perspective or large chunk-size filter constitute 60% and those who prefer both patterns are 25%. Some people, on the other hand, may also prefer one type initially but accept the other type of chunk size as a second preference (Bailey, cited in Charvet 1997).

6.1 'Specific' Meta Program

Students who prefer small chunk-size information are known to have a 'specific' meta program. They speak in detail and give exact names and descriptions. They also use nouns and adjectives frequently. In addition, they give long explanations and expect the teacher to use specific details. However, they cannot read between the lines; therefore, they need a clear picture presented to them. Obviously, they perform well when asked about details such as true–false and multiple-choice questions. They like to write in detail and give long composition pieces. On the other hand, they cannot perceive the whole and have difficulty identifying priorities (Charvet 1998). Further, they are frustrated when others do not pay attention to them when they speak.

To cater for these students, it is advisable to explain concepts in detail and use exact names of places and people. It is recommended to follow a sequential presentation of the lesson, use detailed information (Woodsmall 1988), and use precise details with "modifiers, adverbs and adjectives" (Charvet 1997: 96). Therefore, when giving instructions, teachers should be specific and explain the steps in detail. Moreover, in order to pace the language of the detailed-oriented student, they should match the chunk size of the person speaking. Qualifiers that should be used are: "exactly, specifically, precisely, first, second, in the first place, then, next" (Woodsmall 1988: 20).

6.2 'Global' Meta Program

Students who prefer the global meta program are inclined toward generalities, overviews and summaries. They are comfortable when information presented to them is in large chunks. They are even comfortable with abstract concepts. Furthermore, they talk in general to the extent that people may not understand what they are saying. They do not present information in sequence; rather, they tend to do this in random order. Hence their sentences are short and they will interrupt others if they speak in detail to ask them to be brief. Eventually, they get bored when they are given detailed explanations. They also hate to memorize details and they perform well on general questions of the essay type (James and Woodsmall 1988; Woodsmall 1988; Charvet 1997; Woodsmall and Woodsmall 1998; Hall and Bodenhamer 2005).

Teachers who strive to cater for this group of students should present a summary of the lesson and avoid details. They should also try not to speak in sequence, make sure they use general nouns rather than specific names and "leave out the details and multiple qualifiers" (Charvet 1997: 98). Furthermore, when giving instructions, it is recommended to present them in general terms. Pacing these students requires using general language like: "generally, overview, big picture, framework, basis, foundation" (Woodsmall 1988: 20), 'the big picture', 'the main idea', 'essentially', 'the important thing is', 'in general' and 'concepts'.

7 Conclusion

While knowing meta programs can assist teachers in predicting the behaviors of their students, it is useful to understand that there is no good or bad way in filtering information. In addition, meta programs are not intended for labeling people, since people are not their behaviour. It is also important to remember that meta programs change with time and context. Moreover, the person's emotional state is also a factor that affects his or her meta programs within a given context. It is also important to understand that people are not one program or the other. It is correct to say that people prefer this program over the other one or tend to adopt a combination of both depending on contextual factors. It is useful to remember too that Meta programs have varying degrees of influence in different contexts. Communication becomes more effective when educators use the learners' thinking styles to convey their messages. Hall and Belnap (2004: 212–213) clarify this by saying:

> By simply learning to notice and match the person's meta-programs in our own communications, we have an express road for getting 'on the same channel' (...) When we identify and pace meta-programs in such contexts as teaching (...), we make our communication maximally effective. Why? Because we, in essence, use the other person's style of thinking and reasoning to package our message. This makes it easier for them to hear and understand. It allows us to adapt to their way of 'making sense' of things.

While it requires time an effort to identify single students' preferred meta programs, it is useful to assume that students prefer different information filters and cater for these differences when dealing with the class as a whole. On the other hand, it is feasible to figure out preferred meta programs when working with a small group or coaching individual students. Alternatively, Revell and Norman (1999) advise teachers to help their students understand their meta programs by themselves. There is danger in this in that students may perceive themselves as disadvantaged and helpless.

In a classroom context, and as several of the meta programs are represented evenly according to statistics, it is useful to use both types of pacing language preferences equally even if a teacher does not know about every student's preferences. To make it clear, while there is specific pacing language that is suitable for each type, it is sufficient to use a combination type of pacing language. Students who prefer a certain type will respond to the part that suits them and delete or ignore the unwanted information that is not suitable to their preferred type.

References

Bandler, R., and J. Grinder. 1975. *The structure of magic 1. A book about language and therapy.* California: Science and Behavior Books.

Charvet, S.R. 1997. *Words that change minds: Mastering the language of influence.* Dubuque: Kendall/Hunt Publishing Company.

Hall, M., and B. Belnap. 2004. *The sourcebook of magic: A comprehensive guide to NLP change patterns.* Wales: Crown House Publishing Ltd.

Hall, M., and B.G. Bodenhamer. 2005. *Figuring out people: Design engineering with meta-programs.* Wales: Crown House Publishing Ltd.

James, T., and D. Shephard. 2002. *Presenting magically: Transforming your stage presence with NLP*. Bancyfelin: Crown House Publishing.

James, T., and W. Woodsmall. 1988. *Time line therapy and the basis of personality*. Capitola: Meta Publications.

O'Connor, J., and J. Seymour. 1995. *Introducing neuro linguistic programming: Psychological skills for understanding and influencing people*. London: Thorsons.

Revell, J., and S. Norman. 1999. *In your hands: NLP in ELT*. London: Saffire Press.

Valentino, A.J. 2000. *Personality selling: Using NLP and the enneagram to understand people and how they are influenced*. Iselin: Vantage Point Publishing.

Woodsmall, W. 1988. *Meta programs*. Vienna: Next Step Press.

Woodsmall, M., and W. Woodsmall. 1998. *People pattern power: The nine keys to business success*. USA: The International Research Institute for Human Typological Studies.

Part III
Affective and Social Factors in Language Learning

The Place of Affect in Second Language Acquisition

Magdalena Kębłowska

Abstract The aim of the article is to show that affective learner characteristics play a crucial role in the process of second language acquisition (SLA). Although often neglected by contemporary linguists, preoccupied with an individual's cognitive capacities, in many instances it is emotions rather than intellect that account for the difficulties students may experience when learning a foreign language. SLA researchers point to motivation, ego-boundaries, anxiety, social distance, and risk-taking among others, as instrumental in the process. Also, numerous classroom-oriented studies corroborate the impact students' emotional states have on their learning. Therefore, care should be taken to create classroom conditions in which learners' positive emotions could be fostered. While the above claim has been emphasized by humanistic psychologists for a few decades now, classroom research shows that teachers often lack either the will or the means to attend to their students' emotional well-being.

1 Affective Factors and Linguistics

According to LeDoux (1996: 25), "minds without emotions are not really minds at all". It is common knowledge that an individual can be characterized by cognitive and affective features. It is also generally known that the cognitive factors are related to one's aptitude, intelligence, or strategies of learning, while the affective variables include a person's motivation and attitude, perception of self-esteem, or the feeling of anxiety. Yet despite scholars' awareness of the existence of the latter,

M. Kębłowska (✉)
Teacher Training College, Adam Mickiewicz University, Poznan, Poland
e-mail: magdalenakeblowska@tlen.pl

M. Pawlak (ed.), *New Perspectives on Individual Differences in Language Learning and Teaching*, Second Language Learning and Teaching,
DOI: 10.1007/978-3-642-20850-8_10, © Springer-Verlag Berlin Heidelberg 2012

the importance of affective factors is not infrequently undermined or ignored by linguists.

Linguistics, broadly defined as the study of language, seems to reject the emotional sphere of a human being as subjective and thus non-scientific. It is, therefore, irrelevant in the process of conscious hypothesis formation and testing, as language acquisition is nowadays described. And it often seems that linguists, and academic teachers among them, do not think much of the learner's emotional states perhaps because they believe an individual's cognitive potential (supposedly superior to affect) is able to deal with any interfering influence from his or her affective domain. We should remember that contemporary linguistics draws on cognitive psychology, which a few decades ago questioned the behaviorist explanation of human language acquisition. While the behaviorist view of language learning mechanism totally rejected the role of the mind, cognitivists have shown a deep belief in the human intellectual potential. This contribution to our understanding of learning processes cannot be overstated; however, cognitivists' preoccupation with the mind may also have led to neglecting the sphere of emotions.

It should be stressed here that an ultimate aim of any branch of linguistics (historical, contrastive, descriptive, etc.) is to better understand language and its subsystems, which should in turn lead to developing more effective means of language teaching (the domain of applied linguistics). If linguistics plays such a fundamental role in language pedagogy and because linguistics cannot be separated from its final pragmatic aim of language teaching, the factors that have an impact on language acquisition should not be depreciated by linguists. As van Lier (1994: 341) suggests, both education and linguistics should be developed through what he calls educational linguistics.

2 Affect and Cognition

Affect can generally be described as aspects of feeling, emotion, mood, or attitude that have an impact on our behavior (Arnold and Brown 1999: 1). The interest in the affective domain began in the late 1970s, when educators became increasingly concerned with the consequences of the preoccupation with cognition in education. According to Goleman (1995), our current 'emotional illiteracy' has arisen as a result of overemphasis on the rational, cognitive functions of our mind since the eighteenth century. Such a situation has produced "selfishness, violence, and a meanness of spirit (that) seem to be rotting the goodness of our communal lives" (Goleman 1995: xii). This is why we should educate the whole student, by trying to appeal to his or her cognitive as well as emotional spheres.

Clearly, affect is not in opposition to the cognitive side of learning, but it has to be stressed that attention to *both domains* is indispensable for an adequate development of an individual. Neither domain can be separated from the other, but they seem to complement each other. The above claim is reflected by the humanistic methods developed in the 1970s and 1980s as well as by more contemporary approaches. For example, the common technique of TPR, based on Asher's TPR Method, aims to activate the learner's body in order to lower potential stress related to classroom language learning and in this way promote more memorable acquisition. Similarly, Suggestopedia attempts to help learners get rid of negative emotions by various means: cozy and comfortable classrooms, changed identities, trust in the teacher-parent. More recent learner-centered approaches call for educating the whole learner, for example by acknowledging his or her multiple intelligences (a cognitive variable) with intrapersonal and inter-personal intelligences (closely related to affect) among them. Thus, emotions should not be treated as extras, but rather as a vital part of a human mental life (Oatley and Jenkins 1996: 122) and physical well-being. As Goleman (1997: 34) shows, negative emotions may make one ill, while positive feelings contribute to health.

Not without significance in the treatment of emotions is the research by Zajonc (1984), in which he shows that "affect (...) has primacy over cognition" (Young 1999a: 18). What is more, brain scientists have found that not only could emotions exist before cognition, but that they could be independent of cognition. Emotions were seen as "the threads that (...) hold mental life together but that were generated, most of the time, unconsciously" (Young 1999a: 18). For this reason, besides the conscious, also the unconscious began to be studied by brain scientists. Some researchers also argue that emotions preceded the development of language in humans (cf. Goleman 1995; Calvin 1996), which may justify the role affect plays in language acquisition.

3 The Role of Affect in Second Language Acquisition

The idea that affect has an impact on language learning was, among others, introduced by Gardner and Lambert (1972), who argued that positive affective variables are not only indispensable in language acquisition, but also that they operate independently of the cognitive factors of aptitude and intelligence. In essence, the influence of affective variables helps explain the difficulty some learners experience in language learning as compared to others. For instance, Taylor (1974) claims that it is affective variables that are responsible for the superiority of child over adult language acquisition. He argues that since both first and second language learners appear to use similar learning strategies, like overgeneralization (a cognitive factor), "at a process level, first and second lan-guage learning seem to be identical" (Taylor 1974: 32), and there is no cognitive explanation of the apparent lack of success of adult learners. In fact, adults' cognitive maturity should be helpful when learning the abstract nature of language. Taylor (1974: 33) concludes that adults' insufficient motivation and empathy, strong ego-boundaries and negative attitudes to L2 community may contribute to the problems they have with foreign language learning.

Among the above affective features, Guiora (1983) emphasizes *ego-boundaries*, which stem from a tremendous role the native language plays in creating an individual's identity. As he explains, "language, native language is the very lifeblood of human self-awareness, it is the carrier of identity, the safe repository of a vast array of affective and cognitive templates making up the total web of personality" (Guiora 1983: 10). Since learning a new language does not merely involve acquiring its lexis, syntax, or phonology, but also assimilating new ways of perceiving and describing the world, the learner has to develop a new identity that would allow him or her to function in this changed reality. Unfortunately, the more mature the learner, the stronger his or her native language ego, the more powerful "in holding (...) (his or her) psychological integrity, in promoting (...) defenses against any attempts on the impermeability of (...) language ego" (Guiora 1983: 8). Those defenses may be responsible for adults' tendency to reject aspects of L2 (e.g., pronunciation) because they do not fit in the patterns of their first language ego.

The influence of affect on adults' native accents is also raised by Hill (1970), who shows that this group of learners is able to master one or more foreign languages even in older age if society approves of it or expects it. The author rejects the completion of cerebral dominance and the onset of puberty (both cognitive in nature) as the only factors responsible for maintaining foreign accents. Based on the studies by Sorenson (1967) and Salisbury (1962), she shows that among some Amazon and Australian tribes where multilingualism is inevitable and socially expected, one or more foreign languages are acquired in adulthood without apparent native accent. Hill (1970: 248) thus stresses the importance of *attitudes* in language learning and concludes that in order to explain adult foreign accents the influence of the social and cultural roles that language and phonation play should be explored.

The significance of learners' attitudes is probably best reflected in Schumann's Acculturation Model of SLA. He posits the existence of the so-called *social distance* between a language learner and the target language community which influences the degree of success in language acquisition and acculturation. Schumann (1976) specifies social distance in terms of perceived dominance of either the target language group or the second language learning group, cohesiveness of the latter, congruence of both groups' cultures, and the attitudes the groups hold towards each other. "In this case, the unconscious, emotionally based social distance felt by the learner would override, or at least interfere with the cognitive processing (...) necessary for acquisition (...). Thus, affect (the feelings associated with not belonging to a particular language group) could short-circuit cognition (the learning process) for certain learners" (Young 1999b: 18–19).

Perhaps the most influential SLA theory that highlights learners' emotional states has been Krashen's Monitor Model. One of the hypotheses constituting the Model, the Affective Filter Hypothesis, ascribes the crucial role in language acquisition to emotions. If the learner is experiencing negative emotions (e.g., anxiety, inhibition, low self-esteem), the filter is high and blocks the inflow of language input into the brain's processing system. In other words, for successful acquisition to take place potential negative feelings have to be minimized. While Krashen does not undermine the significance of cognitive learner characteristics, such as aptitude, he believes they are irrelevant in acquisition and can only influence learning. The learned knowledge, however, is inferior to acquired knowledge and always optional in production. Whereas it is what the learner has acquired that allows him or her to actively perform in L2, learned knowledge acts merely as a monitor checking for well-formedness of what the learner produces. Thus, in this model learning and cognition are subordinated to unconscious acquisition possible only if the right affective environment is created.

The above hypotheses all point to affect as a legitimate participant in language acquisition. However, they would remain pure theory if classroom research did not bear out the instrumental role of emotions in language learning.

4 Affective Factors in the Classroom

It is beyond the scope of the present paper to report on all the available research findings showing the influence of affect on classroom language learning and behavior. Therefore, only selected studies pointing to the role of different affective factors will be discussed here.

Back in the 1970s, two studies were carried out, which showed that learners' emotional states or feelings can be responsible for their linguistic performance. Kleinmann (1977) designed a research project whose aim was to find out how effective contrastive analysis (CA) is in predicting students' avoidance of specific structures. While the results strongly suggest that CA is a reliable predictor of avoidance (i.e., the more difficult the structure—because different from L1—the higher the likelihood of avoidance), the learners' performance showed that besides the strictly linguistic (i.e., the perception of difficulty) also affective factors contribute to their language production. In the study, the grammar "structures which otherwise would be avoided are likely to be produced depending on the affective state of the learner with respect to such variables as confidence, anxiety, and motivational orientation" (Kleinmann 1977: 106). For example, a group of Arabic students learning English avoided the passive, as predicted by CA, but within the group the use of this grammar structure by some learners correlated significantly with facilitating anxiety (Kleinmann 1977: 104). In other words, passive sentences were in fact used by the students who exhibited facilitating anxiety.

Although Chastain's study (1975) is less conclusive, it does shed light on the role of affective variables, specifically anxiety, reserved versus outgoing personality type, and creativity. The author found significant correlations between outgoing personality and higher final grades for the foreign language course. In the case of anxiety, however, the results were not so unambiguous: while the correlation between test anxiety and the final grade for the French audiolingual class was negative, it was positive for German and Spanish taught in the traditional way. Chastain (1975: 160) rightly observes that some concern about a test may be facilitating whereas too much may be inhibiting for learners. Similarly, some types of creativity (e.g., creative imagination and risk-taking) were found to correlate positively with course grades, while others (e.g., innovation or curiosity) negatively. Despite the fact that the course grade may not always equal achievement, it is to an extent indicative of students' ability. And despite the tenuous results of the research, "the evidence supporting the existence and measurability of affective characteristics as they influence grades (...) is strong enough to warrant further study" (Chastain 1975: 160).

In his study of affective learner characteristics as predictors of language learning, Ely (1986: 4) hypothesized that: "(1) affective variables influence a student's voluntary classroom participation and (2) voluntary classroom participation (through various cognitive processes) in turn affects second language proficiency". The data from questionnaires exploring students' Language Class Risk-taking (related to extroversion-introversion), Language Class Sociability (the desire to interact), Language Class Discomfort (related to anxiety), the strength of learners' motivation, attitudes to language class, as well as tests measuring the participants' aptitude and current L2 proficiency corroborated the researcher's hypotheses. Risk-taking appeared to be a positive predictor of voluntary participation whereas discomfort had an indirect impact on participation due to its negative influence on risk-taking. While the author is aware of the limitations of his study (e.g., the need for an experimental design rather than correlations in order to prove causality and the relative subjectivity of self-report as a data collection tool) the results may indicate the role Language Class Risk-taking and Classroom Participation play in learning. Perhaps the most crucial conclusion that follows from the research, though, is that "simply exhorting students to take more risks and participate more may not be effective" (Ely 1986: 23) as shown by the negative causal relationship between discomfort and risktaking. The author is convinced that in order for some students to take linguistic risks, which contributes to developing their language proficiency, they need "to feel more psychologically comfortable and safe in their learning environment" (Ely 1986: 23). Thus, this study again places an individual's emotional comfort at the core of cognitive activity.

The concept of emotional comfort and security as the key to successful language learning has been of interest to many researchers, including those outside the field of ELT or applied linguistics. For example, Sarason (1980) and Schwarzer (1986a) tried to show that *anxiety* considerably interferes with successful learning. Eysenck (1979) associated anxiety with self-related cognition, consisting of excessive self-evaluation, preoccupation with potential failure and others' opinions. Since anxious individuals have to divide their attention between task-related cognition and self-related cognition, their cognitive performance may not be effective. In the same vein, Tobias (1986) offers a very influential model of the effect anxiety has on classroom learning. Like Eysenck (1979), she suggests that anxious students, in contrast to their more relaxed counterparts, are engrossed in "self-directed, derogatory cognition rather than focusing on the task itself. These task-irrelevant thoughts compete with task-relevant ones for limited cognitive resources. Non-anxious individuals tend not to engage in such self-preoccupations, giving them an advantage when the task at hand is taxing" (MacIntyre and Gardner 1991a: 43). Inspired by Tobias (1986); MacIntyre and Gardner (1991a, 1991b, 1994) designed a number of studies whose aim was to find out whether language anxiety does indeed interfere with language learning at the input, processing, and output stages. The results indicate that anxiety disturbs "concentration and the initial processing of linguistic stimuli at the input stage", which means that less information is likely to appear in the anxious individuals' short-term memory (MacIntyre and Gardner 1991b: 529). While the feeling of emotional tension does not seem to affect simple cognitive tasks (e.g., those carried out in students' L1), at the output stage it has a definite negative effect on more complex tasks (e.g., those in the foreign language) requiring retrieval of information stored in long-term memory. Confirming Tobias' claims, the authors conclude that language comprehension, rehearsal, and production are likely to suffer due to anxiety (MacIntyre and Gardner 1991b: 530). Similar conclusions can be drawn from the research into the influence of anxiety on various foreign language skills: reading (e.g., Lee 1999; Saito et al. 1999), listening (e.g., Vogely 1998, 1999; Elkhafaifi 2005), writing (e.g., Cheng et al. 1999; Leki 1999; Cheng 2002), and speaking (e.g., Young 1991; Phillips 1992, 1999; Kitano 2001).

What is more, Gardner and MacIntyre (1992) have postulated the interaction between *language learning strategies* and affective variables, especially motivation. Mihaljevic Djigunovic (2000: 3) summarizes their view by saying that although strategies are cognitive in nature, they "have a motivational basis because they develop from prior experience and the learner has (...) to be motivated to use a strategy". As a result of a study carried out among Croatian EFL primary, secondary, and university students, Mihaljevic Djigunovic (2000) identified the relationships between learners' strategies and the affective factors of anxiety, self-concept, attributions, and motivation. She found out that students who use strategies frequently are characterized by positive self-concept and a relatively high level of motivation. They attribute success in learning to effort as well as to task enjoyment. On the other hand, anxious learners seem to use communication strategies much less frequently but tend to resort to socio-affective ones (like learning with others) (Mihaljevic Djigunovic 2000: 14–24). Considering the role learner strategies play in mastering a language, the above results cannot be overestimated. If we believe that language learning success depends on a conscious use of appropriate strategies, we cannot ignore the affective variables that appear to correlate with them.

Along with strategies, contemporary language pedagogy stresses communicating in the foreign language as both a means and an aim of classroom learning. Therefore, *willingness to communicate* (WTC) has been increasingly recognized as an essential characteristic of a successful language learner. Quoting Richmond and Roach (1992), MacIntyre et al. (2003: 140) claim that "willingness to communicate is the one, overwhelming communication personality construct which permeates every facet of an individual's life and contributes significantly to the social, educational, and organizational achievements of the individual." A number of studies have shown that L1 WTC is related to a person's experiences in communication situations as well as to such factors as anxiety and perceived communicative competence. Similarly, MacIntyre et al. (2003) indicate the negative correlation between perceived competence in L2, anxiety and WTC. The authors hypothesize that anxious learners tend to underestimate their communication skills and thus are less willing to communicate. In other words, it may be anxiety that determines an individual's WTC. In essence, the personality characteristic of WTC and the affective variables that have an impact on it should be relevant to those educators who believe in the value of teaching English as communication and for communicative purposes.

5 Discussion and Conclusions

The aim of the present article was to show that the affective learner characteristics (e.g., anxiety, risk-taking, social distance, motivation, etc.) play an instrumental role in the process of foreign language learning. As indicated by the results of the studies reported on above, affect seems to act as a catalyst: positive emotions may enhance, while negative emotions inhibit learning.

It should also be stressed that the influence of affective variables is both *comprehensive* and *complex*. This can best be illustrated on the example of anxiety, which seems to interfere with all the stages of language acquisition: input, processing, and output. In other words, students' feeling of fear or tension will negatively affect their attention, concentration, the choice of learning strategies, the time they need to process the new material, as well as their ability to retrieve it from memory and their willingness to use it in performance (MacIntyre and Gardner 1994: 286–287). On the other hand, anxiety may have a facilitating effect and cause some learners to use more difficult structures in L2.

We should also bear in mind that of all school subjects, foreign language learning is potentially *the most threatening experience* because learners are expected to present themselves using a language in which they have limited proficiency. For this reason, they are more likely "to embarrass themselves, to frustrate their self-expression, and challenge their self-esteem and sense of identity than in any other learning activity". Since language and self are so closely connected, "an attack on one is an attack on the other" (MacIntyre 1999: 32).

If we assume that foreign language learning can be such a frustrating experience and that emotions are indeed so crucial for cognitive activity, care should be taken to create classroom conditions in which learners' positive feelings could be fostered. While the above claim has been emphasized by humanistic psychologists for a few decades now, classroom research often shows that foreign language students perceive their teachers as unhelpful in this respect, or even responsible for their negative emotions. For example, in Price's (1991) research into foreign language students' experience of anxiety, the subjects mentioned teachers' negative attitude to learners' pronunciation and preoccupation with error-free performance as contributing to classroom stress. In a small-scale study carried out by the author of the present article among proficient learners of English (Kębłowska 2006), the respondents also pointed to teachers' role in creating their anxieties by e.g., setting too high or unrealistic expectations, concentrating on absolute correctness in learners' performance and generally creating an atmosphere of constant testing and evaluation (for a comprehensive account of Polish students' language anxiety, see also Piechurska-Kuciel 2008).

Why is the foreign language classroom potentially anxiety-provoking? There is definitely no single answer to this question, but part of the problem seems to lie in the process of teacher preparation for their future profession. Pre-service teachers themselves are exposed to classroom instruction not infrequently characterized by a high level of negative emotions—after all, they are also taught by linguists who may not pay due attention to affect. Thus, there is an urgent need for teachers, teacher trainers, educational authorities, and all other parties involved firstly, to realize the importance of affect and, secondly, to develop effective strategies of promoting students' well-being in the classroom. Prospective foreign language teachers should not only be trained in linguistics and didactics, but should also participate in workshops raising their awareness of affect in the classroom and developing their interpersonal skills. More importantly, teacher trainers should serve as an example and not treat their students' feelings as irrelevant. After all, we cannot expect trainees to become affect-oriented unless we, their tutors, convince them how much affect matters and teach them how to become affective teachers.

References

Arnold, J., ed. 1999. *Affect in language learning*. Cambridge: Cambridge University Press.

Arnold, J., and H.D. Brown. 1999. A map of the terrain. In ed. J. Arnold, 1–24.

Beaven, B., ed. 2006. *IATEFL harrogate conference selections*. Canterbury: IATEFL.

Calvin, W.H. 1996. *How brains think*. New York: Basic Books.

Chastain, K. 1975. Affective and ability factors in second language acquisition. *Language Learning* 25: 153–161.

Cheng, Y. 2002. Factors associated with foreign language writing anxiety. *Foreign Language Annals* 35: 647–656.

Cheng, Y., E.K. Horwitz, and D. Schallert. 1999. Language anxiety: Differentiating writing and speaking components. *Language Learning* 49: 417–446.

Elkhafaifi, H. 2005. Listening comprehension and anxiety in the Arabic language classroom. *Modern Language Journal* 89: 206–220.

Ely, C.M. 1986. An analysis of discomfort, risk-taking, sociability, and motivation in the L2 classroom. *Language Learning* 36: 1–25.

Eysenck, M.W. 1979. Anxiety, learning and memory: A reconceptualization. *Journal of Research in Personality* 13: 363–385.

Gardner, R.C., and W. Lambert. 1972. *Attitudes and motivation in second language learning*. Rowley: Newbury House.

Gardner, R.C., and P.D. MacIntyre. 1992. A student's contribution to second language learning. Part I: Cognitive variables. *Language Teaching* 25: 211–220.

Goleman, D. 1995. *Emotional intelligence*. New York: Bantam Books.

Goleman, D. 1997. *Healing emotions*. Boston: Shambhala.

Guiora, A. 1983. The dialectic of language acquisition. *Language Learning* 34: 3–12.

Hill, J. 1970. Foreign accents, language acquisition, and cerebral dominance revisited. *Language Learning* 20: 237–248.

Horwitz, E.K., and D.J. Young, eds. 1991. *Language anxiety: From theory and research to classroom implications*. Upper Saddle River: Prentice Hall.

Kębłowska, M. 2006. *The factors contributing to proficient English users' language classroom anxiety*. In ed. B. Beaven, 168–170.

Kitano, K. 2001. Anxiety in the college Japanese language classroom. *Modern Language Journal* 85: 549–566.

Kleinmann, H.H. 1977. Avoidance behavior in adult second language acquisition. *Language Learning* 21: 93–107.

LeDoux, J. 1996. *The emotional brain*. New York: Simon and Schuster.

Lee, J.F. 1999. Clashes in L2 reading: Research versus practice and readers' misconceptions. In ed. D.J. Young, 49–63.

Leki, I. 1999. Techniques for reducing second language writing anxiety. In ed. D.J. Young, 64–88.

MacIntyre, P.D. 1999. Language anxiety: A review of the research for language teachers. In ed. D.J. Young, 24–45.

MacIntyre, P.D., and R.C. Gardner. 1991a. Anxiety and second language learning: Toward a theoretical clarification. In eds. E.K. Horwitz, and D.J. Young, 41–53.

MacIntyre, P.D., and R.C. Gardner. 1991b. Language anxiety: Its relationship to other anxieties and processing in native and second languages. *Language Learning* 41: 513–534.

MacIntyre, P.D., and R.C. Gardner. 1994. The subtle effects of language anxiety on cognitive processing in the second language. *Language Learning* 42: 283–305.

MacIntyre, P.D., S.C. Baker, R. Clement, and L.A. Donovan. 2003. Sex and age effects on willingness to communicate, anxiety, perceived competence, and L2 motivation among junior high school French immersion students. *Language Learning* 53: 137–165.

Mihaljević Djigunović, J. 2000. Language learning strategies and affect. *Centre for Language and Communication Studies Trinity College Dublin Occasional Paper* 59: 1–28.

Oatley, K., and J. Jenkins. 1996. *Understanding emotions*. Cambridge: Blackwell.

Phillips, E.M. 1992. The effects of language anxiety on students' oral test performance and attitudes. *Modern Language Journal* 76: 14–26.

Phillips, E.M. 1999. Decreasing language anxiety: Practical techniques for oral activities. In ed. D.J. Young, 124–143.

Piechurska-Kuciel, E. 2008. *Language anxiety in secondary grammar school students*. Opole: Opole University Press.

Price, M.L. 1991. The subjective experience of foreign language anxiety: Interviews with highly anxious students. In eds. E.K. Horwitz, and D.J. Young, 101–108.

Richmond, V.P., and K.D. Roach. 1992. Willingness to communicate and employee success in U.S. organizations. *Journal of Applied Communication Research* 20: 95–115.

Saito, Y., T.J. Garza, and E.K. Horwitz. 1999. Foreign language reading anxiety. *Modern Language Journal* 83: 202–218.

Salisbury, R.F. 1962. Notes on bilingualism and linguistic change in New Guinea. *Anthropological Linguistics* 4: 1–13.

Sarason, I.G. 1980. *Test anxiety: Theory research and applications*. Hillsdale: Lawrence Erlbaum.

Schumann, J. 1976. Social distance as a factor in second language acquisition. *Language Learning* 26: 135–143.

Schwarzer, R. 1986a. Self-related cognition in anxiety and motivation: An introduction. In ed. R. Schwarzer, 1–17.

Schwarzer, R., ed. 1986b. *Self-related cognition in anxiety and motivation*. Hillsdale: Lawrence Erlbaum.

Sorenson, A. 1967. Multilingualism in the Northwest Amazon. *American Anthropologist* 69: 670–684.

Taylor, B.P. 1974. Toward a theory of language acquisition. *Language Learning* 24: 23–35.

Tobias, S. 1986. Anxiety and cognitive processing in instruction. In ed. R. Schwarzer, 35–54.

van Lier, L. 1994. Forks and hope: Pursuing understanding in different ways. *Applied Linguistics* 15: 328–346.

Vogely, A.J. 1998. Listening comprehension anxiety: Students' reported sources and solutions. *Foreign Language Annals* 31: 67–80.

Vogely, A.J. 1999. Addressing listening comprehension anxiety. In ed. D.J. Young, 106–123.

Young, D.J. 1991. The relationship between anxiety and foreign language oral proficiency ratings. In eds. E.K. Horwitz, and D.J. Young, 57–63.

Young, D.J. 1999a. Affect in foreign language and second language learning: A practical guide to creating a low-anxiety classroom atmosphere. In ed. D.J. Young, 3–9.

Young, D.J. 1999b. A perspective on foreign language learning: From body to mind to emotions. In ed. D.J. Young, 13–23.

Young, D.J., ed. 1999c. *Affect in foreign language and second language learning: A practical guide to creating a low-anxiety classroom atmosphere*. Boston: McGraw-Hill College.

Zajonc, R.B. 1984. On the primacy of affect. *American Psychologist* 39: 117–123.

Language Anxiety Levels in Urban, Suburban and Rural Secondary Grammar School Students

Ewa Piechurska-Kuciel

Abstract The main purpose of this study is to investigate language anxiety levels in Polish secondary grammar school students from urban (N = 223), suburban (N = 48) and rural areas (N = 122). The results show that rural students suffer from significantly higher levels of anxiety over the length of their secondary school education when compared to their urban and suburban peers. These results confirm the findings in the literature of the field, further demonstrating that social and educational deprivation of rural adolescents continues to prevail. However, this study also shows that the language anxiety levels of all the study participants significantly decrease towards the end of their secondary school education, irrespective of their residential location.

1 Introduction

Traditionally, SLA research pays systematic attention to linguistic factors, ignoring the role of social environment in the acquisition process (Firth and Wagner 2007). Also, in Poland the research on the literature in this field is scarce, save an impressive study by Komorowska (1978). Nevertheless, the importance of social factors and language learning in the understanding of the acquisition process has now been fully recognized, and warrants more attention (e.g. Larsen-Freeman 2002). Although the gap between living conditions in the countryside and in the city has almost disappeared, the place of residence is still considered an important factor of social differences in Poland (Czarnecka 1999). As there have been no

E. Piechurska-Kuciel (✉)
Opole University, Opole, Poland
e-mail: epiech@uni.opole.pl

M. Pawlak (ed.), *New Perspectives on Individual Differences in Language Learning and Teaching*, Second Language Learning and Teaching, DOI: 10.1007/978-3-642-20850-8_11, © Springer-Verlag Berlin Heidelberg 2012

studies evaluating the relationship between the child's or adolescent's residential location and the level of language anxiety, for the purpose of the study it is assumed that rural adolescents, who generally exhibit lower academic achievement, may also be prone to a greater occurrence of negative feelings in the foreign language learning process, such as language anxiety.

The aim of this paper is to analyze the role of residential location in forming and sustaining language anxiety in secondary school education. The first part of the article presents a review of literature on the place of residence and language anxiety. This is followed by a presentation and discussion of the results of this empirical study on language anxiety levels in urban, suburban, and rural secondary school students. The final part of the paper outlines implications and recommendations for EFL classroom practice and future studies.

2 Literature Review

2.1 Place of Residence

Residential location, also called place of residence, can be defined as the individual's physical environment characterized by "the complex pattern of conscious and unconscious ideals, beliefs, preferences, feeling, values, goals and behavioural tendencies and skills relevant to this environment" (Proshansky, cited in Kyle et al. (2004: 214)). As an influential social factor (Rybczynska 2004), it shapes the individual's daily duties, ways of spending free time, living conditions, access to mass media, financial situation of the family, and access to after-school activities and education, among other things (Czarnecka 1999).

The rural regions in Poland occupy 90% of the total area of the country. In spite of a less hurried pace, sense of place, and protection of family values attributed to non-urban communities, this environment is identified as having many drawbacks. They are caused by limited access to culture, education, heath services, and poor trade and service industry. Also, the financial situation of rural families appears to be dissatisfactory. Nearly 13% of families who live in the countryside assume their financial situation is bad, while 4% characterize it as tragic (Rybczynska 2004). As a consequence, rural individuals are less likely to access resources of any kind (Yang and Fetsch 2007), from limited service provision in medical assistance to under-funding of rural schools and under-investment in cultural facilities. It is assumed that being born in the countryside causes people to get accustomed to their marginal position, as well as to the marginal position of their environment (Szafraniec 1991), which is also called the *province complex* (Maćko 2008).

Not surprisingly then, rural areas appear to be poorly educated (Rybczynska 2004). The general image of the Polish countryside as an educational environment is one that is relatively disadvantaged, owing to spatial and cultural isolation of rural areas, dispersed family life, the absence of institutional authority, the decaying of traditional folk culture, and urbanization processes (Czarnecka 1999). The majority of the countryside's inhabitants claim to have gained primary or vocational education, whereas there are a small percentage of people with secondary or higher education.

Children raised in the countryside are often overburdened with hard work and daily duties (Czarnecka 1999). What is more, they have limited free time and freedom of action. The majority of parents do not attach importance to education and the way their children spend free time. Those parents tend to attribute this obligation to school or their children rather than themselves. As a result, students who live in rural areas exhibit lower academic achievement (Rybczynska 2004). Apart from that, there is also a greater likelihood of their dropping out of high school (Roscigno and Crowley 2001). Rural schools are worse equipped and there are less experienced teachers (Maćko 2008). Moreover, adolescents from villages have lower expectations concerning going to college and earning high incomes, which may lead to the discouragement of positive behaviors in such students (Shears et al. 2006). The mental development of youth in the countryside is often described to lead to a "civilizational handicap" (Ambrozik 1997: 13). It may then be stated that a rural environment restrains students from considerable educational success and inhibits the learning process.

It should also be added that rural children and adolescents are now described to manifest various kinds of emotional and educational problems. First of all, they are shown to experience significant problems with stress and coping (Atkins 1993), which does not distinguish them from urban individuals (Yang and Fetsch 2007). However, the impact of anxiety in rural areas may be higher than that experienced by similarly anxious children from urban social groups (Lyneham and Rapee 2007). No wonder that rural adolescents claim to live on the borderland of social and cultural life, or even in "cultural emptiness" (Szafraniec 1991: 10).

Unlike the rural environment, urban areas are perceived as in many ways advantageous to the individual. One of the main factors connected with the quality of urban life, as opposed to that of rural life, is a lower level of poverty (Rybczynska 2004). A higher percentage of urban inhabitants claim to have higher or secondary education (Czarnecka 1999). In addition, the urban way of living induces different forms of mental and artistic activity (Kowalski 1983) and requires various abstract, cognitive functions, offering opportunities for diversified social interactions, group work, reading or calculating that may be needed to a lesser extent in the rural environment (Stevenson et al. 1990). These may be the chief reasons why in urban areas there are many people who are fully satisfied with the quality of their lives (Czarnecka 1999).

Children who live in urban areas do not seem to be as overburdened with daily duties, and have more free time than those who live in rural areas. Their living conditions seem to be healthier, with their sleeping time significantly longer (Czarnecka 1999). Every day the responsibilities of metropolitan youths are less demanding and less time consuming, which gives them many opportunities of enjoying their free time (Czarnecka 1999). They can entertain themselves and realize their individual interests, meet their friends, read magazines and books, go to the cinema or play computer games.

Yet urban life is also connected with many threats. The most obvious disadvantages are pollution and an uncaring polity (Greene et al. 2007). Apart from that, there are loose personal networks (Beggs et al. 1996) that are less supportive in the face of problems. Higher crime rates and delinquency (Wells and Weisheit 2004) coexist with higher tolerance toward deviant behaviors (Scheer et al. 2000). Another serious disadvantage of this environment is connected with higher levels of substance abuse and family conflict.

In spite of this, cities and towns seem to provide better educational offerings for students with higher socioeconomic status than for their rural counterparts. Well-equipped metropolitan schools introduce extracurricular activities, language courses, and art and PE classes whose main purpose is to entertain and stimulate the physical, emotional and social development of young people. Nearly one-third of children who live in urban areas participate in after-school activities and private foreign language (FL) lessons, while modern languages are taught in all schools in urban areas. It follows that metropolitan schools offer more opportunities for successful development when compared to rural schools (Hochschild 2003).

The research on the role of residential location undoubtedly shows that the urban environment is favorable for the process of learning (Czarnecka 1999). The findings presented above point to a notable discrepancy between students from rural and small-town areas, as opposed to metropolitan ones. In spite of a less hurried pace, sense of place, and protection of family values attributed to non-urban communities, the students from rural areas may still have serious problems in their educational process. Hence, it may be presumed that foreign language acquisition may offer serious challenges to rural students.

2.2 Language Anxiety

The unique situation of learning a foreign language gives way to the activation of a specific anxiety that in turn affects the quality of the SLA process, called language anxiety. It can be defined as "a distinct complex of self-perceptions, beliefs, feelings, and behaviors related to classroom language learning arising from the uniqueness of the language learning process" (Horwitz et al. 1986: 128).

The conceptual model of language anxiety proposed by MacIntyre and Gardner (1989) states that language anxiety is based on the following interrelated processes involved in oral communication: communication apprehension, test anxiety, and fear of negative evaluation. These anxiety types constitute forms of performance anxiety, because language anxiety mainly deals with performance evaluation within academic and social contexts (Cha 2006). Hence, they constitute a broader social context for foreign language acquisition.

Communication apprehension (also known as stage fright, communication anxiety, or performance anxiety) (Horwitz 2002a) generally refers to a type of anxiety experienced in interpersonal communicative settings (McCroskey 1987). The phenomenon is directly connected with communication avoidance (McCroskey et al. 1985), because individuals who generally fear communication also tend to evade it. Test anxiety is defined as "a situation-specific form of trait anxiety" (Zohar 1998: 330) that pushes an individual to react to threatening situations with psychological, physiological and behavioral responses that are sometimes debilitating (Hancock 1994). This is usually connected with emotional reactions accompanying situations where one's performance is being measured or assessed (McDonald 2001). Fear of negative evaluation is characterized as "an apprehension about others' evaluations, avoidance of evaluative situations, and the expectation that others would evaluate oneself negatively" (Watson and Friend 1969). It is primarily connected with social anxiety, and thus related to low self-esteem (Fleming and Courtney 1984). The three theoretical constructs underpinning the phenomenon of language anxiety lead to the conclusion that an anxious FL learner is excessively concerned with the impression they make with their communication efforts (Gregersen and Horwitz 2002).

A foreign language student experiencing elevated levels of language anxiety assesses the language-learning situation as dangerous. This causes apprehension and fear, especially due to the mismatch between their mature and advanced thoughts and immature and poor language, producing self-consciousness and anxiety (Horwitz et al. 1986). The learner pays selective attention to elements of the learning process associated with danger, and interprets ambiguous situations as threatening, with a tendency to remember only bad experiences, which are later associated with the foreign language. Cognitions about his or her own behavior are negative and full of self-derogatory comments and doubts. This is the reason why focusing on such cognitions rather than on the task (MacIntyre and Gardner 1989) produces deficits in performance. The anxious FL learner is not able to work at full potential because anxiety consumes a part of the working memory capacity, which also implies a greater cognitive effort on his part. Apart from that, such a learner becomes aware of signals from physiological activity, like sweating, trembling or a rapid heart beat (Wade and Tavris 1990). These involuntary and unwanted actions of the body often lead to greater discomfort when confronting the teacher and other students in the classroom. In this way the anxious learner's belief that they are making a negative social impression on others can further culminate in producing more anxiety.

In view of the above considerations the main purpose of this research is to examine the relationship between residential location and language anxiety levels. Hence, for the purpose of the research the following hypothesis is formulated: *Students from villages suffer from significantly higher levels of language anxiety than students from cities and towns.*

3 Method

3.1 Participants

The informants in this study were 393 students from the six secondary grammar schools in Opole, located in southwestern Poland (266 girls and 127 boys). They came from 17 classes (natural groups). At the beginning of the study, when they entered secondary school education, their average age was 16.7, with a minimum of 15 and a maximum of 18. 223 of them lived in the city of Opole, 48 in the surrounding towns, while 122 resided in villages.

3.2 Instruments

There were two basic types of instruments applied in this study: a questionnaire and school records. The questionnaire in the first year of the study included information concerning demographic data: gender (1—male, 2—female), age, place of residence (1—village, up to 2,500 inhabitants, 2—town, from 2,500 to 50,000 inhabitants, 3—over 50,000 inhabitants) and the length of experience with English (number of years). In addition, every year the participants gave their self-assessment of speaking, listening, reading, and writing in English (1—very poor, 2—poor, 3—sufficient, 4—good, 5—very good, 6—excellent).

The questionnaire also included the *Foreign Language Classroom Anxiety Scale* (Horwitz et al. 1986). Its purpose is to assess the degree to which students feel anxious during language classes. Sample items on the scale are as follows: 'I can feel my heart pounding when I'm going to be called on in language class' or 'I keep thinking that the other students are better at languages than I am'. All positive items were key-reversed so that a high score on the scale represented a high anxiety level. The minimum number of points that could be obtained on the scale was 33, while the maximum was 165. The scale's reliability was assessed in terms of Cronbach's alpha coefficient of 0.94.

School records were the other instrument applied in the study. They were used for collecting data concerning the final grades in English the informants received at the end of every school year.

3.3 Procedure

This research design is *longitudinal* with three measurements taken at different points of time (*time-series*) (Graziano and Raulin 1993). It allows for following the same participants for three years (the length of the secondary grammar school study), measuring the levels of language anxiety and self-assessment of independent macro-skills. The data collection procedure took place at three intervention points (Year 1, when the participants were in Grade 1, Year 2: Grade 2, and Year 3: Grade 3) over the length of the participants' secondary school education.

3.4 Analyses

The data were computed by means of the statistical program STATISTICA, with the main operations being descriptive and inferential statistics. The descriptive procedures that summarized the characteristics of the sample were: *means* (arithmetic average) and *standard deviation (SD)*, showing how far individuals vary from the mean.

The inferential statistical procedures applied in the study enabled computing the probability of obtaining a particular pattern of data. Among them there were two types of *the student's t-test,* a test of mean differences between two groups (Graziano and Raulin 1993). The *t*-test for independent groups shows differences between two groups on the measurement of a dependent variable (the between-group variation), for example: differences in language anxiety levels in urban and rural students in consecutive years. The correlated *t*-test measures differences in the measurements of the same variable in a group (e.g. language anxiety levels in rural students). The ANOVA procedure was applied to assess global differences in language anxiety levels among students from cities, towns and villages, as well as their self-assessment of FL study, final grades and the length of FL study.

4 Results

The language anxiety measurements collected in the three years for the three independent groups showed that every year the students from the city got seemingly lower language anxiety scores than students from towns and villages, over the whole course of the study. Furthermore, these levels tended to decline in all the groups in all the measurement points (see Fig. 1).

Descriptive statistics results for other variables showed that over the length of their secondary school study urban students self-assessed their FL abilities highest of all the students. A similar effect was detected for their final grades, but only in Year 1. Later, suburban and rural students seemed to gradually get better grades. As far as the length of FL study was concerned, urban students had the longest experience, while rural ones had the shortest (see Table 1 for descriptive statistics results).

By means of one-way ANOVA, the language anxiety measurements in the three groups were compared. In Year 1 the results of all the three groups were significantly different: $F(2) = 13.74^{***}$, showing that language anxiety was lowest in

Fig. 1 Language anxiety
levels in students from cities,
towns and villages

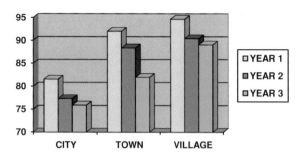

Table 1 Means (M) and standard deviations (SD) of language anxiety and assessment (internal and external) in relation to place of residence

Variable		Urban students (N = 223)		Suburban students (N = 48)		Rural students (N = 122)	
		M	SD	M	SD	M	SD
Language anxiety	Year 1	81.51	23.02	91.98	23.93	94.61	23.72
	Year 2	77.37	22.01	88.35	23.45	90.39	23.05
	Year 3	75.89	23.36	81.92	20.38	89.03	25.20
Self-assessment of FL skills	Year 1	15.76	3.10	14.50	3.32	13.89	3.31
	Year 2	16.13	2.92	14.60	3.60	14.84	3.06
	Year 3	16.28	2.91	15.35	3.28	14.65	2.94
Final grades	Year 1	3.92	0.95	3.69	1.01	3.88	0.91
	Year 2	3.82	1.01	3.71	1.11	4.05	0.92
	Year 3	4.18	0.94	3.96	1.11	4.27	0.86
Length of FL study	Year 1	6.79	2.77	6.08	2.71	3.95	2.41

students from the city and highest in students from villages. In Year 2 similar results were obtained: $F(2) = 14.89^{***}$, as well as in Year 3: $F(2) = 12.28^{***}$ (see Table 3). A closer examination of language anxiety levels revealed that there were no significant differences in language anxiety levels in city and town dwellers in the three years of secondary school study ($t_{\text{Year 1}} = 0.65, p = 0.52; t_{\text{Year 2}} = 52, p = 0.61; t_{\text{Year 3}} = 1.74, p = 0.08$). Nevertheless, such differences existed when it came to the comparison of students from cities and villages ($t_{\text{Year 1}} = 5.00^{***}, p = 0.00; t_{\text{Year 2}} = 5.17^{***}, p = 0.00; t_{\text{Year 3}} = 4.86^{***}, p = 0.00$), or between students from towns and villages ($t_{\text{Year 1}} = 2.84^{**}, p = 0.00; t_{\text{Year 2}} = 3.10^{**}, p = 0.00; t_{\text{Year 3}} = 1.66, p = 0.10$).

In the next step the decrease of language anxiety levels in the three groups was examined. The results revealed that language anxiety levels in rural and urban students were similar, with a significant drop after the beginning of secondary school study and a stabilizing trend towards its end. It should be added that a different pattern is observed in the development of language anxiety in suburban students, whose language anxiety levels significantly dropped only towards the end of the secondary school education (see Table 2 for the summary of within-group results).

Table 2 Within-group differences in language anxiety levels in urban, suburban and rural students

	Urban students (N = 223)	Suburban students (N = 48)	Rural students (N = 122)
Year 1 × Year 2	t (222) = 3.65***, p = 0.00	t (47) = 1.51, p = 0.14	t (121) = 2.90**, p = 0.00
Year 2 × Year 3	t (222) = 1.35, p = 0.18	t (47) = 3.06**, p = 0.00	t (121) = 0.84, p = 0.40

* <0.05; ** <0.01; *** <0.001

Table 3 Between-group differences in urban, suburban and rural students

	Year of study	F(2)	p
Language anxiety levels	Year 1	13.74***	0.00
	Year 2	14.89***	0.00
	Year 3	12.28***	0.00
Self-assessment of FL skills	Year 1	14.24***	0.00
	Year 2	9.59***	0.00
	Year 3	12.05***	0.00
Final grades	Year 1	1.23	0.29
	Year 2	2.89	0.06
	Year 3	2.01	0.13
Length of FL study	Year 1	45.31***	0.00

As far as self-assessment of FL skills was concerned, the comparison of final grades did not render statistically significant differences. In addition, students from villages reported the shortest language experience (see Table 3 for a summary of the group comparisons).

5 Discussion

The purpose of this research was to examine the role of residential location in the development of language anxiety levels in secondary grammar school students. In accordance with the hypothesis formulated for the purpose of the study: *students from villages suffer from significantly higher levels of language anxiety than students from cities and towns*, the research results show that the levels of language anxiety in rural students are significantly higher than those of urban students. As far as the comparison between students from villages and towns is concerned, a similar regularity is identified. Thus, the above hypothesis can be fully corroborated.

These findings confirm the disadvantageous position of students from areas of lower density, who receive their secondary grammar school education in metropolitan areas. The difficulties they face are mostly connected with the necessity to adapt to the different cognitive and social demands placed on them in the urban setting, inducing a different way of living. This may have a large impact on rural children and adolescents, who may suffer from various kinds of emotional and educational problems as a consequence of this type of transition.

Apart from the shift from a rural to urban context, village and small town students also experience school transition, which brings on additional psychosocial or behavioral difficulties (Pedersen 2005). Generally, changing schools seems to induce significant levels of strain by forcing adolescents to take novel educational and social roles. The new surroundings may impose severe cognitive and educational demands and cause significant levels of negative emotions. These results point to a notable disadvantage in students from rural and small-town areas. Aside from that, in the new surroundings rural students may experience feelings of 'otherness' and lack a sense of belonging, which may add to their alienation.[1] Another serious consequence of such a transition is the sudden deterioration of academic achievement, such as school grades (Silverthorn et al. 2005), which may be particularly severe in urban areas.

Apart from these difficulties rural students must cope with, there is also the problem of the physical distance between their home and school, which demands a longer commute, depriving them of proper study time. Additionally, such students may be unable to develop stronger bonds with their peers due to their lack of time, which may otherwise help them to accommodate to the new environment faster. Finally, there are the demands made by the foreign language learning process.

Against the background of the negative impact an urban educational and social setting may place on the rural adolescent, high language anxiety levels appear a likely finding. To start, rural and small-town adolescents have a significantly lower exposure to foreign languages. This finding can be attributed to several reasons, from a higher poverty level connected with under-investment in educational needs, to lower parental support in the sphere of educational needs. Moreover, it seems that the mere physical distance between their place of residence and school may worsen the adaptive behaviors of rural students, who are deprived of a greater contact with foreign languages through cinemas, language schools, and private tutors. In consequence, rural students' overall FL study processes can be negatively affected by their shorter exposure and fewer contact hours when compared to those of their urban peers.

Several other clear patterns can be identified in the development of language anxiety scores obtained by learners from cities, small towns and villages throughout the length of their secondary school education. Primarily, it should be mentioned that in the first measurement (Year 1) the levels of language anxiety are highest in all the participants of the study, irrespective of their residential location. This result can be explained by several causes. Primarily, it should be pointed out that the first measurement was taken at the beginning of secondary school education, when all the students had just experienced school transition, inducing severe stress levels (de Bruyn 2005). Nevertheless, in the next year (Year 2) a

---

[1] Hanna Komorowska, personal communication (February 22, 2008).

significant decrease in language anxiety levels is observed in all the study participants. This finding implies that all the students managed to adapt to the language-learning situation in the new surroundings. Even students from villages exhibited significantly lower levels of language anxiety. Nevertheless, their affective reactions were still strongest in relation to the measurements observed in urban and suburban students. The last measurement of language anxiety levels (Year 3) demonstrates similar findings, with the reservation that language anxiety levels of both rural and metropolitan students do not show any decrease, while the results of suburban students remain at the same level.

These results corroborate the theoretical model of the development of language anxiety proposed by MacIntyre and Gardner (1989). According to it, at the beginning of the language-learning process language anxiety is at the highest level due to the learner's insufficient experience with the FL learning process. In the course of time, when proficiency and experience in the FL increase, anxiety starts declining "in a consistent manner" (MacIntyre and Gardner 1991: 111) because the learner's growing FL mastery is connected with the more successful language use (Mihaljevic Djigunovic 2004). This is the reason why in all the study participants, those from villages (rural areas), small towns (suburban) and cities (urban), language anxiety levels significantly and regularly decrease, virtually irrespective of their residential location.

It follows that the place of residence does not negatively affect the growing mastery of the foreign language, or the adaptive behaviors that help the students cope with emotional challenges the foreign language learning process may offer, which is an optimistic finding. Nevertheless, it should be stressed that the language anxiety levels experienced by students from villages are invariably highest of all measurements taken throughout the three years of secondary school experience. This means that the place of residence remains a significant predictor of language anxiety in secondary school students, because the initial significant discrepancies identified in the three groups (urban-suburban-rural) remain stable throughout the length of secondary school education, in spite of growing FL mastery.

It is worth adding that the external (final grades) and internal (self-assessment) analysis of the students' FL abilities renders further support for the hypothesis of the study. As far as self-assessment of the four skills is concerned, it appears that over the length of the secondary grammar school study urban students perceive their abilities to speak, listen, read and write at a significantly higher level than rural students. This result confirms the inferiority complex of students from the country, because the examination of final grades does not reveal any significant differences, which means that all the three groups of students tend to get similar final grades. This result can be explained by the fact that external assessment is not as sensitive as internal assessment to affective drawbacks, such as language anxiety.

To sum up, residential location is found to be a notable correlate of language anxiety, pointing to a negative relationship between the population density in a given area and language anxiety. It follows that language anxiety scores are highest in students from rural areas (villages) and lowest in students from cities (urban areas). Even so, all students share similar abilities in coping with their anxiety in the FL classroom because the decrease in their language anxiety is significant towards the end of secondary grammar school education due to their growing FL mastery.

6 Implications and Recommendations

The implications of the research mostly concentrate on possible intervention practices performed by the FL teacher. It follows that the teacher should be especially sensitive to the needs of students who come from rural areas while trying to accommodate them in mainstream education. With their lack of previous FL experience, such students undoubtedly require more time and effort. In this situation, a friendly atmosphere in the classroom, an approachable teacher and supportive classmates may be considered undeniably valuable assets for a rural student.

In addition, one should be aware of the fact that such students may not have much time to practice outside school, which is usually a crucial requirement in the process of gaining FL mastery. This is the reason why careful planning and effective work in the classroom is of paramount importance. Moreover, the FL teacher should also bear in mind that effective instruction should also focus on developing more positive attitudes to language learning in rural students. In this way they may have a chance to be effectively assisted in planning their future career in various environments where the knowledge of a foreign language may be considered a notable advantage. These interventions may aid students in attaining personal satisfaction and more successful future prospects.

The study offers many interesting paths for upcoming research. One direction may concern broadening the investigation of the phenomenon of anxiety in the foreign language classroom from the perspective of residential location, which—so far—has not been fully explored. First of all, it is worth shedding more light on possible gender differences within this scope of study. It may be interesting to examine possible differences in study habits and language anxiety levels in girls and boys from rural and metropolitan areas. Another path in research on anxiety may refer to the application of other research designs, apart from the one used here. Although experimental designs offer the greatest degree of control, they are extremely difficult to apply in the case of language anxiety studies. Thus descriptive studies or even case studies still offer a valuable insight into the understanding of cognitive and emotional processes in students from various residential locations and their experience of anxiety in the process of foreign language acquisition.

This study is certainly not free from any limitations. One of them may be the uneven number of participants in each group (urban-suburban-rural). Dividing students into two more distinctive opposite groups (urban versus rural) may render more transparent material for group comparisons. Apart from that, no information concerning study habits was acquired. This might have shed more light on the learner profiles.

In spite of the rather pessimistic observations about high anxiety levels in rural students venturing to study a foreign language, it is vital to point out there are good chances for such students to master a new language irrespective of their residential location (*vide* final grades). It seems, then, that many performance problems are rooted in affective disturbances. Consequently, all parties concerned (parents, students and their peers) need to be educated on ways of coping with anxiety (e.g. how to ask for help, whom to ask, and how to manage problems), as well as on applying suitable affective strategies involving knowledge of oneself as a learner. In this way, by changing the individual's thinking, emotions can be altered to become more positive and facilitate the SLA process.

References

Ambrozik, W.A. 1997. *Dewiacje wychowawcze w środowisku wiejskim* [*Educational deviations in the rural environment*]. Poznań: Eruditus.

Atkins, F.D. 1993. Stress and coping among Missouri rural and urban children. *Journal of Rural Health* 9: 50–56.

Beggs, J.J., V.A. Haines, and J.S. Hurlbert. 1996. Revisiting the rural–urban contrast: Personal networks in nonmetropolitan and metropolitan settings. *Rural Sociology* 61: 306–325.

Cha, H. 2006. Korean elementary ESOL students' English language anxiety and defense mechanism in the ESOL and mainstream classes: Theoretical and pedagogical implications for TESOL. http://etd.lib.fsu.edu/theses/available/etd-04022006-035500/.

Czarnecka, S. 1999. Aspiracje edukacyjne i zawodowe młodzieży wiejskiej—drogi i bariery na przełomie XX i XXI wieku [Educational and vocational aspirations of rural youth—at the turn of the 21st century]. In eds. S. Czarnecka, Z. Jakubowski, and S. Podoliński, 19–163.

Czarnecka, S., Z. Jakubowski, and S. Podoliński, eds. 1999. *Szkoła wiejska—dziecko wiejskie. Realia i perspektywy* [*The rural school—the rural child. Reality and perspectives*]. Częstochowa: Wydawnictwo Wyższej Szkoły Pedagogicznej w Częstochowie.

de Bruyn, E.H. 2005. Role strain, engagement and academic achievement in early adolescence. *Educational Studies* 31: 15–27.

Firth, A., and J. Wagner. 2007. Second/foreign language learning as a social accomplishment: Elaborations on a reconceptualized SLA. *Modern Language Journal* 91: 800–819.

Fleming, J.S., and B.E. Courtney. 1984. The dimensionality of self-esteem II. Hierarchical facet model for revised measurement scales. *Journal of Personality and Social Psychology* 46: 404–421.

Graziano, A.M., and M.L. Raulin. 1993. *Research methods. A process of inquiry.* New York: HarperCollins College.

Greene, F.J., P. Tracey, and M. Cowling. 2007. Recasting the city into city-regions: Place promotion, competitiveness benchmarking and the quest for urban supremacy. *Growth and Change* 38: 1–22.

Gregersen, T., and E.K. Horwitz. 2002. Language learning and perfectionism: Anxious and non-anxious language learners' reactions to their own oral performance. *Modern Language Journal* 86: 562–570.

Hancock, D.R. 1994. Effects of test anxiety and evaluative threat on students' achievement and motivation. *Journal of Educational Research* 94: 284–291.

Hochschild, J.L. 2003. Social class in public schools. *Journal of Social Issues* 59: 821–840.

Horwitz, B. 2002a. Introduction and overview: The hidden communication problem. In ed. B. Horwitz, 1–25.

Horwitz, B., ed. 2002b. *Communication apprehension: Origins and management.* Canada: Singular Thomson Learning.

Horwitz, E.K., M. Horwitz, and J.A. Cope. 1986. Foreign language classroom anxiety. *Modern Language Journal* 70: 125–132.

Komorowska, H. 1978. *Sukces i niepowodzenie w nauce języka obcego [Success and failure in foreign language learning].* Warszawa: Wydawnictwa Szkolne i Pedagogiczne.

Kowalski, S. 1983. *Podejście systemowe w badaniu środowisk wychowawczych [Systems approach in studies of educational environments].* Łódź: Ossolineum.

Kramsch, C., ed. 2002. *Language acquisition and language socialization: Ecological perspectives.* London: Continuum.

Kraszewski, E., and E. Skorupka-Raczyńska, eds. 2004. *Szanse i zagrożenia dzieci i młodzieży wiejskiej [Chances and threats of rural children and youth].* Kalsk: Gorzów Wielkopolski.

Kyle, G., A. Graefe, R. Manning, and J. Bacon. 2004. Effects of place attachment on users' perceptions of social and environmental conditions in a natural setting. *Journal of Environmental Psychology* 24: 213–225.

Larsen-Freeman, D. 2002. Language acquisition and language use from a chaos/complexity theory perspective. In ed. C. Kramsch, 33–46.

Lyneham, H.J., and R.M. Rapee. 2007. Childhood anxiety in rural and urban areas: Presentation, impact and help seeking. *Australian Journal of Psychology* 59: 108–118.

MacIntyre, P.D., and R.C. Gardner. 1989. Anxiety and second language learning: Toward a theoretical clarification. *Language Learning* 39: 251–275.

MacIntyre, P.D., and R.C. Gardner. 1991. Methods and results in the study of anxiety in language learning: A review of the literature. *Language Learning* 41: 85–117.

Maćko, G. 2008. Wyrównywanie szans edukacyjnych. Poradnik praktyczny [Equalling educational opportunities. A practical guide]. http://www.szkola.szans.pl/pl/indekx2.php?option=com_content&task=view&id=54.

McCroskey, J.C. 1987. Willingness to communicate. In eds. J.C. McCroskey, and J.A. Daly, 129–156.

McCroskey, J.C., and J.A. Daly, eds. 1987. *Personality and interpersonal communication.* Thousand Oaks: Sage.

McCroskey, J.C., J.M. Fayer, and V.P. Richmond. 1985. Don't speak to me in English: Communication apprehension in Puerto Rico. *Communication Quarterly* 33: 185–192.

McDonald, A. 2001. The prevalence and effects of test anxiety in school children. *Educational Psychology* 21: 89–102.

Mihaljević Djigunović, J. 2004. Language anxiety: An important concern in language learning. In eds. N. Murray, and T. Thornz, 42–51.

Murray, N., and T. Thornz, eds. 2004. *Multicultural perspectives on English language and culture.* Tallin: Tallin Pedagogical University.

Pedersen, S. 2005. Urban adolescents' out-of-school activity profiles: Associations with youth, family, and school transition characteristics. *Applied Developmental Science* 9: 107–124.

Roscigno, V.J., and M.L. Crowley. 2001. Rurality, institutional disadvantage, and achievement/attainment. *Rural Sociology* 66: 268–292.

Rybczyńska, D. 2004. Zasoby i ograniczenia rodziny wiejskiej a możliwości rozwojowe dzieci [The reserves and limitations of the rural family and the developmental opportunities of children]. In eds. E. Kraszewski, and E. Skorupka-Raczyńska, 9–18.

Scheer, S.D., L.M. Borden, and J.M. Donnermeyer. 2000. The relationship between family factors and adolescent substance use in rural, suburban, and urban settings. *Social Indicators Research* 78: 453–472.

Shears, J., R.W. Edwards, and L.R. Stanley. 2006. School bonding and substance use in rural communities. *Social Work Research* 30: 6–18.

Silverthorn, N., D.L. DuBois, and G. Crombie. 2005. Self-perceptions of ability and achievement across the high school transition: Investigation of a state-trait model. *Journal of Experimental Education* 73: 193–218.

Stevenson, H.W., C. Chen, and J. Booth. 1990. Influences of schooling and urban–rural residence on gender differences in cognitive abilities and academic achievement. *Sex Roles* 23: 535–551.

Szafraniec, K. 1991. *Młodzież wiejska jako efekt socjalizacji pogranicznej. Między lokalizmem a totalitaryzmem. [The rural youth as the effect of the borderland socialization. Between localism and totalitarianism]*. Warszawa: IRWiR PAN.

Wade, C., and C. Tavris. 1990. *Psychology*. 2nd ed. New York: Harper and Row.

Watson, D., and R. Friend. 1969. Measurement of social-evaluative anxiety. *Journal of Consulting and Clinical Psychology* 33: 448–457.

Wells, L.E., and R.A. Weisheit. 2004. Patterns of rural and urban crime: A county-level comparison. *Criminal Justice Review* 29: 1–22.

Yang, R.K., and R. Fetsch. 2007. The self-esteem of rural children. *Journal of Research in Rural Education* 22: 1–7.

Zohar, D. 1998. An additive model of test anxiety role of exam-specific expectations. *Journal of Educational Psychology* 90: 330–340.

Foreign Language Learners as Teachers: Individual Perceptions of a Teaching Process at the Pre-Service Level

Danuta Gabryś-Barker

Abstract The article presented in this volume is a part of a research project investigating the reflective practices of pre-service teachers of English who are still learners themselves studying to become fully qualified professionals. It aims at investigating their ability to identify significant events, the so-called critical incidents in their first teaching practice experiences, reflect upon them and self-assess their development over a period of one academic year in the form of a diary study. The part of the project discussed here relates to the trainees' perceptions of the teaching profession and themselves as teachers. It tries to establish the belief and value systems of the students and to comment on the origin of those beliefs they hold about the teaching profession. On the basis of their narratives presented in the form of an essay, the extent to which the trainees use their own individual preferences as learners in the way they approach teaching will be discussed as well as the extent to which it is influenced by prior learning experiences in the far past at school and at present at the teacher training college. So the focus of the study is the individual variability of trainee-teachers who are still learners themselves.

1 Introduction

The volume in which this article appears comments extensively on the importance of individual differences in language development: the pace of its progress, the ultimate achievement and impediments individual learners experience or are exposed to due to their individual variability. Contextual variability is also a significant factor

D. Gabryś-Barker (✉)
University of Silesia, Katowice, Poland
e-mail: danutagabrys@hotmail.com

M. Pawlak (ed.), *New Perspectives on Individual Differences in Language Learning and Teaching*, Second Language Learning and Teaching,
DOI: 10.1007/978-3-642-20850-8_12, © Springer-Verlag Berlin Heidelberg 2012

and the teacher is perhaps the most significant of these. Therefore, considerations of what constitutes an individual teacher's perceptions of his or her role and position also need to be reflected upon. This paper discusses the reflections that come from trainees who are about to become qualified teachers of English.

Since the present study deals with subjects who are still language learners in the process of completing their professional qualifications, their individual differences may be considered an important variable in how they see themselves in the role of teachers at the beginning of this professional journey. It may be assumed that, as Kubler LaBoskey (1993 p. 23) puts it:

> (…) novices do not enter teacher education programs as blank slates. After many years in classrooms they have ideas about what teachers do. But these ideas are derived from a student perspective, not a teacher perspective, and thus, they are very likely to be inaccurate, inappropriate or incomplete. Such misconceptions may distort or block any new information presented in the teacher education program. Consequently, teacher educators need to consider the potential influence of student preconceptions on the reflective activities and programs they design and implement.

The fact that students have varied learning experiences will also make them have very different systems of beliefs and values in relation to their own performance in a classroom. This is because "not all prospective teachers enter teacher education program with the same views. Students vary in their pre-intervention beliefs, particularly in the degree of orientation toward growth and inquiry" (Kubler LaBoskey 1993 p. 23).

In order to become aware and to be able to modify the misconceptions held by pre-service teachers entering training programs, reflection is an indispensable tool in this process as it is employed both by the educator and the trainee. This project is concerned with the development of reflectivity in the training of FL teachers. It looks at the trainees' ability to reflect and identify significance in their classroom performance and the perceptions of success and failure (Gabryś-Barker 2009). This paper is a presentation of only a part of the whole project, which aims at addressing the issue of pre-service teachers' beliefs about their role and position in a FL classroom and interpretation of these beliefs in the light of all the factors that contribute to their formation.

2 Beliefs and Their Sources

A lot has been written about the belief systems of teachers and the values they hold; these are very comprehensively presented in the well-known book by Richards and Lockhart (1994 30–31). Just to recapitulate, the authors classify the sources of these into the following groups:

- teachers' individual experiences as foreign language learners;
- teachers' own experience of successfully (or unsuccessfully) applied techniques of teaching in their own context;

- preferred teaching practices and routines in a given institution (*established practice*);
- personally driven preferences (e.g. preferences for more interactive techniques);
- knowledge relating to theories of learning/teaching acquired in the course of training or recently encountered (*educationally-based or research based principles*);
- acceptance of a certain approach or method in teaching (*principles derived from an approach or method*, e.g. the belief in communicative language teaching as the best way to develop communicative skills of learners).

Different sources of beliefs and/or their combination will undoubtedly contribute to a system of convictions observed by an individual teacher in relation to:

- the language taught;
- the specificity of a FL learning process;
- FL teaching as a process;
- the program and syllabus implemented;
- FL teaching as a profession.

Also learners involved in the process of teaching as passive 'receivers' (but also these days seen as active participants and decision-making agents in it) become significant sources for the beliefs their teachers hold. To make the whole dynamics of beliefs even more complex, learners' convictions and their sources clearly have a contributive power to the way classroom processes occur. These beliefs relate to some of the same areas as the teachers' systems but will often be of a more indeterminate and misconceived nature, lacking in expertise and awareness in some cases. Such beliefs will be formed by (Richards and Lockhart 1994 p. 52–57):

- perception of the language learnt and how difficult it is;
- attitude to the TL speakers (positive and negative images and stereotypes);
- nature of language learning in its different areas of competence (skills and different aspects of language knowledge);
- learning experiences of the past at different stages of education;
- attitude and perception of oneself as a person and as a learner;
- individual goals learners strive for in their language learning.

Turning to the profile of the subjects of the study reported in this paper, as pre-service teachers, we will be considering a group of language learners with very little—2 months at most—experience of teaching and a long history of FL learning, approximately 10 or more years of formal instruction in EFL. It may be assumed that learning experiences will be the major source for their perceptions of themselves in their own classrooms at the initial stages of teaching. And that this will shape their perceptions of themselves and their roles as teachers and the way they will subsequently conceptualize those roles.

3 Teacher Roles and Teacher Identity

In the introductory part of his book *Diary of a language teacher*, Appel (1995) sketches out an evolution in the approach to the profession of a teacher. As in other areas of professionalism, also a shift in perceptions in teaching can be observed. Following Schön (1983, 1987), Appel admits that:

> (…) the glamour of professionalism in our society has faded away over the last two decades, because 'experts' are no longer seen as providing relevant answers to the world's problems (…) the professions (be they medicine, architecture, management, law or teaching) have defined the relationship between their academic source disciplines and practice as one "in which rigorous professional practitioners are instrumental problem solvers who select technical means best suited to particular purposes. Rigorous professional practitioners solve well-formed instrumental problems by applying theory and technique derived from systematic, preferably scientific knowledge (Schön 1987, quoted in Appel 1995, p. xii).

This tendency is also reflected in classroom practices as advocated and promoted by modern methodologies in which the teacher is no longer an expert, or at least this may not be his major role. A high degree of autonomy given to learners allows a teacher still to remain a relevant source of knowledge among other sources (the learners themselves for instance). However, the teacher is more often seen as a guide, facilitator, and monitor. Training programs in teacher education fully promote this approach to the teaching profession.

Nevertheless, it has to be remembered that pre-service teachers still come from very traditional teaching contexts (at least in the Polish educational system) and there may be a certain confusion of roles they are confronted with as learners at schools and learners at teacher training institutions. In the reality of a classroom situation they may experience a certain disequilibrium (destabilization), which for a novice may be highly threatening. This feeling of disequilibrium will also result from perceptions of oneself in relation to (Brown 2006 p. 677):

- the person I am;
- the person I want to remain;
- the person I hate to be;
- the teacher I fear to be;
- the teacher I want to be.

In his longitudinal study of novice teachers, based entirely on student voices: on intrapersonal comments (an extended student-written narrative) and interpersonal comments (in-depth personal interviews) made by a trainee student, Brown (2006, p. 676) describes a case study of Merryn, a novice teacher, whose development of teacher identity he observed over a period of time. He says:

> Merryn is threatened by the mergence of multiple identities, and the difficulties this multiplicity invites. The disequilibrium comes from the inability to use the emergence of multiple identities as opportunities to extend the range of choice of action. Instead, the multiple identities associated with the different aspects of the teacher's role are experienced as threats to identificatory coherence (…) Becoming a teacher is experienced as becoming an increasingly fragmented person.

But this will not always be the case. For many students, disequilibrium can contribute to personal and professional growth if seen as not threatening but rather "leading to an expanded, integrated self, more diverse and richer in the possibilities for action that multiple identities afford" (Brown 2006, p. 676). Brown sees a mentor teacher (a trainer) as *the significant other* that can influence a trainee in personal and professional growth by consciously monitoring this experience of disequilibrium a novice inevitably faces in the initial stages of the professional career.

4 The Study

4.1 Focus of the Study

This study looks at the ways in which pre-service teachers see themselves as teachers and comments on where these perceptions come from. Like in the study by Strugielska and Siek-Piskozub (2008), an attempt has been made at classifying the trainees' conceptualizations about teachers and themselves as teachers. This time, however, in contrast to the above-mentioned study, the data are qualitative and not quantitative in nature and solely based on individual student voices, reporting in different ways and styles, with a different degree of depth and sophistication on their attitudes, thoughts and feelings towards their new experiences in the FL classroom.

The major focus of the discussion is the influence of learning experiences the trainees have had in the past at school and their learning experiences now (their language learning as well as the acquisition of professional knowledge), and its relevance to experiential events in their classrooms. Specifically, the discussion will revolve around such issues as:

1. To what extent restoring past and present learning experiences contributes to belief systems of pre-service teachers as FL teachers.
2. To what extent they are capable of conceptualizing themselves in terms of metaphors that create a unified system of beliefs.
3. To what extent theoretical knowledge and teacher training add to their image of themselves and their personal as well as professional development.

It will be of interest to see if there are any more dominant patterns, or whether there is a great variability between these images and systems of beliefs as represented by individual pre-service teachers. An additional purpose of this paper is to take a look at a group of practicing teachers and see if their perceptions differ from those who are at initial stages of teaching, still undergoing their training before becoming fully qualified.

4.2 *Sample, Context and Data Sources*

As mentioned earlier, this paper reports on only part of work in progress carried out with a group of thirty pre-service teachers involved in writing a diary as their diploma work throughout the period of their obligatory teaching practice. The focus of the diary is on *critical incidents* (Tripp 1993) identified by the students during their teaching experiences at the beginning, in the middle and towards the end of their apprentice period in schools. At this moment the trainees have just completed the first stage, that is *My beginnings*. Table 1 presents an overview of the whole project.

For the purposes of this discussion only the introductory part of the diploma work *Me as teacher* is analyzed and used as a data source. It is supplemented by a reflective essay written by the same group of students, this time focusing on the factors that have contributed to their perceptions of a FL teacher, past and present, and their contribution to 'who I am', 'what kind of teacher I am now' and 'who I want to be as a teacher in future', and 'how I conceptualize metaphorically this profession'.

The trainees are also compared with a group of thirty in-service teachers, whose teaching practice, though not very extensive yet, has nevertheless entailed regular employment mostly in public schools. Their experience ranges from two to six years. Consequently, they cannot be claimed to be experienced teachers; rather they are still in the process of developing their didactic style and constantly modifying their perceptions about teaching.

5 Data Presentation and Discussion

5.1 *Me as a Teacher (Beliefs)*

When discussing their system of beliefs about the main role of the teacher, the position students take ranges from a very traditional focusing on the teacher himself as the major agent in the process to teaching/learning seen as a knowledge-giver and expert, through a parent-like figure focusing on the learners as those needing care, to perceptions relating to being a missionary and facing a challenge ('A fighter') (see Table 2).

Commenting on the reflections as presented in Table 2, the trainees' perceptions can be interpreted in the following way:

- *Mission*: The perceptions of trainee teachers of the profession and themselves in this profession reflect both their idealistic attitude, pointing out their vocation to teach, and the significant role teachers play in their learner's lives as 'architects and sculptors', or 'gardeners', contributing not only to their knowledge and language ability but above all, to their personal growth. In this category they also see their own growth in personal as well as in professional terms.

Table 1 The structure of the project (Gabryś-Barker 2009)

Stage	Title	Content	Objective
Introduction	The teaching context	1. Me as teacher 2. My students 3. My school	Presentation of the teaching contexts and learner profile

Chapter I	My beginnings	1. *The first impression*
		  1.1. Diary entry 1
		  1.2. Comments
		2. *Ghosts from the past*
		  2.1. Diary entry 2
		  2.2. Comments
		3. *Checking the borders*
		  3.1. Diary entry 3
		  3.2. Comments
		4. Summary
			Introduction to teaching in the first month of teaching practice.
			Initial self-evaluation (strong and weak points)
			Setting goals

Chapter II	In the middle	Three entries in the mid-period of practicum Summary	The end of the first semester teaching experiences Evaluation of progress
Chapter III	Towards the end	Three entries in the final period of practicum Summary	The third (final stage) of teaching practice Evaluation of progress
Chapter IV	My year at school	1. Introduction (general remarks) 2. Successes 3. Failures 3. A way forward	Self-reflection (a general impression) Highlighting success and failure areas Planning for future
Appendices		Lesson plans, materials used, comments from learners (optional)	Additional information, learner feedback to a novice teacher
Bibliography		References and sources used in analysis of critical incidents	To support the analysis of the entries with theory and research findings

Table 2 Perceptions of teacher's roles

Beliefs: *Teaching is like a*:	Rate (% of subjects)	Success or failure ?	Trainees' comments and evaluation (unedited language)
Mission	27	Predominantly seen as failure (20%)	Giving oneself away amazing period opening new worlds to learners affectivity development of awareness golden rule; be prepared
Challenge	20	Mixed responses, but slight dominance of failure	Learning from students adapting to the situation coping need for results role of code of conduct individual approach
Sharing knowledge	22	Experience of failure	Not discouraging feeling the need for knowledge being tested by pupils a productive period need for cooperation with learners competence
Professionalism (teachers as experts—methods, management and control)	25	Perception of failure	A learning experience need for constant development contradictions between the method used and own beliefs
Acting	2	Mostly seen as both success and failure	Experiential period of experimenting teacher as a source of fun discipline focus
Parenting	2	Seen as inadequate (failure)	Need to establish the right atmosphere and climate in the classroom
Parenting and acting	2	Failure due to lack of knowledge and preparation skills	Harsh reality of the classroom: expect the unexpected

- *Challenge*: Teaching seen as challenge expresses the students' insecurity at not being professional enough yet and lacking experience. This challenge, however, seems motivating and encouraging even in the face of failures which the novices encounter quite frequently in their daily classroom practices.
- *Sharing knowledge* and *professionalism*: Awareness of the need for constant development is registered in the perception of teaching as a profession requiring high qualifications in terms of the knowledge a teacher possesses: subject matter knowledge, knowledge of pedagogy and psychology and the basics of effective

interpersonal communication skills, knowledge of the most effective ways of passing language knowledge on to learners and developing their abilities in language use at the level of methodology of teaching.

- *Acting and parenting*: Some of the subjects chose to comment on their perceptions of themselves as teachers in terms of the roles that seem to them to be significant in a FL classroom. These are the roles of an actor and parent, each of them emphasizing different dimensions of teaching. Acting means being able 'to hide behind a mask', to reach a variety of teaching goals and, as a consequence, to be effective in teaching but also in distancing oneself to what one does. The other role, that of a parent, seems to give importance to achieving an appropriate rapport with the learners which would facilitate their learning and well-being in the classroom by making them feel secure, open and recreating 'being at home' in that context.

5.2 Where Do My Beliefs Come From? (Sources of Beliefs)

In their reflections on 'Where do my beliefs about teaching come from?', the students looked back at their past experiences as learners, at primary and secondary schools. These experiences naturally varied from the most exhilarating to the most disastrous. The trainees also revealed their own selves, their personalities, their interests and their perceptions as they changed with increased experience in the classroom. Here are some comments made by the trainees on the factors significant for the formation of their beliefs about teaching (All the comments are direct quotations from the trainees and their language has in no way been altered):

a. *Restoring past experiences (1)*: *Teachers of the past as models*:

(…) until I met an English teacher who was completely different. Her eyes were sparkling and she was full of life. She showed me that a teacher is somebody who has his/her own life and preferences. Moreover, she was keen on sharing her opinions and experiences with us. It was the moment that I realized how important it is to be yourself and still be able to teach others. Who could I compare a teacher to? Trying to answer this question I thought of a guide leading the group of tourists in some place of tourist attraction (…). When I was a student I remember one teacher whom I could compare to a perfect guide.
The first teacher taught me just vocabulary and structures, without practicing speaking and the second one was bored on our lessons (…) as I came to my first English lesson in a secondary school I was little bit frightened but also for the first time wanted to learn this language, I was motivated. She showed me how to demand, and at the same time, keep learners' positive attitude toward English. I would like to be like my teacher from secondary school and hear my learners saying that I was a great teacher and taught them a lot.
(…) the image of a great teacher I based on my learning experience when teaching children I try to imitate my first English teacher. She still teaches in a private school. (…) The learners treat her as a second mother. They admired her as she is lively and energetic

teacher (…) With a bit of luck I will become such a teacher. I would like to be admired by my learners, not only as a competent user of the language but as a good teacher (full of beans).

As a student (…) I needed time to build up my confidence and become more open-minded. Once I felt secure in the classroom I felt like being in the center of it. I wanted to be just like my teacher. I wanted to be her, actually (…) the pattern of future me. (…) thanks to my English teacher in high school I passed the FCE exam and found out about the teacher training college. I had certain ideas that were actually only bricks scattered around. My English teacher helped me to put them together and create quite a strong wall, resistant to the failures I had to put up with later.

b. *Restoring past experiences (2): Acting contrary to one's own school experience:*

When I was a student at gimnazjum I knew that I am going to be a teacher. Moreover, I knew exactly what kind of teacher I am not going to be. Casting back my mind I recall all those hours that my friends and I spent shivering with fear before chemistry classes, crying because of the embarrassment after English lessons or just sleeping during geography.

I can discern some mistakes made by my own teacher of English (…) I had a teacher who always criticized and mocked her students, which resulted in my avoidance of speaking (…) due to this fact, I attempt to be particularly patient and understanding towards shy students in order to help them overcome the obstacle.

Firstly I believe that my experiences as a student with teachers were rather a caution how not to behave than a good model. I used to perceive teachers as boring, scolding and always dissatisfied people (…).

As a teacher I often remind myself of what I used to experience at school and in this way I can understand my students better.

When I was a child I always looked up to those 'big' people, so wise and talking in such an elaborate and eloquent way (…) As I was growing older I started to treat my teachers more as friends that I could always talk to, ask them to help me (…) My English teacher from high school was, unfortunately, nowhere near being my friend (…) When I started studying at the teacher training college I promised myself that if I happen to teach I will do my best not to turn into my English teacher from high school.

c. *Oneself as a learner and the learner as a human being:*

My experience as a student is not very helpful when I started teaching. Being a good teacher means that we have to remember about students' weaknesses. A student is also a normal human being who needs to talk with you or ask for advice.

The conception of me as a teacher derives from my learning experiences as a student and observations of the process of learning among teenagers at a grammar school. (…). When I see teenagers today, I cast my memory back to the times when I was a teenager myself and observe that they have become more rebellious and un-willing to cooperate with the teacher. My ways of teaching teenagers are similar to those used by my teachers who taught me at grammar school. I use knowledge obtained not only from the teachers but also from my own experiences and studies related to methodology.

Secondly, I am sure that my personality greatly influences my teaching because the way I am is the way I teach. It is always me who teaches. (…) I set my heart in everything I do and it is the same with teaching. As a result, I am often affected by my students and their words. What is more, I am prone to criticism, which is not particularly good in a job of a teacher, so I do my best to be successful.

d. *New experiences and changing perceptions*:

Many people share the opinion that teacher's work is not a big deal. I also used to take it for granted while being a primary and secondary school student. (...) Now I can see myself as an example of perceiving it was totally wrong.

When I became a teacher some of my ideas and values underwent modifications, but I still perceive it as spreading the light. With only one exception—I sometimes wonder who is really the source of the light. Is it me or my students?

I have always wanted to be a teacher. During the past two years I have gained a great experience in teaching children. It came to me as a surprise that the cooperation with the pupils can be so inspiring and motivating.

From the very beginning, from the primary school we make some critical remarks about our teachers. We think that we would do certain things better. I also had similar feelings when I was a pupil. However, when I started teaching, my concept about former teachers and their methods of teaching have changed.

What I have learned is that I shouldn't get discouraged by failure and at the same time too confident because of my successes, as all those experiences create me as a teacher and I hope that next time I stumble, it will be easier to stand up and soldier on.

e. *Other interests*:

Literature influenced my life (...) Teachers of Polish were the only ones who managed to keep my interest during long classes that I had to survive (...). Polish Romantic artists awoke in me a sense of responsibility which I want to face. As a teacher I have a great chance to fulfill myself (A fighter).

f. *Unresolved*:

My beliefs are still unrooted.

5.3 My Metaphors About Teaching (Conceptualizations)

The beliefs expressed by the students are well reflected in the way they conceptualize their profession and picture themselves as teachers. They are represented here as quotations serving as headings in the students' narratives:

- *The story of a little boy, Like an eagle, Practice makes perfect*—these metaphors/sayings emphasize the on-going process of searching for models, best practices, still in the early stages of development, still 'young', 'spreading wings' and experimenting.
- *The lighthouse (a beam of hope), A light in the darkness*—the teacher is seen as someone leading his/her learners from a state of ignorance, inability, lack of knowledge to 'enlightenment', always encouraging learners to find their own ways to achieve their goals.
- *A good guide, On a tour, A long way*—the teacher is conceptualized as a guiding person with knowledge and able to demonstrate what is worth seeing and

learning about; also someone who knows the way: where to go and how to get there.

- *Teacher as an actor, Playing the most important role*—here the emphasis is put on the diversity of roles a teacher needs to be able to play, each of them requiring skill and professionalism and also the ability to distance himself/ herself from the real self and 'hide behind the mask'.
- *A torn Sagittarius, Keep being myself*—in contrast to the previous concept of the teacher as an actor, here some of the trainees believe that only by being true to oneself ('keeping one's own identity') can they become successful teachers and establish a genuine rapport with their learners, always expressing and sharing what they think and feel in the open, discussing their own personal experiences with the learners.
- *All thanks to the greatest builders in the world, Sculpting minds*—here the teaching profession is perceived as creative and artistic (a sculptor, an architect), where learners are seen as the end product of an act of creativity on the part of the teacher. These images should be considered very teacher-centered.
- *Old images, Image of me as a teenager*—this perception highlights the role of past experiences and of restoring the past and giving it its due in one's own practices, perhaps in some re-shaped form but based on the models familiar from one's own school days.
- *A knight errant, A fighter*—these images on the other hand point to the need for changes in the teaching profession, discarding old models and emphasizing the need for taking (almost heroic) steps to effect changes even against all the odds: on a macro level, in the entrenched system of schools themselves and on the micro level, in one's own classroom.

Each of these metaphors/conceptualizations of the teaching profession reflects the positive ambitions the pre-service teachers have towards their future profession. Each implies the need for a teacher's active involvement: both professional and personal, creativity and responsibility and also the courage to be different and the need to go on trying, irrespective of failures and obstacles. The following are some exceptionally positive and encouraging perceptions of teachers to be:

> I believe it is fairly adequate to compare myself to a knight. I am such a type of a teacher who constantly looks for solutions when facing a problem (…) Some of them are very challenging and not easy to use in practice. However, it does not frighten me (…).

How do these trainees compare with those who have more regular and extensive experience, though they are still not at this stage fully developed teachers?

5.4 In-Service Teachers Versus Trainees

The in-service teachers were also asked to reflect upon their perceptions of this profession and the sources of the beliefs they hold about it and which they put into practice in their own classrooms. This was carried out in the form of a narrative text.

There are some significant differences between these two groups, the trainees and in-service teachers. What characterizes the in-service teachers in terms of the content of their reflection on their own classroom practices and experiences is the following:

- More focus on discussing learners than teachers themselves. In the case of trainees there was an almost obsessive need to create a positive image of oneself as a teacher and a person which became the focus of their narratives but also had a key role in the identification of critical incidents (discussed in Gabryś-Barker 2009).
- The need to modify the old, traditional objectives of teaching a foreign language by rules and grammar translation and moving towards communicative needs, hence the development of speaking skills as the major instructional issue. This is also seen by the trainees as the most significant aspect of FL instruction.
- Motivating learners and creating their system of values since home is seen as very negligent in this respect, parents seem totally detached from school and uninterested in its workings. On the other hand, the role of home and parents was never mentioned by the trainees as teacher's allies (or their enemies for that matter); hence it may be assumed that it was not considered an important factor for this group of subjects.
- An individualized approach to learners, based on their needs and individual profiles (with emphasis placed on a special care student). This was also seen as equally important by the trainees.

Also in pinpointing the factors that shaped their approach to the teaching profession and, as a consequence, their classroom practices, the in-service teachers looked both at external factors and those deriving directly from their own needs and idiosyncratic experiences. The external factors which seem to be very strong in the comments made by the in-service teachers and which were scarcely ever pointed out by the group of pre-service teachers are:

- the social environment and social background of learners: where they come from, who they are and who their parents are and what system of values they instill in their children (if any at all); there is a strong emphasis placed on diversification of approaches here according to the context of teaching and teacher's roles;
- the objectives of a particular educational context (a specific school) with regard to its social standing and prestige, which went wholly unregarded by the trainees;
- the role of supervisors, the head of the school and educational authorities in general as entities imposing certain measures to be taken and rules to be followed;
- the external constraints imposed by the institution on how to teach, what to teach and how to behave as a teacher were seen as factors taken account of in

approaching teaching and often causing one to act against one's own individual beliefs by in-services, demonstrating a contradiction between externally and internally-driven factors.

Internal factors which are conceived as shaping these teachers' images of themselves as they are or are aiming/struggling to be, relate to:

- their experience as students and the way they were taught in training institutions (TTC—teacher training colleges) and not so much in the early educational context of the primary and secondary school; college teachers are seen by this group of teachers as models of language instructors in terms of language and professional competence; in this respect, trainee teachers emphasize more TTC teachers' professional knowledge rather than seeing them as models of FL instructional practices to be followed;
- knowledge gathered as a result of their TTC program of studies which is seen to constitute 'half of the success', also highlighted and even more strongly, in the comments made by the trainees;
- their own experience of school ('facing reality') as the major factor in forming beliefs, which the trainees still lack but are fully aware of their significance;
- the developmental character which leads to the testing of pedagogical theory in the first year of teaching contributes most significantly to teaching approaches and beliefs;
- the need to take security measures by establishing one's own routines and individual ways, which in the case of pre-service teachers was described as giving up a democratic, friendly manner of teaching when confronted with the reality of the classroom, and taking up a more authoritarian stance somewhat against their own beliefs;
- copying or rejecting the models of the past with almost equally strong emphasis, that is, admiration for or discouragement by previous teachers when relating to the far-past (school); the in-services are more critical of the past than the trainees, who also seem to have a stronger positive memory of their teachers at school; this of course may be due to very sharp changes in approach to teaching foreign languages, moving away from the traditional teacher-dominated class-room (the negative experience of in-service teachers) to learner-centered and more autonomous context (the positive experience of trainees).

It seems surprising that both groups of teachers do not reflect upon themselves as language learners. No transfer of learning, understood as one's individual way of approaching a FL learning situation (Gabryś-Barker 2008) seems to be a significant variable for the subjects in forming their system of beliefs about the nature of the teaching process. In the case of such an extensive learning history, it may be safely assumed that these teachers (both groups) developed their own set of strategies for learning and that their experience of success (for they are amongst the best examples of stories of success in language learning) would contribute to their beliefs about teaching, constituting first-hand experience that could be shared with their learners.

Clearly, similarities and differences between these two groups are experiential. Exposure to the realities of a classroom and a school, and the pedagogical tasks to be performed by pre-service and in-service teachers are very different. Their positions in a school hierarchy and functioning are different. Different types of awareness are present. But they have one thing in common and it is the need to reflect, develop and change. This is very encouraging in view of the fact that, generally speaking, experienced teachers are heavily criticized for becoming routinised. Maybe a new generation of teachers is growing?

6 Final Comments

What was discussed earlier in this article, and illustrated with heart-felt comments from the trainees, can be recapitulated in brief as the main findings. The main beliefs expressed about teaching are seen as (in order of frequency):

- a mission to be accomplished;
- a highly specialist job requiring professionalism;
- sharing of knowledge developed through study and experience;
- performing a well-prepared role.

These systems of beliefs can be conceptualized as metaphors of a victorious battle, a lighthouse showing the way in difficulties, a guided tour or acting on the stage. At the same time, these systems of beliefs derive from:

- models of former teachers that the trainees recover from their memory, mostly at the primary and secondary level—positive examples and, as such, copied by the trainees in their own classrooms, but also negative and, as such, rejected by them;
- one's personality features which determine preferred styles of management and interaction with the learners;
- the new teaching experiences of trainees.

What seems most important in these narratives is that all the trainees who expressed their views see themselves as involved in a developmental process of becoming: becoming more aware and more reflective, more creative and able to share their knowledge and also themselves as people with their own learners, revealing a very strong need to reflect on themselves in their own classrooms. Developing an awareness of this need and a willingness to reflect are the first steps in developing the ability to reflect.

References

Appel, J. 1995. *Diary of a language teacher*. London: Heinemann.

Arabski, J., D. Gabryś-Barker, and A. Łyda, eds. 2008. *PASE Papers* 2007. *Studies in language and methodology of teaching foreign languages*. 2 vols. Katowice: University of Silesia Press.

Barker A., D. Callahan, and A. Ferreira, eds. 2009. Success and failure. *Essays from the 29th APEAA conference at the Aveiro university*, 17-19th April 2008. Aveiro: University of Aveiro press.

Brown, T. 2006. Negotiating psychological disturbance in pre-service teacher education. *Teaching and Teacher Education* 22: 675–689.

Gabryś-Barker, D. 2008. *The role of transfer of learning (TL) in multilingual instruction and development*. Katowice: University of Silesia Press (forthcoming).

Gabryś-Barker, D. 2009. Critical incidents in foreign language instruction: Pre-service teachers' perceptions of success and failure. In eds. A. Barker, D. Callahan, and A. Ferreira, 303–316.

Calderhead, J., and P. Gates, eds. 1993. *Conceptualizing reflection in teacher development*. London/Washington: The falmer Press.

Kubler LaBoskey, V. 1993. A conceptual framework for reflection in pre-service teacher education. In eds. J. Calderhead, and P. Gates, 23–38.

Richards, J., and C. Lockhart. 1994. *Reflective teaching in second language classrooms*. Cambridge: Cambridge University Press.

Schön, D. 1983. *The reflective practitioner. How professionals think in action*. London: Maurice Temple Smith.

Schön, D. 1987. *Educating the reflective practitioner*. San Francisco: Jossey-Bass.

Strugielska, A., and T. Siek-Piskozub. 2008. The teaching/learning experience at the university level: A case study in educational discourse. In eds. J. Arabski, D. Gabryś-Barker, and A. Łyda, 485–498.

Tripp, D. 1993. *Critical incidents in teaching. Developing professional judgement*. London: Routledge.

The Dynamic Nature of a Tertiary Learner's Foreign Language Self-Concepts

Sarah Mercer

Abstract Domain-specific self-concept has been shown to play a decisive role in successful learning and to be positively related to key psychological factors and learning outcomes, such as interest, motivation, goal setting, strategy use, persistence and self-regulated learning. Little research has been carried out into self-concept within SLA and Foreign language learning, although some studies have considered related self-constructs, such as self-esteem and self-efficacy. Its relative absence is, however, surprising if one considers the potentially important role played by the self in foreign language learning compared to other subjects. This article presents part of a PhD study investigating the EFL self-concept of a single, tertiary-level, advanced learner and considers the extent to which it appears to be dynamic. The findings emerging from the analysis reveal that this learner's FL self-concepts appear to encompass both stable and dynamic elements, a finding which supports research results elsewhere. The analysis shows how the construct's dynamic nature may vary depending on the domain-specificity and/or centrality of the self-beliefs concerned, the initial level of self-concept at the outset, and various other psychological processes, such as attributions, self-protection and self-verification strategies. It concludes by considering the implications of the findings for research and pedagogy.

1 Introduction: Self-concept as an Individual Difference

Foreign language learning (FLL) is acknowledged as being a complex undertaking that can potentially be influenced by a vast myriad of factors, both personal and contextual (Oxford 2002), as evinced by many models of language learning

S. Mercer (✉)
University of Graz, Graz, Austria
e-mail: sas_mercer@yahoo.com

M. Pawlak (ed.), *New Perspectives on Individual Differences in Language Learning and Teaching*, Second Language Learning and Teaching, DOI: 10.1007/978-3-642-20850-8_13, © Springer-Verlag Berlin Heidelberg 2012

(see e.g. Clément 1980; Gardner 1985; Schumann 1986; Dörnyei 1994; Oxford and Shearin 1994; MacIntyre et al. 1998; Dörnyei 2005). Focusing on the personal individual variables, it has become clear that the *self* in various guises can play an important role in how an individual approaches and copes with the experience of learning a foreign language (see e.g. Cohen and Norst 1989; Gardner and MacInytre 1993; Ehrman and Oxford 1995; MacIntyre et al. 2002; Ehrman et al. 2003; Dörnyei 2005).

Two particular self-constructs, namely *self-efficacy* and *self-esteem*, have received some attention in SLA (see e.g. Oxford and Nyikos 1989; Ehrman and Oxford 1995; Chamot et al. 1996; Yang 1999; Rubio 2007). However, there is also a third self-construct, namely *self-concept*, which has been ascribed a significant role in general academic learning within the field of psychology, (see e.g. McCombs and Marzano 1990; Wigfield and Karpathian 1991; Hattie 1992; Marsh and Yeung 1997; Muijs 1997; Skaalvik and Valas 1999; Green et al. 2006), but which has been somewhat neglected by SLA.

A person's self-concept consists of the beliefs one has about oneself, or, as (Hamlyn 1983, p. 241) expresses it, "the picture of oneself". Self-concept appears to function in domain-specific terms (Marsh et al. 1988), i.e. self-beliefs are grouped to reflect a particular field or area. It is viewed as "containing both cognitive and affective elements", (Mercer 2008, p. 183) and concerns an individual's self-perceptions in a particular domain, such as learning EFL.

2 Purpose of the Study

This article will briefly describe research carried out as part of a PhD study investigating the self-concept in a FLL context. It aims at casting light on the specific nature of this individual psychological construct in the FLL context, in particular the extent to which it appears to be dynamic.

Given the absence of research into self-concept in SLA and the rather contradictory findings concerning the dynamic nature of self-concept (see e.g. Markus and Kunda 1986; Markus and Wurf 1987; Harter 2006), it was decided to carry out an initial exploratory study aimed at generating ideas and hypotheses which could be investigated in further research. It was thus felt that a single, longitudinal case study would be best suited to providing sufficiently in-depth, rich, holistic and contextualised data that would enable any potential changes in this psychological construct to emerge (Yin 2003).

3 The Case Study in This Programme of Research

The participant in this particular case study was a volunteer, female student who, at the outset of the study, was 20 years old. She was studying two languages, English as her major and Italian as her minor, in order to become a teacher at a university in southern Austria. I will refer to her throughout this paper as Joana.

Joana already had quite a high level of spoken English at the beginning of the study. I would judge her English to have been high B2, low C1 according to the European Common Framework of Reference.[1] Consequently, it can be assumed that she had the meta-language skills to cope with taking part in this research and expressing herself fully in English.

The data were mostly generated through in-depth, informal interviews which extended over a 22-month period, but were also supplemented by 3 written texts which the participant wrote for weeks when we were unable to meet for an interview. As Shapka and Keating (2005, p. 93) claim that a one year period is most likely to be insufficient to track noticeable changes in the self-concept, it was hoped that the extended period of time for this study would enable any potential, even subtle, changes in her self-concepts to be revealed.

4 Findings

In the data, Joana displays evidence of two clear and distinct FL self-concepts, her English as a foreign language (EFL) self-concept and her Italian as a foreign language (IFL) self-concept. Although the two are clearly linked, they are quite distinct. In Joana's case, her EFL self-concept is the most complex, highly developed and strongest, most positive of the two FL self-concepts. In contrast, her IFL self-concept is generally less positive and, at the outset of the study, is initially less detailed and complex in terms of content. Aspects of both FL self-concepts will be considered in establishing the extent to which her FL self-concepts may be dynamic.

4.1 Stable Aspects of Joana's FL Self-Concepts

It is perhaps worth beginning by establishing which aspects of Joana's foreign language (FL) self-concepts did not appear to change over time. The first and most salient stable aspect concerns her global EFL self-concept and her positive relationship with the language. In her very first session she states:

> (...) I really love English and I'm into English (...) I think English was always my favourite or has always been my favourite language (#1: 28-29; 40-41).[2]

---

[1] See http://www.coe.int/t/dg4/linguistic/Source/Framework_EN.pdf (p. 24) (Access date: 28.10.07).

[2] Referencing conventions concerning data extracts: 'J' is used to refer to Joana's case study data. The first number (#1) refers to the number of the primary document from which the extract is taken. These run chronologically with #1 being the first and #24 being the final interview. The following numbers in the reference (28–29) are the line numbers of the data extract. Readers interested in the data in more detail should contact the author directly. The same extract may be used more than once to illustrate different aspects of the analysis.

She continually expresses her positive feelings towards English throughout the period of data collection, and this appears to be a stable aspect of her EFL self-concept, e.g.:

> My feelings towards English. It will always be my sort of number one or my favourite (J#15: 781–782). (J#16: 1168–1170).
> (…) it wouldn't change my attitude towards English anyway because I absolutely love English and that will never change

And indeed in our final session she concludes:

> Well, my relationship to English hasn't changed much in the sense that I'm still totally in love with that language (J#24: 283–284).

Another self-belief present in both her FL self-concepts that did not appear to change was her feeling that she is an open, talkative, sociable person:

> I am a very sociable person (J#4: 1620).
> I'm very communicative (J#5: 1405).
> I am a very sociable person (…) I am a very chatty person (J#24: 781; 894).

It is important to note that this belief about herself appears across both her FL self-concepts and also her general academic self-concept. Its presence in several different domains suggests that it may represent a central, 'core' self-belief for Joana (Harter 2006). Thus, it raises the question as to whether the relative 'centrality' of a self-belief to one's self-concept network, in other words its presence in several domains, may affect the degree to which it may be stable/dynamic (cf. Markus and Wurf 1987).

Another self-belief present across several domains that is important for Joana and which seems to remain unchanged during the research period concerns her belief that she is "an active person" (see e.g. J#5: 697), as the data below illustrate:

> I'm, I'm like my dad and my dad, I mean he has built a house, he is an active person and I think I am a little bit like him, I need activity, I think I'm not a person who can stay in all the time in just studying, studying, studying (J#6: 541–545).
> Because I am so, I don't know, I need to move, I need to do something. I just, I am not that person who can sit down for hours but absolutely not (J#20: 179–182).

This belief is closely related to how she approaches language learning and the kind of learner she perceives herself to be both in her foreign languages and in general academic terms, e.g.:

> A bookworm, yeah that's it, a bookworm. I'm just not that type of person, I'm much too physical or active, I'm like my dad who likes to do something and I, it's still at university, I do a lot, then there was the Latin course, I think I just need exercise even if I go out or something, it doesn't matter. Or if I talk with people in English, that's still exercise. That's actively taking part in something but sitting down and reading, I can't do that or I can not, I don't know I'm just not a regular reader, that's just not me (J#13: 785–793).

This self-belief about being an 'active' person was again shared across several domains, including both her FL self-concepts, and appeared to be an established, central, 'core' part of her self-belief system which remained stable.

4.2 Dynamic Aspects of Joana's FL Self-Concepts

Several aspects of Joana's FL self-concepts did appear to change across the 22-month period. The first noticeable change in Joana's self-concept network concerns her general attitude towards reading and perception of herself as a 'reader'. At the outset, Joana stressed that she was not a reader and had never enjoyed reading in any language:

> And I really like the language but I'm not a reader, I've never been a reader, I used to read comics to sort of lift up my German[3] in Primary School, really I used to read comics like (...) really hundreds of comics because I couldn't read books, I just couldn't do it (J#1: 758–763).

This belief about herself not being a reader was shared across all her language-related domains. She explained her dislike of reading by her understanding of it as a 'passive' activity in contrast to her self-belief as 'an active person', as discussed earlier in the previous section:

> A bookworm, yeah that's it, a bookworm. I'm just not that type of person, I'm much too physical or active (...) Or if I talk with people in English, that's still exercise. That's actively taking part in something but sitting down and reading, I can't do that (...) (J#13: 785–786; 789–792).

The contrast she made between a 'passive reader' type of person and herself as an 'active person' remained consistent throughout.

However, following the period of time together with her boyfriend who was an avid reader and her stay abroad in Italy when she explains she had more spare time to read, her perception of herself as a reader appeared to change:

> I started to enjoy reading because I had the time to read (J#24: 654–656).
> I'd never thought in a million years I'd become a reader but now I actually. I think I am reader now which is amazing because I used to learn German just by reading comics because I couldn't face books (J#24: 2222–2225).

However, on closer examination of the data, I would question whether, although her reading habits appear to have changed in terms of behavioural patterns, her actual belief about herself as a 'reader type of person' has fundamentally changed. Although she unequivocally states in the final interview, as can be seen above, that she now considers herself to be a reader, in the same interview she once again contrasts a 'bookish, passive' type of person with a more 'sociable, active' person such as herself. As has been shown above, her view of herself as an 'active' person was a strong, consistent element of her self-beliefs across several domains that remained stable across the research period and consequently, there seems to be some discrepancy:

> (...) I need that personal link by people I like, you know, people I like. I am not that type of student that reads books, goes to university, studies at home, you know, in their room (...) (J#24: 775–778).

---

[3] German = L1.

I am not, I wouldn't say I am a totally academic person. Ahm, I'd say I am a mixture. I like being active, I enjoy even working, doing manual work or working in a pub or just interacting with people and talking and chatting (J#24: 802–806).

Thus, it seems as if the reported change in respect to herself as a reader cannot be seen as supplanting or replacing her previous self in this respect, although there are clear signs of development with respect possibly to her actual reading habits. There remains a discrepancy between her reported self-perceptions of change and possible actual changes in her core self-concept. This raises the question of how aware learners are of changes in their self-concepts and suggests care must be taken with self-report data.

Turning our attention now specifically to Joana's *EFL self-concept*, the first noticeable change that appears to have taken place concerns her belief about her accent and pronunciation in English. Her feelings noticeably change from a preference for American pronunciation towards a British accent, as can be seen from the chronological extracts from her data below:

I do like British English too but I just feel more comfortable with the other accent (J#2: 208–209).
Because I don't want to lose that American accent and I'm always trying to stick to that (J#3: 770–771).

J[4]   Yeah, I feel like I'm really getting into the British accent. I really, I can really but I don't, I don't mind, I don't mind getting into it anymore
S   No?
J   I have really changed. I don't know why?
S   What's changed or do you know why?
J   I don't know but I can hear me talking English and I can hear me talking more in a British way than in an American way and it's getting on and on (...) I can't speak like before anymore, it's gone, it's like washed away. I can't even, if I'd like to or I'd love to, you know copy it, I couldn't, it's so strange, it's really weird. I thought I'd never lose it but it's like gone (J#9: 398–410; 415–419).

I don't know if you can, if you are able to tell. I think it's a bit more British or neutral now. It's neutral, a bit more neutral than it used to be and I don't like the, oh my god, I was appalled by the Americans I listened to talking in Florence. It was just awful, I thought, how could I have ever liked this accent? It's so bad (J#24: 1154–1159)

It is interesting to note that pronunciation as a skill is of paramount importance to Joana and represents a strong recurrent theme throughout the data. As some researchers have concluded that pronunciation is linked to a learner's identity and relationship to the language (see e.g. Stevick 1978; Jenkins 2006), this makes any changes in self-beliefs concerning pronunciation particularly interesting and raises questions about the potentially 'special' nature of pronunciation with respect to a learner's sense of self.

The only other aspect of her EFL self-concept which appears to change concerns her self-beliefs about writing in English. The first time she explicitly

---

[4] J = Joana; S = Sarah (Researcher).

mentioned her self-concept concerning herself as a writer in English was immediately prior to her mid-term exam in written English when she was talking about preparing for the exams. Her statement implies a high degree of confidence in this domain:

> I mean 'Varieties of Written English', I guess I'll make that, that won't be a big problem (J#5: 61–62).

In the next session, she initially does not mention the exam but makes the first slightly negative statement about her written English:

> I should do more for written English because I know that's my weak point too (…) even if I if I'm not good at written English at the moment or I'm not doing that good (J#6: 915–917; 919–921).

As I knew from our previous sessions that she would have received her grade for the exam by then, I was able to ask her specifically about this, and she explained that she had 'nearly failed' the written exam:

> J   I think that I was brought down by the Varieties the midterm test.
> S   Okay.
> J   Because I had, okay, for me it is a really bad grade to have a four[5] plus and it is a really, for me that is really bad, it's almost like five, or I mean even if it is a four plus, it's not a three right or it's, it's nothing (…) and I just had a few (…) I thought I'd go there and I won't have any problems because I know all these phrases and I can do it (…)
> (…)
> S   And if you're being honest, what did you expect to get?
> J   A two or a three to be honest. I didn't expect it would be that bad (…) (J#6: 956–964; 970–972; 982–985).

Interestingly, her self-concept with respect to her writing in English improves again, and, some weeks later, she has rationalised the result in the following way:

> S   And you feel confident about your English again because you were a bit kind of worried after your exam, well not worried, but after the exam?
> J   Yeah, a bit affected. Yeah, I think I feel confident because I thought that over again and I thought, okay, what is wrong about that text and I thought I have too many details and the style is quite, the style is not correct. Okay, I can do something for that style but there is, there are no essential mistakes like you know basic mistakes, I haven't got any basic mistakes, so why should I be so worried, it's nothing really, it's nothing really deep or something (J#9: 477–488).

When a learner explains a poor result in this way, it could reflect psychological processes employed by the learner in order to protect their overall self-concept in the EFL domain, particularly in this case given the importance of English as a subject to her (cf. Wigfield and Karpathian 1991; Wigfield and Eccles 2000; Eccles and Wigfield 2002; Harter 2006). Joana also appears to engage in processes of 'compartmentalisation' (Showers 1992) by which she 'isolates' the 'near

---

[5] In Austria the grading system is from 1 to 5: 1 is the best grade and 5 is a fail.

failure' to the domain of writing, possibly in order to protect and maintain her overall positive EFL self-concept.

However, as she progresses and finishes the course with a '3', her EFL self-concept in this respect appears to change yet again, and she explicitly begins to mention her perceived weaknesses with written English again:

S   Yeah. What about the way you view yourself as an English learner has that changed?
J   I know now, completely, I'm completely sure that my oral and my writing skills, they really vary a lot.
(...)
J   (...) now in English it's probably, I should have, I know I would be, I know I would be a lot better in writing if I had read more. I'm just not a reader but I think I can still improve on writing a lot and it has to do a lot of practice and I know that, you know the more often you write and the more often you use things, you know, the easier it gets, although you do not read, although you're not a regular reader (J#13: 775–785).
(...)   my writing skills are really not the best (J#15: 352).

Interestingly, her feelings and beliefs about her abilities in written English then began to improve again, and towards the end of the research period, although she still felt somewhat less confident about her written English than her spoken English, she clearly felt more positive than she had at the mid-way stage of the research study:

> I am sure, you know, my writing abilities or whatever, you know, like this term, ahm, I've improved a lot even in terms of my writing but I am still not, I still don't feel comfortable writing a narrative or writing something, you know, professional like a literary text, I've always felt more comfortable, you know, speaking English than writing English. That hasn't really changed that much although I really feel much more comfortable than before or much more secure, much more self-confident (J#20: 651-659).

As indicated earlier, Joana's overall EFL self-concept remained positive throughout, and the experiences in the written course appeared to only temporarily alter her self-beliefs with respect to writing. In fact, it is interesting to note how her EFL writing self-concept appeared to fluctuate and go through a series of highs and lows across the research period, eventually re-adjusting back to virtually its original, relatively positive state.

However, none of the changes in her EFL self-concept were as striking as those that can be seen in her *IFL self-concept*. Given her stay of 6 months in Italy part way through the research period, it is perhaps not surprising that Joana feels that this experience has had a considerable impact on her IFL self-concept in terms of increased proficiency and affective changes in her motivation and attitude towards Italian. This would be expected from the stay abroad literature (see e.g. Meara 1994; Freed 1995a; Coleman 1997) and also from self-concept research concerning periods of transition or major life events which can affect your self-concept (see e.g. Wigfield et al. 1991; Harter et al. 1992; McAdams et al. 2001; Mercer 2007).

On a more global level, it can be seen how her overall IFL self-concept changes during the research period. At the outset, she feels there is a large imbalance between her English and Italian and her preference is clearly for English. Although this remains her favourite of the two languages, there is a noticeable shift with respect to her Italian, as the data below indicate:

> I thought okay my Italian is not as good as my English (J#1: 132–133).
>
> So, I'd say, yeah, I do love Italian now, I really adore the language and I really enjoy speaking it, I enjoy using it, I can, you know, I notice that when I text someone or when I write an email I am much quicker and there is no problem of thinking about vocabulary, it's just there. You know, and that's what happened to my English a long time ago I think, so, well, I was just waiting for that last boost of knowing in Italian (…) I think it's more equal now (J#24: 294–303; 2421).

It is important to note that the changes in her feelings towards and self-concept in Italian begin to change before her stay abroad in Italy. Although the changes are less dramatic, the developments in her IFL self-concept can nevertheless clearly be observed beforehand:

> Well, in Italian I feel like I'm improving a lot at the moment because I'm working hard on it (J#6: 860-862).
>
> I have 6 h of language courses in Italian now, so I'm going to be really. Put a lot of effort into it and I'm actually, I feel it now already that I'm on the way to, you know, on my way to getting really, really better, to improving a lot this term in Italian. Definitely better (J#16: 497–501).
>
> Yeah, and I think I'm making a lot of progress in Italian. I understand a lot more vocabulary (…) I just, I'm just getting better and better and I can feel it and it's really good compared to the last term (J#19: 48–50; 65–66).

It is perhaps also important to note that Joana makes internal attributions for her perceived progress in Italian. It is worth considering whether the fact that a learner makes internal or external attributions for perceived changes in ability may also affect the extent to which a change in the related self-concept may occur and persist (cf. Weiner 1986; Williams et al. 2001). Thus, if a learner believes they can improve through hard work and practice, then any improvements in actual achievement are likely to be internally attributed and could lead to more lasting changes in the related self-concept. The relationship between learners' attribution processes and their self-concepts suggests a rich area for further research (cf. Marsh 1984; Marsh et al. 1984; Marsh 1986; Weiner 1986; Simpson et al. 1996).

At the specific skill level within her IFL self-concept, a noticeable change takes place concerning Joana's self-beliefs about her spoken Italian. The following extracts illustrate the changes in her IFL self-concept in this area, which again also began before she went to Italy around the time of interview J#22:

> I just feel so, I don't know, self-conscious when it comes to talking Italian (J#4: 1653–1654).
>
> (…) in the spoken course I don't feel confident (J#9: 143–144).
>
> Yeah, and I've already noticed that even my spoken abilities are progressing right now (…) (J#21: 45–46).
>
> With time and practice my confidence speaking Italian was raised significantly and I started to believe in myself as a speaker of the language (J#23: 45–47).
>
> I am speaking Italian, I've got no problem, I can walk up to an Italian person and chat to them and I've no problem with that anymore which is really nice (J#24: 1066–1068).

Joana also refers to perceived changes in her IFL self-concept in very specific terms at the language skill and task level. All the following extracts are taken from the final interview, J#24, following her stay in Italy:

J   First of all I think my trip to Italy has influenced me a lot in many ways concerning my Italian, concerning my language skills (...)

(...)

J   I learned without noticing consciously that I'm learning, so right now I can watch an Italian movie without a problem, I, you know, just turn on the TV and it's no problem. I just watched one two days ago and it was really nice because I thought, wow, I can actually understand everything and I don't have to struggle and, you know, listen so carefully and (...)

S   And was that different before you went to Italy?

J   Yeah, totally, totally because my ability of understanding things has increased a lot.

(...)

J   I can actually speak fluently, I can send an email without looking a hundred words up in the dictionary.

(...)

J   In Italian my pronunciation has got a lot better. More natural, more fluent. I don't have to think about it. It just comes out more naturally.

(...)

J   Comprehension, pronunciation, oral skills, reading also, so reading an Italian book now is not a huge problem anymore but it used to be difficult and, you know, it's also concentration wise. It doesn't take that much concentration anymore (J#24: 19–20; 29–39; 300–302; 1122–1124; 1677–1680).

As has been seen, Joana's IFL self-concept seemed to change quite noticeably in virtually all language skill areas following her stay in Italy, however, it should also be remembered that central, 'core' beliefs about herself as an IFL learner, such as being 'an active' and 'sociable' language learner, as elucidated above in sect. 4.1, appeared to remain stable. This raises the question as to whether the aspects which may remain more stable may be the 'core' aspects of one's self-concept, whereas more 'peripheral', less central aspects of the self-concept may be more susceptible to change (cf. Harter 2006). These findings also suggest that the more 'peripheral' aspects of one's self-concept are more likely to be connected to actual ability. It is finally worth noting that as her IFL self-concept was weaker and less developed at the outset of the study than her EFL self-concept, the potential for change may fundamentally have been greater.

4.3 Short-Term Temporary Changes to Joana's Fl Self-Concepts

Finally, there were other more short-term, temporary changes in Joana's self-concept that were perceptible in the data over short periods of time or at particular individual points in time. All of these changes were linked to time of day/year, mood, tiredness, or feeling unwell or nervous, as can be seen from the following excerpts:

(...) so sometimes I have bad days speaking English and sometimes I have good days, it depends really on my, probably whole mood, the whole mood I'm in or whatever. And today I feel like I cannt really talk in English or I can't think of vocabulary and it's hard for me today but I notice right away, so (...) (J#3: 233–237).

Yeah, so I had quite some fun and then you know, when you're awake again it depends a lot on your, like today I feel like I can speak very fluently and there are other days where you make pronunciation mistakes, or like I am tired now but I just, I'm just in the mood of talking, so it's no problem (J#18: 322-327).

Joana generally appears to have a strong positive self-concept concerning speaking in English, but, as seen with these examples, she does not feel equally positive about this aspect of her English at all times and in all contexts. Interestingly, most of these temporary changes are linked to speaking, which may be due to the 'online' nature of speaking as a skill and could also be linked to Joana's sensitivity concerning this skill, given the importance she assigns to it. These changes were also all expressed in terms of ability and could reflect a 'working' self-concept of the moment which differs to her established 'core', more stable self-concept in the domain (Markus and Wurf 1987). It is possible that a learner may have a 'working/online' self-concept that could be affected by temporary factors, such as mood, illness or tiredness, which do not directly affect their core self-concept. Clearly, there could be serious implications of this finding for research methodologies, especially those which rely on single-point data collection methods.

5 Conclusions and Implications

In these data, Joana's FL self-concepts show signs of containing both stable and dynamic elements (cf. Markus and Kunda 1986). On the whole, her overall EFL self-concept seems to remain stable throughout, even in spite of negative feedback in regard to writing in the language. It is worth considering whether its stability results from its already positive, highly developed nature at the outset which possibly offered less potential for change (cf. Young and Mroczek 2003). In addition, self-beliefs that were shared across several domains also appeared to remain stable. It was suggested that such beliefs may constitute 'core' self-beliefs which may be more developed and central to an individual's sense of self and thus more resilient to change (cf. Harter 2006). It was further proposed that the more 'peripheral' aspects of the self-concept, possibly those most closely tied to ability, were the most likely aspects to change (cf. Markus and Wurf 1987).

However, despite the stability in her overall EFL self-concept, certain aspects of her EFL self-concept did appear to change, albeit the changes were subtle and occurred gradually over an extended period of time. Interestingly, her self-concept with respect to writing in EFL seemed to go through a series of highs and lows during the 22-month period and ultimately seemed to return to a level similar to the beginning of the project. It was noted that with respect to her EFL writing self-concept, Joana may have engaged in a series of self-protection or self-verification processes, such as 'compartmentalisation', which may have affected the extent to which her self-concept changed or remained stable. Her EFL self-concept also appeared to change in respect to pronunciation. It is worth considering whether pronunciation may be special in terms of its relation to the self and identity. Additionally, as the changes in her EFL self-concept took place within specific aspects of the more global EFL domain, it seems to confirm findings from other research (Shavelson and Bolus 1982; Young and Mroczek 2003; Harter 2006) that the more domain-specific aspects of the self-concept network may be more susceptible to change than the more global aspects.

In terms of the dynamic aspects of her FL self-concepts, her overall IFL self-concept changed most notably. Possible reasons for this are that it was much weaker and less developed at the outset of the study than her EFL self-concept and as she gained in proficiency and had many critical experiences involving the language during the period, the potential for change was greater. It was also noted that her IFL self-concept changed on a global level, as well as in very specific aspects of the IFL domain on both the skill and specific task level. Although she attributes the greater changes in her IFL self-concept to her extended stay in Italy, it is important to note that there were perceptible changes in her IFL self-concept prior to the stay abroad; a finding which suggests encouraging implications for the potential of pedagogy to affect an individual's self-concept in a domain. It was suggested that it may also be worth noting that Joana made internal attributions for her perceived development and this too may affect the extent to which a self-concept may change.

In terms of research methodologies, the temporary changes which were detected in her 'working' self-concept of the moment suggest that what learners may report about their self-concepts may vary depending on contextual factors, and thus care must be taken with single-point studies which may be accessing a learner's working self-concept of the moment, rather than their core self-concept (cf. Markus and Wurf 1987). Additionally, as with all longitudinal studies, it must be remembered that it is not clear to what extent any of the changes in her FL self-concepts will remain following the end of the research period. Indeed, the findings concerning her EFL writing self-concept serve to illustrate the non-permanency of any potential changes and the potential for fluctuations in reported self-concepts. Given the variation in the findings across differing aspects of her FL self-concepts, it suggests that research methodologies investigating the potentially dynamic nature of FL learner self-concepts would need to be designed in a way which would enable the subtleties and diversity this appears to involve to be revealed.

In terms of pedagogical implications, the findings suggest that if certain aspects of the self-concept are dynamic, then there may be potential to help learners to develop positive but realistic self-concepts in these areas. However, educators need to be realistic about what can be affected and how lasting any changes may be (cf. O'Mara et al. 2006). It must be remembered that the extent to which an aspect of the self-concept is dynamic may depend on a host of complex factors and psychological processes which it is beyond the scope of this paper to discuss fully. Thus, any possible interventions are unlikely to straight-forwardly lead to changes in the self-concept and any changes which do occur may be subtle and take place gradually over a considerable length of time. Further research is therefore needed to elucidate the questions and suggestions generated by this initial, exploratory study about the dynamic nature of FL learner self-concepts and the factors which may affect this.

References

Chamot, A.U., S. Barnhart, P. El-Dinary, and J. Robbins. 1996. High school foreign language students' perceptions of language learning strategy use and self-efficacy, Unpublished report. National Foreign Language Resource Centre, Georgetown University.

Clément, R. 1980. Ethnicity, contact and communicative competence in a second language. In eds. H. Giles, W.P. Robinson, and P.M. Smith, 47–154.

Cohen, Y., and M.J. Norst. 1989. Fear, dependence and loss of self-esteem: Affective barriers in second language learning among adults. *RELC Journal* 20: 61–77.

Coleman, J.A. 1997. Residence abroad within language study. *Language Teaching* 30: 1–20.

Dörnyei, Z. 1994. Motivation and motivating in the foreign language classroom. *Modern Language Journal* 78: 273–284.

Dörnyei, Z. 2005. *The psychology of the language learner.* NJ: Lawrence Erlbaum.

Dörnyei, Z., and R. Schmidt, eds. 2001. *Motivation and second language acquisition.* Honolulu: University of Hawaii.

Eccles, J., and A. Wigfield. 2002. Motivational beliefs, values, and goals. *Annual Review of Psychology* 53: 109–132.

Ehrman, M.E., and R.L. Oxford. 1995. Cognition plus: Correlates of language learning success. *Modern Language Journal* 79: 67–89.

Ehrman, M.E., B.L. Leaver, and R.L. Oxford. 2003. A brief overview of individual differences in second language learning. *System* 31: 313–330.

Freed, B.F. 1995. Language learning and study abroad. In ed. B.F. Freed, 3–33.

Freed, B.F., ed. 1995. *Second language acquisition in a study abroad context.* Philadelphia: John Benjamins.

Gardner, R.C. 1985. *Social psychology and second language learning: The roles of attitudes and motivation.* London: Edward Arnold.

Gardner, R.C., and P.D. MacIntyre. 1993. A student's contributions to second-language learning. Part II: Affective variables. *Language Teaching* 26: 1–11.

Giles, H., W.P. Robinson, and P.M. Smith, eds. 1980. *Language: Social psychological perspectives.* Pergamon: Oxford.

Green, J., G. Nelson, A.J. Martin, and H. Marsh. 2006. The causal ordering of self-concept and academic motivation and its effect on academic achievement. *International Education Journal* 7: 534–546.

Hamlyn, D.W. 1983. *Perception, learning and the self: Essays in the philosophy of psychology.* London: Routledge.

Harter, S. 2006. The self. In eds. W. Damon, and R.M. Lerner, 505–570.

Harter, S., N.R. Whitesell, and P. Kowalski. 1992. Individual differences in the effects of educational transitions on young adolescent's perceptions of competence and motivational orientation. *American Educational Research Journal* 29: 777–807.

Hattie, J.A. 1992. *Self-concept.* NJ: Lawrence Erlbaum.

Hoboken, N.J. 2006. Handbook of child psychology, vol 3, Social, emotional, and personality development. In eds. W. Damon, and R.M. Lerner. NJ: Wiley.

Jenkins, J. 2006. English pronunciation and second language speaker identity. In eds. T. Omoniyi, and G. White, 75–91.

Kaplan, R.B., ed. 2002. *The Oxford handbook of applied linguistics.* Oxford: Oxford University Press.

MacIntyre, P.D., R. Clément, Z. Dörnyei, and K.A. Noels. 1998. Conceptualizing willingness to communicate in a L2: A situational model of L2 confidence and affiliation. *Modern Language Journal* 82: 545–562.

MacIntyre, P.D., S.C. Baker, R. Clément, and L.A. Donovan. 2002. Sex and age effects on willingness to communicate, anxiety, perceived competence, and L2 motivation among junior high school French immersion students. *Language Learning* 52: 537–564.

Markus, H., and Z. Kunda. 1986. Stability and malleability of the self-concept. *Journal of Personality and Social Psychology* 51: 858–866.

Markus, H., and E. Wurf. 1987. The dynamic self-concept: A social-psychological perspective. *Annual Review of Psychology* 38: 299–337.

Marsh, H.W. 1984. Relations among dimensions of self attribution, dimensions of self-concept, and academic achievements. *Journal of Educational Psychology* 76: 1291–1308.

Marsh, H.W. 1986. Self-serving effect (bias?) in academic attributions: Its relation to academic achievement and self-concept. *Journal of Educational Psychology* 78: 190–200.

Marsh, H.W., and A.S. Yeung. 1997. Causal effects of academic self-concept on academic achievement: Structural equation models of longitudinal data. *Journal of Educational Psychology* 89: 41–54.

Marsh, H.W., L. Cairns, J. Relich, J. Barnes, and R.L. Debus. 1984. The relationship between dimensions of self-attribution and dimensions of self-concept. *Journal of Educational Psychology* 76: 3–32.

Marsh, H.W., B.M. Byrne, and R.J. Shavelson. 1988. A multifaceted academic self-concept: Its hierarchical structure and its relation to academic achievement. *Journal of Educational Psychology* 80: 366–380.

McAdams, D.P., R. Josselson, and A. Lieblich, eds. 2001. *Turns in the road: Narrative studies of lives in transition*. Washington: APA.

McCombs, B.L., and R.J. Marzano. 1990. Putting the self in self-regulated learning: The self as agent in integrating will and skill. *Educational Psychologist* 25: 51–69.

Meara, P. 1994. The year abroad and its effects. *Language Learning* 10: 32–38.

Mercer, S. 2007. Critical experiences in language learner development. In eds. M. Reitbauer, N. Campbell, S. Mercer, and R. Vaupetitsch, 147–157.

Mercer, S. 2008. Key concepts in ELT: Learner self-beliefs. *ELT Journal* 62: 182–183.

Muijs, R.D. 1997. Predictors of academic achievement and academic self-concept—a longitudinal perspective. *British Journal of Educational Psychology* 67: 263–277.

O'Mara, A.J., H.W. Marsh, R.G. Craven, and R.L. Debus. 2006. Do self-concept interventions make a difference? A synergistic blend of construct validation and meta-analysis. *Educational Psychologist* 41: 181–206.

Omoniyi, T., and G. White, eds. 2006. *The sociolinguistics of identity*. London: Continuum.

Oxford, R.L. 2002. Sources of variation in language learning. In ed. R.B. Kaplan, 245–252.

Oxford, R.L., and M. Nyikos. 1989. Variables affecting the choice of language learning strategies by university students. *Modern Language Journal* 73: 291–300.

Oxford, R.L., and J. Shearin. 1994. Language learning motivation: Expanding the theoretical framework. *Modern Language Journal* 78: 12–28.

Reitbauer, M., N. Campbell, S. Mercer, and S. Vaupetitsch, eds. 2007. *Contexts of English in use: Past and present*. Wien: Braumüller.

Rubio, F., ed. 2007. *Self-esteem and foreign language learning*. Newcastle: Cambridge Scholars Publishing.

Schumann, J.H. 1986. Research on the acculturation model for second language acquisition. *Journal of Multilingual and Multicultural Development* 7: 379–392.

Shapka, J.D., and D.P. Keating. 2005. Structure and change in self-concept during adolescence. *Canadian Journal of Behavioural Science* 37: 83–96.

Shavelson, R.J., and R. Bolus. 1982. Self-concept: The interplay of theory and methods. *Journal of Educational Psychology* 74: 3–17.

Showers, C. 1992. Compartmentalization of positive and negative self-knowledge: Keeping bad apples out of the bunch. *Journal of Personality and Social Psychology* 62: 1036–1049.

Simpson, S.M., B.G. Licht, R.K. Wagner, and S.R. Stader. 1996. Organization of children's academic ability-related self-perceptions. *Journal of Educational Psychology* 88: 387–396.

Skaalvik, E.M., and H. Valas. 1999. Relations among achievement, self-concept and motivation in mathematics and language arts: A longitudinal study. *Journal of Experimental Education* 67: 135–149.

Stevick, E.W. 1978. Toward a practical philosophy of pronunciation: Another view. *TESOL Quarterly* 12: 145–150.

Weiner, B. 1986. *An attribution theory of motivation and emotion.* New York: Springer.

Wigfield, A., and J. Eccles. 2000. Expectancy-value theory of achievement motivation. *Contemporary Educational Psychology* 25: 68–81.

Wigfield, A., and M. Karpathian. 1991. Who am I and what can I do? Children's self-concepts and motivation in achievement situations. *Educational Psychologist* 26: 233–261.

Wigfield, A., J.S. Eccles, D. MacIver, D.A. Reuman, and C. Midgley. 1991. Transitions during early adolescence: Changes in children's domain-specific self-perceptions and general self-esteem across the transition to junior high school. *Developmental Psychology* 27: 552–565.

Williams, M., R.L. Burden, and S. Al-Baharna. 2001. Making sense of success and failure: The role of the individual in motivation theory. In eds. Z. Dörnyei, and R. Schmidt, 171–184.

Yang, N.-D. 1999. The relationship between EFL learners' beliefs and learning strategy use. *System* 27: 515–535.

Yin, R.K. 2003. *Case study research: Design and methods.* Thousand Oaks: Sage.

Young, J.F., and D.K. Mroczek. 2003. Predicting intraindividual self-concept trajectories during adolescence. *Journal of Adolescence* 26: 586–600.

Motivation Research and SLA: Bringing it into the Classroom

Eowyn Crisfield and Joanna White

Abstract This study addresses the variable of motivation, which is of prime concern to EFL/ESL teachers. Specifically, it was undertaken to assess the hypothesized association between student-perceived course *usefulness* and interest/motivation level in mandatory general and specific purposes (ESP) English second language courses. The study was conducted at one Canadian post-secondary institution over three semesters (N = 615). The participants were enrolled in four course levels and two fields of study. Data collection was undertaken using a one-page questionnaire consisting of ten Likert-scale questions and two-short answer questions. The results indicate that ratings of usefulness and interest are significantly higher for ESP than general ESL courses. Furthermore, there is a significant relationship between usefulness and interest. This relationship varies significantly by level, but not by field of study. The confirmation of a connection between usefulness and interest is pertinent to any adult ESL/EFL situation, particularly in situations where the courses are mandatory and the students therefore not necessarily intrinsically motivated. As interest has already been established as a precursor for motivation, it follows that increasing the usefulness of content would also increase motivation for this target population.

1 Introduction

As any language teacher can tell you, keeping students motivated is one of the most important elements of a successful language class. Unmotivated students tend not to actively participate in the classroom and thereby lose out on learning

E. Crisfield (✉) · J. White
Concordia University, Montreal, Canada
e-mail: ecrisfield@yahoo.ca

M. Pawlak (ed.), *New Perspectives on Individual Differences in Language Learning and Teaching*, Second Language Learning and Teaching, DOI: 10.1007/978-3-642-20850-8_14, © Springer-Verlag Berlin Heidelberg 2012

opportunities. This being the case, what is being done in the area of motivation research to help teachers in their quest to increase student motivation? Second language teachers seeking to improve their knowledge in this area have a host of theories and studies at their disposal. They can examine social–psychological theories, need theories, instrumentality theories, equity theories or reinforcement theories, just to name a few. However, research dealing with second language acquisition has not always been easily transferable to second or foreign language classroom pedagogy. While this may not seem immediately problematic from a research perspective, when one considers that a central goal of SLA research is to illuminate and improve second and foreign language pedagogy (Dörnyei 2001a; McGroarty 2001), it becomes clear that greater effort must be made to translate theory into practice: "From a practicing teacher's point of view, the most pressing question related to motivation is not *what* motivation is but rather *how* it can be increased. It is an unflattering indication of the detachment of research from classroom practice that very little work has been done in the L2 field to devise and test motivational strategies systematically" (Dörnyei 2001a:. 51).

This study is based on Dörnyei's tripartite model of motivation and takes its cues from the Learning-Situation Level, which is the area in which teachers have the most opportunity to affect the motivation level of their students. Dörnyei draws from a variety of theories to create a tripartite model for investigating SLA motivation. This model contains elements of motivation that affect L2 learning in a format which shows their relevance to the L2 classroom. Using this model (Table 1), teachers can clearly identify the different areas of motivation, as well as factors that have potential to affect the motivational level of their students.

2 Interest, Relevance and Motivation

As Schiefele (2001: 172) points out, "(…) and if it is agreed that the content of learning is the main source of being intrinsically motivated to learn, then it follows that interest is the central condition of intrinsic motivation to learn". This study builds on the pre-established relationships between interest, relevance and motivation. Until the middle of the twentieth century, the concept of motivation was investigated mainly under the umbrella term of interest and most psychologists maintained that the most important motivational factor was interest (Krapp 1999; Pintrich and Schunk 2002). In studies investigating the interest-achievement relationship, interest has been found to have a significant effect on both the quantity and quality of learning. In addition, results of reviews and meta-analysis show strong evidence for a general positive relationship between interest, intrinsic motivation, and academic learning (Schiefele 2001).

In educational contexts, interest is used as a central term for obvious reasons. Teachers wish to interest their students in the subject matter they teach. In their view, motivated students are those who appear to enjoy the content being taught. Keller's education-based Motivational-Design model (Keller 1983) includes four

Table 1 Components of foreign language learning (Dörnyei 1994: 28)

Level	Motivational components
Language Level	Integrative motivational subsystem
	Instrumental motivational subsystem
Learner Level	Need for self-achievement
	Self-confidence
	• Language use anxiety
	• Perceived L2 competence
	• Causal attributions
	• Self-efficacy
Learning Situation Level	
Course specific motivational	Interest
Components	Relevance
	Expectancy
	Satisfaction
Teacher-specific motivational	Affiliative motive
Components	Authority type
	Direct socialization of student motivation
	• Modeling
	• Task presentation
	• Feedback
Group-specific motivational	Goal-orientedness
Components	Norm and reward system
	Group cohesion
	Classroom goal structure

motivational components: interest, relevance, expectancy, satisfaction. These general categories subsume more specific elements of motivation and are meant to be a guideline for improving curriculum design to optimize motivation. The first two elements of this model are of particular importance for this study. Firstly, according to Keller, interest must be stimulated in order to increase attention and active-learning behaviours. The pedagogical difficulty here lies in the fact that it is a considerable challenge to stimulate interest in a large class of students with widely varying personalities and interests (Brophy 1998; Covington 1999). Most ESL/EFL curricula make some attempt to tap into student interest, but they are hindered by these factors.

The second element, relevance, has also been investigated in terms of potential for increasing student motivation. In fact some curricula, including LSP and CBI are based on this hypothesis. Research has supported the supposition that students can find content relevant without finding it interesting (Valentine and Repath-Martos 1997) and that there is a demonstrated relationship between increased relevance and increased motivation (Frymier and Shulman 1995). Thus, relevance also offers possibilities for pedagogical intervention to increase motivation.

3 Context of Study

In order to understand the motivational and pedagogical context for this study, it is necessary to understand the Quebec Cégep system. The acronym CEGEP stands for 'collège d'enseignement général et professionnel' (College of General and Professional Education) and is often transformed to the proper noun 'Cégep'. The education system in the province of Québec is unique in its approach to secondary and post-secondary education. Students complete their secondary studies in 5 years. Students wishing to go to university are *required* to complete 2 years of general studies at a Cégep. Students who do not wish to go to university *may choose* to do a three-year career program, known as a 'technique', at a Cégep. Students in the pre-university and technical programs attend the same institutions and many of the same classes. Each program has two components: General Education, and Specific Education. All students, regardless of their orientation or program, must take the same General Education Courses. The General Education courses are further divided into three sections: Formation Générale Commune (A-Block), Formation Génerale Propre (B-Block) and Formation Génerale Complémentaire (C-Block—electives). The Specific Education courses are specialized by program. The goal of this structure is to provide all students with a well-rounded education.

The General Education courses include two mandatory ESL courses. The Ministère de l'éducation (MEQ) is responsible for providing the curriculum guidelines for all Cégep programs. In the ESL courses, students are placed into one of four levels (100—mis-a-niveau, 101—intermediate, 102—upper-intermediate and 103—advanced), and after completing their first course (A-Block), they move horizontally to their second course (B-Block) at the same level.

The A-Block course is part of General Education. Students from all disciplines and types of programs are in the same class. The B-Block course is meant to be complementary to the students' Specific Education, that is, to be linked to their field of study or future profession in some way. At the Cégep where this study was undertaken, the B-Block courses are divided into two groups: Pre-university or Technical. The exception to this is the 103-level (bilingual). There are not enough students at this level to allow for multiple courses, so the pre-university and technical students are in the B-Block together. In the other levels, the A-Block/B-Block system allows teachers some flexibility in making the courses specific for the technical/pre-U groups, but it does not allow for highly specialized courses.

4 Research Questions

As Chambers (1999: 37) points out, "if the teacher is to motivate pupils to learn, then relevance has to be the red thread permeating activities. If pupils fail to see the relationship between the activity and the world in which they live, then the point of the activity is likely to be lost on them". The goal of this study is to investigate the perceptions of Cégep students regarding the A-Block and B-Block English courses. The pedagogical goal of the B-Block courses is directly linked to the learning situation variable of *relevance* in Dörnyei's tripartite model of L2 motivation (Dörnyei 1994), in that the curriculum is designed to be relevant to their future studies and/or careers. Keller (1983) identified *relevance* and *interest* as major determinants of motivation, both of which are necessary for sustained motivation. He further refined relevance to include *instrumental needs*. By this, he is suggesting that the most basic need is for students to find a match between what they are learning in the course and what they believe they need to learn. This idea is also supported by Chambers (1999), who claims that relevance is essential in that students must see a relationship between instructional activities and their own world in order to be motivated. Working from this, the variable being investigated in this study is not the entire concept of *relevance*, which is quite broad, but an element of *relevance* that is identified as *usefulness*. In the broader sense, relevance applies to anything that the students find germane to their lives, whether linked to their studies or not. *Usefulness*, as employed for the purposes of this study, applies to content that can be perceived as directly useful to the students' future studies or career, therefore meeting an instrumental need.

One of the two main issues investigated in this study is the students' perceptions of the relevance of the A- and B-Block English courses. The teachers of B-Block courses plan their courses with the mandate of making the content 'useful' to the students in their future studies and careers, as dictated by the MEQ guidelines. Since no needs-based analyses are done in Cégeps, it is possible that there may be different interpretations of *usefulness* on the part of the students and the teachers. This in turn may lead to discrepancies between the actual curriculum and the students' perceptions of *usefulness*, relevance and applicability. The second issue that this study endeavors to clarify is the possible motivational aspects of *usefulness*, by attempting to discern whether the students' perceptions of usefulness affect their interest level in the A-Block and B-Block courses. If, as has previously been supported by research in other areas of education, interest can be directly linked to motivation (Keller 1983; Maehr 1984; Brophy 1987), then student levels of interest in their ESL course can be seen to be linked to motivation as well. In addition, the study will investigate the extent to which course level (100, 101, 102, 103) and/or field of study (Pre-university or Technical) have a bearing on students' perceptions of usefulness or interest in the A- and B-Block English courses. Students in technical programs have chosen their career, and are within 2 years of finishing their studies when they take their B-Block course. Conversely, students who are in a pre-university program have not necessarily chosen a career yet and have several more years of schooling ahead of them before entering the workforce. For this reason, it is possible that students in technical programs are able to see the practical applications of the course content in their chosen field more clearly than those in pre-university programs, which could in turn increase interest. Finally, it could be hypothesized that students in different levels have differing perceptions due to their ability to handle field-specific activities. These issues have led to four research questions:

1. Do students have the same perceptions of *usefulness* of course content of A-Block and B-Block regarding preparing them to use English in their future studies/career?
2. Is there a relationship between perceptions of usefulness and interest?
3. Do technical program students demonstrate greater perceptions of the usefulness of and interest in the B-Block courses over A-Block courses when compared to pre-university students?
4. Do the students at all levels have the same perceptions of the usefulness of and interest in the B-Block courses?

5 Method

A study of B-Block Cégep students was undertaken to assess the hypothesized association between student-perceived course *usefulness* and interest/motivation level. Specifically, the study evaluated student perceptions of the usefulness, in terms of relevance and applicability to future careers or studies, of A- versus B-Block English courses and the relationship between the perceived usefulness of and student interest in these courses. The study was conducted at one Montréal-area Cégep over three semesters.

5.1 Participants and Procedures

Potentially eligible participants for this study included all students who were enrolled in level 100 (mis-a-niveau), 101(intermediate), 102 (upper-intermediate) and 103 (advanced) B-Block English courses at the Cégep investigated in this study during the data collection periods. The three rounds of data collection resulted in three samples of participants: 177 (28.8% of total participants) from the fall of 2001, 161 (26.2%) from the winter 2002 semester and 277 (45.0%) from the winter 2003 semester. The three sets of data were combined, as there were no apparent differences between the students included in each of the three samples or the B-Block courses given in each of the three semesters. Data collection was conducted during the 13th or 14th week of each semester and therefore at the same point in the course curriculum. During the remaining class or classes, students took their final exams. Since the B-Block course was nearly completed by the time the students filled out the questionnaires, they were able to compare it to their A-Block course.

There were no pedagogical changes made to the B-Block courses between the fall and winter terms. There were no modifications to the questionnaire and study procedures from one data collection to the next. Thus, the final combined sample of study participants included 615 students who were in the final weeks of their B-Block courses. This represents the majority of the B-Block students in each semester, but not the full count, as not all teachers were able to collect data from their students, due to time constraints.

Of the 615 participating students, 131 (21.3%) were enrolled in the B-Block level 100, 177 (28.8%) in level 101, 273 (44.4%) were enrolled in the B-Block level 102 and 34 (5.5%) in level 103. Three hundred and fifty-two (57.2%) of students were in a Pre-University program compared to 221 in a Technical (35.9%) program. Forty-two (6.8%) students did not indicate their program of study.

Teacher participation was limited to assistance with data collection. The researcher undertaking the study has taught at this Cégep and therefore has the requisite knowledge of curriculum in the A- and B-Block courses. All teachers engaged in B-Block English courses—levels 100 through 103 inclusively—during the study time period were asked to encourage their students to participate in the study. After three semesters of data collection, there were eight participating teachers spread over four levels of courses. The teachers were instructed to inform the students that the questionnaire was not a course-evaluation and would not be seen or used in any way by the classroom teacher. This was done in order to minimize any potential bias in student response due to a belief that their survey answers would have an impact on their final course grades. The completed questionnaires were placed by the students in a designated envelope, which was then sealed and given directly to the researcher.

5.2 Materials and Measurement

Data collection was undertaken by means of a one-page questionnaire designed by the researcher for the purposes of this study. The survey is in French, which is the language of instruction at the Cégep and the first language of the majority of the students. Student responses were anonymous—students were not required to provide any identifying information on their completed surveys. The questionnaire consisted of ten Likert-scale type questions and two short-answer questions. Four response choices were provided for each of the Likert-scale questions: *pas du tout* (or *rien*), *peu*, *assez* and *beaucoup*. These responses were coded on an ordinal numeric scale of zero to three, with zero representing *pas du tout/rien*, one representing *peu*, two representing *assez*, and three representing *beaucoup*. Questions one through five and six through ten were to be answered regarding the A-Block and B-Block courses respectively.

The Likert-scale questions were constructed with certain key points in mind, namely, to measure student perceptions of various aspects of course usefulness, as well as their level of interest in the A- and B-Block English courses. Questions 2 (A-Block) and 7 (B-Block) ask students to provide judgments of the usefulness of the skills they have acquired in each course. Student ratings of course usefulness as measured by the relevance of course materials are recorded on questions 3 (A-Block) and 8 (B-Block). Questions 5 and 10 ask for student judgments of course usefulness in terms of the future applicability of their acquired knowledge. Students rate their interest level in each course on questions 4 and 9. Questions 1 and 6 ask students to rate how much they have learned in each course; these questions have not been analyzed for the current study. The other eight Likert scale questions were analyzed quantitatively. The two short answer questions asked for students' perceptions of how they will (or will not) use English in their future studies or career and which English course they preferred and why.

6 Data Analysis

The same questionnaire was used to elicit quantitative and qualitative data from all three data cohorts. The three cohorts were collected over three terms. This was done in order to maximize the sample size, as well as to ensure an adequate variety of participating teachers. Quantitative measurements included the students' self-reported: 1) estimate of amount learned in each course, 2) judgments towards the content of the A-Block and B-Block courses in terms of relevance, applicability and usefulness, and 3) assessment of interest in each course. For the purposes of this article, the results relating to the qualitative data will not be reported on.

6.1 Exclusions

Participants who did not respond to all questions were only excluded from the data analysis on the items where data were missing; they were not excluded from the other analyses. All respondents were included in the samples for the following reason: The focus of the study was on the B-Block curriculum, and all respondents were completing the B-Block course in the Cégep under study. As the A-Block curriculum remains stable across Cégeps, it was not considered necessary, therefore, to exclude any students who had taken their A-Block course at another Cégep from the samples. In contrast, respondents who did not indicate a field of study were excluded from the analyses involving field of study, as it was not possible without this information to place them in the pre-university or technical categories.

6.2 Analysis Procedures

Data entry and descriptive and statistical analyses of the quantitative data obtained in this study were conducted using SPSS Version 11 (SPSS Inc., Chicago, IL., 2003). Missing values were not replaced in the data. In the case of a missing response to any one question, the student was excluded from that analysis.

Sections 1 and 2 of the survey included five items each, scored on a four-point scale. Items 1 and 6 were rated as *rien* (nothing) = 0, *peu* (little) = 1, *assez* (enough) = 2 and *beaucoup* (a lot) = 3. Items 2–5 and 7–10 were rated as *pas du tout* (not at all) = 0, *peu* (little) = 1, *assez* (enough) = 2 and *beaucoup* (a lot) = 3.

Differences in student judgments on the three items measuring usefulness of the A- versus B-Block courses were tested for statistical significance using the Wilcoxon Signed-Ranks test. After establishing the internal reliability of the items measuring usefulness by calculating the Chronbach's alpha coefficient, the three usefulness items were then combined and used in all further analyses.

The hypothesized association between course usefulness and student interest level was examined and tested using Spearman's rho correlations. The mean of the three usefulness items was correlated with the students' ranking of interest in the course. This analysis was conducted within and not between Blocks, thus the associations of interest and usefulness were tested for each Block separately, with no comparisons made of A-versus B-Block. The numeric value of the Spearman's rho correlation coefficient provides an estimate of the strength of the relationship between two factors.

Two-way mixed analysis of variance (ANOVA) and one-way ANOVA procedures were used to assess potential differences in student-ranked course usefulness and interest level by program (Pre-University or Technical) and by course level (100, 101, 102, 103) respectively.

7 Results

The findings are reported for each research question in their original order. The three discrete elements of *usefulness* (relevance, applicability and usefulness) were combined to become the variable called *overall course usefulness*. This was based on a Cronbach's alpha of 0.7 273 for the A-Block course items (2, 3 and 5) and 0.7 988 for the B-Block course items (7, 8 and 10). Results higher than 0.7 000 are acceptable in scales of this size (Dörnyei, 2001b; Dörnyei and Csizér 2002). Because nine separate statistical analyses were conducted, increasing the probability of a Type I error, Bonferroni's procedure was used and resulted in an operational alpha level of 0.005 (0.05/9).

Research question 1: Do students have the same perceptions of usefulness of course content of A-Block and B-Block regarding preparing them to use English in their future studies/career?
The rationale behind this question was to verify the extent to which the surveyed students recognized the underlying design of the usefulness of the B-Block course curriculum and also to confirm the researcher's definition of *usefulness* as being "that which is relevant and applicable to the students' future studies and/or career". Student-perceived *usefulness* of course content, as assessed using the

Table 2 Comparison of student-perceived usefulness of A-Block versus B-Block, mean values of student rankings of course usefulness

Measurement	N	Mean (SD)	Minimum	Maximum
Relevance of course material				
A-Block (Q3)	610	1.52 (0.85)	0.00	3.00
B-Block (Q8)	608	2.08 (0.78)	0.00	3.00
Future applicability				
A-Block (Q5)	608	1.69 (0.75)	0.00	3.00
B-Block (Q10)	613	2.08 (0.75)	0.00	3.00
Course usefulness				
A-Block (Q2)	609	1.80 (0.72)	0.00	3.00
B-Block (Q7)	611	2.18 (0.70)	0.00	3.00
Overall course usefulness				
A-Block (Q2, 3, 5)	600	1.67 (0.62)	0.00	3.00
B-Block (Q7, 8, 10)	603	2.12 (0.63)	0.00	3.00

three measurements of usefulness, was greater for the B-Block English course than for the A-Block.

Table 2 shows the mean values and standard deviations of the student rankings of relevance of course materials, future applicability and overall usefulness. The mean differences between these course usefulness ratings were all statistically significant. Given that the differences are significant between all three pairs of items, the answer to the first research question is affirmative. The students do indeed report perceptions of B-Block course as being more useful than the A-Block course. In addition, the strength of the mean reliability coefficients provided by the Cronbach's alpha scores for the two sets of variables lends credence to the use of the term *usefulness* in the manner defined above. Of the three variables, the greatest difference was noted between relevance of A- versus B-Block content ($z = -12.31$, $p < 0.005$), followed by applicability ($z = -11.10$, $p < 0.005$), and then usefulness ($z = -10.71$, $p < 0.005$).

Research question 2: Is there a relationship between perceptions of usefulness and interest?

The aim of this question was to identify the motivational consequences of *usefulness*. As previous research has shown that increased interest in subject matter is linked to increased motivation (Covington 1999; Krapp 1999; Schiefele 2001), the variables of usefulness and interest were analyzed to verify that such a relationship exists in the context of this study. This was done using the combined overall usefulness mean scores (questions 2, 3 and 5 for A-Block and 7, 8 and 10 for B-Block), and the question rating interest in the course (question 4 for A-Block and 9 for B-Block).

When the hypothesized association of student-perceived course usefulness and interest level was examined, a significant relationship was found (Table 3). For both the A- and B-Block courses, there was a statistically significant positive association between the level of student interest in the course and the degree to

Measurement		Mean (SD)
Interest in course		
A-Block	579	1.75 (0.66)
B-Block	582	1.91 (0.67)
Overall course usefulness		
A-Block	600	1.67 (0.62)
B-Block	603	2.12 (0.63)

Table 3 Mean values of student interest level and student perceived usefulness of the A-Block and B-Block courses

which they perceived the course to be useful, as assessed by the usefulness measure. This indicates that, as the ranking of course usefulness rose, so did interest level. As shown by the numeric value of the correlation coefficient, these associations were stronger for the B-Block (rho = 0.567) than for the A-Block course (rho = 0.501).

Consequently, the answer to the second research question is also affirmative. There is a demonstrated link between perceptions of usefulness of the course and interest. This is in line with educational theory that claims that in order for students' interest in an academic subject to increase, the content must be seen to be useful or relevant to them (Keller 1983; Brophy 1998).

Research question 3: Do technical program students demonstrate greater perceptions of the usefulness of and interest in B-Block courses over A-Block courses when compared to pre-university students?
A two-way mixed ANOVA was used to compare students' perceptions of A-Block courses to B-Block courses and to identify potential differences in their perceptions of course usefulness by stream of study — Pre-University or Technical. No significant differences were noted between the Technical and Pre-University students in terms of their judgments of course usefulness. Irrespective of course of study, however, all students perceived B-Block courses to be significantly more useful than A-Block courses.

A two-way mixed ANOVA was also used to investigate differences between fields in terms of expressed interest in the A- and B-Block courses. As shown in Table 4, no significant differences were found between the Pre-university and Technical students in terms of ratings of interest. However, both groups of students rated the B-Block course as significantly more interesting than the A-Block course.

The answer to both parts of the third research question then is negative. The students in technical programs showed no greater rating of either usefulness of or interest in the B-Block course than the pre-university students.

Research question 4: Do students at all levels have the same perceptions of usefulness of and interest in B-Block courses?
Potential differences in student perceptions of course usefulness and interest by course level were assessed through comparison of the mean rankings for each measure of course usefulness and were tested using a one-way ANOVA. The results of the one-way ANOVA for usefulness revealed that there are statistically significant differences in usefulness ratings between levels. Results from a

Table 4 Two-way mixed ANOVA for interest

Source	SS	df	MS	F	p
Between subjects					
Group	4.18	1	4.18	4.83	0.028
Error	491.18	567	0.87		
Within subjects					
A to B	6.58	1	6.58	20.69	0.000
AB x Group	0.16	1	0.16	0.50	0.479
Error	180.40	567	0.32		

Table 5 Tukey HSD post hoc tests—usefulness by level

Mean	Level	102	100	101	103
2.00	102				
2.16	100				
2.21	101	*			
2.40	103	*			

*$p < 0.05$

Table 6 Tukey HSD post hoc tests—interest by level

Mean	Level	102	100	101	103
1.63	102				
1.89	100	*			
1.92	101	*			
2.32	103	*	*	*	

*$p < 0.05$

post-hoc Tukey test (Table 5) show statistically significant differences in the usefulness rating between the students enrolled in course level 101 and 102, with the 101 students rating the usefulness of the B-Block course significantly higher than the 102 level students. The 103 level students also rated the B-Block course as significantly more useful than the 102 level students. Overall, the 102 level students assessed the B-Block course with the lowest rating of usefulness of the four levels. There were no significant results pertaining to the level 100 students.

The one-way ANOVA for interest also indicated significantly different ratings of interest between levels. Tukey post-hoc tests (Table 6) reveal that the 103 level students rate the B-Block course significantly higher in terms of interest than the other three levels. In addition, the level 100 and 101 students rate course interest higher than the level 102 students. Again, the level 102 students show the lowest ratings of interest of the four levels. The rankings of interest are identical to the rankings of usefulness, in descending order: level 103, 101, 100, 102.

The answer to the final question, then, is that the students at different levels do not have the same perceptions of the usefulness of and interest in the B-Block course. While the results were not identical for the two variables, it is interesting to note that the levels rated both interest and usefulness in the same manner within groups.

8 Discussion and Implications

The results of this study contribute to our understanding of ESL/EFL pedagogy and the factors that may influence motivation in English for specific purposes contexts. The findings are largely applicable to curriculum developers in any post-secondary educational institutions where students are required to successfully complete second or foreign language courses in order to graduate. The confirmation of a link between usefulness and interest is important in that it provides support for one element of the Learning Level in Dörnyei's model of motivation. Not only is this important in terms of advancing our understanding of motivation, it also offers practical applications in the L2 classroom, an element that has been lacking in most motivation research to date. In addition, the results provide support for the role that teachers can play in motivation research in SLA.

The findings confirm that there is a link between usefulness, as a sub-category of relevance, and interest, and suggest that usefulness of content may contribute to increasing interest, and therefore motivation, in ESL students. This applies to students of all levels, although to varying degrees. Therefore, the findings support the implementation of curricula designed to be relevant and useful to ESL/EFL students' future careers or studies.

This study was designed to gather information relative to one element of Dörnyei's tripartite SLA model for motivation (Table 1). It was successful in doing this, and it also provided information pertaining to other theories of motivation. In terms of Dörnyei's Learning Situation Level, this study has given evidence that two of the identified variables, interest and relevance, as defined by *usefulness*, are related. The students who participated in this study showed a pattern of preference for a course with content that was useful to them, and this in turn was linked with increased interest in the course. Given that interest is widely considered an indicator of motivation (Covington 1999; Krapp 1999), it would appear that usefulness is linked with an increase in the students' motivation. The results are in line with other studies with similar goals. The findings of the present study may be interpreted to mean that interest, and therefore motivation, can be increased through usefulness of content rather than through interest in content.

The results also indicate some interesting links to other motivation theories. The element of content usefulness is, by definition, part of the instrumentality category of motivation in the socio-educational model. It is clear that potential usefulness of the activities in terms of future studies/career correlated with increased interest in the participating students. Therefore, it can be considered that, at least for these students, instrumental motives did have an effect on their motivation. This is an important result, notably as the research took place in Quebec, where the dominance of the integrative motive was first established [see, for example, Gardner and Lambert (1959); Gardner, Clément et al. (1979). This study did not allow for comparison of the instrumental nature of usefulness with respect to the students' level of integrativeness. Despite this, it does support work conducted elsewhere which encourages a closer look at the strength of the instrumental motive (Dörnyei and Csizér 2002; Irie 2003). This also supports the links that Noels et al. (2000) have found between instrumental motivation and external regulation. The students who participated in this study fall into the external regulation category in that they are taking ESL courses because they are obligatory for finishing their chosen diplomas. The fact that they are motivated by an instrumental factor, usefulness, supports the notion that instrumentality is a valid paradigm to enhance motivation in students who are required to take second language courses. In this case, whether intrinsic motivation is superior to extrinsic motivation is a moot point as the students who are in obligatory classes are not there due to intrinsic motivation. Therefore, teachers can only work within the instrumentality paradigm to increase motivation.

Although he has proposed several new paths for research, Dörnyei himself has mentioned that the main weakness of motivation research in SLA in the last decade is lack of empirical support for new theories. This study then is a step in the right direction in terms of finding evidence to support Dörnyei's Motivational Components model for SLA motivation. While achieving its main goal of supporting a focus on the usefulness of content to increase motivation in obligatory SLA contexts, the study also demonstrates links to other motivational theories. This corroborates the idea that motivation research in SLA should not be based on only one theory, but rather needs to refer to a variety of theories in order to respond to the needs of SL teachers. This study also confirms the author's position that SLA research can have practical implications for classroom teachers and provides guidance for these teachers in developing and implementing their curricula.

References

Ames, R.E., and C.E. Ames, eds. 1984. *Research on motivation in education*. Vol. 1. Orlando: Academic Press.

Brophy, J. 1987. *On motivating students. Occasional Paper No. 101*. East Lansing: Michigan Institute for Research on Teaching, Michigan State University.

Brophy, J. 1998. *Motivating students to learn*. Boston: McGraw-Hill.

Chambers, G.N. 1999. *Motivating language learners*. Clevedon: Multilingual Matters.

Collins, J.M., and W. Messick, eds. 2001. *Intelligence and personality: Bridging the gap in theory and measurement*. Mahwah: Lawrence Erlbaum.

Covington, M.V. 1999. Caring about learning: The nature and nurturing of subject-matter appreciation. *Educational Psychologist* 34: 127–136.

Dörnyei, Z. 1994. Motivation and motivating in the foreign language classroom. *Modern Language Journal* 78: 273–284.

Dörnyei, Z. 2001a. New themes and approaches in second language motivation research. *Annual Review of Applied Linguistics* 21: 43–59.

Dörnyei, Z. 2001b. *Teaching and researching motivation*. Harlow: Pearson Education Limited.

Dörnyei, Z., and K. Csizér. 2002. Some dynamics of language attitudes and motivation: Results of a longitudinal nationwide survey. *Applied Linguistics* 23: 421–462.

Dörnyei, A., and R.W. Schmidt, eds. 2001. *Motivation and second language acquisition (Technical Report #23)*. Manoa: Second Language Teaching and Curriculum Center, Honolulu University of Hawai'i.

Frymier, A.B., and G. Shulman. 1995. What's in it for me? Increasing content relevance to enhance students' motivation. *Communication Education* 44: 40–50.

Gardner, R.C., and W.E. Lambert. 1959. Motivational variables in second language acquisition. *Canadian Journal of Psychology* 13: 266–272.

Gardner, R.C., R. Clément, P.C. Smythe, and C.L. Smythe. 1979. *Attitudes and motivation test battery: Revised manual. Research Bulletin No.* 15. London/Ontario: University of Western Ontario.

Irie, K. 2003. What do we know about the language learning motivation of university students in Japan? Some patterns in survey studies. *JALT Journal* 25: 86–100.

Keller, J. 1983. Motivational design of instruction. In ed. C.M. Reigeluth, 289–320.

Krapp, A. 1999. Interest, motivation and learning: An educational-psychological perspective. *European Journal of Psychology of Education* 14: 23–40.

Maehr, M.L. 1984. Meaning and motivation: Toward a theory of personal investment. In eds. R.E. Ames, and C.E. Ames, 115–144.

McGroarty, M. 2001. Situating second language motivation. In eds. A. Dörnyei, and R.W. Schmidt, 69–92.

Noels, K.A., L.G. Pelletier, R. Clément, and R.J. Vallerand. 2000. Why are you learning a second language? Motivational orientations and self-determination theory. *Language Learning* 50: 57–85.

Pintrich, P.R., and D.H. Schunk, eds. 2002. *Motivation in education*. 2nd ed. Upper Saddle River: Merrill Prentice Hall.

Reigeluth, C.M., ed. 1983. *Instructional design theories and models*. Hillside: Lawrence Erlbaum.

Schiefele, U. 2001. The role of interest in motivation and learning. In eds. J.M. Collis, and W. Messick, 163–194.

Snow, M.A., and D. Brinton, eds. 1997. *The content-based classroom: Perspectives on integrating language and content*. White Plains: Longman.

Valentine, J.F., and L.M. Repath-Martos. 1997. How relevant is relevance? In eds. M.A. Snow, and D. Brinton, 233–247.

An Overview of L2 Motivation Research in Hungary

Kata Csizér

Abstract The aim of this article is to introduce the Hungarian L2 motivation scene in detail. Hungary is a monolingual country, where people do not speak foreign languages unless they learn them at school, hence the need for L2 motivation research became apparent in the late 1980s when after nearly 40 years of communist rule, the privileged status of the Russian language, as the first and often only foreign language to be learnt, was abolished overnight. The results of research projects carried out in the past 20 years are presented in this article in terms of four distinct learners' groups: young learners, secondary school students, university students and adult language learners. As for the research directions having received considerable attention in Hungary, they can be summarized as follows: the influence of language- and language-related attitudes on L2 motivation within diverse geographical and educational settings; the impact of intercultural contact on L2 motivation; the issues related to students' selves and their relationship with L2 learning; age-related differences in L2 learning and motivation; and the role of English as a increasingly global language and its impact on L2 motivation. Concerning possible future research directions, researchers should consider taking a more classroom-oriented focus and investigate the motivational impact of the micro-context within which students are actually learning L2s, they should also concentrate on special needs students; and longitudinal research projects should investigate the dynamic nature of L2 motivation.

K. Csizér (✉)
Eötvös University, Budapest, Hungary
e-mail: weinkata@yahoo.com

M. Pawlak (ed.), *New Perspectives on Individual Differences in Language Learning and Teaching*, Second Language Learning and Teaching, DOI: 10.1007/978-3-642-20850-8_15, © Springer-Verlag Berlin Heidelberg 2012

1 Introduction

Many conditions are required to learn a foreign language (L2) successfully. Among others, one needs to have good teachers and a lot of input in and/or outside the classroom; language learning aptitude and learning strategies also play a significant role but without being motivated, little success awaits students on the long avenue of language learning. No wonder, therefore, that defining and exploring L2 motivation and researching the characteristics of motivated learners occupy an important place on the research agendas of both applied linguistics and language pedagogy. The importance of such research is even more pronounced in countries like Hungary, where the large majority of the population is monolingual (Central Statistical Office 2004) and people do not speak foreign languages unless they learn them at school. This significant role of L2 motivation research in Hungary is reflected by the fact that a large number of empirical projects were carried out in the last 20 years, most of which were published in international journals as well as in Hungarian pedagogical publications, yet no summary has been offered before on what L2 motivation research achieved in Hungary and what research directions should be explored in future studies. The present summary intends to fill this niche.

This article has five major parts. First, the Hungarian context is described, then the most important motivation research results are summarized in terms of four large learning groups: young learners, secondary school students (between the ages of 14 and 18), university students and adult learners. Finally, the concluding chapter will provide a brief summary of the investigated themes as well as some future research directions will be pinpointed.

Some disclaimers should be added at this point. Although in this article I have concentrated on the Hungarian research scene in general, I have only highlighted those studies whose results have also been published in English-language journals in order to provide the audience of this book with accessible references on the Hungarian L2 motivation situation. In addition, as the emphasis was placed on Hungary and Hungarian research results, I have focused less on how these findings relate to similar issues in various language learning contexts and settings outside Hungary.

2 The Hungarian Context

All the research projects discussed below should be seen against the background of the effects of the major socio-political changes Hungary underwent in the past circa 20 years following the collapse of the communist rule in the late 1980s. The post-communist society was transformed into an open, market-oriented democracy, which officially joined the European Union in the spring of 2004 (see Andorka et al. 1990, 1998, for detailed sociological analyses in English). The language-related consequences of these changes included the abolition of the compulsory status of Russian within the education system, the spread of the availability of foreign language television and cultural products, and the increase of mainly Western European influences in terms of tourism and economic relationships. The co-occurrence of such powerful processes created a particularly interesting 'research laboratory' for studying learners' L2 learning dispositions to various languages in the early 1990s (Dörnyei et al. 2006).

In order to understand the consequences of these changes, one has to keep in mind that fact that Hungary is a monolingual country, that is, most people do not speak a second language unless they succeed to learn a foreign language at school. From 1949 to 1988/1989, Russian was a compulsory second language at all levels of the school system. Apart from various problems identified with the quick introduction of Russian into the curriculum in the early 1950s (e.g. improper training of Russian teachers), it should also be added that people lacked the motivation to learn the language for obvious reasons: it represented the oppressive power, therefore, positive attitudes towards the language, its culture and speakers could not be easily developed. Hence, most of the people did not master the Russian language despite long years of training.

In 1989, the compulsory status of Russian was abolished overnight and the situation in the state education with regard to L2 teaching changed abruptly. English and German took over Russian surprisingly quickly at each level of the education system. In 1993 only 14% of all secondary school students were learning Russian, with close to 80% studying English or German, and by the end of the 1990s Russian completely disappeared from secondary education in Hungary (Vágó 2000).

As for the expansion of foreign language learning within the Hungarian secondary education, the process has shown signs of stagnation since 2000. Without a designated compulsory foreign language to be learnt, in the majority of the schools two foreign languages are offered: English and German, with more than 50% of students opting for English at secondary grammar schools, while at secondary vocational schools students learning German outnumber students taking up English. The second position of German is not threatened by other languages as only around ten percent of the grammar school population learns other languages and this percentage is even lower at vocational schools (Vágó 2006). On a more negative note, Vágó's (2006) data have also revealed that despite the fact that early start (i.e. starting L2 learning at the age of six or seven) is rather prevalent at Hungarian primary schools, two-thirds of students entering Year nine will start foreign language learning from scratch because of the lack of appropriate level learning groups, which obviously hinders achievement in the long run.

Despite several reform efforts concerning L2 learning in the state education system (for an overview in Hungarian see Vágó 2007), the foreign language knowledge of the Hungarian population, as Fodor and Peluau (2003) summarize, is rather poor. The overwhelming majority of Hungarians are monolingual; only about 10–12 percent of the population claim to be able to speak a foreign language and less than 5% can express themselves in two languages. The main languages learned are English and German with about 500,000 learners each; the third foreign language, French, is way behind these two frontrunners with only about 50,000 learners. This indicates that compulsory education might not provide students with sufficient L2 knowledge, which makes L2 motivation research even more pressing within the framework of the Hungarian educational system (Vágó 2007).

3 Young Learners (Aged 6–14)

Several studies concentrated on the motivational dispositions of young learners in Hungary both in the qualitative and quantitative research method paradigms. Young learners' motivational characteristics are important because as instruction starts early at most Hungarian schools (Vágó 2007), one should be acquainted with how initial language learning motivation is taking shape as the initial formation of attitudes and motivational dispositions affect learning patterns later in life (Nikolov 2000).

As for qualitative results, Nikolov's (1999) longitudinal study stands out in Hungary. The researcher carried out a long-term ethnographic study investigating the motivational patterns of three groups of children (aged 6–14) in Pécs between 1977 and 1995. Based on the results obtained by having her pupils answer open-ended questions, Nikolov concluded that children participating in the study were mainly motivated by factors associated with the classroom situation (i.e. positive attitudes towards the learning context and the teacher as well as intrinsically motivated activities, tasks, and materials). Traces of instrumental motivation (i.e. learning the language for pragmatic gains) emerged among older children but no integrative motives were detected, that is, students did not mention that positive attitudes to the L2 communities motivate them to put more effort into language learning. These results, as we will see below, are quite in contrast with Dörnyei and his associates' quantitative findings, which might be explained by the effect of the different research methods or the fact that Nikolov investigated the emerging motives of her own students as well as the level of internalization of the various motives and not generalized motives affecting students' learning behavior (Dörnyei 2005). The uniqueness of Nikolov's work, however, is underlined by the fact that I know of no other longitudinal projects that set out to investigate young learners' motivation within early foreign language programs in Hungary.

Dörnyei et al. (2006) study employed three cross-sectional data collections spanning from 1993 to 2004 involving over 13,000 students with the main aim of investigating 13/14 year-old primary school students' motivational profiles in terms of five target languages: English, German, French, Italian and Russian. Several issues were investigated in the research project; the most important ones included the popularity of the various foreign languages in terms of students' attitudes and language choice over time and the internal structure of L2 motivation. One of the most notable results of this research showed that English became the dominant foreign language for the Hungarian population examined, while

German was losing its appeal and its status as a regional lingua franca. Despite the fact that Hungary is a relatively small country, a marked regional variation was detected in the availability of the various target languages and, to a lesser degree, in students' language choice preferences and their intended learning effort. The results of the study also indicated that students used the same mental framework or schema to appraise the various target languages in terms of five broad, interrelated dimensions: *integrativeness* (reflecting a general positive outlook on the L2 and its culture), *instrumentality* (relating to the utilitarian benefits one might enjoy if he or she speaks the language), *vitality of the community* (concerning the perceived importance and wealth of the L2 communities in question), *attitudes towards L2 speakers/community* (concerning attitudes towards actually meeting L2 speakers and traveling to their country) and *cultural interest* (describing appreciation of cultural products associated with the particular L2 and conveyed by the media). Out of these latent dimensions, *integrativeness* seemed to be the most important one in terms of shaping students' motivated learning behavior (Csizér and Dörnyei 2005).

As a follow-up to the above study, Csizér and Kormos (2008b) (see also Dörnyei and Csizér 2005, 2007) investigated the differences in the motivational and inter-cultural contact measures as well as determinants of motivated behavior between learners of English and German. The questionnaire survey utilized a nationwide sample of 1,777 Hungarian primary school children aged between 13 and 14 studying English and German. The results indicated that students of English had a more positive attitude towards the native speakers of the language they studied than learners of German, and children who studied English had a higher level of linguistic self-confidence, invested more energy into language learning and received more support from their environment than students of German. The findings also revealed that learners of English experienced more frequent direct written means and contact through media products than learners of German. Students with high levels of motivational intensity engaged in various types of inter-cultural contact more frequently than students who invested less energy into language learning. The results also showed that inter-cultural contact, even if not frequently experienced, played a far more important and complex role in language learning than assumed in earlier studies of the field.

4 Secondary School Students (Aged 14–18)

One of the first studies that examined secondary school students' L2 motivation in Hungary was Clément et al. (1994) investigation of grade 11 students' attitudes, anxiety and motivation towards learning English as well as their perception of classroom atmosphere and group cohesion. At that time, this study was considered unique for several reasons. First, it provided results very similar to Gardner's studies in Canada as analysis revealed a latent variable comparable to Gardner's integrativeness (Gardner 1985, 2001, 2006), which consisted of five elements:

attitudes toward the British, motivational intensity, attitudes toward Americans, students' need to achieve and identification orientation (Gardner 1985). Second, linguistic self-confidence emerged as another important variable shaping students' motivated learning behavior, which provided support to Clément's work in Canada (Clément 1980). In addition, it was revealed that there was a third significant element of L2 motivation: the appraisal of the classroom environment. The results indicated that the more cohesive a group seemed to be, the more motivated students were to learn the language, which for the first time in L2 motivation research highlighted the fact that if language learning took place in a classroom environment, the group dynamical processes could not be excluded from the equation. The importance of the group dynamical processes in L2 motivation was indeed reiterated by Csizér and Kormos (2008a), who found that the positive role of the teacher and success in the group also affected motivated learning behavior in a beneficial way. Despite the findings of these two studies, there is a clear lack of data in connection with group dynamical aspects and their impact on L2 motivation, and, therefore, the full assessment of how various aspects of group dynamics influence learning in various instructional contexts is still awaited. In Hungary, for example, the traditional methods involving focus on grammar and translation and frontal teaching are prevalent in a large number of foreign language classes (Intensive Language Preparation Research Group 2004, 2005), hence the group dynamical processes might be less relevant in these classes than in contexts where the teaching practice is more group- and student-centered.

A second theme in L2 motivation research investigated within secondary education in Hungary includes the exploration of task motivation, which, in recent years, has been seen as a highly promising classroom-based research direction explaining why students behave as they do in a specific learning situation where they are carrying out a specific task (Dörnyei 1996, 2002; Julkunen 2001). Kormos and Dörnyei's (2004) project involved 44 secondary school students enrolled in two different grammar schools in Budapest, who were asked to perform an oral argumentative task. As part of their data analysis, Kormos and Dörnyei tested the relationship between several linguistic and motivational variables. Their results indicated that when both the quantity and quality of task execution were compared, motivation influenced the quantity of talk and not how well students executed the task, hence, they concluded that "motivation seemed to function as a driving force that made students actively engage in a task, but it played a limited role determining the quality of the outcome" (p. 15). In addition, results also revealed the positive attitudes to the language course, more precisely, the teacher, teaching materials and teaching methods related to the quality of students' performance. Despite these promising and enlightening results, it has to be noted that as the findings came from a relatively small sample from one particular location in Hungary, further qualitative and quantitative studies are required to investigate task motivation and its effects on students' behavior, performance and achievement.

The most recent research efforts in Hungary concentrated on the testing of a new motivational framework put forward by Dörnyei (2005), called the

L2 Motivational Self System. This model consists of three main components: *Ideal L2 Self*, *Ought-to L2 Self* and the *L2 Learning Experience*, in which the *Ideal L2 Self* describes one's ideal self-image expressing the wish to become a competent L2 speaker; the *Ought-to L2 Self* contains "attributes that one believes one ought to possess (i.e. various duties, obligations, or responsibilities) in order to avoid possible negative outcomes" (Dörnyei 2005, p. 106), and L2 *learning experience* covers "situation specific motives related to the immediate learning environment and experience" (2005: 106). The results based on structural equation modeling revealed that in the case of secondary school students ($N = 202$), it was only Ideal L2 Self and L2 Learning Experience that contributed significantly to motivated learning behavior (Csizér and Kormos 2009). This indicated that a strong self-concept, which expressed students' self-perceptions and their confidence about succeeding in the learning task should not only be assumed to be a predictor variable, but even a pre-requisite for achieving a particular learning goal (for a review see Zimmerman 1989; Zimmerman and Schunk 2007). The results also suggested that international posture (that is positive attitudes to English as an international language) was highly related to students' idealized images of themselves, hence, these data corroborated previous investigations that have shown both in Asian settings (e.g. Lamb 2004; Warden and Lin 2000; Yashima 2000, 2002) and in Hungary (Kormos and Csizér 2008) that students' attitude to the role of English in our globalized world was not only a highly important driving force in L2 learning, but it also contributed to students' future images of themselves as successful language learners. In addition, our finding that knowledge orientation (i.e. to learn English in order to become more knowledgeable) contributed positively to attitudes related to international English showed that for Hungarian learners, English served as an important tool for gaining knowledge about the world around them via the information channels provided by globalized mass media such as the Internet. It seems therefore that in the Hungarian setting, the students' views about the global significance of English do not act as an extrinsic motivating factor, but are internalized motives that are very strongly related to the students' L2 self-concept.

As for the third component of Dörnyei's model, the L2 learning experience, it was highlighted in previous research in the field of L2 learning motivation that classroom factors including the teacher exerted an important influence on what learning experiences students had and how much effort they were willing to invest in language learning (Nikolov 1999). Csizér and Kormos (2009) also revealed that although it seemed to be imperative that students had an intrinsic interest in learning an L2 and had a strong L2 self-concept, the role of the language learning situation was also essential. Positive attitudes to the learning context and the teacher as well as motivating activities, tasks, and teaching materials seemed to influence both the learners' self-concept as well as how enthusiastically they studied English. Thus, our findings underline the importance of Dörnyei's (2001) argument that it is largely the teachers' responsibility to motivate students, and their role in terms of maintaining students' motivation cannot be overlooked in secondary education.

5 University Students (Aged 18 and Above)

The number of studies into the motivational profiles of university students in Hungary is rather limited. I am only aware of two investigations carried out by my colleagues and myself that deal with how non-language majors and English-majors see their motivation to learn English. The first study involved the testing of above outlined L2 Motivational Self-System (Dörnyei 2005) with the help of a sample drawn from several universities and colleges in Budapest (Csizér and Kormos 2008b). Our data revealed that there were only minor differences between the motivational set-up concerning students' self images and their learning experiences of secondary school and university students. One such difference was that for the secondary school sample the Ought-to self dimension of Dörnyei's model did not contribute to motivated learning behavior in a significant way but its role became more pronounced and significant for university students. In line with Higgins' (1987) self-discrepancy theory, which indicated that one's ought-to self is primarily shaped by significant others, we could conclude that in the investigated setting for students in tertiary education, the Ought-to L2 self was entirely socially constructed, that is, students' views of what attributes they should possess to meet the expectations of their environment were formed based on the attitudes of their immediate learning environment, which, in the case of young adults, primarily originated from the students' parents.

Another difference between younger learners and university students concerned the Ideal L2 self, as it proved to have a stronger effect on motivated learning behavior in the case of university students than for secondary school students. If we consider the students' self-concept in general, we can see that students' self-images go through considerable changes in the period of adolescence (Carlson 1965), and therefore their Ideal L2 Self is also under transformation at this age. University students, however, are in a period of their lives when they have a fairly stable self-image, but it is still flexible (Carlson 1965); therefore the L2 self can easily form part of their self-image. As for the formation of the Ideal L2 self, this can be influenced by several factors not yet investigated in L2 motivation research. For example, the significant differences in students' future image of themselves as competent speakers of English might also be due to the fact that secondary school students experience a limited amount of contact with speakers of English, and thus do not yet perceive the high importance of being able to use English in the future. The finding that for secondary school students the role of the Ideal L2 self was less pronounced than that of language learning experience, whereas for university students these two factors were of equal importance (for details, see Kormos and Csizér 2008), might also be explained by hypothesizing that for secondary school students, English was just another subject at school; therefore, L2 learning experiences gained in the classroom had a great effect on how much effort students were willing to invest in language learning. For university students, attitudes to language learning might be somewhat less important, as their relatively stronger and more developed L2 concept might potentially compensate even for the negative experiences of the learning situation.

As for the language learning motivation of English majors, in a mixed method study, Kormos et al. (2008) revealed that the motivational profiles of students majoring in English at Eötvös University in Budapest possessed a number of ambivalent features. In the first phase, the interview data indicated that the respondents had very favorable attitudes to the language itself, had relatively strong instrumental motives and attached significant importance to the role of English in today's globalized world. Moreover, their main goal was to attain a very high level of competence in English, to have good oral skills and knowledge of the language that could be used in everyday communication. All these characteristics suggest that students would invest a lot of energy in language learning and be satisfied with the process of their learning. In the second phase of the investigation, the questionnaire and interview data, however, demonstrated that this was not the case. The majority of students acknowledged that if there was no external pressure on them (such as having to pass a language proficiency exam), they did almost nothing to maintain or improve their language competence. They did not appear to use a sufficient number of learning strategies, which indicated a low level of learner autonomy. In other words, the English language students participating in this study placed responsibility on the university for their learning. The language learning experiences of the students also indicated that they had high expectations of the university which the institution could not and would not be able to meet. The lack of sufficient data, however, does not allow for a further analysis into how these discrepancies influence language majors' learning selves and how the L2 experience shapes students' Ideal and Ought-to L2 selves.

6 Adult Learners (Beyond Tertiary Education)

As the introductory chapter outlined the foreign language situation in the late 1980s and early 1990s, there was an increased interest in learning Western languages (Dörnyei 1990). This interest was reflected by the appearance of the first private schools in the 1980s and around the change of the regime in 1989, private language schools started to mushroom as a direct result of the language needs becoming more apparent to the general population (Dörnyei 1990). These language schools catered for the needs of the (young) adult professional population, whose members badly needed the knowledge of a Western language in order to acquire better positions on the labor market as the presence of and contact with foreign companies grew. The first systematic study into L2 motivation in the late 1980s involved these young adult professionals who were clearly dissatisfied with the language learning opportunities offered by the state educational system at the time. Dörnyei's (1990) study employed Robert Gardner's motivational paradigm as a blueprint and operationalised latent dimensions relating to integrative and instrumental motivation. Dörnyei's (1990) results suggested a very interesting phenomenon in connection with the relationship of motivational profiles and language learning goals for young adults, as those students who intended to reach beyond an intermediate level in their L2 studies showed a higher level of integrative motivation than those without such an aim. As Dörnyei (2005) often describes the Ideal L2 self as the reinterpretation of integrative motivation, these early results might also strengthen the claim that without a pronounced (and perhaps idealized) self image the level of L2 motivation will be less strong and goals will be more immediate. In addition, however, these idealized selves should always be compared to students' actual selves and if the distance is too broad between the two types of self images effort would be seen useless and students' L2 motivation, in turn, will not be sufficient to achieve long-term success.

After this initial study, the language learning motivation of adult learners has been largely ignored in Hungary, as most of the researchers felt more compelled to work within primary and secondary school settings in order to enhance the efficiency of teaching and learning for school-aged students. However, as dissatisfaction grew with the various aspects of foreign language instruction in the state education system (Nikolov 1999), it became necessary to investigate the possible sources of demotivation. Marianne Nikolov (2001), Nikolov and Nagy (2003) carried out a mixed method project concerning the language learning dispositions of unsuccessful adult learners in order to find out what factors might contribute to students' lack of L2 motivation and why students might lose their motivation during the learning process. Her study concluded that classroom-related processes, more specifically teachers, played an important role in shaping students' dispositions, motivation and achievement and therefore inappropriate methods and lack of motivating teaching practice would thwart the learning process (Nikolov 2001; Nikolov and Nagy 2003).

Kormos and Csizér's (2008) study employed a more positive perspective and investigated successful adult learners' motivational profiles with the help of Dörnyei's L2 Motivational Self System. We found that for adult learners, language-related attitudes and Ideal L2 self variables played almost equal roles in shaping learning behavior and they explained around 40% of the variation in motivated behavior, whereas for learners in secondary and tertiary education, language learning attitudes were slightly more important than the Ideal L2 self. This finding might be explained with reference to the fact that the language learning attitudes of younger students were primarily based on classroom experience and were largely shaped by teachers (see e.g. Nikolov 1999), whereas older students had clear goals with language learning, which were already incorporated in their Ideal L2 self and were less dependent on their teacher and classroom experiences. In addition, structural equation modeling revealed that adult learners' self-images were highly dependent on their views of the international role of the English language, that is, those learners who accepted the fact that English was increasingly becoming a global language and had positive attitudes towards this global role reported more positive self-image and, in turn, a higher level of motivated learning behavior (Kormos and Csizér 2008). These results further reinforce the overall feasibility of Dörnyei's (2005) L2 Motivational Self System but the slight difference between learners' groups indicates that the actual importance of the three components (Ideal L2 self, Ought-to L2 self and L2 learning experience) might vary for different learners' groups in various contexts.

7 Conclusion

It is a generally accepted fact that language learning motivation is a crucial contributor to L2 learning success in all educational contexts (Dörnyei 2005). The present overview has intended to introduce the Hungarian research scene by describing the most important results with the aim of providing implications that might be relevant in other European contexts as well.

The emerging major themes in L2 motivation research in Hungary, in my view, not only satiate local interest but also place this country on the international scene of mainstream L2 motivation research. The research directions having received considerable attention in Hungary can be summarized as follows:

- the influence of language—and language—related attitudes on L2 motivation within diverse geographical and educational settings;
- the impact of intercultural contact on L2 motivation;
- the issues related to students' selves and their relationship with L2 learning;
- age-related differences in L2 learning and motivation; and
- the role of English as a increasingly global language and its impact on L2 motivation.

The list might seem impressive but it is far from complete. First, as the vast majority of the results cited above come from studies employing a macro perspective, that is, those motivational dimensions were focused on that were generalizable across various learning situations and stable motives stemming from a succession of the students' past experiences in the social world were targeted, and considerably less attention was paid to situation-specific motives that were rooted in the L2 learners' immediate learning environment. Future research activities in Hungary should definitely take a more classroom-oriented focus and investigate the motivational impact of the micro-context within which students are actually learning L2s. Second, most of the studies presented here have used a cross-sectional design and only few of them explored motivation over time, that is, how students' motivational dispositions might change in the course of their learning carrier. Despite the fact that most researchers would agree on the dynamical nature of L2 motivation (see Dörnyei 2005, for an overview), hardly any Hungarian studies touched upon the true longitudinal nature of the motivational processes. Third, all of the studies summarized above have drawn samples from students studying within general, mainstream educational settings and the motivational profiles of special needs students' have been largely ignored (Kormos and Kontra 2008). Fourth, several researchers in the L2 motivation paradigm call our attention to the fact that studies, frameworks and models in general educational psychology might and should be incorporated into the L2 motivation research agenda (Dörnyei 2005), but this call has mostly been ignored in Hungary, largely because the training of foreign language researchers lacks a marked interdisciplinary approach, therefore, the gap between research in educational psychology and foreign language education cannot be bridged. Taking into account these shortcomings of L2 motivation research in our country, it can be concluded that there are still a number of L2 motivation questions to be investigated in Hungary but the past 20 years of solid research might be relevant not only for Hungarian researchers and educators but for colleagues working outside Hungary as well.

References

Andorka, R., T. Kolosi, and Gy. Vukovics. 1990. *Social report*. Budapest: TÁRKI-Századvég.

Andorka, R., T. Kolosi, and Gy. Vukovics. 1998. *Social report*. Budapest: TÁRKI-Századvég.

Carlson, R. 1965. Stability and change in the adolescent's self-image. *Child Development* 36: 659–666.

Central Statistical Office. 2004. *Census 2001: Ethnic minorities in Hungary*. Budapest: Central Statistical Office.

Clément, R. 1980. Ethnicity, contact and communicative competence in a second language. In eds. H.M. Giles, W.P. Robinson, and P.M. Smith, 147–154.

Clément, R., Z. Dörnyei, and K.A. Noels. 1994. Motivation, self-confidence, and group cohesion in the foreign language classroom. *Language Learning* 44: 417–448.

Csizér, K., and Z. Dörnyei. 2005. Language learners' motivational profiles and their motivated learning behavior. *Language Learning* 55: 613–659.

Csizér, K., and J. Kormos. 2008a. An overview of Hungarian secondary school students' foreign language motivation. In ed. H.V. Knudsen, 65–87.

Csizér K., and J. Kormos. 2008b. The relationship of inter-cultural contact and language learning motivation among Hungarian students of English and German. *Journal of Multilingual and Multicultural Development* 29: 30–48.

Csizér, K., and J. Kormos. 2009. Learning experiences, selves and motivated learning behaviour: A comparative analysis of structural models for Hungarian secondary and university learners of English. In eds. Z. Dörnyei, and E. Ushioda, 98–119.

Dörnyei, Z. 1990. Conceptualizing motivation in foreign-language learning. *Language Learning* 40: 45–78.

Dörnyei, Z. 1996. Moving language learning motivation to a larger platform for theory and practice. In ed. R.L. Oxford, 71–80.

Dörnyei, Z. 2001. *Motivational strategies*. Cambridge: Cambridge University Press.

Dörnyei, Z. 2002. Motivational basis of language learning tasks. In eds. Z. Dörnyei, P. Robinson, and P. Skehan, 137–158.

Dörnyei, Z. 2005. *The psychology of the language learner: Individual differences in second language acquisition*. Mahwah: Lawrence Erlbaum.

Dörnyei, Z., and K. Csizér. 2005. The effects of intercultural contact and tourism on language attitudes and language learning motivation. *Journal of Language and Social Psychology* 24: 1–31.

Dörnyei, Z., and M. Schmidt, eds. 2001. *Motivation and second language acquisition* (Technical Report #23). Honolulu: The University of Hawai'i, Second Language and Curriculum Center.

Dörnyei, Z., and E. Ushioda, eds. 2009. *Motivation, language identity and the L2 self*. Clevedon: Multilingual Matters.

Dörnyei, Z., P. Robinson, and P. Skehan, eds. 2002. *Individual differences in second language acquisition*. Amsterdam: John Benjamins.

Dörnyei, Z., K. Csizér, and N. Németh. 2006. *Motivational dynamics, language attitudes and language globalisation: A Hungarian perspective*. Clevedon: Multilingual Matters.

Fodor, F., and S. Perluau. 2003. Language geostrategy in eastern and central Europe: Assessment and perspectives. In eds. J. Maurais, and M.A. Morris, 85–98.

Gardner, R.C. 1985. *Social psychology and second language learning: The role of attitudes and motivation*. London: Edward Arnold.

Gardner, R.C. 2001. Integrative motivation and second language acquisition. In eds. Z. Dörnyei, and R. Schmidt, 1–19.

Gardner, R.C. 2006. The socio-educational model of second language acquisition: A research paradigm. *EUROSLA Yearbook* 6: 237–260.

Giles, H.M., W.P. Robinson, and P.M. Smith, eds. 1980. *Language: Social psychological perspectives*. Oxford: Pergamon.

Halász, G., and J. Lannert, eds. 2000. *Education in Hungary* 2000. Budapest: Országos Közoktatási Intézet.

Higgins, E.T. 1987. Self-discrepancy: A theory relating self and affect. *Psychological Review* 94: 319–340.

Intensive Language Preparation Research Group. 2004. Report on the results of the survey of students in intensive language preparation programs in the fall semester of 2004/2005 academic year [In Hungarian]. On-line. http://www.om.hu/letolt/vilagnyelv/ om_nyek_jelentes_2004_osz.pdf.

Intensive Language Preparation Research Group. 2005. Report on the results of the survey of students in intensive language preparation programs in the spring semester of 2004/2005 academic year [In Hungarian]. On-line. http://www.om.hu/letolt/vilagnyelv/ om_nyek_jelentes_2005_tavasz.pdf.

Julkunen, K. 2001. Situation- and task-specific motivation in foreign language learning. In eds. Z. Dörnyei, and R. Schmidt, 29–41.

Knudsen, H.V., ed. 2008. *Secondary school education*. NY: Nova Science Publishers.

Kormos, J., and K. Csizér. 2007. An interview study of inter-ethnic contact and its role in language learning in a foreign language environment. *System* 35: 241–258.

Kormos, J., and K. Csizér. 2008. Age-related differences in the motivation of learning English as a foreign language: Attitudes, selves and motivated learning behavior. *Language Learning* 58: 327–355.

Kormos, J., and Z. Dörnyei. 2004. The interaction of linguistic and motivational variables in second language task performance. *Zeitschrift für Interkulturellen Fremdsprachenunterricht* [Online] 9.

Kormos, J., and E.H. Kontra, eds. 2008. *Language learners with special needs: An international perspective*. Clevedon: Multiling. Matters.

Kormos, J., K. Csizér, A. Menyhárt, and D. Török. 2008. Great expectations: The motivational profile of Hungarian English majors. *Arts Humanit High Education* 7: 63–80.

Lamb, M. 2004. Integrative motivation in a globalizing world. *System* 32: 3–19.

Lannert, J., I. Vágó, and M.M. Kőrösné, eds. 2006. *Foreign language and digital knowledge of adults* [In Hungarian]. Budapest: Felnőttképzési Intézet.

Maurais, J., and M.A. Morris, eds. 2003. *Languages in a globalising world*. Cambridge: Cambridge University Press.

Moon, J., and M. Nikolov, eds. 2000. *Research into teaching English to young learners: International perspective*. Pécs: University of Pécs.

Nikolov, M., and E. Nagy. 2003. I have been learning for years without success: Adult language learners' experiences [In Hungarian]. *Modern Nyelvoktatás* 9: 14–40.

Nikolov, M. 1999. 'Why do you learn English?' 'Because the teacher is short': A study of Hungarian children's foreign language motivation. *Language Teaching Research* 3: 33–56.

Nikolov, M. 2000. Issues into early foreign language programmes. In eds. J. Moon, and M. Nikolov, 21–48.

Nikolov, M. 2001. A study of unsuccessful language learners. In eds. Z. Dörnyei, and M. Schmidt, 149–169.

Oxford, R.L., ed. 1996. *Language learning motivation: Pathways to the new century (Technical Report #11)*. Honolulu: University of Hawai'i, Second Language Teaching and Curriculum Center.

Schunk, D.H., and B.J. Zimmerman, eds. 2007. *Motivation and self-regulated learning: Theory, research and applications*. New York: Lawrence Erlbaum.

Vágó, I. 2000. The content of education. In eds. G. Halász, and J. Lannert, 169–238.

Vágó, I. 2006. Language learning routes. In eds. J. Lannert, I. Vágó, and M.M. Kőrösné, 59–70.

Vágó, I., ed. 2007. *Focus on language learning* [In Hungarian]. Budapest: OKI.

Warden, C.A., and H.J. Lin. 2000. Existence of integrative motivation in an Asian EFL setting. *Foreign language annals* 33: 535–547.

Yashima, T. 2000. Orientations and motivations in foreign language learning: A study of Japanese college students. *JACET Bulletin* 31: 121–134.

Zimmerman, B.J. 1989. Theories of self-regulated learning and academic achievement. In eds. B.J. Zimmerman, and D.H. Schunk, 1–38.

Zimmerman, B.J., and D.H. Schunk, eds. 1989. *Learning and achievement: Theoretical perspectives*. Berlin: Springer.

Zimmerman, B.J., and C.E. Schunk. 2007. Motivation: An essential dimension of self-regulated learning. In eds. D.H. Schunk, and B.J. Zimmerman, 1–30.

Part IV
Individual Differences in Learning and Teaching Practices

Comprehensible Pragmatics: Where Input and Output Come Together

Andrew D. Cohen

Abstract This chapter relates issues of comprehensible input and comprehensible output to an increasingly prominent field: second-language pragmatics, where the intended meanings often go beyond the literal ones. The chapter will take a close look at what comprehensibility of language at the level of pragmatics actually entails. In looking at both the comprehension and production of pragmatic material, we will consider briefly the negotiation of meaning and conversational repairs—modifications made to the interactional structure of discourse and to words, sounds, and syntax for the purpose of communicating pragmatics. We will first look at what comprehensible input means with regard to pragmatics, whether through language (e.g. lexical items—words and phrases, syntax—e.g. verb tenses, or discourse), through gestures, or through silence. Then we will consider what comprehensible output entails in order that the addressees interpret the intended pragmatics correctly. Finally, we will reflect on the implications for both the learning and teaching of L2 pragmatics in lights of these comprehensibility issues.

1 Introduction

This chapter relates issues of comprehensible input and comprehensible output to an increasingly prominent field: second/foreign-language (L2)[1] pragmatics, where the intended meanings often go beyond the literal ones. Having pragmatic ability,

---

[1] For the purposes of this paper, L2 will serve as a generic label, including both the context where the language is spoken widely and the context where it is not. In principle, pragmatic development in an L2 will be faster in the former context than in the latter, but it depends largely on how the learner makes use of the available resources.

A. D. Cohen (✉)
University of Minnesota, MN, USA
e-mail: adcohen@umn.edu

M. Pawlak (ed.), *New Perspectives on Individual Differences in Language Learning and Teaching*, Second Language Learning and Teaching, DOI: 10.1007/978-3-642-20850-8_16, © Springer-Verlag Berlin Heidelberg 2012

in fact, implies that as listener or reader, you are able to interpret the intended meanings of what is said or written, the assumptions, purposes or goals, and the kinds of actions that are being performed (Yule 1996: 3–4). As speaker, pragmatic ability means that you know how to say what you want to say with the proper politeness, directness, and formality (for instance, in the role of boss, telling an employee that s/he is being laid off; or in the role of teacher, telling a student that his/her work is unacceptable). You also need to know what not to say at all and what to communicate non-verbally. As writer, pragmatic ability means knowing how to write your message intelligibly, again paying attention to level of politeness, directness, formality, and appropriateness of the rhetorical structure of the message (for instance, in the role of employee, composing an e-mail message to your boss requesting a promotion and a raise, or a paid vacation from the boss; or as neighbor, writing a note complaining about late-evening TV noise).

While *native speaker* pragmatic norms will be used as a benchmark for pragmatic ability in this chapter, it needs to be acknowledged that sometimes non-native speakers can be as pragmatically appropriate as or more so than some natives. So where 'native speaker' is used, consider the term to encompass as well those nonnatives who are highly competent when it comes to the pragmatics of the language. The chapter will take a close look at what *comprehensibility of language* at the level of pragmatics actually entails. We will first look at what *comprehensible input* means with regard to pragmatics. We will also consider what *comprehensible output* entails in order that the addressees interpret the intended pragmatics correctly. Finally, we will reflect on the implications for both the learning and teaching of L2 pragmatics in light of these comprehensibility issues.

2 Theoretical Underpinnings for Pragmatic Comprehensibility

So, what needs to happen for nonnatives to achieve success at comprehending and producing language pragmatically? Let us look at the comprehension and production of pragmatic material, and consider briefly the negotiation of meaning and conversational repairs—modifications made to the interactional structure of discourse and to words, sounds, and syntax for the purpose of communicating pragmatics.

Krashen's *input hypothesis* (Krashen 1982) posited that learners' language development follows a relatively predictable pattern or *natural order* whereby they understand input that contains structures a little beyond their current level of competence ($i + 1$). In addition, input becomes more comprehensible with the help of contextual and extralinguistic clues. This approach to acquisition sounds liberating especially in the pragmatics arena, in some ways—in that learners can relax and just absorb, and teachers can decrease their level of explicit instruction. Yet, in reality, applying the input hypothesis in the area of pragmatics is problematic in that much of the pragmatics of a language is not easily acquirable since it is not highly observable. Sometimes, in fact, it is very subtle (e.g. ways to complain in cultures where overt complaining is unacceptable, as in Japan), and other times the pragmatics are clear but the instances of pragmatic use are low-frequency (e.g. what people say at a funeral).

In response to Krashen's input hypothesis, Long (1985, 1996) posited that the input needs to undergo interactional modifications through the negotiation of meaning for learners to gain control of a language. Yet given the demanding nature of communicative interaction for learners at the level of literal meanings, how much more demanding it may become at the level of pragmatics. Still, it could be argued that thrashing issues out in a back and forth with an interlocutor, through email, or through other formats can help learners to acquire pragmatics. Further-more, native speakers may not call learners even on an egregious *faux pas* prag-matically. The reason is that even if they take offense, they may feel uncomfortable about explicitly raising the issue with the learner.

Another refinement of acquisition theories would seem to contribute espe-cially to pragmatics: Schmidt's (1990, 1993, 2001) addition of the *noticing hypothesis*. Schmidt would contend that in order for input to become intake on the road to acquisition, both L2 linguistic forms and contextual factors must be 'noticed'. Although noticing does not necessarily guarantee L2 pragmatic learning, it is claimed to be a necessary condition—that mere exposure to the L2 is unlikely to lead to learners' noticing of pragmatic features and understanding of general pragmatic norms (Kasper and Schmidt 1996; Kasper and Rose 2002). There is evidence especially in the study abroad literature that this is the case—simply going off to another country does not ensure that pragmatics will be acquired (see the review of literature in Cohen and Shively 2007). In fact, Olshtain and Blum-Kulka (1985) constituted some years ago with regard to positive politeness strategies in Hebrew that, left to their own devices, it can take L2 learners over 10 years or more to perform pragmatics in a way indistin-guishable from natives.

A final theoretical refinement of the input hypothesis would be Swain's *output hypothesis*. Swain posits that output opportunities are likely to contribute to learners' acquisition of the L2 as the learners notice gaps in their linguistic system and look to the input around them (e.g. a conversational partner) for resource material that can assist them in articulating their message (Swain and Lapkin 1995; Swain 1998). She added that their output also reinforces retention of new infor-mation and enhances fluency. The output hypothesis is consistent with Long's concern for interaction as a means for language development, though in the case of Swain's hypothesis, the interactions can be with fellow learners, and not neces-sarily with natives. She has demonstrated how, for example, learners in a French immersion program and ESL students as well can progress in their learning of the target language by interaction with fellow students around issues of, say, grammar. In terms of pragmatics, however, it may well be that fellow students are not very good models. In fact, what may result in a failed request, for example, to a native speaker may be adequate with a fellow nonnative, especially with someone from the same speech community and sociocultural background.

Table 1 Comprehending the pragmatics of the input

Nature of the input	Proficiency in L2/FL and in other languages	Age, gender, occupation, social status, communities of practice	Former cross-cultural experiences
Language			
Lexical items (words or phrases)	'*Bonjour*' 'No worries'— Australia	The 'in' words and how to use them—'cool', 'sweet', 'bad', etc. Curse words in NZ	
Syntax (e.g. verb tenses)	Conditional in Spanish in a request to a friend		
Discourse	An apology extending over numerous turns in a corpus		Renting a car: 'When was your driver's license issued?'
Gestures	Negative transfer of a gesture from one L2 to another ('Wait' in Hebrew)		
Silence	Silence in the L2 (moments in Japanese; hitchhiking in Israel).		

In considering the role of input, interaction, noticing, and output, we need to bear in mind that learners differ in their learning styles, language strategy repertoires, and motivation for language learning (see Cohen and Weaver 2006). Consequently, what works for one L2 learner in terms of gaining pragmatic awareness and enhanced pragmatic performance may not work for another. Some learners may, for example, benefit from extensive observation of what natives do without much interaction with them, at least during an initial phase. Others may prefer to start interacting from the beginning, without an initial period of observation. Let us first consider what *comprehensible input* with regard to pragmatics might actually mean for learners, and then we will look at what learners need to do to produce *comprehensible output* pragmatically.

3 Comprehending the Pragmatic Messages in the Input

The input could be through language (e.g. through lexical items, syntax, or discourse), though gestures, or through silence. Whether the input is pragmatically comprehensible to the nonnative depends on various factors, such as: (1) the functional proficiency of the nonnative in the target language and in other languages, (2) the age, gender, occupation, social status, and experience of the nonnative in the relevant communities of practice (e.g. talk on the shop floor), and (3) the nonnative's previous multilingual/multicultural experiences. Table 1 relates these factors to a sampling of language and nonverbal behaviors in an effort to illustrate how such factors may contribute to the ease or difficulty which a nonnative has in interpreting the pragmatics of an interaction in a given situation.

For example, to what extent do nonnatives understand the *illocutionary force* or function of *bonjour* in a French-speaking community? The pragmatics of this apparently simple greeting may have subtle pragmatics attached to it, which the less savvy nonnative may miss. An American approaches a man on the street in Martinique, as I did in December of last year, and launches directly into a request for help in interpreting a confusing parking slip issued by a machine and intended to be put on the dashboard of the car. Instead of responding to the man's question (asked in fluent French), he says, *Bonjour*. So an L2 speaker of French needs to know what that *bonjour* means. Perhaps it could possibly mean, 'What? I didn't hear the question'. It most likely meant, 'I was put off by your focusing imme-diately and exclusively on the parking slip, without going through the courtesy of extending a morning greeting'—an instance of negative transfer from US norms for requests of strangers.

As far as he was concerned, before we got into any matters of substance, an initial greeting was in order or even essential. After I greeted him properly, I proceeded to have a nice conversation with this man who was *Martiniquais*, living in Paris for over 40 years and working with the police there. His response to me was, 'No one will be checking parking for the next few days since it is a holiday period'.[2]

The point here with regard to pragmatics is that knowing the word alone is not sufficient in comprehending the L2. It is crucial to know how competent speakers of the language are likely to use this word in such a context. In this instance, his *bonjour* was telling me in no uncertain terms to use a greeting as a segue to further discourse. I was clearly operating from a US-based pragmatics mode and simply transferring this approach to this parking slip situation, rather than asking myself how a native French speaker would do it, observing how they do it, or asking how to do it. While such differences may be very pronounced in the foreign-language situation as in this case (where there were few Americans and little English is spoken), they may be more subtle and even blurred in L2 situations such as when French is spoken in a French-speaking community in the USA. In this intercultural situation, perhaps the need for the greeting first is diminished given the influence of the mainstream language community where 'we get down to business' right away.

Other comprehensible pragmatics problems can be attributed to negative transfer from the L1, overgeneralization of material in the L2, or limited profi-ciency in the L2 (three categories to be elaborated on in the section on pragmat-ically comprehensible output, below). So at the lexical level, the first time a nonnatives hear 'no worries' as used in Australia to mean 'you're welcome', they

---

[2] Claire Kramsch reported in a talk a few years ago a similar experience with a station master in France where she rushed up to him and asked what track a certain train was on, and before he would respond to that query, he responded with *Bonjour, madame?*, in order to signal to her that a preliminary greeting was in order before discussing train locations.

interpret it as an intrusion into their private life and their level of worry. I thanked an Ozzie in Melbourne for holding a men's room door open for me, and when he said 'No worries' in return, at first I wondered why he was 'messing' with my worries. How would he know just how many worries I might have. Then I realized what he intended by his response. At the level of syntax, the nonnative has to correctly interpret the role of grammar (e.g. verb tenses) in pragmatics. It has been seen, for example, that English-speaking study abroaders to Spanish-speaking countries misread their acquaintances' use of the conditional in requests (e.g. *podrias* 'could you…' instead of *puedes* 'can you') as being overly formal (Cohen and Shively 2007). Another language-related issue is that speech acts in real time may not show up in a neat, interpretable fashion, but rather be spread over a number of turns in a lengthy interaction, culminating in something like, 'Well, then, I'm sorry for that' (see Félix-Brasdefer 2006). It may be progressive enough and subtle enough that the nonnative does not even realize that an apology is taking place.

A rather obvious case of miscomprehension would be with a gesture such as the one for 'wait' in Hebrew, which consists of extending the forearm with the fingers and thumb bunched and pointing upwards without moving the hand. It is used to mean, 'Just a second and I'll be with you', or 'Please wait and let me cut in' (when on a bike, in a car or whatever vehicle). Such a gesture does not exist in American English but does (with the hand moving) in European languages and has a different, sometimes obscene, meaning. So seeing this similar version in Europe may wrongly be interpreted as 'wait', when it actually means something obscene.

Finally, the use of silence itself can have a pragmatic function that is lost on a nonnative speaker who is unaware of the norms. So, for example, an American English speaker may interpret silence in a Japanese speaker as meaning that the person is relinquishing the floor when this may not be the case. As chair of a session at an academic meeting, I once led a round of applause for a Japanese speaker of English when I interpreted his extended pause as meaning he had ended his remarks when he had not. Another example of silence would be a somewhat dated example of when hitchhiking was prevalent in Israel, hitchhikers would be expected to remain silent, rather than to entertain the driver with their conversation, which may be the norm in the USA.

With regard to demographic variables and community of practice, pragmatics can play itself out in terms of the 'cool' or 'in' words that people use in communication. Nonnatives may be hard put to correctly interpret just what the use of 'sweet' or 'that rocks' actually means in terms of how formal or informal, friendly or unfriendly the interlocutor is choosing to be. In addition, nonnatives may misinterpret the role of curse words in the discourse. They may find them offensive, without realizing that in the particular community of practice, they serve a crucial role, perhaps providing an important bonding between employer and employee, and among the employees. So, for example, as part of a *Language in the workplace* project at Victoria University of Wellington, Holmes and her colleagues collected over 2,000 interactions in English (mostly L1) in the workplace in New Zealand (Holmes 2003). Extensive analysis of their corpus yielded insights into what was necessary for fitting in and becoming an integrated member of the workplace, with the focus being specifically on small talk, humor, complaints and whinges (i.e. indirect complaints or complaints to the wrong person), and refusals. The findings were that speech acts may be highly indirect and dependent on both the personalities of the interlocutors and on their actual relationship with others in the workplace, sometimes established over long periods of time.

With regard to previous multilingual experiences, the nonnative may come to a situation with expectations based on pragmatic experiences in numerous other speech communities, only to find that the norm for this situation is distinctly and perhaps surprisingly different. Such was the case when my wife and I arrived at the InterRent shack a ways from the airport in Martinique in December of 2007 and the French-speaking clerk asked me when my license was issued. I promptly told her 'February of 2007', reading the date of issue from my Minneapolis driver's license. The clerk then looked very perplexed and informed me that she could not rent me a car since the driver must have at least a year's experience driving before renting a car. What she meant in her question was when I was issued my first driver's license. But that is not what she said. Then what followed, once we determined the misunderstanding, was that she needed to calculate the year that I in fact first started driving, which was probably about 1960, but for safety sake, I just arbitrarily said at age 18, which would mean 45 years ago. She was relieved and then preceded with the rental agreement.

Having laid out a number of possible misunderstandings, the question remains as to the factors which will determine whether pragmatic failure will actually occur in the case of a given individual? Presumably it is more likely to occur among the less proficient and more inexperienced users of the L2, those unfamiliar with the language of the aged or the very young, those less familiar with how the L2 deals with social status, or those with more limited contact with members of certain communities of practice. But let us assume that two speakers have the same degree of background knowledge and exposure to the language. What might contribute to one of them understanding the pragmatics of the situation better than the other one? Learning style preference may play a role, such as the relative introversion of the nonnative. Learners who are more extroverted may be more into their speaking than into careful observation of native-speaker pragmatic behavior. Keen powers of observation may assist learners in getting the pragmatics of a message despite the fact that most of the vocabulary and grammatical structures in the message are incomprehensible to them. They simply take the clues that they perceive (e.g. tone of voice, facial expression, body posture, elaborateness or curtness of the utterance) and intuit or infer the rest from there. Strategy repertoire may also play a role in that some learners select among their strategies that of being more consciously aware of how pragmatics works in the given speech community and specific situation, even to the extent of asking locals whether they have interpreted a speech act correctly or not.

4 Producing Pragmatically Comprehensible Output

What do learners need to do in order for their output to be *comprehensible* pragmatically to their interlocutors? It helps for the nonnatives to accommodate to the local speech community's norms for pragmatic performance, such as in, say, making a request. There are at least five factors that can stand in the way of acceptable accommodation (Ishihara and Cohen 2010), possibly leading to the pragmatically inappropriate output: (1) *negative transfer* of pragmatic behavior from their L1 or some other language they know, (2) *overgeneralization of pragmatic behavior* to a situation where it is inappropriate, (3) *limited L2 grammatical ability*, (4) *the effect of instruction or instructional materials*, and (5) *resistance to target-language norms* for pragmatic behavior (see Table 2).

4.1 Negative Transfer

In this instance, the nonnatives transfer the patterns for how they would conduct the interaction in their L1 or dominant-language speech community, most likely unknowingly but sometimes knowing it is probably wrong but the only thing they know how to do. Let us suppose that a Korean learner of English responds to an American friend's compliment about nice looking clothes saying 'No, that's not true'. Whereas this would be appropriately modest behavior in Korean culture, in USA culture this response to such a compliment may make it sound as if she were flatly rejecting or questioning the friend's judgment, and hence creates a somewhat awkward situation or even sounds insulting. Another example would be when a Japanese student requests that a professor read a paper he wrote by saying, 'Professor, read this paper please'. Such a request may come across as too direct, even though the student said 'please' which would probably make the request polite enough in Japanese.

4.2 Overgeneralization of L2 Norms

Some learners may generalize pragmatic norms acceptable in one situation to another situation where that behavior is not appropriate. So, for example, a Korean learner of American English perceives Americans as being very direct and frank about things, a perception that is reinforced when the American male passenger sitting next to him on a flight shares some intimacies. Consequently, the Korean is surprised when the fellow passenger is clearly reluctant to answer a question about how much he makes a month. While the Korean would not ask that question in his

Table 16.2 Producing pragmatically comprehensible output

Nature of the output	Negative transfer	Overgeneralization of L2 norms	Limited L2 grammatical ability	Effect of instruction or instructional materials	Resistance to local norms
Language					
Phrases	Rejecting a compliment with 'No, that's not true'	Using a formal request or refusal when the given situation calls for greater informality			Avoiding 'Did you eat yet?' as a greeting in Indonesian
Sentences or groups of sentences	Request to read a thesis: 'Dr. X, please read this'	Being overly frank—asking for salary information	Making a request that sounds like an order	Giving the actual reason for a refusal in a situation where it is not appropriate	Avoiding using honorific verbs to speak to or about people of higher status
Gestures		Overusing hand gestures in Italian			
Silence				Using filled pauses too much rather than silence	

home culture, he just assumed that American frankness in discussing intimacies would carry over to other topics as well.

Another example would be that of the American who has heard that Italians talk with their hands so he makes an effort to use a lot of hand gestures to make his points in Italian while studying in Rome. An Italian friend takes him aside to tell him that he is gesturing too much, and also that some of his gestures mean something different from what he intends them to mean.

Yet another example would be of an American study-abroad student who has a sense that Spanish speakers are more formal in their commands. So if she wants a glass of water from her host-family mother, she asks for it in a most polite way, 'Would you be able to give me a glass of water, please'. Her host mother finds her style overly formal since in their Barcelona home they just say the equivalent of 'Water, please' or 'Give me a glass of water, please'. Finally, there is the example of the English-speaking learner of Japanese whose close Japanese friend offers her more food at an informal dinner meal at her apartment. The learner knows an expression, *Iie, kekkoudesu*, an equivalent of 'No thanks' in Japanese and uses it. However, she is unaware that this expression is usually used in formal situations and sounds funny or awkward if directed to a close friend.

4.3 Limited L2 Grammatical Ability

Lack of knowledge of certain grammatical forms, or more likely lack of knowledge of how to use them functionally in a given target-language situation, may inadvertently lead to producing language that is pragmatically gauche. A beginning learner of English, for example, might request that a clerk in a repair shop fix an item, with 'Do this for me now' because the learner has not yet learned how to be more indirect and consequently sound more polite (e.g. 'I was wondering how soon you might be able to repair this for me'). Such a request (interpreted as an order) may, in fact, draw the ire of the clerk, particularly if the nonnative has relatively good pronunciation.

4.4 The Effect of Instruction or Instructional Materials

Learners might also be led to pragmatic failure as a result of somewhat misleading information that they receive either from the teacher or for from the course materials. So, for example, a learner of English may have read in an ESL textbook that Americans tend to give the precise reason for why they cannot attend a party that they are invited to. Yet when the learners do the same, they find that in the particular instance (say, an important work-related party) it may be interpreted as an unacceptable excuse (e.g. 'I can't come because I have a dinner date with a friend'). As another example, an American learner of Japanese may be taught in class to fill a pause with *eeto* (more informal) or *ano* (more formal), and so does his best to fill as many pauses as he can that way. His native-speaking interlocutor is annoyed by this overuse of these pauses and eventually tells the learner that he is filling his pauses too much—that natives prefer to use silence or non-verbal cues more. Whereas in part this could be considered a case of overgeneralization, it originates from instruction regarding the filling of pauses. What is misleading is that in Japanese silence is favored more than in English, and the teacher neglected to point this out as well.

4.5 Resistance to Local L2 Norms

Another source of pragmatic failure may be an intentional desire not to abide by the L2 speech community's norms in the given instance despite having full knowledge of what is expected—which sets this category apart from the other four. So for example, an English-speaking learner of Indonesian hears natives use the equivalent of 'Did you eat yet?' as a regular greeting but avoids using it herself because it does not really seem like a greeting to her. Or an American learner of Japanese has learned the honorific verbs that are required when speaking to or about people of higher status even if they are not present at the time (e.g. asking if the higher-status person has eaten by using *meshiagarimashitika* instead of *tabemashitika*, the non-honorific verb), but refuses to use them, feeling they are excessive.

Obviously whether or not a message leads to pragmatic failure depends not just on the nonnative sender but on the recipient as well. It is possible and often the case that the native speakers of the L2 will go the extra distance to comprehend the nonnative-speaker, even if the nonnative's behavior misses the mark by a long shot in terms of pragmatic appropriateness. In fact, the native-speaking interlocutor often has the wherewithal either to cut the nonnative slack or to lower the boom, depending on factors that may have little to do with whether the intended message was understood. On the other hand, a perceived breach of pragmatic etiquette may itself be enough to result in pragmatic failure for the nonnative. For example, several years ago while I was a visiting professor in New Zealand, a Japanese student who had recently graduated from the department came to my office, put her MA thesis on my desk, and said, 'Dr. Cohen, read this please', an example of negative transfer mentioned above. I hesitated for a moment but then had a visceral reaction and responded, 'No, I won't. I'm on sabbatical here and they don't pay me to do this. Sorry'. I did take a glance at it but no more than that. Had she said, 'Dr. Cohen—I was wondering if you might just take a look at my MA thesis and let me know what you think of…', I may very well have read through it.

5 Strategies for Negotiating Meaning and Making Conversational Repairs

Some learners are better at getting the L2 pragmatics right then are others. Part of it is due to their strategic ability as a language learner in general and especially in terms of their strategic ability with regard to pragmatics (see Cohen 2005). These individuals are strategic both in how they go about learning pragmatics and in their L2 performance so that both their comprehension and production of language are pragmatically appropriate for the given situation. They also have strategies for evaluating metapragmatically how well they understood the pragmatics of a given message and also how effective their pragmatics were in producing a message. Such strategies can make the difference between pragmatic failure and pragmatic success since in some cases nonnatives can take strategic action to avoid pragmatic failure or remediate once it has happened. For example, nonnatives can check to make sure that they interpreted a message (such as a key request from a co-worker) correctly, 'So let me see if I understand your request, George. You want me to speak to the boss on your behalf?' Nonnatives could also include an alerter before a delicate speech act so that the addressee will be lenient in interpreting the intent of the message: 'Hi, George. I want to make apology but not so sure it is OK. I try now…'.

In Krashen's (1982) terms, some nonnatives are better monitor users than others when it comes to pragmatics. In Long's (1985) terms, some nonnatives are better at making sure there is rich interaction that serves to clarify the intended pragmatic meaning in both the input and the output. In part this can be a function of the personality-related style preferences of the learner, such as being more extroverted or more closure-oriented (i.e. less tolerance of ambiguity; see Cohen and Weaver 2006). In Schmidt's (1990) terms, some nonnatives are better at noticing the pragmatic aspects of discourse, both in classroom settings and out in the real world. And there are some nonnatives who more actively create situations where they can check to see if they, in Swain's (1998) terms, are producing output that is comprehensible pragmatically. As I suggested at the outset of this chapter, what works for one L2 learner in terms of gaining pragmatic awareness and enhanced performance may not work for another. Some learners may, for example, benefit from extensive observation of what natives do without actually engaging in interaction with natives very much, while others start interacting extensively from the very start.

6 Conclusion

The purpose for this exploration has been to take a pragmatically-oriented look at both the input and output sides of what is comprehensible. Ideally, this chapter will provide teachers and researchers with ideas for what needs to be considered both pedagogically and from a researcher's perspective in order to better deal with the issues of comprehensibility in the pragmatics arena. So, returning to the question posed at the outset, what needs to happen for nonnatives to achieve success at comprehending and producing language pragmatically? It would appear that part of an L2 learner's pragmatics is acquired without explicit instruction. Nonetheless, as this chapter would suggest, there are numerous pragmatic features that most likely would benefit from explicit instruction (whether from a teacher directly or through a website such as the three posted at http://www.carla.umn.edu/speech-acts/) if the intention is to have the learners achieve relative control over them within a reasonable amount to time.

References

Bardovi-Harlig, K., C. Félix-Brasdefer, and A. Omar, eds. 2006. *Pragmatics and language learning.* 11 vols. Honolulu: National Foreign Language Resource Center, University of Hawai'i, Manoa.

Cohen, A.D. 2005. Strategies for learning and performing L2 speech acts. *Intercultural Pragmatics* 2: 275–301.

Cohen, A.D., and R.L. Shively. 2007. Acquisition of requests and apologies in Spanish and French: Impact of study abroad and strategy-building intervention. *Modern Language Journal* 91: 189–212.

Cohen, A.D., and S.J. Weaver. 2006. *Styles and strategies-based instruction: A teachers' guide.* Minneapolis: Center for advanced research on language acquisition, University of Minnesota.

Doughty C.J., and J. Williams, eds. 1998. *Focus on form in classroom second language acquisition*. Cambridge: Cambridge University Press.

Félix-Brasdefer, C. 2006. Teaching the negotiation of multi-turn speech acts: Using conversation-analytic tools to teach pragmatics in the FL classroom. In eds. K. Bardovi-Harlig, C. Félix-Brasdefer, and A. Omar, 167–197.

Gass, S., and C. Madden, eds. 1985. *Input in second language acquisition Rowley*. MA: Newbury House.

Holmes, J. 2003. Talk at work and 'fitting in': A socio-pragmatic perspective on workplace culture. In ed. G. Wigglesworth, 95–115.

Ishihara, N., and A.D. Cohen. 2010. *Teaching and learning pragmatics: Where language and culture meet*. Harlow: Longman Applied Linguistics, Pearson Education.

Kasper, G., and S. Blum-Kulka, eds. 1993. *Interlanguage pragmatics*. Oxford: Oxford University Press.

Kasper, G., and K. Rose. 2002. *Pragmatic development in a second language*. Malden: Blackwell.

Kasper, G., and R. Schmidt. 1996. Developmental issues in interlanguage pragmatics. *Studies in Second Language Acquisition* 18: 149–169.

Krashen, S.D. 1982. *Principles and practice in second language acquisition*. Oxford: Pergamon.

Long, M.H. 1985. Input and second language acquisition theory. In eds. S. Gass, and C. Madden, 337–393.

Long, M.H. 1996. The role of linguistic environment in second language acquisition. In eds. W.C. Ritchie, and T.K. Bhatia, 413–468.

Olshtain, E., and S. Blum-Kulka. 1985. Degree of approximation: Nonnative reactions to native speech act behavior. In eds. S. Gass, and C. Madden, 303–325.

Ritchie, W.C., and T.K. Bhatia, eds. 1996. *Handbook of second language acquisition*. San Diego: Academic Press.

Robinson, P., ed. 2001. *Cognition and second language instruction*. Cambridge: Cambridge University Press.

Schmidt, R. 1990. The role of consciousness in second language learning. *Applied Linguistics* 11: 129–158.

Schmidt, R. 1993. Consciousness, learning, and interlanguage pragmatics. In eds. G. Kasper, and S. Blum-Kulka, 21–42.

Schmidt, R. 2001. Attention. In ed. P. Robinson, 3–32.

Swain, M. 1998. Focus on form through conscious reflection. In eds. C.J. Doughty, and J. Williams, 64–81.

Swain, M., and S. Lapkin. 1995. Problems in output and the cognitive processes they generate: A step towards second language learning. *Applied Linguistics* 16: 371–391.

Wigglesworth, G., ed. 2003. Marking our difference: Languages in Australia and New Zealand universities. In *Proceedings of Conference on Language Education in Australian and New Zealand universities*. Melbourne: University of Melbourne.

Yule, G. 1996. *Pragmatics*. Oxford: Oxford University Press.

Instructional Mode and the Use
of Grammar Learning Strategies

Mirosław Pawlak

Abstract The scope of research into language learning strategies is impressive, with scholars using various instruments to identify strategic behaviors, proposing competing taxonomies, investigating the variables affecting strategy use, tracing the impact of the application of such devices on language proficiency, and evaluating the effectiveness of strategy training programs. These advances, however, do not apply in equal measure to all language skills and subsystems, and one of such neglected terrains is learning grammar. The present article contributes to the scant body of research in this area by reporting the findings of a study which investigated the use of grammar learning strategies by 142 English philology students at different stages of a BA program. It took as a point of reference a classification of such devices derived from the theoretical framework proposed by Oxford et al. (2007) in which such behaviors are related to three instructional modes in teaching grammar, namely implicit learning with focus on form, explicit inductive learning and explicit deductive learning. Although the analysis of Likert-scale items indicated a high rate of use of grammar learning strategies, especially in the implicit mode, the subjects' responses to an open-ended question did not support such findings, which might be the result of some inherent weaknesses of the data collection instrument. The article closes with some tentative pedagogical recommendations as well as guidelines on how grammar learning strategies could be classified and investigated.

M. Pawlak (✉)
Adam Mickiewicz University, Kalisz, Poland
e-mail: pawlakmi@amu.edu.pl

M. Pawlak (ed.), *New Perspectives on Individual Differences in Language Learning and Teaching*, Second Language Learning and Teaching, DOI: 10.1007/978-3-642-20850-8_17, © Springer-Verlag Berlin Heidelberg 2012

1 Introduction

As can be seen from recent state-of-the art articles and edited collections (e.g. Anderson 2005; Dörnyei 2005; Macaro 2006; Cohen and Macaro 2007; Griffiths 2008a), huge strides have been made in research into language learning strategies in the last three decades. Although there are still heated debates concerning the definition and distinctive features of strategic devices, with some scholars even going as far as to abandon the term *strategy* in favor of *self-regulation* (Dörnyei and Skehan 2003; Dörnyei 2005), numerous empirical investigations carried out to date have provided invaluable insights into different types of strategies, factors influencing their choice and use, their contribution to learning various skills and subsystems as well as the value of strategy training programs (Oxford 2001, 2002; Chamot 2004; Oxford and Schramm 2007; Takeuchi et al. 2007; Rubin 2008; Chamot 2008). At the same time, however, there remain important areas that have been conspicuously neglected by researchers such as grammar, pronunciation or pragmatics, and it is the first of these that is the focus of the present paper.

The lack of interest in how learners go about mastering formal aspects of the target language (TL), which can be ascribed to the promulgation of non-interventionist approaches and subsequently task-based methodologies (Pawlak 2006a), has recently been acknowledged by language learning strategy experts who emphasize the need to pursue this line of enquiry. For example, Oxford et al. (2007, p. 117) point out that "(…) most researchers who have become well known in the L2 learner strategy area, perhaps influenced by the low profile of grammar in the communicative language teaching approach, have either ignored grammar strategies or slid them into the more general 'cognitive strategy' category, thereby unwittingly hiding these strategies from view". Anderson, in turn, writes that "(…) the role of strategies in the teaching of L2 grammar has focused more on the teacher's pedagogic strategies than on learner's strategies for learning the grammar of a language", adding that "[w]hat is greatly lacking in the research are studies that specifically target the identification of learning strategies that L2 learners use to learn grammar and to understand the elements of grammar" (2005, p. 766). Also the present author has argued that "(…) the most immediate challenge for researchers must be identification and classification of grammar learning strategies because only in this way will we be able to seek cause-effect relationships, establish correlations or make comparisons between studies" (Pawlak 2008a, p. 123).

The study reported in this paper sought to implement such guidelines by investigating the application of grammar learning strategies (GLS) by advanced learners of English, adopting as a point of reference the theoretical framework and classification proposed by Oxford et al. (2007) which relates the use of these devices to the mode of instruction used by the teacher. At the outset, an overview of previous studies dealing with GLS will be provided, and the taxonomy employed in the analysis of the data will be outlined and evaluated. This will be followed by the description of the subjects, the instrument of data collection and the procedures used in the analysis, as well as the presentation, discussion and interpretation of the findings. Finally, an attempt will be made to propose recommendations for classroom practice and offer suggestions concerning the directions, design and methodology of future research endeavors in the area of grammar learning strategies.

2 Overview of Research into Grammar Learning Strategies

As mentioned above, there is a striking paucity of studies investigating the use of grammar learning strategies, with researchers primarily focusing on the identification and description of such devices with the help of existing taxonomies rather than attempting to devise a separate classification, explore the factors underlying the use of specific behaviors, examine its impact on learning outcomes or determine the benefits of strategies-based instruction in this area. The relevant studies can be divided into two groups, depending on whether GLS were investigated alongside other strategies with a view to describing the overall repertoire of such devices used by a particular group of learners, an approach typical of much earlier research, or, rather, they focused exclusively on GLS, a trend evident in the latest empirical investigations. As regards the former, the importance of learning grammar was emphasized in the outcomes of the *good language learner studies* carried out in the 1970s and 1980s, where emphasis was laid on the necessity of choosing appropriate techniques in effectively confronting this challenge. Rubin (1975), for example, found that successful learners are prepared to attend not only to meaning but also to form, Stern (1975, 1983) underscored the role of explicit learning, Naiman et al. (1996/1978) included in their list the strategy of realizing language as a system, whereas G. Ellis and Sinclair (1986) argued that good learners are interested in how the target language works. Strategies for learning grammar were also identified in the studies conducted in the 1980s which provided a basis for two influential classifications of strategic devices proposed by O'Malley and Chamot (1990) and Oxford (1990), but in neither of these were they given the prominence they deserve. In the Polish context, valuable insights into the use of GLS were offered by Droździał-Szelest (1997) who sought to identify and evaluate the whole spectrum of language learning strategies used by secondary school students. She classified the strategic behaviors using O'Malley and Chamot's (1990) taxonomy and found a clear predominance of cognitive strategies such as deduction, with metacognitive strategies, typically in the form of selective attention, being considerably less frequent, and socioaffective strategies not being mentioned at all. The conclusions she reached are particularly germane to the discussion in the present paper, which is evident in the following comment: "Generally, the strategies used by the students were not very original. However, they seem to accurately reflect the general tendency in language teaching in Polish schools (...) Thus, the strategies are quite informative about the mode of instruction used by individual teachers in their classrooms" (1997, p. 123).

Finally, Griffiths (2008a) found that one of the characteristics of individuals who make the most rapid progress in language learning, identified on the basis of the level they represented, is that they report frequently using strategic devices to improve their knowledge of grammar.

When it comes to the research projects designed to specifically target grammar learning strategies, they can be further subdivided into such that seek to identify, describe and evaluate the GLS favored or used by specific groups of learners, and such that set out to explore factors affecting strategy use as well as the relationship between the application of GLS and success in learning grammar. A potentially fruitful line of enquiry falling into the first category, which is seldom referred to in the SLA learning strategy literature, is represented by empirical investigations of strategic devices employed to assign gender to nouns in the mother tongue or additional languages (e.g. Karmiloff-Smith 1979; Stevens 1984; Cain, Weber-Olsen and Smith 1987; Oliphant 1997). Such strategies can be divided into *morphophonological* (e.g. word endings), *semantic* (i.e. natural gender of the referent) or *syntactic* (e.g. derivational suffixes), depending on individuals' sensitivity to different kinds of cues (Oxford et al. 2007). More in line with mainstream strategy research, Fortune (1992) explored learners' opinions about various types of self-study grammar practice exercises and found that although most of his respondents manifested a preference for deductive activities, plentiful opportunities to engage in induction generated increased support for tasks encouraging this mode of learning. More recently, Bade (2008) investigated the attitudes towards grammar learning displayed by ESL students in New Zealand, with their responses to open-ended questions not only showing an overwhelming desire to concentrate on accuracy and have their errors corrected but also speaking to the diversity of GLS applied. There are also research projects that have investigated the use of grammar learning strategies by Polish learners of English at different educational levels and, as such, they are of particular relevance to our discussion. One of them was undertaken by Mystkowska-Wiertelak (2008a) who employed a modified version of Oxford's (1990) Strategy Inventory for Language Learning (SILL) with upper secondary school students. She found, in contrast to the results reported by Droździał-Szelest (1997), that it was metacognitive strategies that were most often used, followed by compensation, social, memory, cognitive and affective strategies. Pawlak (2008a), in turn, demonstrated in a longitudinal diary study that highly proficient English Department students were aware of the need to deploy various GLS, but most of them still manifested a propensity to use traditional cognitive strategies such as formal practice, thus emulating the instructional modes favored by their grammar teachers and taking heed of examination requirements. Worth mentioning is also the attempt made by Pawlak (2009a, 2009b, 2010, in press) to devise a comprehensive classification of GLS and to construct on this basis a research tool that can be used to measure the application of these strategic devices, as well as initial implementation of the two in research projects.

As regards the relationships between GLS and other variables, invaluable insights have come once again from research into gender assignment referred to in the previous paragraph, with the use of strategies hinging upon such factors as learners' age, developmental stage, the nature of L1 and L2 as well as the differences between them, and, in the case of multilingual individuals, also the number of additional languages studied and their characteristics (Oxford et al. 2007). Although pertinent studies are still few and far between, similar issues have recently started to be addressed in general language learning strategy research. One example is the study conducted by Tilfarlioğlu (2005) who investigated the relationship between the use of GLS by Turkish students and their attainment, reporting that there were no differences in the frequency with which successful and unsuccessful learners drew upon these devices but showing that strategy choice was a function of such variables as gender, length of study or educational background. Mystkowska-Wiertelak (2008a), in turn, discovered that the frequency with which these strategies were used depended on learners' age. As for the beneficial effects of the application of GLS, a connection between the employment of such devices and improved outcomes in learning grammar has been reported for upper secondary school learners and English Department students (Mystkowska-Wiertelak 2008a, 2008b). A positive relationship between the application of GLS and attainment in the latter group was also found by Pawlak (2009b), with the caveat that the correlation was weak and limited only to strategies involved in explicit deductive learning (see Sect. 3). While such findings are far from conclusive, they do provide some tentative support for implementing strategies-based instruction in this area.

As can be seen from this overview, despite undeniable advances that have been made in recent years, research into grammar learning strategies remains in its infancy not only because of the blatant scarcity of pertinent empirical investigations but also their limited scope as well as the fragmentary and at times conflicting findings. Equally important, the studies described above frequently relied on quite diverse research methodologies and collected data on strategy use in very different ways, which is perhaps not overly surprising given the fact that many of them targeted the overall repertoire of strategic devices and researchers have not yet devised appropriate tools for the study of GLS. Nevertheless, if we wish to extend our knowledge of this crucial area and be in a position to offer viable pedagogical guidelines, it is indispensable to compare and evaluate the findings of various studies, and this can only be accomplished with the help of a valid and reliable instrument of collecting data on GLS use. The first step in developing such a tool, however, should logically involve drawing up a taxonomy of strategic behaviors of this kind and it is one such attempt that has informed the present study and will be the focus of the subsequent section.

3 Classification of Grammar Learning Strategies as a Function of Instructional Mode

The research project reported below drew upon a taxonomy of grammar learning strategies proposed by Oxford et al. (2007: 117) who define such devices as "actions or thoughts that learners consciously employ to make language learning or/and language use easier, more effective, more efficient and more enjoyable".

They seek to relate specific GLS to the instructional approaches teachers use to deal with grammar, repeatedly emphasizing, however, that "learning does not always follow the path intended by an instructional mode or by the teaching; and learners' grammar strategies frequently appear independently of the goals and beliefs of the teacher" (2007, p. 129). On the basis of recent SLA literature on form-focused instruction (e.g. Doughty 2003; DeKeyser 2003; Ellis 2006), they make a distinction between *implicit* and *explicit* approaches. The former are further subdivided into *focus on meaning* (i.e. complete avoidance of grammar in the classroom) and *focus on form* (i.e. attention to form takes place in communicative tasks in response to learner difficulty in expressing the intended meaning), whereas the latter comprise *focus on forms—explicit inductive mode* (i.e. learners are overtly instructed to pay attention to form and discover rules for themselves) and *focus on forms—explicit deductive mode* (i.e. rules and associated structures are presented to learners who are requested to apply them in specific instances). Since the inherent feature of *focus on meaning* is that it eschews any type of attention to formal aspects of the TL, it is difficult to talk about the application of GLS in this case and, thus, no strategic behaviors are listed for this mode, which, obviously, does not mean that learners do not use them. For the remaining three categories, Oxford et al. (2007) provide lists of concrete strategic devices such as the following:

(1) *implicit L2 learning that includes focus on form*: noticing structures that cause problems with communication, paying attention to how more proficient people say things and then imitating, keeping a notebook of new structures that seem important or frequent, etc.;

(2) *explicit inductive L2 learning*: participating in rule-discovery discussions in class, creating one's own hypotheses about how the target structures operate and then testing them, listening carefully for teacher feedback about the structures used, etc.;

(3) *explicit deductive L2 learning*: previewing a lesson to identify the key structures to be covered, making up sentences using the rule, scheduling grammar reviews by massing them closely at first and then spreading them out, etc.

Despite the fact that Oxford et al. (2007) stop short of actually using the word 'classification' to refer to the strategic options they describe, they argue that the division can function as a theoretical framework for studying the ways in which learners approach learning grammar.

What should be emphasized at this point is that classifying grammar learning strategies according to dominant approaches to form-focused instruction is not without its limitations, some of which the present author has highlighted elsewhere (Pawlak 2008a). For one thing, as Oxford et al. (2007) are at pains to underscore, although the use of GLS may be influenced and encouraged by the teacher's instructional choices, it is ultimately the learner who decides if, when and how to learn TL grammar in accordance with his or her own beliefs, expectations and goals. Therefore, a classification of this kind is lacking in that it fails to include a learner perspective and it might not be reflective of classroom reality because, for example, exclusive focus on meaning in a particular lesson will not prevent students from attending to grammatical structures if their beliefs or learning styles dictate that they do so. This problem is further aggravated by the fact that many of the GLS, especially those in the *focus on form category* (input flooding, input enhancement, etc.), are representative of recent trends in grammar teaching and, thus, they might not be used by teachers and are unknown to learners. Another reservation is connected with the fact that, being solely concerned with the mode of form-focused instruction, the framework ignores the existing taxonomies of strategic devices, with the effect that the GLS included in the same category often represent strategies that are fundamentally different in nature. This is evident, for instance, in the case of implicit learning with occasional shifts to form, where the metacognitive strategy of selective attention (i.e. noticing TL structures) is listed alongside the cognitive strategy of analyzing expressions (i.e. considering clues like sound, meaning and form to figure out the gender of a noun) or the social strategy of cooperating with others (i.e. collaborative text reconstruction). On the other hand, if we attempt to assign the different strategic behaviors to the categories included, for example, in Oxford's (1990) taxonomy, it will turn out that most of them are cognitive and metacognitive in nature. Moreover, the latter are rather limited in scope, memory strategies are infrequent, and social, affective and compensation strategies are extremely rare or do not appear at all. While it is obvious that cognitive strategic devices are bound to play a key role in understanding and practicing grammatical structures, other types of GLS also contribute to complete mastery of this language subsystem and should thus be given attention they deserve. Finally, the strategies listed by Oxford et al. (2007) are mainly concerned with noticing, studying or remembering grammar points at the expense of accurately reflecting the efforts learners make to formally practice explicitly taught TL forms, while it is reasonable to assume that the contribution of such devices is hard to overestimate (Pawlak 2008a, 2008b).

Such limitations notwithstanding, the classification based on the theoretical framework proposed by Oxford et al. (2007) is a useful tool in investigations of grammar learning strategies for at least three reasons. Firstly, as Pawlak (2008a) found, there is a close fit between the GLS reported by advanced language learners and their teachers' instructional practices as well as examination requirements, which indicates that using a taxonomy based on the dominant approaches to grammar instruction does not necessarily pose the danger of overlooking many important strategic devices students actually employ. Secondly, the fact that learners may not have experienced some instructional practices and, consequently, fail to employ certain GLS does not mean that such items should be removed from the list. This is because the frequency with which specific devices are reported is reflective of a particular educational reality and can provide invaluable insights for research, teaching and strategy training. Thirdly, and most importantly perhaps, although the picture of GLS use that emerges from such a classification is bound to be impoverished, it does have the potential to contribute to our understanding of how learners go about mastering TL grammar and can serve as a point of departure for scholars interested in the acquisition of this subsystem. It is this rationale that underlay the employment of the taxonomy in the study to which we now turn our attention.

4 Aims, Subjects, Data Collection Instruments and Analytical Procedures

The main aim of the research project was to investigate the use of grammar learning strategies by advanced learners of English as a function of the instructional mode adopted by the teacher as well as to determine whether there are differences in this respect between first, second and third year philology students. In addition, the study was intended to appraise the utility of the taxonomy of GLS based on the theoretical framework put forward by Oxford et al. (2007) and to provide data that could be drawn upon in devising a more comprehensive, valid and reliable classification of the strategic devices learners use when studying grammar. The participants were 142 English Departments students, 67 of whom were in the first year of their BA program, 38 in the second and 37 in the third. At the time the study was carried out, their average experience in learning English was about 10 (9.89) years, with much variation in this respect, as indicated by the high values of standard deviation (2.70) and especially range (17.0). As required by the nature of the program, the students were advanced users of English, representing the B2, C1 or even C2 levels, and they assigned their English proficiency a mean value of 4.02 on a 6-point scale, where 1 indicated the lowest and 6 the highest level. In this case, the group was more homogenous as the standard deviation stood at 0.57, not a single student entered 1 or 2 and as many as 87 (61.27%) chose 4. The subjects were somewhat less optimistic about their command of grammar as measured by expected end-of-semester grades in practical grammar classes, with the average of 3.60 and standard deviation of 0.63. When it comes to their access to English outside school, most of the students (128 or 90.14%) reported that they had such opportunities but mainly mentioned the Internet, television and newspapers rather than contacts with native speakers or other TL users.

Obviously, there also existed differences between the students in the three years of the program, which is the reason why a comparison of their use of GLS was undertaken in the first place. Quite predictably, the mean length of learning English increased with the level (8.40, 10.08 and 11.19 for the subjects in year 1, 2 and 3, respectively) and so did the average value of self-assessment (3.78 in year 1, 3.92 in year 2 and 4.35 for year 3), although this was only partly true for the mean anticipated end-of-semester grades in practical grammar (3.55 for year 1, 3.46 for year 2 and 3.78 for year 3). It should also be remembered that, in contrast to the first year students, the second and third year subjects had been attending methodology classes in which they had the opportunity to familiarize themselves with different approaches to teaching grammar as well as a myriad of techniques and procedures used for this purpose. Also, by virtue of the fact that the subjects in higher levels had more experience in attending narrowly focused practical grammar classes, they had been required to study grammatical features on their own and had had to prepare for end-of-the-year examinations in which the knowledge of grammar plays a crucial role, it could reasonably be assumed that they must have developed their own ways of dealing with this language subsystem.

The data concerning the application of GLS were collected by means of a questionnaire which provided a combination of factual, attitudinal and behavioral information (Dörnyei 2007). The first part of the survey included both open-ended and closed items in which the respondents were requested to state how long they had been learning English, self-access their proficiency level and comment on their use of English outside the classroom, and which served as a basis for the comments included earlier in this section. More in line with the goals of the study, the subjects were also asked to supply their expected end-of-semester grade in a grammar class, rank the importance of grammar learning on a scale of 1 (lowest) to 6 (highest) as well as to describe their favorite way of studying grammatical structures. The most important part of the instrument, however, was based on the taxonomy proposed by Oxford et al. (2007) and consisted of three groups of Likert-scale items corresponding to different grammar learning strategies under the rubrics of *implicit learning involving focus on form, explicit inductive learning* and *explicit deductive learning.* With a view to avoiding confusion or occurrence of random answers, however, a decision was made to change the wording of some of the GLS by removing such terms as 'dictogloss' or 'input flood'. Without being informed about the rationale for the division or acquainted with the labels of the three groups, the students had to indicate the extent to which a specific statement was true about them on a 5-point scale, where 1 meant that it did not apply to them at all and 5 that it perfectly reflected their thoughts and actions. Thus, the instructions mirrored those used in Oxford's (1990) SILL and the respondents were also told that there were no right or wrong answers on particular items.

The students were asked to complete the questionnaire during their regular classes and they had as much time as they needed to do this, with the procedure taking about 25 minutes. Although the teachers supervising the administration of the instrument did not influence the subjects' responses in any way, on a few occasions they supplied explanations in response to the participants' queries and uncertainties. The data collected in this way were subjected to a combination of quantitative and qualitative analysis depending on the nature of a particular item. The former involved tabulating the means and standard deviations for each question requiring a numerical answer and each statement, with separate calculations being made for each of the three instructional modes, each of the three levels of the program, and the sample as a whole. Additionally, since in most cases the data were not normally distributed, the levels of statistical significance of the differences identified through relevant comparisons were established by means of the non-parametric, two-tailed *Mann–Whitney test*. As for the latter, it applied to the responses provided in open-ended items and consisted in identifying recurring themes and grouping similar ideas related to access to the TL and favorite ways of learning grammar. Also here, however, numerical analysis was employed in the last stage to determine the frequency of reported actions and behaviors.

5 Results and Discussion

Before moving on to the discussion of the reported use of grammar learning strategies, a few comments are in order about the subjects' perceptions of the significance of grammar and their favorite ways of learning it. Given the nature of the program, the considerable requirements the students had to meet and the overall high proficiency level they represented, it should not come as a surprise that most of them recognized the importance of learning English grammar. This is evident in their responses to the question concerning the significance of this language subsystem, where the average was 4.16, with as many as 122 (85.92%) participants entering the value of 3.5 or higher, a finding which largely corroborates the results reported by Pawlak and Droździał-Szelest (2007) in their study of the beliefs about grammar, its learning and teaching held by BA and MA English philology students. It should also be pointed out that the subjects did not vary much in their assessment of the role of the grammatical component since the average standard deviation was relatively low and stood at 0.68. Even though the differences between the three groups were small and not significant, the importance attached to grammar increased with each successive year (4.10 for year 1, 4.18 for year 2 and 4.20 for year 3), which is indicative of a possible pattern that could have become more pronounced had more subjects taken part in the study. In fact, it is reasonable to assume that, despite the weight given to grammar in practical English classes, many first year students may consider it as less important than other subsystems and skills as a consequence of the emphasis that high school curricula and final examination place on communicative ability rather than accuracy. With time, however, as they become familiarized with the intricacies of the TL grammar and are expected to apply complex structures in written and oral production in many classes, they come to appreciate its significance as a tool for attaining greater clarity and precision as well as a recourse which helps them position themselves in the world (cf. Batstone 1994).

Of particular relevance was the open-ended question where the subjects were requested to comment on their favorite way of learning English grammar since their responses provided a backdrop against which their reported frequency of use of specific GLS listed as Likert-scale statements could be evaluated, interpreted and verified. Similarly to the findings of Pawlak and Droździał-Szelest (2007) as well as some of the research projects discussed earlier (e.g. Droździał-Szelest 1997; Pawlak 2008a), the subjects reported using a surprisingly limited repertoire of strategies for studying grammatical structures, most of which reflected their concern with rules and their accurate application in highly controlled text-manipulation activities (Ellis 1997). This is visible in the fact that as many as 105 (73.94%) of the students made references to what they described as 'doing exercises' (e.g. multiple-choice, translation, paraphrasing, gap-filling), whereas 72 (50.70%) mentioned studying, analyzing, memorizing or revising. Only 21 (14.79%) of the respondents emphasized the need for more naturalistic practice of the structures taught in comprehension and production (e.g. attending to grammar features when watching television, reading newspapers or browsing the Internet, using them in real communication), and just a handful reported utilizing such strategies as cooperating with others in solving grammar problems, coming up with sentences with a particular feature, highlighting new structures through color or underlining, making charts or keeping a grammar notebook.

Such preoccupation with the mastery of rules and application thereof in traditional exercises was visible in all the three groups, although, somewhat in line with the growing appreciation of the role of grammar in the course of the program, there were differences in this respect, particularly between the first and second year participants (71.64% in year 1, 78.95% in year 2 and 72.97% in year 3 for doing exercises, and 46.27% in year 1, 55.26% in year 2 and 54.05% in year 3 for studying rules). At the same time, the students in year 2 and year 3 were more cognizant of the need to apply grammatical structures in communication (8.96%, 21.05% and 18.92% in years 1, 2 and 3, respectively), which may testify to their greater proficiency, experience and awareness of what it means to know a foreign language. These differences notwithstanding, a crucial finding was that only several respondents mentioned just a few of the GLS included in the subsequent part of the survey and that the strategic devices listed therein did not reflect most of the ways of learning described in the responses to the open-ended question. This is indeed a vital observation which has be kept in mind when discussing the choices the participants made with respect to the Likert-scale items representing grammar learning strategies characteristic of the particular instructional modes in teaching grammar.

Table 1 and Fig. 1 illustrate average frequencies of use of grammar learning strategies reported by the first, second and third year students as well as these three groups combined for the three instructional modes included in Oxford et al.'s (2007) taxonomy. As can be seen from the data and their diagrammatical representation, the mean score for overall strategy use stood at 3.49, which indicates, following Oxford's (1990) interpretation (average of 3.5 or higher), that the subjects employed the GLS at a relatively high rate of frequency.[1] Interestingly, the frequency of use of GLS was the highest in year 2 (3.57), growing by 0.12 in comparison with year 1 (3.45), and then dropping to the previous level in year 3, although neither of these differences reached significance. If we examine the application of strategic devices as a function of instructional mode, it turns out that the average was the highest for implicit learning with focus on form (3.59), followed by explicit deductive learning (3.46) and explicit inductive learning (3.42), with the differences between the first and the remaining two amounting to 0.17 and

---

[1] In her commentary on the SILL, Oxford (1990) recommends that the averages should be rounded off to the nearest tenth, with the effect that 3.4 indicates medium and 3.5 high strategy use. Since in the present study, the scores were rounded to two decimal spaces, an average of 3.49 falls between Oxford's cut-off points, thus posing some interpretation problems. Still, it is logical to assume that, being closer to 3.5 than 3.4, a score like this should be interpreted as evidence for a high rate of frequency of GLS use.

Table 1 Average frequencies of grammar learning strategy use reported by the three groups of students for different instructional modes

Type of GLS	Year I			Year II			Year III			Total		
	M	SD	Rank	M	SD	Rank	M	SD	Rank	M	SD	Rank
Implicit learning with focus on form	3.62	0.94	1	3.63	1.00	1	3.51	0.93	1	**3.59**	**0.96**	**1**
Explicit inductive learning	3.34	1.02	3	3.55	1.16	2	3.36	1.17	3	**3.42**	**1.12**	**3**
Explicit deductive learning	3.39	1.02	2	3.52	1.42	3	3.48	1.36	2	**3.46**	**1.27**	**2**
Total	**3.45**	**0.99**	**–**	**3.57**	**1.19**	**–**	**3.45**	**1.15**	**–**	**3.49**	**1.12**	**–**

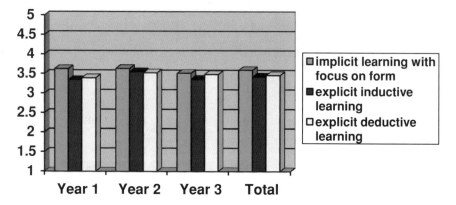

Fig. 1 Average frequencies of grammar learning strategy use as a function of year and instructional mode

0.13, respectively, and being statistically significant ($p < 0.05$).[2] These results were largely mirrored in each of the three groups since the reported frequency GLS use was always highest for implicit learning, with the caveat that only in year 1 did the differences of 0.28 (implicit vs. inductive) and 0.23 (implicit vs. deductive) reach statistical significance.[3] The rank order of strategies only deviated from the general pattern in year 2 where the average for inductive explicit learning slightly exceeded that for deductive explicit learning (0.55 vs. 0.52), but neither these nor

---

[2] The levels of statistical significance were $z = 3.26$ and $p = 0.0011$ and $z = 3.03$ and $p = 0.0025$ for the differences between implicit learning, on the one hand, and explicit inductive and explicit deductive learning, on the other.

[3] The levels of significance were as follows: $z = 3.00$ and $p = 0.0027$ for the difference between implicit learning with focus on form and inductive explicit learning, and $z = 2.82$ and $p = 0.0048$ for the difference between implicit learning with focus on form and deductive explicit learning.

any other comparisons between groups yielded statistically significant differences. When it comes to variability in the application of GLS, the subjects appeared to be quite heterogenous, as evidenced by the fact that the average standard deviation stood at 1.12, with its value being the lowest for implicit learning with focus on form in year 3 (0.93) and the highest for deductive explicit learning in year 2 (1.42). Two findings are particularly noteworthy in this respect, namely: (1) dispersion tended to increase with the year in the BA program (0.99 in year 1, 1.19 in year 2 and 1.15 in year 3), and (2) SD values were always highest for deductive explicit learning (1.02 in year 1, 1.42 in year 2, 1.36 in year 3, and 1.27 overall). Although the differences were small in both cases and should thus be viewed with caution, they are still indicative of an interesting pattern.

One possible interpretation of such findings which immediately comes to mind when we are confronted with the numbers reported above is that there are grounds for optimism since not only did the participants report using the GLS listed at a high rate of frequency but they also appeared to be aware of the need to learn grammatical structures through meaning and message conveyance. In fact, such a conclusion would not be overly surprising in light of the fact that we are dealing here with advanced learners who have considerable experience in studying English, strive to achieve high, perhaps even native-like proficiency levels, and must have been sensitized to various aspects of the language learning process in their practical English, linguistics or methodology classes. On the other hand, however, the findings have to be viewed through the prism of the subjects' responses to the question concerning their favorite ways of learning English grammar presented earlier. Since the range of strategies reported therein was very limited and references to using the structures taught in real communication were few and far between, we should exercise circumspection in interpreting the frequency averages reported for the Likert-scale items. Obviously, it could be argued that, because the open-ended question came first, the participants did not think of all the actions they engaged in the process of learning grammar but, being presented with statements illustrating specific GLS, they were better able to indicate their strategic behaviors. At the same time, if GLS were indeed applied as often as the analysis of the responses to the Likert-scale items would indicate, it is quite logical to assume that the subjects should have mentioned a wide variety of such devices when asked about their favorite ways of learning. By the same token, if strategies characteristic of implicit learning with a focus on form were of particular importance to the participants, we are at a loss to explain why only around 15% reported opting for naturalistic practice in their study of grammar. Moreover, interviews with the students' grammar teachers showed that the instructional techniques associated with some of the GLS listed for the implicit and explicit inductive learning mode (e.g. input flood, input enhancement, collaborative rule discovery, the garden-path technique) were seldom or never used in class, especially in year 1 and 2, which casts doubt on the subjects' readiness to apply the related strategies. All of this shows that the students might have reported higher GLS use than was really the case, either because they felt it was the right thing to do or because they did not wish to admit their ignorance of some of the behaviors. In addition, the fact that most of the GLS that the students enumerated in response to the open-ended question were not included in the three inventories speaks to a potential weakness of the theoretical framework proposed by Oxford et al. (2007), which was in fact signaled in Sect. 3 of this paper.

There are also several other important observations that have to be made concerning the reported frequency of GLS use as a function of the instructional mode and the stage in the BA program. For one thing, the differences between the averages in year 1, 2 and 3, albeit small and statistically insignificant, can perhaps be attributed to the fact that the transition from the first to the second year and in particular the outcomes of the final examination make students convinced of the need to pay more attention to grammar. This pressure is alleviated in the last year, where they become more confident about their abilities, experience fewer problems with this subsystem and have to channel their energies into learning content as well as writing their diploma papers. Although, as noted above, they are still aware of the significance of grammar as such, there might simply be less need for them to apply strategic devices. Secondly, greater emphasis on induction than deduction reported for year 2 might be indicative of the students' efforts to work on grammar in their own time, which is in line with the interpretation offered above. This finding could as well be reflective of teachers' instructional practices since in the second year the focus shifts from introduction of new structures to their consolidation, which warrants greater reliance on discovery activities. Thirdly, the gradual increase in variability of GLS use from year 1 to year 2 and its high level in year 3 might indicate that, in the course of time, students find their own preferred ways of learning grammar, presumably more suitable to their cognitive styles, goals or experiences. Obviously, this is not tantamount to claiming that the GLS they employ are no longer affected by what happens in grammar classes, a relationship for which Pawlak (2008a) provided ample evidence in his diary study. In fact, the interdependence of learners' and teachers' actions also finds support in the results of this research project since, irrespective of the stage of the program, reponses to the open-ended question most often included examples of GLS involved in explicit deductive learning, an instructional mode which is preferred in most English Departments.

Even though the overall average frequencies of GLS use for the whole sample, the three groups of students and the three instructional approaches are revealing, this macroperspective should logically be complemented with a microperspective, where the scores for individual strategy statements listed for each mode are taken into account. Such information is included in Tables 2 through 4, each for one instructional mode, where the cells with results indicating a high rate of use (3.5 or higher) have been shaded and the numbers in rows with statistically significant differences in at least one of the comparisons between year 1, 2 and 3 have been bolded. As can be seen from the last column of Table 2, which presents the mean scores, the frequencies of use of as many as 8 GLS can be regarded as high, with statements 11 ('I notice when someone gives me a corrected version of what I said, listen to how that version differs from my own, and try to improve what I said'), 3 ('I notice (or remember) structures that are repeated often in the text'), and

Table 2 Average frequency of grammar learning strategy use reported for implicit learning involving a focus on form by first, second and third year students as well as all of the subjects

No	Part A: Implicit learning involving focus on form Grammar learning strategy statement	Mean (SD)			
		Year I (N = 67)	Year II (N = 38)	Year III (N = 37)	Total (N = 142)
1.	I notice (or remember) structures that cause me problems with meaning or communication.	3.54 (0.91)	3.39 (1.10)	3.57 (0.96)	3.50 (0.99)
2.	I notice (or remember) structures that are highlighted in the text by italics, boldface, underlining, color-coding, etc.	4.06 (0.87)	4.00 (1.09)	4.16 (0.99)	4.07 (0.98)
3.	I notice (or remember) structures that are repeated often in the text.	4.18 (0.69)	4.18 (0.77)	4.03 (0.87)	4.13 (0.78)
4.	I notice (or remember) structures that are emphasized orally, through pitch, loudness, or repetition.	3.27 (1.01)	3.74 (0.98)	3.35 (1.06)	3.45 (1.02)
5.	I notice (or remember) structures that are repeated extremely frequently in a short time period (e.g. the past tense in a series of stories over the course of a few lessons).	3.78 (0.95)	3.87 (0.88)	3.59 (0.98)	3.75 (0.94)
6.	I notice (or remember) a structure which, when I encounter it, causes me to do something (check a box, etc.).	3.69 (0.87)	3.45 (0.92)	3.81 (0.88)	3.65 (0.89)
7.	When I don't know the gender of a noun, I quickly consider clues like sound, meaning, and form.	3.25 (0.89)	2.97 (1.20)	3.08 (0.86)	3.10 (0.98)
8.	I pay attention to how more proficient people say things and then imitate.	3.73 (0.90)	4.00 (0.70)	3.95 (0.81)	3.89 (0.80)
9.	I work with others to reconstruct texts read by the teacher, which contain many instances of a particular structure.	2.94 (1.09)	2.63 (1.13)	2.11 (0.94)	2.56 (1.05)
10.	I keep a notebook of new structures that seem very important or frequent.	2.87 (1.40)	2.95 (1.51)	2.27 (1.19)	2.70 (1.37)
11.	I notice when someone gives me a corrected version of what I said, listen to how that version differs from my own, and try to improve what I said.	4.25 (0.77)	4.37 (0.75)	4.27 (0.69)	4.30 (0.74)
12.	I compare my speech and writing with that of more proficient people to see how I can improve.	3.87 (0.97)	4.00 (0.99)	3.89 (0.91)	3.92 (0.97)
	Overall average reported frequency	3.62 (0.94)	3.63 (1.00)	3.51 (0.93)	3.59 (0.96)

2 ('I notice (or remember) structures that are highlighted in the text by italics, boldface, underlining, color-coding, etc.') representing the highest averages (4.30, 4.13 and 4.07, respectively). There were two instances, both in year 2 (statements 1 and 6), where the overall high rate of use did not hold for one of the three groups and one, also in year 2 (statement 4), where the average reported frequency was medium but the group frequency was high. Of particular relevance are also the GLS which were used at a low rate of frequency, which, according to Oxford's (1990) criteria, involves the average score of 2.4 or lower. Although this was not the case with any of the totals, the means were below this threshold for statements 9 ('I work with others to reconstruct texts read by the teacher, which contain many instances of a particular structure') and 10 ('I keep a notebook of new structures

that seem very important or frequent') in year 3. As regards the comparisons between the three groups, statistically significant differences were identified for statements 4 (0.47 between year 1 and year 2), and 9 (0.83 between year 1 and year 3 and 0.52 between year 2 and year 3). It is also worthwhile to highlight the differences of 0.68 and 0.36 between year 2 and year 3 for statements 10 and 6, where the results failed to reach significance but came close to the required 0.05 confidence level.[4]

Aside from the reservations concerning the feasibility of such a high frequency of use of this type of GLS that were expressed above, a number of other comments are in order at this point. First, while it does not come as a surprise that such strategies as attending to grammar structures causing problems with communication (1), comparing one's TL production with that of more proficient speakers (8 and 12) or making the most of corrective feedback (11) were frequently reported by the subjects, the fact that the mean scores were so high for those involved in input enhancement (2) and input flood (5) certainly does. If, as noted earlier, these instructional techniques were seldom used in grammar classes and, as some research findings indicate (e.g. Pawlak 2006b), they are unlikely to have often been employed in high school, a question arises as to whether we are dealing here with real or imagined actions, or perhaps some sort of avoidance behavior. It is also interesting that the average in this category is the lowest for third year students who, logically, should have developed the necessary awareness and skills to appreciate the value of learning grammar through communication and take steps which would facilitate this approach. One possible answer is that many such students have reached the point where they focus on meaning rather than form when reading, listening and interacting with others, and another is they were simply more honest in the responses. This could explain, for example, why these participants were less likely to notice and remember structures emphasized orally (4), reconstruct texts read by the teacher (9), or keep a notebook with grammatical structures (10). Even in this group, however, it is quite easy to discern the influence of teachers' instructional practices, which perhaps accounts for the high frequency of the GLS connected with visual input enhancement (2) or application of explicit knowledge in specific task types (6). What should also be noted are the relatively high values of standard deviation for statements where the differences were statistically significant or reached such significance (4, 9 or 10), which indicates that the subjects did not find these GLS equally useful or that some of them were simply more candid about their actions than others.

Moving on to the strategies characteristic of explicit inductive learning, listed together with their mean scores and standard deviations in Table 3, it can be observed that the subjects reported using five of the GLS at a high rate of frequency. This was the case for statements 1, 6, 8, 9 and 10, with the last of these

---

[4] The levels of significance for these statements were as follows: $4-z = -2.32$, $p = 0.0206$ (year 1 vs. year 2), $9-z = 3.62$, $p = 0.0003$ (year 1 vs. year 3) and $z = 2.03$, $p = 0.0419$ (year 2 vs. year 3), $10 - z = 1.90$, $p = 0.0574$ (year 2 vs. year 3), and $6 - z = 1.73$, $p = 0.0835$ (year 2 vs. year 3).

Table 3 Average frequency of grammar learning strategy use reported for explicit inductive learning by first, second and third year students as well as all of the subjects

No	Part B: Explicit inductive learning Grammar learning strategy statement	Mean (SD)			
		Year I (N = 67)	Year II (N = 38)	Year III (N = 37)	Total (N = 142)
1.	Based on all possible clues, I try to discover the underlying rule.	3.51 (0.99)	3.56 (1.02)	3.74 (0.86)	3.60 (0.96)
2.	I participate in rule-discovery discussions in class.	3.18 (1.07)	3.21 (1.10)	3.13 (1.14)	3.17 (1.10)
3.	I write down structures on note cards so that I can think about how they work.	3.42 (1.17)	3.41 (1.35)	2.50 (1.33)	3.11 (1.28)
4.	I keep a notebook of examples of any structure for which I am trying to find the rule.	2.51 (1.16)	2.62 (1.33)	2.00 (1.04)	2.38 (1.18)
5.	I create my own hypotheses about how structures work and check these hypotheses.	2.88 (1.17)	3.41 (1.12)	2.89 (1.25)	3.75 (0.94)
6.	I notice when the teacher leads me into an overgeneralization error (e.g. saying 'I goed'), and then I think about what went wrong.	3.55 (0.86)	3.72 (0.94)	3.68 (1.25)	3.65 (1.02)
7.	I participate in written brainstorming about possible underlying rules.	2.87 (0.98)	2.97 (1.33)	2.97 (1.37)	2.94 (1.23)
8.	I check with others who are more proficient to make sure my rule interpretation is correct.	3.64 (0.93)	3.92 (1.09)	3.92 (1.10)	3.83 (0.04)
9.	After discovering a rule, I try to apply it as soon as possible in a meaningful context.	3.67 (1.04)	4.00 (1.28)	4.26 (1.18)	3.98 (1.17)
10.	I listen carefully for any feedback the teacher gives me about the structures I use.	4.15 (0.84)	4.67 (1.06)	4.53 (1.16)	4.45 (1.02)
	Overall average reported frequency	3,34 (1.02)	3.55 (1.16)	3.36 (1.17)	3.42 (1.12)

('I listen carefully for any feedback the teacher gives me about the structures I use') being by far the most popular and generating the average of 4.45. There was just one strategic behavior which was used at a low rate of frequency by the third year students as well as the whole sample (2.00 and 2.38, respectively) and it had to do with keeping a notebook with examples of a structure for which a rule was being discovered (4). On the whole, such findings are not surprising because using different clues to figure out the rule, checking with more proficient peers whether a generalization is correct, trying to apply a newly discovered rule in a meaningful context or carefully listening for teacher feedback all represent actions which advanced learners of English are likely to engage in. On the other hand, the popularity of keeping a special notebook to facilitate rule discovery is not something that many students are likely to find particularly appealing, regardless of the educational level. What is quite baffling, though, is the high rate of reported use (3.65) of the strategy in which a learner notices that he or she has been led into an overgeneralization error and thinks about what has gone wrong (6), which would be employed in reaction to the *garden path technique* (cf. Herron and

Tomasello 1992). Since this instructional option is not often used in practical grammar classes or in language teaching in general, one might wonder why this statement was given so much recognition. One viable explanation could be that it was simply misunderstood by the students or perhaps entirely alien to them, which, as was the case with the previous category, could have made them opt for what they saw as a safe option.

As regards the statistically significant differences between the respondents in the three groups, they were found for statements 3 (0.92 between year 1 and year 3, and 0.91 between year 2 and year), 4 (0.51 between year 1 and year 2, and 0.62 between year 2 and year 3), 5 (0.53 between year 1 and year 2), 9 (0.59 between year 1 and year 3) and 10 (between year 1 and year 2). There was also a sizable difference (0.52) approaching statistical significance for the comparison between the second and third year students in the case of statement 5.[5] These changes in the frequency of use of individual GLS which grew from year 1 to year 2 only to decrease in year 3 are reflective of a general pattern observed for inductive explicit learning and accounted for earlier in this section. The only deviation from this trend can be seen in statement 9 ('After discovering a rule, I try to apply it as soon as possible in a meaningful context'), where the average increases as a function of experience in the BA program (0.33 from year 1 to year 2 and another 0.26 from year 2 to year 3), which might again result from the third year students being more concerned with meaning rather than form. It should also be noted that the standard deviations for some of the statements are considerable, as is the case, for instance, with the use of note cards (3), keeping a notebook (4), creating hypotheses (5), participating in written brainstorming (7) and applying rules (9). These findings might indicate that the use of induction may hinge upon a variety of individual characteristics, with the effect that the related GLS should not be indiscriminately imposed upon students.

The final group of grammar learning strategies to be discussed here are those involved in explicit deductive learning, the averages and standard deviations for which can be found in Table 4. As can be seen from the data, the use of eight devices was reported at a high rate of frequency, with the greatest mean scores found for those represented by statement 2 ('I pay attention to the rule that the teacher or the book provides'), 3 ('I try to apply the rule carefully and accurately in specific sentences'), 13 ('I remember grammar information by location on a page in the book') and 11 ('I paraphrase rules I am given, because I understand them better in my own words'), standing at 4.07, 3.89, 3.87 and 3.85, respectively. There were three cases in which the overall high frequency was not reflected in individual mean scores in specific years (statements 4, 11 and 14 for year 1), and one in which the individual averages exceeded that for the whole sample (statement 4

---

[5] The levels of statistical significance were as follows: $3 - z = 3.45, p = 0.0006$ (year 1 vs. year 3) and $z = 2.83, p = 0.0046$ (year 2 vs. year 3), $4 - z = 2.46, p = 0.0131$ (year 1 vs. year 3) and $z = 2.06, p = 0.0390$ (year 2 vs. year 3), $5 - z = -2.05, p = 0.0399$ (year 1 vs. year 2) and $z = 1.91, p = 0.0561$ (year 2 vs. year 3), $9 - z = 2.17, p = 0.0302$ (year 1 vs. year 3), and $10 - z = -2.32, p = 0.0203$ (year 1 vs. year 2).

Table 4 Average frequency of grammar learning strategy use reported for explicit deductive learning by first, second and third year students as well as all of the subjects

		Year I (N = 67)	Year II (N =38)	Year III (N = 37)	Total (N = 142)
1.	I preview the lesson to identify the key structures to be covered.	3.12 (1.15)	2.72 (1.26)	2.66 (1.05)	2.83 (1.15)
2.	I pay attention to the rule that the teacher or the book provides.	4.12 (0.69)	3.97 (0.96)	4.11 (0.83)	4.07 (0.83)
3.	I try to apply the rule carefully and accurately in specific sentences.	3.79 (0.91)	3.85 (0.90)	4.03 (0.79)	3.89 (0.87)
4.	I make up new sentences using the rule.	3.30 (1.02)	3.85 (1.04)	3.61 (0.97)	3.49 (1.01)
5.	I check my new sentences (or ask for help) to see if I understand the rule.	3.60 (0.87)	3.79 (0.92)	3.55 (1.03)	3.65 (0.94)
6.	I memorize rules about frequently used linguistic forms/structures (for example, verb endings, singular/plural, noun-pronoun agreement, subject-verb agreement).	3.70 (0.94)	3.77 (1.20)	3.63 (1.08)	3.70 (1.07)
7.	I memorize how structures change their forms (for instance, from a noun to an adjective, form an adjective to an adverb).	3.67 (0.94)	3.51 (1.23)	3.53 (1.13)	3.57 (1.10)
8.	I color-code different grammar categories in my notebook.	3.31 (1.38)	3.08 (1.81)	3.21 (1.74)	3.20 (1.64)
9.	I work with a study partner to apply grammar rules.	2.88 (1.27)	2.72 (1.61)	2.58 (1.50)	2.73 (1.46)
10.	I schedule my grammar reviews by massing them closely at first, then spreading them out.	2.81 (0.86)	2.90 (1.67)	3.18 (1.47)	2.96 (1.32)
11.	I paraphrase rules I am given, because I understand them better in my own words.	3.49 (1.01)	4.10 (1.55)	3.97 (1.59)	3.85 (1.38)
12.	I make grammar charts.	2.66 (1.15)	2.97 (1.95)	2.79 (1.96)	2.81 (1.69)
13.	I remember grammar information by location on a page in the book.	3.69 (1.26)	3.97 (1.91)	3.95 (1.96)	3.87 (1.71)
14.	I use newly learnt rules/structures in context as soon as possible.	3.33 (0.86)	4.03 (1.91)	4.03 (1.90)	3.78 (1.56)
	Overall average reported frequency	3.39 (1.02)	3.52 (1.42)	3.48 (1.36)	3.46 (1.27)

in year 2 and year 3). Interestingly, none of the remaining GLS listed proved to be used at a low rate of frequency and the only statements with mean scores lower than 3.00 were 1 ('I preview a grammar lesson to identify the key structures to be covered'), 9 ('I work with a study partner to apply grammar rules') and 12 ('I make grammar charts'). Such results are obviously not surprising given the fact that the reported frequency of use of strategies was second highest for explicit deductive learning (see Table 1 above) and that this instructional mode is the most common irrespective of the educational level or the type of language program. It should also be noted that many of the most frequently reported GLS are compatible with the instructional approach which constitutes the staple of grammar teaching in most classrooms. This is the still ubiquitous PPP sequence, where learners are first asked to pay attention to rules, memorize generalizations and exceptions, then they have to apply them in specific sentences and check their solutions, and, in the last stage, they are requested to use the structures in context (cf. Pawlak 2006b). By contrast, metacognitive and social strategic devices, such as previewing the lesson to identify the most important points (1), planning the learning process (10) or collaborating with a study partner (9), are used less frequently, which is also reflective of the Polish educational reality. Another crucial finding is the high level of variability in the use of some GLS, with the greatest values of standard deviation observed for statements 13 (1.71), 12 (1.69) and 8 (1.64). What these devices have in common is that they embody highly specific cognitive strategies of remembering grammar information by location on a page, making grammar charts and color-coding grammatical categories, the application of which is closely related to dominant cognitive and learning styles, and thus subject to much individual variation. A similar interpretation applies to learning with a partner (9), paraphrasing rules (11) or scheduling grammar reviews, for which SD values were also high.

If we examine the differences in reported strategy use between the three groups, it turns out that they were sizable enough to reach statistical significance in the case of statement 1 (0.46 between year 1 and year 3), 4 (0.55 between year 1 and year 2), 11 (0.61 between year 1 and year 2) and 14 (0.70 between year 1 and year 2 and 0.70 between year 1 and year 3). Attention should also be given to the difference between year 1 and year 2 in statement 1 (0.40) as well as that between year 1 and year 3 in statement 11 (0.48), where the level of significance was approached.[6] Generally speaking, in all of these statements and as well as in most of those for which no statistically significant differences were found, we can see a tendency for the second year students to become more dependent on GLS in the explicit deductive learning mode whereas the opposite is true for the third year students, albeit on a much smaller scale. Such trends can be accounted for by first year students' realization of the importance of grammar and third year students' greater preoccupation with meaning rather than form, an explanation that is consistent with the interpretation of the findings for the remaining two instructional modes. In fact, more frequent application of strategies typical of explicit deductive learning may indicate greater overall concern with grammar and does not preclude extensive use of GLS involved in explicit inductive learning, particularly if these are often used in practical grammar classes. If we accept such an interpretation as plausible, quite intriguing are the average frequencies for the strategies of previewing lesson content (1), memorizing how structures change

---

[6] The following levels of statistical significance were obtained for these statements: $1 - z = 2.04$, $p = 0.0411$ (year 1 vs. year 3) and $z = 1.39$, $p = 0.1632$ (year 1 vs. year 2), $4 - z = -2.47$, $p = 0.0136$ (year 1 vs. year 2), $11 - z = -2.51$, $p = 0.0119$ (year 1 vs. year 2) and $z = 1.31$, $p = 0.1886$ (year 1 vs. year 3), and $14 - z = -2.04$, $p = 0.0417$ (year 1 vs. year 2) and $z = -2.21$, $p = 0.0269$ (year 1 vs. year 3).

their form (7), color-coding grammatical categories (8) and collaborating with a partner (9), where the opposite, although not always statistically significant, tendency was observed. It could reasonably be argued, however, that as students gradually cover the major areas of English grammar and become more proficient, there are fewer opportunities for them to employ the first two of these GLS, whereas the application of the other two hinges upon their individual learning styles.

6 Conclusions, Pedagogical Implications and Directions for Future Research

The main aim of the present paper was to augment the scarce body of literature dealing with strategies that language learners use when studying and practicing grammatical structures by exploring the application of such devices by advanced learners of English. As the foregoing discussion has demonstrated, the participants reported using the GLS listed in the three parts of the questionnaire as Likert-scale statements at a relatively high rate of frequency and, what is particularly surprising, their responses indicated that they most often drew upon strategies characteristic of implicit learning involving focus on form. Such findings, however, stood in contrast to the outcomes of the analysis of the subjects' responses to an open-ended item in which they were requested to comment on their favorite ways of learning grammar. Here, in line with the results of most of the previous studies, the repertoire of the reported strategies was extremely limited, mostly quite traditional strategic devices were mentioned and the need for naturalistic practice was recognized by just about 15% of the students, all of which casts doubt on the average frequencies calculated for the Likert-scale items. In fact, it seems that in many cases the students may have wished to paint themselves in a favorable light, stipulating that the behaviors listed were beneficial or, to play it safe, reporting the use of GLS they were unfamiliar with. Much less surprising was the finding that the use of GLS, particularly those involved in explicit inductive and deductive learning, increased in year 2 only to decrease in year 3, which may indicate growing concern with grammar in second year students and a shift of emphasis from form to meaning in the last stage of the BA program. Equally predictable was the observation that there was a marked preference for the use of some GLS related to deductive instruction, which can be viewed as the default approach to grammar teaching in Polish schools, and that variability increased with the level in the program as students gradually identified their preferred ways of learning. The analysis of individual strategic statements listed for the three instructional modes, in turn, provided further evidence that the subjects reported a high rate of use of GLS which they had little opportunity to apply, confirmed the impact of instructional techniques on strategy choice, and showed that the application of strategic devices may be subject to much individual variation, presumably as a function of different learning styles.

These findings provide a basis for a handful of tentative pedagogic proposals which mainly apply to grammar instruction in foreign languages departments, but can also be of relevance to language teachers in other types of programs or at lower educational levels. For one thing, the interdependence of teaching techniques and learning strategies points to the need of stressing the communicative dimension of grammar, with the effect that students will not only report using the structures taught in authentic comprehension and production but also actively seek learning opportunities of this kind and take full advantage of them. Equally indispensable is a comprehensive, systematic and meticulously planned program in the course of which learners would be acquainted with various GLS, with the caveat that it should be part of more general strategy training, which, in turn, should be just one component of a broader policy of fostering learner autonomy (cf. Pawlak 2008a). What teachers have to bear in mind, however, is that the choice of a particular strategy is often a very individual matter, hinging upon beliefs and expectations, prior learning experiences and, most importantly, the dominant cognitive and learning styles. Therefore, it does not make sense to impose specific GLS on learners, as is often the case with strategies involved in induction, but, rather, present them with a range of options from which the most beneficial, suitable or useful devices can be selected.

The research project also intended to appraise the utility of a data collection instrument based on the theoretical framework proposed by Oxford et al. (2007), in which grammar learning strategies are clustered together according to whether they involve implicit learning with focus on form, explicit inductive learning or explicit deductive learning. The discrepancies described above show that many of the doubts raised in Sect. 3 are warranted in that the inventories include behaviors which are likely to be unknown to respondents but fail to reflect strategies that learners most often report when queried about their favorite ways of learning grammar. Other shortcomings include excessive focus on GLS needed to notice, remember and understand grammar structures, insufficient emphasis on some categories of strategic behaviors, as well as lack of opportunity for students to comment at some length on the use of specific devices. As the findings of this study demonstrate, however, this does not mean that the theoretical framework as such should be abandoned or that the tool constructed on its basis is useless and should be avoided in future research projects. Rather, such problems only indicate that there is an urgent need to design better data collection instruments which would provide comprehensive, valid and reliable data on the application of GLS in different groups of learners. Until such instruments become available and have been carefully validated, though, there is no reason why the tool used in the present study, perhaps with some modifications, should not continue to be employed to collect data on GLS, its main strength being the recognition of the relationship between learners' strategic devices and teachers' instructional practices.

This said, it should be emphasized that the main task for theorists and researchers is to devise a classification of GLS which would give justice to the full range of strategies learners fall back upon when studying grammar, as only then will it be possible to take the further step of evaluating specific actions, exploring the impact of various factors on strategy choice, and appraising the effects of training programs. In the view of the present author, a taxonomy of this kind should combine one of the existing divisions of learning strategies, such as that put forward by Cohen and Dörnyei (2002), and one of the current classifications of techniques and procedures in teaching grammar, such as that described by Ellis (1997) and Pawlak (2006a). A data collection instrument constructed on the basis of such a taxonomy would consequently include Likert-scale items related to metacognitive, affective, social and cognitive strategies, with the last group reflecting the possible instructional options. Clearly, the tool would have to provide both quantitative and qualitative data, and be subject to constant modifications in response to empirical data on strategy use gleaned from various sources (cf. Pawlak 2008b). In fact, efforts to devise and implement such a classification and research instrument are already under way (Pawlak 2009a, 2010, in press), but it has to be emphasized that that the research they have inspired is still in its infancy. While the study reported in this article is admittedly limited in scope and does not meet many of the criteria listed above, it is undoubtedly a step in the right direction as it deepens our understanding of how advanced learners grapple with the challenge of mastering target language grammar.

References

Anderson, N. 2005. L2 learning strategies. In ed. E. Hinkel, 757–771.

Bade, M. 2008. Grammar and good language learners. In ed. C. Griffiths, 74–184.

Batstone, R. 1994. *Grammar*. Oxford: Oxford University Press.

Cain, J., M. Weber-Olsen, and R. Smith. 1987. Acquisition strategies in a first and second language: Are they the same? *Journal of Child Language* 14: 333–352.

Carter, R., and D. Nunan, eds. 2001. *The Cambridge guide to teaching English to speakers of other languages*. Cambridge: Cambridge University Press.

Chamot, A.U. 2004. Issues in language learning strategy research and teaching. *Electronic Journal of Foreign Language Teaching* 1: 12–25.

Chamot, A.U. 2008. Strategy instruction and good language learners. In ed. C. Griffiths, 266–281.

Cohen, A.D., and Z. Dörnyei. 2002. Focus on the language learner: Motivation, styles and strategies. In ed. N. Schmitt, 170–190.

Cohen, A.D., and E. Macaro, eds. 2007. *Language learner strategies*. Oxford: Oxford University Press.

DeKeyser, R. 2003. Implicit and explicit learning. In eds. C.J. Doughty, and M.H. Long, 313–348.

Dörnyei, Z. 2005. *The psychology of the language learner: Individual differences in second language acquisition*. Mahwah: Erlbaum.

Dörnyei, Z. 2007. *Research methods in applied linguistics*. Oxford: Oxford University Press.

Dörnyei, Z., and P. Skehan. 2003. Individual differences in second language learning. In eds. C.J. Doughty, and M.H. Long, 589–630.

Doughty, C.J. 2003. Instructed SLA. In eds. C.J. Doughty, and M.H. Long, 256–310.

Doughty, C.J., and M.H. Long, eds. 2003. *The handbook of second language acquisition*. Oxford: Blackwell.

Droździał-Szelest, K. 1997. *Language learning strategies in the process of acquiring a foreign language*. Poznań: Motivex.

Ellis, R. 1997. *SLA research and language teaching*. Oxford: Oxford University Press.

Ellis, R. 2006. Current issues in the teaching of grammar: An SLA perspective. *TESOL Quarterly* 40: 83–107.

Ellis, G., and B. Sinclair. 1986. *Learning to learn English: A course in learner training*. Cambridge: Cambridge University Press.

Fisiak, J., ed. 2006. *English language, literature and culture*. Poznań: Adam Mickiewicz University Press.

Fortune, A. 1992. Self-study grammar practice: Learners' views and preferences. *ELT Journal* 46: 160–171.

Griffiths, C. 2008a. Strategies and good language learners. In ed. C. Griffiths, 83–98.

Griffiths, C., ed. 2008b. *Lessons from good language learners*. Cambridge: Cambridge University Press.

Herron, C., and M. Tomasello. 1992. Acquiring grammatical structures by guided induction. *French Review* 65: 708–718.

Hinkel, E., ed. 2005. *Handbook of research in second language teaching and learning*. Mahwah: Lawrence Erlbaum.

Johnson, K., ed. 2008. *Expertise in second language learning and teaching*. New York: Palgrave Macmillan.

Karmiloff-Smith, A. 1979. *A functional approach to child language*. Cambridge: Cambridge University Press.

Macaro, E. 2006. Strategies for language learning and for language use: Revising the theoretical framework. *Modern Language Journal* 90: 320–337.

Mystkowska-Wiertelak, A. 2008a. The use of grammar learning strategies among secondary school students. In ed. M. Pawlak, 139–148.

Mystkowska-Wiertelak, A. 2008b. "Rozwijanie autonomii przy użyciu Europejskiego portfolio językowego a podnoszenie poziomu poprawności gramatycznej". [Developing autonomy with the help of the European Language Portfolio and enhancing the level of grammatical accuracy]. In ed. M. Pawlak, 197–206.

Naiman, N., M. Fröhlich, H.H. Stern, and A. Todesco. 1996 (1978). The good language learner. Clevedon: Multilingual Matters.

O'Malley, J.M., and A.U. Chamot. 1990. *Learning strategies in second language acquisition*. Cambridge: Cambridge University Press.

Oliphant, K. 1997. Acquisition of grammatical gender in Italian as a foreign language (Net Work #7). Honolulu: University of Hawaii. http://nflrc.hawaii.edu/NetWorks/NW07/NW07.pdf.

Oxford, R.L. 1990. *Language learning strategies: What every teacher should know*. Boston: Heinle.

Oxford, R.L. 2001. Language learning strategies. In eds. R. Carter, and D. Nunan, 166–172.

Oxford, R.L. 2002. Language learning strategies in a nutshell: Update and ESL suggestions. In eds. J.C. Richards, and W.A. Renandya, 124–132.

Oxford, R.L., and K. Schramm. 2007. Bridging the gap between psychological and sociocultural perspectives on L2 learner strategies. In eds. A.D. Cohen, and E. Macaro, 47–68.

Oxford. R.L., K. Rang Lee, and G. Park. 2007. L2 grammar strategies: The Second Cinderella and beyond. In eds. A.D. Cohen, and E. Macaro, 117–139.

Pawlak, M. 2006a. *The place of form-focused instruction in the foreign language classroom*. Kalisz – Poznań: Adam Mickiewicz University Press.

Pawlak, M. 2006b. Teaching grammar in Polish schools: Facing the reality. In ed. J. Fisiak, 63–72.

Pawlak, M., ed. 2007. Exploring focus on form in language teaching (Special issue of Studies in Pedagogy and Fine Arts 7). Poznań – Kalisz: Adam Mickiewicz University Press.

Pawlak, M. 2008a. Advanced learners' use of strategies for learning grammar: A diary study. In ed. M. Pawlak, 109–125.

Pawlak, M. 2008b. Strategie uczenia się gramatyki–próba klasyfikacji [Grammar learning strategies: Towards a classification]. Paper presented during the Second Conference "Język–Poznanie–Zachowanie" [Language–Cognition–Behavior], Łódź, Poland.

Pawlak, M., ed. 2008c. *Investigating English language learning and teaching.* Poznań–Kalisz: Adam Mickiewicz University Press.

Pawlak, M., ed. 2008d. Autonomia w nauce języka obcego – co osiągnęliśmy i dokąd zmierzamy [Autonomy in language learning: Achievements and prospects for the future]. Poznań – Kalisz–Konin: Wydawnictwo UAM i PWSZ w Koninie.

Pawlak, M. 2009a. Investigating grammar learning strategies: In search of appropriate research tools. Paper presented at the 19th Conference of the European Second Language Association, Cork, 2–5 September.

Pawlak, M. 2009b. Grammar learning strategies and language attainment: Seeking a relationship. *Research in Language* 7: 43–60.

Pawlak, M. 2010. The use of grammar learning strategies by advanced learners of English: Identifying the influences, Paper presented at the Annual Conference of the American Association for Applied Linguistics, Atlanta, 6–9 March.

Pawlak, M. In press. Grammar learning strategies: State of the art. In eds. L. Pedrazzini, and A. Nava.

Pawlak, M., and K. Droździał-Szelest. 2007. When I think about grammar... Exploring English department students' beliefs about grammar, grammar learning and grammar teaching. In ed. M. Pawlak, 99–318.

Pedrazzini, L., and A. Nava, eds. In press. Learning and teaching English: Insights from research. Polimetrica, Monza-Milano.

Richards, J.C., and W.A. Renandya, eds. 2002. *Methodology in language teaching: An anthology of current practice.* Cambridge: Cambridge University Press.

Rubin, J. 1975. What the 'Good Language Learner' can teach us. *TESOL Quarterly* 9: 41–51.

Rubin, J. 2008. The expert language learner: A review of good language learner studies and learner strategies. In ed. K. Johnson, 37–63.

Schmitt, N., ed. 2002. *An introduction to applied linguistics.* London: Edward Arnold.

Stern, H.H. 1975. What can we learn from the good language learner? *Canadian Modern Language Review* 31: 304–318.

Stern, H.H. 1983. *Fundamental concepts of language teaching.* Oxford: Oxford University Press.

Stevens, F. 1984. *Strategies for second language acquisition.* Montreal: Eden Press.

Takeuchi, O., C. Griffiths, and D. Coyle. 2007. Applying strategies to contexts: The role of individual, situational, and group differences. In eds. A.D. Cohen, and E. Macaro, 69–92.

Tilfarlioğlu, Y. 2005. An analysis of the relationship between the use of grammar learning strategies and student achievement at English preparatory classes. *Journal of Language and Linguistic Studies* 1: 155–169.

Individual Learner Differences and Accuracy in Foreign Language Pronunciation

Małgorzata Baran-Łucarz

Abstract The paper presents outcomes of studies examining the influence of some cognitive and affective individual learner differences (ILDs) on FL pronunciation acquisition and learning. The first part of the paper reports on early and more contemporary observations made by different researchers (i.e. Purcell 1980; Gonet 2006; Pastuszek-Lipińska 2007). The later fragments are devoted to describing a few experiments carried out in this area by myself. The learner variables whose predictive strength in reference to accuracy in FL pronunciation I examined are the following: sensory modality preference, the extent of Field Independence (FI), attributional style, self-concept, belief in the ability to control some factors affecting success in FL pronunciation learning. Finally, profiles of excellent, very good and very poor learners of English phonetics are provided. Results of these observations encourage us to conclude that FI, auditory preference, and musical talent are significant predictors of a high level in FL pronunciation. Individuals luckily 'programmed' with such ILDs outperform other post-puberty FL users particularly in acquisitional contexts, i.e. when no explicit help is provided. However, it turns out that formal multisensory instruction, systematic practice and phonetic competence allow also learners lacking these innate predisposition to reach equally high levels of FL pronunciation. It must be clarified, though, that this is more probable when learners reveal high motivation (preferably 'aesthetic'), believe in the ability to take control over their progress in learning, and perceive their level and abilities as realistically as possible.

M. Baran-Łucarz (✉)
Institute of English Studies, University of Wroclaw, Wroclaw, Poland
e-mail: mbaran-lucarz@ifa.uni.wroc.pl

M. Pawlak (ed.), *New Perspectives on Individual Differences in Language Learning and Teaching*, Second Language Learning and Teaching, DOI: 10.1007/978-3-642-20850-8_18, © Springer-Verlag Berlin Heidelberg 2012

1 Introduction

Pronunciation is an aspect that foreign language (FL) students usually show great concern for, irrelevant of their level, age and educational background. Although nativelike accuracy is not a must in the case of average learners, it should be aimed at by some groups of FL users, e.g. FL teachers. What can contribute not only to our better understanding of the model of FL pronunciation acquisition, but also make our instruction more effective are studies examining the influence of individual learner differences (ILDs) on the rate and success in FL learning and acquisition. The paper reports on outcomes of several observations carried out in this area among adult FL learners, followed by an attempt to find some common ground.

2 Review of Literature on Predictors of Accuracy in FL Pronunciation

2.1 Suter (1976), Purcell and Suter (1980)

Among earlier studies on determinants of accuracy in FL pronunciation is the one carried out by Suter (1976). It involved a group of 61 Arabic, Persian, Japanese and Thai students studying English at one of the Universities in the United States. Not only did the subjects have a chance to pick up the target language (TL) pronunciation living in the English-speaking country, but they were also provided with some explicit phonetic training. The participants' free speech was evaluated on a six-point scale by 14 judges representing an average native speaker of English (presumably American English).

The first statistical analyses showed that 12 out of 20 factors correlated significantly with the level of TL pronunciation accuracy. The determinant that was found to be the most important was native language. Among the variables whose influence on pronunciation proved to be insignificant were the following: allegiance to old culture, sex, motivational types (economic and social prestige motivation), amount of formal training on pronunciation, extroversion, amount of formal learning of English, and the number of known FLs.

However, the use of more advanced statistical tools (Purcell and Suter 1980) led to the conclusion that only 4 variables account for the differences in FL pronunciation accuracy. The regression analysis showed that *first language, aptitude for oral mimicry,* the *number of years* spent in the TL country and months of *residing with native speakers* of English, and strength of *concern for pronunciation* altogether explained 67.3% of variance. The authors close the discussion of results stating the following (Purcell and Suter 1980: 286):

> The variables which turn out to be important seem to be those which the teachers have the least influence on (...). The present study indicates that the attainments of accurate

pronunciation in a second language is a matter substantially beyond the control of educators. In Krashen's terms, the important variables determining pronunciation accuracy in English are all acquisition variables; formal learning is almost entirely out of picture.

2.2 Gonet (2006)

More recently, a pilot study conducted among 10 adult Polish learners of English "whose pronunciation is generally considered exceptionally good" has been carried out (Gonet 2006: 71). Such subjects were found among junior and senior university and college phonetics teachers and among university students or graduates. So as to discover which "intrinsic learner characteristics" and "external situational characteristics" guarantee success at FL pronunciation, the researcher designed a questionnaire, in which "the respondents were asked to specify on a four-grade scale, how well a given characteristic reflected their attitude, temperament, quality, disposition or experience" (2006: 71). The use of advanced statistics, such as cross-question consistency, two-way ANOVA, post-hoc confidence interval testing, allowed to build a hierarchy of variables responsible for exceptionally high levels of accuracy in FL pronunciation. At the top of the list was *motivation*, followed in descending order by *auditory sensitivity*, ability of *self-evaluation*, backed up by *knowledge of theoretical phonetics*. As the author of the study claims, it is surprising that such variables as the choice of teaching methods and techniques, correction, and contact with authentic TL were found "at the bottom of the scale" (2006: 70).

2.3 Pastuszek-Lipińska (2007)

Valuable data have been provided by Pastuszek-Lipińska (2007), who devoted her study to finding out whether *musical talent* can aid in achieving highest levels in FL pronunciation. Numerous experiments have already proven that brains of musicians and non-musicians vary in terms of anatomy and function (Münte et al. 2002). These outcomes allow to speculate that "intensive musical training may generate changes in the human brain, and thus also alter the processing of sounds" (Pastuszek-Lipińska 2007: 12). Some studies testing these hypotheses were carried out by Dodane (2000), who compared second language production of children that had no music lessons with those who received musical training. Results of one of the experiments proved that musically trained children were significantly better at perception of intonation and FL melody, and at phonetic contrasts than those who were not offered any music classes, which stresses the value of music education at pre-puberty. The research of Alexander, Wong, and Bradlow (2005) showed that American-English-speaking musicians were better at identifying and discriminating lexical tones than non-musicians, proving that "experience with music pitch processing may facilitate the processing of lexical pitches" (Pastuszek-Lipińska 2007: 12).

Finally, the author of the article reports on her own study carried out among 106 musician and non-musician native speakers of Polish. Their task was to repeat stimuli created synthetically in five different languages, which demanded quick processing of the stimuli. The performance was assessed by native speakers of these FLs, and analysed from the acoustic, phonetic and statistical perspective. The results proved that musicians outperformed non-musicians, i.e. they could produce more sentences and strings of words with fewer errors, and their pronunciation was considered by the judges more nativelike than that of their friends who had no musical training.

3 Sensory Modality Preferences and Accuracy in FL Pronunciation

The concept of sensory modality preferences, embracing auditory, visual, kinesthetic and tactile styles, is well-known to all interested in SLA studies and FL teaching. The division refers not only to one's most comfortable, and thus dominating, perceptive channel, which determines sensitivity to and ability to notice various stimuli from the outside world. Since these different modes belong to one of the dimensions of cognitive style, they are also considered to be various manners of holding the perceived stimuli in the short-term memory, and storing and retrieving them from long-term memory. Taking into account the fact that in the case of some individuals the most natural, effortless and specialized mode of perception is through the auditory channel, we may presuppose that they find it easier to master FL pronunciation than those whose dominating styles are other than auditory. We may assume that their advantage will be most visible in natural settings and classroom learning where no help in the form of formal instruction is provided.

To find out if auditory style is one of the components of talent for acquiring FL pronunciation, an empirical study involving 50 Polish high school learners of English was conducted (Baran 2000). The subjects were from 17 to 19 years old and represented pre-intermediate (N = 23), intermediate (N = 12), and upper-intermediate (N = 15) levels of English. Their sensory modality preference was diagnosed with the use of the *Barsch Learning-Style Inventory* (Davis and Nur 1994) translated into Polish. Since there were only a few students revealing a dominant kinesthetic sensory mode, and no generalizations could be made, their results were not analyzed in this experiment. The subjects were classified either as visual learners (N = 28), auditory learners (N = 10), or those that showed no preference for the auditory or visual mode (N = 12).

The pronunciation of the students was assessed on the basis of performance on 4 tasks—free speech (subtest D), dialogue reading (subtest C), reading a set of minimal pairs (subtest B), and a perception test on minimal pairs (subtest A). To evaluate their pronunciation of English as objectively as possible an atomistic approach was used, i.e. points were distributed for several vowels, consonants, word stress, prominent and weak syllables, and intonation contours. Since it was crucial to control any formal instruction on pronunciation that might have been offered to the subjects, a questionnaire allowing to gather all the necessary information on this matter was used, supported by interviews with the students and their teachers.

Having evaluated the pronunciation of every subject on each test, the means and standard deviations were computed for three proficiency levels, with the distinction between the auditory, visual, and no-preference group. It appeared that not even once were the scores achieved by visual perceivers the highest. In 3 subtests the means of visual students were the lowest. On the whole, the highest mean scores were achieved 6 times by auditory perceivers, and 6 times by the no-preference group. Moreover, in the case of free speech and dialogue reading, in which monitoring pronunciation was the most difficult, the auditory learners outperformed not only the visual and no-preference groups who were at the same level of proficiency, but also those that were one level higher.

Due to the scarce number of auditory dominant subjects, the group was combined with the students showing no strong modality preference. Finally, at each level there were two classes, which made it possible to use the t-test. The Kolmogorow and Bartlett tests proved that the scores in each group were normally distributed and the variances for the scores of the two groups equal. For all three proficiency levels, the t test calculated at $\alpha = 0.05$ allowed to conclude that people revealing an auditory style and no preference in these modes reach significantly higher levels of accuracy in FL pronunciation than visual learners when no formal instruction on this aspect is offered.

However, the lack of such an inborn predisposition to pick up FL phonetics can be compensated by explicit teaching, in which the instructor provides the learners with a wide variety of presentation techniques and exercises, adjusting them to the students' preferred channels of perception. Examples of such activities are offered, for example, by Bukowski (2003) and Wrembel (2007a), Wrembel (2007b). Other interesting suggestions can be found in Wrembel (2007a: 39), who is for a holistic approach in pronunciation training, which consists in applying "multisensory modes of presentation and practice". Additionally, she anticipates that FL pronunciation teaching can be more effective when "cross-channel reinforcements" are used, an example of which is associating TL sounds and their symbols with color.

4 FD/FI and Accuracy in FL Pronunciation

4.1 FD/FI and FL Pronunciation Acquisition

Field-dependence (FD)/field-independence (FI) is one of the dimensions of cognitive style that refers to one's preferred manners of perceiving, organizing, analyzing and recalling information and experience. Analysis of the characteristics of people revealing these two styles provide a basis for hypothesizing that FI post-puberty FL learners will reach higher levels of accuracy in pronunciation than the FDs when exposure to the TL is not supported with any formal instruction on this aspect. Let us look at some of the features of this cognitive style dimension that constitute the ground for such premises.

First of all, experiments in which the Embedded Figures Test (EFT) is applied show that the more FI and less FD one is, the easier one finds it to "'break up' an organized field in order to separate out a part of it" (Witkin et al. 1971: 5). In other words, FD people show more passiveness, which reveals itself in perceiving the field as it is rather than via analysis of its components. Thus, it seems that when picking up FL pronunciation is concerned, FI individuals are in a better position already at the input stage, since the ability to notice, isolate, discern, and disembed discrete elements (e.g. FL segments, syllables, word stress) from larger perceptive wholes (words and sentences) is an ability that might help perceive the minute features of a FL accent.

It has been also observed that FD/FI people differ in terms of how they approach ambiguous material, i.e. new (lacking or having insufficient cues) or complex (containing too many cues that need to be taken into consideration) material. While FI individuals easily and spontaneously introduce organizing structures by themselves, FD people need external sources of reference. An example of such ambiguous input filled with novelty that requires structuralizing is undoubtedly FL pronunciation.

Furthermore, we may assume that the operations taking place at the central processing stage, such as separating the essential elements from the unimportant ones, making quick and numerous comparisons, identifying certain components, and exploring relationships between them in order to infer and induce patterns and rules will be more effectively realized by FI individuals. People revealing more FD will find these operations more difficult due to their lower level of fluid intelligence, poorer short-term memory, difficulties with access to and retrieval from long-term memory, and smaller range and pace of simultaneous information processing (Nosal 1990).

Finally, the output stage, i.e. speaking, requires carrying out and controlling several cognitive processes simultaneously. Most of the attention and consciousness is focused on meaning, and the last aspect one usually thinks about and is capable of controlling is pronunciation. Consequently, we may assume that the slower pace and smaller range of these parallel operations in the case of FDs will deteriorate the correctness of their pronunciation.

It is also some features of psychological differentiation, embracing such areas as sense of self as separate identity, controls and defences that may put the FD individuals in an unfavourable position when it comes to FL pronunciation acquisition. One of defensive behaviours of the FDs is ignoring and not taking in stimuli that are unpleasant and uncomfortable for the individual, an example of which might be some features of the TL phonological system. Their defences determine what "enters into consciousness and what is put aside" (Witkin et al. 1971: 9). All in all, the thought and perception of FD people is not kept discrete from feelings.

4.2 FD and FL Pronunciation Learning

We may hypothesize that FD individuals can achieve much higher levels of accuracy in FL pronunciation when exposure is supported by explicit phonetic training. In formal learning the instructor performs the role of the external source of reference that FDs need so much, and thus can help these individuals at all stages of information processing.

First of all, in the case of FD individuals we may expect learning to bring better results than acquisition, since the FL phonological material in acquisitional settings, which is usually ambiguous and lacks clear structure is now provided in an organized manner. The difficulties with noticing and disembeding smaller bits from larger units can be compensated in teaching by making certain aspect of pronunciation salient, and by providing them in the form of sequentially parceled bits of information.

Moreover, it is advantageous for the FD learners that they are not left on their own to rely on the inductive and analytical abilities needed for identifying patterns, but can find support and guidance in the teacher or other learners. They will feel even more comfortable if the teacher chooses the deductive approach and allows them to take the role of a spectator, rather than of a hypothesis-former and explorer (Nebelkopf and Dreyer 1973; Witkin et al. 1977).

To enable the students to produce utterances with 'good' pronunciation without the need to control this aspect at the output stage, proper habits have to be built. What can help in forming them is raising the learners' phonological meta-awareness and intensive practice. In the case of FD individuals who are so sensitive to reinforcement and approval seeking (Nosal 1990), it seems vital to offer them a lot of controlled operations, i.e. plenty of reinforcement, feedback and correction. Furthermore, psychological profiles of the FDs suggest that their progress may be faster when provided with cooperative rather than competitive settings, social cues, humour and fantasy. Finally, since thinking and perception of the FDs are so strongly influenced and regulated by emotions, we may presuppose that better results will be achieved when learning takes place in a friendly atmosphere and the affective filter is kept at a low level.

4.3 Results of Studies on FD/FI and FL Pronunciation Accuracy

To find out if the extent of FI is a predictor of success in FL pronunciation acquisition and/or learning an empirical study was carried out (Baran 2003, 2004). It involved 96 adults (first-year students of the Institute of English Studies and Teacher Training College in Wrocław, Poland) whose pronunciation was evaluated twice—before a course in phonetics and after 8 months of phonetic training. The samples collected before the subjects started studying at one of the institutes exemplified their pronunciation resulting from acquisition. One of the question-naires distributed among them allowed the researcher to control for formal instruction on pronunciation that might have been offered prior to the course of phonetics. Pronunciation recorded on the second occasion was a result of exposure supported by conscious study and systematic practise of the features of English pronunciation.

During the course the analytic-linguistic approach of pronunciation teaching was used. The students were offered various presentation techniques, such as verbal descriptions of articulators, identification of the place and manner of sound articulation, visual representations showing the position and movement of the organs of speech while producing the FL segments, and comparisons between the TL and L1 phonological systems. The students were provided with a wide variety of controlled practice activities, and numerous examples of authentic FL materials (songs, films, recordings of interviews).

The cognitive style of the learners was measured with the standardized Group Embedded Figures Test (Witkin et al. 1971). Samples of pronunciation were gathered while performing two tasks, i.e. reading a list of words, which allowed for more monitoring of pronunciation, and reading a humorous dialogue, in which pronunciation was difficult to control. An atomistic evaluation was conducted by 5 raters, who assessed the level of correctness of pronouncing the majority of English segments and several features of connected speech (e.g. weak forms, assimilation, deletion of schwa, coalescence). Additionally, it was supported by a holistic assessment carried out by 3 native speakers of English.

The outcomes of the study showed that there is a statistically significant moderate relationship between pronunciation accuracy resulting from acquisition degree of FI (Pearson $r = 0.30$, $\alpha < 0.05$). Additionally, the results of a multiple regression analysis demonstrated that from 7% (in the case of more controlled tasks) to 8% (in tasks allowing less monitoring) of the variance in pronunciation accuracy resulting from acquisition can be accounted for by the degree of FI.

Apart from this cognitive style dimension, it is the imitation skills that entered the model computed by the multiple regression analysis. Together the two vari-ables accounted for 19% of the variance in learners' pronunciation accuracy scores. The two-predictor model adds support to Purcell and Suter's (1980) observations. While the researchers found that *aptitude for oral mimicry* explained about 14% of the variance in pronunciation accuracy, in my study this skill accounted for 10% to 13% of the variance depending on the type of task, i.e. how much monitoring was allowed.

However, after the subjects of the study underwent the course in phonetics, in the case of dialogue reading the FI students were by no means better than the FD ones (the computed correlation coefficient between pronunciation accuracy and extent of FI was non-significant). A multiple regression analysis showed that 28% of variance in the subjects' pronunciation was accounted for by perceptive skills and phonetic competence. FI did not enter the model.

Moreover, the use of appropriate statistics (Spearman rho test and ANOVA) showed that the amount of progress made during a one-year course in phonetics is not significantly correlated with the extent of FI. Furthermore, it turned out that it was actually the FD learners who made the most distinct progress when offered explicit help.

Similar outcomes were achieved by Elliott (1995a), who searching for predictors of successful FL pronunciation examined a group of 66 adult learners of Spanish. His study showed that accuracy in this FL aspect was not related to gender, travels abroad, other FLs spoken, academic achievements, overall level of Spanish, or having relatives in the TL country. What most strongly affected the level of pronunciation was concern for pronunciation. The second most significant factor was FI, which accounted for from 6% to 7% of variability in pronunciation accuracy. It is also Elliott (1995b) who found out that when FD individuals receive formal instruction on pronunciation, particularly multimodal instruction, the extent of FI does not influence accuracy in this aspect.

4.4 FD, Phonetic Meta-Awareness, and Accuracy in FL Pronunciation

Further observations were carried out to see whether indeed phonetic competence supported by systematic pronunciation training allow FD students to reach the highest levels of accuracy in this FL aspect (Baran 2006). This time progress in the pronunciation of English post-alveolar fricatives and affricates was observed in the case of 46 grown-up teacher trainees, among whom 22% were FI and 78% were FD. The subjects belonged to three different groups in which treatment varied. Group 3 was offered only formal instruction and proved to have high phonetic competence after training; Group 2 was provided only with intensive practice without explicit information about the ways to pronounce the segments; in Group 1 the analytic-linguistic approach was used, i.e. intensive practice was supported by formal instruction offered with the application of various tools.

The subjects' pronunciation of the post-alveolar sounds was assessed when performing the following tasks allowing various use of monitor: description of a picture, reading a text with focus on meaning, and reading well-known dialogues used during the course. Their phonetic competence was tested by two tasks, i.e. recognizing from among several facial diagrams the ones representing the moment of production of post-alveolar fricatives and affricates, and describing in a detailed manner their place and manner of articulation in comparison to Polish counterpart sounds.

It turned out that the FD learners had poorest results in Group 2, where no formal instruction was provided. Over 41% of the FD students in the more controlled tasks and over 50% of these subjects in the case of picture description received 0 points for their pronunciation of the practised segments. More significant progress was visible in the case of FD students who were offered only formal instruction and encouraged to work on the sounds by themselves at home. When it comes to dialogue reading, only one learner's pronunciation was credited with 0 points and 56% of the individuals received a maximum number of points. For the communicative task one person attained 1 point, while 45%—a maximum amount of points. However, the best outcomes were found in Group 1, where the whole group of FDs after the treatment obtained the highest possible scores.

5 Attribution Theory and Accuracy in FL Pronunciation

According to constructivists, attainments in learning, e.g. FLs, are determined more by one's *self-concept*, that is by how individuals perceive themselves as learners, than by their real affective, cognitive and personality profiles (Williams and Burden 1997). The Attribution Theory explains that we differ significantly in what we attribute our successes and failures to (Weiner 1986). While some look for justifications of good and/or poor results of academic success in external factors, such as luck and task difficulty, others consider the reasons to be internal factors, i.e. innate abilities and effort put in learning. It is claimed that people vary in the extent to which they perceive these attributions as stable and controllable.

To see if Attribution Theory may explain the level one reaches in FL pronunciation, a group of 65 students from a teacher training college and English philology filled out a questionnaire, in which they were asked about possible reasons of their success/difficulties with English pronunciation, and the extent to which they believed these factors were controllable (Baran-Łucarz 2008). So as to be able to observe any tendencies and common ground at various levels, the students were classified respectively as excellent, very good, good, very poor, and poor. The subjects were placed in one of the groups depending on how well they did (how close their English pronunciation was to that of English native speakers) on two tasks: reading a text and free speech.

One of the first interesting observations concerned the issue of self-image. While the excellent and very good subjects considered their level in pronunciation lower than it actually was, the great majority of the poor and very poor students overestimated their pronunciation (only 2 students out of 19 believed their level was 'at the border of good and poor'; the rest assumed they spoke with 'good' pronunciation). What is even more surprising is that 50% of the (very) poor subjects claimed that FL pronunciation is easy to learn. Moreover, 60% of thought think they had a capability to assess properly their own pronunciation, which most probably was not true. The same subjects justified their 'good' and not 'very good' accent by the limited time devoted to pronunciation practice. Only half of this group attributed their difficulties with pronunciation to too little effort put into working on this FL aspect. It was also 50% who claimed their lower level was due to the circumstances being against them. Furthermore, the belief about the extent of controllability and stability of certain factors varied across different levels. While the excellent, very good and good subjects considered numerous factors to be under their control, many poor and very poor students thought that circumstances and time devoted to practising pronunciation were frequently uncontrollable. It is also their interest in pronunciation, ways of and effort put into working on improving this FL aspect that, as they claimed, not always depended on them (for exact data see Baran-Łucarz 2008). The outcomes of this study show that indeed such ILDs as false self-concepts and beliefs about FL pronunciation learning might be responsible for slower pace of progress and lower ultimate level of FL pronunciation.

6 Profiles of Excellent, Very Good, and Very Poor FL Pronunciation Learners

From among about 150 advanced learners of English studying at the Institute of English Studies and the Teacher Training College in Wrocław 13 subjects, among whom there were excellent, very good and very poor FL pronunciation learners were diagnosed on several cognitive preferences, attribution style, strength and type of motivation, and strategies used (Baran-Łucarz 2007). It is vital to underline that all the students had undergone regular phonetic training, and thus their level of pronunciation was shaped both by acquisition and learning.

The major criteria according to which the subjects' level in pronunciation was assessed were correctness of segments, transfer from L1, consistency in using one of the chosen accents, the pronunciation of words commonly mispronounced by Poles and of some suprasegmentals. The participants were evaluated when reading a list of words and a text, and delivering a speech. Their phonological knowledge on various phonetic and phonological issues was assessed on a regular basis with a few written tests.

Several standardized instruments were applied to find out the cognitive characteristics of the subjects (for details see Baran-Łucarz 2007). Moreover, an introductory questionnaire was designed to, among others, control their possible longer stays in English-speaking countries before the critical period, and find out about their motivation and strategies applied consciously to improve their pronunciation. Finally, an instrument was designed to examine the students' attribution style and their opinions on the controllability of attributes for success in FL pronunciation learning.

A detailed look at the profiles of exceptionally good pronunciation learners allows us to conclude that they owe success to an ideal combination of cognitive traits, among which FI, high musical intelligence and talent, and right brain dominance seem to be the most crucial. Such a blend of innate traits freed the students from the necessity to work intensively on pronunciation. It is vital to add that these inborn qualities were supported by strong intrinsic motivation, extensive exposure to authentic spoken language, good phonetic knowledge, and a strong belief that one is in control of progress in learning.

The characteristics of the students representing a very high and very low level of pronunciation show that the gift for music and preference for auditory style are decisive factors. When it comes to the extent of FI, it has been observed again that even strongly FD learners can have very good FL pronunciation when exposure is supported by explicit teaching. Nonetheless, looking at the profiles of the very poor pronunciation achievers we may conclude that a high degree of FI is not sufficient to gain good accent. This leads us to the issue of motivation.

Interestingly, 3 subjects with a very low level of pronunciation showed a very strong desire to achieve a nativelike English accent. This time, however, unlike in the case of the earlier groups, the subjects were evidently motivated instrumentally. While the subjects with an excellent and very good command of TL phonetics would claim e.g. 'I simply love the sound of RP', none of the learners with poor pronunciation responded that this aspect is a source of pleasant aesthetic experience or fascination. Their reasons for their concern for pronunciation were rather pragmatic. Among their justifications were the following ones: 'it allows the speaker to be more communicative', 'a FL teacher should be a good model for the learners', or 'it will help me get a better job'.

Moreover, it turned out that the students showing poor pronunciation did not prove to be too proficient and frequent users of cognitive, metacognitive or affective strategies. It is also their knowledge that was at a low and very low level. What appears to be another important obstacle in achieving good FL pronunciation is their inability to evaluate their skills realistically. Despite the low marks from tests, most of the very poor learners considered their phonetic knowledge to be 'quite good' and their level of pronunciation 'good' or 'rather poor' but not 'poor' or 'very poor'. They were also typical externalisers, blaming outside factors for not being able to achieve the highest levels of FL pronunciation, and believed to have little control of their learning.

7 Summing up

Since researchers choose to observe the influence of different ILDs on FL pronunciation accuracy, and use various instruments and statistical tools, it is not easy to conclude which learner variables are the strongest predictors of success in this aspect. Additionally, what makes generalizations difficult is the fact that while in some observations the subjects' level of pronunciation is a result only of acquisition, in others——mainly of learning. Finally, many experiments involve people who have had a chance to live in the TL community and to support the acquisition by conscious formal studying. Still, despite these difficulties some regularities can be observed.

First of all, irrelevant of the setting in which the TL is mastered, the level in pronunciation seems to be determined by some special ability labelled differently by various researchers, i.e. 'aptitude for oral mimicry', 'auditory sensitivity', 'imitation skills'. One may, however, wonder whether this indeed can be considered an ILD or rather a skill resulting from being predisposed with certain inborn set of characteristics.

Another learner variable determining the level of FL pronunciation is motivation, called by some 'concern for pronunciation', or 'attitudes'. Interestingly, it is not only strength of concern/motivation that determines one's success, but also its type. The observations of learners revealing different levels in FL pronunciation (Baran-Łucarz 2007) show that aesthetic motives lead to more nativelike skills than pragmatic ones.

Moreover, we may risk a statement that the influence of learner variables on the accuracy in FL pronunciation is more visible and more important in the case of acquisition rather than formal learning. Among the most important inborn determinants of success in this FL aspect seem to be musical intelligence/talent, auditory style and FI. However, when the learner is provided with presentation techniques and exercises referring to various modes and intelligences, and with help in the process of noticing, attention steering, inferring and identifying features of the TL phonological system, the students showing other preferences are not doomed to have a low level of pronunciation. Still, they will have to put more effort in the process of learning and need more time to achieve the same results as their gifted friends. What will level the differences between them and the talented students is sound phonological knowledge and conscious use of a wide variety of strategies to practise pronunciation. Thus, unlike what Purcell and Suter (1980: 286) claimed, explicit instruction and practice, particularly when adjusted to the students' preferences, are not at all "out of picture".

Finally, what appears to slow down progress in FL phonetics and needs to be taken care of by the teacher is the false, overestimated (or probably also underestimated) perception of one's self-efficacy, the belief in one's success being dependent more on external than internal factors, and the assumption that they are uncontrollable.

Outcomes of many other studies show that the list of learner variables affecting accuracy in FL pronunciation include many more factors than the ones described in this paper. Among them are age, attracting the attention of most researchers, affective (attitudes, inhibition, anxiety) and personality variables (empathy, intuition, ego-permeability) (for a detailed report see e.g. Leather and James 1991).

References

Alexander, J.A., P.C.M. Wong, and A.R. Bradlow. 2005. Lexical tone perception in musicians and non-musicians. Proceedings of the Interspeech 2005–Eurospeech, 9th European Conference on Speech Communication and Technology. Lisbon, Portugal.

Baran, M. 2000. Cognitive style as a predictor of success in FL pronunciation learning. In ed. B. Rozwadowska, 1–12.

Baran, M. 2003. Field independence as a predictor of success in foreign language pronunciation acquisition and learning. Unpublished doctoral dissertation, University of Wrocław, Wrocław.

Baran, M. 2004. Field independence as a predictor of success in FL pronunciation acquisition and learning. In eds. W. Sobkowiak, and E. Waniek-Klimczak, 11–19.

Baran, M. 2006. Wiedza fonetyczna a postęp w wymowie języka obcego. Zależność/niezależność od pola danych jako zmienna modyfikująca. [Phonetic knowledge and progress in foreign language pronunciation. Field-dependence/independence as an intervening variable]. In eds E. Waniek-Kilmczak, and W. Sobkowiak, 23–37.

Baran-Łucarz, M. 2007. Profiles of excellent, very good, and very poor foreign language pronunciation learners. In ed. M. Wrembel, 5–10.

Baran-Łucarz, M. 2008. Teoria Atrybucji w odniesieniu do uczenia się wymowy języka obcego. [Attribution Theory and learning foreign language pronunciation]. In eds. A. Michońska-Stadnik, and Z. Wąsik, 13–25.

Bukowski, D. 2003. Multisensory modes of teaching and learning phonetics—a few practical suggestions. In eds. E. Waniek Klimczak, and W. Sobkowiak, 11–30.

Davis, E., and H. Nur. 1994. Helping teachers and students understand learning styles. *English Teaching Forum* 32: 12–19.

Dodane, C. 2000. l'apprentissage precoce d'une langue etrangere:une silution pour la maitrise de l'intonation et de la prnunciation? In ed. Guimbretire, 229–248.

Elliott, A.R. 1995a. Field independence/dependence, hemispheric specialization, and attitude in relation to pronunciation accuracy in Spanish as a foreign language. *Modern Language Journal* 79: 357–371.

Elliott, A.R. 1995b. Foreign language phonology: Field independence, attitude, and the success of formal instruction in Spanish pronunciation. *Modern Language Journal* 79: 530–542.

Gonet, W. 2006. Success in the acquisition of English phonetics by Poles (a pilot study). In eds. W. Sobkowiak, and E. Waniek Klimczak, 70–88.

Leather, J., and A. James, 1991. The acquisition of second language speech. *Studies in Second Language Acquisition* 13: 305–341.

Michońska-Stadnik, A., and Z. Wąsik, eds. 2008. Nowe spojrzenia na motywację w dydaktyce języków obcych. [New perspectives on motivation in foreign language pedagogy]. Wrocław: Philological School of Higher Education Press.

Münte, T.F., E. Altenmüller, and L. Jancke. 2002. The musician's brain as a model of of neuroplaticity. *Nature Reviews. Neuroscience* 3: 473–478.

Nebelkopf, E.B., and A.S. Dreyer. 1973. Continuous-discontinuous concept attainment as a function of individual differences in cognitive style. *Perceptual and Motor Skills* 36: 655–662.

Nosal, C.S. 1990. *Psychologiczne modele umysłu [Psychological models of the mind].* Warszawa: Państwowe Wydawnictwo Naukowe.

Pastuszek-Lipińska, B. 2007. Does music education affect second language acquisition? Implications for pronunciation pedagogy. In ed. M. Wrembel, 11–13.

Purcell, E., and R. Suter. 1980. Predictors of pronunciation accuracy: A reexamination. *Language Learning* 30: 271–287.

Rozwadowska, B., ed. 2000. PASE papers in language studies: The proceedings of the 8th Annual Conference of the Polish Association for the Study of English. Aksel s.c, Wrocław.

Sobkowiak, W., and E. Waniek-Klimczak, eds. 2004. Zeszyty Naukowe Państwowej Wyższej Szkoły Zawodowej w Koninie 1/2004 (4). Materiały z konferencji "Dydaktyka fonetyki języka obcego w Polsce", Mikorzyn k. Konina 10–12 maja 2004. Wydawnictwo PWSZ w Koninie, Konin.

Sobkowiak, W., and E. Waniek Klimczak, eds. 2006. Dydaktyka fonetyki języka obcego w Polsce. [Pedagogy of foreign language pronunciation in Poland]. PWSZ w Koninie, Konin.

Suter, R.W. 1976. Predictors of pronunciation accuracy in second language learning. *Language Learning* 26: 233–253.

Waniek Klimczak, E., and W. Sobkowiak, eds. 2003. Zeszyty Naukowe Państwowej Wyższej Szkoły Zawodowej w Płocku. Neofilologia, tom V, Dydaktyka Fonetyki Języka Obcego. Wydawnictwo PWSZ w Płocku, Płock.

Waniek-Kilmczak, E., and W. Sobkowiak, eds. 2006. Zeszyty Naukowe Państwowej Wyższej Szkoły Zawodowej w Płocku. Neofilologia, tom VIII, Dydaktyka Fonetyki Języka Obcego. Wydawnictwo PWSZ w Płocku, Płock.

Weiner, B. 1986. *An attributional theory of motivation and emotion.* New York: Springer-Verlag.

Williams, M., and R.L. Burden. 1997. *Psychology for language teachers.* Cambridge: Cambridge University Press.

Witkin, H.A., P.K. Oltman, E. Raskin, and S.A. Karp. 1971. *A manual for the embedded figures test*. Palo Alto, CA: Consulting Psychologists Press, Inc.

Witkin, H.A., C.A. Moore, D.R. Goodenough, and P.W. Cox. 1977. Field-dependent and field-independent cognitive styles and their educational implications. *Review of Educational Research* 47: 1–64.

Wrembel, M. 2007a. In search of cross-modal reinforcements in the acquisition of L2 practical phonetics. In ed. Wrembel, 39–43.

Wrembel, M., ed. 2007b. IATEFL Pronunciation special interest Group speak out! A special issue 'From Poland with Phon' (38), December 2007.

Quantitative and Qualitative Perspectives on Individual Differences in Error Correction Preferences

Zhou Chunhong and Carol Griffiths

Abstract Questions surrounding the issue of error in language development have long been controversial. To this day there has been no generally accepted definition of exactly what an error is, or how precisely it is related to 'correct' or 'native' language. Theories of the role of error in language development range from a bad habit which must be rigidly corrected to avoid fossilisation on the one hand, to a sign of progress in the development of the learner's interlanguage on the other. As for the role of error correction in practice, this has varied from being seen positively as an essential part of the teacher's role to being viewed negatively as a useless and even harmful waste of time. If theorists and practitioners cannot agree about basic issues surrounding the concept of error in language development, what about the learner? The fact is that, theoretical and practical controversies notwithstanding, corrective feedback is conducted in language classrooms across the globe day after day. What do individual students, that is those on the receiving end, think about error correction? What kind of error correction do they find useful, who do they think should carry out this correction, when and how? How do their perceptions relate to successful language learning outcomes? In order to explore these questions, the study reported in this chapter was undertaken using a questionnaire to gather data regarding students' error correction preferences which were then correlated with end-of-course scores to investigate whether any of the individual preferences were related to success in language learning. In addition, qualitative comments were gathered from the questionnaire forms and selected students were interviewed in order to explore individual perceptions. The chapter concludes by suggesting pedagogical implications of the findings and making suggestions for further research.

Z. Chunhong
Ti Yu Da Xue, Beijing Sports University, Beijing, China

C. Griffiths (✉)
Kim Il Sung University, Pyongyang, Korea
e-mail: carolgriffiths5@gmail.com

M. Pawlak (ed.), *New Perspectives on Individual Differences in Language Learning and Teaching*, Second Language Learning and Teaching,
DOI: 10.1007/978-3-642-20850-8_19, © Springer-Verlag Berlin Heidelberg 2012

1 Background

Questions surrounding the issue of error in language development have long been controversial. To this day there has been no generally accepted definition of exactly what an error is (Ellis and Barkhuizen 2005; Roberts and Griffiths 2008), or how precisely it is related to 'correct' or 'native' language (James 1998; Lennon 1991). Corder (1967) made a distinction between *errors* and *mistakes*, the former being a linguistic deviation resulting from lack of knowledge and the latter being a temporary slip which can often be self-corrected by learners themselves. Although this distinction can be useful for some purposes, in reality the dividing line between an error and a mistake as per Corder's definition is often far from clear, and frequently results in the two terms being used more or less synonymously, adding still further to the ongoing lack of definitional clarity.

However, the fact that error has been and remains so difficult to define has not inhibited firm views relating to them being promoted over the years. On the one hand, behaviourists viewed errors as bad habits which must be rigidly corrected to avoid fossilisation (Skinner 1957). On the other hand, building on Chomsky (1959) cognitive views of language development, Corder (1967) viewed errors as a sign of progress in the development of what Selinker (1972) termed the learner's *interlanguage*.

As for the role of error correction, this has varied from being seen negatively as a useless and even harmful waste of time from which learners do not benefit (for instance Krashen 1977; Truscott 1996). On the other hand, error correction is viewed positively as an essential part of the teacher's role from which learners are capable of learning (for instance McLaughlin et al. 1983; Ur 1996; Harmer 1998, 2001).

Corrective feedback is often categorised according to when it is provided, how it is provided, and who provides it. Questions regarding when it is given include:

- *Immediately or delayed*—should learners receive corrective feedback straight away after an error has been made or should feedback be left until some time later? Debate on this question includes the arguments that immediate feedback helps to avoid the danger of fossilisation, but interrupts communication; whereas delayed feedback allows communication to proceed but is less meaningful once the immediate error situation has passed.
- *Always or as appropriate*—should every single error be corrected without fail, or should it be left to a teacher's judgement to decide when feedback is appropriate given criteria such as learning or communicative purpose as well as individual student variables such as shyness and motivation?

Options regarding how corrective feedback should be dealt with include:

- *Directly or indirectly*—should the learner be informed directly of an error and of the correct form, or should the feedback be less obvious, for instance by means of a recast, such as:

Student: Does class start at 30 past 1?
Teacher: Yes, class starts at 1:30.

- *Publicly versus privately*—should corrective feedback be given in front of classmates or others or be given on a one-to-one basis? If given publicly, feedback can be immediate, and may also benefit others in the class, although it may threaten individual confidence and result in withdrawal and demotivation. If it is private, the realities of most classrooms dictate that feedback will be delayed, perhaps considerably so, thereby losing a lot of its impact; however, private feedback may be gentler on fragile egos.

As for who should carry out error correction, the options most commonly considered involve the teacher, a student's peers, or students correcting their own errors. Some of the issues involved here include:

- *Teacher-correction*—error correction is often considered to be one of a teacher's basic professional responsibilities, and is frequently expected by students and demanded by the learning institution. Teachers themselves, however, are often ambivalent about this area of their work, discouraged because they see the same errors being repeated again and again, even after many hours spent on corrective feedback. Because they often see such a low return on the time invested in error correction, teachers sometimes prefer to play down this aspect of their role.
- *Self-correction*—ideally, of course, students should be able to look over their own work and correct their own errors. The ability to do this reliably, however, pre-supposes a reasonably high level of proficiency, which is often not the case for students still developing knowledge of a new language. Furthermore, students often lack confidence or are unwilling to spend a lot of time on self-correction since they regard this as the teacher's job. Encouraging students to be more self-critical, however, may well be useful in terms of promoting autonomy, which has been shown to be a characteristic of good language learners (for instance, Cotterall 2008).
- *Peer-correction*—sometimes instead of, or in addition to, self-correction, students may be asked to correct each other's errors. The benefits of such an approach might include the possibility that students may learn from others' mistakes. The disadvantages, however, include the fact that students often regard each other's advice with suspicion, considering that they are no more likely to be correct than themselves. Nevertheless, peer correction can provide another avenue for consideration of error, and help to reduce teacher dependence.

As we can see, theorists and practitioners have many areas of disagreement about basic issues surrounding the concept of error and the place of error correction in language development. So, what about the learner? The fact is that, theoretical and practical controversies notwithstanding, the teaching and learning of language goes on in classrooms across the globe day after day, and teachers continue correcting 'errors' (however they may be defined, viewed or categorised) frequently oblivious to the controversy engendered. What, then, do individual students, that is those on the receiving end, think about error correction? What kinds of error correction do they find useful, or do they agree that it is unhelpful and a waste of time? When and how do they think their errors should be corrected, and who do they think should carry out this correction, if at all? Surely these are essential questions which are asked all too infrequently!

Griffiths and Zhou (2008) used a questionnaire based on the error correction types explained above to gather information regarding students' error correction preferences. These data were correlated with end-of-course scores to investigate whether any of the expressed preferences were related to success in language learning. They found that the highest mean preference was expressed for immediate correction of errors (mean = 4.53), with quite a strong average rating also being accorded to being corrected always (mean = 4.33). The lowest mean preference was for public correction (mean = 3.42), with a preference for direct correction scoring somewhat higher (mean = 4.32). As for who should carry out the correction, the strongest preference was clearly for the teacher (mean = 4.63), with peer-correction and self-correction rating considerably lower (mean = 3.95 and 3.87, respectively). Only a preference for immediate correction was significantly correlated (Spearman) with end-of-semester scores ($r = 0.242$, $p < 0.05$). In other words, those who did well on the course tended to rate immediate correction highly.

In addition to the quantitative data summarised above, qualitative comments were also gathered from the individual questionnaire forms and selected students were interviewed in order to further explore individual perceptions. These individual preferences were briefly reported in Griffiths and Zhou (2008) but they will be given more exemplification and further discussion in this chapter.

2 The Study

Conducted at a university in Beijing, China, the study involved 105 freshman English Major students who were asked to complete a questionnaire (see Appendix) regarding their error correction preferences. The students participating in the questionnaire were assembled and the questionnaire forms handed out, completed and returned during this time. The students were supervised by the authors, who explained the purpose of the research in both English and Chinese and answered any questions. Students were asked to rate seven types of error correction (immediate, always, direct, public, teacher, self, peer) according to their individual preferences on a 5-point Likert scale from 5 = strongly positive to 1 = strongly negative. Students were also encouraged to add any personal comments they might have about error correction types in the spaces provided.

At the end of the semester, after the final scores were available, the top five and the bottom five students were invited to a semi-structured interview and asked the following questions:

- How important is error correction for improving your English?
- Can you give details about types of error correction you like or do not like?
- Can you give reasons for your error correction preferences?
- Can you give examples of error corrections in class?
- How do you think error correction should be carried out?
- Which errors should be corrected?

In addition to statistical analysis of the quantitative data summarised in the background section of this paper (see Griffiths and Zhou 2008 for more detail), the students' comments which they added to the questionnaires as well as the interview data were examined for useful insights into individual differences in error correction preferences.

2.1 Results: Questionnaire Comments

Since the aggregated quantitative results from the questionnaires have been reported elsewhere (Griffiths and Zhou 2008) and summarised above, this report will elaborate on the qualitative comments added to the questionnaires and expand coverage of the interviews in order to further explore individual student perceptions regarding error correction practices.

It was clear from the questionnaire results that most students wanted their errors corrected immediately (mean = 4.53). Individual comments included:

> Errors corrected immediately can leave me a deep impression on my mind.
> If the error correction is delayed, the errors will be soon forgotten.
> Correcting my errors immediately can help me realize errors as soon as possible.
> I always can't discover my errors myself, so I need somebody to point them out immediately.

Some students saw immediate correction as a way to make rapid progress:

> Correct my errors immediately can help me improve my English a lot in a short time. It's efficient.

Others made comments which would seem to support the behaviourists' warnings about fossilisation:

> If errors not corrected immediately, when I am accustomed to the errors, it's hard to correct them.

Still others seemed to espouse a communicative philosophy:

> I prefer errors to be corrected immediately, but don't interrupt my speech, or I would forget what I'm going to say.
> Being corrected always was also given a reasonably high rating by the students (mean = 4.33).

Comments included:

> Of course faults should be corrected every time.
> The more, the better.

Others, however, were less positive about being always corrected:

> Every time may too many times. Some errors may be corrected but some may not.
> It'll discourage me and lose the interest about English.
> Will lose confidence.

Direct correction was also given a reasonably high rating by students (mean = 4.32):

> Correcting directly can let me make sure if I made mistakes, and I can correct it as soon as possible.
> I can remember the right answers profoundly.
> Only direct correction can make us know exactly what your error is.
> It's OK. Pointing out directly makes you an deep impression on it.
> It is a good way to correct my mistakes. Indirectly ways make me puzzled.

The least preferred error correction method was public correction (mean = 3.42). Students holding a negative attitude toward public correction considered that correcting their errors publicly could produce embarrassment, anger, inhibition, shame and feelings of inferiority and cause them to lose face, confidence and self-esteem. They wrote on their questionnaires:

> If I am corrected publicly everyone will stare at me, so I don't like it.
> It'll make me in trouble and have a little shame.
> I think it's impolite and it makes myself feel shameful.
> Maybe in public, we'll feel nervous about making a mistake, and if my errors to be corrected publicly many times, it'll destroy my confidence.

Some students regarded their errors as private and did not want them to become public knowledge:

> I don't want others to know my mistakes.
> I will feel a little shy and I think the teacher should correct me out of class.

Four out of 105 students, however, strongly approved of public correction and believed that although it made them lose face, public correction helped them keep their errors deep in mind and avoid repeated errors. Three of them commented:

> Error is not shameful. Knowing error but not correcting them is shameful.
> Enjoying losing face and then I can remember the mistake deeply.
> It may make me lose my face. But in this way, I can remember it deeply and may not forget forever.

The mean end-of-semester score of these four students was 90 points, less than the class average (91.53 points).

As to who should carry out the error correction (teacher, self and peers), most of the students preferred their teacher to correct their errors (mean = 4.63) because they strongly believed that their teacher was professional and experienced and possessed profound knowledge about the English language so their correction must be right and could be done in an appropriate way. Furthermore, they believed it is the teacher's responsibility to correct the students' errors. They commented:

> I think teacher has a wide knowledge and they could help me correct my errors and give
> me some useful advice.
> The teacher is very professional. They know English better than us and they are familiar
> with us.
> I think teacher ought to correct me. It's teacher's responsibility.
> Teachers have the most professional explanation about the mistakes you made.
> Teacher can correct me in a right way.
> It may seem powerful.
> Teacher is the most suitable person to correct our errors.

At the other end of the scale, the lowest rating was for self-correction (average = 3.87). As students commented on the questionnaire:

> I think finding mistakes by myself is difficult so I think it is not the best method for me to
> improve my English.
> How can I do it by myself? If I can I won't make the mistake! But maybe some mistakes
> we made are without consciousness.
> I often can't find my errors, if I can, I also don't know how to correct it.
> I don't think errors can be found immediately by myself.

The rating for peer-correction was only slightly higher (mean = 3.95) than for self-correction, although some students regarded correction by peers as useful:

> My peers is around me, they can always correct immediately.
> With helping others, your own oral English will be improved.
> We fell relaxed when our peers try to correct me, not as serious as teachers.
> I'd like to be corrected by everyone.

There were quite a few reservations about peer correction, however:

> Though my peers have different ideas, still I think they are not professional, I'd rather not
> to ask them for help.
> We are in the same level, so we can't point out all the errors.
> Sometimes I find they doesn't pronounce accurately, but I feel grateful for they would like
> to help me.
> I will listen to them, but not means I will accept the advises.

2.2 Results: Interviews

Without exception, all the students who were interviewed believed that error correction was important. As one interviewee unequivocally put it, 'error correction is very important, it's bad for me to make mistakes'. Furthermore, all interviewees were in agreement regarding the importance of immediate correction. They considered that delayed corrections would cause repeated errors and unconsciously form bad habits.

Although some of the interviewees claimed not to mind public correction, most were less confident. One of the students suggested error corrections should be done softly with a gentle attitude and humour and teachers should be careful about the students' self-esteem. Most of the interviewees did not mind being corrected by anybody but one regarded peers as unqualified. Another expressed lack of confidence with self-correction: 'but nobody tells me and I don't know how to correct them'.

When asked what errors should be corrected, most of the students answered that grammatical errors, pronunciation and vocabulary choice errors were most vital. Practical suggestions for how error correction should be carried out included that the teacher should note down grammar and vocabulary errors and discuss them later. For pronunciation, some suggested that students could use the pronunciation function on their electronic dictionaries.

3 Discussion

In spite of critics such as Krashen (for instance 1977) and Truscott (1996), the students in this study clearly indicated that they wanted to be corrected and felt that corrective feedback is important in order for them to make progress in their language development. Without this correction, they felt they were likely to make mistakes which they would not know how to correct and which might become fossilised.

Also emerging clearly from the data is the students' preference for immediate correction, which was found to be the only type of feedback positively correlated with successful course outcomes. Students prefer their errors to be corrected without delay so that they can recognize where they have gone wrong and avoid repeating their errors. It would seem logical that the strong preference expressed for immediate correction should also be matched by a relatively high score for being corrected always. Presumably, if students are confident that their errors are always corrected, they will feel more secure in the belief that future language output will be correct.

However, although students express a strong preference for immediate correction, their comments reveal that they may feel ashamed, embarrassed and stressed when corrected publicly. Of course, the reality of a classroom situation is that it is in fact impossible to correct students immediately without doing it in front of their classmates, but there is no indication in any of the comments, either on the questionnaires or in the interviews, that students are aware of this inconsistency or have any suggestions to make as to how it can be resolved. The four students who, against the general trend, supported public correction are interesting both in terms of their reasons (making a deep impression) and also considering that that their scores were below average. Might this suggest, perhaps, that public correction does not play a positive role in improving students' English competence, in spite of the fact that some students (perhaps masochistically?) give it a high rating—or maybe they just do not care and therefore do not have the same investment of pride as their more successful classmates. Direct correction is another category which was given a reasonably high preference rating. Presumably, direct correction is clear and unambiguous, and leaves the learner in no doubt about what is correct and what is not.

As to who should carry out the corrections, the qualitative data resulting from the interviews and the comments derived from the students' questionnaires showed that teachers were the most frequently preferred to carry out corrective feedback. These students regarded error correction as the teachers' responsibility and expected them to cope with it with good humour and a soft and gentle attitude which did not destroy the students' confidence and self-esteem. These findings accord with Harmer's (1998, 2001) observations that error correction is considered an indispensable part of the teacher's role which students expect to receive. Cathcart and Olsen (1976) also note that learners want to be corrected by their teachers and would like more correction than they are often provided with. The students' comments on the teachers' corrections also reveal strong confidence in their teachers and in their ability to give accurate, appropriate, professional and knowledgeable corrective feedback.

Students were much less positive, however, about self-correction and peer-correction. Although Van Lier (1988) suggests that self-correction is less likely than other types of correction to lead to a negative affective response, students obviously find it too difficult. Indeed, it is difficult to disagree with the student who argues that if s/he could correct the error him/herself, s/he would not have made the error in the first place! And although Ellis (1994) recommends that self-repair is more beneficial to acquisition than other-repairs, this study did not find a significant correlation between self-correction and end-of-semester results. Peer-correction was also given quite a low rating, and many of the comments indicated a low level of confidence in the reliability of corrective feedback provided by peers.

As for which errors should be corrected, perhaps predictably, students suggested that grammatical, vocabulary and pronunciation errors should be treated. Although at one time grammar and vocabulary were not seen as important components of a communicative approach, in more recent years, they have both been recognised for the part they have to play in language development (e.g. Bade 2008; Moir and Nation 2008). Likewise, although the teaching of 'correct' pronunciation can be problematic (e.g. Brown 2008), research seems to indicate that students are generally anxious to acquire what they perceive as 'good' pronunciation (e.g. Sokhieva 2005).

Regarding how errors might be corrected, of course, the student suggestion concerning noting grammar and vocabulary errors for later discussion contradicts the generally expressed preference for immediate feedback. Furthermore, how reliable a model of pronunciation provided by an electronic dictionary might be is probably open to question, but perhaps better than nothing.

4 Implications for the Teaching/Learning Situation

The clearest finding to emerge from this study is that students want to receive corrective feedback on their language output. They do not regard it as a waste of time. On the contrary, they regard correction as essential to their progress in language development. This would seem to indicate to teachers that correction should be seen as part of their professional responsibilities towards their students.

By far the strongest preference was expressed for immediate correction. Teachers should therefore make every effort to give feedback as quickly as possible. Although rapid marking of written work may not always be easy given a busy teaching schedule, teachers should be aware that delayed feedback lessens the effectiveness of the time they put in. Immediate feedback on errors needs to be tempered by the awareness that too much negative feedback may cause loss of confidence and embarrassment, and that, therefore, caution and sensitivity are required when giving public correction in order to avoid withdrawal and preserve motivation.

Although some strong arguments have been presented over the years for getting students to correct their own or their peers' errors, this study shows a clear preference for teacher correction, which is seen as authoritative and reliable. Perhaps this is not to suggest, however, that attempts to get students to correct their own or each other's errors should be totally abandoned. It is quite possible that, if students can be trained to examine their own language output more critically, they might well avoid many of the errors that they do in fact make. Evidence to support this possibility might be found in the often observed phenomenon that if students are presented with their own errors as an exercise, they are frequently perfectly capable of identifying and correcting what is wrong. Likewise, it is often possible for students to identify their peers' errors when they cannot correct their own, and that mutual learning might result from such an exercise. It would seem, nevertheless, that the main corrective feedback role remains with teachers who need, therefore, to equip themselves with the knowledge which may be required to perform this function well.

The suggestion regarding noting down errors of grammar and vocabulary and dealing with them later is, of course, a fairly standard technique commonly employed by many teachers. Although the feedback provided is not immediate, it can be put into practice fairly soon after the completion of an exercise and helps to remove the embarrassment associated with direct public correction as well as avoiding interrupting the flow of a communicative activity thereby compromising the development of fluency. In order to further alleviate potential negative affective response by students, teachers often disguise the details which would help to identify the student who made the error while leaving the actual error intact.

The value of electronic dictionaries is, of course, a much debated issue, along with issues regarding teacher pronunciation since teachers may display a wide variety of accents. Given the lack of consensus on this question, it is difficult to make any strong recommendation beyond suggesting that, when correcting pronunciation, teachers should remember that there is often more than one possible correct answer.

5 Questions for Further Research

The current study has produced some interesting findings regarding individual differences in error correction preferences, especially in relation to when correction should be carried out (that is, whether it should be immediate or delayed, always or as appropriate), how it should be conducted (that is, should it be public or private, direct or indirect) and who should provide the feedback (teacher, self or peers). Nevertheless, there remain a number of further avenues for useful research:

1. The current study was conducted among freshmen English Major students in a university in Beijing, China, a system which is generally considered traditional in its approach and authority oriented. Are the same results obtained from other students in different situations?
2. Do the findings of this study apply to students with other individual differences, for instance regarding age, gender or national/cultural background? Although this study did not consider error correction preferences in relation to individual variables such as personality, style, motivation, autonomy or strategy use, these could also form the basis of interesting research initiatives (for more discussion on these variables, see Griffiths 2008).
3. What useful teaching strategies can be developed for dealing with some of the problem areas highlighted by this research? For instance, how can public correction be done in such a way as not to reduce confidence and the willingness to participate? How can teacher dependence be reduced and student autonomy promoted?

6 Conclusion

Although the definition of error remains controversial and error correction is sometimes viewed as a waste of time or even harmful, the students in this study were in no doubt that corrective feedback is important to them. Although they do not like public correction, and expect this to be done gently and with good humour, they find immediate correction most useful, since this provides feedback while the error is still fresh in their minds and before it has developed into a habit which can be hard to break. The person from whom they most appreciate corrective feedback is their teacher, whom they generally regard as knowledgeable and authoritative; and in general they lacked confidence both in their own ability to locate errors and in the reliability of their peers to provide accurate corrective feedback.

Although questions regarding error remain hotly debated, the reality is that corrective feedback is practised in millions of classrooms the world over day after day and huge numbers of students are affected by the practice. The current article has looked at the issue mainly from the individual student's perspective. Although there were individual variations in preference for one type of corrective feedback or another, for when, how and by whom it should be done, at no stage was there any suggestion that students did not want to be corrected. On the contrary, students regarded correction of their errors as a basic area of teacher responsibility and essential if they were to make sound progress in their language development.

Appendix

A questionnaire on correction preferences
Please fill in the following form to indicate the ways you prefer your errors to be corrected. Please use the following scale: 5 = strongly positive, 4 = positive, 3 = neither positive nor negative, 2 = negative, and 1 = strongly negative.

I like my errors to be corrected	5	4	3	2	1	Comments
Immediately						
Directly						
Publicly						
Always						
By my teacher						
By myself						
By my peers						

References

Bade, M. 2008. Grammar and good language learners. In ed. C. Griffiths, 174–184.
Brown, A. 2008. Pronunciation and good language learners. In ed. C. Griffiths, 197–207.
Brown, H., C. Yorio, and R. Crymes, eds. 1977. *On TESOL' 77*. Washington: TESOL.
Cathcart, R., and J. Olsen. 1976. Teachers' and students' preferences for correction of classroom errors. In eds. J. Fanselow, and R. Crymes, 41–53.
Chomsky, N. 1959. Review of *Verbal behaviour* by B.F. Skinner. *Language* 35: 26–58.
Corder, S. 1967. The significance of learner errors. *International Review of Applied Linguistics* 5: 161–170.
Cotterall, S. 2008. Autonomy and good language learners. In ed. C. Griffiths, 110–120.
Ellis, R. 1994. *The study of second language acquisition*. Oxford: Oxford University Press.
Ellis, R., and G. Barkhuizen. 2005. *Analyzing learner language*. Oxford: Oxford University Press.
Fanselow, J., and R. Crymes, eds. 1975. *On TESOL'76*. Washington: TESOL.
Griffiths, C., ed. 2008. *Lessons from good language learners*. Cambridge: Cambridge University Press.
Griffiths, C., and C. Zhou. 2008. Researching error correction in China: Procedure, product and pitfalls. In ed. M. Pawlak, 127–137.
Harmer, J. 1998. *How to teach English*. London: Longman.
Harmer, J. 2001. *The practice of English language teaching*. 3rd ed. Harlow: Pearson Education.
James, C. 1998. *Errors in language learning and use*: *Exploring error analysis*. London: Longman.
Krashen, S. 1977. Some issues relating to the monitor model. In eds. H. Brown, C. Yorio, and R. Crymes, 144–158.

Lennon, P. 1991. Error: Some problems of definition, identification and distinction. *Applied Linguistics* 12: 180–196.

Major, J., and J. Howard, eds. 2005. *CLESOL 2004: Refereed conference proceedings of the 9th community languages and English for speakers of other languages conference (CD publication)*. Christchurch: CLESOL.

McLaughlin, B., T. Rossman, and B. McLeod. 1983. Second language learning: An information-processing perspective. *Language Learning* 33: 135–158.

Moir, J., and P. Nation. 2008. Vocabulary and good language learners. In ed. C. Griffiths, 159–173.

Pawlak, M., ed. 2008. *Investigating English language learning and teaching*. Poznań–Kalisz: Adam Mickiewicz University Press.

Roberts, M., and C. Griffiths. 2008. Error correction and good language learners. In ed. C. Griffiths, 282–293.

Selinker, L. 1972. Interlanguage. *International Review of Applied Linguistics* 10: 209–230.

Skinner, B. 1957. *Verbal behavior*. New York: Appleton-Century-Crofts.

Sokhieva, F. 2005. Pronunciation teaching through reflective pronunciation projects. In eds. J. Major, and J. Howard.

Truscott, J. 1996. The case against grammar correction in L2 writing classes. *Language Learning* 46: 327–369.

Ur, P. 1996. *A course in language teaching*. Cambridge: Cambridge University Press.

Van Lier, L. 1988. *The classroom and the language learner*. London: Longman.

Individual Differences in Dictionary Strategy Use

Luciana Pedrazzini and Andrea Nava

Abstract In the past 25 years there has been a flurry of interest in the complex nature of dictionary use, and researchers have devised taxonomies of strategies which aim to describe the process of looking up a word according to different purposes. Most research has focused on identifying and isolating specific strategies across large groups of users, with a view to validating existing taxonomies of dictionary use strategies. By contrast, there appears to be a paucity of research investigating the complexity and the interconnectedness of factors that have a bearing on the *individual user*'s strategic behaviour in dictionary use, which, we would like to argue, is only possible through an in-depth qualitative case study approach. This article reports on an exploratory case study which has involved three first-year Modern Languages students at three different levels of competence (ranging from B1 to B2). The three participants were asked to carry out four tasks for receptive and productive use of a monolingual dictionary (*Longman Dictionary of Contemporary English* 2003). In order to tap the participants' thought processes, we asked them to engage in concurrent verbalization. The experiment was video and audio recorded and the students' verbalizations were subsequently transcribed. Data analysis has shown how individual strategy use is correlated with each participant's English language proficiency and their degree of language awareness.

L. Pedrazzini (✉) · A. Nava
University of Milan, Milan, Italy
e-mail: luciana.pedrazzini@unimi.it

A. Nava
e-mail: andrea.nava@unimi.it

M. Pawlak (ed.), *New Perspectives on Individual Differences in Language Learning and Teaching*, Second Language Learning and Teaching, DOI: 10.1007/978-3-642-20850-8_20, © Springer-Verlag Berlin Heidelberg 2012

1 Introduction

Enquiry into the users and uses of learners' dictionaries had its starting point in the late 1970s and since then it has been conducted in several countries with different aims and methodology.[1] Research has highlighted the need to observe dictionary users as they actually apply specific look up skills (Neubach and Cohen 1988: 2). The results have singled out what can interestingly be defined as a 'paradox':

> On the one hand, there is the high value that users customarily place on their dictionaries—especially monolingual learners' dictionaries—and on the other the quite widespread ignorance of their structure, content, and possible functions (Cowie 1999: 182).

Several studies have shown evidence of "a wide gap between a student's perception of the dictionary's value and its actual usefulness as an aid to learning" (Cowie 1999: 184). In consideration of the complex nature of dictionary use, researchers have devised steps (Scholfield 1999) and taxonomies of strategies which aim to describe the process of looking up a word according to different purposes (e.g. Nesi 2003). Researchers have also focused on identifying and isolating specific skills or strategies across large groups of users, with a view to validating existing taxonomies of dictionary use strategies (e.g. Winkler 2001).

In contrast to most studies carried out so far, there appears to be a paucity of research investigating the complexity and the interconnectedness of factors that have a bearing on the *individual user's* strategic behaviour in dictionary use (Wingate 2004) which, we would like to argue, is only possible through an in-depth qualitative case study approach. This article reports on an exploratory case study which has aimed to identify the factors that impinge on individual differences in the use of a monolingual learner's dictionary by three first-year Modern Languages students at three different levels of competence (ranging from B1 to B2). In order to tap the participants' thought processes as they applied specific look up skills, we asked them to engage in concurrent verbalization, which was video and audio recorded and subsequently transcribed.

In the first part of the article we will briefly review the main areas of investigation into EFL learners' dictionary use and aspects of research methodology concerning methods of data collection. The second part will provide a critical overview of recent studies on dictionary strategy use. In the final part of the paper our exploratory study will be described and the main findings that emerged from data analysis will be illustrated and commented upon.

---

[1] See Nesi (2000), Humblé (2001), Hartmann (2003) for a review of the main studies on learners' dictionary use.

2 Research Into Dictionary Use: Some Methodological Issues

Studies on dictionary use can be described according to four main areas of investigation: (a) the specific categories of linguistic information perceived as important by particular groups of dictionary users; (b) the users' assumptions and expectations in using the dictionary; (c) the language activities in support of which a dictionary is used; (d) the reference skills which users have developed, or need to develop, to use their dictionaries more effectively, with the subsequent evaluation of the teaching programmes or aids designed to enhance these skills (Cowie 1999: 177).

In his review of the main methodological issues in dictionary user research, Tono (2003: 396) stresses the need for "a systematic study of the way in which various variables interact when dictionary users consult a dictionary which contains complex information". Dictionary use is generally recognized as a very complex cognitive process, being characterized "by a very personal intellectual experience, happening in a particular social and cultural setting which can be better understood by the interpretative perspective". For this reason, individual differences in look-up skills and habits are virtually impossible to investigate in large scale research, and it would then be suggested that

> in-depth study of the individual dictionary user as part of a small-scale research project can have special value if it is conducted by the researcher in such a way that it reveals micro-concepts such as individual perspectives, personal constructs, and definitions of situations in relation to dictionary use in a particular environment (Tono 2003: 401).

Nesi (2000: 3–56) tackles further aspects of research methodology analysing the main studies on dictionary use according to three methods of data collection, i.e. questionnaire, test and observation-based. She argues that, whereas in questionnaire-based research the results are often a measure of the respondents' perceptions, rather than an objective fact, test-based research tends to focus on the end-product of dictionary use. Similarly, Humblé (2001: 43–44) sees two main problems with the use of questionnaires: the first is due to the assumption that the subjects have a specific knowledge of linguistic concepts such as those used in questionnaires (e.g. do the subjects really know what an 'idiom' is?); the second might arise from the assumption that the participants are being honest (e.g. are they saying here what they do, or what they think they do?). Conversely, observation-based investigation is concerned with generating hypotheses, rather than testing them. As Nesi (2000: 53) explains, "it is ethnomethodological and holistic, because it sets out to observe natural dictionary use, rather than contrived behaviour taking place in a controlled experimental setting". Moreover, it is focused on the process by which results are achieved and tries to tap the possible causes of any unsatisfactory results highlighting the attitudes and strategies of dictionary users. Observation-based techniques can indeed be considered a very effective way to describe learner behaviour. As Tono (2003: 403) remarks, "their particular strength lies in their attention to the subtlety and complexity of the case in its own right".

Among observation-based techniques, retrospections (also called 'stimulated recall') by students and students' 'thinking aloud' protocols have frequently been used in research on dictionary use.[2] Both techniques require the verbalization of the student's thoughts in relation to a specific task and appear to be effective in clarifying the very nature of their cognitive processes providing unique insights into individual strategic behaviour.[3] Our particular interest in observing the different use of strategies in dictionary use (cf. *infra*) has made us consider think-aloud a particularly suitable method of data collection. One of the main advantages is that the participants are involved in the concurrent vocalization of their 'inner speech' without being asked for any analysis or explanation. In this way, the sequence of thoughts mediating the completion of a task is not interrupted or altered and should thus reflect the participant's cognitive processes. Since providing a think-aloud commentary is not a natural process, participants need some training to get them accustomed to thinking aloud. In addition to that, "it is vital that researchers give participants clear instructions that do not lead them to provide speculation on their metalinguistic reasoning" (Leow and Morgan-Short 2004: 37).[4] The resulting verbal protocol is then recorded, transcribed and analysed. According to Nesi (2000: 36), data analysis may indeed appear to be the most time-consuming stage, especially when we attempt to categorise look-up strategies that vary with each individual subject.

3 Research On Dictionary Strategy Use

Studies investigating the reference skills used by students while carrying out language tasks have revealed that subjects lack basic strategies for successful consultation and have emphasised the importance of training them to use the dictionary more effectively (among the most recent research studies, cf. Cowie 1999; Bishop 2000; Nesi 2000; Winkler 2001; Chi 2003; Nesi 2003; Wingate 2004). In this regard, Cowie (1999: 188) poses a fundamental question, that is "can we really be sure that performance errors are due to inadequate skills, rather than

---

[2] Cf. Nesi (2000) for a review of studies on the use of both the bilingual and the monolingual dictionary which have used the think-aloud techniques; cf. also Wingate (2004).

[3] Dörnyei (2007: 147) points out that the main difference between these two types of introspection lies in the timing: the retrospective interview or report happens after the task has been completed, whereas the think-aloud technique is applied real-time, concurrently to the examined task/process.

[4] Leow and Morgan-Short (2004: 37) address the issue of 'reactivity'—"the act of thinking aloud may trigger changes in learners' cognitive processes while performing the task" and conclude that the potential impact of reactivity in studies that employ concurrent verbalization procedures remains to be empirically tested in the Second Language Acquistion field.

deficiencies in the dictionaries used?" Most studies in his review seem to confirm that poor standards of retrieval can be wholly or largely due to low levels of skill. Moreover, the discrepancies in the levels of reference skills seem to be related to the type of task set rather than the individual level of language ability, especially when subjects are asked to deal with polysemous entries, compounds and collocations (Cowie 1999: 191). In a study carried out with intermediate university students Wingate (2004: 7–9) confirms the findings of previous studies and reports that the most common strategy across three dictionary types was "searching for an equivalent that could replace the unknown word in the reading text (...) but the scanning rarely went beyond the first or second meaning in long entries". A difference in strategy use according to the type of dictionary was that "the users of the bilingual dictionary were more inclined to give up the search if a suitable meaning could not be found immediately". Nesi (2000: 120), on the other hand, finds no significant difference between the groups using three different monolingual dictionaries, "regarding the number of words they looked up, the average time they took to read the dictionary entries, and the number of correct sentences they produced after look-up". Her findings seem to suggest that there is little difference in *intelligibility* between the different defining styles of the dictionary used. Humblé (2001) shifts his attention to the learners' difficulties in using a dictionary and calls for a qualitative type of research aimed at studying the processes involved in using the dictionary for decoding and encoding purposes and ascertaining what the precise users' needs are. This would encourage research to take a step forward in order to identify the necessary characteristics that would make the dictionary a better reference tool for learners.

Data on processes involved in dictionary use have been systematically categorised in taxonomies of reference skills which a university-level language student might need in order to use dictionaries effectively (Scholfield 1999; Nesi 2000; Nation 2001; Nesi 2003). These taxonomies have also been used in empirical studies which compare the use of different types of dictionaries by students of different language levels involved in different types of tasks.[5] For instance, Nesi (2003: 370–372) groups the dictionary skills in her taxonomy chronologically, that is representing the stages in the process of dictionary use, starting with the choice of which dictionary is available for consultation, moving on to the stages of locating and interpreting the information, and ending with the application and recording of dictionary information. Each stage includes a number of micro skills, giving an idea of the possible operations carried out before, during and after the consultation.

---

[5] For example, Bishop (2000) carried out research with students of the Open University with the aim of devising guidelines for using bilingual dictionaries; Winkler (2001) investigated how EFL learners use a learners' dictionary in book form and on CD-ROM; Nesi and Haill (2002) reported on an investigation into the dictionary-using habits of students at a British university over a period of three years; Wingate (2004) studied three groups of students using monolingual and bilingual dictionaries.

This type of taxonomy of dictionary skills can undoubtedly be a useful reference tool for carrying out a research study. However, the linearity and sequentiality of these micro-skills may not reflect accurately the complexity of the actual consultation process, which seems to require an integrated and simultaneous use of strategies (strategy cluster).[6] Data analysis in one of the first detailed studies on processing strategies in the use of dictionaries (Neubach and Cohen 1988: 6) indeed revealed "a variety of strategies and outcomes" both at the point when students were first confronted with the task and during and after the search. We should expect, for instance, that throughout the whole process of looking up a derived form, a learner will probably have to locate it first, interpret morphological information or any restrictive labels related to it; then he/she will also have to read and interpret the definition and derive some relevant information from examples; finally he/she will have to verify and apply the looked up information to the context of use provided by the task. These operations may not necessarily occur in a chronological or sequential order but are more likely to take place according to a sequence reflecting each learner's online decision taking and his or her cognitive and metacognitive processes. According to Macaro (2006: 328), there is some evidence that

> the orchestration of clusters of strategies, that is choosing and evaluating from a range of strategies, is more effective than linear deployment of several strategies. (…) In a dictionary cluster (…) metacognition would monitor and evaluate the cognitive strategies being deployed.

It is also worth considering that in most studies on dictionary use the terms *skill* and *strategy* tend to be used interchangeably, with some preference for *skill*, perhaps to highlight the 'practical' and 'operational' features of the consultation more than the 'cognitive' ones. The term *skill* also seems to imply that this specific ability can be acquired by the learner almost mechanically after some training and is aimed at a practical outcome, that is an efficient consultation. In this regard, Chi (2003: 355–356) argues that the ways to make reference tools more accessible, transparent and easy to understand and use, such as introductions or special sections to explain what the dictionary offers and how to look up words or separate dictionary workbooks to train users how to use the dictionary rely on the assumption that "users have the ability to take the initiative and are willing to practise the activities". As research findings have revealed, this assumption may be somehow 'optimistic'. In addition to that, we would argue that the term *skill* does not completely assume the potential aspects of strategic behaviour which may lead to a successful or an unsuccessful consultation:

> Even though checking a word in a dictionary is usually performed in a routine, largely mechanical manner, to think of research into the steps of dictionary use as dwelling on the

---

[6] With reference to the findings from studies within developmental psychology, Macaro (2006: 327) concludes that "for a strategy to be effective in promoting learning or improved performance, it must be combined with other strategies either simultaneously or in sequence, thus forming strategy clusters".

obvious is to give the lie to the complexity of the strategies involved (Szczepaniak 2003: 192).

As we will try to prove in the data analysis of our study (cf. *infra*), the deployment of an array of specific cognitive and metacognitive strategies required in dictionary consultation is also influenced by other relevant factors, such as the learners' mother tongue and culture, sex, their language ability, their general cognitive processing, their autonomy in learning, their motivation, their beliefs on the choice and usefulness of the dictionary itself.[7]

Finally, lists and taxonomies of skills or strategies in dictionary use do not seem to highlight sufficiently the key importance of those specific strategies which allow the learner to make the required connection between the choice and interpretation of the information in the entry and the specific requirements for the completion of a task. As Szczepaniak (2003: 193) points out, "context and dictionary are used in a back-and-forth way" to attain the aim of the look-up process, that is "to understand the information given in the chosen subentry, and somehow to combine this with the meaning of the text where the unknown was met" (Scholfield 1999: 28). Humblé (2001: 97) considers this issue from a different perspective suggesting that dictionaries should include specific sections in which the information is presented to the learner in different ways to facilitate either decoding or encoding.[8] This would help the learners identify the information in the entry just for decoding purposes, such as understanding the meaning of a word, without dealing necessarily with the burden of information which is more relevant to an encoding task, such as choosing the most appropriate word for a writing task. In order to respond to the learners' specific needs, he also makes a distinction between the possible problems encountered by beginners and by advanced learners in the decoding and encoding look up processes which would call for different ways of dealing with polysemy and collocation.

---

[7] Cf. Dörnyei (2005: 171) for a review of research in the area of learner variation in strategy use. Macaro (2006: 320–321) states that a body of evidence coming from learner strategy research has led scholars to make claims such as: (a) strategy use seems to correlate with different aspects of language learning success and motivation; (b) there are group and individual differences in learner strategy use; (c) learner strategy training can be effective if it is carried out over an extended period of time and if it includes a focus on metacognition.

[8] When decoding–reading–one is dealing with the meaning of a lexical item. An encoding learner needs more information than a decoding learner and the information is of a different nature. When encoding learners look up a word whose meaning they already know to some extent. They may want to confirm this meaning, but their main interest is usage, a combination of syntax and collocation (Humblé 2001: 63–66). Nation (2001: 283–288) suggests making a similar distinction in his dictionary skill taxonomy according to whether the dictionary is used for receptive use (with listening and reading) or for productive use (with speaking and writing).

4 The Study

4.1 Research Design and Methodology

The exploratory study which we are going to report on in the rest of the paper has grown out of the need we have as teachers of Modern Languages undergraduates in a large state university in Italy to make students aware of the range of existing EFL self-access materials and help them develop effective and efficient self-study skills (Pedrazzini and Nava 2008). Given that we are firmly committed to the philosophy that 'teaching begins with learning' (Larsen-Freeman 2008), i.e. pedagogic practice must be rooted in knowledge about learning processes, it was imperative that we found out more about our learners' processes of using a monolingual dictionary before awareness raising and strategy training programmes could be devised. The main research question that the study attempted to answer is as follows:

What factors impact on Italian EFL learners' choice of different strategies in using a monolingual learner's dictionary while they are carrying out vocabulary tasks?

Our overarching aim was not to come up with an inventory of dictionary use strategies (exhaustive taxonomies are available in the literature, as was pointed out earlier) but rather to try to shed some light on the factors that underlie the *variability* in dictionary use processes among Italian EFL learners.

The three participants of the study were Italian native speakers who had just completed their first year of a Modern Languages degree at the University of Milan. They had taken practical language improvement classes, but had not taken part in any dedicated dictionary use training programme. At the start of their degree, they had been placed into three levels of English proficiency (roughly corresponding to CEF levels B1, B1+, B2). Prior to the experiment, they were administered a questionnaire designed to collect information about their language learning background and experience in using monolingual and bilingual dictionaries.

During the experiment, the three participants were asked to carry out four tasks for receptive and productive use of a monolingual dictionary for EFL learners (*Longman Dictionary of Contemporary English* 2003). The Longman dictionary was chosen as it is widely available in Italy and often recommended in English courses in both secondary schools and universities. The four tasks were meant to target different aspects of vocabulary knowledge and use in context and had been designed according to the typical format of dictionary training activities found in existing dictionary workbooks. The first task targeted knowledge and use of polysemy. Participants were asked to complete a number of sentences, using adjectives which are synonyms of 'bad'

1. My son suffered a very _____ injury playing football.
2. She is a fairly _____ learner of languages.

In the second task, participants had to reconstruct collocational pairs featuring degree modifiers by selecting the correct option among three alternatives:

1. I'm sorry, I _____ forgot to pass your message on.
   fully hardly completely
2. I don't think you _____ appreciate how serious the situation is.
   fully strongly completely

The third task asked participants to discriminate among the different meanings and grammatical forms of a word ('limp'). They were provided with four sentences containing 'limp' and had to explain the meaning of this word as used in the specific contexts, and write other sentences in which 'limp' had similar meanings:

1. He limped slightly and looked tired.
2. His arms were hanging limply by the sides.

The final task focused participants on issues of grammatical accuracy and usage– they were supposed to edit a short text by spotting and correcting a mistake in each of the sentences that made up the text:

I wish speak to the manager. The service has been terrible.
First of all, I had troubles getting a menu at all.
Ten minutes after we'd arrived, we hadn't still been given a menu.

In carrying out the tasks, the participants were instructed to follow three steps:

1. Read the instructions and the text of the tasks.
2. Attempt the tasks without relying on the dictionary.
3. Use the monolingual dictionary provided.

In order for the researchers to tap the participants' thought processes, the subjects were asked to engage in concurrent verbalization. As was mentioned above, this is a technique which involves 'thinking aloud', in other words verbalizing one's thoughts the moment one is aware of them (Ericsson and Simon 1993). The 'think aloud' technique has been criticized for possibly distorting thinking processes, especially when participants are asked to verbalize their thoughts retrospectively, or in a language other than their first language, or when they are asked to analyze their thoughts as they report them. None of these demands were placed on the participants of this study, nor were any time constraints imposed.

To familiarise the participants with 'thinking aloud', a short training session was provided prior to the start of the actual experiment. The participants were given two activities to choose from according to their personal preference: an anagram and a partially-completed jigsaw puzzle; all three chose the jigsaw. The experiment was video and audio recorded and the students' verbalizations were subsequently transcribed.

Data analysis involved close reading of the verbal protocols and the development of cross-sectional indexing categories. The process of coding and classifying data was greatly enhanced by the use of existing taxonomies of dictionary use strategies, such as those developed by Nesi (2003) and Nation (2001). The findings that will be summarised and commented upon in the next section will chiefly refer to the participants' use of the monolingual dictionary in carrying out the first of the four tasks.

4.2 Findings: Using a Monolingual Dictionary

In order to contextualise the discussion of the findings related to our research question, we shall first provide brief profiles of each of the three participants in which we will highlight the types of dictionary use strategies they relied on at different stages of the experiment. We will then single out and comment on the factors that appear to have led to individual differences in the three participants' use of the dictionary.

4.2.1 Alessandra

Alessandra displayed the behaviour typical of a student at a low-intermediate (B1) level of competence who still has some difficulty in coping with a language task. The dictionary would have been a very useful resource to overcome some of her language problems if she had been able to draw upon sound dictionary use skills. However, the analysis of her performance showed that she tended to rely on the use of a limited number of strategies which were often of little help in tackling the tasks in the experiment.

Alessandra appeared to have great difficulty in decoding the input sentences from the tasks and thus constantly referred to the dictionary–she even checked the meanings of words she appeared to be familiar with. The effort required by this intense look up activity often resulted in her attention being diverted away from the tasks. To make sure she understood every single word from the tasks (and the dictionary), Alessandra also relied on L1 translation. This procedure proved to be a double-edged sword, as it led her to adopt a word-by-word decoding approach, which often caused her to ignore contextual information and to fail to grasp the specific meaning that a given word acquired in the context of the task input sentences. Alessandra was sometimes also misled by false friends (for example, she interpreted 'injury' as the equivalent of the Italian word 'ingiuria', which actually corresponds to the English 'abuse').

In carrying out the first task, Alessandra had no difficulty locating the main entry for the keyword ('bad'), but was not able to match the correct subentries with the different meanings of 'bad' embodied in the input sentences. She also failed to grasp the function of the 'signpost' labels which introduce the subentries in the Longman dictionary, and mistook them for synonyms of the headword. As a result, she produced unacceptable sentence completions:

She is fairly *no skill* learner of languages.
There was a *not good* smell coming from the drains.

It would appear that Alessandra resorted to what in the literature has been termed a *kidrule strategy*–the selection of familiar segments from the entry which are treated as equivalents for the target word.[9]

The analysis also highlighted the fact that Alessandra lacked awareness of the phenomenon of collocation. She did not view the sequences 'synonym of 'bad' + noun' as possible collocation patterns; as a consequence, although she often looked up the noun component of these sequences in the dictionary, she only did so at the decoding stage of the task–when her aim was to grasp the meaning of these words by interpreting the entry definitions. For example, if she had looked up 'injury' (from the first input sentence in task one: My son suffered a very _____ injury playing football) at the encoding stage of the task, she would have come across 'serious injury' in the Collocation box and just below more useful examples:

She was taken to hospital with *serious* head *injuries*.
He suffered *horrific injuries* in the attack.

4.2.2 Francesca

Francesca had an intermediate (B1+) level of English proficiency. While she did not refer to the dictionary as often as Alessandra did, like Alessandra she did not attempt the tasks on her own first, but went for the dictionary straightaway. She appeared to be quite good at finding her bearings within the entries but did not analyse each definition or example systematically—her typical approach was to focus on the first few options provided by the dictionary.

In carrying out the first task, she looked up 'bad' in the dictionary, bypassed the main entry information and homed in straightaway on the Word Focus box at the end of the entry, which she exploited to find synonyms to fill in the blanks in the task sentences. However, she seemed to have difficulty interpreting the information gleaned from the box and applying it to the task at hand. Indeed, while she showed awareness of the fact that words may often be polysemous, she did not seem to have cognizance of the phenomenon of collocation. As a result, she selected synonyms on the basis of her familiarity with some of the items, their resemblance to Italian words and a vague 'feel for the language'. She was quite happy to rely on these hunches and did not carry out further dictionary searches to test her hypotheses. For instance, she selected the adjective 'awful' to complete the first sentence in task one: 'My son suffered a very *awful* injury playing football',

---

[9] This strategy was originally described in a study carried out with 10–11-year old children by Miller and Gildea (1987) in order to discover the kinds of mistakes native speakers of English attending schools in the United States make when looking up words. A detailed description of this study can be found in Nesi (2000: 42–46).

justifying her choice with the comment that it 'sounded right' to her. It could be argued that Francesca made 'sham use' of the dictionary (Müllich 1990; Nesi 2000: 40). This involves a "failure on the part of users to assimilate new and unexpected dictionary information"–learners only read enough of the entry to confirm a preconceived idea and take a final decision simply on the grounds of personal association.

In addition to having little awareness of collocational features of words, Francesca often failed to identify the correct grammatical class of the items in the tasks and did not seem to be aware of the fact that grammatical information is provided systematically for each headword in the Longman dictionary. As a consequence, she was often led down the garden path in her dictionary searches– an example is when, having failed to pick up on the fact that 'slightly' is an adverb, she associated it with the headword for the verb 'slight' and the definition 'to offend someone by treating them rudely or without respect'.

4.2.3 Roberta

Roberta was the most proficient (B2) English speaker of the three participants and also appeared to be the most adept at making good use of the dictionary. While the other two participants chiefly relied on the dictionary to decode unfamiliar words, Roberta appeared to be aware of a wider range of possible uses of this tool. She moved back-and-forth from the task to the dictionary, adapting her look up strategies to the different stages of the process of solving the tasks. However, as required by the task instructions, Roberta always tried to tap her knowledge of the language and apply it to the tasks before resorting to the dictionary. Although she never explicitly referred to the notion of collocation, she developed her own theory that words that share some semantic features tend to have the same collocates. Hence, she came across the collocation 'serious accident' in the dictionary and concluded that 'serious' might be the correct synonym of 'bad' to put in the sentence 'My son suffered a very _____ injury playing football' as 'injury' is semantically related to 'accident'. She thus displayed an implicit awareness of the phenomenon of collocation. Roberta's heuristics was not, however, always applied systematically. Indeed, Roberta sometimes fell back on the same strategies employed by the two less proficient participants–in one case, she used one of the 'signposts' in the entry for 'bad' as a synonym and produced the sentence 'She is a fairly *not good* learner'.

4.2.4 Discussion

Having sketched a profile of the three participants, we would like to return to our research question: what main factors led to individual differences in the partici- pants' dictionary use strategies? The factors that we will consider are intrinsic to the participants (their level of English proficiency and their degree of general language awareness) or reside in the dictionary itself (e.g. whether information on collocations was featured in the entries).

The first factor that emerged as significant was the participants' level of general English proficiency. Indeed, data analysis showed that the higher the participants' mastery of English, the more sophisticated was their use of the dictionary. While Alessandra and Francesca chiefly viewed the dictionary as a decoding tool, Roberta, the participant with the highest level of English, used it during both the decoding and the encoding stage of the tasks. Alessandra spent a considerable amount of time decoding the input from the tasks, resorting to the same general look up approach throughout the four tasks: she painstakingly went through the entry information in a sequential order, often translating both the task input and the definition and examples from the dictionary. By contrast, Roberta had no problems decoding the input and was more selective in the way she sifted through the information in the dictionary. It could be argued that as Alessandra had to use her attentional resources to carry out the rather low-level input decoding process, she had little attentional space left to devote to higher order metacognitive processes needed to manage dictionary use effectively and efficiently.

Another factor that may have accounted for individual differences in dictionary use strategies was the degree of general language awareness, e.g. metalinguistic awareness, that the participants possessed. Lack of awareness of the phenomenon of collocations led Alessandra and Francesca to focus their dictionary searches on one only of the items in collocational pairs, thus diminishing their chances of successfully reconstructing the pairs. Likewise, Francesca's difficulty in pin-pointing the grammatical class of some of the words in the task input not only hampered her decoding of it but also caused her to waste valuable time in her dictionary look up process. Unlike the other two participants, Roberta appeared to have implicit awareness of collocation; as was mentioned above, she used this awareness to devise a heuristics which enabled her to draw analogies between collocations in the dictionary examples and those in the tasks. This strategy was not, however, applied consistently. It could be hypothesised that if Roberta had possessed explicit awareness of the nature and workings of collocation, she might have deployed her strategic competence more systematically.

Data analysis also seemed to suggest that personality factors may have had a bearing on the participants' strategic behaviour. However, as no standardised measure of the participants' personality traits was undertaken, the remarks that will be made here should be viewed as 'hunches' and avenues for possible future investigation. One possible feature of the participants' personality that appeared to have contributed to individual differences in dictionary use was their willingness (or lack thereof) to take risks and to cope with uncertainty. Both Francesca and Roberta were often happy to rely upon their 'feel for the language' and thus carried out a significantly lower number of dictionary searches than Alessandra. However, unlike Roberta, Francesca obviously still had serious shortcomings in her English proficiency–although she admitted that she was not sure about the use of some of the words, she sometimes decided not to seek help from the dictionary but rather made do with her partial knowledge. One factor that led Francesca to restrict her use of the dictionary might arguably have been an overall (personality-related) risk-taking aptitude, although, as was pointed out earlier, given that no objective measure of the participants' personality traits is available, this hypothesis remains unverified.

The final factor that we would like to comment on is not intrinsic to the participants themselves but relates to the dictionary. Some features of the dictionary that was used in the experiment appeared to hinder rather than facilitate dictionary use for some of the participants. For example, given her relatively low-level English proficiency, Alessandra was routinely sidetracked by the 'signposts' which introduce subentries in the Longman dictionary. Their aim is to provide a shortcut to the different meanings and uses of the headwords; however, the fact that they feature different types of information (synonyms, labels for semantic fields etc.) proved confusing for a relatively inexperienced English user like Alessandra, and led her to undertake a laborious process of analysis of subentry definitions and examples.

Although the inclusion of information about synonyms and antonyms is an important breakthrough of recent pedagogical lexicography, this information appears to be of little use if it is not provided in tandem with information about collocational patterns. The Word focus box for 'bad' in the Longman dictionary only provides register labels for synonyms which are too general for learners to be able to discriminate their different uses. This shortcoming caused the participants who had little awareness of the collocational nature of language to often fall back on translation, and select those options which bore resemblance to Italian words.

5 Conclusion

Initial findings from our study have confirmed that dictionary use implies a very complex process in which various variables interact during the consultation. Recent insights into language learning strategies have highlighted some key features which may provide theoretical support to future developments in dictionary use research. A change in perspective has taken place:

> (…) strategic learning is a far more complex issue than thought before and therefore simply focusing on the surface 'manifestations'—i.e. the tactics and techniques that strategic learners actually employ—does not do the topic justice (Dörnyei 2005: 195).

Focus has thus shifted from the *product* (strategies) to the *process* in order to show learners' actual "strategic efforts to manage their own achievement through specific beliefs and processes". These mechanisms are more related to what has been defined as *self-regulation*, that is "a multidimensional construct, including cognitive, metacognitive, motivational, behavioural, and environmental processes" (Dörnyei 2005: 191). In this light, future investigations into dictionary use may reveal more effectively the interplay of individual difference factors in relation to a number of "integrated and interrelated microprocesses", such as "strategic planning, monitoring and metacognition, strategic tactics and operations, outcome expectations, goal orientation, evaluation and self-reflection" (Dörnyei 2005: 192). This will be possible mainly through observation-based research, particularly techniques which require the verbalization of the student's thoughts in relation to a specific dictionary task.

Although the study was limited in scope, it has provided some evidence of the importance of systematic dictionary use training. Language proficiency beyond an intermediate level appears to be a necessary but not *sufficient* condition for effective dictionary use. Indeed, despite being more confident than the other participants in interpreting and using the dictionary information, Roberta, by far the most proficient English speaker, was not always consistent in the way she deployed her strategic knowledge. This finding is in keeping with recent research into expertise in language learning and teaching. According to this research, what characterises experienced non-expert skill users is a degree of haphazardness in performing the skill effectively and efficiently (Johnson 2002, 2008). Roberta, albeit the most experienced dictionary user of the three participants, was nevertheless not yet an 'expert' and would therefore probably benefit–alongside the other participants–from focused dictionary use training. Dictionary training, however, is unlikely to prove effective if it is not conducted alongside a general language awareness raising programme. As was pointed out earlier, many of the problems the participants of our study came up against in using the dictionary whilst carrying out the tasks stemmed from their low degree of metalinguistic knowledge.

The study has also shown that deployment of strategic competence may also be hindered by deficiencies in the structure of the dictionary entry and the wording of definitions which, in spite of the degree of sophistication pedagogical lexicography has achieved in recent years, still appear to characterize existing monolingual learner's dictionaries.

References

Beaven, B., ed. 2008. *IATEFL 2007 Aberdeen Conference Selection*. Canterbury: IATEFL.
Bishop, G. 2000. Developing learner strategies in the use of dictionaries as a productive language learning tool. *Language Learning* 22: 58–62.
Chi, A. 2003. Teaching dictionary skills in the classroom. In ed. R.R.K. Hartmann, 355–369.
Cowie, A. 1999. *English dictionaries for foreign learners. A history*. Oxford: Clarendon Press.
Dörnyei, Z. 2005. *The psychology of the language learner*. Mahwah: Lawrence Erlbaum.
Dörnyei, Z. 2007. *Research methods in applied linguistics*. Oxford: Oxford University Press.
Ericsson, K., and H. Simon. 1993. *Protocol analysis: Verbal reports as data* (revised edition). Cambridge: MIT Press.
Hartmann, R.R.K., ed. 2003. *Lexicography. Critical concepts*. 1 vols. London: Routledge.
Humblé, P. 2001. *Dictionaries and language learners*. Frankfurt: Haag and Herchen.
Johnson, K. 2002. *Designing language teaching tasks*. London: Palgrave Macmillan.

Johnson, K., ed. 2008. *Expertise in second language learning and teaching*. London: Palgrave Macmillan.

Larsen-Freeman, D. 2008. Teaching begins with learning. Paper presented at the University of Milan, April 14.

Leow, R., and K. Morgan-Short. 2004. To think aloud or not to think aloud: The issue of reactivity in SLA research methodology. *Studies in Second Language Acquisition* 26: 35–57.

Macaro, E. 2006. Strategies for language learning and for language use: Revising the theoretical framework. *Modern Language Journal* 90: 320–337.

Miller, G.A., and P.M. Gildea. 1987. How children learn words. *Scientific American* 257: 94–99.

Müllich, H. 1990. *Die Definition ist blöd!' Herübersetzen mit dem einsprachigen Wörterbuch. Das französische und englische Lernerwörterbuch in der Hand der deutschen Schüler*. Tübingen: Max Niemeyer.

Nation, I.S.P. 2001. *Learning vocabulary in another language*. Cambridge: Cambridge University Press.

Nesi, H. 2000. *The use and abuse of EFL dictionaries*. Tübingen: Max Niemeyer.

Nesi, H. 2003. The specification of dictionary reference skills in higher education. In ed. R.R.K. Hartmann, 370–393.

Nesi, H., and R. Haill. 2002. A study of dictionary use by international students at a British university. *International Journal of Lexicography* 15: 277–305.

Neubach, A., and A.D. Cohen. 1988. Processing strategies and problems encountered in the use of dictionaries. *Journal of the Dictionary Society of North America* 10: 1–19.

Pedrazzini, L., and A. Nava. 2008. How do they actually use the dictionary? In ed. B. Beaven, 183–185.

Scholfield, P. 1999. Dictionary use in reception. *International Journal of Lexicography* 12: 13–34.

Szczepaniak, R. 2003. What users do with dictionaries in situation of comprehension deficit: An empirical study. *Studia Anglica Posnaniensia* 39: 191–232.

Tono, Y. 2003. Research on dictionary use: Methodological considerations. In ed. R.R.K. Hartmann, 394–412.

Wingate, U. 2004. Dictionary use—the need to teach strategies. *Language Learning* 29: 5–11.

Winkler, B. 2001. Students working with an English learners' dictionary on CD-Rom. *Papers from the ITMELT 2001 Conference*.

Part V
Learners with Special Needs in Foreign Language Education

Gifted Visually Impaired Children Learning Foreign Languages

Małgorzata Jedynak

Abstract Giftedness and visual impairment may seem to be the concepts standing in opposition. The former is considered positive exceptionality while the latter refers to some form of disability. However, regardless of a disability, giftedness is a unique characteristic that may appear in every individual. There is an agreement among the researchers that there is a genetic factor that determines giftedness (Begley 2003). Yet, it has not been discovered to what extent the factor may be modified and how important it is (Recent research has identified at least five genes that occur more frequently in people with high IQ score, however, it is still not known how these genes affect performance (Begley 2003)). An impact of environment has not been completely rejected and there is an ongoing debate on the superiority of nurture over nature The child's early pre-school experiences may make the difference between 'bright/talented' and 'gifted', regardless the child's disability. A visual impairment is undoubtedly a factor that needs to be considered while comparing the ability development of sighted and blind children. Thus, the application of the same framework for giftedness comparison analysis cannot be put in place. There is a need to work out a separate framework for visually impaired children learning foreign languages who follow a different path to ability mastery. The paper discusses giftedness as a single exceptionality, its perception by foreign language classroom teachers and a distinction between giftedness and talent. Then it explores the combined characteristics of visual impairment and giftedness, gives the screening checklist for measuring linguistic giftedness in visually impaired learners. It closes with the recommendations for foreign language teachers on nurturing environment that should value individual differences.

M. Jedynak (✉)
Institue of English Studies, University of Wrocław, Wrocław, Poland
e-mail: gosiajedynak@poczta.onet.pl

M. Pawlak (ed.), *New Perspectives on Individual Differences in Language Learning and Teaching*, Second Language Learning and Teaching, DOI: 10.1007/978-3-642-20850-8_21, © Springer-Verlag Berlin Heidelberg 2012

1 The Concept of Giftedness

1.1 Characteristics of Giftedness

The researchers agree upon the point that giftedness is determined by genes (Begley 2003). Early in the twentieth century, giftedness was considered an equivalent of high intelligence described as intelligence score above 130. Psychologists measured a general ability, but in fact they were measuring how a person applied what he had learned. Such an approach could not satisfy all the people since it did not account for original brilliance of Thomas Edison or Albert Einstein who were not successful in school. Thus, a definition of giftedness needed to be modified. Marland (1972) describes a government-sponsored study aimed at examining a status of gifted learners in public schools. Only four percent of them had special programs designed by schools. Marland's study offers a definition of giftedness that may be treated as a model. Gifted children are those identified by professionally qualified people who, by virtue of outstanding abilities, are capable of high performance. They also require the differentiated educational programs and services beyond those normally provided by the regular school program in order to realize their contribution to self and society. Marland (1972) outlined six main areas in which children may demonstrate their giftedness:

1. General intellectual ability.
2. Specific academic aptitude.
3. Creative or productive thinking.
4. Leadership ability.
5. Visual and performing arts.
6. Psychomotor ability.

As we can see, giftedness in Marland's division is not just restricted to intellectual ability. The areas he identified have been broadened even further by Gardner (1993) who put forward a term of multiple intelligences.[1] It is worth noticing that the above characteristics of giftedness may also apply to visually impaired child learners.

Munro (2002) provided important insights into the learning process of gifted learners. Table 1 presents a comparative analysis of the learning process in gifted and other students. Renzulli (1986), in turn, made an attempt to identify the processes associated with giftedness. He defined giftedness as the product of three interacting clusters of traits that can be applied to any area of human potential: above average intellectual ability, high levels of creativity and high levels of task

---

[1] Gardner (1993) refers in his book to linguistic, logical/mathematical, visual/spatial, musical/ rhyming, bodily/kinesthetic, interpersonal, intrapersonal, and naturalist intelligence. Goleman (1995) added yet one more kind of intelligence: emotional intelligence based on the new theories about how the human brain works.

Table 1 Learning new ideas in gifted and other students (Munro 2002: 2)

Learning new ideas most students	Gifted students
Need a challenge or reason for learning they: – differ in their motivation to learn: whether they are self-motivated or motivated by others; motivation to learn ranges from extrinsic to intrinsic; – differ in their motives for learning; their purpose can be to: (1) reproduce or memorize information (superficial or shallow motives), (2) take ideas apart (deep motives), (3) learn ideas to satisfy external criteria, get good marks (achieving motive).	*Need a challenge or reason for learning* they: – learn well by having their knowledge challenged, by being able to frame up questions that they pursue; – are more likely to show intrinsic motivation to learn; they resist extrinsic motivational orientation; – are more likely to show deep motives for learning, to want to take ideas apart, question and extend them by linking with what they know; they often resist learning for superficial or achieving motives.
Need to know where they will end up – need to be assisted to see the goals.	– learn well by forming an impression of where they will end up, see their goals.
Make links with and use what they know about topic – they link the information with what they know about a topic in different ways by: (1) talking to themselves about the ideas, build ideas in linguistic ways, (2) thinking scientifically about the information, (3) forming images or mental pictures about the information, (4) thinking of the key actions and using this to learn; – differ in how fast and efficiently they handle information; – differ in what they know about how to learn, how to think, their thinking or learning strategies; – use what they feel about themselves as learners of the ideas (self-efficacy); – identify what they do not know about the topic; – recode what they know to match the teaching.	– can have superior existing knowledge of a topic that is better differentiated and elaborated in a range of forms: (1) verbal, abstract, semantic form (verbally gifted), (2) imagery, experiential form (visual spatial gifted), (3) scientific-mathematical form (scientifically gifted), (4) musical form; – learn in idiosyncratic ways; they are often not easily programmed externally and need to align what they know with teaching; – process information faster and efficiently, show cognitive efficiency, e.g. memory span, show higher efficacy in elementary processes that determine more complex processes; – are curious, good at questioning a topic or the ideas they will learn about; – need to have the opportunity to recode what they know to match the teaching; – often set unrealistically high standards and goals for themselves.

commitment. At this stage, it is worth making a distinction between giftedness and talent since the two terms are frequently confused.

After having analyzed how gifted students learn, it is useful to look at how they develop intellectually as it allows for their early identification. Gifted children differ qualitatively in how they develop thinking. The order of stages is consistent, but they organize their knowledge differently. They move through stages faster (Lempers et al. 1987; Hix 1990) of up to two years (Carter 1985). Moderate and highly gifted children do not differ in speed and can do at least one formal operations task by age nine or ten. In formal operations gifted learners show domain specificity.

An interesting issue to be considered is a discussion about giftedness is metacognition. It describes how students become responsible learners regulating their own learning and performance. According to Borkowski (1996), self-regulation is the highest level of metacognitive activity. It includes monitoring or self-checking, planning or goal-setting, and attending and rehearsing. Gifted learners use self-regulatory strategies such as defining, focusing, persisting, guiding, copying, correcting, reinforcing and solving.

1.2 Giftedness Versus Talent

At a brainstorm activity with the students of English Studies Department, the participants were not always successful in listing the features that are typical of *gifted* and *talented or bright learners*.[2] According to Munro (2002: 23), an operational definition that differentiates between gifted and talented learners is following: talented learners are these who display exceptional creative ability in areas in which they have been explicitly taught while gifted learners also possess this ability but in areas in which they have not been explicitly taught. In other words, the term giftedness is used to refer to natural abilities that have not been developed or shaped by educational processes (the aptitudes or gifts). The term talent, in turn, refers to the superior mastery of abilities or skills of knowledge that have been developed through educative processes, to a level that can be described as superior.

In order to classify a child as a gifted or talented learner one needs to define a term of creative ability. For Munro (2002) an outcome of thinking is creative when it shows high level understanding, rather than low level interpretation or application, the person has taken the ideas apart. It also shows novel connections between ideas and a person solves problems in unusual or novel ways.

1.3 Teachers' Beliefs About Giftedness

Munro (2002: 1) noticed that classroom teachers frequently have inappropriate beliefs about gifted learners and their learning process. This, in turn, has an impact on the way they recognize these learners and teach them. The stereotypes held by some teachers do not reflect the diversity of giftedness and do not make a distinction between giftedness and talent. They also do not take into consideration how gifted students operate in a classroom setting and how they actually learn.

---

[2] The students were requested to categorize the features of giftedness and talent in two columns. The task turned out to be difficult as the students confused the two terms.

Thus, there is a need for classroom teachers to extend their knowledge on how to teach the gifted learner. The teaching process should include differentiation and elaboration of regular topics, allowing the gifted learning processes to evolve. The latter refers to enhancing students' intrinsic motivation. Teachers should know a range of curriculum and pedagogic options available to them and the situations in which they may apply each solution, i.e. when to use vertical knowledge extension and accelerate the learning process and when to use horizontal broadening introducing more background related to a discussed concept.

Munro (2002: 1) also mentions the need of 'programming' that includes helping gifted students to be 'programmed' by teachers in a way that is based on meaning rather than rote and to pave the programming themselves. The ability of providing specific feedback to these students is also stressed. Feedback should not be based on making comparisons with other peers. Effective feedback should target the knowledge that is in place and challenge further learning through open-ended questions. Teachers of gifted learners should also possess the knowledge on how to advise and counsel both the students and their parents. Counseling helps them understand and use exceptionality to advantage. Gifted learning capacities are related to a social and cultural context. Teachers' task should be to make gifted learners understand in what way their exceptionality may influence interactions with other peers, help them learn in a group and deal with worries about cultural issues (cf. Munro 2000: 2).

2 Issues Relevant to Gifted Visually Impaired Learners

2.1 Giftedness and Disability

According to the Education for All Handicapped Act (1975) or in any of the ensuring amendments that function in the United States, giftedness is not regarded as 'handicap' (Bishop 2004: 166). Therefore, children who were diagnosed to be gifted in some way are not eligible for special education unless they also have some additional disability. Special education service is only available to children with physical/sensory, intellectual, emotional deficits, or in the case of very young children, some forms of delays. Probably by default, many books on disabilities list giftedness among multiple disabilities. It may be due to the fact that there appears no other place to put it. One may usually find a brief paragraph about it and is directed to other sources for further information.

Giftedness is a characteristic that may co-exist with other characteristics or disabilities. Fetzer (2000): 44 noticed that there might be a correlation between giftedness and learning disability. In his article he posed a question "What do Albert Einstein, Thomas Edison, Leonardo DaVinci, Walt Disney, Whoopi Goldberg, Lindsay Wagner, and Robin Williams have in common? All are reported to have learning disabilities." A question that arises here is whether giftedness may be observed in children who are visually impaired and whose cognitive abilities are restrained by the total lack of vision.[3] Since the number of gifted children is small no research has been done on how to provide optimal learning opportunities to the gifted blind children.

Having considered that giftedness may be observed only in two percent of the school population (cf. Johnsen 1986; Johnsen and Corn 1989) and visual impairment is present in about .1 percent of children one may conclude that a group of children with both exceptionalities is very small. The teachers working in the school for the visually impaired recall some gifted children, though in their teaching career these learners were definitely exceptional cases.[4] In Johnsen's studies the blind children suffering from retinoblastoma were found to have a very high level of intelligence.[5] They were reported to have exceptional spatial perception skills despite having no eyes.[6]

2.2 Problems with Identification of Giftedness in Visually Impaired Learners

Though Marland's definition of giftedness gives the main characteristics of the gifted children, it is difficult to identify learners who are born gifted and visually impaired. Frequently, the children who display dual exceptionalities tend to go unidentified due to three reasons:

1. Teachers and parents focus more on visual impairment than on the child's giftedness.
2. Some visually impaired children may also have other disabilities such as a disability to learn. They are often considered underachievers in one domain and their giftedness in other areas tends to remain unidentified.
3. In some visually impaired children their giftedness tends to be unidentified because they are expected to function at a grade level and not to surpass other peers in a classroom.

Professionals involved in the assessment of such learners need to be skilled in identifying giftedness that may be masked in some individuals. In the identification process an assessor should gather evidence of giftedness by collecting data

---

[3] Throughout the paper I will use the term *visually impaired learner* or *visually impaired child* to refer to his/her total lack of vision.

[4] One of the teachers working in the school for the visually impaired children remembers a fifteen year old learner who was a polyglot. He knew five languages almost at a native-like level though he was given formal instruction only in two of them. He was also perceived as a mathematical genius. At the age of ten he managed to learn on his own how to play the piano.

[5] Retinoblastoma is a tumor of the eyes.

[6] It may be presumed that these unusual perception skills are related to the brain's ability to retrieve visual information committed to memory before enucleating.

in various areas. The evidence should show that a given learner displays academic aptitude and superior achievement, probably in areas outside of school, superior cognitive or reasoning ability, creative or productive thinking in areas of interest, and finally high level of intrinsic motivation to learn in areas of interest. A problematic issue related to identification of gifted learners is that they are not always prepared to display their knowledge. It is even more problematic with visually impaired learners who may be inhibited and less likely to show their outstanding abilities. Thus, a diagnostician should have an extensive knowledge on testing such learners to optimize the chance that they provide him with the evidence for their exceptionality. A diagnostician should, for instance, apply interactive/dynamic evaluation for identification. In this approach the individual's knowledge in one area is assessed while supporting his knowledge in other areas. The role of an examiner is to assist the learner to do assessment tasks and to take note of all the conditions under which the learner's ability to display knowledge is facilitated. The effects of misdiagnosis can be severe for learners. If they are left unidentified or misdiagnosed that may be provided with inappropriate instruction by teachers. As a consequence, the gifted visually impaired learner may become alienated from education.

There are no universally accepted procedures of giftedness identification for visually impaired children, especially those under the age of six. What can be found in the literature are developmental scales based on sighted norms. Such scales do not necessarily refer to any characteristics of giftedness. Furthermore, in early childhood there may be no signs of giftedness as it is still in its formative period. One may assume that despite the absence of vision characteristics of giftedness are universal, on condition there are no other disabilities.

2.3 Screening Checklist for Giftedness in Foreign Language Learning

In order to categorize a learner one needs a valid and reliable test to support the pupil's giftedness. Johnson (1987) and Bishop (2004) describe screening tests that may be used for visually impaired children; however, they do not refer to these signs of giftedness that a pupil may display in the area of foreign language learning. During my teaching practice in the school for the blind, I identified a congenitally blind twelve-year-old student who appeared to be very bright at English.[7] Although he was never taught any learning or communication strategies, he managed perfectly to apply them in practice. Other teachers recognized his outstanding problem-solving skills, especially in science. There was a need to design some objective tools to evaluate the boy's abilities. For the purpose of my

---

[7] The boy lost his vision at the sixteen months after a vaccination. At present he attends the residential school for the blind children in Wrocław, Poland.

study I developed a checklist relevant to giftedness in foreign language learning. I also collected different types of data: observations, interviews with the subject, achievement test scores obtained from his English teacher and grade transcripts to make sure that the procedures or sequence of data collection will be as neutral as possible. The checklist below includes the possible indicators of giftedness in visually impaired children learning foreign languages. Three types of responses may emerge in the course of the procedure: a given behavior may never occur, occasionally, or frequently which is an indicator of characteristic giftedness.

1. The child displays a high level of curiosity; the child wants to know 'how' and 'why' L2 is used.
2. The child originates many ideas from one stimulus.
3. The child's responses in a foreign language are original.
4. The child displays high analytical skills; the child compares L1 to L2, notices similarities and differences.
5. The child uses a foreign language appropriately and meaningfully.
6. The child has advanced L2 vocabulary for age and grade level.
7. The child understands multiple word uses and plays on words both in his/her native language and a foreign language.
8. The child responds to explanations better than orders.
9. The child becomes impatient when a teacher's explanation is confusing and vague.
10. The child is a perfectionist, gets annoyed when he cannot get a right lexical or grammatical item.
11. The child may prefer the company of adults (teachers, parents, older children) to peers.
12. The child has a highly developed imaginary world. It may be often noticed in a role-play activity (very difficult to achieve by the blind learners).
13. The child has the ability to concentrate intensely when an activity is of interest.
14. The child is sensorily sensitive; the child may have preferences and dislikes for specific L2 sounds, phrases, sentences, intonation.
15. The child may become fixated on a specific topic, usually acquires a high level of knowledge about the target language, its customs and culture. One may have an impression as if he/she lived in the world related to his/her interests (e.g. American baseball, the British royal family).
16. The child memorizes L2 words exceptionally quickly.
17. The child displays quick mastery and recall of facts.
18. The child represents accelerated academic achievement in a foreign language in relation to peers.
19. The child's scores are in average or high average against sighted peers learning the same material.
20. The child wants to be independent while doing a task.
21. The child is opened to new activities introduced by a teacher; wants to try new things such as new technologies for the blind learning foreign languages.

22. The child becomes very excited about learning a foreign language; perceives learning as being fun.

The procedure described allowed me to identify eighteen out of all the points included in the checklist. At the interview conducted both in Polish and in a foreign language, namely English, the twelve year old boy turned out to be self-confident and outspoken. With his knowledge on many topics related to the English culture, his advanced and sophisticated vocabulary he would undoubtedly surpass many sighted peers of his age. In his quest for knowledge related to the target language he had never been guided by his mother or anyone from a family. His portfolio accessed by the tutor provides evidence for his exceptionality. The boy was involved in various projects with the counterparts from other schools for the blind in Norway and Great Britain. He acted as a translator for teachers and participated in language contests. By means of the same screening checklist the author diagnosed other children in the school for the blind. In the two groups of twelve and thirteen year olds none of the learners scored more than five points.

2.4 Implications for Teachers and Parents of Gifted Visually Impaired Children

The gifted visually impaired learners have been in public and residential schools. If they are early and properly identified by screening checklists and other procedures mentioned above, and consequently a special approach is taken towards them, they may achieve success in a foreign language. This success may guarantee a visually impaired person an access to various professions such as a foreign language teacher or a simultaneous interpreter. Much responsibility lies in a teacher who should focus on those skills that will enable the visually impaired student to access the gifted curriculum. Among these are communication skills including Braille if indicated and the use of technology. The teacher of the visually impaired student can help him/her become his/her own advocate, and introduce the techniques in a classroom that facilitate the student's ability to solve problems and make decisions independently.

Bishop (2004): 174 made a point that there are two layers of the provision of services to visually impaired students that may be gifted. The first one is called 'growing the potential' and applies to preschool children. The boy described in Sect. 2.3 would probably never be identified as a gifted foreign language learner but for different experiences in his early childhood that provided opportunities for giftedness development. Kay (2000): 293, in Bishop (2004) calls these children 'at promise' as opposed to the negative 'at risk'. Since even an infant or a toddler may have a potential to be gifted in one way or another, it is essential to intervene at the right time. Many visually impaired infants and toddlers can reach the developmental milestones on time or within a normal range if they are provided with early intervention. The children, who are visually impaired and gifted at the same time, are even more likely to achieve all the milestones normally as they usually have a high level of motivation. The second layer mentioned by Bishop (2004): 174 refers to 'realizing the potential' of the visually impaired child to make it develop. School-aged children present a special challenge. Many schools do not have gifted programs since that are not required by law to have them. These programs that exist only provide opportunities for acceleration and advanced studies. In practice, they include some extra work that is assigned to the gifted students to make them occupied in a class. However, the gifted visually impaired student needs more than extra work to keep him involved in the learning process.

A well designed gifted program should offer more than a creative learning opportunity. It should value individual differences and pay attention to learning styles. Moreover, it should concentrate on the learner's individual potential and encourage compensatory learning strategies. Corn (1986) noticed that good gifted programs often provide career exposure, mentors, and leadership opportunities.

It seems advisable for the foreign language teacher who teaches gifted visually impaired children to answer the following questions prior to program development:

1. How does the child learn (specific learning processes he/she implements)?
2. What does the child learn (his/her learning outcome)?
3. Why does the child learn (learning style and characteristics of his/her motivation)?
4. What are the child's interpersonal interactions during learning (cultural influences on learning)?
5. What is his/her self-perception and self-efficacy as learners?
6. What is the comparative rate of development of his/her knowledge overall?

Having answered all these questions, the teacher is ready to develop the individualized learning/teaching program implementing various techniques enhancing the linguistic giftedness in the visually impaired learner. Table 2 presents some guidelines for the language teachers on how to approach and develop the gifted behavior in a classroom.

3 Final Thoughts

As has been pointed out above, one can identify the characteristics of giftedness in both sighted and visually impaired learners, though different screening checklists need to be applied. There are still many questions related to gifted learners that are left without answers. Do gifted sighted and visually impaired learners differ in the use of learning strategies? or Do parents of gifted learners model and foster metacognitive strategies more than parents of normal ability children especially during problem solving?

Table 2 Guidelines for language teachers teaching gifted visually impaired learners (based on Munro 2000: 3)

Guidelines	How to do it? What to say?
Help learners understand their giftedness	– not all children need to learn in the same way, though some people may think they should; – they may be strong in some areas but not in others; – some peers may not understand what they know or say.
Encourage learners' pursuit for knowledge	– help them deal with boredom and disengagement from learning; – help them see open-ended aspects of the ideas; – make up games involving the ideas; – encourage them to teach you about the ideas; – provide opportunities for the self-driven aspects of pursuing knowledge; – encourage self-selection of learning materials; – foster interest in problem solving contexts e.g. climate change; – help them communicate with similar minded students using the Internet; – involve them in situations outside of regular school e.g. pen pals with native speakers.
Help learners extend and integrate their knowledge	– teach them ways of researching topics of interest; – let them investigate real problems in everyday life; – help them see tasks as open-ended challenges; – provide suitable role models for learning e.g. mentors.
Help learners manage their learning effectively	– let them use their independence in functional ways; – present ideas as challenges or problems; – give them time to operate independently; – teach them to improve how they learn.
Help them improve their social interaction skills	– point to common things they have with peers; – learn various ways of showing their peers what they know in acceptable ways; – learn the skills necessary for joining in peer group activities; – understand that not all children think in the same way; – set up situations in which they engage in group problem-solving and sharing activities.

References

Begley, S. 2003. Light cast on darkling gene. *Discover* 8: 85–96.

Bishop, V. 2004. *Teaching visually impaired children.* Springfield: Charles Thomas Publisher Ltd.

Borkowski, J.G. 1996. Metacognition: Theory or chapter heading? *Learning and Individual Differences* 8: 391–402.

Carter, K.R. 1985. Cognitive development of intellectually gifted: A Piagetian perspective. *Roeper Review* 7: 180–184.

Corn, A. 1986. Gifted students who have a visual handicap: Can we meet their educational needs? *Education of the Visually Handicapped* 18: 71–84.

Fetzer, E.A. 2000. The gifted/learning disabled child: A guide for teachers and parents. *Gifted Child Today* 23: 44–53.

Gardner, H. 1993. *Frames of mind: The theory of multiple intelligences*. New York: Bantam Books.

Goleman, D. 1995. *Emotional intelligence*. New York: Bantam Books.

Hix, B.O. 1990. The relationship between the conservation response and giftedness in first grade children. An educational field problem research project report. Unpublished masters thesis, Mercer university. ERIC Document Reproduction Service No. ED 3222689.

Johnsen, S. 1986. Who are the gifted? A dilemma in search of a solution. *Education of the Visually Handicapped* 18: 54–70.

Johnsen, S., and A. Corn. 1989. The past, present, and future of education for gifted children with sensory and/or physical disabilities. *Roeper Review* 12: 13–23.

Johnson, L. 1987. Teaching the visually impaired gifted youngster. *Journal of Visual Impairment and Blindness* 81: 51–52.

Kay, K., ed. 2000. *Uniquely gifted: Identifying and meeting the needs of the twice exceptional student*. NH: Avocus Publishing Inc.

Lempersm, J., L. Block, M. Scott, and D. Draper. 1987. The relationship between psychometric brightness and cognitive development precocity in gifted preschoolers. *Merrill Palmer Quarterly* 38: 489–503.

Marland, S. 1972. *Education and the gifted and talented*. Washington: Commission.

Munro, J. 2000. Understanding and identifying gifted learning disabled students. http://www.edfac.unimelb.edu.au/eldi/selage/documents/GLT- Defininggiftedness.pdf.

Munro, J. 2002. How gifted students learn: Mapping research into effective teaching. Article available online. http://www.edfac.unimelb.edu.au/eldi/selage/documents/glmodel-Howgiftedstud.pdf.

Renzulli, J.S. 1986. The three-ring conception of giftedness: A developmental model for creative productivity. In eds. R.J. Sternberg, and J.E. Davidson, 53–92.

Sternberg, R.J., and J.E. Davidson, eds. 1986. *Conceptions of giftedness*. Cambridge: Cambridge University Press.

Individual Differences in Language Learners with Dyslexia

Joanna Nijakowska

Abstract Developmental dyslexia is defined as a lifelong difficulty in processing linguistic information, marked with noticeable inter- and intra-difference with regard to behavioral facets. It has been described as a learning disability—specific difficulty in acquiring the ability to read and spell. This neurodevelopmental condition can be best understood when perceived from a dimensional rather than categorical perspective, in that way the view of dyslexia as a delay or a difference is promoted. Thus reading ability can be illustrated in a form of a continuum, indicating the existence of substantial individual differences. In comparison with their non-dyslexic peers learners with dyslexia can be expected to occupy rather the bottom end of this continuum. However, the way dyslexia leaves its imprint on behavior considerably varies across individuals. Differences between students with dyslexia manifest themselves in the range (various sets and constellations of behavioral manifestations—symptoms) and intensity of difficulties. In addition, throughout life symptoms of dyslexia observable in a given person undergo dynamic changes under the influence of education, effectiveness of therapeutic activities, and efficiency of compensatory strategies. Thus some features of dyslexia alter with age—characteristic symptoms tend to be evident but then can diminish or disappear at given points in development, while other difficulties can prevail into adulthood. The article discusses the most characteristic behavioral manifestations of dyslexia and their dynamic character.

J. Nijakowska (✉)
Chair of Pragmatics, University of Łódź, Łódź, Poland
e-mail: jnijak@wp.pl

M. Pawlak (ed.), *New Perspectives on Individual Differences in Language Learning and Teaching*, Second Language Learning and Teaching, DOI: 10.1007/978-3-642-20850-8_22, © Springer-Verlag Berlin Heidelberg 2012

1 Background

Developmental dyslexia is as a lifetime and chronic difficulty in processing linguistic information. It has been classically defined as a learning disability,[1] specific language-based disorder constitutional in origin and characterized by problems in single word decoding usually stemming from insufficient phonological processing. These specific difficulties in learning to read and spell do not result from generalized developmental disability or sensory impairment and can be perceived as surprising and unexpected with reference to age as well as cognitive and academic abilities. This discrepancy between potential and scholastic achievement is often evident in individuals with dyslexia. Conventional methods of teaching literacy skills which prove effective as relates to other individuals do not seem to bring equally satisfying results in the cases of students with dyslexia, who, at the same time considerably frequently prove to be talented high-achievers in other academic disciplines (Bogdanowicz 1999; Reid 1998).

Researching a neurodevelopmental disorder such as dyslexia invites application of a developmental perspective. Such an approach entails comparing a typical development of a reading skill with the way learners with dyslexia acquire it. In this way, perceived from a dimensional standpoint, dyslexia can be described as a delay or a difference (rather than a deficit or a disorder) in reading development, while reading ability as such can be illustrated in a form of continuum, which naturally implies the existence of considerable variability and individual differences in the skill development. The intensity and range of dyslexic difficulties would vary and learners with dyslexia would occupy different points more towards the bottom end of the proposed continuum. Despite an obvious difficulty to specify an arbitrary cut-off point on the continuum after reaching which one would qualify to be diagnosed to have dyslexia, categorical descriptions of the disorder are commonly used as well (Hulme and Snowling 2009).

Understanding dyslexia in dimensional terms and viewing it as a delay in development of the reading skill modifies the way we look at the improvement. Improvement and development are dynamic processes characterised by change and can be operationalised as the movement up along the continuum. This naturally brings about alterations in the way dyslexia manifests itself in behavior. Particular symptoms are usually observable at the beginning of formal reading instruction and later get reduced or can disappear completely. This does not mean that the underlying problem (usually poor phonological processing) vanishes (Frith 2008). Other signs, for instance spelling difficulty, more persistently prevail into adulthood. It is important to note that symptoms of dyslexia change in the course

---

[1] In recent publications and educational discourse regarding dyslexia and other specific learning differences (SpLDs) (e.g. dyspraxia, dyscalculia, ADHD, Asperger syndrome) the term *learning difference* is promoted over the terms *learning disability* or *disorder*. It is stressed that individuals with SpLDs should be treated as different rather than deficient with regard to certain skills and abilities (Kormos and Smith, in press).

of time and development, however one never grows out of dyslexia. As a result of compensation activities and learning one can become able to successfully deal with the formerly problematic tasks and move up along the continuum of the reading ability. This is where the categorical labels (*having* or *not having dyslexia*) become questionable, while a dimensional description offers a more plausible explanation. Namely, dyslexia constitutes as a life-long condition, marked with noticeable inter- and intra-difference with regard to behavioral facets.

The most characteristic symptom of dyslexia is the fundamental difficulty in the acquisition of skilful word decoding (reading) and encoding (spelling), causing that individuals with dyslexia tend to lag behind their peers with reference to literacy development. Children with dyslexia experience selective difficulty in language processing, with phonological awareness constituting a major area of difference. Dyslexic phonological representations of speech sounds, necessary for skilful spoken word recognition and production, are of poor quality, they tend to be inaccurately specified and indistinct (Goswami 2000; Snowling 2001). Learning to read requires grasping the relations between the spelling patterns and their pronunciations (the alphabetic principle)—an ability to map letter strings of printed words (orthography) on phonemic sequences that spoken words are built of (phonology). Children with dyslexia have noticeable trouble in establishing these connections as well as in generalizing their knowledge in order to read unfamiliar words (Lundberg and Hoien 2001; Snowling 2001).

It is worth noting here that qualitative differences in literacy acquisition are dependent to a great extent on the orthographic system (degree of consistency in mapping letters onto sounds) (Davies et al. 2007; Seymour et al. 2003). Typical, model course of development of a reading skill differs across languages, especially with regard to early reading strategies, and so do the predictors of reading success and behavioral manifestations (symptoms) of dyslexia (Bogdanowicz and Krasowicz-Kupis 2005; Krasowicz-Kupis and Bryant 2004; Sochacka 2004). The more transparent the sound-letter mapping system of a language, the fewer difficulties it poses on individuals with dyslexia learning to read in it, irrespective of the fact whether it is a native, a second or a foreign language (Goswami 2000; Hanley et al. 2004; Lundberg 2002; Reid and Fawcett 2004; Snowling and Caravolas 2007; Wimmer 1993; Ziegler et al. 2003). Students with dyslexia would most probably find Italian, Spanish, Greek or Turkish easier to learn than for example English or French. In shallow orthographic systems phonological deficit is less apparent and dyslexic difficulties concern mainly the speed of word identification and text processing (Vellutino et al. 2004).

A plausible bond between problems with native language learning and difficulties in foreign language study has been put forward. Successful foreign language learning draws on intact language skills and foreign language acquisition will be blocked by any physiological or biological deterrents that handicap the learning of one's native language, as it is in the case of dyslexia (Sparks et al. 1995, 2006). Strong native language competence fosters foreign language acquisition, while poor native language codes can considerably impede the degree of proficiency in a foreign language. The underlying core phonological deficit, responsible for a delay in reading development in one's native language, substantially influences acquisition of any consecutive languages. Phonological awareness and phonological processing abilities are believed to be transferred between languages. It means that the level of phonological competence in one language, native or foreign, can be useful in predicting individual differences as regards an ability to recognize words in both languages. This knowledge seems especially important when diagnosis towards reading difficulties is attempted in children from multilingual and multicultural backgrounds (Geva 2000).

Similarly to the reading ability, foreign language competence should be perceived from a dimensional rather than categorical perspective (*knows* or *does not know* a foreign language). Foreign language ability can be represented on a continuum, with foreign language learning difficulties ranging from mild to severe. Most students with dyslexia can be expected to occupy the bottom part—the more severe end of the continuum. The placement would depend on the type and severity of the disorder (strength of the phonological skills in particular) and the characteristics of the phonological/orthographic system of a language (Sparks 2001, 2006; Sparks et al. 2003, 2008). It can be assumed that some students with dyslexia are well capable of achieving average and above average results in foreign language study (even though most of them would most probably demonstrate varying degrees of difficulty), while others, despite undeniable progress, would still slightly lag behind their peers who do not have dyslexia (Nijakowska 2008, 2010; Sparks and Miller 2000).

Dyslexia can be characterized by multitude of behavioral manifestations and impressive variance as to the areas of difficulty and strength across individuals. Students with dyslexia demonstrate diversified sets or clusters of difficulties. There exist substantial individual differences as relates to the ease and pace of acquisition of the ability to read and spell in the native and consecutive languages in students with dyslexia. These differences manifest themselves in various constellations of behavioral manifestations which undergo dynamic changes over time throughout one's life and determine the placement on the continuum of the reading ability. The remaining part of the article is devoted to specifying the symptoms considered to be characteristic for different developmental stages.

2 Lifelong Character of Dyslexia

Dyslexia is a lifetime condition, thus individuals qualified to have dyslexia experience specific difficulties in print processing in childhood through their adolescent years into adulthood (Downey et al. 2000; Gregg et al. 2005; Oren and Breznitz 2005). Behavioral facets of dyslexia vary across individuals and substantial inter- and intra-individual variance makes the overall picture of dyslexia quite complex (Krasowicz-Kupis 2008). In addition, throughout life symptoms of dyslexia manifest in a given individual change dynamically under the influence of education, effectiveness of therapeutic activities, and efficiency of compensatory strategies. Thus some signs of dyslexia alter with age—characteristic features tend to be evident but then can diminish or disappear at given points in development, while other disorders prevail into adulthood (Bogdanowicz 1999; Snowling 2001).

The most fundamental symptom of dyslexia seems to be a pronounced and persistent difficulty in the acquisition of skilful word decoding (reading) and encoding (spelling). Decoding and encoding are interrelated, they can be collectively perceived as print processing or mechanical aspect of reading and spelling ability (Szczerbiński 2007). Reading difficulties are frequently accompanied by poor spelling. Phonological processing disorders, by definition, constitute a characteristic trait of dyslexia, while linguistic functioning with reference to syntactic, semantic or pragmatic levels may well be within average. All the other symptoms associated with dyslexia discussed in the following sections have been reported to exist in some individuals with dyslexia, so they can, but by no means have to, go along with basic reading impairment. These symptoms may form manifold diversified sets specific to each child. Moreover, their intensity varies as well (Krasowicz-Kupis 2008).

2.1 Risk for Dyslexia

Multiple areas of weakness and warning signs, which to certain extent foreshadow specific difficulties in learning to read and spell, can be identified in children before or at the beginning of their school education (Bogdanowicz 2002; Johnson et al. 2001; Ott 1997). Poor performance identified in post-infantile and pre-school stages with reference to late development of speech, poor phonological skills or late development of motor ability indicates the risk for dyslexia and considerably high probability of later learning difficulties (Bogdanowicz 2002; Ott 1997). Children with these early signs frequently demonstrate isolated difficulties in learning to read and spell with the commencement of school education and formal literacy instruction.

Children with hereditary transmission—coming from families with history of dyslexia (Snowling et al. 2007), children from pathological pregnancy and delivery as well as prematurely born, children showing speech delay, ambidextrousness or left-handedness, and partial/fragmentary disorders of psychomotor development belong to the group of children at risk for dyslexia. Pupils who might not have explicitly demonstrated any signs of developmental delay in very young age but immediately with the onset of formal instruction they clearly begin to experience intensified difficulties in literacy acquisition qualify to the at risk group (Bogdanowicz 2002).

Characteristic signs have been described and organized into detailed inventories by several authors (Bogdanowicz 1999, 2002, 2003; Bogdanowicz and Adryjanek 2004; Ott 1997; Tomaszewska 2001). The more of the symptoms listed below one observes in a particular child, the greater the likelihood of the risk for the learning difficulties. Attention of caretakers should focus on the following spheres of child development and activity: language functions and speech, sequencing (including both visual and auditory sequential memory), fine and gross motor skills, visual functions and visual-motor coordination, orientation in body schemata, space and time, and, last but not least, reading and spelling competence. Failure in noticing, recognizing and reacting to unusual, poor performance of young children within these areas may result in far-reaching consequences as regards their educational careers.

As already indicated, individual differences among regular readers as well as children with dyslexia can be, to a considerable extent, explained by the level of adeptness in phonological processing. Children with dyslexia face marked difficulties in the ability to form phonological representations before they make a start with reading instruction and they are disadvantaged in comparison to normally developing children, since their representations are much less specified and stable (Snowling 2000). As a result also their ability to map orthography on phonology can be hindered. Language impairment can be manifest in several ways, for example, late development of speech, word-naming problems, word mispronunciations, jumbling words, difficulties with rhyme and alliteration, and also poor use of syntax (inappropriate word order and ungrammatical forms). Other problematic aspects include poor memorization of nursery rhymes, short poems and songs, below-standard aptitude to repeat messages and follow a series of instructions, and a tendency to use circumlocutions. Toughness in remembering names and common sequences (e.g. the alphabet, days of the week, months of the year) and retrieving them from memory is also unexceptional. Sound discrimination and manipulation, including blending, sequencing, adding, and deleting tasks usually poses tangible hardness as well.

Enduring below-standard abilities to decode words, encountered at the beginning of school education, qualify as symptoms of the risk for dyslexia. Reading tends to be slow, laborious and so time-consuming that even if accuracy approaches acceptable standards, comprehension habitually gets limited. A commonly observed behavior is a tendency towards skipping certain fragments, repeating lines, and loosing a place in the text. What is more, instead of being properly read (decoded) words are often guessed drawing on the first letter, syllable or an overall appearance of a word, or substituted with a semantic counterpart ('was' for 'lived,' 'car' for 'bus'). Unsurprisingly, decoding seems to be rather tiresome, it involves a great deal of time and arrests most attention, which altogether results in possible comprehension hurdle. In addition, reading is often characterized by noticeably awkward intonation.

As regards spelling ability, some young learners at risk for dyslexia routinely commit numerous mistakes in rewriting and dictation; they continually find it difficult, in comparison to other children, to remember and properly distinguish between the language sounds and their corresponding graphic symbols—letters. At times they also use mirror images of letters and often write down words awkwardly, for instance in reverse direction—from the right to the left. Omission, insertion, displacement, condensation, rotation, reversal, substitution, and guessing typically constitute types of errors which are principally committed by children with dyslexia in reading and spelling (Kaja 2001; Levinson 1980; Ott 1997). Thus, letters, parts of words, syllables, and whole words are often omitted or inappropriately inserted. Bizarrely, skipped elements can resurface in distant parts of the same sentence and letters or syllables of successive words can be condensed and read as new words. Handwriting can be hardly legible and full of corrections, while rate of writing tends to be uncommonly slow.

Poor automatisation (Fawcett and Nicolson 1999, 2001, 2004) of gross motor skills (arms and legs) also constitutes symptomatic behavior and involves lack of a crawling stage, awkwardness in keeping balance, laboriousness in hopping, catching, throwing or kicking a ball, frequent bumping into people and objects, knocking things over or dropping them, struggling to learn to ride a bicycle, to swim or to dance. Consequently, playground games may cause problems, which can be additionally intensified by the use of commands such as left/right, up/down, backwards/forwards, in front of/behind. Poor co-ordination when climbing ropes, standing on one leg or walking along the bench are yet another signs. Late development of fine motor skills (fingers and hands) leads to low dexterity in using cutlery, scissors, rubber, tracing, dressing up, tying up shoe laces, buttoning a shirt, manipulating small objects (building blocks), and, last but not least, drawing and writing (due to an awkward grip of a pencil).

Disorders of visual function and visual-motor coordination concern poor grapho-motor activity, difficulty arranging building blocks or puzzles according to a given pattern and drawing. In addition, poor ability to remember letter shapes, to distinguish between similar shapes (geometric figures or letters, e.g. m-n, l-t) or letters of similar shape but different position in space (p-d-g-b), low graphic level of drawings and written work as well as mirror writing are frequently observable. Children at risk for dyslexia may experience problems in orientation in body schemata and space, they often become confused when discriminating right from left, moreover, they can exhibit low-level orientation in time (yesterday, tomorrow, later, earlier) and poor concentration.

2.2 Symptoms of Dyslexia in Older Individuals

Certain symptoms described above with regard to younger children are no longer apparent in older individuals—learners of higher grades of primary school, secondary school students and adults—but some other difficulties invariably persist. In addition, new areas of difficulty, for example, problems in foreign language learning or in undertaking sports with success may emerge. Other problematic domains include geography (reading maps; directions), arithmetic, geometry, chemistry, music (musical notation), biology (complex terminology) or history (dates, names, chronology), to mention just a few.

Considerably frequently intensified reading difficulties largely attenuate and what consistently remains unchanged is a slow rate of reading and generally negative attitude towards the activity of reading as such. Still, intensity, types and prevalence of reading errors would certainly depend on the orthographic depth of a given language and adopted reading strategies (Ziegler and Goswami 2005, 2006). It appears that the strategy of inferring meaning from contextual cues facilitates high-standard reading comprehension in some adult dyslexic readers. While, rather poor accuracy still seems to prevail in single word and pseudo-word decoding. It is a commonly observed fact that even though reading accuracy gains of students with dyslexia indeed get greater as they progress in school, they continually show low-grade reading and spelling fluency. In fact, college students with and without dyslexia can be best discriminated between by reading fluency level (Gregg et al. 2005).

Generally, among adults with dyslexia there are readers who, despite intensified difficulties experienced during literacy acquisition, are capable of achieving average and above-average reading proficiency and they access higher education facilities with ease. However, cases of individuals whose compensation mechanisms did not prevent failure in developing sufficient reading skills are not rare. Their educational careers are frequently hampered by substantial struggle in adapting to common formal schooling requirements. Still, even those adults who demonstrate comparatively high reading performance because they managed to compensate for their dyslexic difficulties are characterized by relatively stable cognitive profile, with predominant phonological processing difficulties. The phonological representations they demonstrate often prove inadequate and forming new ones does not come without considerable effort as well (Snowling and Nation 1997).

Similarly to reading, the number of specific spelling mistakes such as, for example, additions, deletions or substitutions of parts of words, or reversals may slightly diminish with age and education, however, reiterative orthographic mistakes (difficulty choosing appropriate spelling choice for a given sound, being especially discernable in deep orthographies) notably prevail. Telling apart similar sounds and writing dictations remains a demanding task both in terms of recognizing individual sounds in the right sequence as well as applying the phoneme–grapheme conversion rules.

The most frequently observed categories of spelling errors involve three types. First, a given spelling trial is phonologically incorrect—the phonological structure of a word is disturbed, thus also the corresponding orthographic mapping is inaccurate for the targeted word. Second, a spelling attempt is phonologically accurate but orthographically inappropriate; it can be decoded and the phonological structure of a word is maintained, however the choice of sound-to-letter mappings is incorrect (e.g. 'rein' for 'rain,' 'eeg' for 'egg'). The final category of spelling errors involves skipping tiny elements, such as diacritical marks, or confusing letters similar in shape (Pietras 2007, 2008). Krasowicz-Kupis (2008) suggests that, in fact, it seems to be the overall number rather than a particular type that is more important in evaluation of dyslexic spelling ability, thus the total number of errors should be taken as an indicator of dyslexic spelling difficulty.

While with regard to qualitative analysis, indeed, a broad division into phonologically accurate or inaccurate spellings is recommended.

The following are examples of dyslexic spelling attempts with skipped, added or changed letters, syllables or parts of words: 'trick' for 'tick,' 'walk' for 'walking,' 'sudly' for 'suddenly,' 'rember' for 'remember,' 'amt' for 'amount,' 'merember' for 'remember,' 'tow' for 'two,' 'pakr' for 'park,' 'sitesr' for 'sister.' Individuals with dyslexia tend to demonstrate a conspicuous difficulty in dividing sentences into words—or to keep word boundaries, for instance 'a nother' for 'another,' 'firstones' for 'first ones,' 'halfanhour' for 'half an hour.' In similar vein, dividing words into syllables and constituent phonemes as well as differentiating between similar sounds proves problematic, as a consequence targeted words are often misrepresented graphically. Every now and then phonetic spelling (e.g. 'yoos' for 'use,' 'wokt' for 'walked,' 'mendid' for 'mended') but also bizarre and inconsistent spelling, unusual sequencing of letters, or multiple efforts at spelling a target word (e.g. 'schule,' 'skchool,' 'school') may occur in a given piece of dyslexic writing. At times the way individual words are spelled can be so distorted that it is virtually impossible to decode them.

Poor ability to distinguish between letters of similar shape and to rewrite texts correctly is characteristic rather for younger children, however, on occasion also some older students with dyslexia can continually demonstrate these symptoms. Reduced ability to discriminate and remember letter shapes usually refers to letters similar in shape (a-o, m-n, l-t, hence 'cat' for 'cot,' 'moon' for 'noon') as well as letters similar in shape but differing in their position in space—(p-g-b-d; m-w, n-u, hence 'bady' for 'baby,' 'dot' for 'got,' 'brown' for 'drown,' 'pig' for 'dig,' 'pug' for 'bud'). Inverting words dynamically ('no' for 'on,' 'was' for 'saw,' 'dog' for 'god,' 'gip' for 'pig'), neglecting diacritical marks and misusing lower and upper case letters ('daDDy' for 'daddy') can be sometimes noticed.

In older individuals with dyslexia low level of precision of hand and finger movement (fine motor skills), responsible for unintelligible handwriting and rather poor drawing, can be occasionally reported. Slow and messy written work, subject to numerous corrections may stem from an awkward grip of a pen. In addition, co-movements of other parts of the body (legs, tongue) can be observed during writing. Poorly formed and inappropriately connected letters which may as well drift of the intended angle, direction, and spatial position constitute a characteristic feature. Finally, details such as periods, commas, capitals, are very often omitted, spaces between letters and words can be irregular, and lines can be continually skipped. However, handwriting may be surprisingly neat as well but, at the same time, writing speed gets considerably reduced. Largely, an ability to organize and compose a piece of writing seems to be below standard in terms of accuracy, content and time-efficiency, unlike frequent advanced oral capability (Bogdanowicz and Adryjanek 2004).

Even though language deficit in dyslexia is by definition connected with poor phonological abilities, in some cases it may also incorporate lowered morphological, syntactic and/or syntactic abilities, which supplement disordered phonological processing. Students with dyslexia have been reported to produce ungrammatical utterances, especially with regard to applying phrases which describe spatial relations. Comprehension and retrieval of abstract and complex sentences, in particular those composed of multiple clauses, such as relative or subordinate clauses, frequently poses difficulty on learners with dyslexia (Borkowska 1997, 1998; Krasowicz-Kupis 2003, 2006; Oszwa 2000; Schneider 1999). A subtle deficit on the semantic level of language processing can lead to construal of poorly organized narrative discourse (e.g. in the situation of describing a picture and telling a story), which is characterized by considerably simpler, shorter, or incomplete episodic structure. Difficulties in identifying the setting of a story (characters, time, and place), the main plot, and the resolution have also been noticed in individuals with dyslexia. Basic information in the story can be omitted or deformed in the utterances formed; the most often neglected elements involve the identification of characters and the sphere of spatial–temporal relations. As a consequence, narrative discourse constructed from reduced number of pieces of information becomes markedly less communicative. Moreover, some learners with dyslexia often encounter fair difficulties, with a tendency to increase with age, in accommodating discourse to the social situation that they find themselves in Borkowska (1998), Krasowicz (1997).

Poor gross motor skills and deficient balance, which creates an impression of the overall clumsiness and does not help them in undertaking sport activities, can be displayed by some older students with dyslexia. For that reason they may find the PE classes least enjoyable. In addition, poor orientation in space and body schemata is frequently observed. Sometimes adults with dyslexia fail in distinguishing left from right and finding their way in the unknown place, not to mention getting on a wrong bus because of erroneous perception of the position of figures (e.g. 69 for 96). Proper time management, which involves organizing time efficiently as well as remembering dates and events, particularly in chronological order, seems to be challenging and may pose noticeable burden on these individuals. Doing simple mental mathematical calculations or using multiplication tables may seem obscure as well. Some adults with dyslexia describe themselves as being disorganized and forgetful throughout life, which can probably be attributed to poor concentration abilities. As children they may often fail to recall their homework, while as adults they admit letting slip telephone numbers, messages, names, appointments and dates. In addition, they report misarticulating multi-syllabic words, mispronouncing names and surnames, often being lost for words, committing spelling mistakes, and avoiding reading. All in all, activities such as driving a car, especially in an unfamiliar area, filling the forms, learning the sequences of movements in the aerobics or dance class, quickly retrieving information from memory—all constitute examples of possible areas of perplexity for adults with dyslexia, who are otherwise perceived as intelligent, talented and creative people (Bogdanowicz 2003; Bogdanowicz and Adryjanek 2004; Bogdanowicz and Krasowicz-Kupis 2005).

It needs highlighting that individuals with dyslexia can manifest certainly not all but only diversified sets or clusters of the difficulties described above. Variance as to the areas and severity of problems, levels of creativeness, talents and strengths or sporting faculties across learners with dyslexia is remarkably excessive.

All in all, dyslexia is a life-long condition, whose symptoms differ and change from pre-school age (risk for dyslexia) to adulthood as a function of development and education. There exist marked differences in development of the reading skill between students, both these with and without dyslexia. However, early difficulties can substantially decrease and get compensated through the remedial activities, on condition that sufficient attention, time and training is provided. Spelling difficulties tend to be much more common and persistent in childhood through adolescence to adulthood, despite familiarity with the orthographic rules. Thus, even in adulthood spelling would be expected to remain a painful task, while typically fluent reading is usually an attainable goal. It needs stressing that isolated difficulties in literacy acquisition, which are evident at the beginning of school education, can be responsible for slowed down and distorted progress in many areas of school curriculum and beyond it and almost invariably grow into the global learning difficulty if they are not timely and correctly diagnosed, and then subject to appropriate pedagogical intervention.

References

Bogdanowicz, M. 1999. Specyficzne trudności w czytaniu i pisaniu [Specific difficulties in reading and writing]. In eds. T. Gałkowski, and G. Jastrzębowska, 815–859.

Bogdanowicz, M. 2002. *Ryzyko dysleksji: Problem i diagnozowanie [Risk of dyslexia: Problem and diagnosis]*. Gdańsk: Wydawnictwo Harmonia.

Bogdanowicz, M. 2003. Specyficzne trudności w czytaniu i pisaniu [Specific difficulties in reading and writing]. In eds. T. Gałkowski, and G. Jastrzębowska, 491–535.

Bogdanowicz, M., and A. Adryjanek. 2004. Uczeń z dysleksją w szkole: poradnik nie tylko dla polonistów [A learner with dyslexia in school: A guide not only for teachers of Polish]. Gdynia: Wydawnictwo Pedagogiczne Operon.

Bogdanowicz, M., and G. Krasowicz-Kupis. 2005. Czytanie i pisanie jako formy komunikacji językowej [Reading and writing as forms of language communication]. In eds. T. Gałkowski, E. Szeląg, and G. Jastrzębowska, 986–1015.

Bogdanowicz, M., and M. Smolen, eds. 2004. *Dysleksja w kontekście nauczania języków obcych [Dyslexia in foreign language teaching context]*. Gdańsk: Wydawnictwo Harmonia.

Borkowska, A. 1997. Zaburzenia językowe u dzieci z trudnościami w czytaniu i pisaniu [Language disorders in children with reading and spelling difficulties]. In eds. A. Herzyk, and D. Kądzielawa, 269–292.

Borkowska, A. 1998. *Analiza dyskursu narracyjnego u dzieci z dysleksją rozwojową [The analysis of narrative discourse in dyslexic children]*. Lublin: Wydawnictwo Uniwersytetu Marii Curie-Skłodowskiej.

Borkowska, A., and E.M. Szepietowska, eds. 2000. *Diagnoza neuropsychologiczna: Metodologia i metodyka [Neuropsychological assessment: Methodology and practice]*. Lublin: Wydawnictwo Uniwersytetu Marii Curie-Skłodowskiej.

Davies, R., F. Cuetos, and R.M. Glez-Seijas. 2007. Reading development and dyslexia in a transparent orthography: Survey of Spanish children. *Annals of Dyslexia* 57: 179–198.

Downey, D.M., L.E. Snyder, and B. Hill. 2000. College students with dyslexia: Persistent linguistic deficits and foreign language learning. *Dyslexia* 6: 101–111.

Fawcett, A.J., and R.I. Nicolson. 1999. Performance of dyslexic children on cerebellar and cognitive tests. *Journal of Motor Behaviour* 31: 68–78.

Fawcett, A.J., and R.I. Nicolson. 2001. Dyslexia: The role of the cerebellum. In ed. A.J. Fawcett, 89–105.

Fawcett, A.J. ed. 2001. *Dyslexia: Theory and good practice*. London: Whurr Publishers.

Fawcett, A.J., and R.I. Nicolson. 2004. Dyslexia: The role of the cerebellum. In eds. G. Reid, and A.J. Fawcett, 25–47.

Frith, U. 2008. Rozwiązywanie paradoksów dysleksji [Resolving the paradoxes of dyslexia]. In eds. G. Reid, and J. Wearmouth, 71–102.

Gałkowski, T., and G. Jastrzębowska, eds. 1999. *Logopedia: pytania i odpowiedzi [Logopedics: Questions and answers]*. Opole: Wydawnictwo Uniwersytetu Opolskiego.

Gałkowski, T., and G. Jastrzębowska, eds. 2003. *Logopedia: Pytania i odpowiedzi [Logopedics: Questions and answers]* (revised and extended 2nd ed.). Opole: Wydawnictwo Uniwersytetu Opolskiego.

Gałkowski T., E. Szeląg, and G. Jastrzębowska, eds. 2005. *Podstawy neurologopedii (Introduction to neurologopedics)*. Opole: Wydawnictwo Uniwersytetu Opolskiego.

Gaskell, M.G., ed. 2007. *The Oxford handbook of psycholinguistics*. Oxford: Oxford University Press.

Geva, E. 2000. Issues in the assessment of reading disabilities in L2 children—beliefs and research evidence. *Dyslexia* 6: 13–28.

Goswami, U. 2000. Phonological representations, reading development and dyslexia: Towards a cross-linguistic theoretical framework. *Dyslexia* 6: 133–151.

Gregg, N., C. Hoy, D.A. Flaherty, P. Norris, C. Coleman, M. Davis, and M. Jordan. 2005. Decoding and spelling accommodations for postsecondary students with dyslexia—It's more than processing speed. *Learning Disabilities: A Contemporary Journal* 3(2): 1–17.

Hanley, J.R., J. Masterson, L.H. Spencer, and D. Evans. 2004. How long do the advantages of learning to read a transparent orthography last? An investigation of the reading skills and reading impairment of Welsh children at 10 years of age. *The Quarterly Journal of Experimental Psychology* 57A(8): 1393–1410.

Herzyk, A., and D. Kądzielawa, eds. 1997. *Związek mózg–zachowanie w ujęciu neuropsychologii klinicznej [The relation between brain and behaviour from the perspective of clinical neuropsychology]*. Lublin: Wydawnictwo Uniwersytetu Marii Curie-Skłodowskiej.

Hulme, C., and M.J. Snowling, eds. 1997. *Dyslexia: Biology, cognition and intervention*. London: Whurr Publishers.

Hulme, C., and M. Snowling. 2009. *Developmental disorders of language learning and cognition*. Oxford/Malden: Wiley-Blackwell.

Johnson, M., L. Peer, and R. Lee. 2001. Pre-school children and dyslexia: Policy, identification and intervention. In ed. A.J. Fawcett, 231–255.

Kaja, B. 2001. *Zarys terapii dziecka [An outline of child threapy]*. Bydgoszcz: Wydawnictwo Akademii Bydgoskiej.

Kaja, B., ed. 2003. *Diagnoza dysleksji [Assessment of dyslexia]*. Bydgoszcz: Wydawnictwo Akademii Bydgoskiej im. Kazimierza Wielkiego.

Kormos, J., and A.M. Smith. In press *Teaching languages to students with specific learning difficulties*. Bristol: Multilingual Matters.

Kormos, J., and E.H. Kontra, eds. 2008. *Language learners with special needs: An international perspective*. Bristol: Multilingual Matters.

Kostka-Szymańska, M., and G. Krasowicz-Kupis, eds. 2007. *Dysleksja: Problem znany czy nieznany? [Dyslexia: Familiar or unfamiliar problem?]*. Lublin: Wydawnictwo UMCS.

Krasowicz, G. 1997. *Język, czytanie i dysleksja [Language, reading and dyslexia]*. Lublin: Agencja Wydawniczo-Handlowa AD.

Krasowicz-Kupis, G. 2003. Językowe, ale nie fonologiczne deficyty w dysleksji [Linguistic but not phonological deficits in dyslexia]. In ed. B. Kaja, 95–118.

Krasowicz-Kupis, G. 2006. Dysleksja a rozwój mowy i języka [Dyslexia vs. speech and language development]. In ed. G. Krasowicz-Kupis, 53–69.

Krasowicz-Kupis, G., ed. 2006. *Dysleksja rozwojowa: Perspektywa psychologiczna [Developmental dyslexia: Psychological perspective]*. Gdańsk: Wydawnictwo Harmonia.

Krasowicz-Kupis, G. 2008. *Psychologia dysleksji [Psychology of dyslexia]*. Warszawa: Wydawnictwo Naukowe PWN.

Krasowicz-Kupis, G., and P.E. Bryant. 2004. Świadomość językowa dzieci polskich i angielskich a czytanie [Linguistic awareness of Polish and English children vs. reading]. In eds. M. Bogdanowicz, and M. Smoleń, 36–63.

Levinson, H.N. 1980. *A solution to the riddle dyslexia*. New York: Springer.

Lundberg, I. 2002. Second language learning and reading with additional load of dyslexia. *Annals of Dyslexia* 52: 165–187.

Lundberg, I., and T. Hoien. 2001. Dyslexia and phonology. In ed. A.J. Fawcett, 109–123.

Nijakowska, J. 2008. An experiment with direct multisensory instruction in teaching word reading and spelling to Polish dyslexic learners of English. In eds. J. Kormos, and E.H. Kontra, 130–157.

Nijakowska, J. 2010. *Dyslexia in the foreign language classroom*. Bristol: Multilingual Matters.

Oren, R., and Z. Breznitz. 2005. Reading processes in L1 and L2 among dyslexics compared to regular bilingual readers: Behavioral and electrophysiological evidence. *Journal of Neurolinguistics* 18: 127–151.

Oszwa, U. 2000. Analiza przejawów agramatyzmu u dzieci z dysleksją rozwojową [Analysis of agrammatisms in dyslexic children]. In eds. A. Borkowska, and E.M. Szepietowska, 289–306.

Ott, P. 1997. *How to detect and manage dyslexia: A reference and resource manual*. Oxford: Heinemann Educational Publishers.

Pietras, I. 2007. O klasyfikacji błędów w dysortografii [Error typology in dysorthography]. In eds. M. Kostka-Szymańska, and G. Krasowicz-Kupis, 81–92.

Pietras, I. 2008. *Dysortografia—uwarunkowania psychologiczne [Dysorthography—psychological underpinnings]*. Gdańsk: Wydawnictwo Harmonia.

Reid, G. 1998. *Dyslexia: A practitioner's handbook*. Chichester: Wiley.

Reid, G., and A.J. Fawcett. 2004. An overview of developments in dyslexia. In eds. G. Reid, and A.J. Fawcett, 3–19.

Reid, G., and A.J. Fawcett, eds. 2004. *Dyslexia in context: Research, policy and practice*. London: Whurr Publishers.

Reid, G., and J. Wearmouth, eds. 2008. *Dysleksja: teoria i praktyka [Dyslexia and literacy: theory and practice]*. Gdańskie Wydawnictwo Psychologiczne, Gdańsk.

Schneider, E. 1999. *Multisensory structured metacognitive instruction: An approach to teaching a foreign language to at-risk students*. Frankfurt am Main: Peter Lang.

Seymour, P.H.K., M. Aro, and J.M. Erskine. 2003. Foundation literacy acquisition in European orthographies. *British Journal of Psychology* 94: 143–174.

Snowling, M.J. 2000. *Dyslexia*. Oxford: Blackwell Publishers.

Snowling, M.J. 2001. From language to reading and dyslexia. *Dyslexia* 7(1): 37–46.

Snowling, M.J., and M. Caravolas. 2007. Developmental dyslexia. In ed. M.G. Gaskell, 667–683.

Snowling, M.J, and K. Nation. 1997. Language, phonology and learning to read. In eds. C. Hulme, and M.J. Snowling, 153–166.

Snowling, M.J., V. Muter, and J. Carrol. 2007. Children at family risk of dyslexia: A follow-up in early adolescence. *Journal of Child Psychology and Psychiatry* 48(6): 609–618.

Sochacka, K. 2004. *Rozwój umiejętności czytania [Development of reading ability]*. Białystok: Trans Humana.

Sparks, R. 2001. Foreign language learning problems of students classified as learning disabled and non-learning disabled: Is there a difference? *Topics in Language Disorders* 21(1): 38–54.

Sparks, R. 2006. Is there a 'disability' for learning a foreign language? *Journal of Learning Disabilities* 39(6): 544–557.

Sparks, R., and K.S. Miller. 2000. Teaching a foreign language using multisensory structured language techniques to at-risk learners: A review. *Dyslexia* 6: 124–132.

Sparks, R., L. Ganschow, and J. Patton. 1995. Prediction of performance in first-year foreign language courses: Connections between native and foreign language learning. *Journal of Educational Psychology* 87: 638–655.

Sparks, R., L. Philips, and J. Javorsky. 2003. Students classified as LD who petitioned for or fulfilled the foreign language requirement—Are they different? A replication study. *Journal of Learning Disabilities* 36(4): 348–362.

Sparks, R., J. Patton, L. Ganschow, N. Humbach, and J. Javorsky. 2006. Native language predictions of foreign language proficiency and foreign language aptitude. *Annals of Dyslexia* 56(1): 129–160.

Sparks, R., N. Humbach, and J. Javorsky. 2008. Individual and longitudinal differences among high- and low-achieving, LD and ADHD L2 learners. *Learning and Individual Differences* 8: 29–43.

Szczerbiński, M. 2007. Dysleksja rozwojowa: próba definicji [Developmental dyslexia: an attempt at defining]. In eds. M. Kostka-Szymańska, and G. Krasowicz-Kupis, 48–70.

Tomaszewska, A. 2001. *Prawo do nauki dziecka z dysleksją rozwojową w świadomości nauczycieli* [*Teachers' awareness of dyslexic children's right to learn*]. Kraków: Oficyna Wydawnicza 'Impuls'.

Vellutino, F.R., J.M. Fletcher, M.J. Snowling, and D.M. Scanlon. 2004. Specific reading disability (dyslexia): what have we learned in the past four decades? *Journal of Child Psychology and Psychiatry* 45(1): 2–40.

Wimmer, H. 1993. Characteristics of developmental dyslexia in a regular reading system. *Applied Psycholinguistics* 14: 1–33.

Ziegler, J.C., and U. Goswami. 2005. Reading acquisition, developmental dyslexia, and skilled reading across languages: A psycholinguistic grain size theory. *Psychological Bulletin* 131: 3–29.

Ziegler, J.C., and U. Goswami. 2006. Becoming literate in different languages: Similar problems, different solutions. *Developmental Science* 9(5): 426–453.

Ziegler, J., C. Perry, A. Ma-Wyatt, D. Ladner, and G. Schulte-Korne. 2003. Developmental dyslexia in different languages: Language-specific or universal? *Journal of Experimental Child Psychology* 86: 169–193.

Printed by Printforce, the Netherlands